# Canadian Criminology Today

**Frank Schmalleger**

*The Justice Research Association*

**Rebecca Volk**

*Algonquin College*

## Theories and Applications

Prentice
Hall

**Toronto**

**Canadian Cataloguing in Publication Data**

Schmalleger, Frank
    Canadian criminology today : theories and applications

Includes index.
ISBN 0-13-081072-X

Criminology. 2. Criminology—Canada. I. Volk, Rebecca. II. Title.

HV6025.S34 2001       364       C00-931889-5

Chapter opening photo credits: p. 1, The Canadian Press/Guelph Mercury; p. 40, The Canadian Press/Ryan Remiorz; p. 74, Bohdan Hyrnewych, Stock Boston; p. 102, The Granger Collection; p. 133, Ian Turner/Spooner, Gamma-Liaison, Inc.; p. 165, Photofest; p. 197, The Canadian Press/Winnipeg Free Press/Boris Minkevich; p. 229, Ken Hawkins/Stock South/Uniphoto/PNI; p. 267, AP/Wide World Photos; p. 293, Illustration, Mark Yankus; p. 327, The Canadian Press/Tom Hanson; p. 352, Photofest.

Quotation on p. 94 from *Behind the Bars—Experiences in Crime* by Patrick J. Desroches (Toronto: Canadian Scholars' Press, 1996), pp. 27–28. Used by permission.

ISBN 0-13-081072-X

Vice President, Editorial Director: Michael Young
Editor-in-Chief: David Stover
Marketing Manager: Sophia Fortier
Signing Representative: Samantha Scully
Developmental Editor: Marta Tomins
Production Editor: Avivah Wargon
Copy Editor: Craig Wilson
Production Coordinator: Wendy Moran
Page Layout: Joan M. Wilson
Photo Research: Susan Wallace-Cox
Art Director: Mary Opper
Interior Design: Lisa LaPointe
Cover Design:  Lisa LaPointe
Cover Image:  PhotoDisc

Original English-language edition, entitled *Criminology Today: An Integrative Introduction,* published by Prentice-Hall, Inc., a division of Pearson Education, Upper Saddle River, NJ. Copyright © 1999, 1996 by Prentice Hall, Inc. This edition is authorized for sale in Canada only.

5      05 04 03

Printed and bound in Canada

Statistics Canada information is used with the permission of the Minister of Industry, as Minister responsible for Statistics Canada. Information on the availability of the wide range of data from Statistics Canada can be obtained from Statistics Canada's Regional Offices, its World Wide Web site at **http://www.statcan.ca** and its toll-free access number, 1-800-263-1136.

To my wife, Harmonie,
whose loving spirit and close friendship
have been my constant inspiration.

And to my daughter, Nicole, whom I will always cherish.

—F.S.

To Martin, Monica, and Aaron.

—R.V.

# Contents

# Preface

More than a quarter century ago, the great criminologist Austin Turk began the preface to his book *Criminality and Legal Order* with these words[1]:

> Embarrassment provided much of the initial push that led to the writing of this book. I was embarrassed at my lack of good answers when confronted by students who wondered, somewhat irreverently, why criminology is "such a confused mish-mash." … Some of these students were especially bothered by the "unreality" of criminological studies, by which they meant the lack of sustained attention to connections between the theories and statistics about crime, and what they heard every day about relations among social conflicts, political maneuvers, and law violation and enforcement.

Much has changed since Turk's time, yet much remains the same. Far more criminological studies have been proposed and conducted. All levels of government—federal, provincial/territorial, and municipal—have placed crime near the top of their political agendas. Although crime statistics are actually showing some decline, the Canadian public's perception is different. Recent opinion polls show that public confidence in our criminal justice system is low, especially in the area of youth justice.

Crime is still with us as we enter the twenty-first century. The question that must be answered is, *Why?* Why, despite all the theorizing and studies, can we not "solve" the crime puzzle? Do some people behave violently because they are "born violent"? Or, is their exposure to violence in childhood responsible? Why does the affluent businessperson engage in insider trading while the young person living in a high-crime neighbourhood remains crime-free? What is it that motivates one person and not another to violate the social norms? And, does this motivation vary according to the type of law broken? This text sets out to examine a number of the theories that attempt to answer these and other questions.

The complexity of crime and criminal behaviour is fascinating. Because of the ever-increasing interest in crime and its causation, today's market is full of introductory criminology texts. What makes *Canadian Criminology Today: Theories and Applications* different from all the other texts that deal with the same subject matter? The following list highlights the important differences:

- *Canadian Criminology Today* has been adapted from Frank Schmalleger's pace-setting text to reflect the realities of crime and criminal activity in Canada.
- *Canadian Criminology Today* meets the needs of students preparing for careers in the Canadian criminal justice system. Its focus on the explanations of crime and deviance as well as their application to "real life" examples of criminal behaviour reflects the learning outcomes of introductory criminology courses.
- *Canadian Criminology Today* emphasizes the wide variety of interdisciplinary academic perspectives that contribute to a thorough understanding of the crime problem.

1. Austin Turk, *Criminality and Legal Order* (Chicago: Rand McNally, 1969), p.vii.

- *Canadian Criminology Today* is up to date. It addresses the latest social issues and discusses innovative criminological perspectives within a well-grounded and traditional theoretical framework.
- *Canadian Criminology Today* is socially relevant. It contrasts contemporary issues of crime and social order with existing and proposed crime-control policies.
- *Canadian Criminology Today* is interesting and easy to read. It is written for today's student and makes use of images from the news, stories that grab the reader's attention, and study tools such as learning outcomes, marginal definitions, and a glossary to reinforce student learning.
- *Canadian Criminology Today* is applied. It stresses the consequences of criminology theory for social policy, and describes the practical issues associated with understanding and controlling crime. Canadian social policies focusing on prevention, treatment, rehabilitation, and victim restoration are all discussed.
- *Canadian Criminology Today* is thematic. It builds on the divergence between the social problems viewpoint and the social responsibility perspective. In so doing, it highlights the central issue facing criminologists today: whether crime should be addressed as a matter of individual responsibility and accountability or treated as a symptom of a dysfunctional society.

The thematic approach of *Canadian Criminology Today* is dualistic. On the one hand, it presents a social problems framework, which holds that crime may be a manifestation of underlying cultural issues such as poverty, discrimination, and the breakdown of traditional social institutions. On the other hand, it contrasts the social problems approach with a social responsibility perspective, which claims that individuals are fundamentally responsible for their own behaviour and maintains that they choose crime over other, more law-abiding courses of action. The thematic contrast is an important one, for it provides students with a useful framework for integrating the voluminous material contained within the field of criminology.

Contrasting the two perspectives, as this book does, provides fertile ground for discussion and debate, allowing students to better understand the central issues defining contemporary criminology and to reach their own conclusions about the value of criminology theory.

The hope is that today's students will find *Canadian Criminology Today* relevant, interesting, and informative. It is designed to assist them in understanding the reasons and motivations behind criminal and deviant behaviour, to allow them to draw their own conclusions about the most effective ways to treat such behaviour and, ultimately, to prepare them for their future careers within the criminal justice system. After all, it is only by understanding the problem of crime and criminal behaviour that we can ever hope to come close to solving it.

*Canadian Criminology Today: Theories and Applications* retains the organizational features of the U.S. second edition, *Criminology Today: An Integrative Introduction,* which have made it one of the most popular and accessible introductory criminology texts.

Most importantly, *Canadian Criminology Today: Theories and Applications* has been adapted to reflect that the nature of crime and criminals in Canada is very different from that of our American neighbours. Canadian references to media stories, social policies and programs, statistics, legislation, and Weblinks are used throughout the text.

# Changes to the Canadian Edition

The major changes to the Canadian edition are as follows:

- replacing American case studies and news stories with Canadian examples;
- streamlining (e.g., three parts instead of four and twelve chapters instead of fourteen) to replace the detailed discussion of specific types of crime found in the American edition with a focus on criminology theories and their everyday application to the reality of crime and criminals in Canada;
- expanding the discussion of data collection in a stand-alone chapter;
- extending the "amounts and types of crime" discussion to include the application of the theories considered earlier in the text to this reality (a lot of books don't make this connection, and students are left trying to link the "dry, irrelevant" theory to the reality surrounding them);
- reorganizing theories into categories more consistent with the Canadian approach to the discipline; and
- satisfying learning outcomes for such courses as the Criminology course in the Police Foundations Program in Ontario.

*Canadian Criminology Today: Theories and Application* is divided into three parts.

**Part 1: The Crime Picture** provides an introduction to the subject of criminology.

Chapter 1, What Is Criminology? includes a brief look at theoretical perspectives in criminology.

Chapter 2, Crime Statistics reflects the Canadian reality of the collection and dissemination of crime data.

Chapter 3, Research Methods and Theory Development concentrates on the role of research and includes a comprehensive list of professional journals publishing criminological research.

**Part 2: Crime Causation** broadens the focus on the predominant theoretical explanations of criminal behaviour.

Chapter 4, The Classical Thinkers includes Canadian examples and policy case studies.

Chapter 5, Biological Roots of Behaviour provides a thorough examination of biological theories as they may relate to crime and crime causation.

Chapter 6, Psychological and Psychiatric Foundations of Criminal Behaviour includes an in-depth look at the insanity defence as it applies in Canada.

Chapter 7, Crime and the Role of the Social Environment emphasizes the social structural perspective of sociological crime theories.

Chapter 8, The Meaning of Crime: Social Process Perspectives takes a detailed look at current directions in victimology in the Canadian setting including police, court, correctional, and parole-based programs for victims of crime.

Chapter 9, Social Conflict and Crime is new to this edition and concentrates on the major theories found within the social conflict perspective.

**Part 3: Crime in the Modern World and the Response to It.**

Chapter 10, Patterns of Crime is a new chapter that provides an overview of the extent and types of crime in Canada. Also new are the sections of this chapter that tie together the theoretical explanations of crime discussed in Part 2 with these realities.

Chapter 11, Criminology and Social Policy examines a number of important Canadian legislative responses to crime including The Firearms Act, The National Strategy on Community Safety and Crime Prevention, Crime Prevention through Environmental Design, and the proposed Youth Criminal Justice Act.

Chapter 12, Future Directions in Criminology examines Canadian leadership in the area of restorative justice and geographic profiling. It also includes a summary of organized crime groups and activities in Canada.

## Supplements

A variety of instructor's and student supplements enhance the teaching and learning experience provided by the text.

The *Instructor's Manual with Test Item File and Transparency Masters* (ISBN 0-13-083159-X) provides useful teaching resources and a comprehensive test bank.

The *Computerized Test Manager* (Windows, ISBN 0-13-083157-3) provides hundreds of objective test questions in an easy-to-use software package.

Criminology/criminal justice Web sites: **www.prenhall.com/schmalleger** and **www.prenticehall.ca/winterdyk**.

As well, adopters of *Canadian Criminology Today* may find useful the supplements originally developed in conjunction with U.S. editions of the text: the *Student Study Guide* and the *ABC News Video Library*.

# Acknowledgments

## For the U.S. Edition

A book like *Criminology Today* draws upon the talents and resources of many people, and is the end result of much previous effort. This text could not have been written without the groundwork laid by previous criminologists, academicians, and researchers; hence, a hearty "thank you" is due everyone who has contributed to the development of the field of criminology throughout the years, and especially those theorists, authors, and social commentators who are cited in this book. Without their work the field would be that much poorer. I would like to thank, as well, all the adopters—professors and students alike—of my previous textbooks, for they have given me the encouragement and fostered the steadfastness required to write this new edition of *Criminology Today*.

The Prentice Hall team whom I have come to know so well, and who have worked so professionally with me on this and other projects deserves a special thanks. The team includes Neil Marquardt, Denise Brown, Frank Mortimer, Jr., Marianne Frasco, and Jean Auman. My thanks also to cover designer Joe Sengotta, and interior designer Patrice Sheridan, whose efforts have helped make *Criminology Today* both attractive and visually appealing. In addition, I would like to thank Lori Harvey and the rest of the Carlisle Publishers Services team for their commitment and attention to this project.

The many manuscript reviewers are due a special "thank you" for helping me stick to important themes when I might otherwise have strayed, and for their guidance in matters of detail. I am especially thankful to supplements author Gordon Armstrong for the quality products he has created, and for his exceptional ability to intuitively build upon concepts in the text. Thanks also to Bob Winslow at California State University–San Diego for insight and encouragement on a number of important issues; and to Richard Guymon at Maplewoods Community College, to Debra Kelley at Virginia's Longwood College, and Stephen J. Schoenthaler for their valuable suggestions in the preparation of this new edition.

This book has benefited greatly from the quick accessibility of information and other resources that are available through online services such as America Online, and in various locations on the Internet's World Wide Web. I am grateful to the many information providers who, although they are too numerous to list, have helped establish such useful resources.

I am thankful as well for the assistance of Bill Tafoya and Nancy Carnes, both with the FBI (Bill is now retired); David Beatty, Director of Public Affairs with the National Victim Center; Kris Rose at the National Criminal Justice Reference Service; Marilyn Marbrook and Michael Rand at the Office of Justice Programs; Mark Reading at DEA; and Barbara Maxwell at *USA Today*.

Last, but by no means least, I wish to thank my family—my wife, Harmonie; daughter, Nicole; son, Jason; and mother, Margaret—for their personal help and encouragement.

*Frank Schmalleger*

## For the Canadian Edition

I am grateful for all the help and support I received during the development of this textbook. First and foremost, I want to thank my family, especially my husband, Martin Thornell, and my children, Monica and Aaron, whose positive outlook and humour sustained me throughout this project. To my parents goes my gratitude for teaching me to look for the good in everyone.

I owe a special debt of thanks to the team at Pearson Education Canada. Thanks to David Stover for having faith in my ability to take on this project and to Marta Tomins and Avivah Wargon for their gentle encouragement and boundless patience with my rookie foibles. Craig Wilson and Joe Zingrone provided superb editorial insights, for which I am grateful. Thanks to all those who reviewed the manuscript and offered helpful comments: Gina Antonacci, Humber College; Paul Atkinson, Sir Sandford Fleming College; R.E. Pritchard, Fanshawe College; Ken Smith, Confederation College; Ray Czajkowski, Mohawk College; and special thanks to Vicki Ryckman, Lambton College, and Oliver Stoetzer, Fanshawe College.

I would be remiss if I did not acknowledge the many students I have taught and learned with over the years; their enthusiasm encouraged me to take on this challenge. Finally, I want to recognize the men, women, and youth in conflict with the law whom I have worked with, as they have opened my eyes to the frailty of the human condition.

*Rebecca Volk*

# About the Authors

Frank Schmalleger, Ph.D., Director
The Justice Research Association

Frank Schmalleger, Ph.D., is director of The Justice Research Association (JRA), a private consulting firm and "think-tank" focusing on issues of crime and justice. The Justice Research Association, which is based in Hilton Head Island, South Carolina, serves the needs of the nation's civil and criminal justice planners and administrators through workshops, conferences, and grant writing and program evaluation support. JRA also supports the Criminal Justice Distance Learning Consortium (CJDLC), which can be found on the web at **http://cjentral.com/cjdlc**.

Dr. Schmalleger holds degrees from the University of Notre Dame and the Ohio State University, having earned both a master's (1970) and a doctorate in sociology (1974) from Ohio State University with a special emphasis in criminology. From 1976 to 1994 he taught criminal justice courses at the University of North Carolina at Pembroke. For the last sixteen of those years he chaired the university's Department of Sociology, Social Work, and Criminal Justice. As an adjunct professor with Webster University in St. Louis, Missouri, Schmalleger helped develop the university's graduate program in security administration and loss prevention. He taught courses in that curriculum for more than a decade. Schmalleger has also taught in the New School for Social Research's online graduate program, helping to build the world's first electronic classrooms in support of distance learning through computer telecommunications. An avid Web surfer, Schmalleger is also the creator of award-winning World Wide Web sites, including one which supports this textbook (**http://www.prenhall.com/cjcentral**).

Frank Schmalleger is the author of numerous articles and many books, including the widely used *Criminal Justice Today: An Introductory Text for the 21st Century* (Prentice-Hall), now in its fifth edition; *Criminal Justice: A Brief Introduction* (Prentice-Hall, 1999); *Crime and the Justice System in America: An Encyclopedia* (Greenwood Publishing Group, 1997); *Trial of the Century: People of the State of California vs. Orenthal James Simpsons* (Prentice-Hall, 1996); *Computers in Criminal Justice* (Wyndham Hall Press, 1991); *Career Paths: A Guide to Jobs in Federal Law Enforcement* (Regents/Prentice-Hall, 1994); *Criminal Justice Ethics* (Greenwood Press, 1991); *Finding Criminal Justice in the Library* (Wyndham Hall Press, 1991); *Ethics in Criminal Justice* (Wyndham Hall Press, 1990); *A History of Corrections* (Foundations Press of Notre Dame, 1983); and *The Social Basis of Criminal Justice* (University Press of America, 1981). Schmalleger is also founding editor of the journal *The Justice Professional*.

Schmalleger's philosophy of both teaching and writing can be summed up in these words: "In order to communicate knowledge we must first catch, then hold, a person's interest—be it student, colleague, or policy-maker. Our writing, our speaking, and our teaching must be relevant to the problems facing people today, and they must—in some way—help solve those problems."

Rebecca Volk, M.A., professor at Algonquin College of Applied Arts and Technology

Rebecca Volk is a coordinator and professor in the Police Foundations Program at Algonquin College of Applied Arts and Technology in Ottawa, Ontario. She holds a bachelor's degree in political science from Queen's University and an applied master's degree in criminology from the University of Ottawa.

In addition to teaching, Volk's professional criminological experience has included involvement with a variety of offender aftercare and advocacy agencies, federal and provincial correctional institutions and residential centres, legal aid services, and various police agencies. She serves on the boards of several organizations devoted to assisting the disadvantaged, some of whom are in conflict with the law.

## CHAPTER 1

# What Is Criminology?

Rather than attributing crime and all that is evil to a relatively small group of people, I am saying that crime and socially harmful behaviour is widely (although not evenly) dispersed in society.

—THOMAS GABOR[1]

Much is already known about the phenomenon of crime. Further development in theoretical criminology will result primarily from making sense out of what we already know.

—GEORGE B. VOLD AND THOMAS J. BERNARD[2]

## LEARNING OUTCOMES

After reading this chapter, you should be able to:

- Understand what criminology is and what criminologists do

- Recognize the difference between criminal and deviant acts and appreciate the complexity of this distinction

- Distinguish between the three perspectives of theoretical criminology

- Understand the distinction between the social problems and social responsibility perspectives regarding crime causation

## IMPORTANT TERMS

| | | |
|---|---|---|
| crime | deviance | conflict perspective |
| civil law | criminologist | social policies |
| criminal law | criminology | V-chip |
| indictable offence | criminality | social problems |
| summary conviction | criminal justice | perspective |
| offence | theory | social responsibility |
| hybrid offence | general theory | perspective |
| administrative law | unicausal | social relativity |
| statute | integrated theory | criminal justice system |
| criminalize | consensus model | socialization |
| common law | pluralistic perspective | phenomenology |
| statutory law | | |

# Introduction

Senseless murder is the kind of crime that everyone fears. On November 14, 1997, this fear became a reality for Reena Virk, 14, when she joined a group of friends to "hang out" on a Friday night at a park in Victoria, British Columbia known as "The Gorge," overlooking a saltwater inlet. She called her parents from a convenience store at 9:45 P.M. to say she was on her way home; her parents never saw her again. Several days later, police received a tip that Virk had been murdered, and they rounded up and arrested eight teens. Six girls were charged with aggravated assault. Kelly Ellard and Warren Glowatski were charged with second-degree murder. All the accused were between 14 and 16 years of age. It was over a week after she went missing that Reena Virk's body was found half-submerged in the water at the base of The Gorge.[3]

From her birth on March 10, 1983, Reena Virk had been the darling of an extended family within the 5 000-strong Indo-Canadian community in Victoria. As she approached adolescence, Virk felt the tight-knit extended family beginning to stifle her; she wanted friends her own age and of her own choosing. She became frustrated and angry with her family when they disapproved of the friends she began associating with. Virk disliked her parents' strict rules, such as a 9 P.M. curfew. She rebelled and left her parental home. She drifted between her grandparents' home and various shelters and group homes. Although she kept in touch with her mother by telephone, at the time of her death Virk had gone from a strictly supervised situation to one in which she set her own limits. One of her pastimes included spending hours with friends at The Gorge.

According to media accounts, seven girls and one boy surrounded Virk at the park as she sat on a stone wall. Kelly Ellard stubbed her cigarette on Virk's forehead, accusing her of taking her address book and spreading rumours about her. Virk tried to run away, but the group caught her as she attempted to climb the stairs leading to a bridge spanning the gorge; they bent her over the rail and beat her. Warren Glowatski repeatedly kicked her in the head. Virk broke free and stumbled across the bridge, where she was again attacked by the group of teens. Pulled down to the water's edge, Virk was repeatedly punched and kicked; Ellard rammed her head into a tree with such force that Virk eventually fell on her face, unconscious. Ellard then grabbed Virk's hair, pulled her head backward, and administered a karate chop to her windpipe. Ellard smoked a cigarette and held Virk's head under the water with her foot until she drowned. Pathologist Dr. Laurel Gray stated that the injuries to Virk's brain, head, liver, and other vital organs were similar to those suffered by victims of motor vehicle accidents.

As the profiles of Warren Glowatski and Kelly Ellard emerged, it became clear that they did not really seem to appreciate the seriousness of their actions. Glowatski was described as a typical "98-pound weakling" who insisted that he had played only a minor role in Virk's death. He claimed that he thought Ellard was going to rob Virk and that his participation in the beating was to that end. Testifying that he left before Virk drowned, he stated, "I didn't know she was going to die."

When police arrested Kelly Ellard for the murder of Reena Virk, her immediate response was, "Oh, my God," and then she laughed. While she appeared cold and calculating at times, Ellard frequently lapsed into childlike behaviour, promising to stay in her room for the rest of her life if she was allowed to go home. She admitted pushing Virk, whom she had just met for the first time, but insisted that other girls were responsible for her death. Amazingly, Ellard claimed later that the last time she saw Virk she appeared drunk, because she couldn't walk straight. She suggested that Virk probably fell into the water and drowned as a result of her intoxicated state.

The six girls charged with aggravated assault were found guilty and received sentences ranging from 60 days to 1 year in jail. Both Ellard and Glowatski were tried as adults and were convicted of second-degree murder and sentenced to life imprisonment. Ellard is eligible for parole after 5 years, while Glowatski can be considered for parole after 7 years.

The troubling thing about Reena Virk's death, however, is not so much *how* she was killed, but *why* she died. Reena Virk's mother, Suman Virk, expressed rage and sorrow that some of the youths stood around and watched her daughter being attacked and did nothing to help her.

Fourteen-year-old Reena Virk was punched, kicked, and eventually drowned by a group of teenage peers. What do murders like this have to say about the condition of Canadian society today?
*The Canadian Press/Chuck Stoody*

# What Is Crime?

Canadians and the Canadian mass media display a penchant for closely following gruesome and spectacular crimes, such as the murder of Reena Virk, and for thoroughly documenting the violent deaths of celebrities and other well-known individuals. Canadian accessibility to the American mass media also means that Canadians are inundated with news of criminal activities in the United States, which seem to be more frequent and sensational than similar events in Canada. For example, the 1997 murders of fashion designer Gianni Versace and Ennis Cosby (son of entertainer Bill Cosby), the 1996 killing of 6-year-old starlet JonBenet Ramsey, and the 1993 murder of basketball great Michael Jordan's father (James Jordan) on a North Carolina roadside, all received much press coverage. The alleged misdeeds of other celebrities such as O.J. Simpson, Michael Jackson, Snoop Doggy Dogg, and Michael Tyson seemed to attract even more attention. Canadian examples include the serial killings committed by Clifford Olson between 1980 and 1981, the mass murder of 14 female students in Montreal in 1989, and the heinous murders of Leslie Mahaffy and Kristen French at the hands of Paul Bernardo and Karla Holmoka in 1992. Gillian Guess became somewhat of a Canadian celebrity in 1996 when she was charged with obstruction of justice. As a juror in a 1995 murder trial in British Columbia, Ms. Guess had established a sexual relationship with one of the accused, who was subsequently acquitted. It was the first time in North America or the Commonwealth that this had ever happened!

**Crime** human conduct in violation of the criminal laws of a jurisdiction that has the power to make such laws, and for which there is some form of authorized sanction.

Of course, not all misdeeds are crimes. **Crime,** simply defined, is human conduct in violation of the criminal laws of a jurisdiction that has the power to make such laws. Without a law that circumscribes a particular form of behaviour, there can be no crime, no matter how deviant or socially repugnant the behaviour in question may be.

A recent case from Australia well illustrates the principle that without a law defining an activity as illegal, there can be no crime. In 1997, an Australian court acquitted Aboriginal activist John Kelly of "making a demand with menaces"—an offence under Australian law that is similar to the crime of extortion. Kelly was charged by prosecutors with trying to extort $10 000 (Australian) by threatening to "point the bone," or place a death curse, on a well-known Australian comedian.[4] Northern Territory Supreme Court Judge Steven Bailey directed a jury to acquit Kelly after a three-day trial, saying that "there was no evidence of unlawful conduct" in the Aboriginal activity of "pointing the bone" and that any threat made on the basis of such activity was essentially meaningless.[5] Had Kelly threatened to kill the comedian with a gun, the judge would probably have found otherwise. As in this case, however, the laws of most states would make it difficult or impossible to convict someone of assault charges for putting a voodoo curse on another person, or for burning an effigy of the person in a "black magic" ritual.

The notion of crime as behaviour that violates the law derives from earlier work by criminologists, who defined crime as "an intentional act in violation of the criminal law ... committed without defence or excuse, and penalized by the state as a felony or misdemeanor."[6] Edwin Sutherland,[7] one of the best-known criminologists of the last century, said of crime that its "essential characteristic ... is that it is behavior which is prohibited by the State as an injury to the State and against which the State may react ... by punishment."

In the study of criminology, three major forms of the law must be distinguished: civil, criminal, and administrative. **Civil law** deals with arrangements between individuals, such as contracts and claims to property. It exists primarily for the purpose of enforcing private rights. In contrast, **criminal law** regulates actions that have the potential to harm interests of the state. Because the state is made up of citizens, acts that are harmful to citizens of the state are fundamentally criminal in nature. Hence, although serious crimes with identifiable victims—such as murder and sexual assault—are clearly criminal, offences that have no obvious victims, such as drug use, gambling, and prostitution, may also be regulated by the criminal law because they detract from the quality of life of citizens or decrease social order.

Serious criminal offences are referred to as **indictable offences** and include murder, robbery, sexual assault, hostage-taking, perjury, and passing counterfeit money, among others. Less serious crimes or misdemeanours, such as making indecent telephone calls, being found in a common bawdy house, causing a disturbance in or near a public place, and loitering on private property at night, are known as **summary conviction offences**. **Hybrid offences** (dual-procedure offences) constitute a third category of criminal offence and include pointing a firearm, driving while disqualified, and uttering death threats. They may be tried as either indictable or summary conviction offences. The decision on how to treat a hybrid offence is made by the Crown attorney and is based on the circumstances surrounding the offence and the accused.

**Administrative law** regulates many daily business activities. Violation of such regulations generally results in warnings or fines, depending on their adjudged severity. For example, decisions of the British Columbia Criminal Injuries Compensation Board or the Ontario Workers' Compensation Board constitute part of administrative case law.

Although the legalistic approach to crime—which sees crime solely as conduct in violation of the criminal law—is useful in the study of criminology, it is also limiting. Those who adhere to a legalistic perspective insist that the nature of crime cannot be separated from the nature of law, as the one explicitly defines the other. Not recognized by any legalistic definition of crime, however, is the social, moral, and individual significance of fundamentally immoral forms of behaviour. Simply put, some activities not contravened by **statute** nonetheless call out for a societal response, sometimes leading commentators to proclaim "that ought to be a crime!" or "there ought to be a law against that!" Some suggest that "crime is primarily an offense against human relationships, and secondarily a violation of a law—since laws are written to protect safety and fairness in human relationships."[8]

Practically speaking, however, the legalistic perspective is persuasive. In most places, no one can be arrested for any particular conduct, no matter how atrocious, unless a law on the books criminalizes that particular activity.[9] Similarly, according to Canadian judicial principles, a new law cannot retroactively apply to past behaviour. Only those prohibited acts that are committed after the effective date of any new statute can be prosecuted as crimes. Hence, if the manufacture and sale of tobacco products should one day be declared criminal, individuals who are today engaged in the "tobacco trade" could not be prosecuted under it. Only if they continued their (now illegal) behaviour, would they be subject to lawful sanction.

One serious shortcoming of the legalistic approach to crime is that it yields the moral high ground to powerful individuals who are able to influence the making of laws and the imposition of criminal definitions on lawbreakers. By making their own laws,

**Civil law** body of law that regulates arrangements between individuals, such as contracts and claims to property.

**Criminal law** body of law that regulates actions which have the potential to harm interests of the state.

**Indictable offence** a serious criminal offence; specifically, one that carries a prison sentence of 14 years or longer.

**Summary conviction offence** a criminal offence that is less serious than an indictable offence; one that carries a maximum penalty of 6 months in jail.

**Hybrid offence** a criminal offence that can be classified as indictable or as a summary conviction; the classification is usually made by the Crown attorney.

**Administrative law** regulates many daily business activities. Violation of such regulations generally results in warnings or fines, depending upon their adjudged severity.

**Statute** a formal written enactment of a legislative body.

**Criminalize** to make
illegal.

**Common law** law
originating from usage
and custom rather than
from written statutes.
The term refers to
nonstatutory customs,
traditions, and
precedents that help
guide judicial decision-
making.

**Statutory law** law in the
form of statutes or
formal written strictures,
made by a legislature or
governing body with the
power to make law.

powerful but immoral individuals may escape the label "criminal." Although democratic societies such as Canada would seem to be immune from such abuses of the legislative process, history demonstrates otherwise. In Chapter 7, we will explore this issue
further and focus on the process of criminalization, the method used to **criminalize**
some forms of behaviour—make them illegal—while other forms remain legitimate.

The legalistic definition of crime also suffers from its seeming lack of recognition
of the fact that formalized laws have not always existed. Undoubtedly, much immoral
behaviour occurred even in the distant past, and contemporary laws probably now
regulate most such behaviour. English **common law,** for example, upon which much
Canadian **statutory law** is based, judged behaviour in terms of usage and custom
rather than against written statutes. Although Canada has enacted a comprehensive
federal legal code, it still adheres to the common law tradition. The exception to this is
Quebec provincial law, which operates under the civil law system used in many conti-
nental European countries. Dating back to law of the Romans, the modern civil law
system is based on the Napoleonic Code of the early nineteenth century. Common law
is discussed in more detail in Chapter 4.

Changes in the law will undoubtedly continue to occur, perhaps even legitimizing
former so-called crimes or recognizing that fundamentally moral forms of behaviour
have been unduly criminalized. Over the last decade, for example, the federal government, along with members of the general public, have debated the virtues of euthanasia. In 1993, Sue Rodriguez, a 42-year-old British Columbia woman, challenged before
the Supreme Court of Canada the statute that criminalizes the act of assisted suicide.
Suffering a slow and painful death from amyotrophic lateral sclerosis (ALS), also
known as "Lou Gehrig disease," Ms. Rodriguez felt that the law forbidding her to have
someone assist her in her death violated her rights under the Canadian Charter of
Rights and Freedoms. She lost her bid and committed suicide 2 years later.

The debate over assisted suicide
highlights the changing nature of criminal
activity. Sue Rodriguez used her personal
situation to attempt to get the Supreme
Court to strike down section 241(b) of
the Criminal Code of Canada, which
makes it illegal to assist someone in
committing suicide. She was
unsuccessful and the law stands.
*The Canadian Press/Chuck Stoody.*

Dr. Jack Kevorkian, perhaps the best known American pro-euthanasia activist of modern times, has been waging a crusade to legalize doctor-assisted suicide for terminally ill individuals. In mid-1997, Kevorkian publicly acknowledged having helped a total of 45 people kill themselves.[10] Kevorkian has been tried and acquitted three times on charges related to the deaths of five people in Michigan. In a challenge to law enforcement officials in Michigan, Kevorkian convinced CBS Television to air a videotape he had made showing his involvement in the assisted suicide of Thomas Youk. Three days later, on April 13, 1999, Kevorkian was arrested and charged with second-degree murder. He was convicted and received a sentence of incarceration for 10 to 25 years. He is currently appealing his case.

Recognizing the difficulties that attend euthanasia, Kevorkian has said publicly that "the whole controversy" over assisted suicides could be resolved by certifying doctors to perform assisted suicides. "All we have to do to solve the whole controversy is have the medical profession come forward [and] lay the guidelines down. The guidelines [should] say only certain doctors can do it, and if you don't, we're going to punish you."[11]

Practical considerations can also force reevaluation of existing laws. Arguments for the decriminalization of "soft" drugs such as marijuana, for example, have included the belief that increasing penalties for drug use does little to halt or even substantially slow the flow of drugs. In fact, some argue that criminalization unnecessarily puts a lucrative trade into the hands of organized crime, since it is the criminal status of drugs, not drugs themselves, that causes the crime. Further, proponents of the legalization of drugs argue that valuable enforcement resources are diverted away from the attack on other more serious forms of crime.[12]

### *theory* v e r s u s *reality*   *Should Assisted Suicide Remain Illegal?*

On September 30, 1993, in a 5 to 4 decision, the Supreme Court of Canada upheld the constitutionality of the law banning assisted suicide (section 241(b) of the Criminal Code of Canada). In *Rodriguez v British Columbia (Attorney General)*, lawyers for Sue Rodriguez argued that the law violated the right to equal benefit of the law (section 15) and the right to life, liberty, and security of the person (section 7) protected in the Canadian Charter of Rights and Freedoms. In essence, Ms. Rodriguez argued that the law prohibiting assisted suicide violated her right to equality, since it prevents persons who are physically unable to end their lives unassisted from choosing suicide when that option is available to other members of the public (attempting suicide was decriminalized in Canada in 1972). She also argued that the assisted suicide law infringed on her personal autonomy, or the protection of the dignity and privacy of individuals with respect to decisions concerning their own bodies.

The Supreme Court disagreed. The majority judgment advanced the following argument:

Assisted suicide, outlawed under the common law, has been prohibited by Parliament since the adoption of Canada's first Criminal Code. The long-standing blanket prohibition in section 214(b), which

▶

fulfills the government's objective of protecting the vulnerable, is grounded in the state interest in protecting life and reflects the state policy that human life should not be depreciated by allowing human life to be taken.

The dissenting minority held that:

Section 7 of the Charter, which grants Canadians a constitutional right to life, liberty and the security of the person, is a provision which emphasizes the innate dignity of human existence. Dying is an integral part of living and, as a part of life, is entitled to the protection of s. 7. It follows that the right to die with dignity should be as well protected as any other aspect of the right to life. State prohibitions that would force a dreadful, painful death on a rational but incapacitated terminally ill patient are an affront to human dignity.

Similarly, in 1997 the United States Supreme Court upheld the constitutionality of two laws prohibiting assisted suicide. Although the Court ruled that terminally ill people do not have a constitutionally protected right to assisted suicide, it did nothing to bar the individual states from legalizing the process. Some jurisdictions, led by the state of Oregon, have legalized doctor-assisted suicide under prescribed conditions.[13]

### DISCUSSION QUESTIONS

1. What is crime? Is assisted suicide a crime? What about doctor-assisted suicide? Why or why not?
2. Who is Dr. Jack Kevorkian (discussed elsewhere in this chapter)? Is he a criminal? Why or why not?
3. Are there any activities that are not against the law which you think should be criminal? If so, what are they?
4. Are there any activities that are against the law but that you think should not be illegal? If so, what are they?

## Crime and Deviance

**Deviance** behaviour that violates social norms or is statistically different from the "average."

From a broader point of view, most crimes can be regarded as deviant forms of behaviour, that is, as behaviours that are in some way abnormal. Abnormality, **deviance,** and crime, however, are concepts that do not always easily mesh. Some forms of deviance are not criminal, and the reverse is equally true. Deviant styles of dress, for example, although perhaps outlandish to the majority, are not circumscribed by criminal law, unless (perhaps) decency statutes are violated by a lack of clothing. Even in such cases, laws are subject to interpretation and may be modified as social norms change over time. For example, in December 1996 the Court of Appeal in Ontario overturned the conviction of Gwen Jacobs, who had been charged with committing an indecent act after she walked topless down a city street on a hot summer's day in 1991. The three judges on the panel ruled that there had to be a sexual connotation for the act to be considered indecent, and they found that Jacobs had no such motivation.

Deviance is relevant to the social context within which it occurs, as these bathers on an Italian nude beach show. Why is public nudity against the law in most Canadian jurisdictions? *Lucas/The Image Works.*

This case holds special interest for students of criminology because it highlights the role that societal interpretation plays in defining a criminal offence. Some forms of behaviour are quite common but are still against the law. Speeding on provincial highways, for example, although probably something that most motorists engage in occasionally, is illegal. Complicating matters further is the fact that some forms of behaviour are illegal in some jurisdictions but not in others. Panhandling and the activities of "squeegie kids," for example, violate provincial statutes in some provinces but not in others.

## Parents Guilty of Lesser Charge in Son's Death

Do parents have the right to deny medical treatment for their children because of their religious beliefs? As the following story shows, religious beliefs are not a defence when a child dies.

Parents whose religious beliefs kept them from seeking treatment for their gravely ill 14-year-old son were found not guilty Wednesday of criminal negligence causing death.

But Steven Shippy, 44, and his wife, Ruth, 36, were convicted of failing to provide the necessities of life.

Calahan Shippy died at home Dec. 30, 1998, from complications of diabetes. The parents said they didn't know he had diabetes and thought he had the flu.

The Shippys belong to the Followers of Christ based in Oregon City, Ore. The sect believes illness is cured by prayer and anointing oil.

▶

The Shippys on their family homestead northwest of Red Deer, Alberta. *The Report*

After the verdict, the boy's father said he believes he has the right not to seek medical help for his eight children.

The parents will be sentenced June 26 in Red Deer Court of Queen's Bench.

Crown prosecutor Ian Fraser told Justice Douglas Sirrs he will not seek a jail term.

Sirrs said he was troubled by the case.

He said the family and other sect members in the area showed a wilful blindness and an ignorance of medical issues.

"I have little doubt they are caring and responsible parents with their children," he said.

"Calahan was emaciated to the point where he looked like a starving victim from the Holocaust."

Harold Grinde, a supporter of the family, said it was a case of religious discrimination.

## DISCUSSION QUESTIONS

1. The parents in this story each received a three-year suspended sentence for failing to provide the necessities of life. Do think this sentence is justified? Why or why not?

2. Should a person's religious beliefs be controlled by law? If so, what limits should the law specify?

SOURCE: *Edmonton Journal*, Thursday, June 8, 2000, p. A8. Reprinted with permission of the Canadian Press

# What Do Criminologists Do?

A typical dictionary definition of a **criminologist** is "one who studies crime, criminals, and criminal behaviour."[14] People who have graduate degrees in the field of criminology or criminal justice from an accredited university often refer to themselves as criminologists. Some criminologists hold degrees in related fields such as sociology and political science and have specialized in the study and control of crime and deviance. Many criminologists either teach criminology or criminology-related subjects in institutions of higher learning, including universities and community colleges. Many criminology professors are involved in research or writing projects, by which they strive to advance criminological knowledge. Other criminologists are strictly researchers and work for federal agencies such as the Department of Justice, the Solicitor General of Canada, or the Canadian Centre for Justice Statistics.

The results of criminological research in Canada and the United States are generally published in journals such as the *Canadian Journal of Criminology,* (the official publication of the Canadian Criminal Justice Association), the *Canadian Journal of Law and Society,* the *Canadian Journal of Women and the Law, Criminology* (the official publication of the American Society of Criminology), *Theoretical Criminology, Crime and Delinquency, Social Problems,* and *Victimology.*[15] International English-language journals are numerous and include the *Australian and New Zealand Journal of Criminology,* and the *British Journal of Criminology.*

The term *criminologist* may also be applied to persons who have earned undergraduate degrees in the field. These degrees may provide entree into police investigative or support work, probation and parole agencies, court-support activities, and correctional (prison) work. Forensics laboratory technicians, ballistics experts, computer crime investigators, polygraph operators, crime-scene photographers, and prison program directors are examples of the kinds of jobs available to criminologists. Criminologists also work for government agencies interested in the development of effective social policies intended to deter or combat crime.

Private security provides another career track for individuals interested in criminology. The number of personnel employed by private security agencies today is one-third greater than that of public law enforcement agencies, and the gap is widening.[16] Increasing competition for employment means that many upper- and middle-level private managers working for private security firms hold criminology or criminal justice degrees.

A similar trend is emerging in the field of public policing. While most Canadian police services require applicants to have a minimum of grade 12 education, by 1996, 81 percent of police officers in Canada had attained levels of education greater than this minimum. Of these, 35 percent had a community college diploma, while 14 percent had a university degree. The remainder had attended some type of post-secondary institution.[17]

Of course, criminologists have various alternatives. Many with undergraduate degrees in criminology or criminal justice go on to law school. Some teach high school while others become private investigators. Many criminologists provide civic

**Criminologist** one who is trained in the field of criminology; also, one who studies crime, criminals, and criminal behaviour.

organizations (such as victims' assistance and justice advocacy groups) with much needed expertise, a few work for politicians and legislative bodies, and some appear on talk shows to debate the pros and cons of various kinds of social policies designed to "fight" crime. Some criminologists even write books such as this one!

## What Is Criminology?

The attempt to understand crime predates written history. Prehistoric evidence, including skeletal remains showing signs of primitive cranial surgery, seem to indicate that preliterate people explained deviant behaviour in terms of spirit possession. Primitive "surgery" was an attempt to release unwanted spiritual influences. In the thousands of years since, many other theoretical perspectives on crime have been advanced. This book describes various criminological theories and covers some of the more popular ones in detail.

Before beginning any earnest discussion, however, it is necessary to define the term *criminology*. As our earlier discussion of the nature of crime and deviance indicates, criminologists must not only deal with a complex subject matter—consisting of a broad range of illegal behaviours committed by frequently unknown or uncooperative individuals—they must also manage their work under changing conditions mandated by ongoing revisions of the law and fluctuating social policy. All this leads to considerable difficulties in defining the subject matter under study. Nonetheless, definitions of criminology abound.

Edwin Sutherland suggested that criminology consists of three "principal divisions": (1) the sociology of law, (2) scientific analysis of the causes of crime, and (3) crime control.[18] Another well-known criminologist, Clarence Ray Jeffery, similarly sees three components of the field: (1) detection (of the offender), (2) treatment, and (3) explaining crime and criminal behaviour.[19] Criminology can also be defined as "an interdisciplinary study of the various bodies of knowledge, which focuses on the etiology of crime [or the construction of theories to describe, explain or predict criminal behaviour], the behavior of criminals, and the policies and practices of crime control."[20]

For our purposes, we will use a definition that brings together the works of previous writers but that also recognizes the increasingly professional status of the criminological enterprise. Throughout this book, then, we will view **criminology** as an interdisciplinary profession built around the scientific study of crime and criminal behaviour, including their manifestations, causes, legal aspects, and control. As this definition indicates, criminology includes consideration of possible solutions to the problem of crime. Hence, this text will describe treatment strategies and social policy initiatives that have grown out of the existing array of theoretical explanations for crime.

Our definition is in keeping with the work of another outstanding criminologist of the twentieth century, who has written that the purpose of criminology is to offer well-researched and objective answers to four basic questions: (1) "Why do crime rates vary?" (2) "Why do individuals differ as to **criminality**?" (3) "Why is there variation in reactions to crime?" and (4) "What are the possible means of controlling criminality?"[21]

As a field of study, criminology in its present form is primarily a social scientific discipline. Contemporary criminologists generally recognize, however, that their field

**Criminology** an interdisciplinary profession built around the scientific study of crime and criminal behaviour, including their form, causes, legal aspects, and control.

**Criminality** a behavioural predisposition that disproportionately favours criminal activity.

Criminology examines the causes of crime and seeks ways to prevent or control it. Criminal justice examines the criminal justice system, including police, courts, and corrections. How do the two disciplines complement one another? *D. Greco/The Image Works.*

is interdisciplinary; that is, it draws upon other disciplines to provide an integrated approach to understanding the problem of crime in contemporary society and to advance solutions to the problems crime creates. Hence, biology, sociology, political science, psychology, economics, medicine, psychiatry, law, philosophy, and numerous other fields all have something to offer the student of criminology, as do the tools provided by statistics, computer science, and other forms of scientific and data analysis.

It is important, however, to note that although criminology may be interdisciplinary in its approach to the subject matter of crime, few existing explanations for criminal behaviour have been successfully integrated. Just as physicists today are seeking a unified field theory to explain the wide variety of observable forms of matter and energy, criminologists have yet to develop a generally accepted integrated approach to crime and criminal behaviour that can explain the many diverse forms of criminality while also leading to effective social policies in the area of crime control. The attempt to construct criminological theories of relevance is made all the more difficult because, as discussed earlier, the phenomenon under study—crime—is subject to arbitrary and sometimes unpredictable legalistic and definitional changes.

Not only must a successfully integrated criminology bring together the contributions of various theoretical perspectives and disciplines, it must also—if it is to have any relevance—blend the practical requirements of our nation's judicial system with emotional and rational calls for morality and justice. Should capital punishment, for example, be reinstated? If so, on what basis? Is it because it is a type of vengeance, and therefore deserved? Or, can we continue to say that it is unjustified because many sociological studies have shown that it does little to reduce the rate of serious crime such as murder? Just what do we mean by *justice,* and what can criminological studies tell us—if anything—about what is just and what is unjust?

The editors of the relatively new journal, *Theoretical Criminology,*[22] which began publication in 1997, tell us in their inaugural issue that "criminology has always been somewhat of a haphazardly-assembled umbrella-like structure which nevertheless usefully shelters a variety of theoretical interests that are espoused and employed by different disciplinary, methodological and political traditions." In other words, while the field of criminology can benefit from the wide variety of ideas available from a multiplicity of perspectives, all of which seek to understand the phenomenon we call "crime," cross-discipline collaboration can be quite difficult.

As the earlier definition of *criminology* indicates, however, it is more than a field of study or a collection of theories—it is also a profession.[23] Some of the primary purposes of the criminology profession have been identified in the following manner: "Controlling crime through prevention, rehabilitation, and deterrence and ensuring that the criminal justice system reflects the high aspiration we have as a society of 'justice for all,' characterize the principal goals that in my judgment motivate the work of our field."[24]

**Criminal justice** the scientific study of crime, the criminal law, and components of the criminal justice system, including the police, courts, and corrections.

Notably, criminology also contributes to the discipline of **criminal justice,** which emphasizes application of the criminal law and study of the components of the justice system, especially the police, courts, and corrections. As one author stated, "criminology gives prominence to questions about the *causes of criminality,* while the *control of lawbreaking* is at the heart of criminal justice."[25]

## Theoretical Criminology

Theoretical criminology, a subfield of general criminology, is the variety of criminology most often found in community colleges and universities. Theoretical criminology, rather than simply describing crime and its occurrence, posits explanations for criminal behaviour. As Edwin Sutherland stated, "[t]he problem in criminology is to explain the criminality of behavior. ... However, an explanation of criminal behavior should be a specific part of [a] general theory of behavior and its task should be to differentiate criminal from noncriminal behavior."[26]

**Theory** a series of interrelated propositions that attempt to describe, explain, predict, and ultimately to control some class of events. A theory gains explanatory power from inherent logical consistency and is "tested" by how well it describes and predicts reality.

To explain and understand crime, criminologists have developed many theories. A **theory,** at least in its ideal form, is made up of clearly stated propositions that posit relationships, often of a causal sort, between events and things under study. An old Roman theory, for example, proposed that insanity is caused by the influence of the moon, and may even follow its cycles—hence the term *lunacy.*

**General theory** one that attempts to explain all (or at least most) forms of criminal conduct through a single, overarching approach.

Theories attempt to provide us with explanatory power and help us to understand the phenomenon under study. The more applicable a theory is found to be, the more generalizable it is from one specific instance to others—in other words, the more it can be applied to other situations. A **general theory** of crime is one that attempts to explain all (or at least most) forms of criminal conduct through a single, overarching approach. Unfortunately, often "[t]heories in criminology tend to be unclear and lacking in justifiable generality."[27] When we consider the wide range of behaviours regarded as criminal—from murder, through drug use, to white-collar and computer crime—it seems difficult to imagine one theory that can explain them all, or which might even explain the same type of behaviour under varying circumstances. Still, many past theoretical approaches to crime causation were **unicausal** while attempting to be all-inclusive.

**Unicausal** having one cause. Unicausal theories posit only one source for all that they attempt to explain.

That is, the approaches posited a single, identifiable source for all serious deviant and criminal behaviour.

An **integrated theory,** in contrast to a general theory, does not necessarily attempt to explain all criminality but is distinguishable by the fact that it merges (or attempts to merge) concepts drawn from different sources. Put another way, "An integrative criminology … seeks to bring together the diverse bodies of knowledge that represent the full array of disciplines that study crime."[28] Hence, integrated theories provide potentially wider explanatory power than narrower formulations. Recognizing that no one theory can explain all criminal behaviour, it has been noted that, "The basic idea of theoretical integration is straightforward; it concerns the combinations of single theories or elements of those theories into a more comprehensive argument. At the same time, it would be well to note that in practice, integration is a matter of degree: some theorists have combined or integrated more concepts or theoretical elements than have others."[29]

Both theoretical integration and the general applicability of criminological theories to a wide variety of law-violating behaviour are intuitively appealing concepts. Even far more limited attempts at criminological theorizing, however, often face daunting challenges. To date, "criminologists have not managed to articulate a large collection of relatively formalized arguments in a general or integrated form."[30] Hence, although we will use the word *theory* in describing the many explanations for crime covered by this book, it should be recognized that the word is only loosely applicable to some of the perspectives we will discuss.

As we shall learn in Chapter 3, many social scientists insist that to be considered *theories,* explanations must consist of sets of clearly stated, logically interrelated, and measurable propositions. The fact that only a few of the theories described in this book rise above the level of organized conjecture—and those offer only limited generalizability and have rarely been integrated—is one of the greatest failures of criminology today.

**Integrated theory** an explanatory perspective that merges (or attempts to merge) concepts drawn from different sources.

## Theoretical Perspectives in Criminology

What starting point do criminologists use when developing their theories? Does the way in which a criminologist views the social order have any impact on the theory of crime and criminal behaviour he or she posits? There are three generally accepted perspectives within criminology, each of which maintains its own view of what constitutes crime and, by definition, criminal behaviour. Known as the *consensus perspective,* the *pluralistic perspective,* and the *conflict perspective,* each sees the relationship between the law and the social order somewhat differently. A criminologist's choice of perspective can influence his or her approach in explaining the causes of crime and criminal behaviour and, in turn, his or her suggestions for their prevention or control.

### The Consensus Perspective

The **consensus model** of social organization is built around the notion that most members of society agree on what is right and wrong, and that the various elements

**Consensus model** an analytical perspective on social organization holding that most members of society agree as to what is right and what is wrong and that the various elements of society work together in unison toward a common and shared vision of the greater good.

of society—including institutions such as churches, schools, government agencies, and businesses—work together toward a common and shared vision of the greater good. According to Raymond J. Michalowski, whose excellent analytical work is used to describe each of the three major approaches discussed in this section, the consensus perspective is characterized by four principles[31]:

- A belief in the existence of core values. The consensus perspective holds that commonly shared notions of right and wrong characterize the majority of society's members.
- The notion that laws reflect the collective will of the people. Law is seen as the result of a consensus, achieved through legislative action, and represents a kind of social conscience.
- The assumption that the law serves all people equally. From the consensus point of view, the law not only embodies a shared view of justice, but is itself perceived to be just in its application.
- The idea that those who violate the law represent a unique subgroup with some distinguishing features. The consensus approach holds that law violators must somehow be improperly socialized, psychologically defective, or suffer from some other lapse which leaves them unable to participate in what is otherwise widespread agreement on values and behaviour.

The consensus perspective was operative in North American politics and characterized much social scientific thought throughout the early 1900s. It found its greatest champion in Roscoe Pound, former dean of the Harvard School of Law. Pound developed the notion that the law is a tool for engineering society. The law, Pound said, meets the needs of men and women living together in society and can be used to fashion society's characteristics and major features. Pound distilled his ideas into a set of jural postulates. Such postulates, Pound claimed, explain the existence and form of all laws insofar as laws reflect shared needs. Pound's postulates read as follows[32]:

- In civilized society men and women[33] must be able to assume that others will commit no intentional aggressions upon them.
- In civilized society men and women must be able to assume that they may control for beneficial purposes what they have discovered and appropriated to their own use, what they have created by their own labor, and what they have acquired under the existing social and economic order.
- In civilized society men and women must be able to assume that those with whom they deal in the general intercourse of society will act in good faith and hence

   1. Will make good reasonable expectations that their promises or other conduct will reasonably create.
   2. Will carry out their undertakings according to the expectations which the moral sentiment of the community attaches thereto.
   3. Will restore specifically or by equivalent what comes to them by mistake or unanticipated or (via a) not fully intended situation whereby they receive at another's expense what they could not reasonably have expected to receive under the circumstances.

- In civilized society men and women must be able to assume that those who are engaged in some course of conduct will act with due care not to cause an unreasonable risk of injury upon others.
- In civilized society men and women must be able to assume that those who maintain things likely to get out of hand or to escape and do damage will restrain them or keep them within their proper bounds.

## The Pluralistic Perspective

Contrary to the assumptions made by consensus thinkers, however, it has become quite plain to most observers of the contemporary social scene that not everyone agrees on what the law should say. Society today is rife with examples of conflicting values and ideals. Consensus is hard to find. Modern debates centre on issues such as abortion, euthanasia, the death penalty, the purpose of criminal justice agencies in a diverse society, social justice, the rights and responsibilities of minorities and other under-represented groups, women's issues, the proper role of education, economic policy, social welfare, the function of the military in a changing world, environmental concerns, and appropriate uses of high technology. As many contemporary public forums would indicate, there exists within Canada today a great diversity of social groups, each with its own point of view regarding what is right and what is wrong, and each with its own agenda.

Such a situation is described by some writers as pluralistic. A **pluralistic perspective** mirrors the thought that a multiplicity of values and beliefs exists in any complex society and that different social groups will each have their own set of beliefs, interests, and values. A crucial element of this perspective, however, is the assumption that although different viewpoints exist, most individuals agree on the usefulness of law as a formal means of dispute resolution. Hence, from a pluralistic perspective the law, rather than reflecting common values, exists as a peacekeeping tool that allows officials and agencies within the government to settle disputes effectively between individuals and among groups. It also assumes that whatever settlement is reached will be acceptable to all parties because of their agreement on the fundamental role of law in dispute settlement. The basic principles of the pluralist perspective include the following notions[34]:

**Pluralistic perspective** an analytical approach to social organization holding that a multiplicity of values and beliefs exist in any complex society but that most social actors agree on the usefulness of law as a formal means of dispute resolution.

- Society consists of many and diverse social groups. Differences in age, gender, sexual preference, ethnicity, and the like often provide the basis for much naturally occurring diversity.
- Each group has its own characteristic set of values, beliefs, and interests. Variety in gender, sexual orientation, economic status, ethnicity, and other forms of diversity produce interests which may unite like-minded individuals but which may also place them in natural opposition to other social groups.
- A general agreement exists on the usefulness of formalized laws as a mechanism for dispute resolution. People and groups accept the role of law in the settlement of disputes and accord decisions reached within the legal framework at least a modicum of respect.

- The legal system is value neutral. That is, the legal system is itself thought to be free of petty disputes or above the level of general contentiousness which may characterize relationships between groups.
- The legal system is concerned with the best interests of society. Legislators, judges, prosecutors, attorneys, police officers, and correctional officials are assumed to perform idealized functions that are beyond the reach of interest groups. Hence, such official functionaries can be trusted to act in accordance with the greater good, to remain unbiased, and to maintain a value-free system for the enforcement of laws.

According to the pluralistic perspective, conflict is essentially resolved through the peacekeeping activities of unbiased government officials exercising objective legal authority.

## The Conflict Perspective

**Conflict perspective** an analytical perspective on social organization holding that conflict is a fundamental aspect of social life itself and can never be fully resolved.

A third point of view, the **conflict perspective,** maintains that conflict is a fundamental aspect of social life itself that can never be fully resolved. At best, according to this perspective, formal agencies of social control merely coerce the unempowered or the disenfranchised to comply with the rules established by those in power. From the conflict point of view, laws become a tool of the powerful, useful in keeping others from wresting control over important social institutions. Social order, rather than being the result of any consensus or process of dispute resolution, rests upon the exercise of power through law. Those in power must work ceaselessly to remain there, although the structure they impose on society—including patterns of wealth-building that they define as acceptable and circumstances under which they authorize the exercise of legal power and military might—gives them all the advantages they are likely to need. The conflict perspective can be described in terms of the following key elements[35]:

- Society is made up of diverse social groups. As in the pluralistic perspective, diversity is thought to be based on distinctions that people hold to be significant, such as gender, sexual orientation, social class, and the like.
- Each group holds to differing definitions of right and wrong. Moralistic conceptions and behavioural standards vary from group to group.
- Conflict between groups is unavoidable. Conflict is based on differences held to be socially significant (such as ethnicity, gender, and social class) and is unavoidable because groups defined on the basis of these characteristics compete for power, wealth, and other forms of recognition.
- The fundamental nature of group conflict centres on the exercise of political power. Political power is the key to the accumulation of wealth and to other forms of power.
- Law is a tool of power and furthers the interests of those powerful enough to make it. Laws allow those in control to gain what they define (through the law) as legitimate access to scarce resources and to deny (through the law) such access to the politically disenfranchised.
- Those in power are inevitably interested in maintaining their power against those who would usurp it. The powerful strive to keep their power.

# Criminology and Social Policy

Of potentially broader importance than theory testing are **social policies** based on research findings. In a document entitled *Safer Communities* by the Departments of Justice and the Solicitor General of Canada, for example, the role of the mass media in encouraging violence among young people is examined. High profile cases have caused many to blame the media for creating a current culture of violence. The television series *Mighty Morphin' Power Rangers* was dropped from a number of television networks in Canada after a 5-year-old girl in Norway was beaten senseless in 1994 by 3 young boys and left to freeze to death. In 1993 in the United States, a mother claimed that the Music Television (MTV) cartoon *Beavis and Butt-Head* had prompted her 5-year-old son to set a fire that killed his 2-year-old sister.[36] Experts on research into violence on television claim that scenes of violence occur 6 times per hour on average in prime time evening shows, while children's programming averages between 20 and 25 violent scenes per hour.[37]

In September 1995, the Canadian Radio-Television and Telecommunications Commission (CRTC) opened public hearings to tackle the issue of violence on television. The CRTC-approved guidelines that emerged forbid the broadcasting of shows with violence that is gratuitous or made to look glamorous and stipulated that scenes of violence intended for adult audiences cannot be telecast between 6 A.M. and 9 P.M.[38]

The creation of the **V-chip** by Canadian electrical engineering professor Tim Collins allows parents to block certain television programs or scenes. Canada is considering legislation that would require all new television sets to have V-chips built in. The United States enacted similar legislation in 1996.[39]

Copycat violence has also been attributed to films. Touchstone Pictures, for example, reedited the movie *The Program,* cutting scenes in which drunken football players test their nerve by lying end to end in the middle of a highway. Several young men who apparently copied the stunt were either killed or critically injured. Commenting on the incidents, a Touchstone spokesperson said, "[w]hile the scene in the movie in no way advocates this irresponsible activity, it is impossible for us to ignore that someone may have recklessly chosen to imitate it. ..."[40] The *Safer Communities* document bemoans the fact that television doesn't do more to influence public opinion in positive ways. "This medium has the most powerful ability to shape our perceptions," it states. "It can educate its audience, combat stereotypes, provide models of pro-social behaviour and attitudes. But for the most part television, and other media too, have not picked up the challenge."[41]

Professional criminologists are themselves acutely aware of the need to link sound social policy to the objective findings of well-conducted criminological research. At a recent meeting of North American criminologists, the need to forge just such a link was emphasized. At the meeting, criminologists were told that they are crucial to "the generation of knowledge that is useful in dealing with crime and the operation of the criminal justice system, and then helping public officials to use that knowledge intelligently and effectively. ... [S]o little is known about the causes of crime and about the effects of criminal justice policy on crime that new insights about the criminal justice system can often be extremely revealing and can eventually change the way people think about the crime problem or about the criminal justice system."[42]

**Social policies** government initiatives, programs, and plans intended to address problems in society. The National Strategy on Community Safety and Crime Prevention, for example, is a kind of generic (large-scale) social policy—one consisting of many smaller programs.

**V-chip** a device that enables viewers to program their televisions to block out content with a common rating. It is intended for use against violent or sexually explicit programming.

## Social Policy and the Fear of Crime

Fear of crime remains pervasive in contemporary Canada. A 1997 national Angus Reid/CTV News poll found that most Canadians believe that crime has been on the increase in their communities.[43] Of those polled, 59 percent perceived an increase in crime over the past 5 years; this was down slightly from the 68 percent in 1994 and consistent with the public's perception in 1990 (57%). This concern was especially marked in western Canada, where 30 percent of British Columbians saw a "great increase" in crime. The same poll found that 21 percent of Canadians surveyed feared being a victim of crime in their own community, with 5 percent harbouring a "great deal" of fear and 16 percent a "fair amount" of fear. When asked to name the most important problems in their community, 22 percent of the respondents named crime and related issues as "top of mind." This figure ranged from 10 percent in Atlantic Canada and Quebec to 42 percent in British Columbia.

The poll also examined public confidence in the Canadian justice system, finding that 86 percent of respondents felt that they are at least "somewhat confident" in their local police (37% "very confident"). Canadians were less pleased with the courts—52 percent expressed "overall confidence" compared to 47 percent who were "not very confident" or "not at all confident" in the operation of the courts. A modest majority surveyed expressed a lack of faith in the prison system (54% "not very/not at all confident"), while 72 percent expressed "little/no confidence" in the parole system.

Fear of crime is not necessarily related to the actual incidence of crime, however, as crime rates (discussed in detail in Chapter 2) have actually declined in recent years. Even if fear of crime has reached "unreasonable" levels when objectively compared with the actual incidence of criminal activity, however, fear remains an important determinant of public policy. Hence, government agendas promising to lower crime rates, and that call for changes in the conditions that produce crime, can be quite successful politically for those who promote them in an environment where fear of crime is high.[44]

According to pollsters, fear of crime is a consistent concern among Canadians. Given recent statistics showing falling crime rates, is such fear realistic? *H. Darr Beisner/USA Today.*

# Justice for the People, By the People

Cornwall citizens thought too many young offenders were slipping through the cracks. so they took matters into their own hands.

In 1993, the people in this scrappy blue-collar city made a pact with themselves: We will punish the minor crimes of our young people ourselves—we are, henceforth, the jury.

For six years now, average citizens—real estate agents, gas-bar owners, hospital administrators, a newspaper editor—have sat on a panel that hands out sentences under the regular court system's alternative measures program.

In practice, it means young offenders can avoid a criminal record if they agree to a set of conditions imposed, within guidelines, by one of their fellow citizens.

As Wayne Kyte likes to put it, there is no "they" in this justice system.

"What this program has really done is say that the 'they' are us," says Mr. Kyte, executive director of Laurencrest, a 16-bed young offender residence that administers the program for the three surrounding counties.

The Ontario government is so impressed that yesterday it announced the creation of five other youth justice committees, including one in Ottawa, modelled after the one in Cornwall.

Mr. Kyte said one of the main reasons the Cornwall committee was created was because of the cigarette-smuggling crisis in the early 1990s. He said wayward teenagers were carrying contraband across the American border, getting caught and ending up with absolute discharges or suspended sentences.

As more youths appeared on the docket, there was a widely held perception, Mr. Kyte says, that the Young Offenders Act was simply not working. "A lot of kids were embracing the idea that crime pays."

The idea emerged that justice would be better served if it could be seen to be done.

Bonnie Fitzpatrick, a mother of four, is a ReMax real estate agent. She is one of 12 people on a rotating panel of citizens who decide, with the help of a case worker, what kind of penalty a young offender should get.

The cases are rounded up so that about a dozen are dealt with one day a month. There can be from one to four panel members present for the sentencing.

Typically, Ms. Fitzpatrick would meet with the youth, his or her parents and the caseworker, usually within a few weeks of the offence. She would be permitted to ask questions to ascertain the offender's level of contrition and the appropriate payback.

"If he stands there and has a 'you can't touch me' attitude, then you have to do something stronger," says Ms. Fitzpatrick.

The alternative measures program also avoids repeated court trips. The program is designed to have the penalty discussed and handed down in one visit. There is no avenue of appeal.

"I think (offenders) feel better" after talking about their act and freely accepting a penalty, says Ms. Fitzpatrick. "I've had parents come back to me, four, five, six months later, and say, "Thank you.""

The legal powers of committee members are limited, though the government has announced it is giving the committees a couple of new options, such as imposing curfews, suspending a driver's licence and orders forbidding association with certain people.

"It's been fantastic," says Mr. Kyte. "It's worked out beyond our wildest dreams." The statistics bear him out.

▶

Of 358 offenders who came before the citizens' committee since 1993, only six have needed to repeat the program and 36, or 10 percent, eventually had another conviction.

The bulk of the cases (245) involved theft, while 16 involved trespassing and 15 were redirected mischief charges.

Offenders wrote apologies in 310 of the cases; did community service work in 168; and 143 were ordered to write essays.

Christine Lapensée owns a MacEwen Petroleum outlet in Cornwall. She knows first-hand the impact of shoplifting on a small business.

If shopkeepers are willing—but they usually aren't—the offender can be sent back to do work in the store, be made to write an essay on the impacts of theft or asked to make financial restitution.

Christine Lapensée says young offenders "get lost in the system."
*Ottawa Citizen/Kelly Egan*

"It deals with the matter almost immediately," says Ms. Lapensée. "[The offender] has to deal with it right away."

In the regular court system, she points out, the offender gets lost in a lengthy round of remands, pre-trial hearings and legal manoeuvering. "They get lost in the system."

Both Ms. Lapensée and Ms. Fitzpatrick say it's been valuable to hear from young people themselves why and how they got into trouble.

The new pilot committees will handle such crimes as theft, false pretences, fraud, possession of stolen property and causing a disturbance. They will not deal with break-and-enters, joy-riding, weapons offences or assaults.

The Crown attorneys will still have control over which route an offender will take, although police will now be given some discretion.

Offenders choosing the alternative measures route must, in writing, accept responsibility for their actions.

Should they refuse to perform their community service or opt out at any stage, they are to be returned to the regular court system.

The Ottawa committee is to be operating in the fall.

Mr. Kyte says it's easy to find committee members, often working through service clubs. They are given a training session. If anything, he says the problem is making sure the members are busy enough, since they only meet once a month.

## DISCUSSION QUESTIONS

1. Do you believe that citizens should take an active role in sentencing offenders through programs like the one described in this article? Why or why not?
2. What kinds of citizen involvement in the youth justice system can you envision that are not discussed in this article?
3. What kinds of government policies might further the role of citizen involvement in dealing with youth crime? How might such policies be crafted so as to ensure meaningful cooperation between citizen volunteers and formal agencies of justice?

SOURCE: Kelly Egan, "Justice for the People, by the People," *Ottawa Citizen*, February 5, 1999, p. C3. Reprinted with permission.

# The Theme of This Book

This book builds on a social policy theme by contrasting two popular perspectives (see Figure 1.1). One point of view, termed the **social problems perspective**, holds that crime is a manifestation of underlying social problems such as poverty, discrimination, the breakdown of traditional social institutions, the poor quality of formal education available to some, pervasive family violence experienced during the formative years, and inadequate socialization practices that leave young people without the fundamental values necessary to contribute meaningfully to the society in which they live. Advocates of the social problems perspective advance solutions based on what is, in effect, a public health model which says that crime needs to be addressed much like a public health concern.

Proponents of this perspective typically foresee solutions to the crime problem as coming in the form of large-scale government expenditures in support of social programs designed to address the issues that lie at the root of crime. They often look to legislatively enhanced social, educational, occupational, and other opportunities as offering programmatic solutions to ameliorate most causes of crime. The social problems approach to crime is characteristic of what social scientists term a *macro* approach. Instances of individual behaviour (crimes) are portrayed as arising out of widespread and contributory social conditions that enmesh unwitting individuals in a causal nexus of uncontrollable social forces.

**Social problems perspective** the belief that crime is a manifestation of underlying social problems such as poverty, discrimination, pervasive family violence, inadequate socialization practices, and the breakdown of traditional social institutions.

## Figure 1.1

### *The Theme of this Book*
*Social Problems versus Social Responsibility*

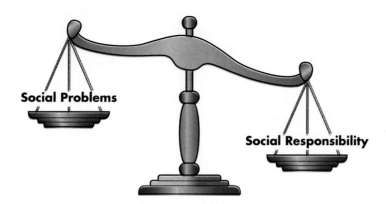

At the core of today's thinking about crime exists a crucial distinction between those who believe that *crime is a matter of individual responsibility* (the social responsibility perspective), and those who emphasize that *crime is a manifestation of underlying social problems* beyond the control of individuals (the social problems viewpoint).

In 1993, the Parliamentary Standing Committee on Justice and the Solicitor General tabled a report entitled *Crime Prevention in Canada: Towards a National Strategy.* The report recommended the implementation of a "National Strategy on Community Safety and Crime Prevention" focused on developing new plans to look at the causes of crime and to develop partnerships with communities across the country to carry out crime prevention activities. Phase I of the National Strategy (1994–1997) saw the creation of the National Crime Prevention Council, whose mandate was the promotion of crime prevention through social development, with particular emphasis on early prevention programs targeting children and youth. The Council identified a number of factors that place children and youth at risk of engaging in criminal behaviour. These included child poverty, inadequate living conditions, inconsistent and uncaring parenting, childhood traumas such as physical and sexual abuse, family breakdown, racism and other forms of discrimination, difficulties in school, delinquent friends, and living in situations where there is alcohol, drug, and other kinds of substance abuse. Phase II (since 1997) is building on the work done by the Council and focuses on helping communities develop programs and partnerships to reduce crime and victimization. In addition to focusing on children and youth, this phase places priority on Aboriginal people and on women's personal safety.[45] An overview of the National Strategy on Community Safety and Crime Prevention is presented on page 26, and a detailed examination can be found in Chapter 11.

A contrasting perspective lays the cause of crime squarely at the feet of individual perpetrators. This point of view holds that individuals are fundamentally responsible for their own behaviour and maintains that they choose crime over other, more law-abiding courses of action. Perpetrators may choose crime, advocates of this perspective say, because it is exciting, it offers illicit pleasures and the companionship of like-minded thrill seekers, or because it is simply less demanding than conformity. This viewpoint, which we shall call the **social responsibility perspective,** tends to become increasingly popular in times when the fear of crime rises. Advocates of the social responsibility perspective, with their emphasis on individual choice, tend to believe that social programs do little to solve the problem of crime because, they say, a certain number of crime-prone individuals, for a variety of personalized reasons, will always make irresponsible choices. Hence, advocates of the social responsibility approach suggest crime reduction strategies based on firm punishments, imprisonment, individualized rehabilitation, increased security, and a wider use of police powers. The social responsibility perspective characteristically emphasizes a form of *micro* analysis that tends to focus on individual offenders and their unique biology, psychology, background, and immediate life experiences. A note about wording is in order: although this perspective might also be termed the *individual responsibility perspective,* because it stresses individual responsibility above all else, we've chosen to use the term *social responsibility perspective* instead, as it holds that individuals must be ultimately responsible to the social group of which they are a part, and that they should be held accountable by group standards if they are not. In short, this perspective is one characterized by societal demands for the exercise of individual responsibility.

**Social responsibility
perspective** the belief
that individuals are
fundamentally
responsible for their own
behaviour and that they
choose crime over other,
more law-abiding
courses of action.

The contrast between the social problems and social responsibility perspectives came to the fore in the 1997 trial of Jesse Timmendequas, a previously convicted sex offender and admitted killer of 7-year-old Megan Kanka.[46] The defence for Timmendequas centred on his claims of repeated sexual abuse by his father as he was growing up—an experience his attorneys said left him helplessly attracted sexually to young children. The jury hearing the case rejected Timmendequas' abuse defence, found him guilty of killing Kanka, and recommended that he be sentenced to die. In summing up the feelings of many of those present, prosecutor Kathryn Flicker noted that "Timmendequas' childhood was not a bed of roses." But, she asked, "where does individual responsibility fit into the whole scheme? He was responsible as an adult, as we all are."[47]

In Canada, the social problems perspective has been in the forefront of national thinking. The 1997 Angus Reid/CTV News poll cited earlier indicates that Canadians attach the greatest weight to the "social development" approach for crime prevention. A total of 84 percent of those polled indicated that a "much higher/somewhat higher priority" should be given to social development as a means of crime prevention. Forty-one percent placed a "much higher priority" on enhanced law and order efforts, while thirty-six percent wanted a "much higher priority" given to community crime prevention programs.[48]

There has been some emphasis placed on the social responsibility perspective in Canada as well. Our American neighbours to the south have been waging a "war on crime" since 1994, with the introduction of the Violent Crime Control and Law Enforcement Act. It expanded the number of capital crimes under federal law from a handful of offences to fifty-two.[49] The law also made $8.8 billion (U.S.) available to municipalities to put 100 000 new police officers on the streets, and allocated $7.9 billion (U.S.) for states to build and operate prisons and incarceration alternatives such as boot camps. A subchapter of the 1994 Violent Crime Control Act created a federal "Three Strikes and You're Out" law, mandating life imprisonment for criminals convicted of three violent federal felonies or drug offences. Similarly, the law increased or created new penalties for over 70 federal criminal offences, primarily covering violent crimes, drug trafficking, and gun crimes.

Some segments of Canadian society have echoed the American call for a get-tough approach to crime. Pressure on legislators has resulted in proceeds-of-crime legislation that increases police authority to seize goods suspected of being purchased with the proceeds of crime, firearms legislation that attempts to restrict the circulation of illegal firearms and their use in the commission of crimes, and proposed amendments to the Young Offenders Act that would see tougher sanctions for youth who break the law (see Chapter 11 for an in-depth look at some of this legislation). Individual provinces have "gotten tough" on crime and criminals. Alberta and Ontario, for example, have opened U.S.-model boot camps for young offenders, and Ontario recently proposed parental-responsibility legislation that would hold parents of children under 18 financially responsible for property damage committed by their children.

## *theory versus reality* — *Crime Prevention through Social Development*

This book builds upon a theme that contrasts the social problems perspective on crime with another approach called "social responsibility." An example of the social problems perspective is seen in the federal government's National Strategy on Community Safety and Crime Prevention. Introduced in 1994, the federal government now invests $32 million annually in this initiative. A summary of the National Strategy follows.

### THE NATIONAL STRATEGY ON COMMUNITY SAFETY AND CRIME PREVENTION

#### Phase I

The National Strategy on Community Safety and Crime Prevention is designed to help Canadians create safer communities, by supporting community-based crime prevention efforts, enhancing communities' knowledge and experience with respect to crime prevention and fostering partnerships and collaboration.

The Government of Canada launched Phase I of the National Strategy in 1994. This phase provided a framework for federal efforts to support community safety and crime prevention; encouraged federal, provincial and territorial cooperation; and emphasized the mobilization of Canadians to take action at the community level to prevent crime. As part of Phase I, the federal government created the National Crime Prevention Council (1994–1997), made up of 25 individuals—child development experts, community advocates, academics, social workers, lawyers, police officers, doctors and business people—who volunteered their time to develop a plan to deal with the underlying causes of crime.

Promoting crime prevention through social development, the former Council focused on children and youth and developed models for dealing with the early prevention of criminal behaviour. These models showed that children need adequate care throughout their early lives, and this extends to what happens before they are born. Above all else, children need good parenting. At the same time, there is a need to eliminate, to the extent possible, known risk factors in children's lives, such as abuse, poverty, and drug and alcohol abuse. We know that children grow up to be good citizens when they have had the benefit of developing in a nurturing family and community environment.

#### Phase II

Building on the excellent work of the former Council, Phase II of the National Strategy aims to increase individual and community safety by equipping Canadians with the knowledge, skills and resources they need to advance crime prevention efforts in their communities. The National Strategy adopts a social development approach, placing a particular emphasis on children, youth, women and Aboriginal peoples.

▶

The objectives of the National Strategy are:

- to promote the integrated action of key governmental and non-governmental partners to reduce crime and victimization;
- to assist communities in developing and implementing community-based solutions to problems that contribute to crime and victimization, particularly as they affect children, youth, women and Aboriginal people; and
- to increase public awareness of and support for effective approaches to crime prevention.

Crime prevention through social development (CPSD) is a long-term, proactive approach. It is directed at removing those personal, social and economic factors that lead some individuals to engage in criminal acts or to become victims of crime. This approach aims at strengthening the quality of life for individuals, families and communities. CPSD is intended to increase positive attitudes or behaviours in individuals by influencing their experiences in areas such as family life, education, employment, housing or recreation.

The National Strategy is investing in projects that address risk factors in people's lives, such as abuse, violence, poor parenting, and drug and alcohol abuse.

## The Government of Canada believes that action must take place at the community level.

It is the people who live, work and play in a community who understand their area's resources, problems, unique needs and capacities.

With an investment of $32 million annually, the National Strategy enables the Government of Canada to help communities develop programs and partnerships that will prevent crime in the first place.

The National Strategy priority groups are:

### Children and Youth

The best way to deal with the underlying causes of crime and victimization is to provide children, youth and their families with targeted support and resources. It is recognized that community safety and positive social development of children and youth are linked.

### Aboriginal People

Many Aboriginal communities experience disproportionately high rates of violence, victimization and poverty due partially to geographical and cultural isolation. Funding under the National Strategy will complement *Gathering Strength: Canada's Aboriginal Action Plan*, contributing to improvements in health and public safety, and investment in people and economic development.

### Women's Personal Security

Studies have reported that one-half of Canadian women have experienced at least one incident of violence since the age of 16. Fear of crime is a particularly important issue for women because it restricts their freedom to participate fully in society. Initiatives are required to improve women's personal security and to reduce victimization and fear of crime.

▶

**OTHER FEDERAL PROGRAMS CONTRIBUTING TO
CRIME PREVENTION**

Phase II of the National Strategy on Community Safety and Crime Prevention is complemented by other government initiatives, especially those aimed at children and youth. These include:

- Youth Justice Renewal Strategy
- National Children's Agenda
- Community Action Plan for Children
- Canada Prenatal Nutrition Program
- Youth Employment Strategy
- Millennium Scholarship Fund
- Federal Action Plan on Gender Equality
- Family Violence Initiative
- *Gathering Strength: Canada's Aboriginal Action Plan*—the federal government's response to the final report of the Royal Commission on Aboriginal Peoples
- Aboriginal Justice Initiative
- First Nations Policing Policy
- Aboriginal Head Start

### DISCUSSION QUESTIONS

1. What are the major differences between the social problems and the social responsibility perspectives on crime?
2. Which perspective do you find personally most appealing? Why?
3. Which perspective is closest to the social development model of crime prevention discussed here?
4. Do you believe that the social development model is applicable to the crime problem? Can crime be effectively prevented or reduced using this approach? Why or why not?

SOURCE: National Crime Prevention Centre Web site, www.crime-prevention.org. Reprinted with permission of the National Crime Prevention Centre.

# The Social Context of Crime

Crime does not occur in a vacuum. Every crime has a quasi-unique set of causes, consequences, and participants. Crime affects some people more than others, having a special impact on those who are direct participants in the act itself—offenders, victims, police officers, bystanders, and so on. Crime, in general, provokes reactions from the individuals it victimizes, from concerned groups of citizens, from the criminal justice system, and sometimes from society as a whole, which manifests its concerns through the creation of social policy. Reactions to crime, from the everyday to the precedent-setting, may colour the course of future criminal events.[50]

In this book, we shall attempt to identify and examine some of the many social, psychological, economic, biological, and other causes of crime while simultaneously expounding on the many differing perspectives that have been advanced to explain both crime and criminality. An example of differing perspectives can be found in an upcoming box in this chapter entitled, "The Murder of John Lennon." The box provides insight into the motivation of Mark David Chapman (Lennon's killer) and shows that the assumptions we, as outsiders to the event itself, make about the genesis of criminal purpose are not always correct. As the box reveals, popular conceptions of criminal motivation are typically shaped by media portrayals of offender motivation, which often fail to take into consideration the felt experiences of the law violator. By identifying and studying this diversity of perspectives on criminality, we will discover the characteristic disjuncture among victims, offenders, the justice system, and society as to the significance each assigns to the behaviour in question—and, often, to its motivation. It will not be unusual to find, for example, that sociological or psychological initiatives assigned to offenders by theorists and others are not identified with by the offenders.

Another example of misattribution can be seen in the case of Damian Williams, the African-American sentenced in December 1993 to 10 years in prison for beating Caucasian truck driver Reginald Denny during the Los Angeles riots. Most reporters and many attorneys assumed that Williams was motivated during the beating by his knowledge of verdicts of innocence that had been returned earlier that same day in the state trial of California police officers accused of beating African-American motorist Rodney King—an incident whose capture on videotape galvanized the United States and Canada. An infuriated Williams, the media supposed (and reported), attacked Denny in response to frustrations he felt at a justice system that seemed to protect Caucasians at the expense of African-Americans. Williams, however, told a reporter at his sentencing that he knew nothing about the verdicts and was just caught up in the riots. "Maybe other people knew about [the King verdict], but I wasn't aware of it until later … I was just caught up in the rapture," Williams said.[51]

## *theory* versus *reality* — *The Murder of John Lennon*

At 10:50 P.M. on December 8, 1980, Mark David Chapman, 25, killed famous musician and former Beatle John Lennon. Lennon, who was returning home from a recording session with his wife, Yoko Ono, died in a hail of bullets fired from Chapman's .38-caliber pistol. As a musical luminary, John Lennon was well known to the world. Even his private life—from his residence in the exclusive Dakota Apartments in New York City to his dietary preferences and investment portfolios—was the subject of popular news stories and media exposés.

Following Lennon's death, the public generally assumed that Chapman had chosen his murderous course of action due to innate, albeit perverted, needs fed by a twisted rationale—specifically, to become famous by killing a celebrity. In similar assassination attempts involving Gerald Ford, Ronald Reagan, and others, the media has assumed much the same type of motivation. News stories have communicated to the public the image of would-be assassins sparked by the desire to make headlines and see their names become household words. To assign such motivation to the killers of famous

▶

people is understandable from the media perspective. Many of the people encountered by newscasters and writers in daily work have an obvious interest in seeing their names in print. Constant experiences with such people do much to convince byline authors and narrators that the drive for glory is a major motivator of human behaviour.

Such "pop psychology," however, probably does not provide an accurate assessment of the motivation of most assassins. We know from recent conversations with Chapman that he, at least, was driven by a different mindset. In an interview 10 years after the killing (the first one he gave since the shooting), Chapman related a story of twisted emotions and evil whisperings inside his own head. Just before the shooting, the unemployed Chapman, living in Hawaii, had gotten married. Faced with a difficult financial situation and rising debts, he became enraged by what he perceived as Lennon's "phoniness." Lennon, he reasoned, had become rich singing about the virtues of the common person, yet Lennon himself lived in luxury made possible by wealth far beyond the reach of Chapman and others like him. According to Chapman, "He [Lennon] had told us to imagine. . . . He had told us not to be greedy. And I had believed!" In effect, Chapman shifted responsibility for his own failure onto Lennon. For that, he reasoned, Lennon must pay. In preparation for the killing, Chapman would record his own voice over Lennon's songs, screaming such things as, "John Lennon must die! John Lennon is a phony." Once a born-again Christian, Chapman turned to Satanism and prayed for demons to enter his body so that he could have the strength to carry out the mission he had set for himself.

Today, says Chapman, he has changed. Much of his time behind bars is spent writing religious tracts and other stories, with inspiration drawn from verses Lennon made famous. Chapman became eligible for parole in the year 2000, but his request to be released was turned down.

## DISCUSSION QUESTIONS

1. Why did Chapman kill Lennon? Will we ever be sure of his true motivation? How can we be certain we have uncovered it?
2. Was Chapman insane at the time of the killing? What does *insanity* mean in this context? How can it be determined?
3. Should Chapman be released from custody? Why or why not?

SOURCE: Jack Jones, "Decade Later, Killer Prays to be Forgiven," *USA Today,* December 3, 1990, p. 1A.

## Making Sense of Crime: The Causes and Consequences of the Criminal Event

This book is built around the fact that criminal activity is diversely created and variously interpreted. In other words, *crime, like other social events and experiences, is fundamentally a social construction.*[52] To say that crime is a social construction is not to lessen the impact of the victimization experiences which all too many people undergo in our society every day. Nor does such a statement trivialize the significance of crime prevention efforts or the activities of members of the criminal justice system. Likewise, it does not underplay the costs of crime to individual victims and to society as a whole. It does, however, recognize that although a given instance of criminal behaviour may have many causes, it also carries with it many different kinds of meaning—at least one for offenders, another (generally quite different meaning, of course) for victims, and still another for agents of the criminal justice system. Similarly, a plethora of social interest groups, from victims' advocates, through prisoner "rights" and gun control organizations, all interpret the significance of lawbreaking behaviour from unique points of view—and each arrives at different conclusions as to what should be done about the so-called crime problem.

For these reasons, we have chosen to apply the concept of **social relativity** to the study of criminality.[53] Social relativity refers to the fact that social events are differently interpreted according to the cultural experiences and personal interests of the initiator, the observer, or the recipient of that behaviour. Hence, as a social phenomenon, crime means different things to the offender, to the criminologist who studies it, to the police officer who investigates it, and to the victim who experiences it firsthand.

Figure 1.2 (page 32) illustrates the causes and consequences of crime in rudimentary diagrammatic form. The figure consists of a foreground, describing those features that immediately determine the nature of the criminal event (including responses to the event as it is transpiring), and a background, in which generic contributions to crime can be seen with interpretations of the event after it has taken place. We call the background causes of crime "contributions" and use the word "inputs" to signify the more immediate propensities and predispositions of the actors involved in the situation. Inputs also include the physical features of the setting in which a specific crime takes place. Both background contributions and immediate inputs contribute to and shape the criminal event. The more or less immediate results or consequences of crime are termed "outputs," while the term "interpretations" appears in the diagram to indicate that any crime has a lasting impact both on surviving participants and on society.

As Figure 1.2 shows, the criminal event is ultimately a result of the coming together of inputs provided by the offender, the victim, society, and the justice system.

Offenders bring with them certain background features, such as personal life experiences, a peculiar biology (insofar as they are unique organisms), a distinct personality, personal values and beliefs, and various kinds of skills and knowledge (some of which may be useful in the commission of crime). Background contributions to crime can be vitally important. Recent research, for example, tends to cement the existence of a link between child-rearing practices and criminality in later life. Joan McCord,[54] reporting on a 30-year study of family relationships and crime, found that self-confident, nonpunitive, and affectionate mothers tend to insulate their male children from delinquency and, consequently, later criminal activity. Difficulties associated with the birthing process have also been linked to crime in adulthood.[55] Birth trauma and negative familial relationships are but two of the literally thousands of different kinds of experiences individuals may have. Whether individuals who undergo trauma at birth and are deprived of positive maternal experiences will turn to crime depends on many other things, including their own mixture of other experiences and characteristics, the appearance of a suitable victim, failure of the justice system to prevent crime, and the evolution of a social environment in which criminal behaviour is somehow encouraged or valued.

Immediate inputs are contributed to the criminal event by each of the parties identified in Figure 1.2. Foreground contributions by the offender may consist of a particular motivation, a specific intent (in many cases), or a drug-induced state of mind.

**Social relativity** the notion that social events are differently interpreted according to the cultural experiences and personal interests of the initiator, the observer, or the recipient of that behaviour.

Figure 1.2

## The Causes and Consequences of Crime.

Some crimes are especially difficult to understand, no matter how they are viewed. In 1995, for example, the town of Union, South Carolina, was devastated by the trial of Susan Smith. Smith, who originally claimed a carjacker had forced her from her car and driven off with her two young sons still in the vehicle, confessed to the murders of both Alex, 1, and Michael, 3. Smith admitted she drove the car, with her sons still strapped into child safety seats, off a pier and into a nearby lake. An exhaustive 10-day nationwide search for the boys had failed to turn up any significant leads, and the case might have gone unsolved until investigators discovered a letter from Smith's lover saying that he felt unable to accept both her and the children. An autopsy revealed that the children were still alive as the car went into the lake, but that both drowned as the car flipped onto its roof and sunk.

**Criminal justice system**
the various agencies of justice, especially police, courts, and corrections, whose goal it is to apprehend, convict, sanction, and rehabilitate law violators.

Like the offender, the **criminal justice system** also contributes to the criminal event, albeit unwillingly, through its failure to (1) prevent criminal activity, (2) adequately identify specific offenders prior to their involvement in crime, and (3) prevent the early release of convicted criminals who later become repeat offenders. Such background contributions can be seen in prisons (a central component of the justice system) that serve as "schools for crime," fostering anger against society and building a propensity for continued criminality in inmates who have been "turned out." Similarly, the failure of system-sponsored crime prevention programs—ranging from the patrol activities of local police departments to educational and diversionary programs intended to redirect budding offenders—helps to set the stage for the criminal event.

Some crimes are especially difficult to understand. Susan Smith, of Union, South Carolina, confessed to drowning her two young sons, Alex, 1, and Michael, 3, in 1994. The boys are shown in happier times in the photo above. *Spartan Herald Journal/Sygma and American Fast Photo/SABA Press Photos, Inc.*

On the other hand, proper system response may reduce crime. A recent study found that police response (especially arrest) could, under certain demographic conditions, dramatically reduce the incidence of criminal behaviour.[56] Additionally, the study found that arrest "constitutes communication to criminals in general...," further supporting the notion that inputs provided by the justice system have the power to either enhance or reduce the likelihood of criminal occurrences. Immediate inputs provided by the justice system typically consist of features of the situation such as the presence or absence of police officers, the ready availability (or lack thereof) of official assistance, the willingness of police officers to intervene in pre-crime situations, and the response time required for officers to arrive at a crime scene.

Few crimes can occur without a victim. Sometimes the victim is a passive participant in the crime, for example, an innocent person killed by an impaired driver. In such cases, the victim is simply in the wrong place at the wrong time. Even then, however, merely by being present the victim contributes his or her person to the event, thereby increasing the severity of the incident (i.e., the impaired driver who injures no one may still be breaking the law but is committing a far less serious crime than if somebody is killed). Sometimes, however, victims more actively contribute to their own victimization through the appearance of defencelessness (perhaps because of old age, drunkenness, or disability), by failing to take appropriate defensive measures (leaving doors unlocked or forgetting to remove keys from a car's ignition), through an unwise display of wealth (flashing large-denomination bills in a public place), or simply by making other unwise choices (walking down a dark alley in a dangerous section of the city at 2 or 3 A.M., for example). In a recent study of Canadian victimization, Leslie W. Kennedy and David R. Forde found that violent personal victimization "... is contingent on the exposure that comes from following certain lifestyles."[57] This was especially true, they found, "for certain demographic groups, particularly young males." See Chapter 8 for a further discussion on victims of crime.

Although lifestyles may provide the background that fosters victimization, a more active form of victimization characterizes "victims" who initiate criminal activity—such as the barroom brawler who picks a fight but ends up on the receiving end of the ensuing physical violence. Victim-precipitated offences are those that involve active victim participation in the initial stages of a criminal event and that take place when the soon-to-be victim instigates the chain of events that ultimately results in the victimization.

Finally, the general public (termed *society* in Figure 1.2) contributes to the criminal event both formally and informally. Society's formal contributions sometimes take the form of legislation, whereby crime itself is defined. Hence, as we shall discuss in considerable detail in Chapter 11, society structures the criminal event in a most fundamental way by delineating (through legislation and statute) what forms of activity are to be thought of as criminal.

Society's less formal contributions to crime arise out of generic social practices and conditions such as poverty, poor and informal education, various forms of discrimination by which pathways to success are blocked, and the **socialization** process. The process of socialization has an especially important impact on crime causation because it provides the interpretative foundation used to define and understand the significance of particular situations in which we find ourselves, and it is upon those interpretations that we may (or may not) decide to act. Date rape, for example, can occur when a man concludes that his date "owes" him something for the money he has spent on her. That feeling, however inappropriate from the point of view of the victim and the justice system, probably has its roots in early learned experiences—including values communicated from television, the movies, and popular music—about gender-related roles under such circumstances. In other words, society, through the divergent values and expectations it places upon people, property, and behaviour under particular conditions, may provide the motivational basis for many offences.

The contributions society makes to the backgrounds of both offender and victim (and to the structure of the justice system), and the influences each in turn have upon the general social order, provide for a kind of "feedback loop" in our vision of crime (the loop is not shown in Figure 1.2 for fear of unnecessarily complicating it). Through socialization, for example, individuals learn about the dangers of criminal victimization; but when victimization occurs and is publicized, it reinforces the socialization process, leading to an increased wariness of others, and so on. An example can be seen in the fact that children throughout Canada are routinely taught to avoid strangers and to be suspicious of people they do not know. A few decades ago, avoiding strangers was not ordinarily communicated to children, but entered cultural awareness following a number of horrendous and well-publicized crimes involving child victims. It is now a shared part of the socialization process experienced by countless Canadian children every day.

The contributions made by society to crime are complex and far reaching. Some say that the content of the mass media (television, newspapers, popular music, etc.) can lead to crime by exposing young people to inappropriate role models and to the kinds of activity—violence and unbridled sexuality, for example—that encourage criminality.

Society's foreground contributions to crime largely emanate from the distribution of resources and the accessibility of services, which are often the direct result of economic conditions. A study of the availability of medical resources (especially quality hospital emergency services)[58] found that serious assaults may "become" homicides when such resources are lacking but that homicides can be prevented through the effective utilization of capable medical technology. Hence, societal decisions leading to the distribution and placement of advanced medical support equipment and personnel can effectively lower homicide rates in selected geographic areas. Of course, homicide rates will be higher in areas where such equipment is not readily available. According to the study, "The causes of homicide transcend the mere social world of the combatants."[59]

**Socialization** the lifelong process of social experience whereby individuals acquire the cultural patterns of their society.

The moments immediately preceding any crime are rife with possibilities. When all the inputs brought to the situation by all those present coalesce into activity that violates the criminal law, a crime occurs. Together, the elements, experiences, and propensities brought to the situation by the offender and the victim, and those that are contributed to the pending event by society and the justice system, precipitate and decide the nature, course, and eventual outcome of the criminal event. It is important to note that some of the inputs brought to the situation may be inhibiting; that is, they may tend to reduce the likelihood or severity of criminal behaviour.

As mentioned earlier, the causes of crime, however well documented, tell only half the criminological story. Each and every crime has consequences. Although the immediate consequences of crime may be relatively obvious for those parties directly involved (e.g., the offender and the victim), crime also indirectly impacts society and the justice system. Figure 1.2 terms the immediate effects of crime *outputs*. As with the causes of crime, however, the real impact of such outputs is mediated by perceptual filters, resulting in what the figure terms *interpretations*. Boxes in the figure labelled with the word *interpretation* indicate that after a crime has taken place each party to the event must make sense out of what has transpired. Such interpretations consist of cognitive, emotional, and (ultimately) behavioural reactions to the criminal event.

Interpretations are ongoing. They happen before, during, and after the criminal event, and are undertaken by all those associated with it. An interesting and detailed study of the interpretive activity of personnel in the criminal justice system documented what happens when callers reach the 911 dispatcher on police emergency lines.[60] Because many prank calls and calls for information are made to 911 operators, the operator must judge the seriousness of every call that comes through. What the caller says was found to be only a small part of the informational cues that the dispatcher seeks to interpret prior to assigning the call to a particular response (or nonresponse) category. Honest calls for help may go unanswered if the operator misinterprets the call. Hence, quite early on in the criminal event, the potential exists for a crucial representative of the justice system to misinterpret important cues and conclude that no crime is taking place.

Other interpretative activities are at least as significant. The justice system, taken as a whole, must decide guilt or innocence and attempt to deal effectively with convicted offenders. Victims must attempt to make sense of their victimizations in such a way as to allow them to testify in court (if need be) and to pick up the pieces of their crime-shattered lives. The offender must come to terms with oneself and decide whether to avoid prosecution (if escape, for example, is possible), accept blame, or deny responsibility. Whatever the outcome of these more narrowly focused interpretative activities, society—because of the cumulative impact of individual instances of criminal behaviour—will also face tough decisions through its courts and lawmaking agencies. Societal-level decision-making may revolve around the implementation of policies designed to stem future instances of criminal behaviour, the revision of criminal codes, or the elimination of unpopular laws.

Our perspective takes a double-barrelled view of the social event called *crime*. We will (1) consistently attempt to identify the multiplicity of causes giving rise to criminal behaviour, and (2) highlight the processes involved in the continual and ongoing interpretation and redefinition of the crime phenomenon. Such a perspective has been variously termed *interpretive sociology, phenomenological psychology,* or *symbolic interactionism,* depending not only on the subject matter to which it has been applied, but also on the scholarly era in which it has predominated. From this perspective, crime can be viewed as an emergent phenomenon—one that arises out of the complex interrelationships between victim, offender, and the social order. The advantages of a **phenomenological** perspective come in accurately assessing and communicating the personal and social underpinnings, as well as the consequences, of crime. As one criminologist recently explained, "An understanding of crime and criminality as constructed from the immediate interactions of criminals, control agents, victims, and others, and therefore as emerging from a tangled experiential web of situated dangers and situated pleasures, certainly refocuses theories of criminal causality on the criminal moment."[61] The chapters that follow employ the integrative perspective advocated here to analyze criminal events and to show how various theoretical approaches can be woven into a consistent explanation of crime.

**Phenomenology** the study of the contents of human consciousness without regard to external conventions or prior assumptions.

## The Primacy of Sociology

Like many other criminology texts, this book recognizes the contributions made by numerous disciplines to the study of crime and crime causation, including biology, psychology, and political science. It is important to recognize, however, that the primary perspective from which most contemporary criminologists operate is a sociological one. Today's dominant theoretical understandings of criminal behaviour are routinely couched in the language of social science, especially within the framework of sociological theory. The social problems versus social responsibility theme, around which this book is built, is in keeping with such a tradition. The phenomenological perspective, discussed in the last few paragraphs, also falls squarely within a sociological framework and, as mentioned earlier, is frequently referred to as *phenomenological sociology.*

The primacy of the sociological perspective in today's criminological enterprise recognizes the fact that crime, as a subject of study, is a social phenomenon. Central to any study of crime must be the social context of the criminal event, which brings victims and criminals together.[62] Hence, contemporary criminology rests upon a sound tradition of social scientific investigation into the nature of crime and criminal behaviour that is rooted in European and North American sociological traditions that are now well over 200 years old.[63] Although sociological explanations for crime will be discussed throughout this text—and especially in Chapters 7, 8, and 9—it is important for today's students to realize at the outset that the sociological perspective forms the contemporary foundation of the discipline of criminology.

While sociological theories continue to develop, new and emerging perspectives ask to be recognized. The role of biology in explaining criminal tendencies, for example, appears to be gaining strength as the mapping of human DNA grows.

Whatever new insights may develop over the coming years, it is likely that the sociological perspective will continue to dominate the field of criminology for decades to come. Such dominance is rooted in the fact that crime—regardless of all the causative nuances that may be identified in its development—occurs within the context of the social world. As such, the primary significance of crime and of criminal behaviour is fundamentally social in nature, and any control over crime must stem from effective social policy.

## Summary

As we enter the twenty-first century, contemporary criminologists face the daunting task of reconciling an extensive and diverse collection of theoretical explanations for criminal behaviour. All these perspectives aim to assist in understanding the social phenomenon of crime—a phenomenon that is itself open to interpretation and which runs the gamut from petty offences to major infractions of the criminal law. At the very least, we should recognize that explanations for criminal behaviour rest on shaky ground, insofar as the subject matter they seek to interpret contains many different forms of behaviour, each of which is subject to personal, political, and definitional vagaries.

## Discussion Questions

1. This book emphasizes a social problems versus social responsibility theme. Describe both perspectives. How might social policy decisions based upon these perspectives vary?

2. What is crime? What is the difference between crime and deviance? How might the notion of crime change over time? What impact does the changing nature of crime hold for criminology?

3. Do you believe that assisted suicide should be legalized? Why or why not? What do such crimes as assisted suicide have to tell us about the nature of the law and about crime in general?

4. Do you think that policy-makers should address crime as a matter of individual responsibility and accountability, or do you think that crime is truly a symptom of a dysfunctional society? Why?

5. Describe the various participants in a criminal event. How does each contribute to a definition of the event?

6. This chapter recognizes the primacy of the sociological perspective in today's criminological thought. Why is the sociological perspective especially important in studying crime? What other perspectives might be relevant? Why?

# Weblinks

**www.library.utoronto.ca/libraries_crim/centre/centre.htm**

The University of Toronto Centre of Criminology. Research and instruction on a broad range of crime, order, and social control issues.

**www.sfu.ca/criminology/**

Simon Fraser University, School of Criminology. Offers graduate programs in criminology, as do the Universities of Ottawa, Toronto, and Montreal.

**www.acjnet.org/acjeng.html**

Access to Justice Network. The Access to Justice Network (ACJNet) is an electronic community that brings together people, information, and educational resources on Canadian justice and legal issues.

## CHAPTER 2

# Crime Statistics

Who does what? When? How often? These are the perennial questions about crime. There is no scarcity of answers. Indeed, there is a surplus. The problem is that the answers seldom satisfy. Dissatisfaction follows from the fact that our measures of crime are of doubtful accuracy.

—JOHN HAGEN [1]

## LEARNING OUTCOMES

After reading this chapter, you should be able to:

● Understand the usefulness and limitations of crime data

● Recognize the various methods used to collect and disseminate crime data

● Identify the predominant social dimensions of crime

● Assess various explanations for the correlation between specific social dimensions and criminal behaviour.

**IMPORTANT NAMES**

Thomas Robert
  Malthus

André Michel Guerry
  Adolphe Quételet

John Braithwaite

**IMPORTANT TERMS**

demographics
statistical school
Uniform Crime Report
  (UCR)

Victimization Survey
crime rate
dark figure of crime

self-report study
correlation
correlates of crime

# Introduction

Wesley "Pop" Honeywood, 94, knows little about statistics—but he is familiar with crime. Over the years, Honeywood, who lives in the United States, has been arrested forty-six times and has been imprisoned on eight occasions since 1946.

Honeywood's troubles with the law began at the close of World War II when he and a couple of friends stole a bomber and flew it over Italy for fun. After landing, Honeywood was arrested by military police, did a brief stint in jail, and received a dishonourable discharge from the army.

Not long ago, the geriatric career criminal stood before a criminal-court judge, awaiting sentencing after pleading guilty to charges of armed assault and possession of a firearm. The incident grew out of Honeywood's liking for grapes, which he had watched ripen in his neighbour's yard at the end of the summer. Finally, unable to resist the temptation any longer, Honeywood helped himself to bunches of the fruit. When confronted by the neighbour, Honeywood pulled a gun and threatened the man.

Because of all the crimes he's committed, Honeywood now faces sentencing as a habitual offender and could be sent to prison for 60 years. Making matters worse is the fact that Honeywood was on probation for the attempted sexual assault of a 7-year-old girl when he was arrested for the grape theft. And age hasn't mellowed him. Honeywood admits shooting a man in the buttocks in 1989, but claims self-defence. The case never went to trial.

Honeywood says he is not afraid of a prison sentence. "I can do it," he smiles. "I've been locked up a whole lot of times here, but they turn me loose every time."

The sentencing judge worries about his age and the fact that he probably won't survive a long prison stay. But, he says, "[t]he first duty is to protect the public. If he is a 94-year-old that is a danger to the public and he has to go to jail, so be it."

Honeywood, however, wishes he would have plea bargained. "I wish they would give me house arrest," he says. "I don't go nowhere, but stay home. My lawyer says he [the judge] might put me in an old folks home." Even if he goes to prison, Honeywood figures he may beat the odds. His father lived to be 113.

# A History of Crime Statistics

Pop Honeywood is a statistical anomaly. Few people are involved in crime past middle age. Fewer still ever reach Honeywood's stage in life. Statistical data from the Canadian Centre for Justice Statistics show that the likelihood of crime commission declines with age. Persons 65 years of age and older, for example, commit fewer than 1 percent of all crimes, and the proportion of crimes committed by those over age 90 is so small that it cannot be meaningfully expressed as a percentage of total crime.

Although the gathering of crime statistics is a relatively new phenomenon, population statistics have been collected periodically since pre-Roman times. Old Testament accounts of enumerations of the Hebrews, for example, provide evidence of Middle Eastern census-taking thousands of years ago. In like manner, The New Testament describes how the family of Jesus had to return home to be counted during an official census—providing evidence of routine census-taking during the time of Christ. The lustrum, which was a ceremonial purification of the entire ancient Roman population after census-taking, leads historians to conclude that Roman population counts were made every 5 years. Centuries later, the *Doomsday Book,* created by order of William the Conqueror in 1085 to 1086, provided a written survey of English landowners and their property. Other evidence shows that primitive societies around the world also took periodic counts of their members. The Incas, for example, a pre-Columbian Indian empire in western South America, required successive census reports to be recorded on knotted strings called *quipas.*

Although census-taking has occurred throughout history, inferences based on statistical **demographics** appear to be a product of the last 200 years. In 1798, the English economist **Thomas Robert Malthus** (1766–1834) published his *Essay on the Principle of Population as It Affects the Future Improvement of Society,* in which he described a worldwide future of warfare, crime, and starvation. The human population, Malthus predicted, would grow exponentially over the following decades or centuries, leading to a shortage of needed resources, especially food. Conflict on both the interpersonal and international levels would be the result, Malthus claimed, as individuals and groups competed for survival.

**Demographics** the characteristics of population groups, usually expressed in statistical form.

## Adolphe Quételet and André Michel Guerry

As a direct result of Malthusian thought, investigators throughout Europe began to gather "moral statistics," or social enumerations which they thought may prove useful in measuring the degree to which crime and conflict existed in societies of the period. Such statistics were scrutinized in hopes of gauging "the moral health of nations"—a phrase commonly used throughout the period. One of the first such investigators was **André Michel Guerry** (1802–1866), who calculated per capita crime rates throughout various French provinces in the early 1800s.

In 1835, the Belgian astronomer and mathematician **Adolphe Quételet** (1796–1864) published a statistical analysis of crime in a number of European countries, including Belgium, France, and Holland. Quételet set for himself the goal of assessing the degree to which crime rates vary with climate, sex, and age. He noticed what is still obvious to criminal statisticians today—that crime changes with the seasons, with many violent crimes showing an increase during the hot summer months and property crimes increasing in frequency during colder parts of the year. As a consequence of these observations, Quételet proposed what he called the "thermic law." According to thermic law, Quételet claimed, morality undergoes seasonal variation—a proposal that stimulated widespread debate in its day.[2]

The first officially published crime statistics appeared in London's *Gazette* beginning in 1828 and France's 1825 *Compte generale*. Soon comparisons (or what contemporary statisticians call *correlations*) began to be calculated between economic conditions and the rates of various types of crime. From a study of English statistical data covering the years 1810 to 1847, Joseph Fletcher concluded that prison commitments increased as the price of wheat rose. In like fashion, the German writer Gerog von Mayr, whose data covered the years 1836 to 1861, discovered that the rate of theft increased with the price of rye in Bavaria.

The work of statisticians such as Guerry and Quételet formed the historical basis for what has been called the **statistical school** of criminology. The statistical school foreshadowed the development of both sociological criminology and the ecological school, perspectives which are discussed in considerable detail later in this book.

**Statistical school** a criminological perspective with roots in the early 1800s that seeks to uncover correlations between crime rates and other types of demographic data.

# Usefulness of Crime Statistics

How many assaults were committed last year in Canada? Who committed them? Who were the most likely to be victims? What part of the country had the highest rate of assault? Why?

These are the types of questions frequently asked not only by those with a particular interest in the study of crime and criminals but also by members of the general public. Crime statistics help provide answers to these and other questions and paint a picture of the reality of crime in this country. Often the first step toward solving a problem is understanding it, and this certainly applies to the problem of crime. Criminologists, students of criminology, and interested members of the public must understand the crime problem before any serious attempts at controlling or preventing it can be made. Crime statistics and data can be useful toward this end, in a number of ways.

Crime data assist in describing the nature and extent of crime, which is necessary to develop effective crime control policies. These policies, in turn, are usually responses to public pressure. Since it is the public who is the major player in reporting crime, the types of crime they report reflects those issues most concerning them. By providing descriptive information about criminal activity, crime data serve as a gauge of the community's well-being.

Chapter 3 provides a discussion of the usefulness of theory development in the study of crime and criminals. Crime data provide the empirical data to support the hypotheses developed by criminologists, who attempt to explain the phenomenon of crime and criminals. The crime data ultimately provide the test for theoretical assertions.

Just as crime statistics are used as a basis for developing social policy, they are also crucial in evaluating that policy. Whether or not young offender "boot camps" will reduce the amount of youth crime or federal firearms registration legislation will reduce the amount of violent crime committed with a firearm will ultimately be assessed through an analysis of the data (see Chapter 11 for an in-depth look at these and other

Canadians are especially fearful of violent crime. Here police investigate the scene of a fatal shooting of a bank teller during an armed robbery. Is the public's perception of the amounts and types of crime borne out by official statistics? *The Canadian Press/Toronto Star/Ron Bull.*

crime-control initiatives). Program evaluation is often difficult to do well and many such evaluations fall prey to the cost factor. Some programs are introduced largely because they are more cost-effective than conventional approaches, yet they may not achieve the desired result of reducing crime. Likewise, some programs that successfully reduce crime are shelved because they are seen as too expensive.

Most criminologists agree that the prevention of crime is generally considered preferable to its punishment. Prevention, in turn, is largely based on prediction. What types of people are most likely to commit what types of crime and why? Where will they commit them? Criminologists and others use crime data to help provide answers to these questions. The Canadian Crime Prevention Through Environmental Design model (CPTED) is based on the theory that the proper design and effective use of a physical space can help reduce the incidence of crime in that area. This theory, in turn, is based on crime data showing that crime occurs more often in areas where the opportunities for criminal activity are greatest (see Chapters 7 and 11 for a further description of the CPTED model).

It is important to note that predicting criminal activity and behaviour is an inexact science open to numerous pitfalls. In the early part of the twentieth century, for example, Cesare Lombroso believe he could predict future criminal behaviour based on an individual's physical characteristics such as the size of his ears or the shape of his nose. In the search for a "quick fix" to the crime problem, some people subscribed to such predictors. For others, prediction models for crime and criminal behaviour are about as accurate as "flipping a coin."[3]

Finally, crime data are useful in providing a picture of risk. Public perceptions of the amount and types of crime are often inconsistent with reality. Crime statistics are useful in assessing the risk to various segments of the population. For example, does one's sex, age, or social class have any bearing on his or her risk of becoming a victim of crime or of becoming involved in criminal behaviour? The study of risk assessment, with crime data used as its basis, is a growing area of interest within criminology, relying heavily on crime data as a basis.

# Sources of Crime Statistics

Compilation of crime statistics has continued apace ever since crime-related data began to be gathered over a century ago. Crime statistics in Canada are reported in two major surveys: the **Uniform Crime Reporting** system (UCR) and the **Victimization Survey**, conducted through the General Social Surveys. Both fall under the auspices of Canada's national statistics department, Statistics Canada. In 1981, the Canadian Centre for Justice Statistics was created as a satellite of Statistics Canada, through the cooperation of the federal and provincial governments. See Box 2.1 for a detailed look at the Canadian Centre for Justice Statistics.

It is important to realize at the outset that these two types of data differ. Because of the differences in methodology and crime coverage, the two approaches examine the nation's crime reality from somewhat different perspectives, and results are not strictly comparable. Nevertheless, the two surveys can complement one another, and each is certainly useful in providing an overall picture of criminal activity. The two surveys are compared in detail later in the chapter.

**Uniform Crime Report (UCR)** a summation of crime statistics tallied annually by the Canadian Centre for Justice Statistics (CCJS) and consisting primarily of data on crimes reported to the police.

**Victimization Survey** first conducted as the Canadian Urban Victimization Survey in 1981 by Statistics Canada and then every 5 years since 1988 as part of the General Social Survey. It provides data on surveyed households reporting that they had been affected by crime.

## The Canadian Centre For Justice Statistics

**BOX 2.1**

As the collection of crime data became more formalized through the introduction of the Uniform Crime Reports in the 1960s and Victimization and Self-Report Surveys in the 1970s, it became apparent that Canada needed a national centre for the collection, collation, and dissemination of this data. The creation of the Canadian Centre for Justice Statistics (CCJS) in 1981 was a result of a decade of numerous task forces and ongoing federal/provincial negotiations around this issue. By 1985, the CCJS had evolved as the administrative arm of Canada's National Justice Statistics Initiative (NJSI), whose mandate is to "provide information to the justice community and the public on the nature and extent of crime and the administration of justice in Canada".[4] It is through the CCJS that the NJSI produces statistical information to be used to support the legislative, policy, management, and research agenda of the Canadian government and inform the public.

As such, the CCJS is subdivided into program areas, including law enforcement, courts, legal aid, corrections, and juvenile justice. Each of these program areas collect and collate data to examine the incidence of crime and criminal activity in Canada in areas such as homicide, street prostitution, criminal harassment, weapons and violent crime, motor vehicle crimes and impaired driving, and violent youth crime. The work of the Centre also includes compiling information on other aspects of the criminal justice system, including justice-system expenditures, prisons and corrections data, probation and parole populations, inmate profiles, public perceptions and fear of crime, criminal justice system personnel figures, and information on the activities of adult and youth courts. This information is made available to the public through a service bulletin known as *Juristat*, which is published periodically throughout the year. *Juristat* and other CCJS reports are made available through the Centre in Ottawa or through a number of Statistics Canada Regional Reference Centres throughout the country. Most public, community college, and university libraries also carry this information in reference departments, under the

▶

▶

call number 85-002. Publications of the CCJS can also be obtained by telephone at 1-800-387-2231, by fax at 1-613-951-6615, or through the Statistics Canada Web site at **www.statcan.ca**. Some statistical information is also available through this Web site.

## The Uniform Crime Reporting System

The Uniform Crime Reporting system (UCR) was initiated in 1961 through the efforts of Statistics Canada and the Canadian Association of Chiefs of Police. The purpose of the system is twofold. It provides a standardized procedure by which police departments across the country can collect information about crimes that come to their attention and then report this information to Statistics Canada, specifically to the Canadian Centre for Justice Statistics (CCJS). The CCJS then collates the raw data and makes it available to the public.

Initial UCR data are structured in terms of six major categories of crime. These include crimes of violence, property crimes, other criminal code offences, federal statutes violations, provincial statutes violations, and municipal bylaw violations. Police record crimes according to these categories and a set of rules specified by Statistics Canada and the Canadian Association of Chiefs of Police and contained in a *Uniform Crime Reporting Manual*. Between 1962 and 1988, the official crime statistics generated from the UCR were based on summarized monthly police reports from police departments across the country. These police reports included the number of incidents and offences reported to police, the number of actual offences, the number of offences cleared, the number of adults charged, the number of youths charged, and the sex of those charged. Known as the Aggregate Uniform Crime Reporting Survey, this system has been criticized on the grounds that aggregated statistics are "less useful for analytic purposes than information based on characteristics of individual crimes."[5]

### Recent Changes to the Uniform Crime Reporting System

Changes in the UCR after 1998 shifted the emphasis of data collection away from summary or aggregate collection to incident-based collection. The new system, known as the Revised UCR Survey or Incident-Based UCR, included changes in the following areas:

- *information on victims:* age, sex, victim/accused relationship, level of injury, type of weapon causing injury, drug and/or alcohol use;
- *information on the accused:* age, sex, type of charges laid or recommended, drug and/or alcohol use; and
- *information on the circumstances of the incident:* type of violation (or crime), target of violation, types of property stolen, dollar value of property affected, dollar value of drugs confiscated, type of weapon present, time and type of location of the incident.[6]

An arson fire. Arson causes millions of dollars' worth of property damage yearly. Are UCR statistics on arson accurate? *The Canadian Press/Calgary Herald/Ted Jacob.*

The Revised UCR was fully implemented in 1992 but to date only includes data from 169 police departments, or 46 percent of the national volume of reported crime. The incidents recorded in the most recent UCR are distributed as follows: 41 percent from Quebec, 35 percent from Ontario, 12 percent from Alberta, 8 percent from British Columbia, 3 percent from Saskatchewan, and 1 percent from New Brunswick.[7]

The UCR also records offences cleared by charge or otherwise and rates of crime. The phrase *offences cleared by charge* refers to an offence that is closed when police have formally charged a person or when there is sufficient evidence to lay a charge against an identified person, even if that person has not been apprehended by police. *Offences cleared otherwise* refers to cases in which police cannot charge a person even if they have identified a suspect and have enough evidence to support the laying of a charge. Examples include cases of diplomatic immunity, instances in which the complainant declines to proceed with charges against the accused, or cases where the alleged offender dies before being formally charged.[8] The *clearance rate* indicates the proportion

**Crime rate** crime per
capita based on the
number of recorded
crimes calculated per
100 000 population.

of incidents that are cleared by charge or otherwise for different types of offences, compared to the total number of actual incidents.

The **crime rate** used in the UCR is based on a population of 100 000. By taking into account population, the crime picture is standardized across the country in any given year. For example, in 1998, the total number of recorded violent crimes was 295 369. The rate of crimes of violence was 975, based on a 1998 Canadian total population of 30 300 422 taken from 1998 census numbers. This crime rate was calculated as follows:

$$\frac{\text{\# of reported violent crimes}}{\text{total population}} \times 100\ 000$$

$$\frac{295\ 369 \text{ violent crimes reported}}{30\ 300\ 422 \text{ total population}} \times 100\ 000 = 975$$

Thus, we see that there were 975 violent crime incidents per 100 000 population in Canada in 1998. If we consider a specific type of violent crime, such as homicide, and apply the same procedure, the equation would look like this:

$$\frac{555 \text{ homicides reported}}{30\ 300\ 422 \text{ total population}} \times 100\ 000 = 1.8$$

This tells us that there were approximately 2 homicides for every 100 000 Canadians in 1999.[9] A summary of the UCR findings for 1998 is reproduced in Box 2.2.

## Highlights of the 1998 UCR
BOX 2.2

- Canada's police-reported crime rate decreased for the seventh year in a row in 1998, falling 4%. The 1998 rate was the lowest rate since 1979.
- With the exception of Newfoundland (+3%) and Saskatchewan (+2%), all provinces reported a decline in their crime rate. Newfoundland reported the lowest crime rate (5 803 incidents per 100 000 population), while Saskatchewan reported the highest (12 403).
- Of the 2.5 million Criminal Code incidents, 12% were violent crimes, 56% were property crimes, and the remaining 32% were other offences such as mischief, disturbing the peace, prostitution and arson.
- The rate of violent crime declined for the sixth consecutive year, down 2%. Despite these recent declines, the violent crime rate was still 12% higher than 10 years ago. All major categories of violent crime decreased in 1998, including homicide (–6%), sexual assault (–6%), assault (–1%), and robbery (–3%).
- There were 555 homicides in 1998, 31 fewer than in the previous year. The homicide rate has generally been falling since the mid-1970s. The 1998 rate of 1.8 homicides per 100 000 population is the lowest in 30 years.
- The property crime rate dropped 7%, continuing the general decline that began in 1991. All major categories of property crime decreased in 1998, including motor vehicle theft (–7%), breaking and entering (–7%), and other theft (–7%).

▶ • Fuelled by an 8% drop in property crimes, the youth crime rate, as measured by the number of youths charged by police, declined 4% in 1998. This rate has generally been decreasing since 1991. The rate of youths charged with violent offences also decreased (−1%) for the third straight year.

SOURCE: S. Tremblay, "Crime Statistics in Canada, 1998," Statistics Canada, *Juristat*, Catalogue No. 85-002, vol. 19, no. 9, p. 1.

## Programmatic Problems with Available Data

The most significant methodological feature of the Uniform Crime Reporting System is indicated by its name. It is a "reporting" system. In other words, only crimes that are reported to the police (or that are discovered by them, or by someone else who then reports them) are included in the statistics compiled by the system. Unless someone complains to the police about a criminal incident, it will go unreported and will not appear in the UCR. Most complaints, of course, are made by victims.

Because UCR data are based on *reported* crime, the system has been criticized for underestimating the true incidence of criminal activity within Canada—a measurement that would also include unreported crimes. Unreported and under-reported criminal activity has been called the "**dark figure of crime**." Some experts say, for example, that sexual assault is the most under-reported crime in the UCR. Reasons for not reporting a crime such as sexual assault are numerous and include (1) fear of the perpetrator; (2) shame, which may carry over from traditional attitudes about sexual behaviour and a woman's role in sexual encounters; (3) fears the victim may have of not being believed; and (4) fear of further participation in the justice system (such as the possibility of the victim's being required to go to court and testify against the offender, thereby exposing herself to potentially embarrassing cross-examination and public scrutiny). Other general reasons cited by victims for failure to report a crime include "fear of revenge," "nothing can be done," "the crime was too minor," or the incident was a "private matter."

**Dark figure of crime** refers to that portion of criminal activity that goes unreported and/or undetected by official sources.

Many other crimes are under-reported as well. Although sexual assault is indeed seriously under-reported (a conclusion drawn from comparison of UCR and Victimization Survey sexual assault statistics), the most seriously under-reported crime may in fact be theft $5 000 and under, because the theft of small items may never make it into official police reports and may even be forgotten by victims during interviews with Victimization surveyors.

It is interesting to note that changes in public attitude about certain types of crime such as child abuse have resulted in the public's inclination to report these crimes more readily. Does an increase in the number of reported child abuse cases mean that there are more incidents of child abuse occurring or simply that more cases are being reported?

Another concern raised about the accuracy of UCR numbers lies with the way in which police services record and report the criminal activity that is detected. The UCR receives crime data from municipal police departments across Canada as well as from the RCMP, the Ontario Provincial Police, and the Sûreté du Québec (Quebec's provincial police force). To expect that all these police services are recording their crime statistics in an uniform manner is somewhat unrealistic, although the CCJS does work with police agencies on an ongoing basis to detect and resolve any difficulties in the reporting or transmission of data. Nevertheless, there are variations in how the police count crime, resulting from a number of factors. Changes in the number of police services and police officers will most certainly affect the number of detected crimes. Enforcement practices or mandates often vary from police department to police department. If commercial break and enters are a problem in one community, for example, local police will be more vigilant toward this type of criminal activity, which will be reflected in the crime report.

Related to police recording and reporting are methodological concerns with the way the UCR "counts" crime, especially in an incident involving multiple offences. The UCR counts only the most serious offence in the incident. For example, if someone breaks into a store, severely assaults the security personnel, and steals a stereo, only the assault is recorded. The most serious offence is determined by the maximum sentence length; in the scenario just mentioned, although the break and enter and assault both carry a maximum life sentence, the crime against the person is considered more serious and takes precedence over the crime against property. As a result, less serious offences tend to be under-represented by the UCR survey.

Even though for the purposes of counting, crimes against the person take precedence over crimes against property, this is not the case when the crime rate is calculated. Recall that the crime rate is the total number of reported crimes in a given year per 100 000 population. This total includes all categories of crime including federal and provincial statute violations. For example, the number of reported motor vehicle thefts may skyrocket in a given year, while the number of assaults may fall. The resulting overall crime rate for that year would be higher than for the year before because both classifications of crime are assigned the same weight.

Finally, for violent crimes the UCR records the number of incidents in terms of victims. If one person assaults two people, two incidents are recorded. But if two people assault one person, only one incident is recorded. The exception to this scoring rule for violent crime is robbery: one occurrence of robbery is counted as one incident regardless of the number of victims. Since robbery can involve many people who could be considered victims, to count each one would seriously overstate the occurrence of robbery. Thus, the total number of incidents recorded in the UCR is actually equal to the number of victims of violent crimes (other than robbery) plus the number of individual occurrences of nonviolent crimes and robbery.[10]

A final concern with the accuracy of the UCR centres around the legal definition of crime. For example, the renaming and redefinition of rape to sexual assault in 1983 means that a man can be charged for sexually assaulting his wife. The types of behaviour constituting sexual assault have been more clearly defined to include those behaviours from unwanted sexual touching to aggravated sexual assault that endangers the life of the victim. Similarly, amendments to the definition of arson in 1990 now include mischief fires as arson. Both of these redefinitions have broadened the scope of these criminal activities and have resulted in a corresponding increase in the statistical incidence of these crimes.

The consistency of definition is also a concern. Part of the difficulty in measuring child abuse, for example, arises from the fact that there is no apparent consensus as to what constitutes child abuse across Canada at the provincial and territorial level, where child welfare services are organized and delivered. For example, the maximum age of the child to be protected and the policies underlying child protection vary across the country (see Table 2.1). It is estimated that cases of child abuse would double if threats and acts of indecent exposure were added to the definition. As well, the distinction between corporal punishment and physical abuse is not clear, which further thwarts the accurate accounting of child abuse. For the purposes of recording, the CCJS defines child abuse as incidents of physical and sexual assault and homicide where the victim is under 18 years of age.[11]

## Table 2.1
## Provincial/Territorial Child Welfare Legislation

| Province/ Territory | Child's Age as Defined in Child Protection Legislation | Abuse as Defined in Child Protection Legislation | Child Abuse Registry | Witnessing Family Violence: Definition of a Child in Need of Protection |
|---|---|---|---|---|
| NFLD | Under 16 | A child who is physically or sexually abused, physically or emotionally neglected, sexually exploited or in danger of that treatment (Child Welfare Act) | No | A child who is living in a situation where there is severe domestic violence; . . . |
| PEI | Under 18 | Abuse is defined as physical, mental, emotional or sexual mistreatment of the child by a person responsible for his care and well-being (Family and Child Services Act) | No | A child who is living in a situation where there is severe domestic violence; . . . |
| NS | Under 16 | Child has suffered physical, sexual, or emotional harm by the person, or by the person's failure to supervise and protect the child adequately (Children and Family Services Act) | Yes | A child is in need of protective services where the child has suffered physical or emotional harm caused by being exposed to repeated domestic violence by or towards a parent or guardian, and the child's parent or guardian fails or refuses to obtain services or treatment to remedy or alleviate the violence; . . . |
| NB | Under 16 | The security or development of a child is suspected to be in danger if he/she is physically or sexually abused, physically or emotionally neglected, sexually exploited or in danger of such treatment (Family Services Act, 1995) | No | The security and development of the child may be in danger when the child is living in a situation where there is severe domestic violence; . . . |
| QUE | Under 18 | Sexual abuse and physical ill-treatment are the result of an action or failure to act which lead to trauma or physical injury (Youth Protecton Act) | No | No legislation |
| ONT | Under 16 | Child is in need of protection where . . . the child has suffered physical harm . . . been sexually molested . . . been emotionally harmed demonstrated by anxiety, depression, withdrawal, or self-destructive behaviour . . . suffered from a mental, emotional or developmental condition that could impair the child's development (Child and Family Services Act) | Yes | No legislation |
| MAN | Under 18 | Abuse is an act or omission of any person . . . that results in physical injury, emotional disability of a permanent nature, or sexual exploitation of the child with or without the child's consent (Child and Family Services Amendment Act, 1996) | Yes | No legislation |

| Table 2.1 | continued |
|-----------|-----------|

| Province/ Territory | Child's Age as Defined in Child Protection Legislation | Abuse as Defined in Child Protection Legislation | Child Abuse Registry | Witnessing Family Violence: Definition of a Child in Need of Protection |
|---|---|---|---|---|
| SASK | Under 16 | Physical abuse occurs when a parent uses physical means or permits another person to use physical means which result in severe bruising, burns or . . . Sexual abuse involves any parental behaviour which may involve erotic touching . . . emotional neglect or abuse (Child and Family Services Act) | No | The child has been exposed to domestic violence or severe domestic disharmony that is likely to result in physical or emotional harm to the child. |
| ALTA | Under 18 | A child is emotionally injured if there is substantial and observable impairment of the child's mental or emotional functioning . . . physically injured if there is substantial and observable injury to any part of the child's body . . . sexually abused if the child is inappropriately exposed or subjected to sexual contact, activity or behaviour (Child Welfare Act) | No | A child is emotionally injured if there are reasonable and probable grounds to believe that the emotional injury is a result of . . . exposure to domestic violence or severe domestic disharmony. |
| BC | Under 19 | A child needs protection if the child is or is likely to be physically harmed . . . sexually abused or exploited by a parent . . . or by another person if the child's parent is unwilling or unable to protect the child . . . or, if the child is physically harmed because of neglect . . . emotionally harmed . . . deprived of necessary health care . . . (Child, Family and Community Services Act) | No | No legislation |
| YUK | Under 18 | A child is in need of protection if he is abandoned . . . if he is in probable danger of physical or psychological harm . . . if he is cut, burned or physically abused in any other way . . . if he is deprived of necessities of life . . . (Children's Act) | No | No legislation |
| NWT | Under 18 | Child abuse is a condition of physical harm where a child suffers physical injury but does not include reasonable punishment administered by a parent or guardian . . . malnutrition or mental ill-health of a degree that if not remedied could impair growth . . . sexual molestation (Child Welfare Act) | No | No legislation |

SOURCE: Canadian Centre for Justice Statistics, *The Juristat Reader*, 1999, p. 187/Statistics Canada, *Juristat*, Catalogue No. 85-002, vol. 17, no. 11, p. 3.

## Data Gathering Using Victimization Surveys

Victimization surveys differ from the UCR in one especially significant way: rather than depending on reports of crimes to the police, the data contained in victimization surveys consist of information elicited through interviews with members of randomly selected households throughout the country. Hence, these surveys uncover a large number of crimes that may not have been reported, and are therefore regarded by many researchers as a more accurate measure of the actual incidence of crime in Canada than is the UCR.

# Crime and Justice Information on the World Wide Web

A rich repository of crime and justice information can be found on the World Wide Web. One place to start is the Network for Research on Crime and Justice (RCJ-NET), at **www.qsilver.queensu.ca/rcjnet**. The RCJ-NET is a network of academics and senior government officials set up in 1996 to "develop, conduct, and communicate superior quality research on crime and justice, and to provide policy-relevant advice" (see Chapter 3 for an in-depth look at RCJ-NET). This Web site maintains, among other things, a comprehensive list of links, including:

- Access to Justice Network
- Canadian Association of Chiefs of Police
- Correctional Service of Canada
- Criminal Intelligence Service of Canada
- Department of Justice Canada
- Department of the Solicitor General of Canada
- International Centre for the Prevention of Crime
- Law Commission of Canada
- National Clearinghouse on Family Violence
- National Crime Prevention Centre
- Police Futures Group
- Royal Canadian Mounted Police

Many of these sites provide statistics and research on crime, criminals, and victims.

Web sites of criminology departments at various Canadian universities are another good starting point for collecting crime information. Many of these sites provide information on crime, or good links to it.

You might also be interested in information found at the Justice Information Center (JIC), a service of the National Criminal Justice Reference Service (NCJRS) in the United States. Located at **www.ncjrs.org**, the NCJRS maintains an extensive source of information on crime statistics, crime prevention, and research and evaluation in the area of crime control.

A number of significant victimization surveys have been undertaken in Canada. The first, and perhaps the most comprehensive, was the *Canadian Urban Victimization Survey* (CUVS) conducted in 1981 under the auspices of the Solicitor General of Canada. It randomly sampled about 60 000 Canadians over the age of 16 in 7 major cities. In telephone interviews, respondents were asked to describe any victimization experiences they had had in the preceding calendar year. Eight categories of crime were included in the survey: sexual assault, robbery, assault, break and enter, motor vehicle theft, theft of household property, theft of personal property, and vandalism. The survey uncovered over 700 000 personal victimizations and almost 900 000 household victimizations for the calendar year 1981. It also revealed that fewer than 42 percent of these victimizations had been reported to the police or had otherwise come to police attention.[12] The highlights from the CUVS are found in Box 2.3.

Beginning in 1988, Statistics Canada has conducted a Victimization Survey every 5 years, as part of the *General Social Survey* (GSS). The 1993 GSS (the latest one from

## Highlights of the Canadian Urban Victimization Survey (CUVS)

BOX 2.3

- Fewer than 42 percent of all crimes are reported to the police: 62 percent of all sexual assaults go unreported, 55 percent of robberies, 66 percent of assaults, 36 percent of break and enters, 3 percent of motor vehicle thefts, 56 percent of household theft, 22 percent of personal thefts, and 65 percent of incidents of vandalism go unreported.

- Sixty-six percent of respondents said they did not report the crime because they thought it was "too minor," 61 percent because they felt the "police couldn't do anything", and 24 percent because they felt reporting was an "inconvenience."

- Forty percent of respondents felt unsafe in their own neighbourhoods during the evenings, while five percent felt unsafe there during the day.

- Those who reported spending more time outdoors in the evening also reported a greater incidence of victimization.

- Thirty percent of offences against the person occur in the summer months, while 18 percent occur in the winter months.

- The major determinants of fear are: being older, being female, living in an urban setting, and having a lower income.

- Thirty-five percent of personal violent crimes involve the use of a weapon (13% involved guns).

SOURCE: Compiled from Ministry of Solicitor General, *Canadian Urban Victimization Survey* (Ottawa: Ministry of Supply and Services), 1982.

which victimization data are available) sampled a national target population of about 10 000 Canadians over 15 years of age, excluding full-time residents of institutions. Interviews were conducted by telephone over the 12 months of 1993, using random-digit dialling techniques. Respondents were asked about their experiences with the criminal justice system in the previous 12 months and specifically about 8 types of criminal victimization: sexual assault, robbery and attempted robbery, assault, break and enter and attempted break and enter, motor vehicle theft and attempts, attempts at and theft of personal property, attempts at and theft of household property, and vandalism. Respondents were also questioned about their perceptions and fear of crime and their knowledge and perceptions of the criminal justice system. Demographic information about the respondents was also gathered, including age, sex, marital status, as well as educational, occupational, and income levels. Highlights of comparisons between the findings of the 1988 and 1993 surveys are presented in Box 2.4.

Generally, the comparison shows that individual and household victimization rates did not change appreciably in the 5-year period between 1988 and 1993. While a significant proportion of Canadians (about 24%) were affected by one or more of the crimes covered in the 1993 GSS, there is no indication that this proportion has changed since 1988. This unchanged rate of victimization is particularly interesting when compared with the heightened fear of crime reported by Canadians, discussed in Chapter 1.

# Comparison of the Victimization Findings of the 1988 and 1993 General Social Survey (GSS)

BOX 2.4

- According to the General Social Survey (GSS), the 1988 and 1993 rates of victimization are reasonably consistent across crime categories: while the 1988 and 1993 GSS rates of assault remained almost the same, the 1993 rate of robbery/attempt decreased by 31% below the 1988 rate and the rate of personal theft/attempt fell by 14%.

- Violent victimizations were more likely to have been committed by a stranger in 1993 than in 1988. The proportion of robberies/attempts committed by a stranger was greater in 1993 (67%) than in 1988 (45%) and the proportion of assaults committed by a stranger was also larger in 1993 (38%) than in 1988 (27%). Nevertheless, as in 1988, the majority of sexual assaults and assaults in 1993 were perpetrated by offenders known to the victim.

- Factors such as area of residence and gender may increase one's risk of victimization. In both 1988 and 1993, urban dwellers and young Canadians aged 15 to 24 years consistently reported higher rates of violent victimization than rural dwellers and older Canadians.

- According to the General Social Survey, reported rates of break and enters (−7%), motor vehicle or part thefts/attempts (−27%), and vandalism (−13%) were lower in 1993 than in 1988.

- In both 1988 and 1993, rates of household victimizations were consistently lower among rural households than among urban households. In 1988, the rate of total household victimizations was 252 per 1 000 urban households versus 146 per 1 000 rural households. In 1993, rates of total household victimizations were 222 per 1 000 urban households and 133 per 1 000 rural households.

- 1988 and 1993 data show that households with higher incomes experienced greater rates of household crime. In 1988, households with incomes ranging from $40 000 to $59 999 reported the highest rate of total household victimizations of any other income group (296 incidents per 1 000 households). In 1993, households with an income of $60 000 or more reported the highest rate of total household victimizations (254 incidents per 1 000 households).

SOURCE: Statistics Canada, Canadian Centre for Justice Statistics, *A Graphical Overview of Crime and the Administration of Criminal Justice in Canada*, 1996, Catalogue No. 85F0018, pp. 173, 175.

While the CUVS and subsequent CSS have helped to provide a picture of the amounts and types of crime generally in Canada, other surveys have been conducted to look at specific types of crime victims. Most notable among these is the first-ever national *Violence Against Women Survey* (VAWS), undertaken by Statistics Canada in 1993. Over 12 000 women 18 years of age and older were interviewed by telephone about their experiences of physical and sexual violence since the age of 16 and about their perceptions of their personal safety. The findings of the survey indicated significantly more incidents of violence against women than had ever been previously indicated in official UCR numbers. One-half of all Canadian women reported having experienced at least one incident of violence since age 16, and almost one-half reported that this violence had been perpetrated by men known to them. A summary of the findings from the *VAWS* is outlined in Box 2.5.

## Highlights of the Violence Against Women Survey (VAWS)

BOX 2.5

- Fifty percent of all Canadian women have experienced at least one incident of violence since the age of 16.

- Almost 50 percent of women reported violence by men known to them, and 25 percent reported violence by a stranger.

- Twenty-five percent of all women have experienced violence at the hands of a current or past marital partner (includes common-law unions).

- About 15 percent of currently married women reported violence by their spouses; 50 percent of women with previous marriages reported violence by a previous spouse.

- More than 10 percent of women who reported violence in a current marriage have at some point felt their lives were in danger.

- Sixty percent of Canadian women who walk alone in their own area after dark feel "very" or "somewhat" worried doing so.

- Women with violent fathers-in-law are at three times the risk of assault by their partners than are women with non-violent fathers-in-law.

SOURCE: Statistics Canada, "*Violence Against Women Survey*, Highlights," *The Daily*, Catalogue No. 11-001, Nov. 18, 1993, p. 1.

There have been a number of initiatives undertaken at the international level to compare victimization rates from country to country. The most recent, known as the *International Crime Victimization Survey* (ICVS), was conducted in 1996. Canada was one of more than 30 participating countries and had also participated in the previous two studies in 1989 and 1992. The survey was coordinated by the Minister of Justice in the Netherlands and the United Nations Interregional Crime and Justice Research Institute. It set out to provide comparable information on the incidence of victimization around the world. In the 1996 study, persons aged 16 years and older were asked through random telephone sampling for information on 11 offences (robbery/attempted robbery, sexual assault, assaults/threats, theft of personal property, burglary of residence, attempted burglary of residence, theft of motor vehicle, theft from motor vehicle, vandalism to vehicle, theft of motorcycle, theft of bicycle). Respondents were asked when, where, and how often offences had occurred over the previous 5 years; whether offences were reported to police; and whether victimization experiences were considered serious. Respondents were also asked for their opinion on public safety, policing, and sentencing. There was an average of 1 000 to 2 000 persons interviewed per country. Despite some recognized methodological shortcomings, such as the likelihood of fairly large sampling errors, the findings of the survey are interesting. Twenty-five percent of Canadians reported having been victimized within the previous year, which was about average when compared to 10 other Western industrialized countries. A summary of the highlights of this survey can be found in Box 2.6.

# Highlights of the International Crime Victimization Survey (ICVS)

BOX 2.6

- According to the 1996 International Crime Victimization Survey (ICVS), 25 percent of the adult population in Canada reported being victimized in the previous year. In comparison to 10 other western industrialized countries, Canada's figure was about average.

- Results for the five countries that have participated in all three rounds of the ICVS (Canada, England and Wales, Finland, the Netherlands, and the United States) indicate that victimization rates are fairly stable. In the 1996 survey, Canada's overall victimization rate fell slightly to 25 percent, from the 28 percent recorded in both 1989 and 1992. This mirrors the decline in Canada's police-reported crime rates over the past few years.

- Among the group of 11 western industrialized countries, Canadians were most satisfied with their police. In 1996, 80 percent of the population felt the police were doing a good job at controlling crime in their area. The Netherlands, which had the highest victimization rate, ranked their police lowest—only 45 percent of the population felt the police were doing a good job.

- When asked to decide on a sentence for a burglar convicted for a second time, people in Canada, England and Wales, Northern Ireland, Scotland, and the United States chose prison by a wide margin over other sanctions. By contrast, people in Austria, Finland, France, the Netherlands, Sweden, and Switzerland much preferred community service.

- People in Sweden felt safest walking alone in their area after dark: 87 percent of the population felt "very" or "fairly" safe. The figure was lowest for residents of England and Wales (65%). Canada's figure, at 73 percent, was third lowest among 11 countries.

- Fear of a break-in was highest in France, where 53 percent of the population felt the chances were "likely" or "very likely" that they would experience a break-in in the coming year. Canada had the third highest figure (30%), while Finland had the lowest (11%) in the group of 11 countries. Previous burglary victims were more fearful of a break-in than non-victims.

- A majority of households in the western countries are using home security measures. Usage of at least one of seven home security measures was highest in England and Wales (89% of households). In Canada, 78 percent of households reported using at least one of the measures. Special door locks were the most popular measure in nine countries, including Canada.

SOURCE: Statistics Canada, "Criminal Victimization: An International Perspective, Highlights," *Juristat*, Catalogue No. 85-002, vol. 18, no. 6, p. 1.

## Critique of Victimization Surveys

Just as the UCR has been criticized for under-representing the actual incidence of criminal activity in Canada, victimization surveys in general, and the GSS in particular, can be criticized for possible over-reporting of some crimes. It is beyond the purview of a victimization survey to verify the actual occurrence of any of the crimes reported to the interviewers. Hence, no measure exists as to the number of crimes that might be under-reported. Victimization surveys are dependent upon the ability of the respondent to not only recall incidents and their details but also to accurately place them in time. Some respondents provide a more detailed and accurate account of their victimization experience which may, in turn, skew the data. As well, by their nature, victimization surveys exclude data on homicide, kidnapping, so-called "victimless crimes" (public intoxication, prostitution and gambling), impaired driving, drug offences, crimes such as vandalism and theft committed against commercial or public property, and crimes committed against children under the age of 15.

## Comparing Uniform Crime Reporting Surveys and Victimization Surveys

The data generated by the UCR and Victimization Surveys, while based on the same categories of crime, reveal a very different picture. Findings from the UCR are the reports of crimes recorded by the police, who are generally alerted to the crime as a result of a call from a victim. The type and frequency of calls to police change over time and vary according to location. For example, as the community tolerance for sexual assault and family violence declines, victims or witnesses of these crimes may be more willing to report them to authorities, and authorities will be more likely to treat them as crimes.

Victimization surveys, on the other hand, were developed to provide a way of looking at crime from the perspective of individual victims. They describe what has happened to individual Canadians and the way in which these individuals respond to their victimization experiences. Without a doubt, these surveys reveal that many Canadians do not report personal victimizations and suggest the reasons for this.

Despite their divergent foci, UCR and Victimization Surveys can complement one another. Victimization data can help place UCR findings in context. For instance, how much change in official crime data for family violence can be attributed to changes in reporting patterns or police practices? (Police in Ontario and some other provinces are mandated to lay charges against the perpetrator in a domestic assault situation if sufficient evidence exists, regardless of the victim's willingness to concur). How are crime trends a reflection of people's attitudes toward crime and the criminal justice system? While neither UCR nor victimization data can provide comprehensive information about crime, when considered together they are useful in providing a picture of crime and criminal activity in Canada. See Figure 2.1 for a comparison of the UCR and GSS.

## Figure 2.1

## *Differences Between the UCR and GSS*

| UCR | GSS |
|---|---|
| **DATA COLLECTION METHODS:** | |
| Administrative police records | Personal reports from individual citizens |
| Census | Sample survey |
| 100% coverage of all police agencies | Sample of approximately 10 000 persons using random digit dialling sampling technique |
| Data submitted on paper or in machine-readable format | Computer Assisted Telephone Interviewing (CATI); excludes households without telephones |
| National in scope | Excludes Yukon and Northwest Territories |
| Continuous historical file: 1962 onwards | Periodic survey: 1988, 1993, next survey anticipated in the year 2000 |
| All recorded criminal incidents regardless of victims' age | Target population: persons aged 15 and over, excluding full-time residents of institutions |
| Counts only those incidents reported to and recorded by police | Collects crimes reported and not reported to police |
| **SCOPE AND DEFINITIONS:** | |
| Primary unit of count is the criminal incident | Primary unit of count is criminal victimization (at personal and household levels) |
| Nearly 100 crime categories | Eight crime categories |
| "Most Serious Offence" rule results in an undercount of less serious crimes | Statistics are usually reported on a "most serious offence" basis, but counts for every crime type are possible, depending on statistical reliability. |
| Includes attempts | Includes attempts |
| **SOURCES OF ERROR:** | |
| Reporting by the public | Sampling error |
| Processing error, edit failure, non-responding police department | Non-sampling error related to the following: coverage, respondent error (e.g., recall error), non-response, coding, edit and imputation, estimation |
| Police discretion, changes in policy and procedures | |
| Legislative change | |

SOURCE: Statistics Canada, *An Overview of the Differences between Police-Reported and Victim-Reported Crime, 1997*, Catalogue No. 85-542-XPE, p. 6.

# Data Gathering Using Self-Report Studies

**self-report study** a data
collection method
requiring subjects to
reveal their own
participation in criminal
behaviour.

Another approach to the production of data on the amount and types of crime is the **self-report study**. Within the field of criminology, there is a widely held belief that to understand crime, it is important to ask people about their involvement with it. There have been countless self-report studies conducted with various groups of individuals, most notably with youth. The results of the ground-breaking work by Short and Nye[13] led many to believe that traditional police data have the potential to be biased toward certain segments of society, in particular the lower socioeconomic classes. Other gaps between official sources of data and self-report data have been found in the age, sex, and race of the offender. One of the most notable Canadian self-report studies was conducted by LeBlanc and Fréchette during the 1970s and 1980s.[14] Using a list of 39 questions, these researchers questioned a large group of high-risk Montreal youth on a variety of behaviours (the list of questions is reproduced in Table 2.2). LeBlanc and Fréchette hoped to use the results of their surveys to describe delinquent patterns for all high-risk Canadian male youth. Despite methodological shortcomings, including the failure to consider cultural differences between French and English-speaking Canadians and the failure to consider delinquency rates among females, the study was important in its contribution to a general understanding of the crime picture among youth in Canada.

In general, self-report studies are recognized within the field of criminology as one means of counting crime and criminals. When considered in conjunction with other methods of information gathering, self-report studies help provide a more clear and complete picture of crime and who commits it. They are considered to be particularly useful in highlighting the relationship between social class and crime and in uncovering much crime that goes undetected.[15]

## Limitations of Self-Report Studies

Since their acceptance as a legitimate means of examining the reality of crime and criminals, self-report studies have consistently become more sound. Nevertheless, a number of shortcomings continue to exist, largely methodological. For example, the accuracy of this research approach is largely predicated on the honesty and forthrightness of the respondent. Inaccurate answers may result from a number of factors, including the respondent's failure to disclose behaviour or, conversely, to exaggerate behaviour, or the respondent's failure to remember. Often respondents are concerned about confidentiality and anonymity, which is understandable given the information they are being asked to reveal. This, in turn, may affect the way they answer or indeed whether they even participate in the survey. Analyses of self-report studies indicate, for example, that the more offences a respondent has committed, the fewer he/she is likely to admit to. Conversely, those respondents who have committed a lesser number of offences are more likely to admit to them in a self-report survey.

Other methodological limitations include a lack of standardized data collection methods, such as comparable questions, time frames, or geographic areas. In general, however, there seems to be agreement that self-report studies are useful in providing a

## Table 2.2

# Self-Report Questions from the Montreal Youth Study by LeBlanc and Fréchette

**During the past 12 months, did you:**

1. . . . purposely damage or destroy musical instruments, sports supplies, or other school equipment?
2. . . . purposely damage or destroy public or private property that did not belong to you?
3. . . . take some school property worth $5.00 or more?
4. . . . purposely damage school building (windows, walls, . . .)?
5. . . . take a motorcycle and go for a ride without the owner's permission?
6. . . . take a car and go for a ride without the owner's permission?
7. . . . purposely destroy a radio antenna, tires, or other parts of a car?
8. . . . "beat up" someone who hadn't done anything to you?
9. . . . take something from a store without paying?
10. . . . threaten to beat up someone to make him do something he didn't want to do?
11. . . . get into a place (a movie, a game, or a performance) without paying the admission price?
12. . . . use a weapon (stick, knife, gun, rock, . . .) while fighting another person?
13. . . . use stimulants (speed, pep pills, etc. . . .) or hallucinogens (LSD, STP, THC, etc. . . .)?
14. . . . have a fist fight with another person?
15. . . . take something of large value (worth $50.00 or more) that did not belong to you?
16. . . . gamble for money with persons other than your family members?
17. . . . sell any kind of drugs?
18. . . . break into and enter somewhere to take something?
19. . . . carry a weapon (chain, knife, gun, etc. . . .)?
20. . . . take something of some value (between $2.00 and $50.00) that did not belong to you?
21. . . . purposely set a fire in a building or in any other place?
22. . . . take and keep a bicycle that did not belong to you?
23. . . . take something of little value (worth less than $2.00) that did not belong to you?
24. . . . trespass anywhere you were not supposed to go (vacant house, railroad tracks, lumber yard, etc. . . .)?
25. . . . use marijuana or hashish?
26. . . . make anonymous phone calls (not say who you were)?
27. . . . use opiates (heroin, morphine, opium)?
28. . . . send in a false alarm?
29. . . . buy, use or sell something that you knew to be stolen?
30. . . . drive a car without a driver's licence?
31. . . . have sexual relations (other than kissing) with a person of the same sex?
32. . . . skip school without a legitimate excuse?
33. . . . have sexual relations (other than kissing) with a person of the opposite sex?
34. . . . take part in a gang fight between adolescents?
35. . . . run away from home for more than 24 hours?
36. . . . tell your parents (or those who replace them) that you would not do what they ordered you to do?
37. . . . take money from home without permission and with no intention of returning it?
38. . . . get drunk on beer, wine, or other alcoholic beverages?
39. . . . "fool around" at night when you were supposed to be at home?

*SOURCE*: M. LeBlanc and M. Fréchette, *Male Criminal Activity from Childhood through Youth: Multilevel and Developmental Perspectives* (New York: Springer-Verlag, 1989), pp. 195–96, cited in M.A. Jackson and C.T. Griffiths (eds.), *Canadian Criminology: Perspectives on Crime and Criminality* (Toronto: Harcourt, Brace & Company, Canada, 1995), p. 193. Reprinted with permission.

more rounded picture of the criminal, especially when compared with the picture that is often captured in official statistics based on police reports. While the official statistics provide information on tangibles such as the age and sex of an offender, self-report studies serve to reveal characteristics such as education levels, home life, peer group, and general socioeconomic realities of the offender. It has been suggested that this approach could be used to include an examination of those biological and psychological factors that contribute to criminal behaviour, thereby complementing the environmental realities they already help to illuminate. Whether the findings of these self-report studies that target a specific group in a specific time and place can be used to deduce general assumptions about criminals and the crimes they commit is still open to debate.

# The Social Dimensions of Crime

## What Are "Social Dimensions"?

Crime does not occur in a vacuum. It involves real people—human perpetrators and victims. Because society defines certain personal characteristics as especially important, however, it is possible to speak of the "social dimensions of crime," that is, aspects of crime and victimization as they relate to socially significant attributes by which groups are defined, and according to which individuals are assigned group membership. Socially significant attributes include gender, ethnicity or race, age, income or wealth, profession, and social class or standing within society. Such personal characteristics provide criteria by which individuals can be assigned to groups such as "the rich," "the poor," "male," "female," "young," "old," "black," "white," "white-collar worker," "manual labourer," and so on.[16]

We have already alluded briefly to the fact that the UCR, Victimization Surveys, and self-report studies structure the data they gather in ways that reflect socially significant characteristics. The UCR, for example, provides information on reported crimes, which reveals the sex and age of perpetrators. Victimization statistics document the age and sex of crime victims and the educational, occupational and income levels of households reporting victimizations. Self-report studies provide some insight into the age, sex, ethnic background, education levels, social habits, and socioeconomic status of those engaged in delinquent or criminal behaviour.

The social dimensions of crime are said by statisticians to reveal relationships or correlations. A **correlation** is simply a connection or association observed to exist between two measurable variables.

**Correlation** a causal, complementary, or reciprocal relationship between two measurable variables.

Correlations are of two types: positive and negative. If one measurement increases when another, with which it is correlated, does the same, then a positive correlation or positive relationship is said to exist between the two. When one measurement decreases in value as another rises, a negative or inverse correlation has been discovered. Victimization data, for example, show a negative relationship between age and victimization. As people age, victimization rates decline. Hence, although some elderly people do become crime victims, older people as a group tend to be less victimized than younger people. Uniform Crime Report data, on the other hand, show a positive relationship between youth and likelihood of arrest—specifically, between young adulthood and arrest. Young adults, it appears, commit most crimes. Hence, as people age, they tend to be both less likely to be victimized and less likely to become involved in criminal activity.

A word of caution is in order, however. Correlation does not necessarily imply causation. Because two variables appear to be correlated does not mean that they have any influence on one another, or that one causes another to either increase or decrease. Correlations that involve no causal relationship are said to be *spurious*. A study of crime rates, for example, shows that many crimes seem to occur with greater frequency in the summer. Similarly, industry groups tell us that food retailers sell more ice cream in the summer than at any other time. Are we to conclude, then, from the observed correlation between crime rates and ice cream sales, that one in some way causes the other? To do so on the basis of an observed correlation alone would obviously be foolish.

Some observed correlations do appear to shed at least some light on either the root causes of crime or the nature of criminal activity, often referred to as **correlates of crime**. Our discussion now turns to these.

**Correlates of crime** those variables observed to be related to criminal activity such as age, gender, ethnicity and social class

## Age and Crime

If records of persons accused are any guide, criminal activity is associated more with youth than any other stage of life. Year after year, Uniform Crime Reports consistently show that younger persons, from their mid-to-late teens to their early and mid-twenties, account for the bulk of the crime reported in this country. Indeed, age is one of the strongest correlates of criminal behaviour.

In Canada, the correlation between youth and crime varies slightly when considering the type of crime committed. The 1998 UCR indicates that persons accused of violent crimes are older than persons accused of property crimes, with the median age for the former being 29 years and 22 years for the latter.[17] In 1998, 14- to 19-year-olds were the highest risk group for committing both violent and property offences. Nearly 25 percent of persons accused of violent crimes fell within this age bracket, as did more than one in three persons accused of property crimes (see Figure 2.2). It is interesting to note when considering Figure 2.2 that "age-specific" crime rates were calculated using census information as it relates to age distribution. Prior to 1998, the age distribution of accused persons was based on the actual number or persons accused by the police, which did not take into account the age distribution of the entire population.

Despite cautions raised by some American criminologists that an impending demographic shift will result in a substantial increase in crime and especially violent crime,[18–22] a look at the demographic reality in Canada paints a somewhat different picture. According to Statistics Canada, a demographic evolution is occurring in Canada: the so-called "baby boomers" are now aged 30 to 50, fertility rates have declined since 1971 (resulting in fewer children), mortality rates have declined (resulting in increased longevity), and there has been a decreasing proportion of young adults, the group at greatest risk of committing crime. Further possibilities are raised in Box 2.7.

At the same time, the proportion of elderly, who are more fearful of crime, is increasing.[23] Statistics Canada projects that persons aged 0 to 14, a group that decreased significantly from about 45 percent of the population in 1976 to approximately 30 percent in 1996, will continue to decline to a low of about 25 percent by 2041. In comparison, persons aged 65 and over are projected to make up more than 20 percent of the population by 2011 and more than 30 percent by 2041.[24] Figure 2.3 shows the trend in the number of crimes and the number of 15- to 24-year-olds as rates per 100 000 population from 1962 to 1998. Between 1962 and 1978, both lines show a

**Figure 2.2a**

*Age-Specific Rates of Persons Accused of Violent
Crime, Sample of 169 Police Agencies, 1998*

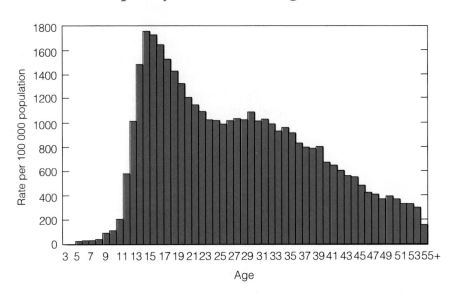

**Figure 2.2b**

*Age-Specific Rates of Persons Accused of Property
Crime, Sample of 169 Police Agencies, 1998*

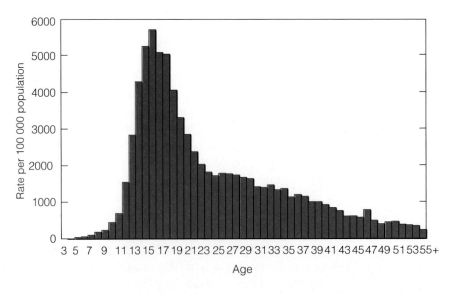

SOURCE: S. Tremblay, "Crime Statistics in Canada, 1998," Statistics Canada, *Juristat*, Catalogue No. 85-002,
vol. 19, no. 9, p. 12.

**Figure 2.3**

*Crime Rate and Demographics, Canada, 1962–1998*

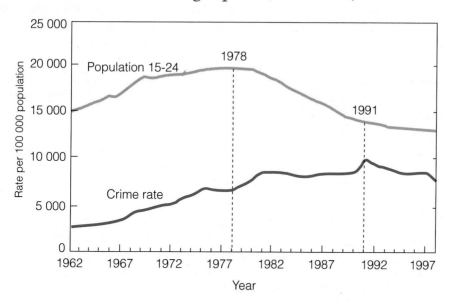

SOURCE: S. Tremblay, "Crime Statistics in Canada, 1998," Statistics Canada, *Juristat*, Catalogue No. 85-002, vol. 19, no. 9, p. 5.

constant increase. While crime continued to increase from 1978 to 1991, however, the rate of 15- to 24-year-olds per 100 000 population decreased. Since 1991, however, both trends have decreased. The crime rate has dropped by 22 percent and the 15- to 24-year-old population by 6 percent. Despite the anomaly of the years between 1978 and 1991, the statistics do seem to indicate a relationship between the trend in the crime rate and the trend in the high-risk offender age group.

Given these demographic realities, crimes committed by the elderly, or geriatric criminality, have sparked much interest among criminologists and the popular media. Movies such as *The Over the Hill Gang* have depicted the exploits of aged criminals. Although in the minority, real-life elderly criminals are not hard to find. The case of Edward Cook, 68, is illustrative. Cook usually works with an elderly female companion and the two are known for showing up in swank jewellery stores, posing as casually dressed tourists. The couple travels with a video camera casually slung over Cook's shoulder. Cook, however, keeps the camera running—recording security devices and showcased valuables throughout the targeted stores. Cook returns after closing hours, deactivates store alarms, and helps himself to the choicest jewels.

Why do older people commit crimes? One author explains it this way: "The reasons older people turn to crime are varied. Some people never retire—from trouble. Others find that retirement gets them into trouble. Boredom and unstructured leisure, fear of the future, frustration over limited finances, family neglect or stress—the same conditions that contribute to teenage crime—can lead seniors to commit desperate or foolish acts."[25]

Some older criminals use their age to advantage. Few people, for example, suspect older people of criminal intent. Hence, potential victims are less likely to be on their guard against crime in the presence of an older offender. Similarly, experience gained from previous criminality, and from life in general, can be turned into assets in the criminal arena. As the old adage goes, "knowledge is power," and whereas social convention holds that wisdom comes with age, so does increased criminal opportunity for those so inclined.

Although conventional street crime may be the bailiwick of the young, the indications are that older offenders are over-represented in other forms of crime, including those that require special skills and knowledge for their commission. Many of these crimes are job related and involve fraud, deception, or business activities that are criminal.

When considering the correlation between age and victimization, Canadian statistics show that Canadians between the ages of 15 and 24 years experience personal victimization at rates nearly twice that of those 24 to 44 years and 7 times that of those aged 45 to 64 years. The younger group is almost eight times as likely as the older groups to be victims of violence and six times as likely to be victims of personal theft.[26] The victimization rate for those 55 years and over was 31 per 100 000 population, compared with 312 per 100 000 for those aged 15 to 24 years.[27] Victimization Survey findings further show that those over 65 years of age are more likely than those who are younger to feel unsafe walking alone at night in their neighbourhoods. Between 1988 and 1993, those who indicated that they felt "very unsafe" walking alone in their neighbourhoods increased from 28 to 38 percent.[28]

Statistics show that children are over-represented as victims of certain types of crimes. While victimization surveys only poll Canadians over 17 years of age, UCR statistics indicate that for offences such as sexual assault, other sexual offences (sexual interference, invitation to sexual touching, sexual exploitation, and incest) and abduction, children under 12 years of age represent 25 percent, 50 percent, and 81 percent, respectively.[29]

## Correlation between Age and Crime

BOX 2.7

Why are age and crime such a strong correlate? Explanations range from the biological, which look at hormonal variables such as higher levels of testosterone in males, to an examination of the social and personal realities existing at various stages of life. Do offenders "grow out of crime" as they mature? Do they develop significant attachments to people, such as spouses and children, or to jobs, that they do not want to risk losing through continued involvement in crime? Do they settle down and no longer see criminal-deviant behaviour as fun or as a means to attain immediate gratification or peer approval? Does the age at which a youth becomes involved in criminal behaviour and is labelled by the criminal justice system as an offender have any bearing on how long his/her criminal career will last? Do some offenders simply grow too tired and physically unable to continue in a criminal lifestyle? There is no simple explanation as to why age and crime are correlated. Keep these questions in mind as you consider the theories of criminal behaviour presented in Chapters 5 to 9. Can the age of the offender be factored into any or all of these theories?

## Gender and Crime

Gender appears so closely linked to most forms of criminal activity that it has been called "the best single predictor of criminality …"[30] Table 2.3 shows degree of involvement in each of the major categories of crime by gender by representing the proportion of male-female involvement in each category. For example, of all the violent crimes in this country in a given year, close to 90 percent are committed by men.

| Table 2.3 | | |
|---|---|---|
| *Male-Female Involvement in Crime: Percentage of Charges by Gender, 1998* | | |
| **Criminal Code Offences** | **Males** | **Females** |
| Violent crimes | 86.2% | 13.8% |
| Property crimes | 77.5% | 22.5% |

SOURCE: Compiled from CANSIM, **www.statcan.ca**.

The apparently low rate of female criminality has been explained by some as primarily due to cultural factors, including early socialization, role expectations, and a reluctance among criminal justice officials to arrest and prosecute women. Others have assumed a biological propensity toward crime and aggression among men that may be lacking in women. These and other issues are addressed in Chapters 5 to 9.

It is important to note, however, that the rate of female criminality, especially relating to property crimes, has increased substantially in Canada since the 1960s. A comparison of the rates of males and females involved in property offences such as serious theft, fraud, and minor theft since 1968 shows that women have become twice as involved in these types of offences in the 1990s. Some criminologists cite *role convergence*, or the adaptation of the role of women to more closely resemble that of men, as an explanation for this. Still others see the significant increases in female involvement in offences such as shoplifting, credit card fraud, and passing bad cheques as a manifestation of the *feminization of poverty*, rather than the convergence of male and female roles.[31] As the number of poor, female, single parents grows, their marginalization may be reflected in increases in certain types of female property crimes.

When women commit crime, they are more often followers than leaders. A 1996 study of women in correctional settings, for example, found that women are far more likely to assume "secondary follower rules during criminal events" than "dominant leadership roles."[32]

Concerning victimization, women are victimized less frequently than are men in most crime categories. Table 2.4 indicates the UCR victimization rates for selected crimes of violence against women. While male victims significantly outnumber female victims in incidents of homicide, attempted murder, assault and robbery, the reality is very different when the victimization rates for sexual assault, criminal harassment, and kidnapping/hostage-taking are considered. Victimization Surveys, the Violence

Female gang members fighting. Although much female criminality has long been overlooked, criminologists are now increasingly aware of gender issues. How does the criminality of men and women appear to differ? *Copaken/Gamma-Liaison, Inc.*

Against Women Survey (VAWS) in particular, indicate that up to one-half of all Canadian women have experienced at least one incident of violence since the age of 16. Specifically, the VAWS findings indicate that 34 percent of women surveyed reported having experienced a physical assault, 39 percent reported having been sexually assaulted, and 15 percent had experienced unwanted sexual touching. Almost one-half of the women surveyed experienced violence by men known to them (boyfriends,

## Table 2.4

### *Adult Victims of Violence by Gender: Selected Incidents, 1998*

|  | Males | Females |
|---|---|---|
| Homicide | 70% | 30% |
| Attempted murder | 75% | 25% |
| Assault (levels 1,2,3) | 49% | 51% |
| Other assaults | 81% | 19% |
| Sexual assault (levels 1,2,3) | 8% | 92% |
| Robbery | 56% | 44% |
| Criminal harassment | 21% | 79% |
| Kidnapping/Hostage-taking | 34% | 66% |

SOURCE: Adapted from S. Tremblay, "Crime Statistics in Canada, 1998," Statistics Canada, *Juristat*, Catalogue No. 85-002, vol. 19, no. 9 (1999).

dates, marital partners, friends, family, neighbours).[33] A detailed examination of some of the current Canadian legislation aimed at assisting victims of crime, female victims in particular, can be found in Chapter 8.

## Ethnicity and Crime

Unlike crime statistics from the United States, Canadian crime statistics do not routinely report on the racial and ethnic makeup of offenders. American statistics tell us that in most crime categories, arrests of African-American offenders is equal to or exceeds arrests of Causcasian offenders. When these numbers take into account the relative proportion of ethnic groups in the American population and calculate the extent to which criminal activity is associated with each, the discrepancy between African-Americans and Causcasians is even greater. For example, while African-Americans are arrested for about 56 percent of all murders committed annually, or slightly over one-half, the murder rate among African-Americans is 10 times greater than it is among Causcasians, since the former account for only one-eighth of the population.[34]

The only official Canadian statistics that report on the correlation between ethnicity and crime derive from studies that consider incarcerated offender or inmate profiles. The number of inmates, however, while accurate, is not representative of the actual number of offenders and offences detected by police. Nevertheless, correctional statistics are useful in shedding light on the reality of ethnicity and crime in Canada. Table 2.5 shows an over-representation of especially Aboriginals and blacks among those inmates serving a federal sentence of incarceration (one that is 2 years or greater).

### Table 2.5

### *1997 Canadian Federal Incarceration Rates, by Racial Group*

| Race | Population Size[a] | Percentage of Population | Number in Prison[b] | Percentage of Prison Population | Prison Rate (per 100 000) |
|---|---|---|---|---|---|
| Caucasian | 24 228 690 | 85.1% | 10 329 | 73.3% | 42.63 |
| Aboriginal | 1 101 955 | 3.9% | 2 037 | 14.5% | 184.85 |
| Black | 573 860 | 2.0% | 840 | 6.0% | 146.37 |
| Asian[c] | 2 070 670 | 7.2% | 334 | 2.4% | 16.13 |
| Other[d] | 552 950 | 2.0% | 551 | 3.9% | 99.64 |
| Total | 28 528 125 | 100.0% | 14 091 | 100.0% | 49.39 |

[a] Canadian population figures are taken from the 1996 Canadian Census. Estimates of the racial minority population are based on a new Census question designed to measure the "visible minority" population of Canada. This "race" question was asked for the first time on the 1996 Census. Information was obtained from the Statistics Canada Web site (**www.statcan.ca**).

[b] Federal prison figures are provided by the Correctional Service of Canada (Solicitor General 1998).

[c] The Asian category includes individuals who identified themselves as either Chinese, Japanese, Korean, South-East Asian, South-Asian, or Filipino.

[d] The "Other" category includes people who identified themselves as Arab/West Asian, Latin American or having a multiple racial background.

SOURCE: Scot Wortley, "A Northern Taboo: Research on Race, Crime, and Criminal Justice in Canada," *Canadian Journal of Criminology*, vol. 41, no. 2, 1999, p. 261.

The reality of Aboriginal over-representation in the Canadian criminal justice system has been studied for some time. A one-day snapshot of inmates in Canada's adult correctional institutions shows that Aboriginal peoples account for 17 percent of all inmates, 14 percent of all inmates in federal facilities, and 18 percent of all inmates in provincial facilities (for those serving 2 years less 1 day). Figure 2.4 illustrates that, across the country, the proportion of Aboriginal inmates is much greater than the proportion of Aboriginal persons in the general population, with the most striking dichotomies occurring in the prairie provinces, the Yukon, and the Northwest Territories. While Aboriginal and non-Aboriginal inmates are convicted for similar types of offences, a larger proportion of Aboriginal inmates are convicted and sentenced to incarceration for crimes against the person, compared with non-Aboriginals (42% vs. 31%, respectively, within provincial institutions and 79% vs. 72%, respectively, in federal institutions).

---

**Figure 2.4**

## *Distribution of Aboriginal Inmates*

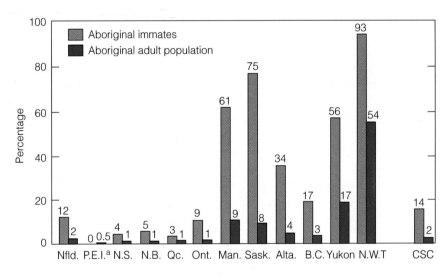

[a]Number of Aboriginal immates too small to be expressed.

SOURCE: Anne Finn, Shelley Trevethon, Gisèle Carrière, and Melanie Kowalski, "Female inmates, Aboriginal Inmates, and Inmates Serving Life Sentences: A One-Day Snapshot," Statistics Canada, *Juristat*, Catalogue No. 85-002, vol. 19, no. 5 (1999), p. 9.

## Social Class and Crime

Prior to 1960, criminologists generally assumed that a correlation existed between social class and crime. They believed that members of lower social classes were more prone to commit crime, and they thought that this propensity applied to all types of criminal activity. In the early 1960s, however, studies of the relationship between social class and crime, which made use of offender self-reports, seemed to show that the relationship between social class and criminality was an artifact of discretionary practices within the criminal justice system.[35] Such studies, especially of teenagers, found that rates of self-reported delinquency and criminality were fairly consistent across various social classes within North American society. Similar studies of white-collar criminality seemed to show that although the nature of criminal activity may vary between classes, members of all social classes had nearly equal tendencies toward criminality. Hence, the apparent penchant for crime among members of the lower social classes was explained partially by the fact that the types of crime traditionally committed by these groups were those most likely to come to the attention of law enforcement officials and be fully prosecuted by the criminal justice system. While there is no doubt that people from all social classes commit crimes, a number of studies point to a significant correlation between lower socioeconomic status and criminal activity, as we shall see below.

In 1978, a comprehensive re-evaluation of 35 previous studies of the relationship between social class and crime concluded that previously claimed links were nonexistent.[36] Publication of the report fuelled further study of the relationship between social class and crime, and in 1981 a seminal article by Australian criminologist **John Braithwaite**—which summarized the results of 224 previous studies on the subject—concluded rather convincingly that members of lower social classes were indeed more prone to commit crime.[37] In contrast to earlier studies, Braithwaite found that "socioeconomic status is one of the very few correlates of criminality which can be taken, on balance, as persuasively supported by a large body of empirical evidence."

Many of the difficulties surrounding research into the relationship between social class and crime appear to stem from a lack of definitional clarity. In the many different studies evaluated by Braithwaite, for example, neither *crime* nor *class* was uniformly defined. Some researchers[38] have similarly suggested that earlier studies may have been seriously flawed by their near-exclusive focus on young people and by their conceptualization of crime in terms of relatively minor offences (truancy, vandalism, etc.). Hence, a lack of concise definitions of the subject matter, combined with inadequate measurement techniques, may have led to misleading results.

Recent Canadian studies of street youth in Toronto and Edmonton found that many came from lower-class families and were on the street because of poor relationships at home and at school. The struggle for survival often resulted in involvement in delinquency and crime.[39]

Canadian correctional statistics record the educational level and employment status of each inmate upon entry into a federal correctional facility. Inasmuch as education and employment can be used as indicators of social class, these statistics reveal that almost one-half of all federally incarcerated inmates have a grade 9 education or less (compared with 19 percent of the adult population) and were unemployed at the time of admission (compared with 10 percent general adult unemployment). For provincial inmates, the corresponding figures are 34 and 55 percent (see Table 2.6).

Are those from the lowest socioeconomic classes also most likely to be victims of crime? Victimization Survey data from the GSS indicate that those households with incomes below $15 000 have the lowest victimization rate, 42 percent lower than those households with incomes of $60 000. Personal victimization figures are quite different, however. Those victims identified as having incomes below $15 000 are 28 percent more likely to become personally victimized. Rates of assault are 43 percent higher and total violent crime is 54 percent higher for this income group.[40]

### Table 2.6

## Educational and Employment Status of Adult Inmates

| Grade Completed | Provincial/<br>Territorial Adult Inmate | Federal<br>Adult Inmate |
| --- | --- | --- |
| 9 or less | 34% | 46% |
| 10 to 11 | 39% | 29% |
| 12 or higher | 27% | 25% |
| **Employment Status*** | | |
| Unemployed | 55% | 43% |
| Employed | 45% | 57% |

*at time of admission to correctional facility

SOURCE: Adapted from Anne Finn, Shelley Trevethon, Gisèle Carrière, and Melanie Kowalski, "Female inmates, Aboriginal Inmates, and Inmates Serving Life Sentences: A One-Day Snapshot," Statistics Canada, *Juristat*, Catalogue No. 85-002, vol. 19 no. 5 (1999), p. 10.

## Summary
Crime statistics have been gathered in one form or another for at least 150 years. Although early data about crime may have been used to assess the moral health of nations, modern-day criminal statistics programs provide a fairly objective picture of crime in Canada and elsewhere. Statistics often form the basis for social policy.

Today, two large-scale government programs collect crime data in Canada. One, the Uniform Crime Reporting system, is administered by Statistics Canada and annually collects information on crimes reported to the police and on charges laid throughout the country. The other, Victimization Surveys conducted as part of the *General Social Survey* every 5 years, is also run by Statistics Canada. These surveys provide reports on the criminal victimization of households and individuals.

As discussed, the social correlates of crime in Canada include age, sex, race, and social class. Although crime statistics do not tell the whole story and other forms of crime need to be recognized, it appears from the best information available that young men are especially over-represented in Canadian crime statistics. Among these men, Aboriginals account for a proportion that is vastly over-representative of their numbers in our population. Recognizing the reality of such involvement should help our society secure a safer future for all its citizens and enhance effective crime prevention efforts.

Other than gender, age, and ethnicity, social class can be a significant indicator of the likelihood of criminal involvement. Suffice it here to say that crimes are committed by members of all social classes. As we will recognize in later chapters, however, powerful classes make the laws and are therefore less apt to have need of breaking them and are probably more committed to preservation of the status quo. Hence, many offenders, especially those arrested for street, property, and crimes of violence, come from the lower social classes.

Some people argue that crime statistics do not justify the degree of fear Canadians express about crime. Others suggest that statistics are misleading and that they do not provide a true picture of crime in Canada. Even though the actual incidence of crime is difficult to measure, crime statistics do provide us with an appreciation for the extent of the problems facing victims of crime, social policy-makers, and law enforcement personnel today.

# Discussion Questions

1. This book emphasizes a social problems versus social responsibility theme. Which perspective, if any, is best supported by a realistic appraisal of the "social dimensions" of crime discussed in this chapter?

2. What are the major differences between the UCR and the Victimization Surveys? Can useful comparisons be made between these two crime indices? If so, of what might such comparisons consist?

3. What is a *crime rate?* How are rates useful?

4. What are the reasons victims don't report crimes to the police? Which crimes appear to be the most under-reported? Why are those crimes so infrequently reported? Which crimes appear to be the most frequently reported? Why are they so often reported?

5. This chapter seems to say that if you are young, male, Aboriginal, undereducated, and unemployed, you have a greater likelihood of becoming involved in criminal activity. What are some of the arguments that might support this "reality?"

# Weblinks

**www.statcan.ca/english/Pgdb/State/justic.htm**
Statistics Canada, Justice and Crime. Current statistics on crime, victims, suspects, the police, and the courts.

**www.canada.justice.gc.ca/**
Department of Justice, Canada. Numerous links to current news and events, programs and services, and general information about Canada's criminal justice system.

**www.csc-scc.gc.ca/**
Correctional Service of Canada. Information on Canadian correctional policy, legislation, research, and publications. Good links to provincial/territorial sites.

**www.npb-cnlc.gc.ca/**
National Parole Board, Canada. Provides useful information on all aspects of parole as well as links to related legislation and statutes.

**www.scc-csc.gc.ca/index_e.htm**
Supreme Court of Canada. History of the Supreme Court, overview of the Canadian judicial system, judgments, information on cases, and frequently asked questions.

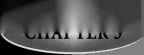

# Research Methods and Theory Development

Criminological research is most frequently concerned with the discovery of the causes of crime and the effect of various methods of treatment.

—HERMANN MANNHEIM[1]

Over the last 10 years, the Canadian federal government has significantly redirected and reduced funding and support for both university and government criminal justice research.

—CHRISTOPHER MURPHY AND PHILIP STENNING[2]

## LEARNING OUTCOMES

After reading this chapter, you should be able to:

- Appreciate the relevance of criminological theory to the study of crime and criminals

- Recognize the role of criminological research in theory development and display an understanding of various research designs

- Identify research limitations, including problems in data collection and analysis

- Recognize the ethical considerations involved in conducting criminological research

- Identify the impact of criminological research on the creation of social policy

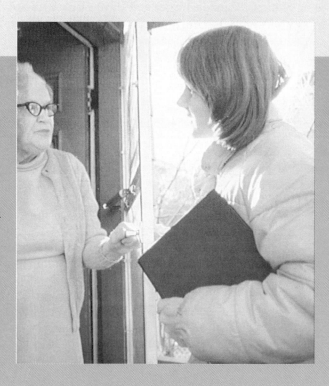

IMPORTANT TERMS

| | | |
|---|---|---|
| hypothesis | internal validity | secondary analysis |
| theory | external validity | intersubjectivity |
| research | controlled experiments | replicability |
| applied research | quasi-experimental | descriptive statistics |
| pure research | designs | inferential statistics |
| primary research | control group | tests of significance |
| secondary research | randomization | quantitative methods |
| variable | survey research | qualitative methods |
| operationalization | case study | *verstehen* |
| research designs | participant observation | data confidentiality |
| confounding effects | self-reports | informed consent |

# Introduction

A recent issue of the *Canadian Journal of Criminology* was devoted entirely to an examination of the state of criminological research in Canada today.[3] The editors, Christopher Murphy and Philip Stenning, express concern at what they perceive to be a significant reduction in the amount of government support for criminological research in this country and the related declining influence of such research on the processes of criminal justice policy-making. They cite the termination of the University Centres of Criminology funding program in 1994, the recent elimination of the research division at the Ministry of the Solicitor General, the severe downsizing of the research branch at the Department of Justice, and the closure of the Canadian Police College research section as evidence of this. Murphy and Stenning invited Canadian criminologists to contribute to the issue with *their* views on the health of criminological research and theory. Writers tackled such subject areas as youth justice, sentencing, corrections, Aboriginal justice issues, race and crime issues, and feminist research.

The response to this invitation was "remarkably vigorous" and varied in its assessment. Many contributors were discouraged about recent federal government attitudes toward criminological research, and many expressed the need for continued empirical research to inform policy development, despite the fact it is now politically unfashionable. The authors concluded that research in criminology should not be allowed to retreat into the ivory towers of academia. They called for "the development of new practices and more productive relationships between those who do research and those involved in the policy development process here."[4]

This chapter, which concerns itself with criminological research methods and theory development, is intended to show to those now embarking upon the study of criminology why modern-day criminology has both validity and purpose—that is, to show how it is applicable to social life in today's world. Were it not, criminological study would be pointless and criminological theorizing fruitless. Happily, because it is built on a scientific approach to the subject matter of crime, criminology has much to offer as we attempt to grapple with the crime problems now facing us. For criminology to realize its full potential, however, more than mere scientific acceptance is necessary. Criminology must become accepted as a policy-making tool, consulted by lawmakers and social planners alike, and respected for what it can tell us about both crime and its prevention.

# The Science of Criminology

Over the past century, criminologists have undertaken the task of building a "scientific criminology," as distinguished from what had been the "armchair criminology" of earlier years. Armchair criminologists offered their ideas to one another as conjecture—fascinating "theories" that could be debated (and sometimes were) ad nauseam. The ruminations of armchair criminologists achieved a considerable degree of popular acclaim through the involvement of distinguished lecturers, the association of such ideas with celebrated bastions of higher learning, and their publication in prestigious forums, but they were rarely founded on anything other than mere speculation.

The ideas of armchair criminologists followed in the intellectual tradition of Christian apologists who busied themselves with debates over questions such as how many angels could fit on the head of a pin, or whether Noah had forgotten to take certain types of insects aboard the ark, but that had made the famous journey by happenstance (why, for example, would anyone take two mosquitoes?). They were the kinds of things one could probably never know with certainty, no matter how much the ideas were debated. Under such circumstances, one person's theory was another's fact and still another's wishful thinking.[5]

Although it is easy to dispense with armchair criminology as the relaxed musings of carefree intellectuals undertaken almost as sport, it is far more difficult to agree on the criteria necessary to move any undertaking into the realm of serious scientific endeavor. Present-day criminology is decidedly more scientific, however, than its intellectual predecessor—which means that it is amenable to objective scrutiny and systematic testing. In fact, the drive to make criminology "scientific" has been a conscious one, beginning with many of the approaches discussed in Chapter 5.

A variety of criteria have been advanced for declaring any endeavor "scientific." Among them are[6]:

- The systematic collection of related facts (as in the building of a database).
- An emphasis on the availability and application of the scientific method.
- "The existence of general laws, a field for experiment or observation ... and control of academic discourse by practical application."
- "The fact that it has been ... accepted into the scientific tradition."
- An "emphasis on a worthwhile subject in need of independent study even if adequate techniques of study are not yet available" (as in the investigation of paranormal phenomena).

Probably all the forgoing could be said of criminology. For one thing, criminologists do gather facts. The mere gathering of facts, however, although it may lead to a descriptive criminology, falls short of offering satisfactory explanations for crime. Hence, most contemporary criminologists are concerned with identifying relationships among the facts they observe, and with attempting to understand the many and diverse causes of crime. This emphasis on unveiling causality moves criminology beyond the merely descriptive into the realm of conjecture and theory-building.

A further emphasis on measurement and objectivity gives contemporary criminology its scientific flavour.

## The Devil Made Her Do It

### Demonic Possession Trial in Dallas

Scientific criminology generally scoffs at claims of supernatural influences in crime commission. As the story that follows shows, however, not everyone is convinced.

Doretha Crawford insists she and her sister didn't gouge out their sister's eyeballs with their fingers. But when a prosecutor asked her Tuesday if her sister had been possessed, she didn't hesitate.

"It wasn't her," Crawford said, describing how her sister, Myra Obasi, 30, while seemingly possessed by a demon, drove wildly, swerved toward huge trucks and tried to run off the road.

"Her whole features changed. Her eyes were big…. She spoke in a man's voice. Mist came out of her mouth. Her teeth were black and scattered. It said it got her, and it was going to get us, too."

In one of the most bizarre cases in recent Texas history, Crawford and her sister, Beverly Johnson, testified in their own defense, saying they didn't blind Obasi in Dallas last March.

Instead, they insist, they fled demons for two days, prayed and sought out ministers, all trying to save their sister.

Obasi, stunning courtroom observers, said she agrees.

A Shreveport, La., schoolteacher who is now totally blind, Obasi testified in a near-whisper, crying occasionally, that she has no idea how she lost her eyeballs. But she insisted her sisters had nothing to do with it.

All three sisters were in the house of Mattye Bradfield, an elderly preacher in southern Dallas, when Obasi was horribly blinded.

But Crawford, 34, and Johnson, 35, testified that they couldn't remember the critical period—a claim prosecutor George West mocked as "stereo memory loss."

Police and prosecutors have said Obasi at first told them the sisters blinded her while trying to "beat the devil" out of her. The tale, by any measure, is a truly hellish one.

Last spring Johnson began having headaches that a doctor could not cure, according to her father, Chester Crawford. Crawford reluctantly told jurors he then took Johnson to see Benny Morgan, a practitioner of "hoodoo," a Christianized version of voodoo.

Prosecutors and police have said the diagnosis was that the family was under attack by demons. Johnson said her father told them later that one of their sisters, living in Houston, was trying to kill them. So when someone wrote the words "BLOOD ROOM" on Obasi's car last March, they fled from Arcadia, La., where the two defendants lived, to Dallas. They turned their five children over to a stranger along the way.

All three sisters say they are firm Christian believers. But prosecutors, who expect to finish the trial today, say they will convince jurors otherwise.

Both women face two to 10 years for aggravated assault.

Sisters: Doretha Crawford, centre, and Beverly Johnson, left, were tried for gouging out Myra Obasi's eyes. Obasi (shown in photo on top right) says her sisters had nothing to do with it. Is a spiritual influence active in certain forms of criminality? *(a) Pat Sullivan/AP/Wide World Photos; (b and c) Ariane Kadoch/The Dallas Morning News.*

## DISCUSSION QUESTIONS

1. Do you believe that the devil plays a role in modern-day crime causation? If so, describe the nature of that role.
2. How might we research whether the devil, or some other supernatural force, is active in influencing crime rates today?

SOURCE: Mark Potok, "Demonic Possession Trial Has Dallas Under Its Spell," *USA Today*, September 21, 1994, p. 8A. Copyright 1994, *USA Today*. Reprinted with permission.

# Theory-Building

Ultimately, the goal of research within criminology is the construction of theories or models that allow for a better understanding of criminal behaviour and that permit the development of strategies intended to address the problem of crime. A theory consists of a set of interrelated propositions that provide a relatively complete form of understanding. Hence, even if we find that crime is higher when the moon is full, we must still ask, "Why?" Is it because the light from full moons makes it possible for those interested in committing crime to see better at night? If so, then we would expect crime to be higher on full moon nights in areas where there is no cloud cover than in areas where clouds obliterate the moon's light. Likewise, cities should show less of a rise in crime during full moons than rural areas and small towns, as city lights effectively minimize the impact of the light of the moon. In any event, a complete lunar theory of crime causation would contain specific propositions about the causal nature of the phenomena involved.

There are many ways to define the word *theory*. One cogent definition comes from Don M. Gottfredson, a well-known criminologist of modern times, who writes that "[t]heories consist of postulates [i.e., assumptions], theoretical constructs, logically derived hypotheses, and definitions. Theories," says Gottfredson, "can be improved steadily through **hypothesis** testing, examination of evidence from observations, revisions of the theory, and repetitions of the cycle, repeatedly modifying the theory in light of the evidence."[7] Another well-known methodologist describes theories this way: "… a theory is a set of related propositions that suggest why events occur in the manner that they do. The propositions that make up theories are of the same form as hypotheses: they consist of concepts and the linkages or relationships between them."[8]

These definitions all have something to offer; however, the definition of the term *theory* that we choose to use in this book combines aspects of them all. For our purposes, then, a **theory** consists of a series of interrelated propositions that attempt to describe, explain, predict, and ultimately control some class of events. Theories gain explanatory power from inherent logical consistency and are "tested" by how well they describe and predict reality. In other words, a good theory provides relatively complete understanding, is supported by observations, and stands up to continued scrutiny.

Theories serve a number of purposes. For one thing, they give meaning to observations. They explain what we see in a particular setting by relating those observations to other things already understood. Hence, a simple example of a theory of physics explains the behaviour of light by saying that light has the properties of both waves and particles. Such a theory is immediately useful, for although we may have trouble conceptualizing the light's essence, we can easily grasp ideas such as "wave" and "particle," both of which we experience in everyday living.

Theories within criminology serve the same purpose as those in the physical sciences, although they are often more difficult to test. Few people, for example, can intuitively understand the motivation of "lust murderers" (a term developed by the Federal Bureau of Investigation in the United States and popularized by some recent movies) or men who sexually abuse and kill women, often sadistically. Most people,

**Hypothesis** 1. an explanation that accounts for a set of facts and that can be tested by further investigation.
2. something that is taken to be true for the purpose of argument or investigation.

**Theory** a series of interrelated propositions that attempt to describe, explain, predict, and ultimately to control some class of events. A theory gains explanatory power from inherent logical consistency and is "tested" by how well it describes and predicts reality.

after all, are not lust murderers, and therefore lack an intellectual starting point in striving to understand what goes on in the minds of those who are. Some psychiatric theories (discussed in Chapter 6) suggest that lust murderers kill because of a deep-seated hatred of women. Hate is something that most minds can grasp, and a vision of lust murder as an extreme example of the age-old battle between the sexes provides an intellectual "handle" that many can appreciate. Hence, theory-building dispenses of the old adage that "it takes one to know one," instead bringing at least the possibility of understanding within the reach of all. Note, however, that although such limited explanations as the one discussed here may provide a degree of understanding, they must still be tested to determine whether they are true.

Theories provide understanding in a number of ways. Kenneth R. Hoover identifies the following four uses of theory in social scientific thinking[9]:

- Theories provide *patterns* for the interpretation of data. Population density, for example, tends to be associated with high crime rates, and maps showing high population density tend to be closely associated with diagrams that reflect rates of crime. Hence, some theorists are quick to suggest, overcrowding increases aggression and therefore crime. "People," says Hoover, "like to think in terms of images, analogies, and patterns; this helps to simplify complex realities and to lighten the burden of thought."
- Theories *link* one study with another. Some years ago, for example, a case study of women's prisons in California found the existence of artificially constructed "families," around which women's lives centered. A similar, but later, study of a Chinese prison also found that family-like groups had been created by female inmates there—prompting some theorists to suggest that women felt a need to nurture and to be nurtured by aspects of social structure, and that they carried such a need with them into prison. The fact that cross-cultural support was found for the suggestion provided a linkage between the two studies which tended to lend further support to the suggestion itself.
- Theories supply frameworks within which concepts and variables acquire *special significance.* The death penalty, for example, although especially significant to individuals condemned to die, acquires special significance when seen as a tool employed by the powerful to keep the powerless under their control.
- Theories allow us to *interpret* the larger meaning of our findings for ourselves and for others. Hence, the death penalty has become a moral issue for many people today, shrouded as it is in ethical considerations and images of national identity and ultimate justice.

## The Role of Research

More important than the claims made by theories and by the theorists who create them are findings of fact that either support those claims or leave them without foundation. Hence, theories, once proposed, need to be tested against the real world through a variety of research strategies, including experimentation and case studies.

Any theory gains credence if activity based on it produces results in keeping with what that theory would predict. Bernard P. Cohen, a seminal thinker on the subject of social scientific theory construction, tells us that "scientific knowledge is theoretical knowledge, and the purpose of methods in science is to enable us to choose among alternative theories."[10]

Knowledge is inevitably built on experience and observation. Hence, the crux of scientific research is data collection. Data collection occurs through a variety of techniques, including direct observation, the use of surveys and interviews, participant observation, and the analysis of existing data sets—all of which will be discussed shortly.

**Research** can be defined as the use of standardized, systematic procedures in the search for knowledge.[11] Some researchers distinguish between applied research and nonapplied or pure research. **Applied research** "consists of scientific inquiry that is designed and carried out with practical application in mind."[12] In applied research, the researcher is working toward some more or less practical goal. It may be the reduction of crime, the efficient compensation of victims of crime, or an evaluation of the effectiveness of policies implemented to solve some specific aspect of the crime problem. **Pure research,** on the other hand, is undertaken simply for the sake of advancing scientific knowledge and is not expected to be immediately relevant.

Another type of research is called secondary research or secondary analysis.[13] It is distinguished from **primary research** in that the latter is characterized by original and direct investigation.[14] **Secondary research**, on the other hand, consists of new evaluations of existing information collected by other researchers.

Scientific research generally proceeds in stages, which can be divided conceptually among (1) problem identification, (2) the development of a research design, (3) a choice of data-gathering techniques, and (4) a review of findings, which often includes statistical analysis.

**Research** the use of standardized, systematic procedures in the search for knowledge.

**Applied research** scientific inquiry that is designed and carried out with practical application in mind.

**Pure research** research undertaken simply for the sake of advancing scientific knowledge.

**Primary research** research characterized by original and direct investigation.

**Secondary research** new evaluations of existing information collected by other researchers.

## Problem Identification

Problem identification, the first step in any research, consists of the naming of a problem or choice of an issue to be studied. Topics may be selected for a variety of reasons. For example, some Canadian criminologists contend that "[t]he growing politicization of the policy development process ... has placed increasing constraints not only on what kinds of criminological research will be supported by governments, but also on who will receive support to do it."[15] It may also be that private foundation monies have become available to support studies in a specific area, perhaps the researcher has a personal interest in a particular issue and wants to learn more, or maybe a professor or teacher has assigned a research project as part of the requirements for successful class completion. Whatever the reason for beginning research, however, the way in which a research problem is stated will help narrow the research focus and serve as a guide to the formulation of data-gathering strategies.

Although some criminological research undertaken today is purely descriptive, the bulk of such research is intended to explore issues of causality—especially the claims made by theories purporting to explain criminal behaviour. As such, much contemporary research in criminology is involved with the testing of hypotheses.

The *Canadian Oxford Dictionary* defines the word *hypothesis* in two ways:

1. "A proposition made as a basis for reasoning, without the assumption of truth …"
2. "a supposition made as a starting point for further investigation from known facts …"

Within the modern scientific tradition, a hypothesis serves both purposes. Some criminologists, as mentioned earlier, have observed what appears to be a correlation, or relationship, between phases of the moon and the rate of crime commission. Such observers may propose the following hypothesis: "The moon causes crime." Although this is a useful starting hypothesis, it needs to be further refined before it can be tested. Specifically, the concepts contained within the hypothesis must be translated into measurable variables. A **variable** is simply a concept that can undergo measurable changes.

Scientific precedent holds that only measurable items can be satisfactorily tested. The process of turning a simple hypothesis into one that is testable is called **operationalization.** An operationalized hypothesis is one that is stated in such a way as to facilitate measurement. It is specific in its terms and in the linkages it proposes. We might, for example, move a step further toward both measurability and specificity in our hypothesis about the relationship between the moon and crime by restating it as follows: "Rates of murder, sexual assault, robbery, and assault rise when the moon's fullness increases, and are highest when the moon is fullest." Now we have specified what we mean by crime (i.e., murder, sexual assault, robbery, and assault), rates of which can be calculated. The degree of the moon's fullness can also be measured. Once we have operationalized a hypothesis and made the concepts it contains measurable, those concepts have, in effect, become variables.

Now that the concepts within our hypothesis are measurable, we can test the hypothesis itself. That is to say, we can observe what happens to crime rates as the moon approaches fullness, as well as what happens when the moon is full, and see whether our observations support our hypothesis. As our dictionary definition tells us, once a hypothesis has been operationalized it is assumed to be true for purposes of testing. It is accepted, for study purposes, until observation proves it untrue, at which point it is said to be rejected. As one renowned researcher stated, "[t]he task of theory-testing … is predominantly one of rejecting inadequate hypotheses."[16]

**Variable** a concept that can undergo measurable changes.

**Operationalization** the process by which concepts are made measurable.

## Research Designs

Research designs structure the research process. They provide a kind of road map to the logic inherent in one's approach to a research problem. They also serve as guides to the systematic collection of data. **Research designs** consist of the logic and structure inherent in any particular approach to data gathering.

A simple study, for example, might be designed to test the assertion that the consumption of refined white sugar promotes aggressive or violent tendencies among men. One could imagine researchers approaching prison officials with the proposal that inmate diets should be altered to exclude all refined sugar. Under the plan, cafeteria cooks would be instructed to prepare meals without using sugar. Noncaloric sweet-

**Research design** the logic and structure inherent in an approach to data gathering.

eners would be substituted for sugar in recipes calling for sugar, and Kool Aid, sweetened iced tea, and carbonated beverages containing sugar would be banned. Likewise the prison canteen would be prohibited from selling items containing sugar for the duration of the experiment.

To determine whether the forced reduction in sugar consumption actually affected inmates' behaviour, researchers might look at the recorded frequency of aggressive incidents occurring within the confines of the prison before the experiment was initiated and compare such data with similar information on such incidents following the introduction of dietary changes. A research design employing this kind of logic can be diagrammed as follows:

$$O_1 \times O_2$$

Here "$O_1$" (termed a *pretest*) refers to the information gathered on inmate aggressiveness prior to the introduction of dietary changes (which themselves are shown as "X," also called the *experimental intervention*), and "$O_2$" (termed the *post-test*) signifies a second set of observations—that occurring after dietary changes have been implemented. Researchers employing a strategy of this type, which is known as a "one-group pretest–post-test" design, would likely examine differences between the two sets of observations, one made before introduction of the experimental intervention and the other after. The difference, they may assume, would show changes in behaviour resulting from changes in diet—in this case the exclusion of refined white sugar.

Although this basic research design well illustrates the logic behind naive experiments, it does not lend good structure to a research undertaking, because it does not eliminate other possible explanations of behavioural change. For example, during the time between the first and second observations inmates may have been exposed to some other influence that reduced their level of aggression. A new minister may have begun preaching effective sermons filled with messages of love and peace to the prison congregation; television cable service to the prison may have been disrupted, lowering the exposure inmates received to violent programming; a new warden may have taken control of the facility, relaxing prison rules and reducing tensions; a transfer or release of especially troublesome inmates, scheduled at some earlier time, may have occurred; a new program of conjugal visitation may have been initiated, creating newfound sexual outlets and reducing inmate tensions; and so on. In fact, the possibilities for rival explanations (i.e., those that rival the explanatory power of the hypothesis under study) are nearly limitless. Rival explanations such as these, called "competing hypotheses" by some researchers and **confounding effects** by others, make the results of any single series of observations uncertain.

## Achieving Validity in Research Designs

Confounding effects, which may invalidate the results of research, are of two general types: those that affect the **internal validity** of research findings and those that limit the ability of researchers to generalize the research findings to other settings—called **external validity.** Often, when external validity is threatened, researchers do not feel confident that interventions that have "worked" under laboratory-like or other special conditions will still be effective when employed in the field. Hence, researchers

**Confounding effects** rival explanations; also called competing hypotheses, which are threats to the internal or external validity of any research design.

**Internal validity** the certainty that experimental interventions did indeed cause the changes observed in the study group; also the control over confounding factors, which tend to invalidate the results of an experiment.

**External validity** the ability to generalize research findings to other settings.

achieving internal validity may be able to demonstrate that diets low in refined white sugar lower the number of instances of overt displays of aggressiveness in a single prison under study. They may not feel confident (for reasons discussed below), however, that similar changes in diet, if implemented in the general nonprison population, would have a similar effect. Most researchers consider internal validity, or the certainty that experimental interventions did indeed cause the changes observed in the study group, the most vital component of any planned research. Without it, considerations of external validity become irrelevant. Factors that routinely threaten the internal validity of a design for research are said to include the following[17]:

- *History:* Specific events that occur between the first and second observations, which may impact measurement. The examples given in the prison study described earlier (the arrival of a new minister or new warden, etc.) are all applicable here.
- *Maturation:* Processes occurring within the respondents or subjects that operate as a result of the passage of time. Fatigue and decreases in response time due to age are examples.
- *Testing:* The effects of taking a test upon the scores of a later testing. When respondents are measured in some way that requires them to respond, they tend to do better (i.e., their scores increase) the next time they are tested. In effect, they have learned how to take the test, or how to be measured, even though they may not have acquired more knowledge about the subject matter which the test intends to measure.
- *Instrumentation:* Changes in measuring instruments, or in survey takers, which occur as a result of time. Batteries wear down, instruments need to be recalibrated, interviewers grow tired or are replaced with others, and so on—all of which can change the nature of the observations made.
- *Statistical regression:* When respondents have been selected for study on the basis of extreme scores (as may be the case with personality inventories), later testing will tend to show a "regression toward the mean," or a return to more average scores, because some extreme scores are inevitably more the result of accident or luck rather than anything else.
- *Differential selection:* Built-in biases result when more than one group of subjects is involved in a study and when the groups being tested are initially somehow different. The random assignment of subjects to test groups greatly reduces the chances that such significant differences will exist.
- *Experimental mortality:* A differential loss of respondents from comparison groups, which may occur when more than one group is being tested (i.e., one group loses members at a greater rate than another group, or certain kinds of members are lost from one group but not from another).

Threats to external validity include the following:

- *Reactive effects of testing:* A pretest may sensitize subjects in such a way that they especially respond to the experimental intervention when it is introduced. Nonpretested subjects (such as those in other locations) may not respond in the same way.

- *Self-selection:* A process whereby subjects are allowed to decide whether they want to participate in a study. Self-selected subjects may be more interested in participation than others, and they may respond more readily to the experimental intervention or treatment.
- *Reactive effects of experimental arrangements:* Persons being surveyed or tested may know that they are part of an experiment and therefore react differently than if they were in more natural settings. Even if they are not aware of their participation in a study, some investigative paraphernalia (such as observers, cameras, and tape recorders) that may be present might change the way in which they behave.
- *Multiple-treatment interference:* Sometimes more than one study is simultaneously conducted on the same persons or group of persons. Under such circumstances "treatments" to which subjects are exposed may interact, changing what would otherwise be the study's results. Multiple-treatment interference may also result from delayed effects, as when a current study is affected by the impact of one that has already been completed.

## Experimental and Quasi-Experimental Research Designs

To amass greater confidence that the changes intentionally introduced into a situation are the real cause of observed variations, it is necessary to achieve some degree of control over factors that threaten internal validity. In the physical sciences, controlled experiments often provide the needed guarantees. **Controlled experiments** are those that attempt to hold conditions (other than the intentionally introduced experimental intervention) constant. In fact, some researchers have defined the word *experiment* simply as controlled observation.

    Whereas constancy of conditions may be possible to achieve within laboratory settings, it is far more difficult to come by in the social world—which by its very nature is in an ongoing state of flux. Hence, although criminologists sometimes employ true experimental designs in the conduct of their research, they are more likely to find it necessary to use quasi-experimental designs or approaches to research that "are deemed worthy of use where better designs are not feasible."[18] **Quasi-experimental designs** are especially valuable when aspects of the social setting are beyond the control of the researcher. The crucial defining feature of quasi-experimental designs is that they give researchers control over *the when and to whom of measurement,* even though others decide the "when and to whom" of exposure to the experimental intervention.

    Sometimes, for example, legislators enact new laws intended to address some aspect of the crime problem, specifying the kinds of crime preventative measures to be employed and what segment of the population is to receive them. Midnight basketball, intended to keep young people off the streets at night, is an example of such legislatively sponsored intervention. The question, of course, is whether money spent in support of such an activity would actually reduce the incidence of street crime committed by youth. Unfortunately, often good research data that could answer the question is unavailable. However, once the programs are in place they can be studied by researchers. Hence, although criminologists were not politically situated so as to be able to enact midnight basketball legislation, they are able to study the effects of such legislation after it has been enacted.

**Controlled experiments** those that attempt to hold conditions (other than the intentionally introduced experimental intervention) constant.

**Quasi-experimental designs** approaches to research that, although less powerful than experimental designs, are deemed worthy of use when better designs are not feasible.

Whether criminologists decide on experimental or quasi-experimental designs to guide their research, they depend on well-considered research strategies to eliminate rival explanations for the effects they observe. One relatively powerful research design frequently employed by criminologists is diagrammed as follows:

$$experimental\ group \qquad O_1 \times O_2$$
$$control\ group \qquad O_3 \quad O_4$$

The meaning of the notation used here is similar to that of the one-shot case study design discussed earlier. This approach, however, called the "pretest–post-test control group design," gains considerable power from the addition of a second group. The second group is called a **control group,** because it is not exposed to the experimental intervention.

Critical to the success of a research design such as this is the use of randomization in assigning subjects to both experimental and control groups. **Randomization** is the process whereby individuals are assigned to study groups without biases or differences resulting from selection. Self-selection is not permitted (when some individuals volunteer for membership in either the experimental or control group), nor are researchers allowed to use personal judgment in assigning subjects to groups.

Control over potential threats to internal validity is achieved by the introduction of a properly selected control group, because it is assumed that both experimental and control groups are essentially the same at the start and that any threats to internal validity will affect both groups equally as the experiment progresses—effectively canceling out when final differences between the two groups are measured. If some particular historical event, for example, affects the experimental group and modifies the measurable characteristics of that group, that event should have the same impact on the control group. Hence, in the previous design, when $O_4$ is subtracted from $O_2$, the remaining observable *net effects* are assumed to be attributable to the experimental intervention.

In the prison study discussed earlier, randomization would require that *all* inmates be systematically but randomly divided into two groups. Random assignments are typically made by using a table of random numbers. In this simple study, however, something as easy as the flip of a coin should suffice. One group, the experimental group, $(O_1)$ would no longer receive refined white sugar in their diets, $(\times)$ while the other (the control group, $O_3$) would continue eating as before. Because, with this one exception in diet, both groups would continue to be exposed to the same environment, it can be assumed that any other influences on the level of violence within the prison will cancel out when final measurements are taken, and that measurable differences in violence between the two groups can be attributed solely to the effects of the experimental variable (in this case, of course, removal of sugar from the diet).

**Control group** a group of experimental subjects that, although the subject of measurement and observation, are not exposed to the experimental intervention.

**Randomization** the process whereby individuals are assigned to study groups without biases or differences resulting from selection.

## Techniques of Data Collection

It is the combination of (1) hypothesis building, (2) operationalization, and (3) systematic observation in the service of hypothesis testing that has made modern-day criminology scientific, and which has facilitated scientific theory-building within the field. Hence, once a research problem has been identified, concepts made measurable,

Social science research within a correctional setting. Inmate surveys may increase our knowledge of crime causation. Specifically, what might such surveys tell us? *Rick Friedman/Black Star.*

and a design for the conduct of the research selected, investigators must decide on the type of data to be gathered and the techniques of data gathering they wish to employ. Ultimately, all research depends on the use of techniques to gather information, or data, for eventual analysis. Like research designs, which structure a researcher's approach to a problem, data-gathering strategies provide approaches to the accumulation of information needed for analysis to occur.

Many first-time researchers select data-gathering techniques on the basis of ease or simplicity. Some choose according to cost or the amount of time required by the techniques themselves. The most important question to consider, however, when beginning to gather information is *whether the data-gathering strategy selected will produce information in a form usable to the researcher.* The kind of information needed depends, of course, on the questions to be answered. Surveys of public opinion as to the desirability of the death penalty, for example, cannot address issues of the punishment's effectiveness as a crime control strategy.

Five major data-gathering strategies typify research in the field of criminology:

*Surveys:* **Survey research** typically involves the use of questionnaires. Respondents may be interviewed in person, over the telephone, or queried via e-mail or fax. Mail surveys are common, although they tend to have a lower response rate than other types of social surveys. The information produced through the use of questionnaires is referred to as *survey data.* Survey data provide the lifeblood of pollsters such as Decima Research, Angus Reid, and CROP (Centre de recherche sur l'opinion publique), who gather data on public opinion, voting preferences, and so forth. Similarly, Statistics Canada data are gathered by survey takers who are trained periodically for that

**Survey research** a social science data-gathering technique involving the use of questionnaires.

purpose. Survey data also inform the Canadian Urban Victimization Survey and result in such publications as *Violence Committed by Strangers, Risk of Personal and Household Victimization,* and other Statistics Canada-related reports produced by the Canadian Centre for Justice Statistics. Surveys have also been used in criminology to assess fear of crime and attitudes toward the police and to discover the extent of unreported crime.

*Case studies:* The **case study** is built around an in-depth investigation into an individual case. The study of one (perhaps notorious) offender, scrutiny of a particular criminal organization, analysis of a prison boot camp, and others may all qualify as case studies. Case studies are useful for what they can tell us to expect about other, similar cases. If study of a street gang, for example, reveals the central role of a few leaders, then we would expect to find a similar organizational style among other gangs of the same kind.

When one individual (termed a *single subject*) is the focus of a case study, the investigation may take the form of a life history. *Life histories* involve gathering as much historical data as possible about a given individual and his or her experiences during early socialization and adulthood. Most life histories are quite subjective due to the fact that they consist primarily of recounts of events by the participants themselves. Life histories may also be gathered on groups of individuals, and similarities in life experience thereby discovered may provide researchers with clues to current behaviour, or with points at which to begin further investigations.

Case studies, although they may suffer from high levels of subjectivity in which feelings cannot be easily separated from fact, provide the opportunity to investigate individual cases—an element that is lacking in both survey research and participant observation.

*Participant observation:* **Participant observation** "involves a variety of strategies in data gathering in which the researcher observes a group by participating, to varying degrees, in the activities of the group."[19] Some participant researchers operate undercover, without revealing their identity as researchers to those whom they are studying, whereas others make their identity and purpose known from the outset of the research endeavor. As one criminologist states, participation observation "means that criminologists must venture inside the immediacy of crime."[20]

One of the earliest and best-known participant observers in the field of criminology was William Foote Whyte, who described his 1943 study of criminal subcultures in a slum district that he called "Cornerville" this way: "My aim was to gain an intimate view of Cornerville life. My first problem, therefore, was to establish myself as a participant in the society so that I would have a position from which to observe. I began by going to live in Cornerville, finding a room with an Italian family. ... It was not enough simply to make the acquaintance of various groups of people. The sort of information that I sought required that I establish intimate social relations. ... This active participation gave me something in common with them so that we had other things to talk about besides the weather. It broke down the social barriers and made it possible for me to be taken into the intimate life of the group."[21]

It is possible to distinguish between at least two additional kinds of participant observation: (1) the participant as observer and (2) the observer as complete participant. When researchers make their presence known to those whom they are observing, without attempting to influence the outcome of their observations or the activities of

**Case study** an investigation into an individual case.

**Participant observation** a variety of strategies in data gathering in which the researcher observes a group by participating, to varying degrees, in the activities of the group.

the group, they fit the category of participants who are observers. When they become complete participants in the group they are observing, however, researchers run the risk of influencing the group's direction. As Whyte explains, "I made it a rule that I should try to avoid influencing the actions of the group. I wanted to observe what the men did under ordinary circumstances; I did not want to lead them into different activities."[22] Even researchers who make their presence known, however, may inadvertently influence the nature and direction of social interaction, because people tend to act differently if they know they are being watched.

Another problem facing the participant observer is that of "going native," or of assuming too close an identification with the subjects or the behaviour under study. Like undercover police officers who at times may be tempted to participate in the illegalities they are supposed to be monitoring, participant researchers may begin to experience feelings of kinship with their subjects. When that happens, all sense of the research perspective may be lost, and serious ethical problems can arise.

On the other hand, some researchers may feel disgust for the subjects of their research. Data gatherers with a particular dislike of drug abuse, for example, may be hard put to maintain their objectivity when working as participant observers within the drug subculture. Hence, as Frank Hagan observes, "[t]he researcher must avoid not only overidentification with the study group, but also aversion to it."[23]

*Self-reporting:* Another subjective data-gathering technique is one that uses **self-reports** to investigate aspects of a problem not otherwise amenable to study. When official records are lacking, for example, research subjects may be asked to record and report rates of otherwise secretive behaviour. Self-reports may prove especially valuable in providing checks on official reports consisting of statistical tabulations gathered through channels such as police departments, hospitals, and social services agencies.

**Self-reports** research investigations of subjects in order to record and report their behaviours.

Self-reports may also be requested of subjects in survey research, and it is for that reason that self-reporting is sometimes considered simply another form of survey research. However, many self-reporting techniques require the maintenance of a diary or personal journal and request vigilant and ongoing observations of one's own behaviour by the subject under study. Hence, sex researchers may ask subjects to maintain an ongoing record of their frequency of intercourse, the variety of sexual techniques employed, and their preference in partners—items of information that are not easy to come by through other means or that cannot be accurately reconstructed from memory.

Self-reporting enters the realm of the purely subjective when it consists of introspection, or personal reflection. Introspective techniques, or those intended to gather data on secretive feelings and felt motivation, are often used by psychologists seeking to assess the mental status of patients. Criminologists, however, have at times used introspective techniques to categorize criminal offenders into types and to initiate the process of developing concepts more amenable to objective study.

*Secondary analysis:* Not all data-gathering techniques are intended to generate new information. **Secondary analysis** entails the reanalysis of existing data, that is, secondhand analysis of data that were gathered for another purpose. Secondary analysis of existing data and using previously acquired information can save researchers a considerable amount of time and expense.

**Secondary analysis** the reanalysis of existing data.

One important source of data for secondary analysis is the Canadian Centre for Justice Statistics, created through the National Justice Statistics Initiative (NJSI) of the federal government of Canada. The mandate of the NJSI is "to provide information to the justice community and the public on the nature and extent of crime and the administration of criminal justice in Canada."[24] Through the Canadian Centre for Justice Statistics, the NCJI is meant to ensure the production of useful information to support legislative, policy, management, and research agendas, and to inform the public. Access to Canadian Centre for Justice Statistics data is open to the public, and data sets are available for sale to individual researchers. (A more detailed look at the Canadian Centre for Justice Statistics is found in Chapter 2.)

The use of secondary data rarely alerts research subjects to the fact that they (or the data they have provided) are being studied, although they may have been so aware when data were first gathered. Hence, secondary analysis, which constitutes one form of unobtrusive research, is said to be *nonreactive*. Although unobtrusive measures include other forms of data collection, the use of archival records in data analysis constitutes a virtual "goldmine of information waiting to be exploited."[25] Nonetheless, it is important to keep in mind that secondary data usually involve the use of information that was collected for a purpose outside of the interests of the current researcher.

## Problems in Data Collection

Scientific data gathering builds on observations of one sort or another. Observation is, of course, not unique to science. Individuals often make personal observations and draw a plethora of intimate conclusions based on what they see or hear. Scientific observation, however, generally occurs under controlled conditions, and must meet the criteria of intersubjectivity and replicability. **Intersubjectivity** requires that, for observations to be valid, independent observers must report seeing the same thing under the same circumstances. "Do you see what I see?" is a question that highlights the central role of intersubjectivity in scientific observation. If observers cannot agree on what they saw, then the raw data necessary for scientific analysis have not been acquired. **Replicability** of observations means that, at least in the field of scientific experimentation, when the same conditions exist the same results can be expected to follow. Hence, valid experiments can be replicated. The same observations made at one time can be had again at a later time if all other conditions are the same.

In the physical sciences, replicability is easy to achieve. Water at sea level, for example, will always boil at 100 degrees Celsius. Anyone can replicate the conditions needed to test such a contention. When replicability cannot be achieved, it casts the validity of observations into doubt. Some years ago, for example, a few scientists claimed to have achieved nuclear fusion at room temperature. Their supposed accomplishment was dubbed "cold fusion" and hailed as a major breakthrough in the production of nuclear energy. When scientists elsewhere, however, attempted to replicate the conditions under which cold fusion was said to occur, they could find no evidence that the initial experimenters were correct. Replicability and intersubjectivity are critical to the scientific enterprise for, as one researcher states, "[s]cience rests its claim to authority upon its firm basis in observable evidence ..."[26]

It is important to recognize, however, that some observations—even those standing up to the tests of intersubjectivity and replicability—can lead to unwarranted conclusions. For example, spirit possession, an explanation for deviance that was

**Intersubjectivity** a scientific principle that requires that independent observers see the same thing under the same circumstances for observations to be regarded as valid.

**Replicability (experimental)** a scientific principle that holds that the same observations made at one time can be had again at a later time if all other conditions are the same.

apparently widely held in primitive times, must have appeared well validated by the positive behavioural changes that became apparent in those who submitted to the surgery called for by the theory—a craniotomy intended to release offending spirits from the head of the afflicted party. The actual cause of behavioural reformation may have been brain infections resulting from unsanitary surgical conditions, slips of the stone knife, or the intensity of pain endured by those undergoing the procedure without anesthetics. To the uncritical observer, however, the theory of spirit possession as a cause of deviance, and cranial surgery as a treatment technique, would probably appear to have been supported by the evidence of induced behavioural change.

Some methodologists note that "[t]heories are as much involved in the determination of fact as facts are in establishing a theory."[27] Theories are intimately involved in the process of data collection. They determine what kinds of data we choose to gather, what we look for in the data itself, and how we interpret the information we have gathered. In short, theories determine what we see, as well as what we ignore. In the late 1700s, for example, when a meteorite shower was reported to the French Academy of Sciences, observers reported that some fragments had struck the ground, causing tremendous explosions. The learned scientists of the academy quickly dismissed these accounts, however, calling them "a superstition unworthy of these enlightened times."[28] Anyone, they said, knows that stones don't fall from the sky.

## Data Analysis

Some data, once collected, are simply archived or stored. Most data, however, are subject to some form of analysis. Data analysis generally involves the use of mathematical techniques intended to uncover correlations between variables, and to assess the likelihood that research findings can be generalized to other settings. Such techniques are called *statistics*, and their use in analyzing data is called *statistical analysis*. Some theorists, for example, posit a link between poverty and crime. Hence, we might suspect that low-income areas would be high-crime areas. Once we specify what we mean by "low income" and "crime" so that they become measurable variables, and gather data on income levels and the incidence of crime in various locales, we are ready to begin the job of data analysis.

Statistical techniques provide tools for summarizing data. They also provide quantitative means for identifying patterns within the data and for determining the degree of correlation that exists between variables. Statistical methods can be divided into two types: descriptive and inferential. **Descriptive statistics** are those that (1) describe, (2) summarize, or (3) highlight the relationships within the data gathered. **Inferential statistics,** on the other hand, attempt to generalize findings by specifying how likely they are to be true for other populations, or in other locales.

Descriptive statistics include measures of central tendency, commonly called the mean, median, and mode. The *mode* refers to the most frequently occurring score or value in any series of observations. If, for example, we measure the age of all young offenders held in a secure young offender facility, it may be that they range in age from 12 to 17, with 16 being the most commonly found age. Sixteen, then, would be the modal age for the population under study.

**Descriptive statistics**
describe, summarize, or highlight the relationships within data gathered.

**Inferential statistics**
specify how likely findings are to be true for other populations, or in other locales.

The *median* defines the midpoint of a data series. Half of the scores will be above the mean and the other half will be below. It may be, for example, that in our study of young offenders, we find equal numbers in each age category. The median age for those held might then be 15.

The mathematical average of all scores within a given population is referred to as the *mean.* The mean is the most commonly used measure of central tendency. It is calculated by simply adding together all the scores (or ages, in our example) and dividing by the total number of observations. Although calculations of the mean, median, and mode will often yield similar results, this will not be the case with populations that are skewed in a particular direction. If our population of young offenders under study, for example, consisted almost entirely of 16-year-olds, then the mode for that population would inevitably be 16, while other measures of central tendency would yield somewhat lower figures.

Other descriptive statistics provide measures of the standard deviation of a population (i.e., the degree of dispersion of scores about the mean) and the degree of correlation or interdependence between variables (i.e., the extent of variation in one that can be expected to follow from a measured change in another). As discussed in Chapter 2 (where the term *correlation* is defined), although the degree of correlation may vary, the direction of correlation can also be described. We say, for example, that if one variable increases whenever another, upon which it is dependent, does the same, a positive correlation or positive relationship exists between the two. When one variable decreases in value as another rises, a negative or inverse correlation exists.

Another statistical technique, one that provides a measure of the likelihood that a study's findings are the results of chance, is commonly found in criminological literature. **Tests of significance** are designed to provide researchers with confidence that their results are in fact true and not the result of sampling error. We may, for example, set out to measure degree of gun ownership. Let's say that the extent of gun ownership in the area under study is actually 50 percent. We have no way of knowing that, of course, until our study is complete. We may decide to use door-to-door surveys of randomly selected households, because cost prohibits us from canvassing all households in the study area. Even if we have made our best survey effort, however, some slight probability remains that the households we have chosen to interview may all be populated by gun owners. Although it is very unlikely, we may, by chance, have excluded those without guns. Assuming that everyone interviewed answers truthfully, we would come away with the mistaken impression that 100 percent of the population in the study area are armed!

The likelihood of faulty findings increases as sample size decreases. Were we to sample only one or two households, we would have little likelihood of determining the actual incidence of gun ownership. The larger the sample size, however, the greater the confidence we can have in our findings. Hence a positive correlation exists between sample size and the degree of confidence we can have in our results. Even so, in most criminological research it is not possible to study all members of a given population, and so samples must be taken. Statistical tests of significance, expressed as a percentage, assess the likelihood that our study findings are due to chance. Hence, a study that reflects a 95 percent confidence level can be interpreted as having a 5 percent likelihood that the results it reports are mere happenstance. In other words, for every hundred such studies, five yield misleading results. The problem, of course, is that it would be impossible to know (without further research) which five that would be!

## Quantitative versus Qualitative Methods

There are some who feel that there has been a tendency in criminology research over the past half century to overemphasize **quantitative methods** or techniques—that is, those that produce measurable results that can be analyzed statistically. To be sure, as such critics would be quick to admit, a considerable degree of intellectual comfort must be achieved in feeling that one is able to reduce complex forms of behaviour and interaction to something countable (as, say, the frequency of an offence). Intellectual comfort of this sort derives from the notion that anything expressible in numbers must somehow be more meaningful than that which is not.

It is crucial to realize, however, that numerical expression is mostly a result of how researchers structure their approach to the subject matter and is rarely inherent in the subject matter itself. Such is especially true in the social sciences, where attitudes, feelings, behaviours, and perceptions of all sorts are subject to quantification by researchers, who impose upon such subjective phenomena artificial techniques for their quantification.

One recent highly quantitative study, for example,[29] reprinted in the journal *Criminology,* reported on the relationship between personality and crime. The study found that "greater delinquent participation was associated with a personality configuration characterized by high Negative Emotionality and Weak Constraint." Although it may seem easy to quantify "delinquent participation" by measuring official arrest statistics (even here, however, official statistics may not be a good measure of delinquent behaviour, as many law violations go undiscovered), imagine the conceptual nightmares associated with trying to make measurable concepts such as "negative emotionality" and "weak constraint." In such studies, even those replete with numerical data derived through the use of carefully constructed questionnaires, questions still remain about precisely what it is that has been measured.

Not everyone who engages in social science research labours under the delusion that everything can and must be quantified. Those who do, however, are said to suffer from the mystique of quantity. As some critics point out, "[t]he failure to recognize this instrumentality of measurement makes for a kind of *mystique of quantity*; which responds to numbers as though they were repositories of occult powers. ... The mystique of quantity is an exaggerated regard for the significance of measurement, just because it is quantitative, without regard either to what has been measured or to what can subsequently be done with the measure."[30] The mystique of quantity treats numbers as having intrinsic scientific value. Unfortunately, this kind of thinking has been popular in the social sciences, where researchers, seeking to make clear their intellectual kinship with physical scientists, have been less than cautious in their enthusiasm for quantification.

*It is ... pathetic to observe how many statistical refinements are wasted on utterly inadequate basic material.*

—HERMANN MANNHEIM[31]

**Qualitative methods,** in contrast to those that are quantitative, produce subjective results or results that are difficult to quantify. Even though their findings are not ex-

**Quantitative methods**
research techniques that produce measurable results.

**Qualitative methods**
research techniques that produce subjective results or results that are difficult to quantify.

pressed numerically, qualitative methods provide yet another set of potentially useful criminological research tools. Qualitative methods are important for the insight they provide into the subjective workings of the criminal mind and the processes by which meaning is accorded to human experience. Introspection, life histories, case studies, and participant observation all contain the potential to yield highly qualitative data.[32]

Consider, for example, how the following personal account of the motivation needed to rob banks provides subjective insights into the life of a young offender that would otherwise be difficult to express[33]:

> I rob banks for the money. I like the excitement and thrills, but I do it for the money. The danger is exciting, but I don't do it for that. I spend my money on drugs—a lot on coke. It really does fly. I don't know where half of it goes. I had an apartment when I was sixteen and I was really proud of it. I bought a bed, a T.V., a 13-foot-long couch worth $1 600. I was proud of myself. I was doing well. I was living with a chick who was 18, but she was just a friend. I'd also spend a lot of money on my family. I'd give some to my sisters. I'd spend a lot on taxis. I'd take them everywhere. On movies and amusement parks. Money is important to me. I never have enough, I always want more. If I was to get a big score, I would want another big score. After awhile you start getting bigger ideas. I've thought about doing an armoured vehicle and I've watched them make deliveries.
>
> It's only a fluke or a set-up that gets you caught. You either get caught cold-cock or you don't get caught at all. If they don't catch us in the first couple of hours, then forget it. They don't have a very good chance. This was the first time I got caught, but I think I learned a lot. Next time it will not be so easy. Once you get caught, everyone goes through a process where they don't want to do it anymore. Then after a couple of months, you're willing to do it again. I'm supposed to have a job when I hit the street, but if I have no job and no money I would do a bank for sure. It's your only means of survival. If I have no job and nowhere to stay, of course I'm going to do a bank. It's what I know. I've been trained to do that.

This passage is taken from an interview with Jules, aged 17. From a French Canadian family of eight brothers and eight sisters, Jules started robbing banks at fifteen. His five older brothers have all been convicted of robbing banks and armoured vehicles. At the time of the interview, Jules was serving an eighteen-month prison sentence for two counts of robbery. He was arrested 5 years later at 22, again for bank robbery, and was sentenced to 15 years in prison.

Although the preceding is a purely personal account, and may hold questions of generalizability for researchers, imagine the difficulties inherent in acquiring this kind of data through the use of survey instruments or other traditional research techniques. Autobiographical accounts, introspection, and many forms of participant observation amount to a kind of phenomenological reporting, in which description leads to understanding and intuition is a better guide to theory-building than volumes of quantifiable data.

In a seminal 1997 article, Jeff Ferrell uses the term ***verstehen*** to describe the kind of subjective understanding that can be achieved by criminologists who immerse

*Verstehen* the kind of subjective understanding that can be achieved by criminologists who immerse themselves into the everyday world of the criminals they study.

An 18-year-old gang member. Some researchers doubt that quantitative methods can adequately assess the subjective experiences of certain kinds of offenders. What is the nature of such "subjective experiences"? *Jim Tynan/Impact Visuals Photo & Graphics, Inc.*

themselves into the everyday world of the criminals they study. Criminological *verstehen,* a term derived from the early writings of sociologist Max Weber, means, according to Ferrell, "a researcher's subjective understandings of crime's situational meanings and emotions—its moments of pleasure and pain, its emergent logic and excitement—within the larger process of research." Ferrell adds, "[i]t further implies that a researcher, through attentiveness and participation, at least can begin to apprehend and appreciate the specific roles and experiences of criminals, crime victims, crime control agents, and others caught up in the day-to-day reality of crime."[34]

A growing number of criminologists believe that qualitative data-gathering strategies represent the future of criminological research. Martin D. Schwartz and David O. Friedrichs say that this initiative is central to postmodern criminology. As discussed in Chapter 12, postmodern criminology builds upon:

1. a method that can reveal starkly how knowledge is constituted, and can uncover pretensions and contradictions of traditional scholarship in the field;
2. a highlighting of the significance of language and signs in the realm of crime and criminal justice; and
3. a source of metaphors and concepts (e.g., "hyperreality") that capture elements of an emerging reality, and the new context and set of conditions in which crime occurs.[35]

"The guiding premise here," say Schwartz and Friedrichs, "is that a postmodernist approach enables us to comprehend at a more appropriate level" than do the more traditional techniques of quantitative criminology, "our knowledge of a dynamic and complex human environment."

# Values and Ethics in the Conduct of Research

Research, especially that conducted within the social sciences, does not occur in a vacuum. Values enter into all stages of the research process, from the selection of the problem to be studied to the choice of strategies to address it. In short, research is never entirely free from preconceptions and biases, although much can be done to limit the impact such biases have on the results of research.

The most effective way of controlling the effects of biases is to be aware of them at the outset of the research. If, for example, researchers know that the project they are working on elicits strong personal feelings but necessitates the use of interviewers, then it would be beneficial to strive to hire interviewers who are relatively free of biases or can control the expression of their feelings. Potential data gatherers might themselves be interviewed to determine their values and the likelihood that they might be tempted to interpret the data they gather or report it in ways that are biased. Similarly, data gatherers who are prejudiced against subgroups of potential respondents can represent a threat to the validity of the research results. The use of such interviewers may "turn off" some respondents, perhaps through racial innuendo, personal style, mannerisms, and so forth.

Of similar importance are ethical issues which, although they may not affect the validity of research results, can have a significant impact on the lives of both researchers and research subjects. The protection of human subjects, privacy, and **data confidentiality**—in which research data are not shared outside of the research environment—are the most important ethical issues facing researchers today. **Informed consent** is a strategy used by researchers to overcome many of the ethical issues inherent in criminological research. Informed consent means that research subjects will be informed as to the nature of the research about to be conducted, their anticipated role in it, and the uses that will be made of the data they provide. Ethics may also require that data derived from personal interviews or the testing of research subjects be anonymous (not associated with the names of individual subjects) and that raw (unanalyzed) data be destroyed after a specified time interval (often at the completion of the research project).

Federal regulations require a plan for the protection of sensitive information as part of grant proposals submitted to federal agencies. Some universities, research organizations, and government agencies have established institutional review boards tasked with examining research proposals before they are submitted to funding organizations to determine whether expectations of ethical conduct have been met. Institutional review boards often consist of other researchers with special knowledge of the kinds of ethical issues involved in criminological research.

Participant observation sometimes entails an especially thorny ethical issue. In other words, should researchers themselves violate the law if their research participation appears to require it? The very nature of participant observation is such that researchers of adult criminal activity may at times find themselves placed in situations where they are expected to "go along with the group" in violating the law. Those researching gang activity, for example, have sometimes been asked to transmit potentially incriminating information to other gang members, to act as drug couriers, and even to

**Data confidentiality** an ethical requirement of social scientific research that stipulates that research data not be shared outside of the research environment.

**Informed consent** an ethical requirement of social scientific research that specifies that research subjects will be informed as to the nature of the research about to be conducted, their anticipated role in it, and the uses to which the data they provide will be put.

commit crimes of violence to help establish territorial claims important to members of the gang. Researchers who refuse may endanger not only their research but themselves. Compliance with the expectations of criminal groups, of course, evokes other kinds of dangers, including the danger of apprehension and prosecution for violations of the criminal law. As one criminologist explains, "criminological (and other) field researchers cannot conveniently distance themselves from their subjects of study, or from the legally uncertain situations in which the subjects may reside, in order to construct safe and 'objective' studies. Instead criminological field research unavoidably entangles those who practice it in complex and ambiguous relations to the subjects and situations of study, to issues of personal and social responsibility, and to law and legality."[36]

Although the dilemma of a participant observer, especially one secretly engaged in research, is a difficult one, some of the best advice on the subject is offered by Frank E. Hagan, who writes: "In self-mediating the potential conflicting roles of the criminal justice researcher, it is incumbent on the investigator to enter the setting with eyes wide open. A decision must be made beforehand on the level of commitment to the research endeavor and the analyst's ability to negotiate the likely role conflicts. Although there are no hard and fast rules … *the researcher's primary role is that of a scientist.*"[37]

Hagan also suggests that a code of ethics should guide all professional criminologists in their research undertakings. This code, says Hagan, would require the researcher to assume the following personal responsibilities[38]:

- Avoid procedures that may harm respondents.
- Honour commitments to respondents and respect reciprocity.
- Exercise objectivity and professional integrity in performing and reporting research.
- Protect confidentiality and privacy of respondents.

---

# Professional Journals Publishing Criminological Research

BOX 3.1

Criminologists often seek to publish the results of their research to share them with others working in the field. A wide range of professional journals in North America publish the work of criminologists, some of which are listed below. Most of these journals are available through community college or university libraries, and a number of them can be accessed through the Internet.

| | |
|---|---|
| American Journal of Criminal Justice | Criminal Justice Review |
| Canadian Journal of Criminology | Criminology |
| Canadian Journal of Law and Society | Federal Probation |
| Canadian Journal of Women and the Law | International Journal of Comparative and |
| Corrections Today | Applied Criminal Justice |
| Crime and Delinquency | Journal of Contemporary Criminal Justice |
| Crime and Social Justice | Journal of Crime and Justice |
| Criminal Justice Ethics | Journal of Criminal Justice Education |

▶

Journal of Criminal Law and Criminology
Journal of Interpersonal Violence
Journal of Police Science and Administration
Journal of Quantitative Criminology
Journal of Research in Crime and Delinquency
Justice Professional
Justice Quarterly
Law and Society Review

Law Now Magazine
RCMP Gazette
Social Forces
Social Problems
Sociology of Criminal Law
The Prison Journal
Theoretical Criminology
Violence and Victims
Victimology

# Social Policy and Criminological Research

Although research in the area of criminology may have much to offer policy-makers, publicly elected officials are often either ignorant of current research or do not heed the advice of professional criminologists, seeking instead to create politically expedient policies. Nowhere is this reality more evident than in the area of Aboriginal justice initiatives in Canada. In an article entitled, "The Impact of Aboriginal Justice Research on Policy: A Marginal Past and an Even More Uncertain Future," Carol LaPrairie writes, "The benefits of research for Aboriginal criminal justice in Canada have scarcely been tapped. There have been some issue-specific activities ... over the past 25 years but research has not systematically been designed and integrated into policy, practice, and project development. Because research is often negatively perceived by Aboriginal people and is of sporadic interest to government, its history of shaping justice projects and influencing policy decision-making has been marginal at best."[39]

LaPrairie concludes that this apparent lack of research impact and integration results from the fact that government legislators equate Aboriginal justice issues with the self-government movement, which has largely served to portray Aboriginal justice problems (such as the over-representation of Aboriginals as offenders in the criminal justice system) as conflicts over race and culture, rooted in a colonial history of conflict and discrimination. She claims that the emphasis of research on the race/cultural issue has failed to consider other possible explanations for problems faced by Aboriginal people, such as "community marginalization, inequity of distribution of community resources, and family breakdown and dysfunction."[40]

Even when excellent research is available to guide policy creation, a realistic appraisal must recognize that criminologists are sometimes as much to blame for counterproductive policies as anyone. The American experience with the "three-strikes" laws provide an example of the kind of dilemma facing criminologists who would influence social policy on the basis of statistical evidence.

"Three-strikes" laws, which became popular with legislatures across the United States over the last decade, require that three-time felons receive lengthy prison sentences (often life without the possibility of parole) following their third conviction. Such laws are built on the notion that "getting tough" on repeat offenders by putting them in prison for long periods should reduce the crime rate. Logic seems to say that lengthy prison sentences for recidivists will reduce crime by removing the most dangerous offenders from society.

A 1997 study of the three-strikes laws in twenty-two states, however, concluded that such legislation typically results in clogged court systems and crowded correctional facilities and encourages three-time felons to take dramatic risks to avoid capture.[41] A wider-based study,[42] dubbed "the most comprehensive study ever of crime prevention,"[43] found that "much of the research on prisons was inadequate or flawed, making it impossible to measure how much crime was actually prevented or deterred by locking up more criminals." More significantly, the central finding of the massive 1997 study was that current government-sponsored crime prevention initiatives are often poorly evaluated, leading to uncertainty over whether funded programs actually "work." Hence, although the three-strikes laws remain popular with the American voting public, and lawmakers have been quick to seize upon get-tough crime prevention policies in the interest of winning votes, solid and consistent research support showing the efficacy of such laws continues to be elusive.

# The Network for Research on Crime and Justice

BOX 3.2

In June 1996, a number of senior criminal justice officials met with academics from a variety of disciplines at Queen's University in Kingston, Ontario to discuss options that would allow policy-makers to respond in a more timely and effective manner to the needs of the criminal justice environment. The result of this one-day conference, entitled "Bridging Policy and Research Agendas in Crime and Justice", was the creation of the Network for Research on Crime and Justice, or RCJ-NET.

With a current membership of about 200 members and a board of directors made up of academics and senior government officials, including the commissioners of both Correctional Service Canada and the RCMP, RCJ-NET seeks to "develop, conduct and communicate superior quality research on crime and justice, and to provide policy-relevant advice." Toward this end, the RCJ-NET serves to promote quality criminal justice research, assists in matching research proposals with the needs of policy- and decision-makers, communicates criminal justice research proposal requests and research results, and allows for open communication and exchange of ideas between researchers and policy-makers.[44]

The RCJ-NET Web site contains summaries of research along with a large number of links to related sites of interest. It is hoped that as the Web site expands, it will become a repository for current criminal justice research planning and findings that will be useful for academics, policy-makers, and students of criminology. The Network for Research on Crime and Justice is located at **www.qsilver.queensu.ca/rcjnet**.

# Summary
Criminology—like its sister disciplines of sociology, psychology, geography, and political science—is a social science that endeavours to apply the techniques of data collection and hypothesis-testing through observation and experimentation. Successful hypothesis-testing can lead to theory-building and to a more complete understanding of the nature of crime and crime causation. Although the scientific framework and its techniques have largely been inherited from the physical sciences—such as chemistry, astronomy, and physics—in which they have been well established for centuries, criminology has been accepted into the scientific tradition by all but the most hard-nosed purists. Even so, criminologists are still game to study aspects of the field that are "in need of study," even where adequate resources (funding) or techniques (for example, the complete mapping of all human chromosomes) are not yet available.

Another component of scientific criminology, the detailed description of crime and related phenomena even where meaningful hypotheses are lacking, is also very much with us. In one descriptive area alone, that of crime statistics (discussed in Chapter 2), so much data have already been gathered that it is unlikely they will ever be completely analyzed.

The fondest hope of many criminologists today is that effective research into the causes of crime, coupled with meaningful evaluations of crime prevention efforts, will one day significantly influence social policy mandates, resulting in legislation and government-sponsored initiatives built on programs demonstrated to be effective.

## Discussion Questions

1. This book emphasizes a social problems versus social responsibility theme. How might a thorough research agenda allow us to decide which perspective is the most fruitful in combating crime?

2. What is a *hypothesis*? What does it mean to operationalize a hypothesis? Why is operationalization necessary?

3. What is a *theory*? Why is the task of criminological theory construction so demanding? How do we know if a theory is any good?

4. Explain experimental research. How might a good research design be diagrammed? What kinds of threats to the validity of research designs can you identify? How can such threats be controlled or eliminated?

5. List and describe the various types of data-gathering strategies discussed in this chapter. Is any one technique "better" than another? Why or why not? Under what kinds of conditions might certain types of data-gathering strategies be most appropriate?

6. What is the difference between qualitative and quantitative research? What are the advantages and disadvantages of each?

# Weblinks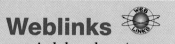

**www.icclr.law.ubc.ca/**

International Centre for Criminal Law Reform & Criminal Justice Policy. A non-profit institute located in Vancouver, British Columbia. Affiliated with the United Nations, its goal is to contribute to national and international efforts to reduce crime and improve justice. Provides an extensive list of research publications.

**www.cprn.com/cprn.html**

Canadian Policy Research Networks. The Canadian Policy Research Networks sets out to inform the public and lead debate on social and economic issues.

**www.ciaj-icaj.ca/index.html**

Canadian Institute for the Administration of Justice (CIAJ). The CIAJ is a national, non-profit organization that seeks to foster improvements in the administration of justice in Canada through discussion and program development.

**www.ccsd.ca/**

Canadian Council on Social Development (CCSD). The CCSD is one of Canada's most authoritative voices promoting better social and economic security for all Canadians. A national, self-supporting, non-profit organization, the CCSD's main product is information, and its main activity is research, focusing on concerns such as income security, employment, poverty, child welfare, pensions, and government social policies.

**www.home.istar.ca/~ccja/**

Canadian Criminal Justice Association (CCJA). The CCJA is a national membership organization dedicated to improving the criminal justice system in Canada.

## CHAPTER 4

# The Classical Thinkers

Nature has placed mankind under the governance of two sovereign masters, pain and pleasure.

—JEREMY BENTHAM[1]

The more promptly and the more closely punishment follows upon the commission of a crime, the more just and useful will it be.

—CESARE BECCARIA[2]

## LEARNING OUTCOMES

After reading this chapter, you should be able to:

- Discuss the relevance of the history of criminology and its early thinkers to current views of crime and criminality
- Recognize the primary elements of the classical school
- Identify modern day practices that embody the principles of the classical school
- Assess the shortcomings of the classical approach

**IMPORTANT NAMES**

Thomas Hobbes        Jean-Jacques Rousseau        Cesare Beccaria
John Locke           Thomas Paine                 Jeremy Bentham
Montesquieu

**IMPORTANT TERMS**

mores                   natural rights           dangerousness
folkways                classical school         individual rights
*mala in se*            deterrence                 advocates
*mala prohibita*        hedonistic calculus      incapacitation
trephination            utilitarianism           specific deterrence
Code of Hammurabi       Panopticon               general deterrence
retribution             neoclassical             recidivism
Twelve Tables             criminology            recidivism rate
common law              individual rights and    capital punishment
the Enlightenment         due process            law and order
social contract         just-deserts model         advocates
natural law

# Introduction

On April 10, 1995, Canada Customs officials seized and confiscated computer disks from John Robin Sharpe that contained a text entitled, "Sam Paloc's Flogging, Fun, and Fortitude—A Collection of Kiddiekink Classics." Sharpe was charged with simple possession of child pornography contrary to section 163.1(4) of the Criminal Code of Canada and possession of child pornography for the purpose of distribution and sale, contrary to s. 163.1(3). Thirteen months later, on May 13, 1996, police again charged Sharpe under sections 163.1(4) and 163.1(3) after confiscating a collection of books, manuscripts, stories, and photographs depicting child pornography from his home near Surrey, British Columbia.

At trial, Sharpe argued that s. 163.1(4) infringed upon his individual freedoms, especially his freedom of expression guaranteed and protected under section 2(b) of the Canadian Charter of Rights and Freedoms. The trial judge, Justice Duncan Shaw, accepted this submission, finding s. 163.1(4) to be unconstitutional. Sharpe was acquitted on the counts of possession. The Crown appealed the court's ruling to the British Columbia Court of Appeal, where it was dismissed. An appeal to the Supreme Court of Canada was heard in early 2000, but no decision has been rendered at the time of writing.

The court's ruling astounded many Canadians and ignited public controversy across the nation. Those who opposed the court's decision protested that the protection of an individual's right to freedom of expression should not come at the expense of public safety, especially that of children. Canadians Against Violence Everywhere Advocating its Termination (CAVEAT), a victim's advocacy group, argued that "the nature of child pornography places it in the category of a violent form of expression or analogous to a violent form of expression, and therefore must be excluded from section 2(b) Charter protection." Child pornography, CAVEAT argued, targets and victimizes the most vulnerable members of society.

Others, like the Canadian Civil Liberties Association (CCLA), believe that the Sharpe case highlights shortcomings surrounding the legal definition of child pornography. The CCLA argued that "in its current form, the law appears capable of imperiling legitimate art." The CCLA cited the case of Toronto artist Eli Langer, who was charged with having created "child pornography" because of a number of drawings he had on display in an art gallery that depicted youngsters in sexual situations. The charges were ultimately withdrawn and Langer's work was deemed by the court to have "artistic merit." In this case, however, the constitutionality of the child pornography law was upheld; the CCLA contends that legitimate artists who deal with such subject matter will continue to risk criminal charges. Indeed, the CCLA points out, those parents who take and keep photographs of their nude babies run a similar risk.

The controversy sparked by the Sharpe case highlights the balancing act the Canadian criminal justice system must play between upholding and protecting the rights of each individual Canadian as enshrined in the Charter of Rights and Freedoms and upholding and protecting the collective rights of Canadian society as a whole as embodied in the Criminal Code and other statutes. Some Canadians argue that an overemphasis on individual rights comes at the expense of the rights of the group. Others fear that the erosion of individual rights may make the state too powerful. This debate has roots in the Enlightenment and the emergence of the classical school of criminology, both of which are discussed in this chapter.

# Major Principles of the Classical School

This brief section serves to summarize the central features of the classical school of criminological thought. Each of the points listed in this discussion can be found elsewhere in this chapter, where they are discussed in more detail. The present cursory overview, however, is intended to provide more than a summation—it is meant to be a guide to the rest of this chapter.

Most classical theories of crime causation make the following basic assumptions:

- Human beings are fundamentally rational, and most human behaviour is the result of free will coupled with rational choice.
- Pain and pleasure are the two central determinants of human behaviour.
- Punishment, a necessary evil, is sometimes required to deter law violators and to serve as an example to others who would also violate the law.
- Root principles of right and wrong are inherent in the nature of things and cannot be denied.
- Society exists to provide benefits to individuals that they would not receive in isolation.
- When men and women band together for the protection offered by society, they forfeit some of the benefits that accrue from living in isolation.
- Certain key rights of individuals are inherent in the nature of things, and governments that contravene those rights should be disbanded.
- Crime disparages the quality of the bond that exists between individuals and society and is therefore an immoral form of behaviour.

# Forerunners of Classical Thought

The notion of crime as a violation of established law did not exist in the most primitive of preliterate societies. The lack of lawmaking bodies, the paucity of formal written laws, and loose social bonds precluded the concept of crime as law violation. All human societies, however, from the simplest to the most advanced, evidence their own widely held notions of right and wrong. Sociologists term such fundamental concepts of morality and propriety as "mores" and "folkways." Mores, folkways, and laws were terms used by William Graham Sumner[3] near the start of the twentieth century to describe the three basic forms of behavioural strictures imposed by social groups upon their members. According to Sumner, mores and folkways govern behaviour in relatively small primitive societies, whereas in large, complex societies they are reinforced and formalized through written laws.

**Mores** consist of proscriptions covering potentially serious violations of a group's values. Murder, sexual assault, and robbery, for example, would probably be repugnant to the mores of any social group. **Folkways,** on the other hand, are simply time-honoured customs, and although they carry the force of tradition, their violation is less likely to threaten the survival of the social group. The fact that North American men have traditionally worn little jewellery illustrates a folkway that has given way in recent years to various types of male adornment, including earrings, gold chains, and even makeup. Mores and folkways, although they may be powerful determinants of behaviour, are nonetheless informal, because only laws, from among Sumner's trinity, have been codified into formal strictures wielded by institutions and created specifically for enforcement purposes.

Another method of categorizing socially proscriptive rules is provided by some criminologists who divide crimes into the dual categories of *mala in se* and *mala prohibita*. Acts that are ***mala in se*** are said to be fundamentally wrong, regardless of the time or place in which they occur. Forcing someone to have sex against his or her will, and the intentional killing of children, are sometimes given as examples of behaviour thought to be *mala in se*. Those who argue for the existence of *mala in se* offences as a useful heuristic category usually point to some fundamental rule, such as religious teachings (the Ten Commandments, the Koran, etc.), to support their belief that some acts are inherently wrong. Such a perspective assumes that uncompromisable standards for human behaviour rest within the very fabric of lived experience.

***Mala prohibita*** offences are those acts that are said to be wrong for the simple reason that they are prohibited. So-called victimless or social order offences such as prostitution, gambling, drug use, and premarital sexual behaviour provide examples of *mala prohibita* offences. The status of such behaviours as *mala prohibita* is further supported by the fact that they are not necessarily crimes in every jurisdiction. Gambling, for example, is legal in parts of Canada, mainly because of the huge revenue potential it holds. Certain types of gambling are being rapidly legalized in many areas while other forms remain illegal. Raffles and games of chance have been legal in Canada since early 1900. Government-regulated lotteries were legalized in 1969 and continue to generate huge sums of money. The late 1980s saw the advent of casinos, and by 1995 several provinces had them.[4]

**Mores** behavioural proscriptions covering potentially serious violations of a group's values. Examples might include strictures against murder, sexual assault, and robbery.

**Folkways** time-honoured customs. Although folkways carry the force of tradition, their violation is unlikely to threaten the survival of the social group.

**Mala in se** acts that are thought to be wrong in and of themselves.

**Mala prohibita** acts that are wrong only because they are prohibited.

## The Demonic Era

Since time began, humankind has been preoccupied with what appears to be an on-going war between good and evil. Evil has often appeared in impersonal guise, as when the great bubonic plague, also known as the Black Death, ravaged Europe and Asia in the fourteenth century, leaving as much as three-quarters of the population dead in a mere span of twenty years. At other times, evil has seemed to wear a human face, as when the Nazi Holocaust claimed millions of Jewish lives during World War II.

Whatever its manifestation, the very presence of evil in the world has begged for interpretation, and sage minds throughout human history have advanced many ex-planations for the evil conditions that individuals and social groups have at times been forced to endure. Some forms of evil, such as the plague and the Holocaust, appear cosmically based, whereas others—including personal victimization, criminality, and singular instances of deviance—are the undeniable result of individual behaviour. Cosmic-level evil has been explained by ideas as diverse as divine punishment, karma, fate, and the vengeful activities of offended gods. Early explanations of personal de-viance ranged from demonic possession to spiritual influences to temptation by fallen angels—and even led to the positing of commerce between humans and supernatural entities such as demons, werewolves, vampires, and ghosts.

Archeologists have unearthed skeletal remains that provide evidence that some early human societies believed outlandish behaviour among individuals was a conse-quence of spirit possession. Carefully unearthed skulls, dated by various techniques to approximately 40 000 years ago, show signs of early cranial surgery, or **trephination,** apparently intended to release evil spirits thought to be residing within the heads of offenders. Such surgical interventions were undoubtedly crude, and probably involved fermented anesthesia along with flint cutting implements.

As discussed in Chapter 3, any theory gains credence if activity based on it pro-duces results in keeping with what that theory would predict. Hence, spirit possession, as an explanation for deviance, probably appeared well validated by positive behav-ioural changes in those "patients" who submitted to the surgery called for by the the-ory. The actual cause of such observed reformation, however, may have been brain infections resulting from unsanitary conditions, accidental slips of the stone knife, or the deterrent power of the pain endured by those undergoing the procedure. Nonethe-less, to the uncritical observer the theory of spirit possession as a cause of deviance, and cranial surgery as a treatment technique, might have appeared to be supported by the "evidence" of low rates of future crime.

**Trephination** a form of surgery, typically involving bone and especially the skull. Early instances of cranial trephination have been taken as evidence for primitive beliefs in spirit possession.

## Early Sources of the Criminal Law

### The Code of Hammurabi

Modern criminal law is the result of a long evolution of legal principles. The **Code of Hammurabi** is one of the first known bodies of law to survive and be available for study today. King Hammurabi ruled the ancient city of Babylon from 1792 to 1750 B.C. and cre-ated a legal code consisting of a set of strictures engraved on stone tablets. The Hammurabi laws were originally intended to establish property and other rights and were crucial to the

**Code of Hammurabi** an early set of laws established by the Babylonian King Hammurabi, who ruled the ancient city from 1792 to 1750 B.C.

continued growth of Babylon as a significant commercial centre. Hammurabi law spoke to issues of theft, property ownership, sexual relationships, and interpersonal violence. As Marvin Wolfgang has observed, "In its day, 1700 B.C., the Hammurabi Code, with its emphasis on **retribution**, amounted to a brilliant advance in penal philosophy mainly because it represented an attempt to keep cruelty within bounds."[5] Prior to the code, captured offenders often faced the most barbarous of punishments, frequently at the hands of revenge-seeking victims, no matter how minor their transgressions had been.

**Retribution** the act of taking revenge upon a criminal perpetrator.

## Early Roman Law

Of considerable significance for our own legal tradition is early Roman law. Roman legions under Emperor Claudius I (10 B.C.–54 A.D.) conquered England in the mid-first century, and Roman authority over "Britannia" was further consolidated by later Roman rulers who built walls and fortifications to keep out the still-hostile Scots. Roman customs, law, and language were forced upon the English population during the succeeding three centuries under the Pax Romana—a peace imposed by the military might of Rome.[6]

Early Roman law derived from the **Twelve Tables**, which were written circa 450 B.C. The tables were a collection of basic rules regulating family, religious, and economic life. They appear to have been based on common and fair practices generally accepted among early tribes which existed prior to the establishment of the Roman Republic. Unfortunately, only fragments of the tables survive today.

**Twelve Tables** early Roman laws written circa 450 B.C. that regulated family, religious, and economic life.

The best known legal period in Roman history occurred during the reign of Emperor Justinian I (527–565 A.D.). By the end of the sixth century, the Roman Empire had declined substantially in size and influence and was near the end of its life. In what may have been an effort to preserve Roman values and traditions, Justinian undertook the laborious process of distilling Roman laws into a set of writings. The Justinian Code, as these writings came to be known, actually consisted of three lengthy legal documents: (1) the Institutes, (2) the Digest, and (3) the Code itself. Justinian's code distinguished between two major legal categories: public and private laws. Public laws dealt with the organization of the Roman state, its Senate, and governmental offices. Private law concerned itself with contracts, personal possessions, the legal status of various types of persons (citizens, free persons, slaves, freedmen, guardians, husbands and wives, and so forth), and injuries to citizens. It contained elements of both our modern civil and criminal law and influenced Western legal thought through the Middle Ages.

## Common Law

Common law forms the basis for much of our modern statutory and case law. It has often been called *the* major source of modern criminal law. **Common law** refers to a traditional body of unwritten legal precedents created through everyday practice and supported by court decisions during the Middle Ages in English society. Common law is so called because it was based on shared traditions and standards rather than on those that varied from one locale to another. As novel situations arose, the declarations of British justices on them became the start for any similar future deliberation. These decisions generally incorporated the customs of society as it operated at the time.

**Common law** a body of unwritten judicial opinion originally based on customary social practices of Anglo-Saxon society during the Middle Ages (also discussed in Chapter 1).

Common law was given considerable legitimacy upon the official declaration by the English King Edward the Confessor (ruled 1042–1066 A.D.) that it was the law of the land. The authority of common law was further reinforced by the decision of William the Conqueror to use popular customs as the basis for judicial action following his subjugation of Britain in 1066.

Eventually, court decisions were recorded and made available to *barristers* (the British word for trial lawyers) and judges. As Howard Abadinsky wrote, "Common law involved the transformation of community rules into a national legal system. The controlling element (was) precedent."[7] Today, common law forms the basis of many of the laws on the books in English-speaking countries around the world.

## The Magna Carta

The Magna Carta (literally, "great charter") is another important source of modern laws and legal procedure. The Magna Carta was signed on June 15, 1215, by King John of England at Runnymede, under pressure from British barons who took advantage of John's military defeats at the hands of Pope Innocent III and King Philip Augustus of France. The barons demanded a pledge from the king to respect their traditional rights and forced the king to agree to be bound by law.

At the time of its signing, the Magna Carta, although 63 chapters in length, was little more than a feudal document listing specific royal concessions.[8] Its original purpose was to ensure feudal rights and to guarantee that the king could not encroach on the privileges claimed by landowning barons. Additionally, the Magna Carta guaranteed the freedom of the church and ensured respect for the customs of towns. Its wording, however, was later interpreted during a judicial revolt in 1613 to support individual rights and jury trials. Sir Edward Coke, chief justice under James I, held that the Magna Carta guaranteed basic liberties for all British citizens. One section of the Magna Carta states that "No free man shall be arrested and imprisoned ... unless by the lawful judgment of his peers and by the law of the land."[9] Section 7 of the Canadian Charter of Rights and Freedoms assures this fundamental right for Canadians today. Similarly, another specific provision of the Magna Carta, designed originally to prohibit the king

The Magna Carta, an important source of modern Western laws and legal procedure. What are some other important sources of modern criminal law? *Corbis-Bettmann.*

from prosecuting the barons without just cause, was expanded into the concept of "due process of law," a fundamental cornerstone of modern legal procedure. Because of these later interpretations, the Magna Carta has been called "the foundation stone of our present liberties."[10]

## The Enlightenment

**The Enlightenment,** also called the Age of Reason, was a highly significant social movement that occurred during the eighteenth century. The Enlightenment built upon ideas developed by seventeenth-century thinkers such as Francis Bacon (1561–1626), Thomas Hobbes (1588–1679), John Locke (1632–1704), René Descartes (1596–1650), Jean-Jacques Rousseau (1712–1778), Baruch Spinoza (1632–1677), and others. Because of their indirect contributions to classical criminological thought, it will be worthwhile briefly discussing the writings of several of these important historical figures.

**Enlightenment, (the)** also known as the Age of Reason. A social movement that arose during the eighteenth century and built upon ideas such as empiricism, rationality, free will, humanism, and natural law.

### Thomas Hobbes (1588–1679)

The English philosopher **Thomas Hobbes** developed what many writers regard as an extremely negative view of human nature and social life, which he described in his momentous work, *Leviathan* (1651). Hobbes described the natural state of men and women as one that is "nasty, brutish, and short." Fear of violent death, he said, forces human beings into a **social contract** with one another to create a state. The state, according to Hobbes, demands the surrender of certain natural rights and submission to the absolute authority of a sovereign, while offering protection and succor to its citizens in return. Although the social contract concept significantly influenced many of Hobbes's contemporaries, much of his writing was condemned for assuming an overly pessimistic view of both human nature and existing governments.

### John Locke (1632–1704)

In 1690, the English philosopher **John Locke** published his *Essay Concerning Human Understanding* (1690), in which he put forth the idea that the natural human condition at birth is akin to that of a blank slate, upon which interpersonal encounters and other experiences indelibly inscribe the traits of personality. In contrast to earlier thinkers, who assumed that people are born with certain innate propensities and even rudimentary intellectual concepts and ideas, Locke ascribed the bulk of adult human qualities to life experiences.

**Social contract** the Enlightenment-era concept that human beings abandon their natural state of individual freedom to join together and form society. Although in the process of forming a social contract individuals surrender some freedoms to society as a whole, government, once formed, is obligated to assume responsibilities toward its citizens and to provide for their protection and welfare.

In the area of social and political thought, Locke further developed the Hobbesian notion of the social contract. Locke contended that human beings, through a social contract, abandon their natural state of individual freedom and lack of interpersonal responsibility to join together and form society. Although individuals surrender some freedoms to society, government, once formed, is obligated to assume responsibilities toward its citizens and to provide for their protection and welfare. According to Locke and other writers, governments should be required to guarantee certain inalienable rights to their citizens, including the right to life, health, liberty, and possessions. A product of his times, during which the dictatorial nature of monarchies and the Roman church were being much disparaged, Locke stressed the duties that governments have toward their citizens, while paying very little attention to the inverse—the responsibilities of individuals to the societies of which they are a part. As a natural consequence of such an emphasis, Locke argued that political revolutions, under some circumstances, might become an obligation incumbent upon citizens.

Locke also developed the notion of checks and balances between divisions of government, a doctrine that was elaborated by the French jurist and political philosopher Charles Louis de Secondat **Montesquieu** (1689–1755). In *The Spirit of Laws* (1748), Montesquieu wove Locke's notions into the concept of a separation of powers between divisions of government. The Canadian parliamentary system is based on these very principles.

### Jean-Jacques Rousseau (1712–1778)

The Swiss-French philosopher and political theorist **Jean-Jacques Rousseau** further advanced the notion of the social contract in his treatise of that name (*Social Contract,* 1762). According to Rousseau, human beings are basically good and fair in their natural state, but historically were corrupted by the introduction of shared concepts and joint activities such as property, agriculture, science, and commerce. As a result, the social contract emerged when civilized people agreed to establish governments and systems of education to correct the problems and inequalities brought on by the rise of civilization.

**Natural law** the philosophical perspective that certain immutable laws are fundamental to human nature and can be readily ascertained through reason. Man-made laws, in contrast, are said to derive from human experience and history—both of which are subject to continual change.

Rousseau also contributed to the notion of **natural law,** a concept originally formulated by St. Thomas Aquinas (1225–1274), Baruch Spinoza (1632–1677), and others to provide an intuitive basis for the defence of ethical principles and morality. Natural law was used by early Christian church leaders as a powerful argument in support of their interests. Submissive to the authority of the church, secular rulers were pressed to reinforce church doctrine in any laws they decreed. Thomas Aquinas, a well-known supporter of natural law, wrote in his *Summa Theologica* that any man-made law that contradicts natural law is corrupt in the eyes of God. Religious practice, which strongly reflected natural law conceptions, was central to the life of early British society. Hence, natural law, as it was understood at the time, was incorporated into English common law throughout the Middle Ages.

Rousseau agreed with earlier writers that certain immutable laws are fundamental to human nature and can be readily ascertained through reason. Man-made law, in contrast, he claimed, derives from human experience and history—both of which are subject to continual change. Hence, man-made law, also termed *positive law,* changes from time to time and from epoch to epoch. Rousseau expanded the concept of natural law to support emerging democratic principles and claimed that certain fundamental human and personal rights were inalienable because they were based on the natural order of things.

**Natural rights** the rights that, according to natural law theorists, individuals retain in the face of government action and interests.

**Thomas Paine** (1737–1809), the English-American political theorist and author of *The Rights of Man* (1791 and 1792), defended the French Revolution, arguing that only democratic institutions could guarantee the **natural rights** of individuals. For example, commentators have cited the "crimes against humanity" committed by Nazis during World War II as indicative of natural law principles. The chilling testimony of

Thomas Paine (1737–1809) was an important contributor to the concept of natural law. What are the central tenets of natural law? *Corbis-Bettmann.*

Rudolf Hess,[11] Hitler's deputy, during the 1945 war crimes trial in Nuremberg, Germany, as he recalled the "Fuehrer's" order to exterminate millions of Jews, indicated the extent of the planned "final solution." Hess testified: "In the summer of 1941 I was summoned to Berlin to Reichsfuehrer SS Himmler to receive personal orders. He told me something to the effect—I do not remember the exact words—that the Fuehrer had given the order for a final solution of the Jewish question. We, the SS, must carry out that order. If it is not carried out now then the Jews will later on destroy the German people. He had chosen Auschwitz on account of its easy access by rail and also because the extensive site offered space for measures ensuring isolation."[12] Who could argue against the premise, natural law supporters ask, that Hitler's final solution to the Jewish "problem" was inherently wrong?

Although the concept of natural law has waned somewhat in influence over the past half century, many people today still maintain that the basis for various existing criminal laws can be found in immutable moral principles, or in some other identifiable aspect of the natural order. The Ten Commandments, "inborn tendencies," the idea of sin, and perceptions of various forms of order in the universe and in the social world have all provided a basis for the assertion that natural law exists. Modern-day advocates of natural law still claim that it comes from outside the social group and that it is knowable through some form of revelation, intuition, or prophecy.

The present debate over abortion is an example of modern-day use of natural law arguments to support both sides in the dispute. Those who oppose abortion claim that an unborn fetus is a person and that he or she is entitled to all the protection that we would give to any other living human being. Such protection, they suggest, is basic and humane and lies in the natural relationship of one human being to another, and within the relationship of a society to its children. These "pro-life" groups are striving for passage of a law, or a reinterpretation of past Supreme Court precedent, that would support their position. Advocates of the present law (which allows abortion upon request under certain conditions) maintain that abortion is a "right" of any pregnant woman because she is the only one who should be in control of her body. Such "pro-choice" groups also claim that the legal system must address the abortion question, but only by way of offering protection to this "natural right" of women.

# The Classical School

As many authors have pointed out, the Enlightenment fuelled the fires of social change, leading eventually to the French and American Revolutions. The Enlightenment—one of the most powerful intellectual initiatives of the last millennium—also inspired other social movements and freed innovative thinkers from the chains of convention. As a direct consequence of Enlightenment thinking, superstitious beliefs were discarded and men and women began to be perceived, for the first time, as self-determining entities possessing a fundamental freedom of choice. Following the Enlightenment, many supernatural explanations for human behaviour fell by the wayside and free will and rational thought came to be recognized as the linchpins of all significant human activity. In effect, the Enlightenment inspired the re-examination of existing doctrines of human behaviour from the point of view of rationalism.

Within criminology, the Enlightenment led to the development of the **classical school** of criminological thought. Crime and deviance, which had been previously explained by reference to mythological influences and spiritual shortcomings, took their place in Enlightenment thought alongside other forms of human activity as products of the exercise of free will. Once man was seen as self-determining, crime came to be explained as a particularly individualized form of evil, or moral wrongdoing fed by personal choice.

## Cesare Beccaria (1738–1794)

**Cesare Beccaria** (whose Italian name was Cesare Bonesana, but who held the title Marchese di Beccaria) was born in Milan, Italy. The eldest of four children, he was trained at Catholic schools and earned a doctor of laws degree by the time he was 20.

In 1764, Beccaria published his *Essay on Crimes and Punishments.*[13] Although the work appeared originally in Italian, it was translated into English in London in 1767. Beccaria's *Essay* consisted of 42 short chapters covering only a few major themes. Beccaria's purpose was not to set forth a theory of crime but to communicate his observations on the laws and justice system of his time. In the *Essay,* Beccaria distilled the notion of the social contract into the idea that "[l]aws are the conditions under which independent and isolated men united to form a society." More than anything else, however, his writings consisted of a philosophy of punishment. Beccaria claimed, for example, that although most criminals are punished based on an assessment of their criminal intent, they should be punished instead based on the degree of injury they cause. The purpose of punishment, he said, should be **deterrence** rather than retribution, and punishment should be imposed to prevent offenders from committing additional crimes. Beccaria saw punishment as a tool to an end and not an end in itself, and crime prevention was more important to him than revenge.

To help prevent crimes, Beccaria argued, adjudication and punishment should both be swift, and once punishment is decreed, it should be certain. In his words, "The more promptly and the more closely punishment follows upon the commission of a

**Classical school** a criminological perspective operative in the late 1700s and early 1800s that had its roots in the Enlightenment. It held that men and women are rational beings, that crime is the result of the exercise of free will, and that punishment can be effective in reducing the incidence of crime, as it negates the pleasure to be derived from crime commission.

**Deterrence** the prevention of crime.

crime, the more just and useful it will be." Punishment that is imposed immediately following crime commission, claimed Beccaria, is connected with the wrongfulness of the offence, both in the mind of the offender and in the minds of others who might see the punishment imposed and thereby learn of the consequences of involvement in criminal activity.

Beccaria concluded that punishment should be only severe enough to outweigh the personal benefits to be derived from crime commission. Any additional punishment, he argued, would be superfluous. Beccaria's concluding words on punishment are telling: "In order for punishment not to be, in every instance, an act of violence of one or of many against a private citizen, it must be essentially public, prompt, necessary, the least possible in the given circumstances, proportionate to the crimes, [and] dictated by the laws."

Beccaria distinguished between three types of crimes—those that threatened the security of the state, those that injured citizens or their property, and those that ran contrary to the social order. Punishment should fit the crime, Beccaria argued, and theft should be punished through fines, personal injury through corporal punishment, and serious crimes against the state (such as inciting revolution) through the death penalty. Beccaria, however, was opposed to the death penalty in most other circumstances, seeing it as a kind of warfare waged by society against its citizens.

Beccaria condemned the torture of suspects, a practice still used in the eighteenth century, saying that it was a device that ensured that weak suspects would incriminate themselves, while strong ones would be found innocent. Torture, he argued, was also unjust, because it punished individuals before they had been found guilty in a court of law. In Beccaria's words, "No man can be called guilty before a judge has sentenced him, nor can society deprive him of public protection before it has been decided that he has in fact violated the conditions under which such protection was accorded him. What right is it then, if not simply that of might, which empowers a judge to inflict punishment on a citizen while doubt still remains as to his guilt or innocence?"

Beccaria's *Essay* also touched upon a variety of other topics. He distinguished, for example, between two types of proof—that which he called "perfect proof," in which there was no possibility of innocence, and "imperfect proof," where some possibility of innocence remained. Beccaria also believed in the efficacy of a jury of one's peers but recommended that half of any jury panel should consist of peers of the victim, whereas the other half should be made up of peers of the accused. Finally, Beccaria wrote that oaths were useless in a court of law, because accused individuals will naturally deny their guilt even if they know themselves to be fully culpable.

Beccaria's ideas were widely recognized as progressive by his contemporaries. His principles were incorporated into the French penal code of 1791 and significantly influenced the justice-related activities of European leaders such as Catherine the Great of Russia, Frederick the Great of Prussia, the Austrian Emperor Joseph II, and the framers of the American Constitution. Perhaps more than anyone else, Beccaria is responsible for the contemporary belief that criminals have control over their behaviour, that they choose to commit crimes, and that they can be deterred by the threat of punishment.

## Jeremy Bentham (1748–1832)

**Jeremy Bentham,**[14] another founding personality of the classical school, wrote in his *Introduction to the Principles of Morals and Legislation* (1789) that "nature has placed mankind under the governance of two sovereign masters, pain and pleasure." To reduce crime or, as Bentham put it, "to prevent the happening of mischief," the pain of crime commission must outweigh the pleasure to be derived from criminal activity. Bentham's claim rested upon his belief, spawned by Enlightenment thought, that human beings are fundamentally rational and that criminals will weigh in their minds the pain of punishment against any pleasures thought likely to be derived from crime commission.

Bentham advocated neither extreme nor cruel punishment—only punishment sufficiently distasteful to the offender that the discomfort experienced would outweigh the pleasure to be derived from criminal activity. Generally, Bentham argued, the more serious the offence the more reward it holds for its perpetrator and, therefore, the more weighty the official response must be. "Pain and pleasure," said Bentham, "are the instruments the legislator has to work with" in controlling antisocial and criminal behaviour.

Bentham's approach has been termed **hedonistic calculus** or **utilitarianism** because of its emphasis on the worth any action holds for an individual undertaking it. As Bentham stated, "[b]y the principle of utility is meant that principle which approves or disapproves of every action whatsoever, according to the tendency which it appears to have to augment or diminish the happiness of the party whose interest is in question; or, what is the same thing … to promote or to oppose that happiness." In other words, Bentham believed that individuals could be expected to weigh, at least intuitively, the consequences of their behaviour before acting, so as to maximize their own pleasure and minimize pain. The value of any pleasure, or the inhibitory tendency of any pain, according to Bentham, could be calculated by its intensity, duration, certainty, and immediacy (or remoteness in time).

**Hedonistic calculus** or **utilitarianism** the belief, first proposed by Jeremy Bentham, that behaviour holds value to any individual undertaking it according to the amount of pleasure or pain that it can be expected to produce for that person.

Jeremy Bentham (1748–1832) whose work is closely associated with the classical school of criminology. What are the key features of the classical school?
*Corbis-Bettmann.*

Bentham claimed that nothing was really new in his pleasure-pain perspective. "Nor is this a novel and unwarranted, any more than it is a useless, theory," he wrote. "In all this there is nothing but what the practice of mankind, wheresoever they have a clear view of their own interest, is perfectly comfortable to. An article of property, an estate in land, for instance, is valuable, on what account? On account of the pleasures of all kinds which it enables a man to produce, and what comes to the same thing the pains of all kinds which it enables him to avert." In fact, Bentham's ideas were not new, but their application to criminology was. In 1739, David Hume distilled the notion of utilitarianism into a philosophical perspective in his book *A Treatise of Human Nature.* Although Hume's central concern was not to explain crime, scholars who followed Hume observed that human behaviour is typically motivated more by self-interest than by anything else.

Like Beccaria, Bentham focused on the potential held by punishment to prevent crime and to act as a deterrent for those considering criminal activity. In any criminal legislation, he wrote, "[t]he evils of punishment must … be made to exceed the advantage of the offence." Bentham distinguished between 11 different types of punishment, as follows:

- *capital punishment,* or death;
- *afflictive punishment,* which includes whipping and starvation;
- *indelible punishment,* such as branding, amputation, and mutilation.
- *ignominious punishment,* such as public punishment involving use of the stocks or pillory;
- *penitential punishment,* whereby an offender might be censured by his or her community;
- *chronic punishment,* such as banishment, exile, and imprisonment;
- *restrictive punishment,* such as licence revocation or administrative sanction;
- *compulsive punishment,* which requires an offender to perform a certain action such as to make restitution or keep in touch with a probation officer;
- *pecuniary punishment,* involving the use of fines;
- *quasi-pecuniary punishment,* in which the offender is denied services that would otherwise be available to him or her; and
- *characteristic punishment,* such as mandating that prison uniforms be worn by incarcerated offenders.

Utilitarianism is a practical philosophy, and Bentham was quite practical in his suggestions about crime prevention. Every citizen, he said, should have their first and last names tattooed on their wrists for the purpose of facilitating police identification. He also recommended creation of a centralized police force focused on crime prevention and control—a recommendation that found life in the English Metropolitan Police Act of 1829, which established London's New Police under the direction of Sir Robert Peel. This model of policing was adopted in the creation of Canada's first national police force, the Dominion Police Force, in 1867.

Bentham's other major contribution to criminology was his suggestion that prisons be designed along the lines of what he called a Panopticon House. The **Panopticon,** as Bentham envisioned it, was to be a circular building with cells along the circumference, each clearly visible from a central location staffed by guards. Bentham recommended that Panopticons should be constructed near or within cities so that they might serve as examples to others of what would happen to them should they

**Panopticon** a prison designed by Jeremy Bentham that was to be a circular building with cells along the circumference, each clearly visible from a central location staffed by guards.

commit crimes. He also wrote that prisons should be managed by contractors who could profit from the labour of prisoners, and that the contractor should "be bound to insure the lives and safe custody of those entrusted to him." Although a Panopticon was never built in Bentham's England, French officials funded a modified version of such a prison, which was eventually built at Lyons, and three prisons modelled after the Panopticon concept were constructed in the United States.

Bentham's critics have been quick to point out that punishments seem often not to work. Even punishments as severe as death appear not to have any effect on the incidence of crimes such as murder (a point that we will discuss in greater detail later in this chapter). Such critics forget Bentham's second tenet, however, which is that for punishment to be effective, "it must be swift and certain." For any punishment to have teeth, Bentham said, it must not only mandate a certain degree of displeasure but must follow almost immediately upon its being decided, and there must be no way of avoiding it.

## Heritage of the Classical School

The classical school was to influence criminological thinking for a long time. It has been instrumental in molding the way in which thinkers on the subject of crime have viewed the topic for more than 200 years. The heritage left by the classical school is still operative today in the following five principles, each of which is a fundamental constituent of modern-day perspectives on crime and human behaviour:

- *The principle of rationality:* Human beings have free will and the actions they undertake are the result of choice.
- *The principle of hedonism:* Pleasure and pain, or reward and punishment, are the major determinants of choice.
- *The principle of punishment:* Criminal punishment is a deterrent to unlawful behaviour, and deterrence is the best justification for punishment.
- *The human rights principle:* Society is made possible by individuals cooperating together. Hence, society owes to its citizens respect for their rights in the face of government action, and for their autonomy insofar as such autonomy can be secured without endangering others or menacing the greater good.
- *The due process principle:* An accused should be presumed innocent until proven otherwise, and an accused should not be subject to punishment prior to guilt being lawfully established.

Some of these concepts are easily recognizable in the Canadian Charter of Rights and Freedoms, the Criminal Code of Canada, and the Young Offenders Act.

## Neoclassical Criminology

The 1970s saw a resurgence of the classical school. The public was becoming more and more frustrated by increasing crime rates and the apparent ineffectiveness of correctional programs designed to rehabilitate offenders. In addition, government policies designed to rectify those social conditions, such as unemployment and poverty, believed to contribute to criminality were viewed as failures. In an often-quoted article entitled, "What Works?" Robert Martinson noted that "[w]ith few and isolated exceptions, the rehabilitative efforts that have been reported so far have had no appreciable effect on recidivism."[15]

In this atmosphere of frustration, some criminologists turned to a revival of the classical tenets of punishment—rational choice and deterrence—as a more effective means of dealing with the crime problem. They advocated a move away from the treatment and rehabilitation practices within correctional institutions and toward more punishment-oriented programs as a more effective way of curtailing future criminality. Some effects of this return to classical criminology are still being reflected in criminal justice policy today.

In essence, two **neoclassical criminology** schools of thought continue to exist. The first continues to build upon ideas inherent in the notion of a social contract and places an emphasis on **individual rights and due process**. This approach emphasizes punishment within a context of the rights of the individual offender. The second type of classical thinking has taken the form of a **just-deserts model**, with a society-wide emphasis on both deterrence and retribution as the twin goals of criminal punishment.

**Neoclassical criminology** a contemporary version of classical criminology which emphasizes deterrence and retribution with reduced emphasis on rehabilitation.

**Individual rights and due process** the notion that criminal offenders have certain rights that must be defended against potential government excesses.

**Just-deserts model** the notion that criminal offenders deserve the punishment they receive at the hands of the law, and that punishments should be appropriate to the type and severity of crime committed.

## Not All Urging Mercy for Teen Facing Flogging

The 1994 "caning" of an American teenager in Singapore provided an example of the continuing popularity of the just-deserts philosophy, as the following story illustrates.

Michael Fay's father pleaded Sunday for the International Red Cross to intervene. Fay's mother begged for leniency. President Clinton said the penalty outweighs the crime.

But when it comes to the case of the Dayton, Ohio, man who may be flogged—six lashes—for spray-painting cars in Singapore, some Americans have no sympathy, and have written Singapore officials to say so.

The punishment—meted out with a 4-foot-long, half-inch-thick split-bamboo rod called a rotan—is "hardly a spanking," says lawyer Theodore Simon, who represents Fay, 18.

When a prisoner is struck, "pieces of skin and flesh fly at each stroke of the rotan," says Simon. If the prisoner faints, he's revived by a doctor so the flogging can continue.

"This is mutilation, basically," says the father, George Fay of Dayton.

The elder Fay said he thinks his son's confession was coerced and he'll ask Singapore President Ong Teng Cheong for clemency. He also intends to get the International Red Cross to attend and monitor the flogging.

Michael Fay was singled out because he's an American, his father says. Fay's mother, Randy Chan, with whom he lives in Singapore, has lobbied for leniency.

Also:

• A worldwide association of meeting planners is threatening to boycott Singapore unless it grants Fay clemency. "We'll hit Singapore in its pocketbook" if Fay is caned, said Troy Johnson of the Arizona-based International Society of Meeting Planners.

▶

Michael Fay, the 18-year-old American teenager who was caned in Singapore in 1994 for spray-painting cars, makes the "sign of the cross" before entering Singapore's High Court. Should Fay have been caned? *Jonathan Drake/Corbis-Bettman.*

- Clinton has called the punishment extreme and has urged Singapore to reconsider.
- Although the sentence has outraged Fay's parents, more than 100 letters and 200 phone calls in support of the punishment have come from Americans, says Chin Hock Seng of the Singapore Embassy.
- "America should be taking lessons from Singapore on how to prevent crime. Hold the line—don't give in," said a letter from Huntington Beach, Calif.
- "Punish hooligans and enjoy the benefits of a safe, clean society!" said a writer from Fresno, Calif.
- "I urge you to … vigorously apply Singapore law to the criminal's rear end," said a writer from Silver Spring, Md.

*Chicago Tribune* columnist Mike Royko wrote that he had received letters "several inches high," and 99% wrote that "yes, hooray, [Fay] should be flogged."

The Dayton *Daily News,* Fay's home-town newspaper, also is getting mail in support of the flogging.

The ordeal began last month when Michael Fay pleaded guilty to a 10-day spree in which he and other foreign students spray-painted and threw eggs, bricks and flower pots at 18 cars. Fay was sentenced to 4 months in prison, a $2 230 fine and flogging with the split-bamboo cane.

A State Department human-rights report last year criticized caning, and Amnesty International has called it a form of torture.

Michael Fay remained in jail in Singapore, awaiting the outcome of his appeal. No date has been set for the punishment.

As most readers will recall, Fay did not receive clemency and was flogged—a punishment referred to as "caning" in Singapore. Due to the American outcry over the event, however, the number of lashes he received was reduced to four. Fay then spent an additional month imprisoned in Singapore before being released and returning to the United States.

► **DISCUSSION QUESTIONS**

1. Do you believe that corporal punishment can be an effective response to crime? Why or why not?
2. Do you believe that the caning of Michael Fay was deserved? Why or why not?
3. Do you believe that independent nations, such as Singapore, should be permitted to implement their own sense of justice without interference from other countries? Why or why not?

SOURCE: Carol J. Castaneda, "Not All Urging Mercy for Teen Facing Flogging," *USA Today*, April 4, 1994, p. 3A. Copyright 1994, *USA Today*. Reprinted with permission.

## Individual Rights and Due Process in Neoclassical Thought

An important legacy of the classical school is found in the principles of human rights and due process. Inherent in these principles is the notion that the individual must be protected against the power and authority of the state. While the social contract dictates that all members of a given society are required to abdicate some of their inherent rights and freedoms, it also mandates that the government has an obligation to provide for the welfare and protection of its citizens. The rights protected in the Canadian Charter of Rights and Freedoms are examples of this obligation. Specifically, the legal rights outlined in sections 7 to 14 of the Charter ensure that individuals charged with a criminal offence by the state are assured the right to be protected against arbitrary detention or imprisonment, to retain legal counsel, to be tried within a reasonable time, to be considered innocent until proven otherwise, and to remain free from cruel and unusual treatment or punishment.

Those who advocate for these and other individual rights cite correctional overcrowding, high rates of recidivism, and increased criminal activity in many areas of society. This school of neoclassical thinkers points out that an increasing emphasis on imprisonment has done little to stem the tide of rising crime. They call for renewed recognition of individual rights in the face of criminal prosecution, and for reduction in the use of imprisonment as a criminal sanction—suggesting that it be employed as a kind of last resort to deal with only the most dangerous offenders. **Dangerousness,** or the likelihood that a given individual will later harm society or others, should be the major determining criterion for government action against the freedom of its citizens, **individual rights advocates** argue. Dangerousness, they suggest, should form the standard against which any need for incapacitation might be judged (see Chapter 6 for a more in-depth discussion of dangerousness). **Incapacitation,** simply put, is the use of imprisonment or other means to reduce the likelihood that an offender will be capable of committing future offences.

Proponents of modern-day incapacitation often distinguish between selective and collective incapacitation. Selective incapacitation is the control of crime through imprisonment of specific individuals who are felt to constitute the greatest risk of committing future crimes. Collective incapacitation, on the other hand, involves the sentencing of offenders according to prior record and the seriousness of the crime committed.

**Dangerousness** the likelihood that a given individual will later harm society or others; it is often measured in terms of **recidivism,** or the likelihood of new crime commission or rearrest for a new crime.

**Individual rights advocates** those who seek to protect personal freedoms in the face of criminal prosecution.

**Incapacitation** the use of imprisonment or other means to reduce the likelihood that an offender will be capable of committing future offences.

Advocates of selective incapacitation as a crime-control strategy point to studies showing that the majority of crimes are perpetrated by a small number of hard-core repeat offenders. The most famous of those studies was conducted by Marvin Wolfgang and focused on 9 000 male individuals born in Philadelphia in 1945. By the time this cohort of men had reached age 18, Wolfgang was able to determine that 627 "chronic recidivists," or repeat offenders, were responsible for the large majority of all serious violent crimes committed by the group. Other, more recent, studies have similarly shown that a small hard core of criminal perpetrators is probably responsible for most criminal activity.[16]

Proponents of collective incapacitation advocate the reformation of sentencing policies to include, for example, mandatory minimum sentences. Such a practice dictates that a sentencing judge must impose a certain minimum penalty at the very least. In Canada, there are very few offences that carry a minimum sanction. Included among them are first- and second-degree murder, the use of a firearm during the commission of an offence, a second conviction for impaired driving, and bookmaking and placing bets on behalf of others (outside a legally sanctioned system).

Such thinking has led to the development of incapacitation as a modern-day treatment philosophy and to the creation of innovative forms of incapacitation that do not require imprisonment—such as home confinement, the use of halfway houses or career training centres for convicted felons, and psychological and/or chemical treatments designed to reduce the likelihood of future crime commissions. Similarly, such thinkers argue, the decriminalization of many offences and the enhancement of social programs designed to combat what they see as the root causes of crime—including poverty, low educational levels, a general lack of skills, and inherent or active discrimination—will lead to a much reduced incidence of crime in the future, making high rates of imprisonment unnecessary.

## Just Deserts and Neoclassical Thought

Modern neoclassical thinkers arguing from the just-deserts perspective contend that if a person is attracted to crime and chooses to violate the law, he or she deserves to be punished since the consequences of the crime were known to the individual before the crime was committed. The old adages, "he got what was coming to him" or "she got her due" well summarize the thinking behind the just-deserts model of criminal sentencing. Just deserts, as discussed earlier in the chapter, refers to the notion that criminal offenders deserve the punishment they receive at the hands of the law, and that any punishment that is imposed should be appropriate to the type and severity of crime committed. The idea of just deserts has long been a part of Western thought, dating back at least to Old Testament times. The Old Testament dictum of "an eye for an eye, and a tooth for a tooth" has been cited by many as divine justification for strict punishments. Some scholars believe, however, that in reality the notion of "an eye for an eye" was intended to reduce the barbarism of existing penalties whereby an aggrieved party might exact the severest of punishments for only minor offences. Even petty offences were often punished by whipping, torture, and sometimes death.

According to the neoclassical perspective, doing justice ultimately comes down to an official meting out of what is deserved. Justice for an individual is nothing more nor less than what that individual deserves when all the circumstances surrounding that person's situation and behaviour are taken into account.

In addition to the notion that a criminal deserves the sanction he or she receives is the belief that the criminal *must* be punished to curtail future criminal behaviour. This notion of deterrence is a hallmark of modern neoclassical thought. In contrast to early thinkers, however, today's neoclassical writers distinguish between deterrence that is specific and that which is general. **Specific deterrence** is a goal of criminal sentencing that seeks to prevent a particular offender from engaging in repeat criminality. **General deterrence,** in contrast, works by way of example and seeks to prevent others from committing crimes similar to the one for which a particular offender is being sentenced.

Following their classical counterparts, modern-day advocates of general deterrence frequently stress that for punishment to be an effective impediment to crime it must be swift, certain, and severe enough to outweigh the rewards flowing from criminal activity. Those who advocate punishment as a deterrent are often frustrated by the complexity of today's criminal justice system and the slow and circuitous manner in which cases are handled and punishments are meted out. Punishments today, even when imposed by a court, are rarely swift in their imposition. If they were, they would follow quickly after sentencing. The wheels of modern criminal justice, however, are relatively slow to grind to a conclusion, given the many delays inherent in judicial proceedings. Similarly, certainty of punishment is anything but a reality. Certain punishments are those which cannot be easily avoided. However, even when punishments are ordered, they are often not carried out—at least not fully.

The recommendation that determinant-sentencing tactics be adopted in Canada is an attempt to address this concern.[17] Determinant sentencing is a strategy that mandates a specified and fixed amount of time to be served for every category of offence. Under determinant sentencing schemes, for example, judges might be required to impose a 7-year sentence on an offender convicted of armed robbery but only a 1-year sentence on those convicted robbers who use no weapon. Determinant sentencing schemes build upon the classical notion that a fixed amount of punishment necessary for deterrence can be calculated and specified. Due process proponents contend that determinant sentences may also reduce sentencing bias since disparity based on race or social status would be eliminated. Canadian judges have voiced the concern that determinant sentencing models limit the amount of discretion or personal judgment they can exercise when meting out a sentence. It is unlikely that these sentencing models will be fully adopted in Canada.

If the neoclassicists are correct, ideally criminal punishments should prevent recidivism. **Recidivism** means, quite simply, the repetition of criminal behaviour by those already involved in crime. Recidivism can also be used to measure the success of a given approach to the problem of crime. When so employed, it is referred to as a **recidivism rate,** expressed as the percentage of convicted offenders who, during a designated period of time after release from a correctional facility, are rearrested for a new crime or a violation of the conditions of their release (known as a "technical violation").

While the public perception is that recidivism rates in Canada are high, the reality is somewhat different. The most recent studies show that recidivism rates range from about 25 to 45 percent, with the rate for those who actually commit a new crime about 13 to 20 percent.[18] What studies do not measure, however, are the numbers of released

**Specific deterrence** a goal of criminal sentencing that seeks to prevent a particular offender from engaging in repeat criminality.

**General deterrence** a goal of criminal sentencing that seeks to prevent others from committing crimes similar to the one for which a particular offender is being sentenced.

**Recidivism** the repetition of criminal behaviour.

**Recidivism rate** the percentage of convicted offenders who have been released from prison and who are later rearrested for a new crime.

offenders who return to crime but are not caught, or who return to crime after their period of supervision.

Punishment is a central feature of both classical and neoclassical thought. Whereas punishment served the ends of deterrence in classical thought, its role in neoclassical thinking has been expanded. It is, for example, but a small step from the concept of just deserts to the concept of retribution. Those who advocate retribution see the primary utility of punishment in its ability to provide revenge. Neoclassical perspectives are experiencing a contemporary resurgence through a new-found emphasis on the wider use of punishment as a criminal deterrent. Zero-tolerance strategies used by police in some Canadian cities represent the get-tough approach to crime, starting with the crackdown on those committing minor infractions such as panhandling and urinating in public.

## Theory in Perspective
### The Classical School and Neoclassical Thinkers

### THE CLASSICAL SCHOOL
A criminological perspective operative in the late 1700s and early 1800s that had its roots in the Enlightenment and that held that men and women are rational beings, that crime is the result of the exercise of free will, and that punishment can be effective in reducing the incidence of crime because it negates the pleasure to be derived from crime commission.

### CLASSICAL CRIMINOLOGY.
The application of classical school principles to problems of crime and justice.
**Period:** 1700s–1880
**Theorists:** Cesare Beccaria, Jeremy Bentham, others
**Concepts:** Free will, deterrence through punishment, social contract, natural law, natural rights, due process, Panopticon

### NEOCLASSICAL CRIMINOLOGY, TYPE I: INDIVIDUAL RIGHTS ADVOCACY.
Involves modern-day application of the classical principles of due process and natural rights to problems of crime in contemporary society.
**Period:** 1960s–present
**Theorists:** Many
**Concepts:** Due process, constitutional rights, incapacitation, dangerousness

### NEOCLASSICAL CRIMINOLOGY, TYPE II: THE LAW AND ORDER SCHOOL.
Involves modern-day application of classical principles to problems of crime and crime control in contemporary society in the guise of "get-tough" social policies.
**Period:** 1970s–present
**Theorists:** Many
**Concepts:** Determinate sentencing, just deserts, specific deterrence, general deterrence

## The Death Penalty

Notions of deterrence, retribution, and just deserts all come together in **capital punishment.** Given the many different philosophies of punishment represented by the death penalty, it is not surprising that so much disagreement exists as to the efficacy of death as a form of criminal sanction. While capital punishment has not been legal in Canada since 1976, many Canadians would like to see its reinstatement. It is practised in many states in the United States and in other parts of the world, such as Japan, Russia, and China.

> **Capital punishment** the legal imposition of a sentence of death upon a convicted offender. Another term for the death penalty.

The extent to which the death penalty acts as a general deterrent has been widely studied. Some researchers[19] have compared murder rates between U.S. states that have eliminated the death penalty and those retaining it, finding little variation in the rate at which murders are committed. Others have looked at variations in murder rates over time in jurisdictions that have eliminated capital punishment, with similar results.[20] A 1988 Texas study provided a comprehensive review of capital punishment by correlating homicide rates with the rate of executions within the state between 1930 and 1986.[21] The study, which was especially important because Texas has been quite active in the capital punishment arena, failed to find any support for the use of death as a deterrent. Opponents of capital punishment frequently cite such studies to claim that the death penalty is ineffective as a deterrent and should be abolished.

Other abolitionist rationales include claims that (1) the death penalty has, at times, been imposed on innocent people, (2) human life is sacred and state-imposed death lowers society to the same moral (or amoral) level as the individual murderer, (3) the death penalty has been (and may still be) imposed in haphazard and discriminatory fashion, and (4) the death penalty is imposed disproportionately upon ethnic minorities.

Advocates of capital punishment generally discount each of these claims, countering with the notion that death is *deserved* by those who commit especially heinous acts, and that anything short of capital punishment under certain circumstances is an injustice in itself. Some people, the claim is made, deserve to die for what they have done. Such arguments evolve from a natural law perspective, and are based on the notion of just deserts as discussed earlier.

## Public Humiliation

The practice of "shaming," or public humiliation, is also a reflection of the notion that offenders must pay. Used widely in the United States, convicted offenders can be ordered by the courts to participate in a number of humiliating activities. Examples include those such as the case of an offender ordered to wear a T-shirt in public advertising his crime. Another had to post a sign on his property announcing his offence. Still another was ordered to take out a newspaper ad detailing her crime.[22]

Some feel the merits of these sentences of public humiliation in deterring the offender from further crime are doubtful, since the end result is more likely degradation than rehabilitation. Not all proponents of shaming see degradation as the sole outcome, however. Australian John Braithwaite and others advocate a policy of "reintegrative shaming," through which offenders begin to understand and recognize their misdeeds and shame themselves. The actual shaming must be brief and controlled and followed by forgiveness, apology, and repentance.[23] Some of the ideas found in this "restorative justice" approach are discussed in Chapter 12.

# Pilot Project A New Tactic on Teen Crime

## Program Focuses on Family of Young Offenders

Can the behaviour of young offenders be changed if caught early enough? Should this process involve strict discipline? As the following article shows, more innovative approaches may also be effective.

Ontario is quietly experimenting with a young offender treatment program that has had astonishing success in the United States, cutting the number of new crimes committed by teenagers by as much as 70 per cent.

The experiment, known as Multi-Systemic Therapy (MST), is based on the theory that sending problem teens to jail and using conventional treatment programs rarely gets results.

Funded by both the provincial and federal governments, the pilot project is labour-intensive. Two probation officers devote hours each week sorting out the problems experienced by young offenders and their families. The cost: $6 800 per family a year.

The alternative—sending problem teens to counselling sessions, treatment facilities and jail—rarely gets proven results.

In the U.S., youths sent to *boot camps*—the controversial alternative launched in Ontario last year—went on to commit 16 per cent more crimes over-all once they were released, several studies have shown.

"The research shows that *boot camps* actually ... result in an increase in crime," said Dr. Alan Leschied of the Family Court Clinic in London, Ont., who is serving as principal investigator for the Ontario experiment.

And the cost is much higher—about $110 000 a year—to keep a young offender in closed custody in Ontario, Leschied said.

Instead, for the past 18 months, therapists from probation offices in Peel Region, London, Ottawa and Barrie have been going into the homes of 83 troubled teens to root out bad behaviour with the help of parents, neighbours and teachers.

Only the worst kids between the ages of 12 and 15 qualify for the program—those classified at "high risk" of committing future crimes.

To ensure a proper comparison with other programs, only half of those recommended for the program, either by judges or parents, receive it, while the rest go into conventional treatment. The participants are selected by lottery.

Case workers visit the families about every second day for three to five months. The focus is on correcting behavioural problems such as aggression or failing to abide by curfews, said Kelly McDonnell, a clinical supervisor for Peel.

If a parent is depressed and can't keep an eye on the teen, then medical help is arranged so that they can overcome it.

"We're not trying to change all of the problems a family has," McDonnell said when the program was outlined recently at the annual conference of the Probation Officers Association of Ontario. "We're just targeting one or two problems to get enough change so they can carry on."

The most conservative studies in the United States have shown the program lowered recidivism by 44 per cent, Leschied said, while other less-controlled studies have pointed to about a 70 per cent drop.

Less Tustin, a policy analyst with the community and social services ministry, said the province is committed to continuing with the project until 2001, but can't yet compare the success of the Ontario program with the U.S. studies.

"At the end of the four years, if this program, in terms of cost effectiveness and lowering recidivism rates, is successful, we will be looking at implementing it across the province," Tustin said.

The program hasn't been without controversy, she noted. Money was shifted from other uses, such as closed custody facilities, to help fund it, and MST staff carry caseloads of two to four clients, compared with the 30 to 50 of most probation officers.

It's also potentially dangerous work, the conference was told.

In London, Ont., case workers tote cellphones, check out the home for escape routes and have perfected a code word to use when phoning supervisors in an emergency without tipping off the family.

"It does truly amaze me the amount of information you can get by being in a family's home every second day," McDonnell said. "You are in there. You are getting to the bottom of the problem."

## DISCUSSION QUESTIONS

1. Can the behaviour of young offenders be changed if caught early enough?

2. Is strict discipline required to bring about this change or are other approaches, such as the MultiSystemic Therapy program, equally effective?

SOURCE: Tracey Tyler, "Pilot Project A New Tactic on Teen Crime. Program Focuses on Family of Young Offenders," *Toronto Star*, November 12, 1998, p. A12. Reprinted with permission of the Toronto Star Syndicate.

# Policy Implications of the Classical School

Much of the practice of criminal justice in North America today is built around a conceptual basis provided by the classical school theorists. The social policy position of today's classical school heirs, however, is complex and anything but clear. On the one hand, that school of today's neoclassical thinkers known as *individual rights advocates* emphasizes individual rights and intuitively defends the prerogatives of individuals against potential government excesses inherent in the social contract. In Canada, the federal government's official stance towards crime and criminals remains tempered by this approach. In 1993, the Standing Committee on Justice and the Solicitor General recommended a move away from the use of imprisonment. Instead, the Committee proposed the development of a national crime prevention strategy as an effective way of dealing with crime. As a result, much focus is placed on the use of prevention programs such as the Community Justice Program, initiated under the auspices of the Royal Canadian Mounted Police.

The direction to the courts in Canada continues to be that incarceration be used only as a last resort in those cases where it is believed that no other course of action will protect the community. This message was very clearly reflected through the passage of Bill C-41 into law in 1996. Among other amendments to the Criminal Code of Canada, this Bill created a new disposition, the Conditional Sentence of Imprisonment. This provision (section 742 of the Criminal Code of Canada), allows the court to order that an offender sentenced to imprisonment serve his or her sentence in the community under supervision. The conditional sentence applies only to sentences of up to 2 years less a day and where there is no minimum sentence. Bill C-41 is specifically designed to reduce the number of admissions to custody.

Those heirs of the classical school who see punishment as the central tenet of criminal justice policy, on the other hand, believe it to be a natural and deserved consequence of criminal activity. Such thinkers call for greater prison capacity and new prison construction. They argue that although punishment theoretically prevents crime, in today's society few criminals are ever effectively punished. These proponents of neoclassical theory, often called **law and order advocates**, frequently seek stiffer criminal laws and increased penalties for criminal activity. They insist on the importance of individual responsibility and claim that law violators should be held unfailingly responsible for their actions. Law and order advocates generally want to ensure that sentences imposed by criminal courts are the sentences served by offenders, and they argue against reduced prison time for whatever reason. Finally, many of today's neoclassical thinkers rally around the death penalty because they believe it is either justified as a natural consequence of specific forms of abhorrent behaviour or because they believe that it will deter others from committing similar crimes in the future. They answer critics who claim that evidence does not support a belief in

**Law and order advocates** those who suggest that, under certain circumstances involving criminal threats to public safety, the interests of society should take precedence over individual rights.

capital punishment as a deterrent by pointing out that death is at least a specific deterrent, if not a general one.

Despite official government proclamations, it appears that the advocates of law and order are gaining a foothold in today's political arena. Many in the country fear crime, and calls for "get-tough-on-crime" policies are often well received by many political constituencies. During the past 15 years, the total number of individuals sentenced to serve all or part of their sentences in a correctional facility has increased by approximately 50 percent, to about 34 000, or approximately 115 people per 100 000 population (see Figure 4.1). Some correctional experts predict that, unless significant sentencing reforms are put in place, the total number of inmates in Canada may increase to 45 000 by the year 2004.[24] By comparison, the prison population in the United States stands at around 1.8 million, or about 600 people per 100 000 population.

Recent Canadian outcry against perceived increases in the amount of violent crime committed by youth has resulted in changes in the legislation used to deal with this group of offenders. The federal government's proposed Youth Criminal Justice Act (1999) reduces the age of adult sentences from 16 to 14 for those young people convicted of serious crimes such as murder and sexual assault, and for repeat offenders. It also allows for the publication of the names of offenders who receive adult sentences. Despite these apparently "tougher" sanctions for violent youth, the Act also specifies that sentences should reflect the seriousness of the offence. See Chapter 11 for an in-depth look at this Act.

The highly publicized case of Michael Fay, an American youth who in 1994 received a prison sentence of four months as well as four lashes after being found guilty of spray-painting cars in Singapore, prompted an international reaction (see boxed article on page 117). In Canada, some law and order proponents, such as Reform Member of Parliament Art Hanger, declared that corporal punishment practices such as caning might work in reducing crime and that Canada should adopt a system of corporal punishment similar to that of Singapore.[25] Alberta and Ontario have adopted "boot-camp" facilities for young offenders. These boot camps do not practise corporal punishment but do impose strict discipline.

In some provinces, consideration has been given to reinstating a model of "chain gang." In 1997, Ontario saw the reintroduction of a program in which inmates are required to clean up litter along major highways. In parts of the United States, inmates working along roads are fitted with electric "stun belts" rather than chains, which can be activated to send 50 000 volts of electricity through an inmate's body.

Other policies that clearly reflect the neoclassical approach of just deserts include the suspension of various inmate privileges in correctional institutions, such as limiting access to television, VCRs, sports activities, weight rooms, and smoking. As well, pressure is being placed on the federal government to mandate the use of consecutive sentences for those convicted of more than one murder or violent sexual offence. If, for example, an offender is found guilty of two murders, he or she would be required to serve two life sentences—one after the other rather than at the same time, or concurrently, which is now the practice.

## Figure 4.1

# Trends in Adult Prison Population Counts, Canada

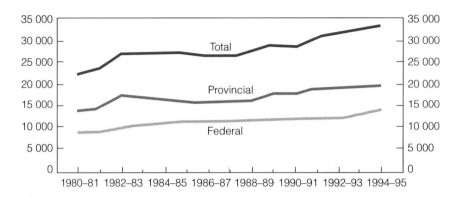

SOURCE: Colin Goff, *Corrections in Canada* (Cincinnati, OH: Anderson Publishing Co., 1999), p. 4. Reprinted with permission of Anderson Publishing Co.

Today's "get-tough-on-crime" approach has led to dramatic increases in Canada's prison population. What are some alternatives to incarceration? *The Canadian Press/Ryan Remiorz.*

The reality in the United States indicates that advocates of law and order currently have the upper hand. In 1994, the U.S. Congress passed the Violent Crime Control and Law Enforcement Act, one of the most far-reaching get-tough-on-crime measures ever seen. The law contains a "three-strikes-and-you're-out" provision that provides for mandatory life sentences after a third felony conviction. It also allocates massive amounts of money ($22 billion) for new prison construction and mandates long prison sentences for violent offenders and for those who use guns during the commission of crimes. The new law also bans many types of semiautomatic assault weapons and authorizes the hiring of thousands of additional police officers across the country. Typical of the current nationwide resurgence of interest in the death penalty, it expands the federal death penalty to nearly 60 offences.

## Critique of Classical Theories

The classical school of thought represents more a philosophy of justice than it does a theory of crime causation. As some writers have observed, however, "[t]he true test of Beccaria's essay can be judged by the influence it has had over time on our justice system."[26] The influence of Beccaria, the Enlightenment, and classical thinkers remains today in the Canadian Charter of Rights and Freedoms, in the get-tough approaches to crime, and in the emphasis on individual rights. The classical school "has left behind a legacy that we see in almost every aspect of our present-day justice system."[27]

Critics charge, however, that the classical school lacks explanatory power over criminal motivation, other than to advance the simple claim that crime is the result of free will and individual choice. Such critics point out that classical theory is bereft of meaningful explanations as to how a choice for or against criminal activity is made. Similarly, classical theory lacks any appreciation for the deeper aspects of personal motivation, including those represented by human biology, psychology, and the social environment. Moreover, the classical school, as originally detailed in the writings of Beccaria and Bentham, lacked any scientific basis for the claims it made. Although neoclassical writers have advanced the scientific foundation of classical claims (through studies such as those showing the effectiveness of particular forms of deterrence), many still defend their way of thinking by reference to philosophical ideals (such as just deserts).

In a world grown accustomed to measuring the success of an idea in terms of its measurable consequences, neoclassical theorists are hard put to defend their philosophies. Citing the fact that boot camp prisons, for example, have not measured up to the claims of reduced recidivism touted by get-tough neoclassical politicians, some writers have called for a return to programs already shown to work. As a critic of increased funding for boot camps recently stated, "If helping nonviolent first offenders get their lives and values together is the goal, then the [funding] for boot camps needs to be redirected to such proven programs as drug counseling, alternative sentences, work furloughs, literacy courses and well-supervised probation."[28]

## Assessing Dangerousness

*Dangerousness* is a difficult concept to comprehend. Indicators of dangerousness have yet to be well defined in the social scientific literature, and legislators who attempt to codify any assessment of future dangerousness often find themselves frustrated. On the individual level, however, dangerousness might be more easily assessed. What follows is a description of the criteria one judge, Lois G. Forer, used in deciding whether an offender needed to spend a long time away from society:

I had my own criteria or guidelines—very different from those established by most states and the federal government—for deciding on a punishment. My primary concern was public safety. The most important question I asked myself was whether the offender could be deterred from committing other crimes. No one can predict with certainty who will or will not commit a crime, but there are indicators most sensible people recognize as danger signals:

- First, was this an irrational crime? If an arsonist sets a fire to collect insurance, that is a crime but also a rational act. Such a person can be deterred by being made to pay for the harm done and the costs to the fire department. However, if the arsonist sets fires just because he likes to see them, it is highly unlikely that he can be stopped from setting others, no matter how high the fine. Imprisonment is advisable even though it may be a first offence.

- Second, was there wanton cruelty? If a robber maims or slashes the victim, there is little likelihood that he can safely be left in the community. If a robber simply displays a gun but does not fire it or harm the victim, then one should consider his life history, provocation, and other circumstances in deciding whether probation is appropriate.

- Third, is this a hostile person? Was his crime one of hatred, and does he show any genuine remorse? Most rapes are acts of hostility, and the vast majority of rapists have a record of numerous sexual assaults. I remember one man who raped his mother. I gave him the maximum sentence under the law—20 years—but with good behaviour, he got out fairly quickly. He immediately raped another elderly woman.

- Fourth, is this a person who knows he is doing wrong but cannot control himself? Typical of such offenders are pedophiles. One child abuser who appeared before me had already been convicted of abusing his first wife's child. I got him on the second wife's child and sentenced him to the maximum. Still, he'll get out with good behaviour, and I shudder to think about the children around him when he does. This is one case in which justice is not tough enough.

By contrast, some people who have committed homicide present very little danger of further violence—although many more do. Once a young man came before me because he had taken aim at a person half a block away and then shot him in the back, killing him. Why did he do it? "I wanted to get me a body." He should never get out.

▶

▶ **DISCUSSION QUESTIONS**

1. How are public safety and criminal punishment related?
2. Do you agree that the criteria used by Judge Forer to identify dangerousness are useful? Why or why not?
3. Do you believe that offenders who are identified as "dangerous" should be treated differently from other offenders? If so, how?

SOURCE: Lois G. Forer, "Justice by the Numbers; Mandatory Sentencing Drove Me from the Bench," *The Washington Monthly*, April 1992, pp. 12–18. Reprinted with permission from *The Washington Monthly*. Copyright by The Washington Monthly Company, 1611 Connecticut Ave., N.W., Washington, D.C. 20009 (202) 462-0128.

# Summary

The Enlightenment, a social and cultural renaissance that occurred throughout the late seventeenth and early eighteenth centuries, proved to be a highly liberating force in the Western world. Enlightenment thinkers established many of the democratic principles that formed the conceptual foundations of Canadian society. Their ideas are still alive today, and significantly shape our understanding of human nature and human behaviour. The twin conceptual prongs around which this textbook is built—social responsibility and individual rights—both have their roots in Enlightenment thought and in the belief in free will it engendered. Notions of deterrence as a goal of justice-system intervention, and of punishment as a worthy consequence of crime, owe much of their contemporary influence to the classical school of criminology. As we begin the twenty-first century, we carry with us an intellectual heritage far older than we may realize.

# Discussion Questions

1. This book emphasizes a social problems versus social responsibility theme. Which perspective is most supported by classical and neoclassical thought? Why?
2. Name the various preclassical thinkers identified by this chapter. What ideas did each contribute to Enlightenment philosophy? What form did those ideas take in classical criminological thought?
3. Define *natural law*. Do you believe that natural law exists? If so, what types of behaviour would be contravened by natural law? If they would not be, why not?
4. What is meant by the idea of a "social contract"? How does the concept of social contract relate to natural law?
5. What were the central concepts that defined the classical school of criminological thought? Which of those concepts are still alive? Where do you see evidence for the survival of those concepts?
6. What are the various philosophies of neoclassical criminology identified by this chapter? Which philosophy appeals most to you? Why? Which is the least attractive? Why?
7. Define *recidivism*. What is a recidivism rate?

## Weblinks

**www.crimetheory.com/**

University of Washington. Good, condensed overview of the predominant criminological theories.

**www.faculty.ncwc.edu/toconnor/301/crimhist.htm**

North Carolina Wesleyan College. Provides a decade-by-decade listing of scholarly works in the fields of criminology and criminal justice.

**www.ccla.org**

Canadian Civil Liberties Association. The CCLA is a lobbying and law reform, non-profit organization dealing with issues of Canadians' fundamental human rights. Good discussions on controversial criminal justice issues provide an individual rights perspective.

**www.lfcc.on.ca/**

Centre for Children and Families in the Justice System of the London Family Court Clinic. This site provides an excellent overview of the MultiSystemic Therapy pilot project undertaken in Ontario from 1997 to 2001.

## CHAPTER 5

# Biological Roots of Behaviour

The evidence is very firm that there is a genetic factor involved in crime.

—SARNOFF A. MEDNICK[1]

Men have always loved to fight. If they didn't love to fight, they wouldn't be men.

—GENERAL GEORGE S. PATTON, JR.[2]

**LEARNING OUTCOMES**

After reading this chapter, you should be able to:

- Recognize the importance of biological explanations of criminal behaviour

- Consider the relationship between human aggression and biological determinants

- Be aware of the research linking genetics and crime

- Recognize the contribution of socio-biology to the study of criminality

- Identify modern day social policy which reflects the biological approach to crime causation

- Assess the shortcomings of the biological theories of criminal behaviour

## IMPORTANT NAMES

| | | |
|---|---|---|
| C. Ray Jeffery | Cesare Lombroso | Richard L. Dugdale |
| Konrad Lorenz | Charles Buckman | Arthur H. Estabrook |
| Charles Darwin | Goring | Henry H. Goddard |
| Franz Joseph Gall | Earnest A. Hooton | Edward O. Wilson |
| Johann Gaspar | Ernst Kretschmer | James Q. Wilson |
| Spurzheim | William H. Sheldon | Richard J. Herrnstein |

## IMPORTANT TERMS

| | | |
|---|---|---|
| biological theories | somatotyping | Kallikak family |
| criminal anthropology | cycloid | eugenics |
| phrenology | endomorph | supermale |
| atavism | mesomorph | monozygotic (MZ) |
| positivism | ectomorph | twins |
| criminaloids | hypoglycemia | sociobiology |
| born criminals | testosterone | paradigm |
| constitutional theories | Juke family | |

# Introduction

The mutilation killing of Maude Moormann by her 36-year-old adoptive son, Robert Henry Moormann, in 1984 was one of the most vicious murders ever to have occurred in Arizona.[3] Moormann's biological mother drowned shortly after his birth in 1948, and he lived with his grandparents for a short while before being turned over to a Catholic social services agency for adoption. As a childless couple, Henry and Maude Moormann adopted the boy at age two and one-half. According to popular accounts, Maude was overly protective of her new son, leaving him ill prepared for encounters with other children. Robert became a notoriously poor student, frequently failing classes and often running away from home. At age 13, he was sent to the Sun School in Phoenix, a shelter for troubled boys, after having been accused of molesting a little girl. While home for Christmas holidays, he hid a .22-caliber pistol under his pillow and shot his mother in the stomach when she sat by his bed to talk with him. The bullet lodged in her liver and surgeons feared to remove it. Though she recovered, Maude Moormann always insisted that the shooting had been an accident. Afterward, Robert was in and out of juvenile facilities for a variety of offences—most centred on sexual maladjustment and the molestation of young girls. By the time he was 18, Moormann had been arrested for accosting yet another girl and had been placed on the drug Mellaril to limit his sexual appetites.

As an adult, Moormann was finally sent to prison for kidnapping and molesting an 8-year-old neighbour girl in 1972. He was paroled in 1979, but soon went back to prison for a parole violation. By 1984 Moorman had entered the prison's furlough program and, on January 12 of that year, was released to visit his mother at a local motel. On that fateful night, Moormann demanded that his mother sign papers that would leave him sole heir to her estate. After she refused, Moormann beat her, tied her to the motel room bed, and suffocated her with a pillow. He then made a brief trip to a convenience store where he bought household cleansers and a variety of knives. Upon returning to the motel room, he cut his mother's body into many pieces, stuffing some in a local trash dumpster and flushing her severed fingers down the toilet so that her remains couldn't be easily identified. Then he meticulously cleaned the room to hide any signs of the murder. He was arrested, however, after arousing the suspicions of a prison guard to whom he had offered a box of flesh-covered raw bones for the guard's dogs. It took a jury only 2 hours to convict him and he was sentenced to death.

Robert Moormann was a poor physical specimen who had been judged unfit for the military draft. He had poor vision and flat feet, and suffered from low reading skills and learning disabilities. One physician, to whom he had been taken as a boy, diagnosed him as suffering from brain-stem trauma—the result of two traffic accidents he had been involved in when young.

Did Moormann's crimes have a biological basis? We may never be sure, however, many biological theories have been advanced to explain criminality. Abnormalities of the brain, genetic predispositions, vitamin deficiencies, an excess of hormones such as testosterone, hypoglycemia (low blood sugar), an overabundance of neurotransmitters such as serotonin, and blood abnormalities are among the many current biological explanations of crime.

The field of criminology has been slow to give credence to biological theories of human behaviour. One reason for this, as noted in Chapter 1, is the fact that criminology's academic roots are firmly grounded in the social sciences. As the well-known biocriminologist **C. Ray Jeffery,** commenting on the historical development of the field, observes, "[t]he term *criminology* was given to a social science approach to crime as developed in sociology. … Sutherland's (1924) text *Criminology* was pure sociology without any biology or psychology; beginning with publication of that text, criminology was offered in sociology departments as a part of sociology separate from biology, psychology, psychiatry and law. … Many of the academicians who call themselves criminologists are sociologists."[4]

Even today, little doubt exists that biological understandings of criminality are out of vogue. In 1992 in the United States, for example, a National Institutes of Health–sponsored conference[5] that was intended to focus on the biological roots of crime was cancelled after critics charged that the meeting would, by virtue of its biological focus, be racist and might intentionally exclude sociological perspectives on the subject. Those opposed to the conference argued that "[t]he primary problems that afflict human beings are not due to their bodies or brains, they are due to the environment. Redefining social problems as public health problems is exactly what was done in Nazi Germany."[6] Three years later, when the conference was finally held at a site selected to discourage demonstrations, C. Ray Jeffery pointed out that "[w]hen ideology replaces rational thought there is little hope for a better understanding of human problems."[7]

"One reason why most criminologists are skeptical about genetic influences on criminal behavior is that it seems improbable that behavior that is defined differently in every society could have a genetic foundation."[8] "In other words," say Lee Ellis and Anthony Walsh, "why would genes affect behavior that is circumscribed by laws that vary from one society to another?" The answer, they maintain, "lies in the fact that in nearly all societies with written criminal statutes, there are a fairly standard set of 'core behavior patterns' that are criminalized."[9] Hence, they conclude, "it is possible to maintain that there is little variation from one society to another in what constitutes criminal behavior."

Unfortunately for the field of criminology, critics of biological investigation into the root causes of crime fail to recognize that the advance of science has never been impeded by objective consideration of alternative points of view. Criticism, made before all the facts are in, does little to advance human understanding. Open inquiry, as C. Ray Jeffery notes, requires objective consideration of all points of view, and an unbiased examination of each for their ability to shed light upon the subject under study. Hence, for an adequate consideration of biological theories as they may relate to crime and crime causation, we need to turn to literature outside of the sociological and psychological mainstream.

## Major Principles of Biological Theories

**Biological theories (of criminology)** maintain that the basic determinants of human behaviour, including criminality, are constitutionally or physiologically based and often inherited.

This brief section serves to summarize the central features of **biological theories** of crime causation. Each of these points can be found elsewhere in this chapter, where they are discussed in more detail. This cursory overview, however, is intended to provide more than a summary—it is meant to be a guide to the rest of this chapter.

Biological theories of crime causation make certain fundamental assumptions. These include the following:

- The brain is the organ of the mind and the locus of personality. In the words of the well-known biocriminologist Clarence Ray Jeffery, "The brain is the organ of behavior; no theory of behavior can ignore neurology and neurochemistry."[10]
- The basic determinants of human behavior, including criminal tendencies, are, to a considerable degree, constitutionally or genetically based.
- Observed gender and racial differences in rates and types of criminality may be at least partially the result of biological differences between the sexes and/or between racially distinct groups.
- The basic determinants of human behaviour, including criminality, may be passed on from generation to generation. In other words, a penchant for crime may be inherited.
- Much of human conduct is fundamentally rooted in instinctive behavioural responses characteristic of biological organisms everywhere. Territoriality, condemnation of adultery, and acquisitiveness are but three examples of behaviour that may be instinctual to human beings.
- The biological roots of human conduct have become increasingly disguised, as modern symbolic forms of indirect expressive behaviour have replaced more primitive and direct ones.
- At least some human behaviour is the result of biological propensities inherited from more primitive developmental stages in the evolutionary process. In other words, some human beings may be further along the evolutionary ladder than others, and their behaviour may reflect that fact.
- The interplay between heredity, biology, and the social environment provides the nexus for any realistic consideration of crime causation.

# Biological Roots of Human Aggression

In 1966, **Konrad Lorenz** published his now famous work *On Aggression.*[11] It was an English-language translation of a 1963 book entitled *Das Sogenannte Bose: Zur Naturgeschichte der Aggression (The Nature of Aggression)* which had originally appeared in German. In his writing, Lorenz described how aggression permeates the animal kingdom and asked, "What is the value of all this fighting?" "In nature," he said, "fighting is such an ever-present process, its behavior mechanisms and weapons are so highly developed and have so obviously arisen under the ... pressure of a species-preserving function, that it is our duty to ask this ... question."[12]

Lorenz accepted the evolutionary thesis of the nineteenth-century biologist **Charles Darwin** that intraspecies aggression favored the strongest and best animals in the reproductive process, but he concluded that aggression served a variety of other purposes as well. Aggression, said Lorenz, ensures an "even distribution of animals of a particular species over an inhabitable area ..."[13] and provides for a defence of the species from predators. Human aggression, he claimed, meets many of the same purposes but can take on covert forms. The drive to acquire wealth and power, for example, that was so characteristic of Western men at the time of his writing, was described by Lorenz as part of the human mating ritual, whereby a man might "win" a prized woman through displays of more civilized forms of what could otherwise be understood as intraspecies aggression.

Charles Darwin (1809–1882), founder of modern evolutionary theory. *Julia Cameron/Corbis-Bettmann.*

In today's enlightened times, such observations may seem to many like mere foolishness. Lorenz's greatest contribution to the study of human behaviour, however, may have been his claim that all human behaviour is, at least to some degree, "adapted instinctive behavior." In other words, much of human conduct, according to Lorenz, is fundamentally rooted in instinctive behavioural responses characteristic of biological organisms everywhere and present within each of us in the form of a biological inheritance from more primitive times. Even rational human thought, claimed Lorenz, derives its motivation and direction from instinctual aspects of human biology. The highest human virtues, such as the value placed on human life, "could not have been achieved without an instinctive appreciation of life and death."[14]

Building upon the root functions of aggression, Lorenz concluded that much of what we today call crime is the result of overcrowded living conditions, such as those experienced by city dwellers, combined with a lack of legitimate opportunity for the effective expression of aggression. Crowding, from this perspective, increases the likelihood of aggression, while contemporary socialization simultaneously works to inhibit it. In the words of Lorenz, "… in one sense we are all psychopaths, for each of us suffers from the necessity of self-imposed control for the good of the community."[15] When people break down, argued Lorenz, they become neurotic or delinquent; crime may be the result of stresses that have been found to typically produce aggression throughout the animal kingdom.

At first blush, Lorenz's explanations, like many of the biologically based theories we will encounter in this chapter, appear more applicable to violent crime than to other forms of criminal offence. However, it is important to recognize that modern frustrations

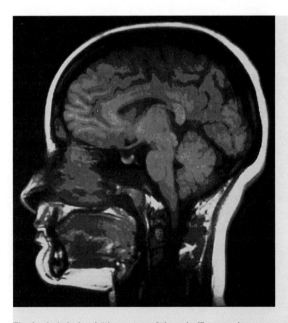

The brain is indeed "the organ of the mind" as modern researchers are continuing to discover. Here a computer-enhanced image shows areas of activity within the brain. Do you think biology may play a role in crime? *Scott Camazsine/Photo Researchers, Inc.*

and concomitant manifestations of aggression may be symbolically, rather than directly, expressed. Hence, the stockbroker who embezzles a client's money, spurred on by the need to provide material goods for an overly acquisitive family, may be just as criminal as the robber who beats his victim and steals her purse to have money to buy liquor.

## Theory in Perspective
### Types of Biological Theories

**BIOLOGICAL THEORIES**

adhere to the principle that the basic determinants of human behaviour, including criminality, are constitutionally or physiologically based and inherited.

**Early Positivism.** These biological approaches built upon evolutionary principles and were the first to apply scientific techniques to the study of crime and criminals. Early positivistic theories saw criminals as throwbacks to earlier evolutionary epochs.
**Period:**     1880s–1930
**Theorists:**  Franz Joseph Gall, Johann Gaspar Spurzheim, Cesare Lombroso, Charles Goring, and Earnest Hooton
**Concepts:**   Phrenology, atavism, born criminals, criminaloids

**Constitutional Theories.** Such biological theories explain criminality by reference to offenders' body types, inheritance, genetics, and/or external observable physical characteristics.
**Period:**     Modern constitutional theories 1960s–present, Classical constitutional theories 1930s–1940s
**Theorists:**  Ernst Kretschmer, William H. Sheldon, Richard Dugdale, Arthur H. Estabrook, Henry H. Goddard
**Concepts:**   Somatotyping, mesomorph, ectomorph, endomorph, XYY supermale, twin studies

**Body Chemistry.** Such biological theories utilize chemical influences, including hormones, food additives, allergies, vitamins, and other chemical substances to explain criminal behaviour.
**Period:**     1940s–present
**Theorists:**  Various
**Concepts:**   Hypoglycemia, vitamins, food allergies, seratonin, PMS, MAOA

**Sociobiology.** A theoretical perspective developed by Edward O. Wilson to include "the systematic study of the biological basis of all social behavior," which is "a branch of evolutionary biology and particularly of modern population biology."
**Period:**     1975–present
**Theorists:**  Edward O. Wilson
**Concepts:**   Altruism, tribalism, survival of the gene pool

# Early Biological Theories

Numerous perspectives on criminal biology predate Lorenz's work. Some of the perspectives fall into the category of criminal anthropology. **Criminal anthropology** is the scientific study of the relationship between human physical characteristics and criminality. One of the earliest criminological anthropologists was **Franz Joseph Gall** (1758–1828). Gall hypothesized, in his theory of **phrenology** (also called *craniology*), that the shape of the human skull was indicative of the personality and could be used to predict criminality. Gall's approach contained four themes:

- The brain is the organ of the mind.
- Particular aspects of personality are associated with specific locations in the brain.
- Portions of the brain that are well developed will cause personality characteristics associated with them to be more prominent in the individual under study, whereas poorly developed brain areas lead to a lack of associated personality characteristics.
- The shape of a person's skull corresponds to the shape of the underlying brain and is therefore indicative of the personality.

Gall was one of the first Western writers to firmly locate the roots of personality in the brain. Prior to his time, it was thought that aspects of personality resided in various organs throughout the body—a fact reflected in linguistic anachronisms surviving into the present day (as, for example, when someone is described as "hard hearted," or as having "a lot of gall," or as thinking with some organ other than the brain). The Greek philosopher Aristotle was said to believe that the brain served no function other than to radiate excess heat from the body. Hence, Gall's perspective, although relatively primitive by today's standards, did much to advance physiological understandings of the mind–body connection in Western thought.

Although Gall never tested his theory, it was widely accepted by many of his contemporaries because it represented something of a shift away from theological perspectives prevalent at the time and a move toward scientific understanding—a trend that was well underway by the time of his writings. Phrenology also provided for systematic evaluation of suspected offenders and was intriguing for its ease of use. One of Gall's students, **Johann Gaspar Spurzheim** (1776–1853), brought phrenological theory to North America and, through a series of lectures and publications on the subject, helped to spread its influence. Phrenology's prestige in North America extended into the twentieth century, finding a place in classification schemes used to evaluate newly admitted prisoners. Even Arthur Conan Doyle's fictional character Sherlock Holmes was described as using phrenology to solve a number of crimes.

## The Positivist School

One of the best known, early scientific biological theorists—nineteenth-century Italian physician **Cesare Lombroso** (1836–1909)—coined the term *atavism* to suggest that criminality was the result of primitive urges which, in modern-day human throw-backs, survived the evolutionary process. He described "the nature of the criminal" as "an atavistic being who reproduces in his person the ferocious instincts of primitive humanity and the inferior animals."[16]

At about this time, Charles Darwin was making a substantial impact on the scientific world with his theory of biological evolution. Darwin proposed that human beings and other contemporary living organisms were the end products of a long evolutionary process governed by rules such as natural selection, survival of the fittest, and so on. Lombroso adapted elements of Darwin's theory to suggest that primitive traits survived in present-day human populations and led to heightened criminal tendencies among individuals who harboured them. Darwin himself had proposed this idea when he wrote: "[w]ith mankind some of the worst dispositions which occasionally without any assignable cause make their appearance in families, may perhaps be reversions to a savage state, from which we are not removed by very many generations."[17]

The atavistic individual, said Lombroso in his now classic work *L'Uomo delin-quente* (1876), was essentially a throwback to a more primitive biological state. According to Lombroso, such an individual, by virtue of possessing a relatively undeveloped brain, is incapable of conforming his behaviour to the rules and expectations of modern complex society. Lombroso has been called the father of modern criminology because he was the first criminologist of note to employ the scientific method—particularly measurement, observation, and attempts at generalization—in his work. Other writers, more specific in their pronouncements, have referred to him as the "father of the Italian School" of criminology.

Lombroso's scientific work consisted of postmortem studies of the bodies of executed offenders, which he conducted with assistants, measuring the bodies in many different ways. The body of one such well-known criminal, named Vilella, provided Lombroso with many of his findings and reinforced his belief that most offenders were genetically predisposed toward criminality. Study of another offender, an Italian soldier Lombroso calls "Misdea" in his writings[18] and who "attacked and killed eight of his superior officers and comrades," supported such conclusions. The use of science and scientific techniques in the service of criminology has been termed ***positivism.***[19] C. Ray Jeffery, offering a somewhat limited definition of the term but one which applies well to Lombroso's work, has said that "the main characteristic of Positivism is its attempt to answer the riddle of criminality by means of scientific studies of the individual offender."[20]

**Positivism** the application of scientific techniques to the study of crime and criminals.

Lombroso claimed to have found a wide variety of bodily features predictive of criminal behaviour. Among them were exceptionally long arms, an index finger as long as the middle finger, fleshy pouches in the cheeks "like those in rodents," eyes that were either abnormally close together or too far apart, large teeth, ears which lacking lobes, prominent cheekbones, a crooked nose, a large amount of body hair, protruding chin, large lips, a nonstandard number of ribs, and eyes of differing colors or hues. Lombroso went so far as to enumerate characteristics of particular types of offenders. Murderers, whom he called "habitual homicides," have, in Lombroso's words, "cold, glassy eyes, immobile and sometimes sanguine and inflamed; the nose, always large, is frequently aquiline or, rather, hooked; the jaws are strong, the cheekbones large, the hair curly, dark, and abundant; the beard is frequently thin, the canine teeth well developed and the lips delicate. ..."[21]

Atavism implies that there are born criminals. Lombroso was continuously re-assessing his estimates of the proportion, from among all offenders, of the born criminal population. At one point, he asserted that fully 90 percent of offenders committed crimes because of atavistic influences. He later revised the figure downward to 70 percent, admitting that normal individuals might be pulled into lives of crime. In addition to the category of the born criminal, Lombroso described other categories of offenders, including the insane, criminaloids, and criminals incited by passion. The insane were said to include mental and moral degenerates, alcoholics, drug addicts, and so forth. **Criminaloids,** also termed occasional criminals, were described as persons who were pulled into breaking the law by virtue of environmental influences. Nevertheless, most criminaloids were seen by Lombroso as exhibiting some degree of atavism and hence were said to "differ from **born criminals** in degree, not in kind." Those who became criminals by virtue of passion were said to have surrendered to intense emotions, including love, jealousy, hatred, or an injured sense of honour.

Although he focused on physical features, Lombroso was not insensitive to behavioural indicators of criminality. In his later writings, he claimed that criminals exhibited acute sight, hearing abilities that were below the norm, an insensitivity to pain, a lack of moral sensibility, cruelty, vindictiveness, impulsiveness, a love of gambling, and a tendency to be tattooed.

In 1893, Lombroso published *The Female Offender.*[22] In that book, he expressed his belief that women exhibit far less anatomical variation than do men but insisted that criminal behaviour among women, as among men, derived from atavistic foundations. Lombroso saw the quintessential female offender, the prostitute, as "the genuine typical representative of criminality. ..."[23] Prostitutes, he said, are acting out atavistic yearnings and returning to a form of behaviour characteristic of humankind's primitive past.

## Evaluations of Atavism

Around the turn of the twentieth century, the English physician **Charles Buckman Goring** (1870–1919), following in Lombroso's positivistic footsteps, conducted a well-controlled statistical study of Lombroso's thesis of atavism. Using newly developed but advanced mathematical techniques to measure the degree of correlation between physiological features and criminal history, Goring examined nearly 3 000 inmates at Turin prison, beginning in 1901. He enlisted the aid of London's Biometric Laboratory to conclude that "the whole fabric of Lombrosian doctrine, judged by the standards of science, is fundamentally unsound."[24] Goring compared the prisoners with students at Oxford and Cambridge Universities, British soldiers, and noncriminal hospital patients, and published his findings in 1913 in his lengthy treatise *The English Convict: A Statistical Study.*[25] The foreword to Goring's book was written by Karl Pearson, who praised Goring for having no particular perspective of his own to advance and who could, he said, therefore objectively evaluate the ideas of others such as Lombroso.

A similar study was conducted between 1927 and 1939 by **Earnest A. Hooton,** a professor of anthropology at Harvard University. In 1939, Hooton published *Crime and the Man,*[26] in which he reported having evaluated 13 873 inmates from 10 states, comparing them along 107 physiological dimensions with 3 203 nonincarcerated

**Criminaloids** a term used by Cesare Lombroso to describe occasional criminals who were pulled into criminality primarily by environmental influences.

**Born criminals** individuals who are born with a genetic predilection toward criminality.

individuals who formed a control group. His sample consisted of 10 953 prison inmates, 2 004 county jail prisoners, 743 criminally insane, 173 "defective delinquents," 1 227 "insane civilians," and 1 976 "sane civilians."

Hooton distinguished between regions of the country, arguing that "states have favorite crimes, just as they have favorite sons." He reported finding physiological features characteristic of specific criminal types in individual states. For example, "Massachusetts criminals," he said, "are notable for thick beards, red-brown hair, dark brown, green-brown and blue-gray eyes, whites of eyes discolored with yellow or brown pigment flecks, rayed pattern of the iris of the eye, external and median folds of the upper eyelids, broad, high nasal roots and bridges, concave nasal profiles, thick nasal tips, right deflections of the nasal septum, thin integumental lips, thin upper membranous lip and thick lower lip, absence of lip seam, some ... protrusion of the jaws, pointed or median chins, much dental decay but few teeth lost, small and soldered or attached ear lobes, and right facial asymmetries."[27] He went on to say that, through a sufficient degree of statistical manipulation, "[w]e finally emerge with differences between the offense groups which are not due to accidents of sampling, are not due to state variations, and are independent of differences between the ages of the offense groups. Thus, in the case of first-degree murder we find the members of that offense group deficient in persons with abundant head hair, deficient in individuals with narrow nasal bridges, presenting an excess of persons with pointed or median chins, and with compressed cheek bones."[28] He also found that first-degree murderers were more "square-shouldered" than other criminals and had larger ear lobes. From findings such as these, he was drawn to the conclusion that "crime is not an exclusively sociological phenomenon, but is also biological."[29]

In writing that "It is impossible to improve and correct environment to a point at which these flawed and degenerate human beings will be able to succeed in honest social competition,"[30] Hooton made it clear that he did not believe that rehabilitation programs could have much effect upon most offenders and suggested banishing them to a remote location. Hooton concluded that criminals showed an overall physiological inferiority to the general population, and that crime was the result of "the impact of environment upon low grade human organisms."[31]

Hooton, an example of whose work is provided in Figure 5.1, was quickly criticized along a number of dimensions. Stephen Schafer, the well-known contemporary criminologist, says "[t]he major criticisms were that his criminal population was not a representative sample of all criminals, that his control group was a fantastic conglomeration of noncriminal civilians, ... that he emphasized selected characteristics and disregarded others, that he gave no convincing evidence that the criminal's 'inferiority' was inherited, and that he failed to explore other important data that were available."[32] Perhaps even more significant, Hooton failed to recognize that members of his noncriminal control group may, in fact, have been involved in crime but had managed to elude capture and processing by the criminal justice system. In other words, it may have been that the most successful criminals did not appear in Hooton's study group of inmates because they had eluded the law, thereby making their way into his supposedly noncriminal control group. His study may have simply demonstrated that "inferior" criminal specimens are the ones who get caught and end up in prison.

### Figure 5.1

## Old American Criminals

### Mosaic of Cranial, Facial, Metric and Morphological Features
### MASSACHUSETTS

Narrowest face
Narrowest jaw
Thick beards
Broad, high nasal roots and bridges
Thick nasal tips
Right deflections of nasal septum
Concave profiles ①
External and median eyefolds ②
Small, attached ear lobes ③
Thin integumental lips ④
Membranous lips--upper thin, lower thick
Lip seams absent
Undershot jaw
Facial prognathism ⑤
Right facial asymmetry ⑥
Median chins

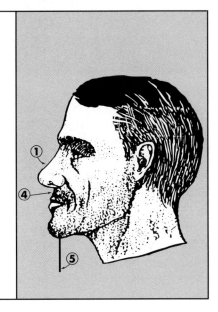

Earnest A. Hooton's "Massachusetts Criminal." Reprinted by permission of the publishers from *Crime and The Man* by Earnest Albert Hooton, Cambridge, Mass: Harvard University Press. Copyright © 1939 by the President and Fellows of Harvard College, renewed 1967 by Mary C. Hooton.

**Constitutional theories** those that explain criminality by reference to offenders' body types, genetics, and/or external observable physical characteristics.

**Somatotyping** the classification of human beings into types according to body build and other physical characteristics.

**Cycloid** a term developed by Ernst Kretschmer to describe a particular relationship between body build and personality type. The cycloid personality, which was associated with a heavyset, soft type of body, was said to vacillate between normality and abnormality.

## Body Types

**Constitutional theories** are those that explain criminality by reference to offenders' body types, genetics, and/or external observable physical characteristics. A constitutional or physiological orientation that found its way into the criminological mainstream during the early and mid-twentieth century was that of body types. Also called **somatotyping,** this perspective was primarily associated with the work of **Ernst Kretschmer** and **William H. Sheldon.** Kretschmer, a professor of psychiatry at the German University of Tubingen, proposed a relationship between body build and personality type and created a rather detailed "biopsychological constitutional typology." Kretschmer's somatotypology revolved around three basic mental categories: cycloids (also called cyclothymes), schizoids (or schizothymes), and displastics. The **cycloid** personality, which was associated with a heavyset, soft type of body according to Kretschmer, vacillated between normality and abnormality. Cycloids were said to lack spontaneity and sophistication, and were thought to commit mostly nonviolent property types of offences. Schizoids, who tended to possess athletic, muscular bodies but, according to Kretschmer, could also be thin and lean, were seen as more likely to be schizophrenic and to commit violent types of offences. Displastics were said to be a mixed group described as highly emotional and often unable to control themselves. Hence, they were thought to commit mostly sexual offences and other crimes of passion.

Influenced by Kretschmer, William H. Sheldon utilized measurement techniques to connect body type with personality.[33] Sheldon felt that Kretschmer had erred in including too large an age range in his work. Therefore, he chose to limit his study to 200 boys between the ages of 15 and 21 at the Hayden Goodwill Institute in Boston. Sheldon concluded that four basic body types characterized the entire group. Each type, described partly in Sheldon's words, is as follows:

- The **endomorph,** who is soft and round and whose "digestive viscera are massive and highly developed" (i.e., the person is overweight and has a large stomach).
- The **mesomorph,** who is athletic and muscular and whose "somatic structures … are in the ascendancy" (i.e., the person has larger bones and considerable muscle mass).
- The **ectomorph,** who is thin and fragile, and who has "long, slender, poorly muscled extremities, with delicate, pipestem bones."
- The balanced type, which is of average build, being neither overweight, thin, nor exceedingly muscular.

Individuals were ranked along each of the three major dimensions (the balanced type was excluded) using a seven-point scale. A score of 1-1-7, for example, would indicate that a person exhibited few characteristics of endomorphology or mesomorphology but was predominantly ectomorphic. Sheldon claimed that varying types of temperament and personalities were closely associated with each of the body types he identified. Ectomorphs were said to be cerebrotonic, or restrained, shy, and inhibited. Endomorphs were viscerotonic, or relaxed and sociable. The mesomorphic, or muscular, body type, however, he said was most likely to be associated with delinquency or somatotonia, which he described as "a predominance of muscular activity and … vigorous bodily assertiveness." William H. Sheldon's work was supported by constitutional studies of juvenile delinquents conducted by Sheldon Glueck and Eleanor Glueck, reported in 1950.[34] The Gluecks compared 500 known delinquents with 500 nondelinquents, and matched both groups on age, general intelligence, ethnical-racial background, and place of residence. Like Sheldon, the Gluecks concluded that mesomorphy was associated with delinquency.

Early biological theorists such as Sheldon, Lombroso, and Gall provide an interesting footnote to the history of criminological thought. Today, however, their work is mostly relegated to the dust bins of academic theorizing. Modern biological theories of crime are far more sophisticated than their early predecessors, and it is to these we now turn.

**Endomorph** a body type originally described as soft and round, or overweight.

**Mesomorph** a body type originally described as athletic and muscular.

**Ectomorph** a body type originally described as thin and fragile, with long, slender, poorly muscled extremities, and delicate bones.

## Chemical and Environmental Precursors of Crime

Recent research in the area of nutrition has produced some limited evidence that the old maxim "You are what you eat!" may contain more than a grain of truth. Biocriminology has made some significant strides in linking violent or disruptive behavior to eating habits, vitamin deficiencies, genetics, inheritance, and other conditions having an effect on body tissue. Studies of nutrition, endocrinology, and environmental contaminants have all contributed to advances in understanding such behaviour.

## Figure 5.2

## *Sheldon's Somatotypes*

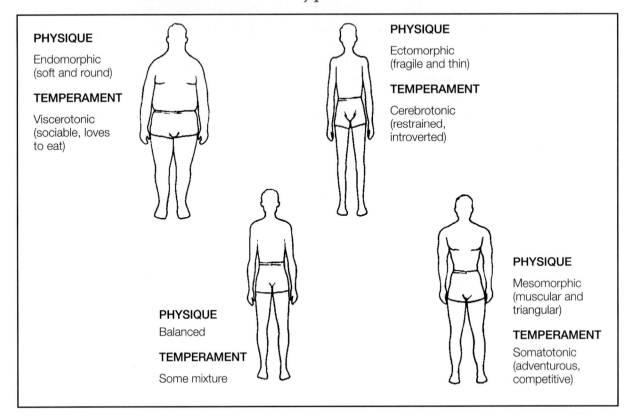

**PHYSIQUE**

Endomorphic
(soft and round)

**TEMPERAMENT**

Viscerotonic
(sociable, loves
to eat)

**PHYSIQUE**

Ectomorphic
(fragile and thin)

**TEMPERAMENT**

Cerebrotonic
(restrained,
introverted)

**PHYSIQUE**

Balanced

**TEMPERAMENT**

Some mixture

**PHYSIQUE**

Mesomorphic
(muscular and
triangular)

**TEMPERAMENT**

Somatotonic
(adventurous,
competitive)

SOURCE: V.F. Sacco and L. W. Kennedy, *The Criminal Event* (Toronto: ITP Nelson, 1994), p.450, as taken from Curt R. Bartol, *Criminal Behaviour: A Psychosocial Approach* (England Cliffs, N.J.: Prentice Hall, 1980).

**Hypoglycemia** a condition characterized by low blood sugar.

One of the first studies to focus on chemical imbalances in the body as a cause of crime was reported in the British medical journal *Lancet* in 1943.[35] Authors of the study linked murder to **hypoglycemia,** or low blood sugar. Low blood sugar, produced by too much insulin in the blood or by near-starvation diets, was said to reduce the mind's capacity to effectively reason or to judge the long-term consequences of behaviour. More recent studies have linked excess consumption of refined white sugar to hyperactivity and aggressiveness. Popular books such as *Sugar Blues* provide guides for individuals seeking to free themselves from the negative effects of excess sugar consumption.

To some degree, even courts have accepted the notion that excess sugar consumption may be linked to crime. In the early 1980s, for example, Dan White, a former San Francisco police officer, was given a reduced sentence after his lawyers convinced the court that their defendant's consumption of massive amounts of refined white sugar had increased his excitability and lowered his ability to make reasoned decisions. White had been convicted of murdering San Francisco Mayor Moscone and City Councilman Harvey Milk during a dispute in the mayor's office. The night before the killings, White stayed awake drinking Coca-Cola and eating many Twinkies.

More than 10 years later, however, a well-conducted study reported in the *New England Journal of Medicine*[36] seemed to contradict the notion that sugar may lead to hyperactivity. Similarly, neither sugar nor artificial sweeteners were shown to have any link to an increase in learning disabilities. In the study, researchers at Vanderbilt University and the University of Iowa varied the diets of supposedly sugar-sensitive youngsters from ones that were high in sugar, to one that was low in sugar but contained the artificial sweetener aspartame. A third experimental diet contained very little sugar but had added saccharin. After surveying parents, teachers, and babysitters and testing the study group for changes in memory, concentration, and math skills, the researchers concluded "[w]e couldn't find any difference in terms of their behavior or their learning on any of the three diets."[37] Hence, to date, the evidence concerning sugar's impact on behaviour is less than clear.

Allergic reactions to common foods have been reported as the cause of violence and homicide by a number of investigators.[38] Some foods—including milk, citrus fruit, chocolate, corn, wheat, and eggs—are said to produce allergic reactions in sensitive individuals, leading to a swelling of the brain and the brain stem. Involvement of the central nervous system in such allergies, it has been suggested, reduces the amount of learning that occurs during childhood and may contribute to delinquency as well as to adult criminal behaviour. Such swelling is also thought to impede the higher faculties, reducing one's sense of morality and creating conditions that support impulsive behaviour.

Some studies have implicated food additives, such as the flavour enhancer monosodium glutamate, dyes, and artificial flavourings in producing criminal violence.[39] Other research[40] has found that coffee and sugar may trigger antisocial behaviour. Researchers were led to these conclusions through finding that inmates consumed considerably greater amounts of coffee, sugar, and processed foods than others.[41] It is, however, unclear whether inmates drink more coffee because of boredom, or whether "excitable" personalities feel a need for the kind of stimulation available through coffee consumption. On the other hand, habitual coffee drinkers in nonprison populations have not been linked to crime, and other studies show no link between the amount of sugar consumed by inmates and hyperactivity.[42] Nonetheless, some prison programs have been designed to limit intake of dietary stimulants through nutritional management and the substitution of artificial sweeteners for refined sugar. Vitamins have also been examined for their impact on delinquency. At least one researcher found that disruptive children consumed far less than optimal levels of vitamins $B_3$ and $B_6$ than did nonproblem youths.[43] Some researchers have suggested that the addition of these vitamins to the diets of children who were deficient in them could control unruly behaviour and improve school performance.

The role of food and diet in causing criminal behaviour, however, has not been well established. Some international health associations have concluded that no convincing scientific relationship between crime and diet has yet been demonstrated.[44] Such groups are becoming concerned that poor nutrition may result from programs intended to have behavioural impacts, such as those that reduce or modify diets in prisons or elsewhere.

In 1997, British researchers Roger D. Masters, Brian Hone, and Anil Doshi published a study[45] purporting to show that industrial and other forms of environmental pollution cause people to commit violent crimes. The study used statistics from the

FBI's Uniform Crime Reporting Program and data from the U.S. Environmental Protection Agency's Toxic Release Inventory. A comparison between the two data sets showed a significant correlation between juvenile crime and high environmental levels of both lead and manganese. Masters and his colleagues suggested an explanation based on a neurotoxicity hypothesis. "According to this approach, toxic pollutants—specifically the toxic metals lead and manganese—cause learning disabilities, an increase in aggressive behavior, and—most importantly—loss of control over impulsive behavior. These traits combine with poverty, social stress, alcohol and drug abuse, individual character, and other social and psychological factors to produce individuals who commit violent crimes."[46]

According to Masters, the presence of excess manganese lowers levels of serotonin and dopamine in the brain—both of which are neurotransmitters associated with impulse control and planning. Masters notes that low blood levels of serotonin are known to cause mood disturbances, poor impulse control, and increases in aggressive behavior. Masters claims that children who are raised from birth on infant formula, and who are not breastfed, will absorb five times as much manganese as breastfed infants. Calcium deficiency is known to increase the absorption of manganese and, says Masters, "a combination of manganese toxicity and calcium deficiency adds up to 'reverse' Prozac."

In support of his thesis, Masters cites other studies, the largest of which was an examination of 1 000 black children in Philadelphia that showed that levels of exposure to lead was a reliable predictor of the number of juvenile offences among the exposed male population, the seriousness of juvenile offences, and the number of adult offences.

According to Masters, toxic metals affect individuals in complex ways. Because lead diminishes a person's normal ability to detoxify poisons, he says, it may heighten the effects of alcohol and drugs. Industrial pollution, automobile traffic, lead-based paints, and aging water delivery systems are all possible sources of contamination. In a recent interview, Masters said: "The presence of pollution is as big a factor [in crime causation] as poverty. ... It's the breakdown of the inhibition mechanism that's the key to violent behavior."[47] When brain chemistry is altered by exposure to heavy metal and other toxins, he said, people lose the natural restraint that holds their violent tendencies in check.

In addition to chemical substances likely to be ingested, other environmental features have also been linked to the likelihood of aggressive behaviour. During the early 1980s, for example, Alexander Schauss and his followers[48] were able to show that the use of a specific shade of the colour pink could have a calming effect on people experiencing feelings of anger and agitation. Findings indicated that exposure to the colour pink produced an endocrine change that had a tranquillizing effect on the muscles. This involuntary effect, said researchers, was not subject to conscious control. As a result of such studies, jail cells in some detention centres were painted pink in hopes that aggressive tendencies among inmates might be reduced. Researchers supported such measures, saying that "the use of pink color in reducing aggression and causing muscular relaxation of inmates is humane and requires no medication or physical force."[49]

A county sheriff in the United States shows off his newly redecorated jail. The jail sports pink walls, a colour that psychologists think may lower the likelihood of aggressive behaviour. The blue teddy bears were the sheriff's idea. How do you think offenders will react? *Sonny Hedgecech*

## Hormones and Criminality

Hormones have also come under scrutiny as potential behavioural determinants. The male sex hormone **testosterone,** for example, has been linked to aggression. Most studies on the subject have consistently shown an apparent relationship between high blood testosterone levels and increased aggressiveness in men. More focused studies have unveiled a direct relationship between the amount of the chemical present and the degree of violence used by sex offenders,[50] while other researchers have linked steroid abuse among bodybuilders to destructive urges and psychosis.[51] Contemporary investigations[52] demonstrate a link between testosterone levels and aggression in teenagers, while others[53] show that adolescent problem behaviour and teenage violence rise in proportion to the amount of testosterone levels in the blood of young men. In 1987, for example, a Swedish researcher, Dan Olweus,[54] reported that boys aged 15 to 17 showed levels of both verbal and physical aggression that correlated with the level of testosterone present in their blood. Olweus also found that boys with higher levels of testosterone "tended to be habitually more impatient and irritable than boys with lower testosterone levels." He concluded that high levels of the hormone led to increased frustration and habitual impatience and irritability.

**Testosterone** the primary male sex hormone; produced in the testes, its function is to control secondary sex characteristics and sexual drive.

Sex hormones, such as testosterone, have been linked to aggressive behaviour. Testosterone also enhances secondary sexual characteristics such as body hair and muscle mass in males. What kinds of crime might be hormonally influenced? *The Kobal Collection.*

In what may be the definitive work to date on the subject, Alan Booth and D. Wayne Osgood[55] conclude that there is a "moderately strong relationship between testosterone and adult deviance,"[55] but suggest that the relationship "is largely mediated by the influence of testosterone on social integration and on prior involvement in juvenile delinquency."[57] In other words, measurably high levels of testosterone in the blood of young men may have some effect on behaviour, but those effects are likely to be moderated by the social environment.

A few limited studies have attempted to measure the effects of testosterone on women. Women's bodies manufacture roughly one-tenth the amount of the hormone secreted by men. Even so, subtle changes in testosterone levels in women have been linked to changes in personality and sexual behaviour.[58] Few such studies exist, however, and their findings should therefore be regarded as inconclusive.

Fluctuations in the level of female hormones, however, may also bear some relationship to law violation. In 1980 a British court exonerated Christine English of charges that she murdered her live-in lover, after English admittedly ran him over with her car after an argument. English's defence rested on the fact that she was suffering from premenstrual syndrome (PMS) at the time of the homicide. An expert witness, Dr. Katharina Dalton, testified at the trial that PMS had caused Ms. English to be "irritable, aggressive, … and confused, with loss of self-control."

Another case[59] involving PMS was decided in 1991 by a Fairfax, Virginia, judge who dismissed drunk driving and other charges against a female orthopedic surgeon named Dr. Geraldine Richter. Richter allegedly kicked and cursed a Virginia state trooper after being stopped for driving erratically; she also admitted to having consumed four glasses of wine. A Breathalyzer test showed her blood-alcohol level to be nearly 0.13 percent—above the 0.10 percent level Virginia law set for such a violation. Charges against Dr. Richter were dismissed after a gynecologist testified on her behalf, saying that the behaviour she exhibited was likely to have been due primarily to PMS.

Although evidence linking PMS to violent and/or criminal behaviour is far from clear, some researchers believe that a drop in serotonin levels in the female brain just prior to menstruation might explain the agitation and irritability sometimes associated with premenstrual syndrome.[60] Serotonin has been called a "behaviour-regulating chemical," and animal studies have demonstrated a link between low levels of the neurotransmitter present in the brain and aggressive behaviour. Monkeys, for example, with low serotonin levels have been found more likely to bite, slap, and chase others of their kind. Studies at the National Institute on Alcohol Abuse and Alcoholism have linked low serotonin levels in humans to impulsive crimes. Men convicted of premeditated murder, for example, have been found to have normal serotonin levels, whereas those convicted of crimes of passion have lower levels.[61]

# Genetics and Crime

## Criminal Families

Some scholars suggest that a penchant for crime may be inherited, and that criminal tendencies are genetically based. Early studies of this type often focused on criminal families, or families that appeared to exhibit criminal tendencies through several generations.

In 1877, **Richard L. Dugdale** (1841–1883) published a study[62] of one such family—the **Juke family.** Dugdale traced the Juke lineage back to a notorious character named Max, a Dutch immigrant who arrived in New York in the early 1700s. Two of Max's sons married into the notorious "Juke family of girls," six sisters, all of whom were said to be illegitimate. Max's male descendants were reputed to be vicious, and one woman named Ada had an especially bad reputation and came to be known as "the mother of criminals." By the time of the study, Dugdale claimed to be able to identify approximately 1 200 of Ada's descendants. He included among their numbers 7 murderers, 60 habitual thieves, 90 or so other criminals, 50 prostitutes, and 280 paupers. Dugdale compared the crime-prone Jukes with another family, the pure-blooded progeny of Jonathan Edwards, a Puritan preacher and one-time president of Princeton University. Descendants of Edwards included American presidents and vice-presidents and many successful bankers and businesspeople. None identified from among the Edwards lineage had had run-ins with the law. In 1915, **Arthur H. Estabrook** published a follow-up to Dugdale's work, in which he identified an additional 715 Juke descendants, including 378 more prostitutes, 170 additional paupers, and 118 other criminals.[63]

**Juke family** a well-known "criminal family" studied by Richard L. Dugdale.

Kallikak family a well-
known "criminal family"
studied by Henry H.
Goddard.

Following in the tradition of family tree researchers, **Henry H. Goddard** (1866–1957) published a study[64] of the **Kallikak family** in 1912. Goddard attempted to place the study of deviant families within an acceptable scientific framework by providing of a kind of control group. For comparison purposes, he used two branches of the same family. One branch began as the result of a sexual liaison between Martin Kallikak, a Revolutionary War soldier, and a barmaid whose name is unknown. As a result of this illegitimate union, a son (Martin, Jr.) was born. After the war, Martin, Sr., returned home and married a righteous Quaker girl, and a second line of descent began. Although the second, legitimate branch, produced only a few minor deviants, the illegitimate line resulted in 262 "feebleminded" births and various other epileptic, alcoholic, and criminal descendants. The term *feebleminded,* which was much in vogue at the time of Goddard's study, was later recast as "mental retardation," whereas people exhibiting similar characteristics today might be referred to as mentally handicapped or mentally challenged. Because feeblemindedness appeared to occur with some predictability in Goddard's study, whereas criminal activity seemed to be only randomly represented among the descendants of either Kallikak line, Goddard concluded that a tendency toward feeblemindedness was inherited but that criminality was not.

Today, the work of Dugdale and Goddard has been discredited.[65] Nevertheless, studies such as these, which focused on inherited mental degeneration, led to the **eugenics** movement of the 1920s and early 1930s, under which mentally handicapped women were frequently sterilized to prevent their bearing additional offspring. In Canada, sexual sterilization laws in Alberta and British Columbia resulted in the sterilization of almost 3 000 citizens between 1928 and 1972. During this period, the legislation targeted not only those with mental illness but also the poor, Native people, unwed mothers, and non–English speaking immigrants.[66]

Eugenics the study of
hereditary improvement
by genetic control.

## The XYY "Supermale"

Recent developments in the field of human genetics have led to the study of the role of chromosomes, and sex-linked chromosomes in particular, in crime causation. The first well-known study[67] of this type was undertaken by Patricia A. Jacobs, a British researcher who in 1965 examined 197 Scottish prisoners for chromosomal abnormalities through a relatively simple blood test known as *karyotyping.*[68] Twelve members of the group displayed chromosomes that were unusual, and seven were found to have an XYY chromosome. "Normal" male individuals possess an XY chromosome structure, and "normal" female individuals are XX. Some other unusual combinations might be XXX, wherein a woman's genetic makeup contains an extra X chromosome, or XXY, also called Klinefelter's syndrome, in which a man might carry an extra X, or female, chromosome. Klinefelter's men often are possessed of male genitalia but are frequently sterile and evidence breast enlargement and intellectual retardation. The XYY man, however, whose incidence in the prison population was placed at around 3.5 percent by Jacobs, was quickly identified as potentially violent and termed a *supermale.*

Supermale a male
individual displaying the
XYY chromosomal
structure.

Following introduction of the supermale notion into popular consciousness, a number of offenders attempted to offer a chromosome-based defence. In 1969, for example, Lawrence E. Hannell, who was adjudged a supermale, was acquitted of murder in Australia on the grounds of insanity.[69] Such a defence, however, did not work for

Richard Speck, another claimed XYY man, convicted of killing eight Chicago nursing students in 1966. It was later learned that Speck did not carry the extra Y chromosome.

To date, there have been nearly 200 studies of XYY males. Although not all researchers agree, taken as a group these studies[70] tend to show that supermales

- are taller than the average male, often standing 6′1″ or more;
- suffer from acne or skin disorders;
- are of less than average intelligence;
- are over-represented in prisons and mental hospitals; and
- come from families with less history of crime or mental illness.

The supermale phenomenon, also called the XYY syndrome, was more sensationalism than fact. Little evidence suggests that XYY men actually commit crimes of greater violence than do other men, although they may commit somewhat more crimes overall. A 1976 Danish study[71] of 4 000 men, which found precisely that, may have helped put the issue to rest. This survey of men born in Copenhagen between 1944 and 1947 also found that the incidence of XYY men was less than 1 percent in the general male population. Other recent researchers have similarly concluded that "studies done thus far are largely in agreement and demonstrate rather conclusively that males of the XYY type are not predictably aggressive."[72]

## Chromosomes and Modern-Day Criminal Families

In 1993, Dutch criminologists caught worldwide attention with their claim that they had uncovered a specific gene with links to criminal behaviour. Geneticist Han Brunner, researcher H. Hilger Ropers, and collaborators studied what media sources called "the Netherlands' most dysfunctional family."[73] Although the unnamed family displayed IQs in the near normal range, they seemed unable to control their impulses and often ended up being arrested for violations of the criminal law. Arrests, however, were always of men. Tracing the family back five generations, Brunner found fourteen men whom he classified as genetically given to criminality. None of the women in the family displayed criminal tendencies, although they were often victimized by their crime-prone male siblings. One brother raped a sister and later stabbed a mental hospital staffer in the chest with a pitchfork. Another tried to run over his supervisor with his car. Two brothers repeatedly started fires, and were classified as arsonists. Another brother frequently crept into his sisters' rooms and forced them to undress at knifepoint.

According to Ropers and Brunner, because men have only one X chromosome they are especially vulnerable to any defective gene. Women, with two X chromosomes, have a kind of backup system in which one defective gene may be compensated for by another wholesome and correctly functioning gene carried in the second X chromosome. After a decade of study, which involved the laboratory filtering of a huge quantity of genetic material in a search for the defective gene, Ropers and Brunner announced that they had isolated the specific mutation that caused the family's criminality. The gene, they said, is one that is responsible for production of an enzyme called monoamine oxidase A (MAOA). This enzyme is crucially involved in the process by which signals are transmitted within the brain. Specifically, MAOA breaks down the chemicals serotonin and noradrenaline. Both are substances that, when found in excess in the brain, have been linked to aggressive behaviour in human beings. Because men with the mutated gene do not produce the enzyme necessary to break down chemical transmitters, researchers surmise, their brains are overwhelmed with stimuli—a situation that results in uncontrollable urges and, ultimately, criminal behaviour.

## Twin Studies

Studies of the criminal tendencies of fraternal and identical twins provide a methodologically sophisticated technique for ferreting out the role of inheritance in crime causation. Fraternal twins (also called dizygotic or DZ twins) develop from different fertilized eggs and share only that genetic material common among siblings. Identical twins (also called **monozygotic** or **MZ twins**) develop from the same egg and carry virtually the same genetic material.

**Monozyotic or MZ twins**, as opposed to dizygotic (or DZ) twins, develop from the same egg and carry virtually the same genetic material.

One of the first studies[74] to link MZ twins to criminality was published in the 1920s by the German physician Johannes Lange. Lange examined only seventeen pairs of fraternal and thirteen pairs of identical twins, but found that in ten of the thirteen identical pairs both twins were criminal, whereas only two of the seventeen fraternal pairs exhibited such similarity. Lange's findings drew considerable attention, even though his sample was small and he was unable to adequately separate environmental influences from genetic ones. The title of his book, *Verbrechen als Schicksal,* whose English translation is *Crime as Destiny,* indicates Lange's firm conviction that criminality has a strong genetic component.

A much larger twin study[75] was begun in 1968 by the European researchers Karl Christiansen and Sarnoff Mednick, who analyzed all twins (3 586 pairs) born on a selected group of Danish islands between 1881 and 1910. Christiansen and Mednick found significant statistical support for the notion that criminal tendencies are inherited and concluded that 52 percent of identical twins and 22 percent of fraternal siblings displayed the same degree of criminality within the twin pair. Such similarities remained apparent even among twins who had been separated at birth and who were raised in substantially different environments.

## Male–Female Differences in Criminality

A number of writers unequivocally recognize that "the male is much more criminalistic than the female."[76] As discussed in Chapter 2, with the exception of crimes such as prostitution and shoplifting, the number of crimes committed by men routinely far exceeds the number of crimes committed by women in almost any category. The data on the extent of male–female criminality in relation to violent crime show a degree of regularity over time. The proportion of homicides committed by men versus women, for example, has remained more or less constant for decades (see Table 5.1). In fact, as the table shows (and contrary to popular expectations), *male* perpetrators appear to be involved in an increasing proportion of murders over the past 32 years. Similarly, the proportion of men murdered by men versus the proportion of women murdered by women has continuously shown a much larger propensity for men to murder one another.

| Table 5.1 |
|-----------|

## Male and Female Murder Perpetrators as a Percentage of All Homicide Suspects, 1966–1998

| 1966 | | 1979 | | 1986 | | 1998 | |
|------|------|------|------|------|------|------|------|
| Male | Female | Male | Female | Male | Female | Male | Female |
| 85.6% | 14.4% | 87.3% | 12.7% | 85.4% | 14.6% | 91.5% | 8.5% |

SOURCES: Adapted from M.A. Jackson and C.T. Griffiths, *Canadian Criminology: Perspectives on Crime and Criminality* (Toronto: Harcourt Brace, 1995), p.149; Statistics Canada, *Homicide Statistics 1979 (cat. 85-209)* (Ottawa: Minister of Supply and Services, 1980); Statistics Canada, *Homicide in Canada 1986: A Statistical Perspective* (Ottawa: Minister of Supply and Services, 1997); and S. Tremblay, "Canadian Crime Statistics, 1988," *Juristat*, vol. 19, no. 9 (Ottawa: Minister of Industry, 1999).

With the exception of crimes against the person, the gap between male and female crime rates has been narrowing in the past 30 years. Overall, the percentage of Criminal Code offences committed by females increased from 9 percent to 18 percent. Increases were seen particularly in offences classified as serious thefts (from 9 to 18%), fraud (from 11 to 29%), and minor theft (from 22 to 34%). Chapter 2 provides additional statistics of this nature.[77]

Interestingly, the situation in the United States is somewhat different. Women are arrested for only 13 percent of all violent crimes and 26 percent of property crimes—proportions that have remained surprisingly constant over the years since the Federal Bureau of Investigation began gathering crime data more than half a century ago. Exceptions include crimes of embezzlement, of drug abuse, and liquor law violations.[78]

In evaluating the criminality of women based on statistics alone, however, there is a danger of misidentifying causal factors operative in the behaviour itself. Although men consistently commit more murders than women, for example, we should not jump to the conclusion that this bit of evidence shows a genetic predisposition toward interpersonal violence in men that is absent in women. To do so would fail to recognize the role of other causal factors. Observable racial variation in crime rates has provided some writers with a basis for claiming that some racial groups are disproportionately criminal—while simultaneously attributing such criminality to a genetic basis. Canadian crime statistics do not routinely report on the racial and ethnic makeup of offenders. Two recent studies of Canadian inmate populations, however, have concluded that offenders from non-Aboriginal, visible, ethnic minorities were under-represented.[79]

The reality for Canadian Aboriginal peoples is quite different. Numerous studies over the years have consistently demonstrated that Aboriginals are over-represented in the criminal justice system. Silverman and Kennedy found that the proportion of Aboriginals involved in homicide is at least five times greater than is their representation in the population.[80] Work by Hyde and LaPrairie indicates that Aboriginal peoples are implicated in more offences involving alcohol, in fewer property offences, and in more violent offences.[81] Again, Chapter 2 provides additional statistics of this nature. By comparison, a look at the statistics in the United States shows that African-Americans are five times more likely than Causcasians to commit murder, three times more likely to commit rape, six times more likely to rob, and twice as likely, on average, to commit any kind of crime.[82]

Such statistics can be inherently misleading because—unlike the undeniable and easily observable biological differences that exist between men and women—racial groupings are defined more by convention than by genetics. In fact, some writers suggest that "pure" racial groups no longer exist, and that even historical racial distinctions were based more on political convention than on significant genetic differences.

The criminality of women (or relative lack thereof) is, in all likelihood, culturally determined to a considerable degree. The consistency of data routinely showing that women are far less likely than men to be involved in most property crimes, however, and less likely still to commit violent crimes, requires recognition. We have already evaluated the role that testosterone may play in increasing the propensity toward violence and aggression among men. A few authors suggest that testosterone is the agent primarily responsible for male criminality and that its relative lack in women leads them to commit fewer crimes. Some evidence supports just such a hypothesis. Studies[83] have shown, for example, that female fetuses exposed to elevated testosterone levels during gestation develop masculine characteristics, including a muscular body build and a demonstrably greater tendency toward aggression later in life. Even so, genetically based behavioural differences between men and women are so overshadowed by aspects of the social environment, including socialization, the learning of culturally prescribed roles, the expectations of others, and so on, that definitive conclusions are difficult to reach.

One recently proposed social-psychological explanation[84] for homicidal behaviour among women, for example, suggests that men who kill tend to do so out of a need to control a situation, whereas women who kill tend to do so because they have lost control over themselves. The theory says that "women as a group are more 'controlled' than men, particularly with respect to their experience and expression of anger." Such control is said to emanate from the fact that "men are always the subjects and women the objects in [a] male-centric universe."[85] As a consequence of our culture's overemphasis on a woman's looks rather than on her performance, the theory says, women internalize a "self-image on the basis of appearance rather than substance of character," resulting in low self-esteem and low self-confidence. Low self-esteem, the argument goes, necessitates greater self-control and results in lower criminality among women. Such a perspective suggests that women tend to commit homicides only when driven "past the brink" of self-control, thus offering an explanation for why homicides committed by women are generally spontaneous rather than planned, why they usually involve the killing of intimates, and why they generally occur in the home. "Women generally view themselves as part of a collective of relationships around them," say one theorist, "and evaluate their self-worth based on the value and success of these relationships."[86] Hence, when relationships break down a woman's self-worth may be negated, resulting in a lessening of control—and homicide may ensue.

## Sociobiology

**Sociobiology** the systematic study of the biological basis of all social behaviour.

In the introduction to his insightful article summarizing sociobiology, Arthur Fisher writes, "[e]very so often, in the long course of scientific progress, a new set of ideas appears, illuminating and redefining what has gone before like a flare bursting over a darkened landscape."[87] To some, **sociobiology**—a theoretical synthesis of biology,

## Violence Linked to Gene Defect:

### Pleasure Deficit May Be the Spark

A gene linked to pleasure-seeking behavior and addictions also may play a role in murder and violence, new research suggests. This pleasure gene normally is involved in the flow of dopamine, a powerful brain chemical that provides people with their sense of well-being. When defective, the gene diminishes dopamine function, driving a person to drink, take drugs or engage in other activities that give dopamine a boost.

Studies suggest people who have a variant of the gene, called "DRD2 A1 allele," are prone to becoming smokers, violent alcoholics, gambling addicts and drug addicts.

"We think they're seeking out ways of fixing the lack of pleasure," says Kenneth Blum, University of Texas Health Science Center, San Antonio. "You might be a pleasure seeker for alcohol, drugs, sex or maybe you get it from violence or murder."

In a study presented Wednesday at an American Psychiatric Association meeting, Blum and 17 researchers found the DRD2 A1 allele in:

- Six of 11 children in a residential treatment program for pathological violence but only one of 30 normal children.
- Half of 109 people diagnosed with "schizoid/avoidant" personality. They are introverted, withdrawn, emotionally cold and distant.

Other research by psychoanalyst Anneliese Pontius, Harvard Medical School, has tied schizoid/avoidant disorder to more than a dozen bizarre murders. She is testing her subjects for the DRD2 A1 variant.

If the findings are confirmed, Blum says problem children could be screened for the gene and given drugs, special diets and other treatments known to boost dopamine.

### DISCUSSION QUESTIONS

1. How might genes that are linked to pleasure-seeking behaviour lead to crime?
2. Should policies be created to reduce potential criminal activity among persons with the DRD2 A1 allele gene? If so, what might they be?

SOURCE: Tim Friend, "Violence Linked to Gene Defect: Pleasure Deficit May be the Spark," *USA Today,* May 9, 1996, p. 1D. Copyright 1997, *USA Today.* Reprinted with permission.

behaviour, and evolutionary ecology—brought to the scientific community by **Edward O. Wilson** in his seminal 1975 work *Sociobiology: The New Synthesis,*[88] holds the promise of just such a new paradigm. In his book, Wilson defined sociobiology as "the systematic study of the biological basis of all social behavior" and as "a branch of evolutionary biology and particularly of modern population biology." Through his

Sociobiologists tell us that certain traits, such as territoriality, are common to both animals and humans. How might territoriality lead to crime? *Paul Lally/Stock Boston.*

entomological study of social insects, especially ants, Wilson demonstrated that particular forms of behaviour could contribute to the long-term survival of the social group. Wilson focused on altruism (selfless, helping behaviour) and found that, contrary to the beliefs of some evolutionary biologists, helping behaviour facilitates the continuity of the gene pool found among altruistic individuals. Wilson's major focus was to show that the primary determinant of behaviour, including human behaviour, was the need to ensure the survival and continuity of genetic material from one generation to the next.

Territoriality, another primary tenet of Wilson's writings, was said to explain much of the conflict seen between and among human beings, including homicide, warfare, and other forms of aggression. In Wilson's words, "[p]art of man's problem is that his intergroup responses are still crude and primitive, and inadequate for the extended extraterritorial relationships that civilization has thrust upon him." The "unhappy result," as Wilson terms it, may be "tribalism," expressed through the contemporary increase of street gangs and racial tension.

The sad results of territoriality, whatever its cause, can be seen in the deadly adventure of 15-year-old Michael Carter and his companions, who ended up in the proverbial wrong place at the wrong time. On June 18, 1997, Carter, from Highland Township, Michigan, and two of his friends hopped a train headed for the town of Holly. The three were looking for a free 10-mile ride on their way to see friends. But they missed their jump-off point, sailed past the town of Holly, and ended up in a run-down inner-city ghetto in the middle of Flint, Michigan, around midnight. Soon the three were surrounded by gang members, led into a secluded area, and shot. Carter died at the scene, while friend Dustin Kaiser, also 15, survived a gunshot wound to the head. The 14-year-old girl who had accompanied the boys was raped and shot in the face, but lived.[89]

As sociobiologists tell us, the violence and aggressiveness associated with territoriality is often reserved for strangers. The approach of sociobiology may explain intragroup aggression—or the violence that occurs within groups—and that which occurs between groups. Wilson writes that his theory suggests that, within the group, "a particularly severe form of aggressiveness should be reserved for actual or suspected adultery. In many human societies," he observes, "where sexual bonding is close and personal knowledge of the behavior of others detailed, adulterers are harshly treated. The sin," he adds, "is regarded to be even worse when offspring are produced."[90] Hence, territoriality and acquisitiveness extend, from a sociobiological perspective, to location, possessions, and even other people. Human laws, says Wilson, are designed to protect genetically based relationships people have with one another as well as their material possessions and their claimed locations in space. Violations of these intuitive relationships result in crime and in official reactions by the legal system.

Wilson's writing propelled researchers into a flurry of studies intended to test the validity of his assertions. One study,[91] for example, found that Indian adult male Hanuman langurs (a type of monkey) routinely killed the young offspring of female langurs with whom they bonded when those offspring had been sired by other male langurs. A Canadian study by Martin Daly and Margo Wilson[92] of violence in the homes of adoptive children found a human parallel in the langur study, showing that stepchildren run a 70 times greater risk of being killed by their adoptive parent(s) than do children living with their natural parents. Some writers concluded that "murderous behavior, warfare, and even genocide were unavoidable correlates of genetic evolution, controlled by the same genes for territorial behavior that had been selected in primate evolution."[93] Others suggested that biological predispositions developed during earlier stages of human evolution colour contemporary criminal activity. Male criminals, for example, tend toward robbery and burglary—crimes in which they can continue to enact their "hunter instincts" developed long ago. The criminality of women, on the other hand, is more typical of "gatherers" when it involves shoplifting, simple theft, and so on.

Human behavioural predilections can be studied in a variety of ways. In the 1989 book *Evolutionary Jurisprudence*,[94] John H. Beckstrom reports on his examination of over 400 legal documents that, he claimed, showed support for Wilson's contentions that humans tend to act so as to preserve territorial claims, the likelihood of successful reproduction, and the continuation of their own particular genetic material. Beckstrom used legal claims and court decisions in his analysis, spanning over 300 years of judicial activity. Other theorists have gone so far as to imply that, among humans, there may be a gene-based tendency to experience guilt and to develop a conscience. Hence, notions of right and wrong, whether embodied in laws or in social convention, may flow from such a naturalistic origin.

As sociobiology began to receive expanded recognition from investigators, most of whom are American, some social scientists began to treat it as "criminology's anti-discipline."[95] Criticisms were quick to come and included charges that

• Sociobiology … fails to convey the overwhelming significance of culture, social learning, and individual experiences in shaping the behaviour of individuals and groups.

- Sociobiology is fundamentally wrong in its depiction of the basic nature of man; there is no credible evidence of genetically based or determined tendencies to act in certain ways.
- Sociobiology is just another empirically unsupported rationale for the authoritative labelling, stigmatization of despised, threatening, powerless minorities.
- Man is so thoroughly different from other animal species, even other primates, that there is no rational basis for the application to man of findings from animal studies.

**Paradigm** an example, model, or theory.

In the words of one observer, "[m]ost criminologists, like most academicians, were wedded to a **paradigm,** and wedded even to the idea of paradigm, the idea that one great problem solution can permit the explanation of nearly all the unexplained variation in the field."[96] In other words, many criminologists were committed to the idea that one theory could explain all that there was to know about crime and its causes. Today, many scholars are beginning to sense the growing need for a new synthesis—for a way to consider the impact of biological theories such as sociobiology along with other long-accepted perspectives such as sociology and psychology.

## Crime and Human Nature: A Contemporary Synthesis

A decade ago Arnold L. Lieber[97] delivered the invited address at the annual meeting of the American Psychological Association in Denver, Colorado. Lieber used the forum to describe his research, which linked phases of the moon to fluctuations in the incidence of violence among human beings. Nights around full moons, according to Lieber, show a significant rise in crime. Although critics found this type of research nonsensical, police officers, hospital personnel, ambulance drivers, and many late-night service providers who heard of Lieber's talk understood what he was describing. Many such individuals, in their own experience, had apparently seen validation of the "full moon thesis."

Shortly after Lieber's presentation, criminologist **James Q. Wilson** and psychologist **Richard J. Herrnstein** teamed up to write *Crime and Human Nature,*[98] a book-length treatise that reiterates many of the arguments proposed by biological criminologists over the past century. Their purpose, at least in part, was to reopen discussion of biological causes of crime. "We want to show," Herrnstein said, "that the pendulum is beginning to swing away from a totally sociological explanation of crime."[99] Their avowed goal was "not to state a case just for genetic factors, but to state a comprehensive theory of crime that draws together all the different factors that cause criminal behavior."

Constitutional factors that Wilson and Herrnstein cite as contributing to crime include the following[100]:

- *Gender:* "Crime," the authors say, "has been predominantly male behavior."
- *Age:* "In general, the tendency to break the law declines throughout life."
- *Body Type:* "A disproportionate number of criminals have a mesomorphic build."

- *Intelligence:* Criminality is said to be clearly and consistently associated with low intelligence.
- *Personality:* Criminals are typically aggressive, impulsive, and cruel.

Although personality, behavioural problems, and intelligence may be related to environment, the authors argue that "each involve some genetic inheritance." Wilson and Herrnstein recognize social factors in the development of personality but suggest that constitutional factors predispose a person to specific types of behaviour, and that societal reactions to such predispositions may determine, to a large degree, the form of continued behaviour. Hence, the interplay between heredity, biology, and the social environment may be the key nexus in any consideration of crime causation.

## Policy Issues

Biological theories of crime causation present unique challenges to policy-makers. According to C. Ray Jeffery, a comprehensive biologically based program of crime prevention and crime control would include

- "Pre- and postnatal care for pregnant women and their infants" to monitor and address potentially detrimental developmental conditions that could lead to heightened aggression and crime later in life.
- Monitoring of children throughout the early stages of their development to identify "early symptoms of behavioral disorder."
- Monitoring of children in their early years to reduce the risk of exposure to violence-inducing experiences such as child abuse and violence committed by other children.
- Neurological examinations, including "CAT, PET, and MRI scans … given when the need is evident."
- Biological research, conducted in our nation's prisons and treatment facilities, that might better identify the root causes of aggression and violence. Laws that prevent the experimental use of prison subjects, the analysis of the bodies of executed prisoners, and other similar types of biological investigations must change, says Jeffery.[101]

Jeffery adds that the fundamental orientation of our legal system must change so as to acknowledge contributions of biological criminologists. Such a change would replace or supplement our current "right to punishment" doctrine with a "right to treatment" philosophy. Jeffery concludes his analysis by saying, "[i]f legal and political barriers prevent us from regarding antisocial behavior as a medical problem, and if we do not permit medical research on criminal behavior, how can we ever solve the crime problem?"[102]

The dangers of an overly large dependence on biological approaches to crime, however, raise the specter of a *1984*-type of Orwellian bogey man in charge of every aspect of human social life, from conception to the grave—and include the possible abortion of defective fetuses, capital punishment in lieu of rehabilitation, and enforced sterilization. Precedent for such fears can be found in cases such as that of

Leilani Muir who, during the 1950s, was placed in Alberta's Provincial Training School for Mental Defectives at the age of 10. Based on a single IQ test, she was labelled a "moron" and, at the age of 14, was sterilized without her consent. The operation was sanctioned under Alberta's Sexual Sterilization Act.

Potential links between race and crime, suggested by some researchers, are especially repugnant to many who criticize biological criminology. Julian Roberts and Thomas Gabor, from the University of Ottawa, observe, "People who accept the view that variations in crime rates reflect genetic factors may also embrace an underlying message about crime prevention. ... Social programs aim to eradicate educational, social, and economic inequities. These efforts can only be undermined by statements stressing the importance of genetic factors in determining criminality."[103] Ronald Walters, a political scientist at Howard University, states that, "[s]eeking the biological and genetic aspects of violence is dangerous to African-American youth. ... When you consider the perception that black people have always been the violent people in this society, it is a short step from this stereotype to using this kind of research for social control."[104] Although biological theories of crime have problems, to entirely ignore the potential contributions of biological theorists does a disservice to the science of criminology and denies the opportunity for compassionate and objective researchers to realistically assist in the process of crime reduction.

In 1997, in an attempt to bring biological theorizing into the criminological mainstream, Lee Ellis and Anthony Walsh expanded on the theme of genetic predispositions, noting that: "In the case of behavior, nearly all of the effects of genes are quite indirect because they are mediated through complex chains of events occurring in the brain. This means that there are almost certainly no genes for something as complex as criminal behavior. Nevertheless, many genes may affect brain functioning in ways that either increase or reduce the chances of individuals learning various complex behavior patterns, including behavior patterns that happen to be so offensive to others that criminal sanctions have been instituted to minimize their recurrence."[105]

## Critique of Biological Theories

An excellent contemporary critique of biological perspectives on crime causation is provided by Glenn D. Walters and Thomas W. White, who contend that "genetic research on crime has been poorly designed, ambiguously reported, and exceedingly inadequate in addressing the relevant issues."[106] Walters and White highlight the following specific shortcomings of studies in the area:

- Few biological studies adequately conceptualize criminality. "Several studies," they say, "have defined criminality on the basis of a single arrest."
- Twin studies, in particular, have sometimes failed to properly establish "whether a pair of twins is monozygotic (MZ) or dizygotic (DZ)." This is because some MZ twins are not identical in appearance, and only a few twin studies have depended on biological testing rather than on a simple evaluation of appearances.
- Problems in estimating the degree of criminality among sample populations are rife in biological (and in many other) studies of criminality. Interview data are

open to interpretation and existing statistical data on the past criminality of offenders are not always properly appreciated.

- Methodological problems abound in many studies that attempt to evaluate the role of genetics in crime. Walters and White mention, among other things, the lack of control or comparison groups, small sample sizes, the dropping out of subjects from study groups, biased sampling techniques, and the use of inappropriate forms of statistical analysis.
- Results obtained in other countries may not be applicable to the country in question. Twin studies conducted in Sweden and Denmark provide an example of this potential lack of generalizability.

Walters and White nevertheless conclude that "[g]enetic factors are undoubtedly correlated with various measures of criminality," but add that "the large number of methodological flaws and limitations in the research should make one cautious in drawing any causal inferences at this point in time."[107]

## Summary

Contemporary criminology has been reluctant to adapt the contributions of biological theories to an understanding of criminality. An objective understanding of any social phenomenon, however, requires clear consideration of all available evidence. Modern proponents of biological perspectives on crime and crime causation point out that the link between the social environment and human behaviour is continuously mediated by the physical brain. Human activity flows from the human mind, and the mind is biologically grounded in the brain. The brain itself is apparently subject to influences from other aspects of the body, such as hormones, neurotransmitters, and the levels of various chemicals in the blood. Such realizations require only a small intellectual leap to the realization that other biological aspects of the human organism may play similar contributory roles in criminal behaviour.

At present, the influence of the environment on human behaviour predominates and studies purporting to have identified biological determinants of behaviour have been thoroughly criticized on methodological and other grounds. For the time being, we must draw the conclusion that while biology provides both a context for and specific precursors to human behaviour, biological predispositions for behaviour in most instances of human interaction are routinely overshadowed by the role of volition, the mechanisms of human thought, and the undeniable influences of socialization and acculturation. Even so, a comprehensive approach to human behaviour must consider the biological precursors of behaviour itself.

## Discussion Questions

1. This book emphasizes a social problems versus social responsibility theme. Which perspective would be most supported by biological theories of crime causation? Why?
2. What are the central features of biological theories of crime? How do such theories differ from other perspectives that attempt to explain the same phenomena?
3. Why have biological approaches to crime causation been out of vogue lately? Do you agree or disagree with those who are critical of such perspectives? Why?

4. Do you agree or disagree with the assertion that " [o]pen inquiry requires objective consideration of all points of view, and an examination of each for their ability to shed light upon the subject under study." Why?

5. What are the social policy implications of biological theories of crime? What Canadian example discussed in this chapter might presage a type of policy based on such theories?

# Weblinks

**www.home.istar.ca/~ccja/angl/cjc.html**
Canadian Journal of Criminology. Provides abstracts of the journal's most current articles.

**www.nejm.org/content/index.asp**
New England Journal of Medicine. Cites numerous articles on the biological effects of conditions such as PMS, hypoglycemia, etc., on behaviour.

**www.crime-times.org/**
*The Crime Times*, which is a non-profit national publication dedicated to exploring the link between biology and violent crime. Links to numerous discussion papers on a wide range of topics.

**www.hyoglycemia.org/**
The Hypoglycemia Support Foundation. This site provides lots of information on the symptoms and effects of low blood sugar levels.

# Psychological and Psychiatric Foundations of Criminal Behaviour

For I have decided to send the feminists, who have always ruined my life, to their maker.

—MARC LEPINE, FROM HIS SUICIDE NOTE FOUND AFTER THE MONTREAL MASSACRE[1]

Society secretly *wants* crime, *needs* crime, and gains definite satisfactions from the present mishandling of it! We condemn crime; we punish offenders for it; but we need it. The crime and punishment ritual is part of our lives!

—KARL MENNINGER[2]

## LEARNING OUTCOMES

After reading this chapter, you should be able to:

● Recognize the contributions of psychology to the understanding of criminal behaviour

● Appreciate the relationship between personality and criminal behaviour

● Recognize the importance of learning theory to an understanding of criminality

● Understand the unique characteristics of those found "not criminally responsible by reason of mental disorder"

● Identify current social policy reflecting the psychological approach to criminal behaviour

IMPORTANT NAMES

Hervey Cleckley          Sigmund Freud          B. F. Skinner
Robert Hare              Albert Bandura         *R. v. Swain*
Hans Eysenck

IMPORTANT TERMS

psychological theories   ego                    punishments
conditioning             superego               insanity
psychopathology          sublimation            McNaughten rule
psychopath               Thanatos               not criminally
sociopath                neurosis                   responsible by
electroencephalogram     psychosis                  reason of mental
    (EEG)                schizophrenics             disorder (NCRMD)
antisocial personality   paranoid               dangerousness
asocial personality          schizophrenics     selective incapacitation
psychiatric              alloplastic adaptation correctional
    criminology          autoplastic adaptation     psychology
forensic psychiatry      social learning theory psychological profiling
psychoanalysis           behaviour theory       Violent Crimes
psychotherapy            operant behaviour          Linkage Analysis
id                       rewards                    System (ViCLAS)

# Introduction

On July 22, 1991, a handcuffed man flagged down a police car in suburban Milwaukee.[3] Officers soon learned that the man was Tracy Edwards, a 32-year-old city resident. The lurid story of homosexual abuse and physical attack that Edwards told led investigators to the apartment of a 31-year-old loner named Jeffrey Dahmer. Dahmer was quickly arrested, and a search of his apartment revealed the body parts of at least 11 people. In a confession to police, Dahmer told of how he had repeatedly lured men to his apartment, murdered them, and then dismembered their bodies. Soon police investigations implicated Dahmer in a 10-year killing spree that spanned several states and may have reached as far as Europe. Edwards, whom Dahmer had met in a shopping mall, explained that he went to Dahmer's apartment because "[h]e (Dahmer) seemed so normal."[4] Sadly, one of Dahmer's victims, a 15-year-old boy, had earlier been discovered by police dazed and bleeding—and was returned to Dahmer's apartment after officers concluded that the situation involved nothing but a dispute between homosexual lovers.

Dahmer pleaded insane as a defence to charges of murder, but an expert witness at his trial, psychiatrist Park Dietz, testified that although Dahmer suffered from various psychological disorders, he could have chosen not to kill. Comparing Dahmer's sexual desires with someone who wants money but chooses not to rob, Dietz said, "[t]he choice is exactly the same. ... The freedom to make it is exactly the same."[5] In contrasting testimony, another expert witness claimed that Dahmer "had uncontrollable urges to kill and have sex with dead bodies. ... "[6] Dahmer was sentenced to 15 consecutive life terms—one each for the murders of 15 men[7]—but was himself murdered by another inmate in late 1994.

CHAPTER 6

167

**Psychological and
Psychiatric
Foundations of
Criminal Behaviour**

Jeffrey Dahmer, perhaps the most infamous serial killer of the twentieth century. What explains the public's seeming fascination with serial killers? *Milwaukee Journal/Sipa Press.*

Also in 1994, in a case that made headlines around the world, Lorena Bobbitt was tried on charges of malicious wounding for admittedly severing her allegedly philandering husband's penis with one stroke from a sharp kitchen knife while he slept. Bobbitt drove away with the severed organ still clutched in her fist and threw it out of her car window onto a grassy field some distance from the couple's apartment. Rescue workers recovered the organ in a predawn search, and it was reattached during hours of microvascular surgery.[8] In defence of her actions she later accused her husband, John, of marital rape. Although he was arrested and charged with raping his wife, a jury voted 12 to 0 to acquit him of all charges.[9]

On the morning immediately following the mutilation, Mrs. Bobbitt had told police that her husband "always [has] an orgasm and he doesn't wait for me. ... I don't think it's fair, so I pulled back the sheets and I did it." The defence attorney in the case, sounding very much like a pop psychologist, explained Mrs. Bobbitt's actions to the jury in these words: "Why did she cut his penis off? Something happened ... that drove her over the edge. If this was sheer jealousy, she'd have cut his throat. But what did she attack? ... The very thing that wounded her."

Finally, in a very violent incident, which has since heightened the public's awareness of violence against women and has resulted in tougher gun control legislation, 14 female students at L'école polytechnique in Montreal were shot to death in 1989 by Marc Lepine, an embittered misogynist. Lepine entered a classroom and shouted, "I want the women," and then, "You're all a bunch of feminists, and I hate feminists."[10] After ordering all the men to leave the room, Lepine shot six women dead. Over the next 20 minutes, the 25-year-old Lepine methodically stalked the cafeteria, the classrooms, and the corridors of the school, leaving 8 other women dead and 13 injured. He finally turned the gun on himself. In the three-page suicide note found in his pocket, Lepine blamed feminists for ruining his life. Lepine's actions were explained by Dr. Renée Fugère, forensic psychiatrist at Montreal's Allan Memorial Institute, as those of a delusional man who repeatedly failed to achieve his ambitions in work—and with women. "Lepine probably did not have the capacity to mourn his failed relationships," she said, "so he kept it inside. Those feelings piled up and finally exploded."[11]

What motivates people to kill or maim—or even to commit other, less serious offences? How can many killers "seem so normal" before their crimes, giving no hints of the atrocities they are about to commit? Serial killer, mass murderer, sexual mutilator, even book thief—all must wrestle, before and after the criminal event, with their personal demons. For answers to questions such as these many people turn to psychological theories. Psychologists are the pundits of the modern age of behaviourism— offering explanations rooted in determinants that lie within *individual actors*. Psychological determinants of deviant or criminal behaviour may be couched in terms of exploitive personality characteristics, poor impulse control, emotional arousal, an immature personality, and so on. Canadian criminal psychologists Don Andrews and James Bonta observe that, "The major sources of theoretical development in criminology have been—and continue to be—psychological. A theory of criminal conduct is weak indeed if uninformed by a general psychology of human behavior".[12] Other writers go so far as to claim that any criminal behaviour is only a symptom of a more fundamental psychiatric disorder.[13]

What is the fundamental distinguishing feature of psychological approaches as opposed to other attempts to explain behaviour? Two contemporary criminologists offer the following insight: "… theories are psychological insofar as they focus on the individual as the unit of analysis. Thus any theory that is concerned with the behavior of individual offenders or which refers to forces or dynamics that motivate individuals to commit crimes would be considered to have a psychological component."[14] Another writer, Curt Bartol, defines psychology as "the science of behavior and mental processes … [p]sychological criminology … is the science of the behavior and mental processes of the criminal. [P]sychological criminology focuses on individual criminal behavior—how it is acquired, evoked, maintained, and modified."[15]

## Major Principles of Psychological Theories

**Psychological theories** those derived from the behavioural sciences and that focus on the individual as the unit of analysis. Psychological theories place the locus of crime causation within the personality of the individual offender.

This brief section serves to summarize the central features of **psychological theories** of crime causation.[16] Each of these points can be found elsewhere in this chapter, where they are discussed in more detail. This cursory overview serves as a guide to the rest of this chapter.

Most psychological theories of crime causation make the following fundamental assumptions:

- The individual is the primary unit of analysis.
- Personality is the major motivational element within individuals, because it is the seat of drives and the source of motives.
- Crimes result from abnormal, dysfunctional, or inappropriate mental processes within the personality.

CHAPTER 6

**169**

**Psychological and
Psychiatric
Foundations of
Criminal Behaviour**

- Criminal behaviour, although condemned by the social group, may be purposeful for the individual insofar as it addresses certain felt needs. Behaviour can be judged "inappropriate" only when measured against external criteria purporting to establish normality.

- Normality is generally defined by social consensus—that is, what the majority of people in any social group agree is "real," appropriate, or typical.

- Defective, or abnormal, mental processes may have a variety of causes, including:
  —a diseased mind;
  —inappropriate learning or improper conditioning;
  —the emulation of inappropriate role models; and
  —adjustment to inner conflicts.

# Early Psychological Theories

A twin thread wove through early psychological theories. One strand emphasized behavioural **conditioning,** the other focused mostly on personality disturbances and diseases of the mind. Together, these two foci constituted the early field of psychological criminology. The concept of conditioned behaviour was popularized through the work of the Russian physiologist Ivan Pavlov (1849–1936), whose work with dogs won the Nobel Prize in physiology and medicine in 1904. The dogs, who salivated when food was presented to them, were always fed in the presence of a ringing bell. Soon, Pavlov found, the dogs would salivate, as if in preparation for eating, when the bell alone was rung—even when no food was present. Hence, salivation, an automatic response to the presence of food, could be conditioned to occur in response to some other stimulus—demonstrating that animal behaviour could be predictably altered through association with external changes arising from the environment surrounding the organism.

The other thread wending its way through early psychological theories was that of mental disease, or **psychopathology.** The concept of psychopathology has been called "one of the most durable, resilient and influential of all criminological ideas."[17] In its original formulation, psychopathology embodied the notion of a diseased mind. It described a particular form of insanity referred to as "moral idiocy," which was thought to have a constitutional, or physiological, basis. The concept is summarized in the words of Nolan Lewis, who wrote during his tenure as director of the New York State Psychiatric Institute and Hospital at Columbia University during World War II that "[t]he criminal, like other people, has lived a life of instinctive drives, of desires, of wishes, of feelings, but one in which his intellect has apparently functioned less effectually as a brake upon certain trends. His constitutional makeup deviates toward the abnormal, leading him into conflicts with the laws of society and its cultural patterns."[18]

**Conditioning** a psychological principle holding that the frequency of any behaviour can be increased or decreased through reward, punishment, and/or association with other stimuli.

**Psychopathology** the study of pathological mental conditions, that is, mental illness.

## The Psychopathic Personality

The term *psychopathy* comes from the Greek words *psyche* (meaning "soul" or "mind") and *pathos* ("suffering" or "illness"). The word appears to have been coined by the nineteenth-century German psychiatrist, Richard von Krafft-Ebing (1840–1902),[19] making

Psychopath or
sociopath a person with
a personality disorder,
especially one
manifested in
aggressively antisocial
behaviour, which is
often said to be the
result of a poorly
developed superego.

its way into English psychiatric literature through the writings of Polish-born American psychiatrist Bernard Glueck (1884–1972)[20] and William Healy (1869–1963).[21] The **psychopath,** also called a **sociopath,** was usually viewed as perversely cruel, often without thought or feeling for his or her victims.[22] By the outbreak of World War II, the role of the psychopathic personality in crime causation had become central to psychological theorizing. In 1944, for example, the well-known psychiatrist David Abrahamsen wrote, "[w]hen we seek to explain the riddle of human conduct in general and of antisocial behavior in particular, the solution must be sought in the personality."[23]

The concept of a psychopathic personality, which by its very definition is asocial, was fully developed by **Hervey Cleckley** in his 1964 book *The Mask of Sanity.*[24] Cleckley described the psychopath as a "moral idiot," or as one who does not feel empathy with others, even though that person may be fully cognizant of what is objectively happening around them. The central defining characteristic of a psychopath is *poverty of affect,* or the inability to accurately imagine how others think and feel. Hence, it becomes possible for a psychopath to inflict pain and engage in acts of cruelty without appreciation for the victim's suffering. Charles Manson, for example, whom some have called a psychopath, once told a television reporter, "I could take this book and beat you to death with it, and I wouldn't feel a thing. It'd be just like walking to the drugstore."

In *The Mask of Sanity,* Cleckley describes numerous characteristics of the psychopathic personality, including the following:

- absence of delusions, hallucinations, or other signs of psychosis;
- inability to feel guilt or shame;
- unreliability;
- chronic lying;
- superficial charm;
- above-average intelligence;
- ongoing antisocial behaviour;
- inability to learn from experience; and
- self-centredness.

According to Cleckley, psychopathic indicators appear early in life, often in the teenage years. They include lying, fighting, stealing, and vandalism. Even earlier signs may be found, according to some authors, in bedwetting, cruelty to animals, sleepwalking, and fire-setting.[25]

**Robert Hare,** from the University of British Columbia, has developed a Psychopathy Checklist—Revised (PCL-R), based on Cleckley's criteria of psychopathy. Intended for use as a diagnostic tool, the PCL-R includes 22 indicators of psychopathy. Individuals are scored from "zero" to "three" for each item, with "zero" indicating not applicable, "one" uncertain, and "two" definitely present. Obviously, the higher the score the more likely that the individual is a psychopath. Currently, the PCL-R is being used to assess both adult and young offenders in Canada.[26]

The terms *psychopath* and *criminal* are not synonymous. Cleckley and others have noted that one can be a psychopath and not a criminal. Individuals manifesting many of the characteristics of a psychopathic personality, however, are likely, sooner or later, to run afoul of the law. As one writer on the topic says, "[t]he impulsivity and aggression, the selfishness in achieving one's own immediate needs, and the disregard for society's rules and laws bring these people to the attention of the criminal justice system."[27] Studies attempting to identify groups of noncriminal psychopaths have been inconclusive.[28]

CHAPTER 6

171

**Psychological and
Psychiatric
Foundations of
Criminal Behaviour**

The causes of psychopathology are unclear. Somatogenic causes, or those based on physiological features of the human organism, are said to include a malfunctioning of the central nervous system characterized by a low state of arousal that drives the sufferer to seek excitement, as well as brain abnormalities that may have been present in most psychopaths since birth. Work by Hare shows that an **electroencephalogram (EEG)** taken of a psychopathic patient is frequently abnormal, reflecting "a malfunction of some ... inhibitory mechanisms," making it unlikely that the psychopath will "learn to inhibit behavior that is likely to lead to punishment."[29] It is difficult, however, to diagnose psychopathology through physiological measurements, since similar EEG patterns also show up in patients with other types of disorders. Psychogenic causes, or those rooted in early interpersonal experiences, are said to include the inability to form attachments to parents or other caregivers early in life, sudden separation from the mother during the first 6 months of life, and other early forms of insecurity. In short, a lack of love, or the sensed inability to unconditionally depend on one central loving figure (typically the mother in most psychological literature), immediately following birth is often posited as a major psychogenic factor contributing to psychopathic development. Other psychogenic causes have been identified to include deficiencies in childhood role playing, the inability to identify with one's parents during childhood and adolescence, and severe rejection by others.

Most studies of psychopaths have involved male subjects. Researchers have focused little on female psychopaths, and it is believed that only a small proportion of all psychopaths are women.[30] What little research there is suggests that female psychopaths possess many of the same definitive characteristics as do their male counterparts, and that they assume their psychopathic roles at similarly early ages.[31] The lifestyles of female psychopaths, however, appear to emphasize sexual misconduct, including lifestyles involving abnormally high levels of sexual activity. Such research, however, can be misleading because cultural expectations of female sexual behaviour inherent in early studies may not always have been in keeping with reality. That is, so little may have been accurately known about female sexual activity to early researchers that the behaviour of women judged to be psychopaths may have actually been far closer to the norm than originally believed.

**Electroencephalogram (EEG)** electrical measurements of brain wave activity.

Charles Manson achieved notoriety because he seemed so difficult to understand. What do you think motivated his crimes? *Corbis-Bettmann.*

## Theory in Perspective
### Types of Psychological and Psychiatric Theories

---

**PSYCHOLOGICAL AND PSYCHIATRIC THEORIES**

Derived from the behavioural sciences and focusing on the *individual* as the unit of analysis.

---

**Psychiatric Criminology,** also known as **Forensic Psychiatry.** Envisions a complex set of drives and motives operating from recesses deep within the personality to determine behaviour.

**Period:** 1930s–present
**Theorists:** Hervey Cleckley, Robert Hare, and others
**Concepts:** Psychopath, sociopath, antisocial, asocial personality

---

**Psychoanalytic Criminology.** A psychiatric approach developed by the Austrian psychiatrist Sigmund Freud that emphasizes the role of personality in human behaviour, and which sees deviant behaviour as the result of a dysfunctional personality.

**Period:** 1920s–present
**Theorists:** Sigmund Freud and others
**Concepts:** Id, ego, superego, sublimation, psychotherapy, Thanatos, neurosis, psychosis, schizophrenia

---

**Frustration-Aggression Theory.** Holds that frustration is a natural consequence of living and a root cause of crime. Criminal behaviour can be a form of adaptation when it results in stress reduction.

**Period:** 1940s–present
**Theorist:** J. Dollard, Albert Bandura, Richard H. Walters, S.M. Halleck
**Concepts:** Frustration, aggression, displacement, catharsis, alloplastic and autoplastic adaptation

---

**Social Learning Theory.** A psychological perspective that says people learn how to behave by modelling themselves after others whom they have the opportunity to observe.

**Period:** 1950s–present
**Theorists:** Albert Bandura and others
**Concepts:** Interpersonal aggression, modelling, disengagement

---

**Behaviour Theory.** A psychological perspective positing that individual behaviour that is rewarded will increase in frequency, while that which is punished will decrease.

**Period:** 1940s–present
**Theorists:** B.F. Skinner and others
**Concepts:** Operant behaviour, conditioning, stimulus-response, reward, punishment

CHAPTER 6

173

**Psychological and
Psychiatric
Foundations of
Criminal Behaviour**

The terms *sociopath* and *psychopath* have fallen into professional disfavour in recent years. By 1968, the American Psychiatric Association's *Diagnostic and Statistical Manual of Mental Disorders*[32] had discontinued use of both terms, replacing them with such jargon as "antisocial" or "asocial" personality. In that year, the APA manual changed to a description of the **antisocial (asocial) personality** type as "individuals who are basically unsocialized and whose behavior pattern brings them repeatedly into conflicts with society. They are incapable of significant loyalty to individuals, groups, or social values. They are grossly selfish, callous, irresponsible, impulsive, and unable to feel guilt or to learn from experience and punishment. Frustration tolerance is low. They tend to blame others or offer plausible rationalization for their behavior."[33] A recent Canadian study of penitentiary inmates in Quebec,[34] which attempts to classify criminal offenders by type of mental disorder, determined that antisocial personalities comprise 46.6 percent of all inmates, while schizophrenics account for 6.3 percent, manic-depressives another 1.6 percent, drug-disordered persons 18.6 percent, depressed individuals 8.1 percent, and alcohol abuse–related suffers another 33.1 percent. A review[35] of 20 such studies found great variation in the degree and type of disorder said to be prevalent among incarcerated offenders. The studies categorized from 0.5 to 26 percent of all inmates as psychotic, 2.4 to 28 percent as mentally subnormal, 5.6 to 70 percent as psychopathic, 2 to 7.9 percent as neurotic, and from 11 to 80 percent of inmates tested as suffering from mental disorders induced by alcoholism or excessive drinking. Generally, however, such studies conclude that few convicted felons are free from mental impairment of one sort or another.

> **Antisocial** or **asocial**
> **personality** refers to
> individuals who are
> basically unsocialized
> and whose behaviour
> pattern brings them
> repeatedly into conflict
> with society.

## Personality Types and Crime

In 1964, a British psychiatrist named **Hans Eysenck** published *Crime and Personality*,[36] a book-length treatise in which he explained crime as the result of fundamental personality characteristics linked to individual central nervous system characteristics. Eysenck described three personality dimensions, each with links to criminality. Psychoticism, which Eysenck said "is believed to be correlated with criminality at all stages,"[37] is defined by characteristics such as a lack of empathy, creativeness, tough-mindedness, and antisociability. Psychoticism, said Eysenck, is also frequently characterized by hallucinations and delusions. Extroverts were described as carefree, dominant, and venturesome—operating with high levels of energy. "The typical extrovert," Eysenck wrote "is sociable, likes parties, has many friends, needs to have people to talk to, and does not like reading or studying by himself."[38] Neuroticism, the third of the personality characteristics Eysenck described, was said to be typical of people who are irrational, shy, moody, and emotional.

According to Eysenck, of these three personality types psychotics are the most likely to be criminal, because they combine high degrees of emotionalism with similarly high levels of extroversion. Individuals with such characteristics, claimed Eysenck, are especially difficult to socialize and to train. Eysenck cited many studies in which children and others who harboured characteristics of psychoticism, extroversion, and neuroticism performed poorly on conditioning tests designed to measure how quickly they would respond appropriately to external stimuli. Conscience, said Eysenck, is fundamentally a conditioned reflex. Therefore, an individual who does not take well to conditioning will not fully develop a conscience and will continue to exhibit the asocial behavioural traits of a very young child.

Eysenck's approach might be termed *biopsychology*, because he claimed that personality traits were fundamentally dependent upon physiology—specifically upon the individual's autonomic nervous system, which Eysenck described as "underlying the behavioral trait of emotionality or neuroticism."[39] Some individuals were said to possess nervous systems that could not handle a great deal of stimulation. Such individuals, like the introvert, shun excitement and are easily trained. They rarely become criminal offenders. Those who possess nervous systems that need stimulation, however, seek excitement and are far more likely to turn to crime. As support for his thesis, Eysenck cited studies of twins showing that identical twins were much more likely than fraternal twins to perform similarly on simple behavioural tests. In particular, Eysenck quoted from the work of J. B. S. Haldane, who was reputed to be a "world-famous geneticist." Haldane, having studied the criminality of 13 sets of identical twins, concluded, "[a]n analysis of the thirteen cases shows not the faintest evidence of freedom of the will in the ordinary sense of the word. A man of a certain constitution, put in a certain environment, will be a criminal. Taking the record of any criminal, we could predict the behavior of a monozygotic twin placed in the same environment. Crime is destiny."[40] Up to two-thirds of all behavioural variance, claimed Eysenck, could be attributed to "a strong genetic basis."

## Early Psychiatric Theories

**Psychiatric criminology** theories derived from the medical sciences, including neurology, and which, like other psychological theories, focus on the individual as the unit of analysis. Psychiatric theories form the basis of psychiatric criminology.

**Forensic psychiatry** that branch of psychiatry having to do with the study of crime and criminality.

Psychological criminology, with its traditional dual emphasis on (1) early forces that shape personality and (2) conditioned behaviour, can be distinguished from **psychiatric criminology,** also known as **forensic psychiatry,** which envisions a complex set of drives and motives operating from hidden recesses deep within the personality to determine behaviour. David Abrahamsen, a psychiatrist writing in 1944, explains crime this way: "[a]ntisocial behavior is a direct expression of an aggression or may be a direct or indirect manifestation of a distorted erotic drive. Crime," said Abrahamsen, "may ... be considered a product of a person's tendencies and the situation of the moment interacting with his mental resistance."[41] The key questions to be answered by psychiatric criminology, according to Abrahamsen, are "[w]hat creates the criminal impulse? What stimulates and gives it direction?" A later forensic psychiatrist[42] answered the question this way: "Every criminal is such by reason of unconscious forces within him. ..." Forensic psychiatry explains crime as being caused by biological and psychological urges mediated through consciousness. Little significance is placed upon the role of the environment external to the individual after the first few formative years of life. Psychiatric theories are derived from the medical sciences, including neurology, and, like other psychological theories, focus on the individual as the unit of analysis.

# Criminal Behaviour as Maladaption

## The Psychoanalytic Perspective

**Psychoanalysis** the theory of human psychology founded by Freud and based on the concepts of the unconscious, resistance, repression, sexuality, and the Oedipus complex.[43]

Perhaps the best known psychiatrist of all time is **Sigmund Freud** (1856–1939). Freud coined the term *psychoanalysis* in 1896 and based an entire theory of human

CHAPTER 6

175

**Psychological and
Psychiatric
Foundations of
Criminal Behaviour**

behaviour on it. From the point of view of psychoanalysis, criminal behaviour is maladaptive, or the product of inadequacies inherent in the offender's personality. Significant inadequacies may result in full-blown mental illness, which in itself can be a direct cause of crime. The psychoanalytic perspective encompasses diverse notions such as personality, neurosis, psychosis, and more specific concepts such as transference, sublimation, and repression. **Psychotherapy,** referred to in its early days as the "talking cure" because it highlighted patient–therapist communication, is the attempt to relieve patients of their mental disorders through the application of psychoanalytical principles and techniques.

According to Freud, the personality is made up of three components—the id, the ego, and the superego—as shown in Figure 6.1. The **id** is that fundamental aspect of the personality from which drives, wishes, urges, and desires emanate. Freud focused primarily on love, aggression, and sex as fundamental drives in any personality. The id is direct and singular in purpose. It operates according to the pleasure principle, seeking full and immediate gratification of its needs. Individuals, however, were said to rarely be fully aware of the urges that percolate up (occasionally into awareness) from the id, because it is a largely unconscious region of the mind. Nonetheless, from the Freudian perspective each of us carries within our id the prerequisite motivation for criminal behaviour. We are, each one of us, potential murderers, sexual aggressors, and thieves—our drives and urges kept in check only by other, controlling aspects of our personalities.

**Psychotherapy** a form of psychiatric treatment based on psychoanalytical principles and techniques.

**Id** the aspect of the personality from which drives, wishes, urges, and desires emanate. More formally, it is the division of the psyche associated with instinctual impulses and demands for immediate satisfaction of primitive needs.[44]

## Figure 6.1

*The Psychoanalytic Structure of Personality*

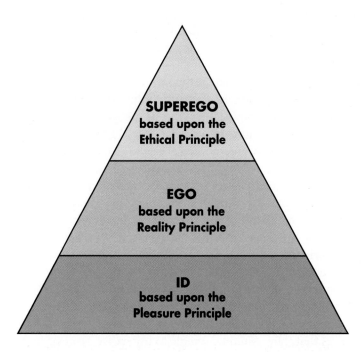

**SUPEREGO**
based upon the
**Ethical Principle**

**EGO**
based upon the
**Reality Principle**

**ID**
based upon the
**Pleasure Principle**

A second component of the personality, the **ego,** is primarily charged with reality testing. Freud's use of the word *ego* should not be confused with popular practice, whereby a person might talk about an "inflated ego" or an "egotistical person." For Freud, the ego was primarily concerned with how objectives might be best accomplished. The ego tends to effect strategies for the individual that maximize pleasure and minimize pain. It lays out the various paths of action that can lead to wish fulfillment. The ego inherently recognizes that it may be necessary to delay gratification to achieve a more fulfilling long-term goal.

The **superego,** the last component of the personality, is much like a moral guide to right and wrong. If properly developed, it assays the ego's plans, dismissing some as morally inappropriate while accepting others as ethically viable. The id of a potential rapist, for example, might be filled with lustful drives, and his ego may develop a variety of alternative plans whereby those drives might be fulfilled, some legal and some illegal. His superego will, however, if the individual's personality is relatively well integrated and the superego is properly developed, turn the individual away from law-violating behaviour based on his sensual desires and guide the ego to select a path of action that is in keeping with social convention. When the dictates of the superego are not followed, feelings of guilt may result. The superego is one of the most misunderstood of Freudian concepts. In addition to elements of conscience, the superego also contains what Freud called the *ego-ideal,* which is a symbolic representation of what society values. The ego-ideal differs from the conscience in that it is less forceful in controlling behaviour in the absence of the likelihood of discovery.

Although Freud wrote little about crime per se, he did spend much of his time attempting to account for a variety of abnormal behaviour, much of which might lead to violations of the criminal law. One way in which a person might be led into crime, according to the perspective of psychoanalysis, is as the result of a poorly developed superego. In the individual without a fully functional superego, the mind is left to fall back on the ego's reality-testing ability. To put it simply, the ego, operating without a moral guide, may select a path of action which, although expedient at the time, violates the law. Individuals suffering from poor superego development are likely to seek immediate gratification without giving a great deal of thought to the long-term consequences of the choices they may make in the moment.

From the Freudian point of view, inadequate sublimation can be another cause of crime. **Sublimation** is the psychological process whereby one item of consciousness comes to be symbolically substituted for another. Sublimation is often a healthy process. Freud held that the many outstanding accomplishments of the human species have been due to sublimation, through which powerful sexual and aggressive drives are channelled into socially constructive activity. However, crime can result from improper sublimation. According to Freud, for example, a man may hate his mother, his hatred being perhaps the faulty by-product of the striving for adult independence. He may, however, be unable to give voice to that hatred directly. Perhaps the mother is too powerful, or the experience of confronting his mother would be too embarrassing for the man. The man may act out his hatred for his mother, however, by attacking other women whom he symbolically substitutes in his mind for the mother figure. Hence, from the Freudian perspective men who beat their wives, become rapists, sexually harass co-workers, or otherwise abuse women may be enacting feelings derived from early life experiences that they would be unable to otherwise express.

CHAPTER 6

177

**Psychological and
Psychiatric
Foundations of
Criminal Behaviour**

Sigmund Freud (1856–1939), examining a manuscript in the office of his Vienna home, circa 1930. *Corbis-Bettmann.*

Sublimation, like many other psychoanalytical concepts, is a slippery idea. Mother hatred, for example, although a plausible explanation for acts of violence by men against women, is difficult to demonstrate, and the link between such hidden feelings and adult action is impossible to prove. Even so, should an offender be so diagnosed it would do little good for him to deny the psychoanalytical explanation assigned to him, because doing so would only result in the professional reproach, "Yes, but you have hidden knowledge of your true feelings from yourself. You are not aware of why you act the way you do!"

Freud also postulated the existence of a death instinct, which he called **Thanatos**. According to Freud, all living things, which he referred to as "animate matter," have a fundamental desire to relax back into an inanimate state, or death. Living, said Freud, takes energy and cunning. Hence death, at least at some level, is an easier choice because it releases the organism from the need for continued expenditure of energy. Thanatos was seen as contributing to many of the advances made by the human species and as underlying a large proportion of individual accomplishments. Were it not for a wish to die, operative at some basic instinctual level, said Freud, few people would have the courage to take risks—and without the assumption of risk, precious little progress is possible in any sphere of life. The notion of an innate death wish has been used to explain why some offenders seem to behave in ways that ensure their eventual capture. Serial killers who send taunting messages to the police, terrorists who tell the media of their planned activities or take credit for public attacks, rapists who "accidentally" leave their wallets at the scene, burglars who break into occupied dwellings may all, for the most part unconsciously, be seeking to be stopped, captured, punished, and even killed.

**Thanatos** a death wish.

**Neurosis** functional
disorders of the mind or
of the emotions
involving anxiety,
phobia, or other
abnormal behaviour.

From the Freudian perspective, **neurosis,** a minor form of mental illness, may also lead to crime. Neurotic individuals are well in touch with reality but may find themselves anxious, fearful of certain situations, or unable to help themselves in others. Fear of heights, for example, may be a neurosis, as may be compulsive handwashing, or eating disorders. A classic example of the compulsive neurotic can be found in the individual who uses paper towels to open doorknobs, refraining from touching the knob directly for fear of picking up germs. Although such behaviour may be unreasonable from the point of view of others, it is reality based (there *are* germs on doorknobs) and, for the individual demonstrating it, probably unavoidable. Most neuroses do not lead to crime. Some, however, can. A few years ago, for example, a man from Iowa was sentenced to nearly 6 years in prison and fined $200 000 for the theft of more than 21 000 rare books from hundreds of libraries.[47] The offender, whose compulsive interest in rare books began at yard sales and with searches in trash dumpsters, may have seen himself as involved in a messianic mission to preserve recorded history. Compulsive shoplifters may also be manifesting another form of neurosis—one in which a powerful need to steal can drive even well-heeled individuals to risk arrest and jail.

## The Psychotic Offender

For many law-abiding citizens, extreme forms of criminal behaviour are often difficult to understand, as the gruesome story of Sandy Charles illustrates.[48] At his trial, it was argued that Charles was responding to delusional beliefs that if he consumed the flesh of another human he would acquire supernatural powers. In July 1995, at the age of 14, Charles lured a 7-year-old playmate into a wooded area near his LaRonge, Saskatchewan home, where he killed and mutilated him. He then cut strips from his victim's flesh and boiled them on a stove. Charged with first-degree murder, Charles pled insanity due to his diagnosed schizophrenia. A jury accepted his defence of insanity and found him not criminally responsible for his actions.

Sandy Charles was found not criminally responsible for the death and mutilation of a playmate. How are these types of offenders dealt with by the Canadian criminal justice system? *The Canadian Press, Saskatoon StarPheonix, Richard Marjan.*

Some seemingly inexplicable forms of criminality may be the result of **psychosis.** Whereas neurotic individuals often face only relatively minor problems in living, psychotic people, according to psychiatric definitions, are out of touch with reality in some fundamental way. They may suffer from hallucinations, delusions, or other breaks with reality. The classic psychotic thinks he is Napoleon, or sees spiders covering what others see only as a bare wall. Individuals suffering from a psychosis are said to be psychotic. Psychoses may be either organic, that is, caused by physical damage to, or abnormalities in, the brain, or functional, that is, those with no known physical cause. Gwynn Nettler says "[t]hought disorder is the hallmark of psychosis ... people are called crazy when, at some extremity, they cannot 'think straight.'"[49] Nettler identifies three characteristics of psychotic individuals: "(1) a grossly distorted conception of reality, (2) moods, and swings of mood, that seem inappropriate to circumstance, and (3) marked inefficiency in getting along with others and caring for oneself."[50] Psychotic persons have also been classified as schizophrenic or paranoid schizophrenic. **Schizophrenics** are said to be characterized by disordered or disjointed thinking, in which the types of logical associations they make are atypical of other people. **Paranoid schizophrenics** suffer from delusions and hallucinations.

Unfortunately, psychiatrists have not been able to agree on definitive schizophrenic criteria that would allow for convenient application of the term. One prominent psychiatrist writes of "how varying ... schizophrenia may appear, ranging from no striking symptoms at all to conspicuous psychotic features. ... Thus on the surface," he continues, "the schizophrenic may appear normal and, to some extent, lead a conventional life."[51] The same author later tells us "[s]chizophrenia is not a clearly defined disease. ... It is characterized rather by a ... kind of alteration of thinking or feeling. ..."[52] At the very least, then, we can safely say that schizophrenia is a disorganization of the personality. In its most extreme form, it may manifest itself by way of hallucinations, delusions, and seemingly irrational behaviour.

With these caveats in mind, it is fair to say that psychoses may lead to crime in a number of ways. In a highly publicized case in Ottawa, Ontario, Jeffrey Arenburg waited outside a local television station and shot and killed well-known sportscaster Brian Smith as he left work. Arenburg, who had a history of paranoid schizophrenia, believed that radio and television stations were broadcasting his thoughts through the fillings in his teeth. His assault on Smith was his attempt to stop these broadcasts.

**Psychosis** a form of mental illness in which sufferers are said to be out of touch with reality.

**Schizophrenics** mentally ill individuals who are out of touch with reality and suffer from disjointed thinking.

**Paranoid schizophrenics** schizophrenic individuals who suffer from delusions and hallucinations.

## The Link Between Frustration and Aggression

In his early writings, Freud suggested that aggressive behaviour was a response to frustration. Aggression toward others, Freud said, is a natural response to frustrating limitations imposed upon a person. The frustration-aggression thesis was later developed more fully in the writings of J. Dollard,[53] Albert Bandura, Richard H. Walters, and others. Dollard's frustration-aggression theory held that although frustration can lead to various forms of behaviour—including regression, sublimation, and aggressive fantasy—direct aggression toward others is its most likely consequence. Because everyone suffers some form of frustration throughout life, beginning with weaning and toilet training, Dollard argued, aggression is a natural consequence of living. Dollard pointed out, however, that aggression could be manifested in socially acceptable ways (perhaps through contact sports, military or law enforcement careers, or simple verbal attacks) and that it could be engaged in vicariously by observing others who are acting violently (as in movies, on television, through popular fiction, and so on). Dollard applied the psychoanalytical term "displacement" to the type of violence that is vented on something or someone not the source of the original frustration and suggested that satisfying one's aggressive urges through observation was a form of "catharsis."

The story of Pierre Lebrun, a former employee of a public transit company, provides us with an example of the frustration-aggression theory as it applies to real-life crime. In April 1999, the 40-year-old Lebrun entered the maintenance garage at a public transportation company in Ottawa and opened fire with a high-powered .30-06–calibre hunting rifle, killing four people and wounding two others before taking his own life. In his suicide note left at his parents' home, Lebrun expressed his anger towards certain former co-workers whom, he claimed, had teased him for a speech impediment. Ironically, none of the men on his "hit list" were victimized. He had been fired by his company several years earlier but his union fought the dismissal and won. Lebrun had resigned from the company 4 months before the killing. It appears he was acting out of the frustrations born of his experiences with his co-workers.[54]

Some psychologists have tried to identify what it is that causes some individuals to displace aggression or to experience it vicariously (through catharsis), while others respond violently and directly toward the immediate source of their frustrations. Andrew Henry and James Short,[55] for example, writing in the 1950s, suggested that child-rearing practices are a major determining factor in such a causal nexus. Restrictive parents who both punish and love their children, said Henry and Short, will engender in their children the ability to suppress outward expressions of aggression. When one parent punishes and the other loves, or when both punish but neither show love, children can be expected to show anger directly and perhaps even immediately, because they will not be threatened with the loss of love. Physical punishment, explained Henry and Short, rarely threatens the loss of love, and children so punished cannot be expected to refrain from direct displays of anger.

In 1960, Stewart Palmer[56] studied murderers and their siblings to determine the degree of frustration they had been exposed to as children. He found that male murderers had experienced much more frustration than their brothers—in fact, more than twice as many frustrating experiences, ranging from difficult births to serious illnesses, childhood beatings, severe toilet training, and negative school experiences, were reported by the murderers than by their law-abiding siblings.

## Crime as Adaptive Behaviour

Some psychiatric perspectives have held that "… crime is a compromise, representing for the individual the most satisfactory method of adjustment to inner conflicts which he cannot express otherwise. Thus, his acting out the crime fulfills a certain aim or purpose."[57] One pressing need of many criminals, according to some psychologists, is the need to be punished—which arises, according to psychiatric theory, from a sense of guilt. Psychiatrists who suggest that the need to be punished is a motivating factor in criminal behaviour are quick to point out that such a need may be a closely guarded

CHAPTER 6

**181**

**Psychological and
Psychiatric
Foundations of
Criminal Behaviour**

secret, unknown even to the offender. Hence, from the psychiatric point of view, many drives, motives, and wishes are unconscious or even repressed by people who harbour them. The concept of repression holds that the human mind may choose to keep certain aspects of itself out of consciousness, possibly because of shame, self-loathing, or a simple lack of adequate introspection. The desire for punishment, however, sometimes comes to the fore. In 1993, for example, Westley Dodd was hanged to death by authorities in the state of Washington for the kidnap, rape, and murder of three little boys 4 years earlier. Dodd, who said he had molested dozens of children over the course of a decade, sought the death penalty after he was convicted, saying he deserved to die and vowing to sue the American Civil Liberties Union (ACLU) or anyone else who sought to save him.[58]

Crime can be adaptive in other ways as well. Some psychiatrists see it as an adaptation to life's stresses. According to Seymour L. Halleck,[59] turning to crime can provide otherwise disenfranchised individuals with a sense of power and purpose. In Halleck's words, "[d]uring the planning and execution of a criminal act the offender is a free man. … The value of this brief taste of freedom cannot be overestimated. Many of the criminal's apparently unreasonable actions are efforts to find a moment of autonomy. …"[60] Halleck says that crime can also provide "excellent rationalizations" for perceived inadequacies—especially for those whose lives have been failures when judged against the benchmarks of the wider society. "The criminal is able to say …, 'I could have been successful if I had not turned to crime. All my troubles have come to me because I have been bad.'"[61] Hence, crime, according to Halleck, provides "a convenient resource for denying, forgetting or ignoring … other inadequacies."

Insofar as the choice of crime reduces stresses that the individual faces by producing changes in the environment (empowerment), it is referred to as an **alloplastic adaptation.** When crime leads to stress reduction as a result of internal changes in beliefs, value systems, and so forth, it is called **autoplastic adaptation.** The offender who

**Alloplastic adaptation**
that form of adjustment resulting from changes in the environment surrounding an individual.

**Autoplastic adaptation**
that form of adjustment resulting from changes within an individual.

Westley Alan Dodd, hanged in 1993 for murdering young boys whom he molested. "People need to know it's the only thing that will stop me," he said of his execution. Might there have been some other alternative?
*Benjamin Benschneider/Seattle Times/Gamma-Liaison, Inc.*

is able to deny responsibility for other failures by turning to crime is said to be seeking autoplastic adaptation. Because other forms of behaviour may also meet many of the same needs as does crime, Halleck points out that an individual may select crime over various other behavioural alternatives only when no reasonable alternatives are available or when criminal behaviour has inherent advantages—as might be the case under instances of economic or social oppression. (That is, individuals who are actively discriminated against may find personal and political significance in violating the laws of the oppressing society.)

In any case, from Halleck's point of view crime "has many advantages even when considered independently of the criminal's conscious or unconscious needs for gratification."[62] In other words, even though crime can be immediately rewarding or intensely pleasureful, says Halleck, such rewards are more "fringe benefits" than anything else. The central significance of criminal behaviour for most offenders is that it "is an action which helps one survive with dignity."[63] Halleck tells us that "[w]e cannot understand the criminal unless we appreciate that his actions are much more than an effort to find a specific gratification."[64] In the final analysis, criminal behaviour is, from Halleck's point of view, a form of adjustment to stress and oppression.

Another approach to stress as a causative agent in crime commission suggests that stress may lead to aggression toward others and toward oneself (i.e., self-destructive behaviour such as suicide, smoking, and abuse of alcohol).[65] This approach attempts to measure stress at the societal level, arguing that although the relationship between stress and aggression has been studied at the individual level, "the neglect of social stress as an explanation for society-to-society differences in aggression may be partially due to a lack of an objective means of comparing the stressfulness of life in different societies ...."[66] Concluding that societal stress levels heighten levels of aggression, it is suggested that social policies should be created to reduce the impact of stressful events such as having to stop work, foreclosing on a mortgage, and dropping out of school.

Finally, we should recognize that perceptions vary, and although criminal behaviour may appear to be a valid choice for some individuals who are seeking viable responses to perceived stresses and oppression, their perceptions may not be wholly accurate. In other words, misperceived stress and oppression may still lead to crime, even when far simpler solutions may be found in a more realistic appraisal of one's situation.

# Social Learning Theory

**Social learning theory** a psychological perspective that says people learn how to behave by modelling themselves after others whom they have the opportunity to observe.

More recently, **Albert Bandura** has attempted to develop a comprehensive **social learning theory** of aggression. Bandura tells us that "[a] complete theory of aggression must explain how aggressive patterns are developed, what provokes people to behave aggressively, and what sustains such actions after they have been initiated."[67] Although everyone is capable of aggression, he says, "[p]eople are not born with ... repertoires of aggressive behavior. They must learn them." He goes on to say, "the specific forms that aggressive behavior takes, the frequency with which it is expressed, the situation in which it is displayed, and the specific targets selected for attack are largely determined by social learning factors." According to Bandura, people learn by observ-

CHAPTER 6
183
**Psychological and
Psychiatric
Foundations of
Criminal Behaviour**

ing others. In some of his early work, Bandura experimented with children who observed adult role models striking inflatable cartoon characters. When the children were observed later, they too exhibited similarly aggressive behaviour toward the models. Bandura also studied violence on television and concluded that "[t]elevision is an effective tutor. Both laboratory and controlled field studies in which young children and adolescents are repeatedly shown either violence or nonviolent fare, disclose that exposure to film violence shapes the form of aggression and typically increases interpersonal aggressiveness in everyday life." A later study,[68] by other researchers, showed that even after 10 years the level of violence engaged in by young adults was directly related to the degree of violent television they had been exposed to as children.

Social learning theory also shows how people can model the behaviour of others. Bandura explained modelling behaviour by reference to the frequent hijacking of domestic airliners to Cuba occurring in the United States in the late 1960s and early 1970s. Such hijackings, Bandura found, followed immediately on the heels of similar incidents in Eastern European nations under Soviet domination. American hijackings, he said, were simply modelling those in Europe, and hijackers in the United States were learning from news accounts of their foreign tutors.

Once aggressive patterns of behaviour have been acquired, it becomes necessary to show how they can be activated. Aggression can be provoked, Bandura suggests, through physical assaults and verbal threats and insults, as well as by thwarting a person's hopes or obstructing his or her goal-seeking behaviour. Deprivation and "adverse reductions in the conditions of life" (a lowered standard of living, the onset of disease, a spouse leaving or caught cheating, etc.) are other potential triggers of aggression. Bandura adds, however, that a human being's ability to foresee the future consequences of present behaviour infuses another dimension into the activation of learned patterns of aggression. That is, aggressive behaviour can be perceived as holding future benefits for individuals exhibiting it. In short, it can be seen as a means to a desired end.

An example of aggression that resulted from thwarted goal-seeking, and which may have been seen as holding future benefits for the boy involved, occurred on August 1, 1991. On that day, Gavin Mandin shot and killed his parents and two sisters.[69] Mandin, who was 15 at the time, waited in the family farmhouse not far from Edmonton, Alberta, for the rest of his family to return from a shopping trip. When the car pulled into the driveway, Mandin sighted through the scope of his pump-action, .22-calibre rifle and fired through a window and screen in the house. A bullet penetrated his father Maurice's temple as he stepped out of the car, killing him instantly. His mother, Susan, still in the car, looked up as another shot crashed through the car's windshield and entered her brain. Mandin then shot his two sisters, Isla, 12, and Janelle, 10, at point-blank range as they sat in the back seat of the car, first in the head and then with the rifle pressed against their chests. Mandin then drove the car with the bodies in it to an area of thick bush nearby. Using ropes and an all-terrain vehicle, Mandin dragged his father's body further into the bush.

By all accounts, Mandin's home life had been normal enough. Mandin was, reportedly, the "apple of his mother's eye" and she would defend him in all circumstances. However, there were signs that Mandin was not as enamoured with his family. Notes found behind Mandin's bed read, "I hate Janelle, I hate Susan, I hate Isla," and "Susan can't make me do anything. I wish she were dead." One particularly disturbing treatise said, "There will come the day when I rule. I will be the leader of the universe.

The body of Gavin's father, Maurice, was found in the bush. By all accounts, Gavin Mandin came from a loving, contented family. Could his actions be seen as stemming from thwarted goals? *The Alberta Report*

All I love and desire will be mine. I will be the most powerful man on earth. I will have all the world it will be my backyard, all my enemies will die by my hand."[70] During his interrogation by RCMP investigators, Mandin cited many reason for his actions. He stated that he was made to clean his room, carry groceries into the house, and wash dishes. He disliked going to church services with the family, so he put a lock on his door to keep them from disturbing him. Mandin told RCMP investigator Corporal Ted Lachuk, "Sometimes, like, I will have something important to say to my mother and she will be sitting down and eating and I will come up to her and say 'mom' and she won't do anything and I'll just keep calling her again and again. One time I called her eight or nine times and she didn't even answer. A couple of times I even tapped her on the shoulder and she ignores me and it really makes me angry." Shortly after being taken into custody, Mandin declared, "I guess I get the house now, eh?" Later he stated that he intended to use a $1 000 bond his mother had saved for him as an investment, to become a "zillionaire."[71]

Returning to Bandura, it is his contention that individuals sometimes become aggressive because they are rewarded for doing so. The early twentieth-century North American concept of a "macho" male figure—virile and masculine— for example, was often associated with the expectation of substantial reward. The macho male figure was the one who won the most respect from his fellows, inevitably came away with the greatest honours (on the playing field, in school, from the community, etc.), and eventually married the most desirable woman. Whether this perception was accurate, it was nonetheless subscribed to by a significant proportion of North American men and, for many decades, served as a guide to daily behaviour.

CHAPTER 6
185
**Psychological and
Psychiatric
Foundations of
Criminal Behaviour**

Another form of reward can flow from aggression. Bandura called it the "reduction of aversive treatment." By this he meant that simply standing up for one's self can improve the way one is treated by others. Oftentimes, for example, standing up to a bully is the most effective way of dealing with the harassment one might otherwise face. Similarly, there is an old saying that "the squeaky wheel gets the grease," and it means, quite simply, that people who are the most demanding will be recognized. Aggressive people often get what they go after.

Bandura recognized that all persons have self-regulatory mechanisms that can ameliorate the tendency toward aggression. People reward or punish themselves, Bandura said, according to internal standards they have for judging their own behaviour. Hence, aggression may be inhibited in people who, for example, value religious, ethical, or moral standards of conduct such as compassion, thoughtfulness, and courtesy. Nonetheless, Bandura concluded, people who devalue aggression may still engage in it through a process he called "disengagement," whereby rationalizations are constructed to overcome internal inhibitions. Disengagement may result from (1) "attributing blame to one's victims," (2) dehumanization through bureaucratization, automation, urbanization, and high social mobility, (3) vindication of aggressive practices by legitimate authorities, and (4) desensitization resulting from repeated exposure to aggression in any of a variety of forms.

Social learning theory has been criticized for lacking comprehensive explanatory power. How, for example, can striking differences in sibling behaviour, when early childhood experiences were likely much the same, be explained? Similarly, why do apparent differences exist between the sexes with regard to degree and type of criminality—irrespective of social background and early learning experiences? More recent versions of social learning theory, sometimes called "cognitive social learning theory,"[72] attempt to account for such differences by hypothesizing that reflection and cognition play a significant role in interpreting what one observes and in determining responses. Hence, few people are likely to behave precisely as others, because they will have their own ideas about what observed behaviour means and about the consequences of emulation.

# Behaviour Theory

**Behaviour theory** has sometimes been called the "stimulus-response approach to human behavior. ... At the heart of behavior theory is the notion that behavior is determined by environmental consequences which it produces for the individual concerned."[73] When an individual's behaviour results in rewards, or in the receipt of feedback which the individual, for whatever reason, regards as rewarding, then it is likely that the behaviour will become more frequent. Under such circumstances, the behaviour in question is said to be reinforced. Conversely, when punishment follows behaviour, chances are that the frequency of that type of behaviour will decrease. The individual's responses are termed **operant behaviour,** because behavioural choices effectively operate upon the surrounding environment to produce consequences for the behaving individual. Similarly, stimuli provided by the environment become behavioural cues that serve to elicit conditioned responses from individuals. Responses are said to be conditioned according to the individual's past experiences,

**Behaviour theory** a psychological perspective positing that individual behaviour that is rewarded will increase in frequency, while that which is punished will decrease.

**Operant behaviour** behaviour that affects the environment in such a way as to produce responses or further behavioural cues.

wherein behavioural consequences effectively defined some forms of behaviour as desirable and others as undesirable. Behaviour theory is often employed by parents seeking to control children through a series of **rewards** and **punishments.** Young children may be punished, for example, with spanking, the loss of a favoured toy (at least for a period of time), a turned-off television, and so forth. Older children are often told what rules they are expected to obey and the rewards that they can anticipate receiving from adherence to those rules. They also know that punishments will follow if they do not obey the rules.

Rewards and punishments have been further divided into four conceptual categories: (1) positive rewards, which increase the frequency of approved behaviour by adding something desirable to the situation—as when a "good" child is given a toy; (2) negative rewards, which increase the frequency of approved behaviour by removing something distressful from the situation—as when a "good" child is permitted to skip the morning's chores; (3) positive punishments, which decrease the frequency of unwanted behaviour by adding something undesirable to the situation—as when a "bad" child is spanked; and (4) negative punishments, which decrease the frequency of unwanted behaviour by removing something desirable from the situation—as when a "bad" child's candy is taken away. According to behaviour theory, it is through the application of rewards and punishments that behaviour is shaped.

Behaviour theory differs from other psychological theories in that the major determinants of behaviour are envisioned as residing in the environment surrounding the individual rather than actually in the individual. Perhaps the best known proponent of behaviour theory is Burrhus Frederic Skinner (1904–1990), popularly referred to as **B. F. Skinner.** Skinner rejected unobservable psychological constructs, focusing instead on patterns of responses to external rewards and stimuli. Skinner did extensive animal research involving behavioural concepts and created the notion of programmed instruction, which allows students to work at their own pace and provides immediate rewards for learning accomplishments.

Although behaviour theory has much to say about the reformation of criminal offenders through the imposition of punishment, the approach is equally significant for its contributions to understanding the genesis of such behaviour. As one writer states, "it is the balance of reinforcement and punishment in an individual's learning history which will dictate the presence or absence of criminal behavior."[74] According to the behavioural model, crime results when individuals "receive tangible rewards (positive reinforcement) for engaging in delinquent and criminal behavior, particularly when no other attractive alternative is available."[75]

A few years ago, for example, Sundahkeh "Ron" Bethune, 15, shot and killed a 26-year-old pizza delivery man who gunned his car motor as Bethune attempted to rob him. Ron, who had been dabbling in the drug trade and who could afford high-priced clothing, jewellery, and other accoutrements of apparent wealth, was esteemed by many other young people in his North Carolina community. When the delivery man tried to run from Ron in front of a group of his friends, Bethune saw no other choice but to kill him. "I just had to show them I wasn't some little punk,"[76] he said afterward in a prison interview. Ron Bethune did not think of the long-term consequences of his behaviour on the night of the killing. All he wanted was to earn the approval of those who were watching him. The crowd's anticipated awestruck response to murder was all the reward Ron needed to pull the trigger that night. He is now serving 5 years for second-degree murder.

CHAPTER 6
**187**
**Psychological and
Psychiatric
Foundations of
Criminal Behaviour**

Behaviour theory has been criticized for ignoring the role that cognition plays in human behaviour. Martyrs, for example, persist in what may be defined by the wider society as undesirable behaviour, even in the face of severe punishment—including the loss of their own lives. No degree of punishment is likely to deter a martyr who answers to some higher call. Similarly, criminals who are punished for official law violations may find that their immediate social group interprets criminal punishment as status enhancing. From the point of view of behaviour theory, criminal punishments are in danger of losing sway over many forms of human behaviour in today's diverse society. Our society's fragmented value system leads to various interpretations of criminal punishments, thereby changing the significance of experiences such as arrest, conviction, and imprisonment. In times past, criminal offenders were often shunned and became social outcasts. Today, in some circles, those who have been judged criminal may find that their new status holds many rewards.

## Insanity and the Law

**Insanity** is a defence allowable in criminal courts. A criminal defendant may be found not guilty by reason of insanity and avoid punitive sanctions even when it is clear that he or she committed a legally circumscribed act. This area of law has been one of endless debate. Legal and psychiatric definitions of insanity or mental disorder rarely coincide. C. Ray Jeffery[78] writes that "[t]hree concepts are confused in the insanity defense": (1) psychiatric, (2) legal, and (3) neurological understandings of mental illness. Even so, psychotic offenders are more likely than most other kinds of criminal wrongdoers to be adjudicated insane or to have their degree of criminal culpability reduced by the courts in recognition of the mental problems they face. The burden of proving a claim of "not guilty by reason of insanity," however, falls upon the defendant.[79] Just as a person is assumed to be innocent at the start of any criminal trial, so too is the person assumed to be sane.

**Insanity (psychological)** persistent mental disorder or derangement.[77]

**Insanity (law)** a legally established inability to understand right from wrong, or to conform one's behaviour to the requirements of the law. Also, a defence allowable in criminal courts.

Insanity can be used as a defence against criminal charges. Lorena Bobbitt sobs on the witness stand before acquittal on charges she severed her husband's penis with a kitchen knife. Bobbitt claimed a kind of irresistible impulse. Should she have been acquitted? *Gary Hershorn/Corbis-Bettmann.*

The Criminal Code of Canada defines mental disorder as a "disease of the mind." Whether a specific condition is a disease of the mind, however, is a question of law. While medical evidence is used to assist a judge in deciding whether the accused suffers a disease of the mind, the Supreme Court of Canada has stated that the protection of public safety must also be considered. For example, if the accused suffers from a recurring condition that may continue to present a danger to the public, then, the Court has ruled, the accused's condition should be treated as a mental disorder.[80] A number of mental disorders are recognized by the courts as diseases of the mind. They include schizophrenia, paranoia, senile dementia, melancholia, various types of epilepsy, and delirium tremens caused by alcohol abuse. However, self-induced states caused by alcohol or drugs, and temporary conditions such as hysteria and concussion, are excluded.[81]

## The McNaughten Rule

Inherent in the discussion of insanity and the law is the concept of criminal responsibility. The roots of this notion are found in British tradition and, in particular, in the case of Daniel McNaughten (also spelled "M'Naughton" and "M'Naghton"). This case was one of the first instances within the Western legal tradition where insanity was accepted as a defence to criminal liability. McNaughten was accused of the 1844 killing of Edward Drummond, the secretary of British Prime Minister Sir Robert Peel. By all accounts, McNaughten had intended to kill Peel, but because he was suffering from mental disorganization shot Drummond instead, mistaking him for Peel. At his trial, the defence presented information to show that McNaughten was suffering from delusions, including the belief that Peel's political party was, in some vague way, persecuting him. The court accepted his lawyer's claims and the defence of insanity was established in Western law. Other jurisdictions were quick to adopt the **McNaughten rule**, as the judge's decision in the case came to be called. The McNaughten rule holds that individuals cannot be held criminally responsible for their actions if at the time of the offence either (1) they did not know what they were doing, or (2) they did not know that what they were doing was wrong.

McNaughten rule a standard for judging legal insanity which requires that offenders did not know what they were doing, or if they did, that they did not know it was wrong.

Today, the McNaughten rule is still followed in Canada when insanity is at issue in criminal cases. Critics of the McNaughten rule say that, although the notion of intent inherent within it appeals well to lawyers, "[i]t is … so alien to current concepts of human behavior that it has been vigorously attacked by psychiatrists. An obvious difficulty with the McNaughten rule is that practically everyone, regardless of the degree of his criminal disturbance, knows the nature and quality and rightness or wrongness of what he is doing."[82]

## Not Criminally Responsible by Reason of Mental Disorder

The Supreme Court decision in *R. v. Swain* in 1991 resulted in an overhaul of the existing legal insanity criteria and practices, most notably automatic and indefinite detention for those found legally insane. In that decision, the Court held not only that "[t]he duty of the trial judge to detain is unqualified by any standard whatsoever" but

CHAPTER 6
**189**
**Psychological and
Psychiatric
Foundations of
Criminal Behaviour**

also that, "[i]nsanity acquitees, … should be detained no longer than necessary to determine whether they are currently dangerous due to their insanity."[83] Bill C-30, which contained the amendments to the Criminal Code (Mental Disorder), was passed by Parliament in 1992. Those previously classified as "not guilty by reason of insanity" are now deemed to be **not criminally responsible by reason of mental disorder** **(NCRMD)**. This new classification reflects the basic principle of Canadian criminal law that to be convicted of a crime, the state must prove not only a wrongful act, but also a guilty mind. In the words of then Minister of Justice Kim Campbell, "The mental disorder provisions of the Criminal Code needed to be updated to reflect the evolution of society and the law. These changes will ensure that individuals are not deprived of their Charter rights. … At the same time, the amendments offer protection of the public from dangerous mentally disordered persons who come into conflict with the law."[84]

Interestingly, other countries use a variety of definitions of legal insanity. In the United States, where the issue falls within the jurisdiction of the individual state, there exist a number of alternatives. In addition to the McNaughten rule, the irresistible impulse test is employed in 18 states and holds that a defendant is not guilty of a criminal offence if the person, by virtue of his or her mental state or psychological condition, was not able to resist committing the action in question. The Durham rule states that an accused is not criminally responsible if his or her unlawful act was the product of mental disease or mental defect, where "disease" is a condition that is capable of improving or deteriorating and "defect" is an unchanging condition that may be congenital or the result of injury or a physical or mental disease. The substantial capacity test blends elements of the McNaughten rule with the irresistible impulse standard. The Brawner rule has been used in some states since 1972 and essentially dictates that the jury is left to constitute insanity. Finally, roughly one-quarter of the U.S. states have adopted the "guilty but mentally ill" (GBMI) standard. A GBMI verdict means that a person can be held responsible for a specific criminal act, even though a degree of mental incompetence may be present in his or her personality. Individuals adjudicated GBMI are, in effect, found guilty of the criminal offence with which they are charged but, because of their mental condition, are generally sent to psychiatric hospitals for treatment rather than to prison.[85]

**Not Criminally
Responsible by Reason of
Mental Disorder (NCRMD)**
a finding that offenders are responsible for committing the offence with which they are charged but, because of their prevailing mental condition, should be sent to a psychiatric hospital for treatment rather than to prison. The maximum length of stay is predetermined.

# Insanity as a Defence

The Criminal Code of Canada permits the defence of insanity, as follows:

| | | |
|---|---|---|
| Defence of Mental Disorder | **16.** (1) | No person is criminally responsible for an act committed or an omission made while suffering from a mental disorder that rendered the person incapable of appreciating the nature and quality of the act or omission or of knowing that it was wrong. |
| Presumption | (2) | Every person is presumed not to suffer from a mental disorder so as to be exempt from criminal responsibility by virtue of subsection (1), until the contrary is proved on the balance of probabilities. |
| Burden of Proof | (3) | The burden of proof that an accused was suffering from a mental disorder so as to be exempt from criminal responsibility is on the party that raises the issue. |

SOURCE: Criminal Code of Canada, R.S.C. 1985, c. C-46, s.16 [as amended S.C. 1991, c. 43, s. 2].

## Provisions for the Hospitalization of Individuals Found "NCRMD"

Part XX.1 of the Criminal Code of Canada makes provisions for the treatment of individuals found NCRMD. The law stipulates that a person found NCRMD must attend a disposition hearing, which can be held by the trial court, or, as is usually the case, be referred to a provincial review board made up of lawyers, psychiatrists, and other appointees. This disposition hearing must be held within 45 days of the NCRMD finding. The NCRMD person may be present at the disposition, may be represented by counsel, and may cross-examine witnesses. The disposition hearings are public and "may be conducted in as informal a manner as is appropriate in the circumstances."[86] The recommendation of the review board for the treatment of the NCRMD individual is expected to reflect the least intrusive or restrictive option consistent with the protection of society. For example, the court or review board might allow someone who committed a theft, who is not dangerous, and who is willing to submit to psychiatric treatment on an outpatient basis to stay at home rather than be sent to a hospital setting. Such a condition would be subject to the supervision of medical staff giving the treatment and to periodic reviews; changes may be effected as required. The review board in such a case would have the authority to revoke this status and order hospitalization, should the person's condition deteriorate.

Bill C-30 further replaces the former practice of indefinite hospitalization under the Warrants of the Lieutenant-Governor with a system of "caps," or maximum periods of deprivation of liberty. The "capping" provides a rough equivalence between the way in which the criminal law treats sane and mentally disordered offenders. For example, in cases of murder the outer limit is life. In cases of offences against the person, the outer limit is 10 years or the maximum penalty stipulated by the Criminal Code, whichever is shorter. For all other offences, the "cap" is the lesser of 2 years or the maximum penalty stipulated by the Criminal Code. Nevertheless, if at the expiration of the "cap" the NCRMD person is still considered a danger, he or she can be involuntarily committed to a secure hospital under the authority of provincial mental health legislation. The initial length of hospitalization is determined by the review boards. Bill C-30 makes a review board mandatory in each province and stipulates that each NCRMD case be reviewed annually. All decisions rendered by the review boards are binding.

Despite public perception, the insanity plea has not been used successfully in a large number of cases in Canada. There are some who argue, however, that the insanity defence is being used more often since the introduction in 1976 of the 25-year minimum life sentence for first-degree murder.[87] Some recent, high-profile cases in which the insanity defence was used successfully include those of André Dallaire, the paranoid schizophrenic who tried unsuccessfully to assassinate Prime Minister Chrétien in June 1996; Dorothy Joudrie, who attempted to murder her husband with five blasts from a shotgun in Calgary in May 1996; and Elizabeth Elliott who, in November 1995 stepped in front of a transport truck on a highway near Perth, Ontario, while carrying her 5-year-old daughter. Elliott's schizophrenia and bipolar disorder had caused her to have religious delusions that were responsible for her behaviour.[88]

CHAPTER 6
**191**
**Psychological and
Psychiatric
Foundations of
Criminal Behaviour**

André Dallaire, a diagnosed paranoid schizophrenic, was declared not criminally responsible for attempting to kill Prime Minister Chrétien in his home. How does the Canadian criminal justice system deal with dangerous people such as Dallaire? *The Canadian Press/Fred Chartrand.*

# Social Policy and Forensic Psychology

Psychological theories continue to evolve. For example, recent research in the field has shown a stability of aggressiveness over time. That is, children who display early disruptive or aggressive behaviour have been found, through the use of studies that follow the same individuals over time,[89] likely to continue their involvement in such behaviour as adults. Some researchers have found that aggressiveness appears to stabilize over time.[90] Children who demonstrate aggressive traits early in life often evidence increasingly frequent episodes of such behaviour until, finally, it becomes a major component of the adolescent or adult personality. From this research, we can conclude that problem children are likely to become problem adults.

Expanding research of this sort holds considerable significance, for those who are attempting to assess dangerousness and identify personal characteristics that would allow for the prediction of dangerousness in individual cases. The ability to accurately predict future dangerousness is of great concern to today's policy-makers. In April 1999, for example, Jean Gerald Dionne, a convicted sex offender, was charged with the kidnapping, forcible confinement, and sexual assault of a teenaged girl. Dionne at the time had a record of assaulting a 58-year-old woman in 1980, of criminal negligence causing death in the drowning of a 2-year-old boy in 1982, and of sexually assaulting an 8-year-old wheelchair-bound girl in 1991.[91]

Can past behaviour predict future behaviour? Do former instances of criminality presage additional ones? Are there other, identifiable, characteristics violent offenders might manifest that could serve as warning signs to criminal justice decision-makers faced with the dilemma of whether to release convicted felons? This, like many other areas, is one in which criminologists are still learning. One recent study[92] found a strong relationship between childhood behavioural difficulties and later problem behaviour. According to authors of the study, "early antisocial behavior is the best predictor of later antisocial behavior. It appears that this rule holds even when the antisocial behavior is measured as early as the preschool period." Using children as young as three, researchers were able to predict later delinquency, leading them to conclude that "some antisocial behavioral characteristics may be components of temperament." A second study,[93] which tracked a sample of male offenders for over 20 years, found that stable, but as yet "unmeasured individual differences" account for the positive association that exists between past criminal behaviour and the likelihood of future recurrence. A 1996 analysis of recidivism studies[94] by Canadians Paul Gendreau, Tracy Little, and Claire Goggin found that criminal history, a history of preadult antisocial behaviour, and "criminogenic needs," which were defined as measurable antisocial thoughts, values, and behaviour, were all predictors of recidivism.

Prediction, however, requires more than generalities. It is one thing to say, for example, that generally speaking 70 percent of children who evidence aggressive behaviour will similarly show violent tendencies later in life, and quite another to be able to predict which specific individuals will engage in future violations of the criminal law. **Selective incapacitation** is a policy based on the notion of career criminality.[95] Career criminals, also termed *habitual offenders,* are people who repeatedly commit violations of the criminal law. Research has shown that only a small percentage of all offenders account for most crimes reported to the police. Some studies have found that as few as 8 percent of all offenders commit as many as 60 serious crimes per year.[96] The strategy of selective incapacitation, however, which depends on accurately identifying potentially dangerous offenders out of existing criminal populations, has been criticized by some authors[97] for yielding a rate of "false positives" of over 60 percent. Potentially violent offenders are not easy to identify, even on the basis of past criminal records, and sentencing individuals to long prison terms simply because they are thought likely to commit crimes in the future would no doubt violate their Charter rights.

In 1996, as part of what the federal government called the High Risk Offender Initiative, Bill C-55 targeted dangerous offenders. Part XXIV of the Criminal Code of Canada deals with dangerous and long-term offenders. The Crown attorney can apply upon conviction (but before sentencing) to have an offender designated as dangerous. The dangerous offender designation brings with it an indefinite or indeterminate sentence of incarceration and a lengthened period of parole ineligibility. One intention of the indeterminate sentence is that these offenders will receive mental and health treatment. Whether or not this happens effectively is debatable. Currently in Canada there are fewer than 200 dangerous offenders. A review of some of these cases by James Bonta and his colleagues revealed that over 90 percent of these offenders were convicted of offences involving sexual aggression.[98]

Definitions of dangerousness are fraught with difficulty because, as some authors have pointed out, "dangerousness is not an objective quality like obesity or brown eyes, rather it is an ascribed quality like trustworthiness." Dangerousness[99] is not necessarily a personality trait that is stable or easily identifiable. Even if it were, recent studies[100] of criminal careers seem to show that involvement in crime decreases with age. Hence,

**Selective incapacitation** a social policy that seeks to protect society by incarcerating those individuals deemed to be the most dangerous.

CHAPTER 6

193

**Psychological and
Psychiatric
Foundations of
Criminal Behaviour**

as one author states, if "criminality declines more or less uniformly with age, then many offenders will be 'over the hill' by the time they are old enough to be plausible candidates for preventive incarceration."[101]

No discussion of social policy as it relates to the insights of criminal psychology would be complete without mention of correctional psychology. **Correctional psychology** is concerned with the diagnosis and classification of offenders, the treatment of correctional populations, and the rehabilitation of inmates and other law violators. Perhaps the most commonly used classification instrument in correctional facilities today is the Minnesota Multiphasic Personality Inventory, better known as the MMPI. Based on results of MMPI inventories, offenders may be assigned to various security levels, differing correctional programs, or a variety of treatment programs. Psychological treatment, when employed, typically takes the form of individual or group counselling. Psychotherapy, guided group interaction, cognitive therapy, behavioural modification, and various forms of interpersonal therapy are representative of the range of techniques used.

**Correctional psychology** that aspect of forensic psychology that is concerned with the diagnosis and classification of offenders, the treatment of correctional populations, and the rehabilitation of inmates and other law violators.

## Social Policy and the Psychology of Criminal Conduct

A practical synthesis of psychological approaches to criminal behaviour is offered by Canadians D. A. Andrews and James Bonta in their 1998 book, *The Psychology of Criminal Conduct*.[102] Andrews and Bonta prefer the term "psychology of criminal conduct," or PCC, to distinguish their point of view from what they call "the weak psychology represented in mainstream sociological criminology and clinical/forensic psychology."[103] Any useful synthesis of contemporary criminal psychology, they claim, should be fundamentally objective and empirical. Clearly they dislike many currently well-accepted perspectives, which they say have "placed higher value on social theory and political ideology than [on] rationality and/or respect for evidence."[104] Specifically, say Andrews and Bonta, "[t]he majority of perspectives on criminal conduct that are most favored in mainstream criminology reduce people to hypothetical fictions whose only interesting characteristics are their location in the social system. Almost without exception …," they write, "the causal significance of social location is presumed to reflect inequality in the distribution of social wealth and power." This kind of theorizing, the authors claim, "is a major preoccupation of mainstream textbook criminology, even though such a focus has failed to significantly advance understanding of criminal conduct."[105]

In *The Psychology of Criminal Conduct*, Andrews and Bonta do not attempt to develop a new behavioural theory but rather ask for the objective application of what is now understood about the psychology of crime and criminal behaviour. Their book is a call for practical coalescence of what is already known of the psychology of criminal offenders. Such coalescence is possible, they say, through the application of readily available, high-quality psychological findings. The authors claim, for example, that from the nearly 500 published reports on "controlled evaluations of community and correctional interventions" it is possible to conclude that treatment reduces recidivism "to at least a mild degree." Further, a detailed consideration of published studies finds that, among other things, targeting higher-risk cases and using treatments outside of formal correctional settings that extend to an offender's family and peers, are all elements of the most effective treatment strategies. Similarly, Andrews and Bonta say, along with objective measures of the success of rehabilitation programs and strategies, effective intervention and treatment services based on the use of psychological assessment instruments that have already demonstrated their validity, empirically established risk factors that can be accurately assessed, and accurately measured community crime rates are all ready and waiting to make a practical psychology of criminal conduct available to today's policy-makers. In the words of Andrews and Bonta, "[t]here exists now an empirically defensible general psychology of criminal conduct (PCC) that is of practical value … it should speak to policy advisors, policy-makers and legislators who must come to see that … human science is not just [a] relic of a positivistic past."[106] The major remaining issue, say the authors, "on which work is only beginning, is how to make use of what works."[107]

# Psychological Profiling

During World War II, psychologists and psychoanalysts were recruited by the U.S. War Department in an attempt to predict future moves enemy forces might make. Psychological and psychoanalytical techniques were applied to the study of Adolph Hitler, the Italian leader Benito Mussolini, the Japanese general and prime minister Tojo Hideki, and other Axis leaders. Such psychological profiling of enemy leaders may have given the Allies the edge in battlefield strategy. Hitler, probably because of his heightened sensitivity to symbols, his strong belief in fate, and his German ancestry (Freud was Austrian), became the central figure analyzed by profilers.

**Psychological profiling**
the attempt to categorize, understand, and predict the behaviour of certain types of offenders based on behavioural clues they provide.

Today, **psychological profiling** is used to assist criminal investigators seeking to better understand individuals wanted for serious offences. Profilers develop a list of typical offender characteristics and other useful principles by analyzing crime scene data in conjunction with interviews and other studies of past offenders. In general, the psychological profiling of criminal offenders is based on the belief that almost any form of conscious behaviour, including each and every behaviour engaged in by the offender during a criminal episode, is symptomatic of an individual's personality. Hence, the way in which a kidnapper approaches his victims, for example, the manner of attack used by a killer, and the specific sexual activities of a rapist, might all help paint a picture of the offender's motivations, personal characteristics, and likely future behaviour. Sometimes psychological profiles can provide clues as to what an offender might do following an attack. Some offenders have been arrested, for example, after returning to the crime scene—a behaviour typically predicted by specific behavioural clues left behind. Remorseful types can be expected to visit the victim's grave, permitting fruitful stakeouts of cemeteries.

In a well-known study[108] of lust murderers (men who kill and often mutilate victims during or following a forced sexual episode), Robert R. Hazelwood and John E. Douglas distinguished between the organized nonsocial and the disorganized asocial types. The organized nonsocial lust murderer was described as exhibiting complete indifference to the interests of society, and as being completely self-centred. He was also said to be "methodical and cunning" as well as "fully

CHAPTER 6

195

**Psychological and
Psychiatric
Foundations of
Criminal Behaviour**

cognizant of the criminality of his act and its impact on society." His counterpart, the disorganized asocial lust murderer, was described this way: "The disorganized asocial lust murderer exhibits primary characteristics of societal aversion. This individual prefers his own company to that of others and would be typified as a loner. He experiences difficulty in negotiating interpersonal relationships and consequently feels rejected and lonely. He lacks the cunning of the nonsocial type and commits the crime in a more frenzied and less methodical manner. The crime is likely to be committed in close proximity to his residence or place of employment, where he feels secure and more at ease."[109]

During the 1980s, the Federal Bureau of Investigation (FBI) in the United States led the movement to develop psychological profiling techniques through its concentration on violent sex offenders and arsonists. Today, the behavioural sciences unit at the FBI Training Academy in Quantico, Virginia continues to focus on serial killers, "lust murderers," domestic terrorists, and the like. The unit's activities were popularized a few years ago by the movie *Silence of the Lambs,* starring Jodie Foster and Anthony Hopkins, which portrayed the activities of a serial killer and enforcement activities designed to stop him. Movies, however, may lead the public to put too much stock in behavioural techniques such as psychological profiling. "It's not the magic bullet of investigations," says retired agent Robert Ressler, "[i]t's simply another tool."[110]

Based on training acquired at the FBI Training Academy, Canadian police officials have developed an automated case linkage system that utilizes some of the behavioural principles used in psychological profiling to identify and track violent serial criminals. The **Violent Crime Linkage Analysis System (ViCLAS)** was introduced in 1995. ViCLAS is a centralized computer bank containing details of more than 40 000 violent crimes, allowing police to recognize patterns among violent offences. In cases of solved or unsolved homicides and sexual assaults, missing persons, and nonparental abductions, police investigators are asked to respond to 263 questions covering details of all aspects of an incident, including victimology, modus operandi, forensics, and behavioural information. While there are some operational glitches still to be worked out, advocates of ViCLAS believe it will serve to facilitate communication between investigators with the common goal of solving serious serial criminal acts and protecting the public from dangerous repeat offenders.

**Violent Crime Linkage Analysis System (ViCLAS)** a centralized computer bank containing details of violent crimes that assists police in recognizing patterns among violent offences and offenders.

# Summary

Psychological and psychiatric theories of criminal behaviour emphasize the role of individual propensities and characteristics in the genesis of criminality. Whether the emphasis is on conditioned behaviour or on the psychoanalytical foundations of human conduct, such approaches ponder the wellsprings of human motivation, desire, and behavioural choice. Unfortunately, legal strictures have prevented psychology from making the kinds of courtroom contributions of which it appears capable. Even so, some theorists now consider the state of psychological criminology sufficiently advanced to allow for the development of a consistent and dependable social policy in the prediction of dangerousness and in the rehabilitation of offenders. Similarly, psychological profiling may soon facilitate informed criminal investigations as well as the prevention of future crime.

## Discussion Questions

1. This book emphasizes a social problems versus social responsibility theme. Which perspective is best supported by psychological theories of crime causation? Why?

2. How do psychological theories of criminal behaviour differ from the other types of theories presented in this book? How do the various psychological and psychiatric approaches presented in this chapter differ from one another?

3. How would the various perspectives discussed in this chapter suggest offenders might be prevented from committing additional offences? How might they be rehabilitated?

4. How can crime be a form of adaptation to one's environment? Why would an individual choose such a form of adaptation over others that might be available?

5. What is the difference, if any, between the antisocial personality and the psychopath?

## Weblinks

**www.hare.org/**

Web page of Dr. Robert Hare, international expert on psychopathy.

**www.soros.org/crime/research_brief__1.html**

The Centre on Crime, Communities, and Culture. The goal of the Centre is to create a better understanding of, and support for, the effective and humane response to criminal behaviour and victimization. Good discussion on mental illness and inmates.

**www.geocities.com/CollegePark/Quad/5889/criminology.htm**

SocioRealm. Online sociology resources from the University of Minnesota, with numerous links to crime-related topics.

# Crime and the Role of the Social Environment

If we would change the amount of crime in the community, we must change the community.

—FRANK TANNENBAUM[1]

In a gang, I understand what I'm supposed to do. In a gang, I have a family. In a gang, I know how to dress, how to walk, how to speak, when to speak, what to say.

—TEENAGED GANG MEMBER[2]

## LEARNING OUTCOMES

After reading this chapter, you should be able to:

- Appreciate the distinctions between the biological/psychological approach and the sociological approach to the study of crime

- Recognize how social rules and structures contribute to criminality

- Distinguish between a number of social-structural theories of criminal behaviour

- Identify modern-day social policy reflecting the social-structural approach

- Assess the shortcomings of the social-structural approach

IMPORTANT NAMES

Robert Park
Ernest Burgess
Clifford Shaw
Henry McKay
Thorsten Sellin

Frederic M. Thraser
Walter B. Miller
Franco Ferracuti
Marvin Wolfgang
Robert K. Merton

Richard Cloward
Lloyd Ohlin
Albert Cohen
Robert Agnew

IMPORTANT TERMS

social structure
social-structural
    theories
social pathology
social disorganization
social ecology
ecological theory
Chicago school of
    criminology
criminology of place

environmental
    criminology
broken windows thesis
defensible space
Crime Prevention
    through
    Environmental
    Design
conduct norms
culture conflict

subculture
subcultural theory
focal concerns
anomie
strain theory
opportunity structure
illegitimate
    opportunity
    structure
reaction formation

# Introduction

In March 1994, police responded to a 911 call reporting a collapsed man on a busy street in Ottawa, Ontario. It soon became apparent that the man had been shot through the chest; he died on the sidewalk before he could be taken to hospital. The incident shocked the nation's capital when details of the case revealed that the victim, Nicholas Battersby, a 27-year-old, British-born engineer, had been shot in a so-called drive-by shooting. An employee at a local high-tech firm, Battersby had simply been out for a stroll at 7:30 in the evening when a bullet from a sawed-off .22-calibre rifle shot from within a Jeep hit him in the chest.

After several days of an intensive police manhunt, three local teens, Rubens Henderson, Brian Raymond, and Cory Cyr were charged with Battersby's murder. All three youths had long records of trouble with the law. Henderson, who had been adopted from a Brazilian orphanage, never really adapted to life in Ottawa. Despite sincere attempts by his mother to provide support, Henderson soon became known as a troublemaker in school. In grade six, he assaulted a student, a teacher, and a vice-principal and was expelled from the school with grades ranging from C to F. He soon acquired a Young Offenders' record, which included break and enter, assault, joyriding in stolen cars, being unlawfully at large, and the use of illicit drugs. His activities brought him into contact with Brian Raymond and Cory Cyr. Raymond was raised by a single mother in a neighbourhood where there was a motorcycle gang clubhouse. Psychologists had used words like "dull' and "borderline" when labelling Raymond's language, math, and reasoning skills. Yet he knew how to hot-wire cars and get his hands on all sorts of drugs. Cory Cyr had spent many of his 16 years in group homes. Two days before the Battersby shooting, he had been released from jail after serving a 30-day sentence for assaulting a youth into unconsciousness after losing a Nintendo game to him. In 1996, Rubens Henderson received a life sentence for second-degree murder, while Cory Cyr and Brian Raymond received 5- and 4-year sentences, respectively, for manslaughter.[3]

CHAPTER 7

**199**
**Crime and the
Role of the Social
Environment**

The motivation behind the killing of Nicholas Battersby is not entirely clear. There is no doubt that the three youths were intoxicated on drugs and alcohol as they rode around in the stolen jeep taking random shots at storefronts and people. What is also certain is that all three had socially deprived backgrounds. They lacked educational achievement and the basic skills needed for success in the modern world. Academic failure, and subcultural values that focused on excitement and greed, dictated the direction their lives were to take—and all but ensured their fateful encounter with Nicholas Battersby.

## Sociological Theories

In contrast to more individualized biological and psychological theories, which have what is called a "micro focus" (discussed in Chapters 5 and 6), sociological approaches utilize a "macro" perspective, stressing behavioural tendencies of group members rather than attempting to predict the behaviour of specific individuals.

Sociological thought has been dominant in behavioural science literature and has influenced criminological theory more significantly than any other perspective during the past half century. This emphasis has probably been due, in part, to a widespread North American concern with social problems, including the women's movement, issues of poverty, and the decline in influence of many traditional social institutions such as government, organized religion, educational institutions, and the family.

Theories classified as sociological can be located in two major categories. One group emphasizes the structure of society (or **social structure**), relationships among social institutions, and the types of behaviour that tend to characterize groups of people. The other group is concerned with the action (or reaction) of society to the offender (or to the victim). That is, they are concerned with the social process—the process of social interaction between society, the victim, and the offender.

This chapter will concentrate on those explanations that fall under the social-structural rubric, while will those theories using the social process as a starting point will be examined in Chapter 8.

**Social structure** the pattern of social organization and the interrelationships between institutions characteristic of a society.

## Major Principles of Social-Structural Perspectives

This brief section serves to summarize the central features of social-structional theories of crime causation. Each of these points can be found elsewhere in this chapter, where they are discussed in more detail. This cursory overview is meant to be a guide to the rest of the chapter.

As this chapter will show, those perspectives on crime causation that have been termed "social-structional" are quite diverse; however, most such perspectives build upon the following fundamental assumptions:

- Social groups, social institutions, the arrangements of society, and social roles all provide the proper focus for criminological study.

- Group dynamics, group organization, and subgroup relationships form the causal nexus out of which crime develops.
- The structure of society and its relative degree of organization or disorganization are important factors contributing to the prevalence of criminal behaviour.
- Although it may be impossible to predict the specific behaviour of a given individual, statistical estimates of group characteristics are possible to achieve. Hence, the probability that a member of a given group will engage in a specific type of crime can be estimated.

Although all sociological perspectives on crime share the foregoing characteristics, particular theories may give greater or lesser weight to the following aspects of social life:

- the clash of norms and values between variously socialized groups;
- the influence of external societal and group forces on individuals;
- the existence of subcultures and varying types of opportunities.

# Social-Structural Perspectives

**Social-structural theories** explain crime by reference to various aspects of the social fabric. They emphasize relationships among social institutions and describe the types of behaviour that tend to characterize *groups* of people as opposed to *individuals.*

**Social pathology** a concept that compares society to a physical organism and sees criminality as an illness.

**Social disorganization** a condition said to exist when a group is faced with social change, uneven development of culture, maladaptiveness, disharmony, conflict, and lack of consensus.

This chapter describes various subtypes of social-structural theory, including (1) ecological approaches, (2) culture conflict, (3) subcultural approaches, and, (4) strain theories. All share some elements in common, and the classification of a theory into one subcategory or another is often more a matter of which aspects a writer chooses to emphasize rather than the result of any clear-cut definitional elements inherent in the perspectives themselves. Most theories in this chapter can also be termed **social-structural theories**, because they explain crime by reference to various aspects of the social fabric. They name the institutional structure of society and the various formal and informal arrangements between social groups as causes of crime and deviance. Environmental influences, socialization, and traditional and accepted patterns of behaviour are all used by social structuralists to portray the criminal as a product of his or her social environment and to depict criminality as a form of acquired behaviour.

The term **social pathology** was often associated with early social-structural theories. Social pathology, a concept prevalent in the criminological literature of a few decades ago, was initially defined as "those human actions which run contrary to the ideals of residential stability, property ownership, sobriety, thrift, habituation to work, small business enterprise, sexual discretion, family solidarity, neighborliness, and discipline of will."[4] It referred simply to behaviour not in keeping with the prevalent norms and values of the social group. Over time, however, the concept of social pathology changed and came to represent the idea that aspects of society may be somehow pathological, or "sick," and may produce deviant behaviour among individuals and groups who live under or are exposed to such social conditions. Social pathology has also been associated with the concept of **social disorganization**,[5] a condition said to exist when a group is faced with "social change, uneven development of culture, maladaptiveness, disharmony, conflict, and lack of consensus. ..."[6]

CHAPTER 7

201
**Crime and the
Role of the Social
Environment**

## Theory in Perspective
### Types of Social-Structural Theories

**SOCIAL-STRUCTURAL THEORIES**

Emphasize relationships between social institutions and describe the types of behaviour that tend to characterize *groups* of people as opposed to *individuals*.

**Ecological Theory or "Chicago School."** Stresses the demographic and geographic aspects of groups and sees the social disorganization that characterizes delinquency areas as a major cause of criminality and of victimization.
**Period:**     1920s–1930s
**Theorists:**   Robert Park, Ernest Burgess, W.I. Thomas, Florian Znaniecki, Clifford Shaw, Henry McKay
**Concepts:**   Demographics, concentric zones, social disorganization, delinquency areas

**Culture Conflict.** Suggests that the root cause of crime can be found in a clash of values between variously socialized groups over what is acceptable as proper behaviour.
**Period:**     1930s
**Theorists:**   Thorsten Sellin and others
**Concepts:**   Conduct norms

**Subcultural Theory.** Highlights violent and delinquent subcultures and emphasizes the contribution made by variously socialized cultural groups to the phenomenon of crime.
**Period:**     1920s–present
**Theorists:**   Frederic M. Thrasher, William Foote Whyte, Walter B. Miller, Gresham Sykes, David Matza, Franco Ferracuti, Marvin Wolfgang, and many others
**Concepts:**   Subculture, socialization, focal concerns, delinquency and drift, techniques of neutralization

**Strain or Anomie Theory.** Posits the disjuncture between socially and subculturally sanctioned means and goals as the cause of criminal behaviour.
**Period:**     1930s–present
**Theorists:**   Robert K. Merton, Richard Cloward, Lloyd Ohlin, Albert Cohen
**Concepts:**   Goals, means, opportunity structures, differential opportunity, reaction formation

## The Chicago School

**Social ecology** an approach to criminological theorizing that attempts to link the structure and organization of any human community to interactions with its localized environment.

Some of the earliest sociological theories to receive widespread recognition can be found in the writings of **Robert Park** and **Ernest Burgess.** In the 1920s and 1930s, Park and Burgess, through their work at the University of Chicago, developed what became known as **social ecology**, or the ecological school of criminology. Social ecology recognizes that crime always shows an uneven geographical distribution. It attempts to explain such variation by the interrelationship between human beings or human groups and their surroundings. As one writer puts it, social ecology is "the attempt to link the structure and organization of any human community to interactions with its localized environment."[7]

The work of Park and Burgess focused on concentric city zones, which were envisioned much like everexpanding circles on a target (see Figure 7.1), wherein diverse populations and behavioural characteristics predominated. Park and Burgess referred to the central business zone as Zone 1 or the Loop, where retail businesses and light manufacturing were typically located. Zone 2, surrounding the city centre, generally contained areas that were in transition from residential areas to business purposes. Zone 3 contained mostly working-class homes, while Zone 4 was occupied by middle-class citizens. Zone 5, consisting largely of suburbs, was called the commuter zone. Early **ecological theories** were formed using 1920s Chicago as a model, hence, the **"Chicago School" of criminology.** Although their applicability to other cities or other time periods may be questionable, such theories pointed out the tendency for criminal activity to be associated with transition zones which, because of the turmoil or social disorganization associated with them, were generally characterized by lower property values, marginal individuals, and a general lack of privacy.

**Ecological theory,** also called the **Chicago School of Criminology** a type of sociological approach that emphasizes demographics (the characteristics of population groups) and geographics (the mapped location of such groups relative to one another) and sees the social disorganization that characterizes delinquency areas as a major cause of criminality and victimization.

Park and Burgess had been strongly influenced by W. I. Thomas and Florian Znaniecki, who described in their book *The Polish Peasant in Europe and America*[8] the problems Polish immigrants faced in the early 1900s when they left their homeland and moved to the cities of America. Thomas and Znaniecki noted how rates of crime rose among people who had been so displaced, and they hypothesized that the cause was the social disorganization resulting from the immigrant's inability to successfully transplant guiding norms and values from their home culture into their new one.

**Clifford Shaw** and **Henry McKay,** other early advocates of the ecological approach, conducted empirical studies of delinquency rates in Chicago. One such study, undertaken in the late 1920s, found that the rate of delinquency among black youths "on the South Side of Chicago decreases regularly by square mile areas, from 19.4 percent in the area adjoining the center of the city, to 3.5 percent in the area 5 miles from the center of the city."[9]

Even at the height of its popularity, the ecological school recognized that American crime patterns might be different from those found elsewhere in the world and that crime zones might exist in city areas other than those surrounding the core. Early comparisons of American, European, and Asian data, for instance, found higher crime rates at the so-called city gates (near-suburban areas providing access to downtown) in Europe and Asia. The greatest contribution the ecological school made to criminological literature can be found in its claim that society, in the form of the community, wields a major influence on human behaviour.[10]

CHAPTER 7

203
Crime and the
Role of the Social
Environment

Figure 7.1

## Chicago's Concentric Zones

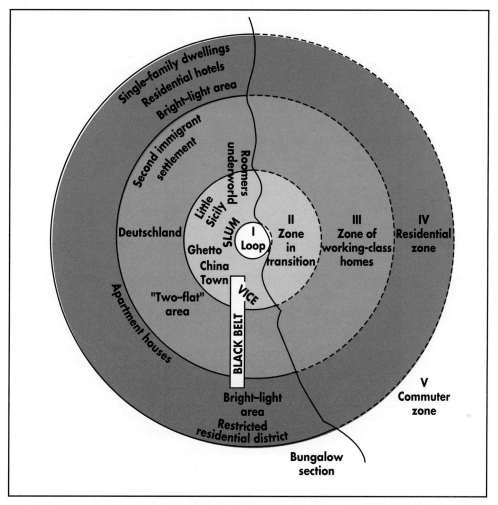

SOURCE: Robert E. Park, Ernest W. Burgess, and R. D. McKenzie, *The City* (Chicago: University of Chicago Press, 1925), p. 55. Copyright © University of Chicago Press. Reprinted with permission.

The work of Canadian Carol LaPrairie, which looks at the reality of high crime rates on some First Nations reserves in Canada, is representative of the ecological approach. In a recent study, LaPrairie concludes that those Aboriginal communities that have remained "institutionally complete" have significantly lower rates of crime compared with those reserves that have experienced rapid change due to economic and cultural pressures.[11] Later studies by LaPrairie used the concepts of social ecology to help explain the variation in rates of incarceration of Aboriginal peoples between the eastern and western provinces. In her comparison of two eastern and two western urban centres, LaPrairie notes significant differences in the degree of integration of the Aboriginal populations. While the eastern centres showed more social integration of inner-city Aboriginal residents, the western cities had displaced most of the Aboriginal population to communities outside the city centres. Not surprisingly, the incarceration rates of Aboriginal peoples is significantly higher in the western centres. LaPrairie's findings recognize the importance of social organization from a social-ecological point of view. The author also stresses the additional need for efforts to stabilize Aboriginal populations within urban centres through the provision of, for example, decent, affordable housing.[12]

Similarly, ecological theorists of the Chicago school formalized the use of two sources of information: (1) official crime and population statistics and (2) ethnographic data. Population statistics, also referred to as demographic data, combined with crime information, provided empirical material that gave scientific weight to ecological investigations. Ethnographic information, gathered in the form of life stories, or ethnographies, described the lives of city inhabitants. By comparing one set of data with the other—demographics with ethnographies—ecological investigators were able to show that life experiences varied from one location to another, and that personal involvement in crime had a strong tendency to be associated with place of residence.

## Critique of the Ecological School

The ecological school, like many sociological approaches to explaining crime, has been criticized for its tendency to forget the individual. By concentrating on the role social institutions and social disorganization play in crime causation, ecological approaches rarely acknowledge the influence of individual psychology, distinctive biology, or personal choice on criminal activity. This sort of criticism was insightfully advanced by W. S. Robinson in a classic 1950 article.[13] Robinson pointed out the "problematic nature of making individual-level inferences on the basis of aggregate data."[14]

Other authors have suggested that ecological theories give too much credence to the notion that location determines crime and delinquency. The nature of any given location changes over time, and evolutions in land-use patterns, such as a movement away from home-ownership and toward rental or low-income housing, for example, may seriously affect the nature of a neighbourhood and the concomitant quality of social organization found there.

Similarly, rates of neighbourhood crime and delinquency may be "an artifact of police decision-making practice"[15] and bear little objective relationship to the actual degree of law violation in an area. Such police bias, should it exist, may seriously mislead researchers into categorizing certain areas as high in crime when, in fact, they may not be.

Another critique of the ecological school can be found in its seeming inability to differentiate between the condition of social disorganization and the things such a condition is said to cause. What, for example, is the difference between social disorganization and high rates of delinquency? Is not delinquency a form of the very thing said to cause it? As Stephen Pfohl has observed, early ecological writers sometimes used the incidence of delinquency as "both an example of disorganization and something caused by disorganization,"[16] making it difficult to gauge the efficacy of their explanatory approach.

Finally, many crimes occur outside of geographic areas said to be characterized by social disorganization. Murder, rape, burglary, incidents of drug use, assault, and so

CHAPTER 7

**205**
**Crime and the
Role of the Social
Environment**

on, all occur in affluent "well-established" neighbourhoods as well as in other parts of a community. Likewise, white-collar, computer, environmental, and other types of crime may actually occur with a greater frequency in socially well-established neighbourhoods than elsewhere. Hence, the ecological approach is clearly not an adequate explanation for all crime, nor of crime.

## The Criminology of Place

Ecological approaches to crime causation have found a modern rebirth in what is now called the "criminology of place." The **criminology of place,** also called **environmental criminology**, is an emerging perspective within the contemporary body of criminological theory that emphasizes the importance of geographic location and architectural features as they are associated with the prevalence of victimization. "Hot spots" of crime, including neighbourhoods, specific streets, and even individual houses and business establishments, have been identified by recent writers. Lawrence Sherman, for example, tells of a study[17] that revealed that 3 percent of places (addresses and intersections) in Minneapolis produce 50 percent of all calls to the police. Crime, says Sherman, although relatively rare, is geographically concentrated.

Another researcher, Rodney Stark, asks "[h]ow is it that neighborhoods can remain the site of high crime and deviance rates despite a complete turnover in their populations? … There must be something about places as such that sustains crime."[18] Stark has developed a theory of deviant neighbourhoods. It consists of 30 propositions, including the following[19]:

1. To the extent that neighbourhoods are dense and poor, homes will be crowded.
2. Where homes are more crowded, there will be a greater tendency to congregate outside the home in places and circumstances that raise levels of temptation and opportunity to deviate.
3. Where homes are more crowded, there will be lower levels of supervision of children.
4. Reduced levels of child supervision will result in poor school achievement, with a consequent reduction in stakes in conformity and an increase in deviant behaviour.
5. Poor, dense neighbourhoods tend to be mixed-use neighbourhoods.
6. Mixed use increases familiarity with and easy access to places offering the opportunity for deviance.

Central to the criminology of place is the **broken windows thesis**[20] which holds that physical deterioration and an increase in unrepaired buildings leads to increased concerns for personal safety among area residents. Heightened concerns, in turn, lead to further decreases in maintenance and repair and to increased delinquency, vandalism, and crime among local residents—which spawns even further deterioration in both a sense of safety and physical deterioration. Offenders from other neighbourhoods are then increasingly attracted by the area's perceived vulnerability.

Even within so-called high-crime neighbourhoods, however, crimes tend to be concentrated at specific locations such as street blocks or multiple-family dwellings. This

**Criminology of place** or **environmental criminology** an emerging perspective that emphasizes the importance of geographic location and architectural features as they are associated with the prevalence of criminal victimization.

**Broken windows thesis** a perspective on crime causation holding that physical deterioration in an area leads to increased concerns for personal safety among area residents and to higher crime rates in that area. The "broken windows" metaphor says that a broken window, left unattended, invites other windows to be broken, which leads to a sense of disorder that breeds fear and serious crime. Hence, by ignoring minor crimes we lose opportunities to repair the first signs of disorder and to hold offenders accountable.

▶

**Defensible space** the range of mechanisms that combine to bring an environment under the control of its residents.

kind of microlevel analysis has also shown, for example, that some units within specific apartment buildings are much more likely to be the site of criminal occurrences than others. Apartments near complex or building entrances appear to be more criminally dangerous, especially if they are not facing other buildings or apartments. Likewise, pedestrian tunnels, unattended parking lots, and convenience stores with clerks stationed in less visible areas are often targeted by criminal offenders.

The criminology of place employs the concept of **defensible space,** a term that evolved out of a conference in 1964 in St. Louis, Missouri.[21] Defensible space has been defined as "a surrogate term for the range of mechanisms—real and symbolic barriers, strongly defined areas of influence, and improved opportunities for surveillance—that combine to bring an environment under the control of its residents."[22] The St. Louis conference, which brought criminologists, police officers, and architects face to face, focused on crime problems characteristic of public housing areas. Findings demonstrated that specific architectural changes that improved barriers, defined boundaries, and removed criminal opportunity could do much to reduce the risk of crime—even in the midst of high-crime neighbourhoods.

The criminology of place holds that location can be as predictive of criminal activity as the lifestyles of victimized individuals or the social features of victimized households. (*Place* has been defined by researchers as "a fixed physical environment that can be seen completely and simultaneously, at least on its surface, by one's naked eyes."[23]) Places can be criminogenic due to the routine activities associated with them. On the other hand, some places host crime because they provide the characteristics that facilitate its commission. In Sherman's study, for example, Minneapolis parks drew "flashers" because they provided "opportunities for concealment" up until the moment when the flasher struck. Changes to the parks, such as moving walkways some distance from trees and shrubbery, can reduce criminal opportunity.

**Crime Prevention Through Environmental Design (CPTED)** a crime prevention model based on the design and use of a physical environment.

Recognizing the criminology of place, the Peel Regional Police Service (Peel is located just west of Toronto), introduced to the Canadian market in the early 1980s a program of **Crime Prevention Through Environmental Design (CPTED)**. It is based on the theory that the proper design and effective use of a physical environment can help reduce the incidence and fear of crime. The CPTED program revolves around three strategies: (1) natural surveillance (keeping potential intruders under observation); (2) natural access control (decreasing the opportunity for crime); and (3) territorial reinforcement (extending a sphere of influence through physical design to develop a sense of ownership by users). In an example cited by Peel Regional Police, a CPTED review of a restaurant recommended the following changes: (1) improvement of sightlines to the outside by removing unnecessary clutter such as bushy plants and promotional material from the take-out window, (2) improvement of sightlines within the restaurant by removing planters that divided the dining room and waiting area, and (3) improvement of lighting by repairing defective ceiling lamps and increasing the number of light fixtures. These changes resulted in a more intimidating and less private target to would-be offenders while also giving staff the ability to better observe potential offenders before a robbery.[24] See Chapter 11 for an in-depth look at the CPTED model.

Sherman points out that "[n]either capital punishment of places (as in arson of crack houses) nor incapacitation of the routine activities of criminal hot spots (as in revocation of liquor licences) seems likely to eliminate crime. But since the routine activities of places may be regulated far more easily than the routine activities of persons, a criminology of place would seem to offer substantial promise for public policy as well as theory."[25]

CHAPTER 7

207
**Crime and the
Role of the Social
Environment**

# Culture Conflict

Fundamental to ecological criminology was the belief that zones of transition, because they tend to be in flux, harbour groups of people whose values are often at odds with those of the larger, surrounding society. This perspective found its clearest expression in the writings of **Thorsten Sellin** in his 1938 book, *Culture Conflict and Crime.*[26] Sellin maintained that the root cause of crime could be found in different values about what is acceptable or proper behaviour. According to Sellin, **conduct norms,** which provide the valuative basis for human behaviour, are acquired early in life through childhood socialization. It is the clash of norms between variously socialized groups that results in crime. Because crime is a violation of laws established by legislative decree, the criminal event itself, from this point of view, is nothing other than a disagreement over what should be acceptable behaviour. For some social groups, what we tend to call crime is simply part of the landscape—something that can be expected to happen to you unless you take steps to protect yourself. From this point of view, those to whom crime happens are not so much victims as they are simply ill prepared.

Sellin also wrote about culture conflict. **Culture conflict** suggests that the root cause of criminality can be found in a clash of values between variously socialized groups over what is acceptable or proper behaviour. In 1997, for example, Danish actress Annette Sorensen was arrested after leaving her toddler in a stroller outside a restaurant while she sat inside with the child's father. Sorensen was charged with endangering the welfare of a child. Her 14-month-old daughter, Liv, was placed in temporary foster care. Sorensen, who was in tears following her arrest, could not understand what had happened. "We do this in Denmark all the time,"[27] the Copenhagen resident told police. Her daughter was soon ordered returned by a city judge, and Sorensen and the child flew home to Denmark, where children are routinely left in strollers outside of restaurants and other public places.[28]

Sellin described two types of culture conflict. The first type, *primary conflict,* arises when a fundamental clash of cultures occurs. Sellin's classic example was that of an immigrant father who kills his daughter's lover following an old-world tradition that demands that a family's honour be kept intact. In Sellin's words, "[a] few years ago, a Sicilian father in New Jersey killed the 16-year-old seducer of his daughter, expressing surprise at his arrest since he had merely defended his family honor in a traditional way. In this case … [t]he conflict was external and occurred between cultural codes or norms. We may assume that where such conflicts occur … norms of one cultural group or area migrate to another and that such conflict will continue so long as the acculturation process has not been completed."[29]

The other type of conflict, called *secondary conflict,* arose, according to Sellin, when smaller cultures within the primary one clashed. So it is that middle-class values, upon which most criminal laws are based, may find fault with inner-city or lower-class norms, resulting in the social phenomenon we call "crime."

In Sellin's day, prostitution and gambling provided plentiful examples of secondary conflict. Many lower-class inner-city groups accepted gambling and prostitution as a way of life—if not for individual members of those groups, then at least as forms of behaviour that were rarely condemned for those choosing to participate in

**Conduct norms** the shared expectations of a social group relative to personal conduct.

**Culture conflict** a sociological perspective on crime that suggests that the root cause of criminality can be found in a clash of values between variously socialized groups over what is acceptable or proper behaviour.

Annette Sorensen, right, is comforted by her friend Mette Vajlo after Sorensen—a Danish citizen—was arrested for leaving her baby unattended on a New York street while she and the baby's father ate dinner. Criminologists tell us that conflict is a pervasive part of everyday life—much of it based on a clash of values built on subcultural differences. Was what Sorensen did "wrong?" *Don Halasy/New York Post/ Corbis-Bettmann.*

them. Today, perhaps drug use and abuse provide more readily understandable examples. For some segments of contemporary society, drug sales have become a source of substantial income, and the conduct norms which typify such groups support at least the relative legitimacy of lives built around the drug trade. In other words, in some parts of Canada, drug dealing is an acceptable form of business. To those who make the laws, however, it is not. It is from the clash of these two opposing viewpoints that conflict, and crime, emerge.

## Subcultural Theory

**Subculture** a collection of values and preferences that is communicated to subcultural participants through a process of socialization.

**Subcultural theory** a sociological perspective that emphasizes the contribution made by variously socialized cultural groups to the phenomenon of crime.

Inherent in the writings of the ecological school is the notion of subculture. Like the larger culture of which it is a part, a **subculture** is a collection of values and preferences that is communicated to subcultural participants through a process of socialization. Subcultures differ from the larger culture in that they claim the allegiance of smaller groups of people. Whereas the wider American culture, for example, may proclaim that hard work and individuality are valuable, a particular subculture may espouse the virtues of deer hunting, male bonding, and recreational alcohol consumption. Although it is fair to say that most subcultures are not at odds with the surrounding culture, some subcultures do not readily conform to the parameters of national culture. Countercultures, which tend to reject and invert the values of the surrounding culture, and criminal subcultures, which may actively espouse deviant activity, represent the other extreme. **Subcultural theory** is a sociological perspective that emphasizes the contribution made by variously socialized cultural groups to the phenomenon of crime.

CHAPTER 7

**209**
**Crime and the
Role of the Social
Environment**

Some of the earliest writings on subcultures can be found in **Frederic M. Thrasher's** 1927 book, *The Gang.*[30] Thrasher studied 1 313 gangs in Chicago. His work, primarily descriptive in nature, led to a typology in which he described different types of gangs. In 1943, William Foote Whyte, drawing on Thrasher, published *Street Corner Society.*[31] Whyte, in describing his 3-year study of the Italian slum he called "Cornerville," further developed the subcultural thesis, showing that lower-class residents of a typical slum could achieve success through the opportunities afforded by slum culture—including racketeering and bookmaking.

## Focal Concerns

In 1958, **Walter B. Miller** attempted to detail the values that drive members of lower-class subcultures into delinquent pursuits. Miller described *lower-class culture* as "a long established, distinctively patterned tradition with an integrity of its own." In Miller's words, "[a] large body of systematically interrelated attitudes, practices, behaviors, and values characteristic of lower-class culture are designed to support and maintain the basic features of the lower-class way of life. In areas where these differ from features of middle-class culture, action oriented to the achievement and maintenance of the lower-class system may violate norms of the middle class and be perceived as deliberately nonconforming. ... This does not mean, however, that violation of the middle-class norm is the dominant component of motivation; it is a byproduct of action primarily oriented to the lower-class system."[32]

In the same article, entitled "Lower Class Culture as a Generating Milieu of Gang Delinquency,"[33] Miller outlined what he termed the **focal concerns** or key values of delinquent subcultures. Such concerns included trouble, toughness, smartness, excitement, fate, and autonomy. Miller concluded that subcultural crime and deviance are not the direct consequences of poverty and lack of opportunity but emanate from specific values characteristic of such subcultures. Just as middle-class concerns with achievement, hard work, and delayed gratification lead to socially acceptable forms of success, said Miller, so too do lower-class concerns provide a path to subculturally recognized success for lower-class youth.

Miller found that trouble "is a dominant feature of lower class culture." Getting into trouble, staying out of trouble, dealing with trouble when it arises become focal points in the lives of many members of lower-class culture. Miller recognized that getting into trouble was not necessarily valued in and of itself but was seen as an oftentimes necessary means to valued ends. In Miller's words, "[for] men, 'trouble' frequently involves fighting or sexual adventures while drinking; for women, sexual involvement with disadvantageous consequences."[34]

Like many theorists of the time, Miller was primarily concerned with the criminality of men. The lower-class masculine concern with toughness which he identified, Miller admitted, may have been a product of the fact that many men in the groups he examined were raised in female-headed families. Miller's "toughness," then, may reflect an almost obsessive concern with masculinity as a reaction to the perceived threat of overidentification with female role models. In words that sound as applicable today as when they were written, Miller tells us, "[t]he genesis of the intense concern over 'toughness' in lower-class culture is probably related to the fact that a significant

**Focal concerns** the key values of any culture, and especially the key values of a delinquent subculture.

proportion of lower-class males are reared in a predominantly female household and lack a consistently present male figure with whom to identify and from whom to learn essential components of a 'male' role. Since women serve as a primary object of identification during the pre-adolescent years, the almost obsessive lower-class concern with 'masculinity' probably resembles a type of compulsive reaction-formation."[35]

Miller described "smartness" as the "capacity to outsmart, outfox, outwit, dupe, take, [or] con another or others and the concomitant capacity to avoid being outwitted, taken or duped oneself. ... In its essence," said Miller, "smartness involves the capacity to achieve a valued entity—material goods, personal status—through a maximum use of mental agility and a minimum of physical effort."

Excitement was seen as a search for thrills—often necessary to overcome the boredom inherent in lower-class lifestyles. Fights, gambling, picking up women, and making the rounds were all described as derivative aspects of the lower-class concern with excitement. "The quest for excitement," said Miller, "finds ... its most vivid expression in the ... recurrent 'night on the town' ... a patterned set of activities in which alcohol, music, and sexual adventuring are major components."

Fate is related to the quest for excitement and to the concept of luck or of being lucky. As Miller stated, "[m]any lower-class persons feel that their lives are subject to a set of forces over which they have relatively little control. These are not ... supernatural forces or ... organized religion ... but relate more to a concept of 'destiny' or man as a pawn. ... This often implicit world view is associated with a conception of the ultimate futility of directed effort toward a goal. ..."

Autonomy, as a focal concern, manifests itself in statements such as "I can take care of myself" or "No one's going to push me around." Autonomy produces behavioural problems from the perspective of middle-class expectations when it surfaces in work environments, public schools, or other social institutions built on expectations of conformity.

Miller's work derived almost entirely from his study of black inner-city delinquents in the Boston area. As such, it may have less relevance to members of lower-class subcultures at other times, or in other places.

## Violent Subcultures

Some subcultures are decidedly violent and are built around violent themes and around values supporting violent activities. In 1967, **Franco Ferracuti** and **Marvin Wolfgang** published their seminal work, *The Subculture of Violence: Toward an Integrated Theory of Criminology,*[36] which drew together many of the sociological perspectives previously advanced to explain delinquency and crime. According to some writers,[37] the work of Wolfgang and Ferracuti "was substantively different from the other subculture theories, perhaps because it was developed almost a decade after delinquent-subculture theories and criminology had developed new concerns." Ferracuti and Wolfgang's main thesis was that violence is a learned form of adaptation to certain problematic life circumstances, and that learning to be violent takes place within the context of a subcultural milieu that emphasizes the advantages of violence over other forms of adaptation. Such subcultures are characterized by songs and stories that glorify violence, by gun ownership, and by rituals tending to stress macho

CHAPTER 7

211

**Crime and the
Role of the Social
Environment**

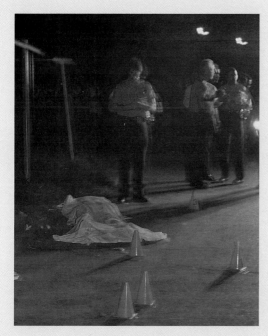

Violent subcultures produce violent acts. Why are some subcultures "violent" while others are not?
*Bryce Lankard.*

models. They are likely to teach that a quick and decisive response to insults is necessary to preserve one's prestige within the group. Subcultural group members have a proclivity for fighting as a means of settling disputes. Subcultures of violence both expect violence from their members and legitimize it when it occurs. In Wolfgang's words, "the use of violence … is not necessarily viewed as illicit conduct, and the users do not have to deal with feelings of guilt about their aggression." In other words, for participants in violent subcultures violence can be a way of life.

Wolfgang and Ferracuti based their conclusions on an analysis of data that showed substantial differences in the rate of homicides between racial groups in the Philadelphia area. At the time of their study, non-Caucasian men had a homicide rate of 41.7 per 100 000, versus only 3.4 for Caucasian men. Statistics on non-Caucasian women showed a homicide rate of 9.3, versus 0.4 for Caucasian women. Explaining these findings, Wolfgang and Ferracuti wrote: "[h]omicide is most prevalent, or the highest rates of homicide occur, among a relatively homogeneous subcultural group in any large urban community. … The value system of this group, as we are contending, constitutes a subculture of violence. From a psychological viewpoint, we might hypothesize that the greater the degree of integration of the individual into this subculture, the higher the probability that his behavior will be violent in a variety of situations."[38]

Wolfgang and Ferracuti extend their theory of subcultural violence with the following "corollary propositions."[39]

1. No subculture can be totally different from or totally in conflict with the society of which it is a part.
2. To establish the existence of a subculture of violence does not require that the actors sharing in these basic value elements should express violence in all situations.

3. The potential resort or willingness to resort to violence in a variety of situations emphasizes the penetrating and diffusive character of this culture theme.
4. The subcultural ethos of violence may be shared by all ages in a subsociety, but this ethos is most prominent in a limited age group, ranging from late adolescence to middle age.
5. The counter-norm is nonviolence.
6. The development of favourable attitudes toward, and the use of, violence in a subculture usually involves learned behaviour and a process of differential learning, association, or identification.
7. The use of violence in a subculture is not necessarily viewed as illicit conduct and the users therefore do not have to deal with feelings of guilt about their aggression.

Canadian researchers have commented on geographical distinctions between violent subcultures in different parts of Canada. National homicide rates have consistently shown a distinct east-to-west/south-to-north upward trend over the last several decades. Homicide rates during this period have been lowest in Newfoundland and highest in British Columbia and two to three times higher in the Yukon and the Northwest Territories than in British Columbia. The reasons for these persistent regional differences are difficult to pinpoint. While certain elements of Canada's social structure (age, ethnicity, economic well-being, etc.) are obvious contributing factors, some researchers suggest that cultural differences among regions of Canada also need to be taken into account. Do the accumulated traditions and shared experiences shaping the values and beliefs of people in different regions contribute to varying levels of violence? Many Canadian researchers believe that this cannot be overlooked.[40]

Regional variations are found in other countries as well. In the United States, for example, a body of criminological literature claims that certain forms of criminal violence are more acceptable in the southern United States than in northern portions of the country.[41] Some writers have also referred to variability in the degree to which interpersonal violence has been accepted in the South over time, whereas others have suggested that violence in the South might be a traditional tool in the service of social order.[42]

The wider culture often recognizes, sometimes begrudgingly and sometimes matter-of-factly, a violent subculture's internal rules. Hence, when one member of such a subculture kills another, the wider society may take the killing less "seriously" than if someone outside the subculture had been killed. As a consequence of this realization, Wolfgang described what he called "wholesale" and "retail" costs for homicide, in which killings that are perceived to occur within a subculture of violence (when both the victim and perpetrator are seen as members of a violent subculture) generally result in a less harsh punishment than do killings that occur outside of the subculture. Punishments, said Wolfgang, relate to the perceived seriousness of the offence, and if members of the subculture within which a crime occurs accept the offence as part of the landscape, so, too, will members of the wider culture that imposes official sanctions on the perpetrator.

Much of the original research into subcultural theory dates back to the 1950s and 1960s. However, the reality of inner-city gangs and violence, especially in the United States but also in Canada, has brought with it a renewed interest in this approach. In his review of the research literature on gangs, Canadian criminologist John Hagan suggests that subcultural theories continue to have a role to play in understanding the serious problems of largely ethnic, urban youth who see themselves as marginalized.[43]

CHAPTER 7

213

**Crime and the
Role of the Social
Environment**

## Critique of Violent Subcultures Theory

Although subcultural approaches are widely accepted within criminology, the notion of a subculture of violence has been questioned. Canadian criminologist Gwynn Nettler criticizes the subculture of violence thesis by insisting that it is tautological, or circular. That is, saying that people fight because they are violent, or that "they are murderous because they live violently" does little to explain their behaviour, according to Nettler. Attributing fighting to "other spheres of violence," he says, may be true, but it is fundamentally "uninformative."[44]

The approach has also been criticized for being racist, because many so-called violent subcultures are said to be populated primarily by minorities. Margaret Anderson says that "[t]he problem with this explanation is that it turns attention away from the relationship of black communities to the larger society and it recreates dominant stereotypes about blacks as violent, aggressive, and fearful. Although it may be true that rates of violence are higher in black communities, this observation does not explain the fact."[45] In sociological jargon, one might say that an observed correlation between race and violence does not necessarily provide a workable explanation for the relationship.

## Murder Showed Gang Would Stop at Nothing

On Sept. 6, 1995, John Wartley Richardson walked out of Millhaven penitentiary in Kingston, Ontario. He'd just turned 24, a hardened and violent Ottawa street thug with a previous conviction for robbery. Now, he was free again after serving part of a 30-month prison term for pimping.

National Parole Board file No. 233185C, obtained by the Citizen, reveals officials had little doubt Mr. Richardson would strike again. In fact, it took just 50 days.

The crime would be murder. The victim would be Sylvain Leduc.

The file shows Mr. Richardson, now 26, has never held a legitimate job. He's been a pimp and a brute, involved in narcotics and the misery of vulnerable, strung-out young women trapped in Ottawa's street sex trade.

In prison, he was sometimes locked in segregation for "negative behaviour." He showed no remorse for anything. An area woman who helped put him away for procuring was so scared afterwards, the file notes, she had police help her relocate to a new town.

In the fall of 1994, Mr. Richardson was rejected for early parole.

"The board is satisfied that reasonable grounds exist to believe that, if released, you are likely to commit an offence involving violence and directs that you not be released."

But 11 months later, parole officials had little choice but to let him go because of a federal statute that grants all but the most dangerous inmates parole after serving two-thirds of their sentences.

"You remain a high risk to reoffend," officials wrote in his file. "Strict adherence to release conditions (including regularly reporting in to authorities) will be required in order to render that risk manageable."

Sylvain Leduc was tortured and killed by members of the Ace Crew gang because he had been disrespectful towards them. Was Sylvain Leduc a victim of a violent subculture? *The Canadian Press/ Ottawa Sun.*

Mr. Richardson, unmanageable as ever, ignored the conditions. He finally met with authorities Jan. 2, 1996, when heavily armed police in Winnipeg arrested him as an armed-and-dangerous fugitive wanted for the Leduc homicide.

A subsequent parole board document added a grim footnote to the file: "The risk you represent is clearly not manageable and the board orders that your statutory release be revoked."

Yesterday, a judge and jury went further. The jury revoked much of what's left of Mr. Richardson's life by finding him guilty of first-degree murder. Justice Douglas Rutherford then shipped him back to a bleak federal cellblock for life, with no chance of parole for at least 25 years. He also sentenced him to an additional 73 years, to be served concurrently, for various other crimes.

Sylvain Leduc was killed because he innocently strayed into the nasty underworld of urban street gangs, where extreme violence and revenge are rewarded with criminal status and power.

Mr. Leduc, 17, offended a dangerous collection of mostly young, black men who called themselves Ace Crew and sold $20-hits of crack cocaine on the streets of Lowertown. His death sentence was sealed with one ugly, unfortunate word: he called them "niggers."

Mr. Leduc's timing was particularly bad. In the fall of 1995, the gang's members were feeling threatened on several fronts.

Police, they worried, might be on to them. And at least one of the teenage girls the gang used for drug-running and sex—she was Mr. Leduc's cousin— wanted out, undermining the group's authority and its all-important reputation on the street. As well, rival drug dealers, they suspected, were muscling in on their turf, on their money.

Ace Crew was, at best, disorganized crime. But in late October 1995, it appeared to be losing its grip on even that existence. And that made it potentially lethal.

Enter John Richardson, fresh out of Millhaven. He was a friend of Mark Williams, the then 19-year-old reputed leader of Ace Crew. Mr. Richardson was just the type of crime consultant who could help the outfit rebuild.

If Ace was struggling, perhaps Mr. Richardson and his pal, Kurton Edwards, 28, could teach the gang a thing or two about becoming so bad, so feared, that people would be afraid to walk the streets of Ottawa.

CHAPTER 7

215

**Crime and the
Role of the Social
Environment**

At least that's how it appeared in the hours leading up to the Leduc murder, as Mr. Richardson regaled the group with violent tales about how notorious U.S. black ghetto gangs ruthlessly maintain their turf. He talked about violence. He talked about retribution. He talked about torture. And he had a gun.

Ace Crew, police believe, has not largely disbanded. Six members and associates have been convicted for various roles in Mr. Leduc's slaying. Another was imprisoned for 11 years for the bold March 1997 shooting of two men inside the crowded Rideau Centre. Five other members and associates, all non-Canadians, have been deported to their native countries because of their criminal activities here.

### DISCUSSION QUESTIONS

1. What subcultural elements (beliefs, behaviour patterns, etc.) may have contributed to Sylvain Leduc's death?

2. Does the subculture of violence thesis help to explain the behaviour of gang members, such as the named Ace Crew who killed Sylvain? If so, how?

3. What explanations, other than a subculture of violence thesis, might be offered to explain the death of Sylvain?

SOURCE: Ian MacLeod, "The Rise and Fall of the Ace Crew: Murder Showed Gang Would Stop at Nothing," *Ottawa Citizen*, April 15, 1998, p. B1. Reprinted with permission.

## Strain Theory

In 1938, **Robert K. Merton** offered what is now regarded as a classic statement of the causes of crime in his concept of **anomie**. *Anomie* is a French word meaning "normlessness," and was popularized by Emile Durkheim in his 1897 book, *Suicide*.[46] Durkheim used the term to explain how a breakdown of predictable social conditions can lead to a feeling of personal loss and dissolution.

**Anomie** a social condition in which norms are uncertain or lacking.

Merton's use of the term was somewhat different. In Merton's writings[47] anomie came to mean a disjunction between socially approved means to success and legitimate goals. This posited strain between goals and means has led to Merton's approach being called **strain theory.** Merton maintained that legitimate goals, involving such things as wealth, status, and personal happiness, were generally defined as desirable for everyone. The widely acceptable means to these goals, however, including education, hard work, financial savings, and so on, were not equally available to all members of society. As a consequence, crime and deviance tended to arise, and individuals felt pressed to succeed in approved terms but were not given the tools necessary for such success. In Merton's words, "[i]t's not how you play the game, it's whether you win."[48] Complicating the picture further, Merton maintained, was the fact that not everyone accepted the legitimacy of socially approved goals. Merton diagrammed possible combinations of goals and means as shown in Figure 7.2, referring to each combination as a "mode of adaptation."

**Strain, or anomie, theory** a sociological approach that posits a disjuncture between socially and subculturally sanctioned means and goals as the cause of criminal behaviour.

## Figure 7.2

### Goals and Means Disjuncture

|  | GOALS | MEANS |
| --- | :---: | :---: |
| Conformity | + | + |
| Innovation | + | − |
| Ritualism | − | + |
| Retreatism | − | − |
| Rebellion | ± | ± |

SOURCE: Robert K. Merton, *Social Theory and Social Structure*, 1968 enlarged edition. Copyright 1967, 1968 by Robert K. Merton. Adapted with permission of the Free Press, a division of Macmillan, Inc.

The initial row in Figure 7.2 signifies acceptance of the goals that society holds as legitimate for everyone, with ready availability of the means approved for achieving those goals. The mode of adaptation associated with this combination of goals and means is called *conformity* and typifies most middle- and upper-class individuals.

*Innovation,* the second form of adaptation, arises when an emphasis on approved goal achievement combines with a lack of opportunity to participate fully in socially acceptable means to success. This form of adaptation is experienced by many lower-class individuals who have been socialized to desire traditional success symbols such as expensive cars, large homes, and big bank accounts, but who do not have ready access to approved means of acquiring them, such as educational opportunity. Innovative behavioural responses, including crime, can be expected to develop when individuals find themselves so deprived. However, in Merton's words, "[p]overty as such, and consequent limitation of opportunity, are not sufficient to induce a conspicuously high rate of criminal behavior. Even the often mentioned 'poverty in the midst of plenty' will not necessarily lead to this result." It is only insofar as those who find themselves in poverty are pressured to achieve material success and the acquisition of other associated symbols of status that innovation results.

Third, *ritualism* describes the form of behaviour arising when members of society participate in socially desirable means, but show little interest in goal achievement. A ritualist may get a good education, work every day in an acceptable occupation, and outwardly appear to be leading a solid middle-class lifestyle. Yet that person may care little for the symbols of success, choosing to live an otherwise independent lifestyle.

*Retreatism* describes the behaviour of those who reject both the socially approved goals and means. They may become dropouts, drug abusers, or homeless, or may participate in alternative lifestyles such as communal living. Such individuals are socially and psychologically often quite separate from the larger society around them.

Merton's last category, *rebellion,* signifies a person, or rebel, who wishes to replace socially approved goals and means with some other system. Political radicals, revolutionaries, and antiestablishment agitators may fit into this category. Merton believed that conformity was the most common mode of adaptation prevalent in society, whereas retreatism was least common.

CHAPTER 7

**217**
**Crime and the
Role of the Social
Environment**

A contemporary application of Merton's strain theory is offered by Margaret Beare in her examination of the increased involvement of Canadian Mohawks in the smuggling of cigarettes in the early 1990s. High taxes on Canadian cigarettes tempted many smokers to turn to cheaper, contraband American cigarettes. In Ontario and Quebec, residents of some First Nations communities along the Canada-U.S. border were the main sources of contraband cigarettes. It is believed that by 1993, more than one-quarter of the cigarettes consumed in Canada had been purchased illegally.[49]

## Differential Opportunity

In the 1960s, **Richard Cloward** and **Lloyd Ohlin** published *Delinquency and Opportunity*.[50] Their book, a report on the nature and activities of juvenile gangs, blended the subcultural thesis with ideas derived from strain theory. Cloward and Ohlin saw socially structured opportunities for success as being of two types: illegitimate and legitimate. They observed that whereas legitimate opportunities were generally available to individuals born into middle-class culture, participants in lower-class subcultures were often denied access to them. As a consequence, the choice of illegitimate opportunities to success were often seen as quite acceptable by participants in so-called illegitimate subcultures.

**Opportunity structure** a path to success. Opportunity structures may be of two types: legitimate and illegitimate.

Cloward and Ohlin used the term **illegitimate opportunity structure** to describe preexisting subcultural paths to success that are not approved of by the wider culture. Where illegitimate paths to success are not already in place, alienated individuals may undertake a process of ideational evolution through which "a collective delinquent solution" or a "delinquent means of achieving success" may be decided upon by members of a gang. Because the two paths to success, legitimate and illegitimate, differ in their availability to members of society, Cloward and Ohlin's perspective has been termed *differential opportunity*.

**Illegitimate opportunity structure** subcultural pathways to success that are disapproved of by the wider society.

According to Cloward and Ohlin, delinquent behaviour may result from the ready availability of illegitimate opportunities with the effective replacement of the norms of the wider culture with expedient subcultural rules. Hence, delinquency and criminality may become "all right" or legitimate in the eyes of gang members and may even form the criteria used by other subcultural participants to judge successful accomplishments. In the words of Cloward and Ohlin, "[a] delinquent subculture is one in which certain forms of delinquent activity are essential requirements for the performance of the dominant roles supported by the subculture."[51] Its "most crucial elements" are the "prescriptions, norms, or rules of conduct that define the activities required of a full-fledged member."[52] "A person attributes legitimacy to a system of rules and corresponding models of behavior," wrote Cloward and Ohlin, "when he accepts them as binding on his conduct."[53] "Delinquents have withdrawn their support from established norms and invested officially forbidden forms of conduct with a claim to legitimacy. ..."[54]

Cloward and Ohlin noted that a delinquent act can be "defined by two essential elements: it is behavior that violates basic norms of the society, and, when officially known, it evokes a judgment by agents of criminal justice that such norms have been violated."[55]

For Cloward and Ohlin, however, crime and deviance were just as normal as any other form of behaviour supported by group socialization. In their words, "deviance and conformity generally result from the same kinds of social conditions …" and "deviance ordinarily represents a search for solutions to problems of adjustment." In their view, deviance is just as much an effort to conform, albeit to subcultural norms and expectations, as is conformity to the norms of the wider society. They added, however, that "[i]t has been our experience that most persons who participate in delinquent subcultures, if not lone offenders, are fully aware of the difference between right and wrong, between conventional behavior and rule-violating behavior. They may not care about the difference, or they may enjoy flouting the rules of the game, or they may have decided that illegitimate practices get them what they want more efficiently than legitimate practices."[56]

Cloward and Ohlin described three types of delinquent subcultures: (1) criminal subcultures, in which criminal role models are readily available for adoption by those being socialized into the subculture; (2) conflict subcultures, in which participants seek status through violence; and (3) retreatist subcultures, where drug use and withdrawal from the wider society predominate. Each subculture was thought to emerge from a larger, all-encompassing "parent" subculture of delinquent values. According to Cloward and Ohlin, delinquent subcultures have at least three identifiable features: (1) "acts of delinquency that reflect subcultural support are likely to recur with great frequency," (2) "access to a successful adult criminal career sometimes results from participation in a delinquent subculture," and (3) "the delinquent subculture imparts to the conduct of its members a high degree of stability and resistance to control or change."[57]

Cloward and Ohlin divided lower-class youth into four types according to their degree of commitment to middle-class values and/or material achievement. Type I youths were said to desire entry to the middle class through improvement in their economic position. Type II youths were seen as desiring entry to the middle class but not improvement in their economic position. Type III youth were portrayed as desiring wealth without entry to the middle class. As a consequence, Type III youths were seen as the most crime prone. Type IV youth were described as dropouts who retreated from the cultural mainstream through drug and alcohol use.

Cloward and Ohlin had a substantial impact on social policy, resulting in government programs designed to change the structures of legitimate opportunities in poor communities. Programs such as Mobilization for Youth, Jobs Corps, and Opportunities for Youth created employment and educational opportunities for deprived youths and were largely based on opportunity theory.

## Reaction Formation

Another criminologist whose work is often associated with both strain theory and the subcultural perspective is **Albert Cohen.** Like Cloward and Ohlin, Cohen's work focused primarily on the gang behaviour of delinquent youth. In Cohen's words, "[w]hen we speak of a delinquent subculture, we speak of a way of life that has somehow become traditional among certain groups in American society. These groups are the boys' gangs that flourish most conspicuously in the 'delinquency neighborhoods' of our larger American cities. The members of these gangs grow up, some to become law-abiding citizens and others to graduate to more professional and adult forms of criminality, but the delinquent tradition is kept alive by the age-groups that succeed them."[58]

CHAPTER 7

**219**
**Crime and the
Role of the Social
Environment**

Cohen argued that youngsters from all backgrounds are generally held account-able to the norms of the wider society through a "middle-class measuring rod" of expectations related to such items as school performance, language proficiency, cleanliness, punctuality, neatness, nonviolent behaviour, and allegiance to other similar standards. Like strain theorists, Cohen noted that unfortunately not everyone is prepared, by virtue of the circumstances surrounding his or her birth and subsequent socialization, for effectively meeting such expectations.

In an examination of vandalism, Cohen[59] found that "nonutilitarian" delinquency, in which things of value are destroyed rather than stolen or otherwise used for financial gain, is the result of middle-class values being turned upside down. Delinquent youths, argued Cohen, who are often alienated from middle-class values and lifestyles through deprivation and limited opportunities, can achieve status among their subcultural peers through vandalism and other forms of delinquent behaviour.

Children, especially those from deprived backgrounds, turn to delinquency, Cohen claimed, because they experience status-frustration when judged by adults and others according to middle-class standards and goals that they are unable to achieve. Because it is nearly impossible for nonmainstream children to succeed in middle-class terms, they may overcome anxiety through the process of reaction formation, in which hostility toward middle-class values develops. Cohen adapted **reaction formation** from psychiatric perspectives, using it to mean "the process in which a person openly rejects that which he wants, or aspires to, but cannot obtain or achieve."[60]

Cohen discovered the roots of delinquent subcultures in what he termed the "collective solution to the problem of status." When youths who experience the same kind of alienation from middle-class ideals band together, they achieve a collective and independent solution and create a delinquent subculture. Cohen wrote, "[t]he delinquent subculture, we suggest, is a way of dealing with the problems of adjustment. ... These problems are chiefly status problems: certain children are denied status in the respectable society because they cannot meet the criteria of the respectable status system. The delinquent subculture deals with these problems by providing criteria of status which these children *can* meet."[61]

Cohen's approach is effectively summarized in a "theoretical scenario" offered by Donald J. Shoemaker,[62] who says that lower-class youths undergo a working-class socialization that combines lower-class values and habits with middle-class success values. Lower-class youth then experience failure in school because they cannot live up to the middle-class norms operative in educational institutions. They suffer a consequent loss of self-esteem and increased feelings of rejection, leading to dropping out of school and "association with delinquent peers." Hostility and resentment toward middle-class standards grow through reaction formation. Finally, such alienated youths achieve status and a sense of improved self-worth through participation in a gang of like-minded peers. Delinquency and crime are the result.

**Reaction formation** the process in which a person openly rejects that which he or she wants, or aspires to, but cannot obtain or achieve.

## Gangs Today

Gangs have become a major source of concern in contemporary North American society, particularly in the United States. Although the writings of investigators such as Cohen, Thrasher, and Cloward and Ohlin focused on the illicit activities of juvenile gangs in inner cities, most gang-related crimes of the period involved vandalism, petty theft, and battles over turf. The ethnic distinctions that gave rise to gang culture in the 1920s through the 1950s in the United States are today largely forgotten. Italian, Hungarian, Polish, and Jewish immigrants, whose children made up many of the early gangs, have been, for the most part, successfully integrated into modern society.

Today's gang members appear more violent, involved with drugs, and intransigent than those studied by early researchers. Although the United States is the nation with the most gangs (and has the best information about them), Canada is not exempt from them. Statistical information about Canadian youth gangs is difficult to obtain, but the Solicitor General of Canada reports that they do exist. Some gangs may have members of one ethnic background, such as the Warriors, an Aboriginal street gang in Winnipeg, Manitoba. Others may be "male" or "female only" gangs, and some are mixed. Gang members can range in age from preteen to adult.[63]

One of the difficulties in determining the amount of gang activity in Canada stems from issues surrounding the definition of "gang" and "gang member." Often small groups of offenders are referred to by law enforcement officials or the media as gangs, even though the members of these groups do not see themselves that way. In a recent study of gangs in the Greater Vancouver area, this concern with definition is addressed and distinctions are made between "criminal business organizations," "street gangs," and "'wanna be' groups." The second phase of the study, known as The Greater Vancouver Gang Study, was started in May 1999 and is concentrating on the emergence, growth, activities, and eventual decline of three Vancouver street gangs. [64]

Information provided by Operation Go Home, a national organization that assists street youth in returning home, has identified a number of characteristics typical of Canadian youth gangs. These include:

- Ages for members range from 14 to 30, with the majority being 17 and 18.
- Most identify with a name (such as Ace Crew or Warriors).
- Many identify with a style of clothing or "colours," while others simply use an identifying bandana or handkerchief.
- Many members are recruited in schools, drop-in centres, or shopping malls, and this recruitment is sometimes forced.
- Male members often recruit girlfriends, who may then become pressured into prostitution.
- Initiation practices vary from none to acts of vandalism or violence.
- Many have their own principles, codes, rituals, and behaviours members must follow. These are not to be shared with anyone outside the gang.[65]

Information about gangs in the United States is much more detailed. A recent national survey[66] found that most gang members (47.8%) were African-American youth, while Hispanic youngsters accounted for 42.7 percent of reported gang members. Asian gang membership constituted 5.2 percent of all gang involvement, while Caucasians accounted for only 4.4 percent of gang members nationwide. A 1996 report estimated a yearly incidence of 580 331 gang-related crimes—a "12-fold increase over the 46 359 gang crimes estimated to have occurred in 1991."[67] The same report estimated the number of juvenile gangs nationwide at 16 643, with memberships totalling 555 181.

CHAPTER 7

221
**Crime and the
Role of the Social
Environment**

Gangs have become a concern in today's society. What social-structural theories might explain the proliferation of gangs and gang-related activity in Canada? *Douglas C. Pizac/AP/Wide World Photos.*

A large-scale project of the National Gang Crime Research Center, known as Project Gangfact, provides a profile of gangs and gang members throughout the United States. The 1996 Gangfact report,[68] based on data collected by 28 researchers in 17 states, showed similar, albeit more detailed, characteristics to the Canadian reality:

- The average age for joining a gang, nationally, is 12.8 years of age.
- Over one-half who joined gangs have tried to quit.
- More than two-thirds of gangs have written rules for members to follow.
- Over one-half of all gangs hold regular weekly meetings.
- Nearly 30 percent of gangs require their members to pay dues.
- Approximately 55 percent of gang members have been recruited by other gang members, while the remainder sought out gang membership.
- Most gang members (79%) said they would leave the gang if given a "second chance in life."
- Four-fifths of gang members reported that their gangs sold crack cocaine.
- Most gangs (70%) are not racially exclusive and consist of members drawn from a variety of ethnic groups.
- One-third of gang members report that they have been able to conceal their gang membership from their parents.
- Most gangs (83%) report having female members, but few allow female members to assume leadership roles.
- Many gang members (40%) report knowing male members of their gangs who had raped females.

# Violent Girls New Crime Wave

Youth crime has traditionally been committed predominantly by males. New studies indicate, however, that more females are becoming involved.

*By Kim Lunman and Laura Shutiak*

CALGARY—Violent acts by young girls—brought sharply home by this week's murder trials in the deaths of Calgary's Isabel Cho, 19, and Victoria's Reena Virk, 14—have become the fastest-growing category of crime in Canada.

The number of teenage girls charged with violent crimes has tripled since 1986, according to the Canadian Centre for Justice Statistics. In all, 5191 female youths aged 12 to 17 were charged with violent crimes—including murder and assault— in 1996, compared with 1728 in 1986, centre figures show. Meanwhile, the number of boys 12 to 17 charged with violent crimes over the same decade doubled to 16 620 from 7547.

"It's not at crisis levels but it is serious," said Sibylle Artz, a Victoria-based expert on violence and teenage girls. "It's serious because people are getting killed."

On Friday, two Victoria girls, 14 and 16, who lured Reena Virk out the night she was beaten and drowned were each sentenced to one year in jail.

Judge Alan Filmer said he was concerned about the futures of the girls, with one displaying "all the elements, quite frankly, of sociopathic conduct."

The two planned to physically confront Ms. Virk, although they didn't think the plan would lead to her death, the judge said. Seven teenaged girls and one boy were charged in Ms. Virk's death.

What happened to Ms. Virk was a horrible example of mob violence set in motion by the actions of the two girls, Judge Filmer said. Ms. Artz, director of the School of Child and Youth Care at the University of Victoria, in part blames the increase in female youth violence on the portrayal of violence by women in movies and television.

"Many of the action-hero movies show that women's power comes from sex and violence—especially violence against other women in competition for men," said Ms. Artz, author of *Sex, Power and the Violent Schoolgirl.* "And this is exactly what young women are doing."

Grant Charles, director of day treatment and research at Woods Homes, a Calgary group home for troubled youth, cautions that statistics can be misleading. "We've dealt with very violent young women for a long time. It's not that the behaviors are new, it's just that we're seeing more of them."

Although the Virk case has made national headlines, other cases nearly as shocking have emerged to surprise law enforcement officers and test community patience, leading to the federal government's recent plan to revamp the Young Offenders Act.

In Alberta, a 13-year-old girl and her 15-year-old boyfriend are charged with murdering the girl's mother in Lethbridge in January. Earlier this week, Edmonton police charged two girls, 14 and 15, following a violent rampage with two boys, aged 13 and 11, for allegedly punching, stabbing and sexually assaulting several victims in two attacks. In Calgary, three women in their early 20s are on trial this week for allegedly beating Ms. Cho to death in a downtown night club.

▶

CHAPTER 7

223

**Crime and the
Role of the Social
Environment**

And in Saskatchewan, two 15-year-old girls are charged with killing the operator of a home for troubled teens in North Battleford.

In Alberta, 668 girls were charged with violent crimes in 1996 compared to 193 charged 10 years ago.

For the next three days, 250 delegates from across Western Canada will discuss violent trends among youth, and possible solutions at a three-day Symposium on Child and Adolescent Violence, starting Sunday in Calgary.

## DISCUSSION QUESTIONS

1. Why is violent crime by young girls increasing?
2. What social-structural theories might be used to explain this phenomenon?

SOURCE: Kim Lunman and Laura Shutiak, "Violent Girls New Crime Wave," *The Calgary Herald*, as cited in the *Ottawa Citizen*, May 10, 1998, p. A6. Reprinted with permission of The Calgary Herald.

Los Angeles is considered to be the "gang capital"[69] of the United States with more than 143 000 juveniles known to be participating in over 1 142 different gangs as of June 1, 1995.[70] During 1994, Los Angeles County saw 779 gang-related homicides, and over 1 711 injuries were directly caused by gang activity.[71] Drugs form the centrepiece of much Los Angeles gang activity, with large quantities of crack—a highly addictive form of cocaine—being produced and sold by many groups.

Contemporary researchers, however, are drawing some new distinctions between gangs and violence. Several years ago, G. David Curry and Irving A. Spergel, in a study of Chicago communities, distinguished between juvenile delinquency and gang-related homicide.[72] They found that communities characterized by high rates of delinquency do not necessarily experience exceptionally high rates of crime or of gang-related homicides. They concluded that although gang activity may be associated with homicide, "gang homicide rates and delinquency rates are ecologically distinct community problems." Gang-related homicide, they found, seems to be well explained by classical theories of social disorganization and is especially prevalent in areas of the city characterized by in-migration and by the "settlement of new immigrant groups." In their study, high rates of juvenile delinquency seemed to correlate more with poverty, which the researchers defined as "social adaptation to chronic deprivation." According to Curry and Spergel, "[s]ocial disorganization and poverty rather than criminal organization and conspiracy may better explain the recent growth and spread of youth gangs to many parts of the country. Moreover, community organization and social opportunity in conjunction with suppression, rather than simply suppression and incapacitation, may be more effective policies in dealing with the social problem."[73] In devising strategies to counter gang activity, policy-makers must remember that many gang members are delinquent before they become associated with gangs and that merely suppressing gangs should not replace other youth crime intervention and prevention strategies.[74]

# General Strain Theory

Strain theory has recently been reformulated by **Robert Agnew**[75] and others into a theory of broader scope, called general strain theory (GST). General strain theory builds on traditional strain theory in several ways. First, it significantly expands the focus of strain theory to include all types of negative relations between an individual and others. Second, GST maintains that strain is likely to have a cumulative effect on delinquency after reaching a certain threshold. Third, general strain theory provides a more comprehensive account of the cognitive, behavioural, and emotional adaptations to strain than do traditional strain approaches. Finally, GST more fully describes the wide variety of factors affecting the choice of delinquent adaptations to strain. According to GST, strain occurs when others do the following: (1) prevent or threaten to prevent an individual from achieving positively valued goals; (2) remove or threaten to remove positively valued stimuli that a person possesses; or (3) present or threaten to present someone with noxious or negatively valued stimuli. Agnew sees the crime-producing effects of strain as cumulative and concludes that whatever form it takes, "[s]train creates a predisposition for delinquency in those cases in which it is chronic or repetitive."[76]

A 1994 study[77] tested some of the assumptions underlying GST through an analysis of American data. It found partial support for GST and discovered that negative relations with adults, feelings of dissatisfaction with friends and school life, and the experience of stressful events (e.g., family dissolution) were positively related to delinquency, as was living in an unpleasant neighbourhood (one beset by social problems and physical deterioration). When conceived of more broadly as exposure to negative stimuli, general strain was found to be significantly related to delinquency.

Contrary to Agnew's hypothesis, however, the study found no evidence that the effects of strain were increased when experienced for longer periods of time nor diminished when adolescents classified that part of their life in which they experienced strain as "unimportant." Consistent with earlier findings,[78] the study also found that feelings of general strain were positively related to later delinquency, regardless of the number of delinquent peers, moral beliefs, self-efficacy, and level of conventional social support. Some support was found for the belief that general strain leads to delinquency by weakening the conventional social bond and strengthening the unconventional bond with delinquent peers.

A recent analysis by Agnew[79] of other strain theories found that all such theories share at least two central explanatory features. Strain theories, Agnew said, (1) focus "explicitly on negative relationships with others; relationships in which the individual is not treated as he or she wants to be treated" and (2) argue that "adolescents are pressured into delinquency by the negative affective states—most notably anger and related emotions—that often result from negative relationships." Agnew also found that strain theories generally describe three different types of negative relationships with others, or forms of "strain": (1) situations in which individuals actively prevent another person from achieving positively valued goals; (2) the intentional removal or threatened removal of something that is positively valued; or (3) the presenting or threatened presenting of negatively valued stimuli.

CHAPTER 7

225

**Crime and the
Role of the Social
Environment**

## Critique of Strain Theory

Merton's original formulation of strain theory, although it has much of value to say about the consequences of unequal opportunity, is probably less applicable to North American society today than it was in the 1930s, because in the last few decades considerable effort has been made toward improving success opportunities for everyone—regardless of ethnic heritage, race, or gender. Hence, it is less likely that individuals today will find themselves without the opportunity for choice, as was the case decades ago. Even so, social programs designed to provide equal opportunity have had little impact on some apparently well-insulated segments of society where even the semblance of participating in "approved means" may be grounds for derision.

General strain theories, like those summarized by Agnew, have more contemporary relevance than Merton's original formulation. As Agnew points out, opportunities to legitimate success may be blocked at many junctures in the life course, resulting in strain, frustration, and anger—all of which may produce law-violating behaviour in those undergoing them.[80]

Travis Hirschi,[81] however, criticizes strain theory for its inability "to locate people suffering from discrepancy" and notes that human beings are naturally optimistic—a fact, he says, that "overrides ... aspiration-expectation disjunction." Hirschi concludes that "[e]xpectations appear to affect delinquency, but they do so regardless of aspirations, and strain notions are neither consistent with nor required by the data."

# Policy Implications

Theoretical approaches that look to the social environment as the root cause of crime point in the direction of social action as a panacea. In the 1930s, for example, Clifford Shaw, in an effort to put his theories into practice, established the Chicago Area Project. The Chicago Area Project attempted to reduce social disorganization in slum neighborhoods through the creation of community committees. Shaw staffed committees with local residents rather than professional social workers. The project had three broad objectives: (1) improving the physical appearance of poor neighbourhoods, (2) providing recreational opportunities for youth, and (3) involving project members directly in the lives of troubled youth through school and courtroom mediation. The program also made use of "curbside counselors," streetwise workers who could serve as positive role models for inner-city youth. Although no effective assessment programs were established to evaluate the Chicago Area Project during the program's tenure, reviewers in 1984 provided a 55 review of the program, declaring it "effective in reducing rates of juvenile delinquency."[82]

Similarly, Mobilization for Youth (MFY), cited earlier in this chapter as an outgrowth of Cloward and Ohlin's theory of differential opportunity, provides a bold example of the treatment implications of social-structural theories. Mobilization for Youth sought not only to provide new opportunities, but also to change the fundamental arrangements of society through direct social action and thereby address the root causes of crime and deviance. Leaders of Mobilization for Youth decided that "[w]hat was needed to overcome ... formidable barriers to opportunity ... was not community organization but community action" that attacked entrenched political interests. Accordingly, MFY promoted "boycotts against schools, protests against welfare policies, rent strikes against 'slum landlords', lawsuits to ensure poor people's rights, and voter registration."[83] A truly unusual government-sponsored program for its time, Mobilization for Youth was eventually disbanded in the face of protests that its mandate was to reduce delinquency, not reform society or test sociological theories.[84]

A contemporary example of social intervention efforts based on sociological theories can be had in the Youth Violence Project: A Community-Based Violence Prevention Project, recently introduced in a Vancouver Island school district. It is a community-based initiative designed to address the problem of youth violence and involves teachers, counsellors, parents, students, and representatives from health and social service agencies. Consisting of 13 individual antiviolence initiatives, it is intended to educate and train students and community members in a preventative approach to violence by helping individuals change their behaviour and acquire skills that enable them to use nonviolent responses in circumstances where violence might previously have been used.[85]

Mobilization for Youth and the Youth Violence Project both stand as examples of the kinds of programs that theorists who focus on the social environment typically seek to implement. Social programs of this sort are intended to change the cultural conditions and societal arrangements that are thought to lead people into crime.

## Critique of Social-Structural Theories

Social-structural theories suffer from one general shortcoming that similarly affects most other perspectives on crime causation. In the words of Canadian criminologist Gwynn Nettler, "the conceptual bias of social scientists emphasizes environments—cultures and structures—as the powerful causes of differential conduct. This bias places an intellectual taboo on looking elsewhere for possible causes as, for example, in physiologies. This taboo is … strongly applied against the possibility that ethnic groups may have genetically transmitted differential physiologies that have relevance for social behavior."[86]

Nettler is telling us that social scientists downplay the causative role of nonsociological factors. Many believe that such factors are important. But, since sociological theorizing has captured most of the academic attention over the past few decades, the role of other causative factors in the etiology of criminal behaviour stands in danger of being shortchanged.

Social-structural approaches also suffer from a seeming inability to explain the behaviour of many, even though they may appear applicable to a few. Moreover, some see the inability of social-structural theories to predict which individuals—or at least what proportion of a given population—will turn to crime, as a crucial failure of such perspectives. Although the large majority of persons growing up in inner-city, poverty-ridden areas, for example, probably experience an inequitable opportunity structure firsthand, only a relatively small number of those people become criminal. It is true that substantially more people living under such conditions may become criminal than those living in other types of social environments. Nonetheless, a large proportion of persons experiencing strain, as well as a large number of persons raised in deviant subcultures, will still embrace noncriminal lifestyles.

CHAPTER 7
227
**Crime and the
Role of the Social
Environment**

In his book, *The Moral Sense,* James Q. Wilson suggests that most people—regardless of socialization experiences and the structural aspects of their social circumstances—may still carry within themselves an inherent sense of fairness and interpersonal morality.[87] If what Wilson suggests is even partially true, then the explanatory power of social-structural theories may be limited by human nature itself.

## Summary

Social-structural theories suggest that the causes of crime lie in the structural arrangements of society and in the way in which social institutions communicate their values to group members. Overall, the concept of subcultures plays an especially important role in sociological theorizing. Even those perspectives that do not speak directly of organized subcultures seem to recognize their significance. These theories also build on the notion that crime may result from blocked opportunities for achieving success.

Because these theories look to the organization of society for their explanatory power, intervention strategies based on them typically argue for the modification of formal or informal group processes—including the educational process and familial and work arrangements—and to the increased availability of legitimate opportunity structures. Social programs may be created under the umbrella of particular sociological theories, as the Youth Violence Project or Mobilization for Youth were.

## Discussion Questions

1. This book emphasizes a social problems versus social responsibility theme. Which of the theoretical perspectives discussed in this chapter best support the social problems approach? Which support the social responsibility approach? Why?
2. Do you believe ecological theories have a valid place in contemporary criminological thinking? Why or why not?
3. How, if at all, does the notion of a "criminology of place" differ from more traditional ecological theories? Do you see the criminology of place approach as capable of offering anything new over traditional approaches? If so, what?
4. What is a violent subculture? Why do some subcultures stress violence? How might participants in a subculture of violence be turned toward less aggressive ways?
5. Compare and contrast the theories discussed in this chapter, citing differences and similarities between and among them. How, for example, does Miller's notion of strain differ from Cloward and Ohlin's idea of opportunity structures? How is it similar?
6. What policy implications do you think the theories discussed in this chapter hold? What kinds of changes in society and in government policy might be based on the theories discussed here? Would they be likely to bring about a reduction in crime?

## Weblinks

**www.discribe.ca/childfind/**
Child Find Canada. Child Find is a volunteer network of registered charitable organizations that provides public education and services related to missing children.

**www.childcybersearch.org/**
Child Cyber Search Canada. Child Cyber Search Canada is Canada's first Internet-based missing children agency. Provides links to police forces across Canada as well as a listing of related missing children sites.

**www.iir.com/nygc/**
National Youth Gang Center. Under the auspices of the U.S. federal government's Office of Juvenile Justice and Delinquency Prevention, the centre provides comprehensive statistical and legislative information about American gang activity.

# The Meaning of Crime: Social Process Perspectives

Deviation is criminal only if effectively reacted to and symbolized as such.

—EDWIN M. LEMERT[1]

The problem of crime always gets reduced to, "What can be done about criminals?" Nobody asks, "What can be done about victims?"

—ROBERT REIFF[2]

## LEARNING OUTCOMES

After reading this chapter, you should be able to:

● Recognize how the process of social interaction between people contributes to criminal behaviour

● Identify and distinguish between a number of social process theories

● Appreciate the importance of an understanding of the victim in the study of crime and criminality

● Identify current social policy initiatives reflecting the social process approach

● Assess the shortcomings of the | social process perspective

IMPORTANT NAMES

Edwin Sutherland
Gresham Sykes
David Matza
Sheldon and Eleanor
    Glueck
John Laub
Robert Sampson

Lawrence E. Cohen
Richard Machalek
Frank Tannenbaum
Edwin M. Lemert
Howard Becker
John Braithwaite
Walter C. Reckless

Travis Hirschi
Michael R. Gottfredson
Hans von Hentig
Benjamin Mendelsohn
Marvin E. Wolfgang
Margaret Fry

IMPORTANT TERMS

social process theories
interactionist
    perspectives
learning theory
differential association
techniques of
    neutralization
life course theories
social capital
cohort analysis
cohort
evolutionary ecology
tagging

primary deviance
secondary deviance
labelling
moral enterprise
stigmatic shaming
reintegrative shaming
containment theory
containment
social control theory
social bond
victimology
victim-proneness
penal couple

victimogenesis
victim-precipitated
    criminal homicide
postcrime victimization
secondary
    victimization
victim/witness assistance
    programs
victim impact statement
restitution
victim fine surcharge

# Introduction

In late 1993, James Hamm found himself at the center of a vicious controversy. Hamm, a convicted murderer, had served 18 years in prison for shooting a man in the head over a drug deal gone bad and was about to enter a state university law school. Hamm had been parolled in June 1992 after Arizona's parole board judged him "rehabilitated." While in prison, Hamm, a former divinity student, earned a bachelor's degree in sociology and had been active in Middle Ground, a prisoner's rights group. While the 45-year-old Hamm worked on getting an education, students at the university were challenging his access to law school, saying that a convicted murderer did not deserve to be admitted. Local politicians claimed, "There are a lot of hard-working young people out there who could not get into law school because he did."[3] Members of the Arizona Board of Regents, which runs the state's public universities, called for a review of policies on admitting ex-convicts to the schools. Nonetheless, Hamm, who scored in the top five percent of all applicants taking the law school admissions test nationwide, seemed to hold excellent promise as a student. In Hamm's words, the controversy surrounding him "touches on feelings about crime, criminals, recidivism, the failure of the criminal justice system … I'm a lightning rod for those feelings,"[4] he said.

The case of James Hamm provides an example of how society's continued reaction to what it defines as criminal behaviour can change the course of an offender's life—often for the worse—even after he has paid his "dues." As some would say, while there

CHAPTER 8

231

**The Meaning
of Crime:
Social Process
Perspectives**

are plenty of ex-cons, there is no such thing as an "ex-ex-con." Or "once a con, always a con." Society, it seems, never forgets.

# Major Principles of Social Process Perspectives

This brief section serves to summarize the central features of social process theories of crime causation. Each of these points can be found elsewhere in this chapter, where they are discussed in more detail. This cursory overview provides a guide to the rest of the chapter.

Most social process theories of crime causation make the following fundamental assumptions:

- The nature of social reality is in flux; what we think of as social reality is a construction—specifically, an artifact of socialization and social interaction. In short, human beings are seen as coproducers of their social worlds.
- The meaning of events and experiences is conferred upon them by the participants in any interaction. Social actors define the situations in which they are involved.
- Meaning is derived from previous learned experiences and is conferred upon experiences in typical and recurring ways.
- Behaviour is criminal insofar as others define it as such and agree to its meaning.
- Criminal behaviour is variously interpreted by the offender, the victim, agents of social control, and society.
- Deviant individuals and criminal offenders achieve their status by virtue of social definition, rather than because of inborn traits.
- Continued criminal activity may be a consequence of limited opportunities for acceptable behaviour, which follow from the negative responses of society to those defined as criminal.
- Career offenders participate in a worldview that differs from the worldview of the conformist and that grants legitimacy to nonconformist activity.

# Social Process Perspectives

The theories discussed in this chapter are typically called **social process theories**, or **interactionist perspectives**, because they emphasize the give-and-take that occurs between an individual and others, including family members, peers, and teachers as well as agents of formal social control such as the police, courts, and correctional organizations. These theories depend upon the action (or reaction) of society to the offender (or the victim) for much of their explanatory power—that is, upon the process of social interaction occurring between the offender and others in society. It is essentially the manner in which this process of socialization occurs that most directly influences the behaviour of an individual and largely determines whether or not he or she becomes criminal. Another term frequently applied to the perspectives outlined in this chapter is interactionist, because the notion of give-and-take implies some activity to which a response is made.

**Social process theories,** also known as **interactionist perspectives,** emphasize the give-and-take that occurs between offender, victim, and society—and specifically between the offender and agents of formal social control such as the police, courts, and correctional organizations.

# Theory in Perspective
## Types of Social Process Theories

**SOCIAL PROCESS THEORIES** also known as **INTERACTIONIST PERSPECTIVES**
Emphasize the give-and-take which occurs between offender, victim, and society—and specifically between the offender and agents of formal social control such as the police, courts, and correctional organizations.

**Differential Association.** Maintains that criminality, like any other form of behaviour, is learned through a process of association with others who communicate criminal values.
**Period:** 1930s–1960s
**Theorists:** Edwin Sutherland and others
**Concepts:** Differential association; crime as learned; techniques of crime; commission, frequency, duration, priority, and intensity of association

**Life Course Theories.** Highlight the development of criminal careers, which are seen as the result of various criminogenic influences that impact individuals throughout the course of their lives.
**Period:** 1930s–present
**Theorists:** Sheldon and Eleanor Glueck, Marvin Wolfgang, John Laub and Robert Sampson, Lawrence E. Cohen and Richard Machalek
**Concepts:** Career criminality, cohorts, social capital, evolutionary ecology

**Labelling.** An interactionist perspective which sees continued crime as a consequence of limited opportunities for acceptable behaviour which follow from the negative responses of society to those defined as offenders.
**Period:** 1938–1940 and 1960s–1980s, 1990s revival
**Theorists:** Frank Tannenbaum, Edwin M. Lemert, Howard Becker, John Braithwaite, and others
**Concepts:** Tagging, labelling, outsiders, moral enterprise, primary and secondary deviance, reintegrative shaming

**Social Control Approaches.** Ask why people obey rules instead of breaking them.
**Period:** 1950s–present
**Theorists:** Walter C. Reckless, Travis Hirschi, Michael R. Gottfredson, and others
**Concepts:** Inner and outer containment, social bond

**Victimology.** The study of victims and their contributory role, if any, in crime causation.
**Period:** 1930s–present
**Theorists:** Hans von Hentig, Benjamin Mendelsohn, Henry Ellenberger, Marvin E. Wolfgang, Margaret Fry, Stephen Schafer
**Concepts:** Victim proneness, penal couple, victim-precipitated homicide, victimogenesis, restitution, victim impact statements, Canadian Statement of Basic Principles of Justice for Victims of Crime

CHAPTER 8

233

**The Meaning
of Crime:
Social Process
Perspectives**

The process of socialization is a complex one. In an attempt to simplify it, the theories in this chapter are divided into three main categories. *Social learning theory* promotes the notion that criminal behaviour is learned through human interaction. *Labelling theory* postulates that some people are labelled criminal by the criminal justice system and by members of society and that this label negatively influences further interactions. Finally, *social control theory* regards interactions with others as a means of controlling one's behaviour, especially if these associations are particularly strong ones.

# Social Learning Theories

## Differential Association

One important perspective on criminality is a form of **learning theory** advanced by **Edwin Sutherland** in 1939. Called **differential association,** Sutherland's thesis was that criminality is learned behaviour, acquired through a process of association with others who communicate criminal values and who may advocate the commission of crimes. All significant human behaviour, according to Sutherland, is learned behaviour, and crime, therefore, is not substantively different from any other form of behaviour.

Although Sutherland died in 1950, the tenth edition of his famous book, *Criminology,* was published in 1978 under the authorship of Donald R. Cressey, a professor at the University of California at Santa Barbara. The 1978 edition of *Criminology* contained the finalized principles of differential association (which, for all practical purposes, were complete as early as 1947). The principles are as follows:

1. *Criminal behaviour is learned.* Sutherland believed that criminal behaviour is learned in the same manner as learning how to read or write. In other words, criminal behaviour is not seen as an inherent character trait.
2. *Criminal behaviour is learned in interaction with other persons in a process of communication.* Sutherland believed that learning criminal behaviour is very much dependent on the association between individuals. Those who are already criminal serve as "teachers" to others.
3. *The principal part of the learning of criminal behaviour occurs within intimate personal groups.* Any individual is influenced by those to whom he or she is closest— family members, peers, and friends. Relationships with these individuals will control the way one sees the world. For example, studies have shown that children who grow up in households where parents abuse alcohol tend to develop the attitudes that support such behaviour.[5] The belief that many young people are pressured by peers to commit illegal acts is inherent in this third principle of Sutherland's. It is the intimate peer group that most significantly influences youth.
4. *When criminal behaviour is learned, the learning includes (a) techniques of committing the crime, which are sometimes very complicated, sometimes very simple, and (b) the specific direction of motives, drives, rationalizations, and attitudes.* Since learning criminal behaviour is like learning any other kind of behaviour, the actual techniques of committing the crime must be taught and learned. Offenders learn from others how to pick locks, get involved in prostitution, obtain and use illicit drugs, or shoplift, for example. In addition to learning the actual techniques of criminal

**Learning theory** the general notion that crime is an acquired form of behaviour, which is learned just as are many other forms of behaviour.

**Differential association** the sociological thesis that criminality, like any other form of behaviour, is learned through a process of association with others who communicate criminal values.

behaviour, Sutherland contended that offenders also learn the attitudes necessary to justify the behaviour. Some of these justifications are discussed later in the chapter under the heading, "Neutralization Techniques."

5. *The specific direction of motives and drives is learned from definitions of the legal codes as favourable or unfavourable.* Sutherland believed that there are a variety of attitudes toward both the legal code and notions of right and wrong behaviour. The attitudes toward criminal behaviour held by the significant people in an individual's life have the greatest impact on the attitudes developed by the individual, through differential association.

6. *A person becomes delinquent because of an excess of definitions favourable to violation of law over definitions unfavourable to violation of law.* Interaction with those people or events that promote a disregard for the law will serve to strengthen and solidify those attitudes in another. For example, if a person spends more time in the company of someone who is constantly stealing compact discs from music stores than with parents who extol the virtues of honesty and respect for the property of others, then disregard for the law becomes reinforced.

7. *Differential associations may vary in frequency, duration, priority, and intensity.* Whether a person learns to disobey the law depends upon the quality of the social interactions experienced. The more often one interacts with a deviant group, the greater the likelihood of learning the behaviour. The length of the interaction also influences the likelihood of learning a given behaviour. Priority has been interpreted to mean the age at which a person first encounters criminality. It is believed that contacts made at an earlier age are likely to have a more significant impact on that person's behaviour than those made later in life. Sutherland referred to intensity as the importance attributed to the people or groups from whom the behaviour is being learned. For example, for many youth at a certain stage of development, peer groups take priority over parents and can significantly influence a young person's behaviour.

8. *The process of learning criminal behaviour by association with criminal and anticriminal patterns involves all of the mechanisms that are involved in any other learning.* Sutherland believed that learning criminal behaviour occurs the same way as learning any other behaviour and does not simply involve imitation.

9. *While criminal behaviour is an expression of general needs and values, it is not explained by those general needs and values, since noncriminal behaviour is an expression of the same needs and values.* This final principle holds that the motive for criminal behaviour is not the same as that for noncriminal behaviour. In other words, the desire for a leather jacket in and of itself does not foster criminal behaviour. Why one will work to earn money to buy the jacket and someone else will steal it is largely determined by the different norms learned through associations with various groups. The learning of deviant norms from deviant groups produces criminal behaviour, according to Sutherland.

Differential association found considerable acceptance among theorists of the mid-twentieth century because it combined then prevalent psychological and sociological principles into a coherent perspective on criminality. Crime as a form of learned behaviour became the catchword of twentieth-century criminology, and biological and other perspectives were essentially abandoned by those involved in the process of theory testing.

CHAPTER 8
235
**The Meaning
of Crime:
Social Process
Perspectives**

Drug use is a type of criminal behaviour that is most often learned through association with peer groups. What specific aspects of drug use need to be learned? *Matt Mendelsohn Photography.*

## Critique of Differential Association

Differential association is not without its critics. Perhaps the most potent criticism is the claim that differential association, because of the way in which Sutherland presented it, is virtually untestable, even though much use has been made of the insights the perspective appears to offer. Other critics also suggest that differential association alone is not a sufficient explanation for crime. If it were, then we might expect correctional officers, for example, to become criminals by virtue of their constant and continued association with prison inmates. Similarly, wrongly imprisoned persons might be expected to turn to crime upon release from confinement. Little evidence suggests that either of these scenarios actually occurs. In effect, differential association does not seem to provide for free choice in individual circumstances, nor for the fact that some individuals, even when surrounded by associates who are committed to lives of crime, are still able to hold onto other, noncriminal, values.

## Neutralization Techniques

Of particular interest to some proponents of differential association is the manner in which various rationalizations are employed by those involved in criminal behaviour. Those who disobey the law are, at least to some degree, participants in the larger culture that surrounds them. How is it, then, that they may choose behavioural alternatives that seemingly negate the norms and values of the larger society? While social learning theorists such as Sutherland and Cressey contend that criminal behaviour is learned through the mastery of techniques, values, and attitudes needed to commit deviant acts, neutralization theory holds that most offenders learn **techniques of neutralization** to allow them to go against conventional values and attitudes. **Gresham Sykes and David Matza** put forth this notion in their 1957 article, "Techniques of Neutralization."[6] Sykes and Matza suggested that offenders can overcome feelings of responsibility when involved in crime commission through the use of the following five types of justifications:

1. *Denial of responsibility,* by pointing to one's background of poverty, abuse, lack of opportunity, and so on. Example: "The trouble I get into is not my fault," or, "They made me do it."
2. *Denial of injury,* by explaining how insurance companies, for example, cover losses. Claims that "everyone does it" or that the specific victim could "afford it" fall into this category. Example: "They're so rich, they'll never miss it."
3. *Denial of the victim,* or justifying the harm done by claiming that the victim, for whatever reason, deserved the victimization. Example: "I only beat up drunks," or, "She had it coming."
4. *Condemning the condemners,* by asserting that authorities are corrupt or responsible for their own victimization. Offenders may also claim that society has made them into what they are, and must now suffer the consequences. Example: "They're worse than we are. They're all on the take," or, "If I don't do it to him, he'll do it to me."
5. *An appeal to higher loyalties,* as in defence of one's family honour, gang, girlfriend, or neighbourhood. Example: "We have to protect ourselves."

In the words of Sykes and Matza, "[i]t is our argument that much delinquency is based on what is essentially an unrecognized extension of defenses to crimes, in the form of justifications for deviance that are seen as valid by the delinquent but not by the legal system or society at large."[7]

A few years later, Matza went on to suggest that delinquents tended to drift into crime when they found that available techniques of neutralization combined with weak or ineffective values espoused by the controlling elements in society. In effect, said Matza, the delinquent "drifts between criminal and conventional action," choosing whichever is the more expedient at the time. By employing techniques of neutralization, delinquents need not be fully alienated from the larger society. When opportunities for crime present themselves, such techniques provide an effective way of overcoming feelings of guilt and allowing for ease of action. Matza used the phrase "soft determinism" to describe drift, saying that delinquents were neither forced to make choices because of fateful experiences early in life, nor were they entirely free to make choices unencumbered by the realities of their situation.

More recent studies have found that whereas "only a small percentage of adolescents generally approve of violence or express indifference to violence … [a] large percentage of adolescents … accept neutralizations justifying the use of violence in particular situations."[8] The acceptance of such justifications by many young people today is seen as supportive of high levels of youth violence. Studies have also found that young people who disapprove of violence but associate with delinquent peers will often use neutralization techniques as justifications for violence in which they personally engage.[9]

CHAPTER 8

237
**The Meaning
of Crime:
Social Process
Perspectives**

## Criminal Careers and Life Course Theory

Criminal careers may develop as the result of various criminogenic influences acting on individuals. Career criminality is frequently explained by **life course theories**, which provide a kind of summary approach incorporating many other sociological perspectives. Most life course theories recognize that criminogenic influences have their greatest impact during the early stages of life. Hence, such perspectives agree with the widely held belief that children are more impressionable than older people, and that the experiences children have shape them for the rest of their lives.

Life course theories are supported by research dating back more than half a century. During the 1930s, for example, **Sheldon** and **Eleanor Glueck** studied the life cycles of delinquent boys. The Gluecks followed the careers of known delinquents in an effort to identify the causes of delinquency. Data were originally collected through psychiatric interviews with subjects, parent and teacher reports, and official records obtained from police, court, and correctional files. Surviving subjects were again interviewed between 1949 and 1965. The Gluecks found that family dynamics played an especially significant role in the development of criminality and observed that "the deeper the roots of childhood maladjustment, the smaller the chance of adult adjustment."[10] Delinquent careers, said the Gluecks, tend to carry over into adulthood and frequently lead to criminal careers.

Several years ago, **John Laub** and **Robert Sampson**[11] reanalyzed the data originally gathered by the Gluecks, and found that children who turn to delinquency are frequently those who have trouble at school and at home, and who have friends already involved in delinquency. Using a sophisticated computerized analysis of the Gluecks' original data, Laub and Sampson identified "turning points" in a criminal career.

**Life course theories** explanations for criminality that recognize that criminogenic influences have their greatest impact during the early stages of life and that hold that experiences children have shape them for the rest of their lives.

People in total institutions share all aspects of their lives and learn attitudes and behaviours from one another—such as these monks in a Buddhist monastery. How is a prison like a monastery?
*Eastcott/Momatiuk/Woodfin Camp & Associates.*

**Social capital** the degree
of positive relationships
with other persons and
social institutions that
individuals build up
over the course of their
lives.

**Cohort analysis** a social
scientific technique that
studies a population that
sharing common
characteristics over time.
Cohort analysis usually
begins at birth and
traces the development
of cohort members until
they reach a certain age.

**Cohort** a group of
individuals sharing
certain significant social
characteristics in
common, such as gender
and time and place of
birth.

**Evolutionary ecology** an
approach to under-
standing crime that
draws attention to the
ways people develop
over the course of their
lives.

Turning points, they found, may occur at any time in such a career, although two especially significant turning points centre on the choice of employment and marriage.
Employers who are willing to give "troublemakers" a chance and marriage partners
who insist on conventional lifestyles can successfully redirect the course of a budding
offender's life, according to these authors. Laub and Sampson also developed the concept of **social capital** to refer to the degree of positive relationships with other persons
and social institutions that individuals build up over the course of their lives. The
greater one's social capital, the less the chance of criminal activity.[12]

Life course theory uses a developmental perspective in the study of criminal careers.
As a consequence, life course researchers frequently use cohort analysis. **Cohort analysis** usually begins at birth and traces the development of a population whose members
share common characteristics until they reach a certain age. One well-known analysis
of a birth **cohort,** undertaken by Marvin Wolfgang during the 1960s, found that a small
nucleus of chronic juvenile offenders accounted for a disproportionately large share of
all juvenile arrests.[13] Wolfgang studied male individuals born in Philadelphia in 1945,
following them until they reached age 18. He concluded that a relatively small number
of violent offenders were responsible for most of the crimes committed by the cohort.
Eighteen percent of cohort members accounted for 52 percent of all arrests. A follow-
up study found that seriousness of offences among the cohort increased in adulthood,
but that the actual number of offences decreased as the cohort aged.[14] Wolfgang's analysis, which is also discussed in Chapter 4, has since been criticized for its lack of a second
cohort, or control group, against which the experiences of the cohort under study could
be compared.[15] More recently, Wolfgang published a cohort analysis of 5 000 individuals born in the Wuchang district of the city of Wuhan in China. The study, from which
preliminary results were published in 1996, utilized Chinese-supplied data to compare
delinquents with nondelinquents. It found "striking differences in school deportment,
achieved level of education, school dropout rate, type of employment, and unemployment rate …"[16] between the two groups.

The ecological perspective on crime control, pioneered by **Lawrence E. Cohen**
and **Richard Machalek,**[17] provides a contemporary example of a life course approach. Like other life course theories, **evolutionary ecology** blends elements of previous perspectives—in this case building upon the approach of social ecology—while
emphasizing developmental pathways encountered early in life. According to Bryan
Vila, "the evolutionary ecological approach … draws attention to the ways people develop over the course of their lives. Experiences and environment early in life," says
Vila, "especially those that affect child development and the transmission of biological traits and family management practices across generations, seem particular important."[18] According to Vila, evolutionary ecology "attempts to explain how people
acquire criminality—a predisposition that disproportionately favors criminal behavior—when and why they express it as crime, how individuals and groups respond to
those crimes, and how all these phenomena interact as a dynamic self-reinforcing system that evolves over time."[19]

One of the most comprehensive studies to date that has attempted to detail life
pathways leading to criminality began in 1986. The study,[20] a cohort analysis, compiled data on 4 500 youths from three distinct but coordinated projects throughout the

CHAPTER 8
239
The Meaning
of Crime:
Social Process
Perspectives

United States. A survey sampled youngsters at high risk for serious delinquency and drug use and found that (1) "the more seriously involved in drugs a youth was, the more seriously that juvenile was involved in delinquency," (2) "greater risks exist for violent offending when a child is physically abused or neglected early in life," (3) students who are not highly committed to school have higher rates of delinquency, (4) "poor family life exacerbates delinquency and drug use," and (5) affiliation with street gangs and illegal gun ownership are both predictive of delinquency. The study also found that "peers who were delinquent or used drugs had a great impact on [other] youth." Perhaps the most significant result of the study was the finding that three separate developmental pathways[21] to delinquency exist. The pathways identified by the study are

1. the *authority conflict pathway,* down which subjects appear to begin quite young (as early as 3 or 4 years of age). "The first step," said the study authors, "was stubborn behavior, followed by defiance around age 11, and authority avoidance—truancy, staying out late at night, or running away."
2. the *covert pathway,* which begins with "minor covert acts such as frequent lying and shoplifting, usually around age 10." Delinquents following this path quickly progress "to acts of property damage, such as firestarting or vandalism, around age 11 or 12, followed by moderate and serious forms of delinquency."
3. the *overt pathway,* in which the first step is marked by minor aggression such as "annoying others and bullying—around age 11 or 12." Bullying was found to escalate into "physical fighting and violence as the juvenile progressed along this pathway."

Another recent study that could potentially produce substantially significant results began in 1990.[22] Project directors describe their ongoing research as "the major criminologic investigation of this century." The study consists of a longitudinal analysis of how individuals, families, institutions, and communities evolve together. It is now "tracing how criminal behavior develops from birth to age 32." Researchers are planning to follow a total of 11 000 individuals in 9 different age groups for 8 years. Final project results are scheduled to be reported in 2002. There are a variety of study methodologies being utilized, including self-reports, individualized tests and examinations, direct observation, the examination of existing records, and reports by informants. Researchers hope to provide answers to the following questions: (1) "How and why do antisocial and criminal behaviors originate?" (2) "What causes some individuals to continue those behaviors?" and (3) "How and why do some individuals cease law-violating behaviors while others continue?"

Life course theories often point to the need for early intervention through nurturant strategies that build self-control through positive socialization. As Vila points out, "[t]here are two main types of nurturant strategies: those that improve early life experiences to forestall the development of strategic styles based on criminality, and those that channel child and adolescent development in an effort to improve the match between individuals and their environment."[23] Nurturant crime control strategies are discussed in more detail in Chapter 11.

## Labelling Theory

An early description of lasting societal reaction to deviance can be found in the work of **Frank Tannenbaum.** Tannenbaum's book, *Crime and the Community,* was published in 1938 and popularized the term *tagging* to explain what happens to offenders following arrest, conviction, and sentencing. Tannenbaum told his readers that crime was essentially the result of "two opposing definitions of the situation," between the delinquent and the community at large. "This conflict over the situation," he said, "is one that arises out of a divergence of values. As the problem develops, the situation gradually becomes redefined. The attitude of the community hardens definitely into a demand for suppression. There is a gradual shift from the definition of the specific acts as evil to a definition of the individual as evil, so that all his acts come to be looked upon with suspicion. … From the community's point of view, the individual who used to do bad and mischievous things has now become a bad and unredeemable human being. … The young delinquent becomes bad because he is defined as bad and because he is not believed if he is good. There is a persistent demand for consistency in character. The community cannot deal with people whom it cannot define."[24]

Tannenbaum used the phrase "dramatization of evil" to explain the process whereby an offender comes to be seen as ultimately and irrevocably "bad." After the process has been completed, Tannenbaum said, the offender "now lives in a different world. He has been tagged. … The process of making the criminal, therefore, is a process of tagging. …" Once a person has been defined as bad, few legitimate opportunities remain open to him or to her. As a consequence, the offender finds that only other people who have been similarly defined by society as bad are available to associate with him or with her. This continued association with negatively defined others leads to continued crime.

Using terminology developed by **Edwin M. Lemert,** it became fashionable to call an offender's initial acts of deviance *primary deviance* and continued acts of deviance, especially those resulting from forced association with other offenders, *secondary deviance.* **Primary deviance,** Lemert pointed out, may be undertaken to solve some immediate problem or to meet the expectations of one's subcultural group. Hence, the robbery of a convenience store by a college student temporarily desperate for tuition money, although not a wise undertaking, may be the first serious criminal offence ever committed by the student. The student may well intend for it to be the last, but if arrest ensues and the student is "tagged" with the status of a criminal, then secondary deviance may occur as a means of adjustment to the negative status. In Lemert's words, "[w]hen a person begins to employ his deviant behavior or a role based upon it as a means of defense, attack, or adjustment to the overt and covert problems created by the consequent societal reaction to him, his deviation is secondary."[25]

**Secondary deviance** becomes especially important because of the forceful role it plays in causing tagged individuals to internalize the negative labels that have been applied to them. Through such a process, labelled individuals assume the role of the deviant. According to Lemert, "[o]bjective evidences of this change will be found in the symbolic appurtenances of the new role, in clothes, speech, posture, and mannerisms, which in some cases heighten social visibility, and which in some cases serve as symbolic cues to professionalization."[26]

**Tagging** the process whereby an individual is negatively defined by agencies of justice.

**Primary deviance** initial deviance often undertaken to deal with transient problems in living.

**Secondary deviance** that which results from official labelling and from association with others who have been so labelled.

The name most often associated with labelling theory is that of **Howard Becker.** In 1963, Becker published *Outsiders: Studies in the Sociology of Deviance,*[27] a work in which the **labelling** perspective found its fullest development. In *Outsiders,* Becker described, among other things, the deviant subculture of jazz musicians and the process by which an individual becomes a marijuana user. His primary focus, however, was to explain how a person becomes labelled an outsider, as "a special kind of person, one who cannot be trusted to live by the rules agreed on by the group."[28] The central fact about deviance, says Becker, is that it is a social product, that "it is created by society." Society creates both deviance and the deviant person by responding to circumscribed behaviours. The person who engages in sanctioned behaviour is, as part of the process, labelled a deviant. In Becker's words, "social groups create deviance by making the rules whose infraction constitutes deviance, and by applying those rules to particular people and labeling them as outsiders. From this point of view, deviance is not a quality of the act the person commits, but rather a consequence of the application by others of rules and sanctions. … The deviant is one to whom that label has been successfully applied."[29]

In developing labelling theory, Becker attempted to explain how some rules come to carry the force of law, while others have less weight or apply only within the context of marginal subcultures. His explanation centred on the concept of **moral enterprise**, a term that he used to encompass all the efforts a particular interest group makes to have its sense of propriety embodied in law. "Rules are the products of someone's initiative," said Becker, "and we can think of the people who exhibit such enterprise as moral entrepreneurs."[30]

An early example of moral enterprise can be found in the Women's Christian Temperance Union (WCTU), a group devoted to the idea of prohibition. The WCTU was highly visible in its widespread fight against alcohol—holding marches and demonstrations, closing drinking establishments, and lobbying legislators. Press coverage of the WCTU's activities swayed many politicians into believing that lawful prohibition of alcoholic beverages was inevitable, and an amendment to the U.S. Constitution soon followed—ushering in the age of prohibition.

While the United States had national prohibition, the situation in Canada was somewhat different. In 1878, the government passed the Dominion Temperance Act, which relegated the decision concerning prohibition to local jurisdictions. In 1901, Prince Edward Island became the first province to vote "dry," but the issue remained a hotly debated one in many other areas of the country. World War I brought virtually national prohibition, and many provinces, including Nova Scotia, Ontario, Alberta, Saskatchewan, and Manitoba, continued to enforce bans on liquor following the war.[31]

Becker claimed that moral enterprise is used similarly to prohibition by other groups seeking to support their own interests with the weight of law. Often the group that is successful at moral enterprise does not represent a popular point of view. The group is simply more effective than others at manoeuvring through the formal bureaucracy that attends the creation of legislation.

Becker was especially interested in describing deviant careers—the processes by which individuals become members of deviant subcultures and take on the attributes associated with the deviant role. Becker argued that most deviance, when it first occurs, is likely to be transitory. That is, it is unlikely to occur again. For example, a youth who shoplifts a candy bar from a convenience store will probably not make a habit out

**Labelling** an interactionist perspective which sees continued crime as a consequence of limited opportunities for acceptable behaviour which follow from the negative responses of society to those defined as offenders.

**Moral enterprise** a term that encompasses all the efforts a particular interest group makes to have its sense of propriety enacted into law.

of this behaviour. However, transitory deviance can be effectively stabilized in a person's behavioural repertoire through the labelling process. If that youth is caught and charged by the police, then he or she becomes known as a "shoplifter" or "young offender." Once a person is labelled "deviant," opportunities for conforming behaviour are seriously reduced. Behavioural opportunities that remain open are primarily deviant ones. Hence, throughout the person's career, the budding deviant increasingly exhibits deviant behaviour, not so much out of choice, but rather because his or her choices are restricted by society. Additionally, successful deviants must acquire the techniques and resources necessary to undertake the deviant act (be it shoplifting larger items or break and enter), and develop the mindset characteristic of others like them. Near the completion of a deviant career, the person who has been labelled a deviant becomes stigmatized by society. He or she internalizes society's negative label, assumes a deviant self-concept, and is likely to become a member of a deviant subgroup. Becker says, "[a] drug addict once told me that the moment she felt she was really 'hooked' was when she realized she no longer had any friends who were not drug addicts."[32] In this way, says Becker, deviance finally becomes a "self-fulfilling prophecy." Labelling, then, is a cause of crime insofar as the actions of society in defining the rule breaker as deviant push the person further in the direction of continued deviance.

Labelling theory contributed a number of unique ideas to the criminological literature. They include the following notions:

1. Deviance is the result of social processes involving the imposition of definitions, rather than the consequence of any quality inherent in human activity itself. In other words, it is society's definition of a given behaviour at a given time and place in history that determines whether or not that behaviour is acceptable.
2. Deviant individuals achieve their status by virtue of social definition rather than because of inborn traits.
3. The reaction of society to deviant behaviour and to actors who engage in such behaviour is the major element in determining the criminality of the person and of the behaviour in question.
4. Negative self-images follow from processing by the formal mechanisms of criminal justice, rather than preceding delinquency.
5. Labelling by society and handling by the justice system tend to perpetuate crime and delinquency rather than reduce it. Those labelled "ex-cons" or "drug addicts" or "young offenders" may experience difficulty finding and holding a job, for example.

Becker's typology of delinquents helped explain the labelling approach. It consisted of those whom he called (1) the pure deviant, (2) the falsely accused deviant, and (3) the secret deviant. The pure deviant is one who commits norm-breaking behaviour and whose behaviour is accurately appraised as such by society. An example might be the burglar who is caught in the act of burglary, then tried and convicted. Such a person, we might say, has gotten what he deserves. The falsely accused individual is one who, in fact, is not guilty, but is labelled deviant nonetheless. The falsely accused category in Becker's typology demonstrates the power of social definition. Innocent people sometimes end up in prison, and one can imagine that the impact of

CHAPTER 8

243
The Meaning
of Crime:
Social Process
Perspectives

conviction and of the experiences that attend prison life can leave the falsely accused with a negative self-concept and with group associations practically indistinguishable from those of the true deviant. In effect, the life of the falsely accused is changed just as thoroughly as is the life of the pure deviant by the process of labelling. Finally, the secret deviant violates social norms, but his or her behaviour is not noticed, and negative societal reactions do not follow. The secret deviant again demonstrates the power of societal reaction—in this case by the very lack of consequences.

Recently, Mike S. Adams proposed a general social learning theory of crime and deviance incorporating components of labelling theory and differential association.[33] Adams contends that "labeling effects are mediated by associations with delinquent peers." He concludes that labelling is not a direct cause of delinquency and crime but "appears to cause delinquency indirectly via the effects of associations with delinquent peer groups." In other words, "the causal chain linking primary to secondary deviance must incorporate links that account for the effects of associations with delinquent [peers]."[34] The transition from primary to secondary deviance is outlined in Box 8.1.

## Critique of Labelling

The labelling approach, although it successfully points to the labelling process as a reason for continued deviance and as a cause of stabilization in deviant identities, does little to explain the origin of crime and deviance. Likewise, few, if any, studies seem to support the basic tenets of the theory. Critics of labelling have pointed to its "lack of firm empirical

## The Deviance Process
BOX 8.1

1. A person commits a deviant/criminal act (if undetected, the act remains primary deviance).
2. Society reacts in a retributive or punitive way.
3. The individual responds by committing more infractions (secondary deviation), which in turn draws additional attention to the criminal. The deviant cycle begins to escalate (e.g., in frequency and/or intensity), a self-fulfilling process.
4. The labelled individual develops more hostility and resentment toward criminal justice agents.
5. Society and the legal system respond by further labelling and stigmatizing the offender.
6. As the individual's options become increasingly restricted, the criminal justice system sees the offender as a problem and the offender sees him- or herself as deviant.
7. The probability for future acts of deviance increases—deviance amplification. Therefore, once labelled and stigmatized, the offender's identity and self-concept evolve around deviance.

### General Model of Labelling Process
Primary deviance → information reaction → continuance of deviance → escalation of response (e.g., stereotyping, rejection, alienation of tagged actor) → more delinquency (secondary deviance) → formal intervention → individual begins to see self as delinquent → self-fulfilling process.

SOURCE: J.A. Winterdyk, *Canadian Criminology* (Toronto: Prentice Hall Canada, 2000), p. 241. Reprinted with permission of Pearson Education Canada.

support for the notion of secondary deviance," and observed that "many studies have not found that delinquents or criminals have a delinquent or criminal self-image."[35]

In addition, there is a lack of unequivocal empirical support for the claim that contact with the justice system is fundamentally detrimental to the personal lives of criminal perpetrators. Although labelling theory suggests that official processing makes a significant contribution to continued criminality, it is questionable whether offenders untouched by the system would forego the rewards of future criminality. Rather, it is the *type* of contact with the criminal justice system that many feel influences the future behaviour of an offender.

## Living in Shame

Labelling theory says that people who commit deviant acts may continue down aberrant pathways because of labels society applies to them. The label of "pedophile" is one of the most stigmatizing and affects more than just the offender, as the following article shows.

When her son was sent to prison for pedophilia, Sheila was plunged into a world of secrecy and loneliness.

Lance, 21, was convicted last year of sexually assaulting an eight-year-old girl and a 10-year-old boy. He was sentenced to 20 months in jail.

"When I first found out he was charged, I was horrified, and immediately thought, 'What have I done wrong?'" says Sheila, who prefers to be identified only as a Lower Mainland teacher.

"I didn't know what to do. It was a nightmare. And because I didn't know what was going on, I wasn't in any kind of position to offer support to my son—who was terrified."

The experience left Sheila feeling isolated and abandoned. She still hasn't told other members of Lance's family—including her ex-husband—about his crime.

"I was feeling so alone. I mean, who could I talk to about this?

"You have a sense of isolation because you cut off all your friends.

"I was worried that everyone would find out. I was worried it would reflect on me and put my job in jeopardy. I have shared with only a few friends.

"Even some of my friends who do understand … their attitude has changed and they stay away. It's like we're all tarred with the same brush.

"People say he's not really a pedophile, and I have to say, 'Yes he is.'"

The system, Sheila says, is just as mystifying to the families of offenders as it is to the victims. For one thing, there are few if any support groups.

"I went to court with my son time after time. I would sit in that courtroom … and I was alone."

Lance, she says, was totally unprepared for the prison system.

"When he was taken into jail you would not believe the harassment from staff, and the filthy comments they made.

"This is a first-time offender, a young kid. He was so frightened.

"The day he was pronounced guilty he wrapped piano wire around his top button. He was afraid he'd end up getting raped because of the hatred towards pedophiles."

▶

CHAPTER 8
245
**The Meaning
of Crime:
Social Process
Perspectives**

It was Lance's first conviction. Sheila believes he had never sexually molested children before.

But she admits he was a difficult child. Being expelled from kindergarten was only the start.

When she divorced Lance's father, things got worse. The next man she married was an alcoholic.

By the time he reached his teens, Lance was stealing and doing drugs.

Finally, in desperation, Sheila had him placed in a foster home.

"It was the hardest thing I've ever done, signing those papers …"

The papers she signed declared that she was legally "abandoning" him. That's the official language of B.C.'s Family Child Services Act, but Sheila insists that was never her intention.

Within weeks, Sheila says, Lance was sexually molested by his foster mother.

Within months he was sexually molesting two other kids in the home, resulting in the two charges of sexual assault.

"She (the foster mother) has admitted it to me," says Sheila.

"We have not pressed charges because my son did not want me to go through any more trauma.

"I have a lot of anger toward her (the foster mom). But I have a lot of guilt because I feel that if I hadn't been with an alcoholic husband, I would have been more aware.

"But Lance himself said, 'Mom, I made those choices, I did those things.'"

That admission, and confrontation with his past, came after months of therapy at Stave Lake, a minimum-security institution near Maple Ridge for sex offenders.

Sheila has nothing but praise for the staff and program. Now she does volunteer work with sex offenders, helping them upgrade their education, and with victims, helping them understand offenders.

Lance was released from prison after six months and has moved away from the Lower Mainland.

He lives with a family, Sheila says, which is aware of his conviction, and he is supervised at all times.

She's anxious for him to get back into counselling, but she says his probation officer won't let him because of his living arrangements.

"They want him to move to a family apartment building where there would be no supervision."

Sheila wonders what kind of life Lance will have.

"I look down the road and I really wonder what chance my son has for having a good, wholesome, healthy life—like having a family.

"I just have to turn it over to God."

## DISCUSSION QUESTIONS

1. How can a label such as "pedophile" affect others associated with the offender? Is there a danger in using such labels?
2. Do you feel any differently about the offender in this story after you know a little about his background and what led him to commit the sexual assaults? Is it possible to separate the offender from the offence?
3. Do you think the names of sexual offenders should be made known to the public? Defend your position.

SOURCE: S. Jiwa and C. Ogilvie, "Living in Shame," *The Province*, February 21, 1993, p. 58.

## Reintegrative Shaming

In what some see as a contemporary offshoot of labelling theory, **John Braithwaite** and colleagues at the Australian National University (ANU) reported initial results of their studies on reintegrative shaming in 1997.[36] Braithwaite compared the effectiveness of traditional court processing of criminal offenders with a restorative justice approach operating in Canberra, Australia known as "diversionary conferencing." The diversionary conferencing approach "consists of an emotionally intense meeting, led by a police officer, between admitted offenders and their supporters, usually family and friends, and the victim of the offense, together with their supporters. In the absence of a direct victim, a representative of the community in which the offence occurred expresses the victim perspective on the events. The group discusses the consequences of the offense for all the parties and then determines what restitution the offenders must comply with to repair the harm for which they are responsible and so avoid going to court."[37]

Called RISE, for Reintegrative Shaming Experiments, the ongoing project is assessing the efficacy of each approach using criteria such as: (1) prevalence and frequency of repeat offending, (2) victim satisfaction with the process, (3) estimated cost savings within the justice process, (4) changes in drinking or drug use behaviour among offenders, and (5) perceptions of procedural justice, fairness, and protection of rights.

At the core of the study is Braithwaite's belief that two different kinds of shame exist. One he calls "stigmatic shaming." **Stigmatic shaming** is thought to destroy the moral bond between the offender and the community. According to Braithwaite, "stigmatic shaming is what American judges employ when they make an offender post a sign on his property saying 'a violent felon lives here' or a bumper sticker on his car saying 'I am a drunk driver.' Stigmatic shaming sets the offender apart as an outcast—often for the rest of the offender's life. By labeling him or her as someone who cannot be trusted to obey the law, stigmatic shaming says the offender is expected to commit more crimes."

The other type of shame, **reintegrative shaming**, is thought to strengthen the moral bond between the offender and the community. This alternative to stigmatic humiliation is meant "to condemn the crime, not the criminal." Through carefully monitored diversionary conferences, Braithwaite hopes to give offenders the opportunity to rejoin the community as law-abiding citizens. To earn the right to a fresh start, says Braithwaite, offenders must express remorse for their past conduct, apologize to any victims, and repair the harm caused by the crime.

Preliminary results from the RISE study support the claimed value of reintegrative shaming. To date, however, most such results are being measured through interviews with offenders following diversionary conferences. Findings show that offenders are far more likely to feel ashamed of their crimes if handled through conferences rather than through formal court processing. See the related discussion in Chapter 12 on restorative justice.

**Stigmatic shaming** that form of shaming, imposed as a sanction by the criminal justice system, that is thought to destroy the moral bond between the offender and the community.

**Reintegrative shaming** that form of shaming, imposed as a sanction by the criminal justice system, that is thought to strengthen the moral bond between the offender and the community.

CHAPTER 8
247
**The Meaning
of Crime:
Social Process
Perspectives**

# Social Control Theories

## Containment Theory

In the 1950s, **Walter C. Reckless** wrote *The Crime Problem*.[38] Reckless tackled head-on the realization that most sociological theories, although conceptually enlightening, offered less than perfect predictability. That is, they lacked the ability to predict precisely which individuals, even those exposed to various "causes" of crime, would become criminal. Reckless thought that the sociological perspectives prevalent at the time offered only half of a comprehensive theoretical framework. Crime, Reckless wrote, was the consequence of social pressures to involve oneself in violations of the law, as well as of failure to resist such pressures. Reckless called his approach **containment theory**, and he compared it with a biological immune response, saying that only some people exposed to a disease actually come down with it. Sickness, like crime, Reckless avowed, results from the failure of control mechanisms—some internal to the person and others external. In the case of sickness, external failures might include unsanitary conditions, the failure of the public health service, the lack of availability of preventative medicine, or the lack of knowledge necessary to make such medicine effective. Still, disease would not result unless the individual's resistance to disease-causing organisms was low or unless the individual was in some other way weak or susceptible to the disease.

**Containment theory** a form of control theory which suggests that a series of both internal and external factors contribute to law-abiding behaviour.

In the case of crime, Reckless wrote, external containment consists of "the holding power of the group." Under most circumstances, Reckless wrote, "[t]he society, the state, the tribe, the village, the family, and other nuclear groups are able to hold the individual within the bounds of the accepted norms and expectations." In addition to setting limits, Reckless saw society as providing individuals with meaningful roles and activities. Such roles were seen as an important factor of *external containment.*

*Inner containment,* said Reckless, "represents the ability of the person to follow the expected norms, to direct himself." Such ability was said to be enhanced by a positive self-image, a focus on socially approved goals, personal aspirations that are in line with reality, a good tolerance for frustration, and a general adherence to the norms and values of society. A person with a positive self-concept can avoid the temptations of crime simply by thinking, "I'm not that kind of person." A focus on approved goals helps keep one on the proverbial straight and narrow path. "Aspirations in line with reality" are simply realistic desires. In other words, if one seriously desires to be the richest person in the world, disappointment will probably result. Even when aspirations are reasonable, however, disappointments will occur—hence the need for a tolerance for frustration. Adherence to the norms and values of the larger society are a basic component of inner containment.

Reckless's containment theory is diagrammed in Figure 8.1. "Pushes toward crime" represents those factors in an individual's background that might propel him or her into criminal behaviour. They include a criminogenic background or upbringing that

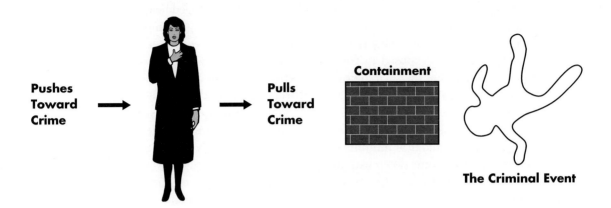

**Figure 8.1**

*A Diagrammatic Representation of Containment Theory*

**Pushes Toward Crime**

**Pulls Toward Crime**

**Containment**

**The Criminal Event**

**Containment** those aspects of the social bond acting to prevent individuals from committing crimes and keep them from engaging in deviance.

**Social control theory** a perspective predicting that when social constraints on antisocial behaviour are weakened or absent, delinquent behaviour emerges. Rather than stressing causative factors in criminal behaviour, control theory asks why people actually obey rules instead of breaking them.

**Social bond** the rather intangible link between individuals and the society of which they are a part; created through the process of socialization.

involves participation in a delinquent subculture, deprivation, biological propensities toward deviant behaviour, and psychological maladjustment. "Pulls toward crime" signifies all the perceived rewards crime may offer, including financial gain, sexual satisfaction, and higher status. "**Containment**" is a stabilizing force and, if effective, blocks such pushes and pulls from leading the individual toward crime.

Reckless believed that inner containment was far more effective than external containment in preventing law violations. In his words, "[a]s social relations become more impersonal, as society becomes more diverse and alienated, as people participate more and more for longer periods of time away from a home base, the self becomes more and more important as a controlling agent."

Containment theory was one of the first social control theories to be proposed. Social control approaches argue that social institutions exercise considerable control over individuals, either directly (as in the case of external containment) or indirectly, perhaps through socialization (as in the case of inner containment). **Social control theory** predicts that when social constraints on antisocial behaviour are weakened or absent, delinquent behaviour will tend to emerge. Rather than stressing causative factors in criminal behaviour, however, social control theories tend to ask why people actually obey rules instead of breaking them.[39]

## Social Bond Theory

Another form of control theory was popularized by **Travis Hirschi** in his 1969 book *Causes of Delinquency*.[40] Hirschi argued that, through successful socialization, a bond forms between individuals and the social group. When that bond is weakened or broken, deviance and crime may result. Hirschi described four components of the **social bond**: attachment, commitment, involvement, and belief.

CHAPTER 8

**249**
**The Meaning
of Crime:
Social Process
Perspectives**

In his writings, Hirschi cites the psychopath as an example of a person whose attachment to society is nearly nonexistent.[41] Other relatively normal individuals may find their attachment to society loosened through "[t]he process of becoming alienated from others [which] often involves or is based on active interpersonal conflict. Such conflict could easily supply," says Hirschi, "a reservoir of socially derived hostility sufficient to account for the aggressiveness of those whose attachments to others have been weakened."

The second component of the social bond—commitment—reflects a person's investment of time and energies into conforming behaviour and the potential loss of rewards that he or she has already gained from that behaviour. In Hirschi's words, "[t]he idea, then, is that the person invests time, energy, himself, in a certain line of activity—say, getting an education, building up a business, acquiring a reputation for virtue. Whenever he considers deviant behavior, he must consider the costs of this deviant behavior, the risk he runs of losing the investment he has made in conventional behavior." For such a traditionally successful person, says Hirschi, "a ten-dollar-holdup is stupidity," because the potential for losing what has already been acquired through commitment to social norms far exceeds what stands to be gained. Recognizing that his approach applies primarily to individuals who have been successfully socialized into conventional society, Hirschi adds, "[t]he concept of commitment assumes that the organization of society is such that the interests of most persons would be endangered if they were to engage in criminal acts."

Involvement, for Hirschi, means "engrossment in conventional activities" and is similar to Reckless's concept of meaningful roles. In explaining the importance of involvement in determining conformity, Hirschi cites the colloquial saying that "idle hands are the devil's workshop." Time and energy, he says, are limited, and, if a person is busy at legitimate pursuits, he or she will have little opportunity for crime and deviance.

Belief is the last of Hirschi's four aspects of the social bond. Hirschi writes that "control theory assumes the existence of a common value system within the society or group whose norms are being violated. … We not only assume the deviant has believed the rules, we assume he believes the rules even as he violates them." How can a person simultaneously believe it is wrong to commit a crime and still commit it? Hirschi's answer is that "[m]any persons do not have an attitude of respect toward the rules of society." That is, although they know the rules exist, they basically do not care. They invest little of their sense of self in moral standards.

In 1990, Hirschi, in collaboration with **Michael R. Gottfredson**, proposed a general theory of crime based on the concepts advanced earlier in control theory.[42] Gottfredson and Hirschi began by asking "What is crime?" Nearly all crimes, they concluded, are mundane, simple, trivial, easy acts aimed at satisfying desires of the moment. Hence, their general theory built on a classical or rational-choice perspective; that is, the belief that crime is a natural consequence of unrestrained human tendencies to seek pleasure and avoid pain. Crime, said Gottfredson and Hirschi, is little more than a subset of general deviant behaviour. Hence, they concluded, crime bears little resemblance to the explanations offered in the media, by law enforcement officials, or by most academic thinkers on the subject.

According to Gottfredson and Hirschi, the offender is neither the diabolical genius of fiction nor the ambitious seeker of the American Dream often portrayed by other social scientists. On the contrary, offenders appear to have little control over their own desires. When personal desires conflict with long-term interests, those who lack self-control often opt for the desires of the moment, thus contravening legal restrictions and becoming involved in crime.[43] Central to Gottfredson and Hirschi's thesis is the belief that a well-developed social bond will result in the creation of effective mechanisms of self-control. As others have noted: "For Gottfredson and Hirschi, self-control is the key concept in the explanation of all forms of crime as well as other types of behavior. Indeed, they believe that all current differences in rates of crime between groups and categories may be explained by differences in the management of self-control."[44] An overview of other integrated theories of crime is found in Chapter 12.

## Victimology: The Study of the Victim

Some people are labelled "criminals" by the justice system and take on a deviant identity. Others, as a consequence of forced entanglements, come to be defined as "victims" and assume the social characteristics appropriate for that role. The process by which one comes to be victimized, the interaction between criminal and victim through which victimization occurs, and the meaning given to victimization after it has occurred all suggest that victimization can be subsumed under a social process perspective on criminality.

Just as criminals have been studied to determine what kinds of social and personal experiences they have, so, too, have criminologists advocated close scrutiny of victims. The development of the field of **victimology**, or the study of victims, has closely paralleled the development of criminology. As was characteristic of the wider body of criminological theory, early victimologists stressed constitutional factors that propelled the victim toward victimization. The adjudged degree of an individual's potential for victimization was termed **victim-proneness.**

One of the earliest writers in the field, **Hans von Hentig**,[45] depicted crime poetically—as a duet played by two. Hans von Hentig appears to have been heavily influenced by a popular German novel of the time, entitled *The Murdered One Is Guilty.*[46] "In a sense," wrote von Hentig, "the victim shapes and moulds the criminal."[47] Comparing the victim and criminal to carnivore and prey, he argued, "In a certain sense, the animals which devour and those that are devoured complement each other. ... To know one we must be acquainted with the complementary partner."[48]

Von Hentig created a typology, or classificatory scheme, of victims based on what he saw as biological or situational weaknesses. Weaknesses could be physically, socially, psychologically, or environmentally based. Anything that puts the potential victim at a disadvantage relative to the criminal predator, constituting "easy prey," so to speak, found a place in his typology. His scheme consisted of the following categories:

**General Classes of Victims**

The young—weak by virtue of age and immaturity

The female—often less physically powerful than the male

The old—incapable of physical defence, and the object of confidence schemes

**Victimology** the study of victims and their contributory role, if any, in crime causation.

**Victim-proneness** the degree of an individual's likelihood of victimization.

CHAPTER 8

251

**The Meaning
of Crime:
Social Process
Perspectives**

Purse snatchers in action. Why do victimologists suggest that some people contribute to their own victimization? *Buu-Turpin/Gamma-Liaison, Inc.*

The mentally defective—unable to think clearly

Immigrants—unsure of the rules of conduct in the surrounding society

Minorities—racial prejudice may lead to victimization or unequal treatment by the agencies of justice

Dull normals—the "born victims of swindlers"

### Psychological Types of Victims

The depressed—submissive by virtue of emotional condition

The acquisitive or greedy—the act of always wanting more propels such individuals into victimization

The wanton or overly sensual—ruled by passion and thoughtlessly seeking pleasure

The lonesome—similar to the acquisitive type of victim, by virtue of wanting companionship or affection

The heartbroken—like the lonesome, if only temporarily

The tormentor—a victim who asks for it, often from his or her own family and friends

Other types include the blocked, exempted, and fighting victims. Blocked victims were those on whom the tables were turned, as in cases when the swindler becomes swindled or the attacker ends up injured. In like fashion, blackmailers often end up dead. Von Hentig also wrote of "victim areas," or parts of the country to which tourists and others with money are drawn. Similarly attracted are the criminals who prey upon them. Recent incidents involving Canadian and other foreign tourists in Florida were presaged by this kind of thinking. Likewise, inner-city areas rich in crime were seen as creating a special relationship between victim and criminal. Criminals in such areas were described as "deleterious mosquitoes. ... [B]ut," wrote von Hentig, "they could not exist if there were no social swamps."[49]

On occasion, said von Hentig, the law creates a victim where there is none at all. The man who visits a prostitute—a willing participant in the offence of prostitution—can, from some perspectives, be classified as a victim. Likewise, the prostitute herself can fall into the category of victim.

Finally, according to von Hentig, in some cases victim and criminal are the same. Arson, burglary, auto theft, and other property crimes in which insurance coverage is sought and false police reports filed are forms of criminal activity that typify such criminals and victims.

Von Hentig used colloquial information, preexisting statistical data, documented individual experiences, and personal observations to support his concepts. Although he did not undertake any empirical research of his own, von Hentig's ideas helped propel the importance of the victim into the forefront of criminological thinking during the 1950s and 1960s.

Some criminologists trace the development of the field of victimology to even earlier writings, including those of **Benjamin Mendelsohn.** In 1937, Mendelsohn, a European defence attorney, published a paper[50] advocating the study of victims. Like von Hentig, Mendelsohn created his own classification of victim types. Mendelsohn's typology was based on the degree of guilt that the victim brought to the criminal event. It included the following six categories:

1. The completely innocent victim. Such a person, said Mendelsohn, is an "ideal victim" in popular perception. In this category, he placed persons victimized while they were unconscious and child victims.
2. Victims with only minor guilt and those victimized due to ignorance. Mendelsohn used the example of a woman who attempts a self-administered abortion and pays with her life.
3. The victim who is just as guilty as the offender, and the voluntary victim. Suicide committed by a couple, solicited euthanasia, and other forms of suicide were included in this category.
4. The victim more guilty than the offender. This category was described as containing persons who provoked the criminal or actively induced their own victimization.
5. The most guilty victim, or the victim "who is guilty alone." Attackers killed by would-be victims in the act of defending themselves were placed into this subgroup.
6. The imaginary victim. Here Mendelsohn allowed for the fact that some individuals file false police reports or believe themselves to have been victimized when in fact they have not been. Senile people, mentally ill individuals, children, and others could fall into this category, he said.

**Penal couple** a term that describes the relationship between victim and criminal. Also, the two individuals most involved in the criminal act—the offender and the victim.

Mendelsohn is generally credited with coining the term *victimology* and developing the concept of the **penal couple**, which describes the relationship between victim and criminal. He also coined the term *victimal* to describe the victim counterpart of the criminal and the word *victimity*, which signified the opposite of criminality. In his writings, Mendelsohn called for the development of victimology as a field of study independent from criminology. He foresaw the creation of an international institute for victimological research as part of the United Nations and called for the creation of an

CHAPTER 8

253
**The Meaning
of Crime:
Social Process
Perspectives**

international society of victimology with its own journal (which he called the *International Review of Victimology*).

In 1954, Henry Ellenberger introduced the concept of **victimogenesis**[51] to explain how persons can undergo life experiences that eventually place them in circumstances that contribute to their future victimization. Just as a criminal experiences events in life that lead to criminality, Ellenberger argued that many victims undergo a process of socialization that results in less caution, a proclivity to associate with possible offenders, an increased likelihood of frequenting places associated with criminal activity, and a generally higher risk of criminal victimization.

In 1957, **Marvin E. Wolfgang** popularized the term **victim-precipitated criminal homicide,** in his study[52] of murders in Philadelphia between 1948 and 1952. "[V]ictim-precipitated cases," said Wolfgang, "are those in which the victim was the first to show and use a deadly weapon, to strike a blow in an altercation—in short, the first to commence the interplay or resort to physical violence."[53] Wolfgang found that victims who brought about their own homicide were more likely than other murder victims to be African-American men with previous police records, especially involving assault, who were killed by stabbing, in a situation where alcohol was present. Significantly, he found, many victim-precipitated homicides were committed by women, often wives. Hence, mate-killing, where threatened wives turn the tables on their abusive husbands, seemed to typify the victim-precipitated criminal homicides that Wolfgang studied.

Some years later Wolfgang, writing in collaboration with Thorsten Sellin,[54] introduced a typology of victims based on victim-offender relationships. They described:

1. Primary victimization—in which an individual falls victim to crime
2. Secondary victimization—in which an impersonal agency such as a business is victimized
3. Tertiary victimization—in which the government or public order is offended, perhaps through regulatory violations
4. Mutual victimization—in which the participants in an offence willingly involve themselves, such as drug sales, gambling, and prostitution
5. No victimization—a category reserved for offences committed by youth that could not be committed by an adult, such as the buying of cigarettes by an underage person

## The Dynamics of Victimization

Some authors[55] have identified a number of procedural models that can be applied to a study of the victimization process, the experience the victim undergoes during and following victimization. The "victims of crime model" developed by Bard and Sangrey[56] postulates that three stages are involved in any victimization: (1) the stage of impact and disorganization, during and immediately following the criminal event; (2) recoil, during which the victim formulates psychological defences and deals with conflicting emotions of guilt, anger, acceptance, and desire for revenge (the state of recoil is said to last from 3 to 8 months); and (3) the reorganizational stage, during which the victim puts his or her life back together and gets on with daily living in a more or less normal fashion. Some victims do not successfully adapt to the victimization experience, and a maladaptive reorganizational stage may last for many years.

**Victimogenesis** the contributory background of a victim as a result of which he or she becomes prone to victimization.

**Victim-precipitated criminal homicide** killing in which the "victim" was the first to commence the interaction or was the first to resort to physical violence.

Another model with applicability to the victimization experience is the "disaster victim's model," originally developed to explain the coping behaviour of victims of natural disasters. This model outlines four stages in the victimization process: (1) preimpact, which describes the state of the victim prior to being victimized; (2) impact, or the stage at which victimization occurs; (3) postimpact, which entails the degree and duration of personal and social disorganization that follows victimization; and (4) behavioural outcome, which describes the victim's adjustment, or lack thereof, to the victimization experience.

Finally, the model developed by Elizabeth Kubler-Ross to describe the stages that dying persons go through has some applicability to the victimization process. Kubler-Ross described a five-part transitional process of denial, anger, bargaining, depression, and acceptance.[57] Victims often either deny the likelihood of their own victimization or believe that "this can't be happening to me." After the victimizing event, many victims feel anger, and some express rage toward their victimizers. Bargaining occurs when victims negotiate with themselves as well as with family members, representatives of the criminal justice community, and social service providers over how the victimization experience should be personally interpreted and about how it should be officially handled. Acceptance occurs when the victim finally acknowledges that victimization has occurred, and the victim makes the adjustments necessary to go on with life. Of course, as in the case of other models, the Kubler-Ross model allows for maladjustment in the final phase as some victims never successfully integrate the victimization experience into their psyches in a way that avoids reduction in the quality of their lives.

## The Victim as a Social Construct

Richard Quinney, whose contribution to the field of criminology is discussed in Chapter 9, argues that the victim is a social construction. That is, the wording of laws, the theoretical explorations of criminologists, and the cultural and institutional arrangements of society all contribute to defining certain social actors as criminals and others as victims. The only real difference between the two, says Quinney, is convention and, one might add, happenstance.

In a 1972 article entitled "Who Is the Victim," Quinney wrote, "... criminologists have tended to share a singular conception of reality. ... Breaking out of the theory of reality that had dominated criminological thought, we would begin to conceive of the victims of police force, the victims of war, the victims of the 'correctional' system, the victims of state violence, the victims of oppression of any sort. Because criminologists have tended to rely on a particular theory of reality, they have excluded these victims."[58] Fundamentally, says Quinney, the concept of victimization relates to one's notion of morality and corresponding understanding of social reality. "To argue," he writes, "that abortion is victimless is to exclude the living fetus as a victim. To regard the person who loses property as a victim is to value the sanctity of private property."

From some points of view, the victim, or at least the degree of victimization, is a cultural artifact. For example, potential murder victims who do not die because they receive prompt medical assistance thwart application of the term *homicide.* In a recent study of the availability of medical resources (especially quality hospital emergency services), William G. Doerner[59] found that serious assaults may "become" homicides where such resources are lacking, but that homicides can be prevented through effective utilization of capable medical technology. Hence, societal decisions on the distribution and placement of advanced medical support equipment and personnel can lower homicide rates in selected geographic areas. In Doerner's words, "the causes of homicide transcend the mere social world of the combatants."[60] This kind of perspective bears more than a passing relationship to the criminology of place, discussed in a box in Chapter 7.

## Critique of Victimology

Victimologists move much of the onus for criminality from the offender to the victim, claiming that the victim's behaviour, appearance, physical or psychological makeup, or circumstances of birth and upbringing contribute significantly to victimization and are, at least to some degree, the cause of the criminal act itself. Although some of these claims may have a certain objective reality, the current political reality of crime—that is, the perception by many Canadians that the country is swamped with far too much crime and the commonly expressed feeling that offenders should be held thoroughly accountable for their actions—seems to dictate a general lack of acceptance for such victimological perspectives.

However, in an article entitled, "The Art of Savage Discovery: How to Blame the Victim," William Ryan explains that most victims of commonplace property and violent crimes are members of the lower class.[61] As a consequence, blaming the victim has become something of a popular undertaking for certain groups in society, in particular the middle and upper classes. According to Ryan, most members of the middle and upper classes sympathize with victims, but they are not about to do anything to change the all too prevalent conditions in society (poverty, unemployment, discrimination, and the like) that generate crime and lead to victimization. "The victim blamer," says Ryan, "is a middle-class person who is doing reasonably well in a material way; he has a good job, a good income, a good house, a good car. Basically, he likes the social system pretty much the way it is. ..." Such people, Ryan says, employ a two-pronged approach to the problem of crime. First, they see victims as fated to be poor, uneducated, and victimized. Second, and somewhat contradictorily, they "want to make the victims less vulnerable, send them back into battle with better weapons, thicker armor, a higher level of morale. ... What weapons," he asks, "... might they have lacked when they went into battle? Job skills? Education? What armor was lacking that might have warded off their wounds? Better values? Habits of thrift and foresight? And what might have ravaged their morale? Apathy? Ignorance? Deviant lower-class culture patterns?" Because the typical middle-class victim-blamer values precisely those attributes that so many lower-class victims lack, says Ryan, he or she is apt to blame the victim for choosing to be ill equipped to deal with the challenges of crime and of criminal victimization itself.

## A History of the Victim

In early times, victims took the law into their own hands. If they were able to apprehend their victimizers, they enacted their own form of revenge and imposed some form of personal retaliation. The Code of Hammurabi (circa 1750 B.C.), one of the earliest known legal codes, required that many offenders make restitution. If the offender could not be found, however, the victim's family was duty bound to care for the needs of the victim. This early period in history has been called the Golden Age of the Victim, because victims were not only well cared for but also had considerable say in imposing punishments upon apprehended offenders.

Eventually, however, crimes came to be understood as offences against society, and the victim was forgotten. By the late Middle Ages the concept of "King's Peace" had emerged, wherein all offences were seen as violations of imperial law. It became the duty of local governments to apprehend, try, and punish offenders, effectively removing the victim from any direct involvement in judicial decision-making. Victims were expected only to provide evidence of a crime and to testify against those who had offended them. Society's moral responsibility toward making victims "whole again" was forgotten, and victims as a class were moved to the periphery of the justice process. Justice for the victim was forgotten, translated instead into the notion of justice for the state.

The situation remained pretty much the same until the 1960s, when renewed interest in the plight of victims led to a resurgence of positive sentiments around the world. Such sentiments were soon translated into a flurry of laws intended to provide compensation to victims of violent crimes.

Compensation for criminal injury is not unknown throughout history. More than 100 years ago, Jeremy Bentham advocated "mandatory restitution, to be paid by a state compensation system, in cases of property crime."[62] Long before that, the Code of Hammurabi specified that

> If a man has committed robbery … that man shall be put to death. If the robber is not caught, the man who has been robbed shall formally declare what he has lost … and the city … shall replace whatever he has lost for him. If it is the life of the owner that is lost, the city or the mayor shall pay one maneth of silver to his kinfolk.

The first modern victim compensation statute was adopted by New Zealand in 1963. Known as the Criminal Injuries Compensation Act, it provided an avenue for claims to be filed by victims of certain specified violent crimes. A three-member board was empowered to make awards to victims. One year later, partially in response to a movement led by the social reformer **Margaret Fry**, Great Britain established a similar board. In 1965, the U.S. state of California passed the first piece of American legislation intended to assist victims of crime, and today all 50 states have passed similar legislation.

The first Canadian criminal injuries compensation plan was created in Saskatchewan in 1967. Currently, a compensation program is available in virtually every province and territory, providing financial compensation for injuries or death resulting from a crime of violence committed by another person. Each provincial compensation program is unique, but all include time limits on the filing of an application and set maximum award amounts per applicant, varying from $5 000 to $30 000. In addition, most plans allow surviving relatives of murder victims, and those

CHAPTER 8

257

**The Meaning
of Crime:
Social Process
Perspectives**

injured while preventing a crime, to qualify for compensation. Payments are not generally awarded, however, for victims with injuries caused by motor vehicle accidents. In all plans, payments for lost wages, medical expenses, and prescription drugs are commonly made. Some provincial plans compensate victims for general damages, including "pain and suffering" caused by the offence. Victims who are responsible in some significant way for their own victimization may receive a lower reward or be disqualified completely. Factors such as intoxication, prior knowledge of the offender's criminalistic tendencies, and provocation of the offender can all result in reduced awards.

Although many tout the benefits of victim compensation programs, recent studies of the effectiveness of government-sponsored compensation programs have found that most crime victims are reluctant to seek compensation and that those who do are generally from households with higher incomes. Frustrations with delays, poor information about the programs, and unmet expectations regarding assistance with psychological and support needs as well as financial needs were also cited as limitations.[63]

## Current Directions in Victimology

Victims experience many hardships extending beyond their original victimization, including the trauma of testifying, uncertainty about their role in the justice process, lost time at work, trial delays, fear of retaliation by the defendant, and a general lack of knowledge of what is expected of them as the wheels of justice grind forward. Problems following from initial victimization are referred to as **postcrime victimization, or secondary victimization.** Police, employer, and spouse insensitivity can all exacerbate the difficulties crime victims face. The bureaucracy of hospitals and social service agencies can also contribute to the victim's sense of continuing victimization.[64]

In recent years, awareness of victims and witnesses of crime has heightened, as has concern for protection of their rights as citizens.[65] In 1983, a Federal Provincial Task Force on Justice for the Victims of Crime made 79 recommendations addressing the needs of victims and the requirements for effective victim services, many of which are in place today. These include provisions within the Criminal Code of Canada that ensure criminal injuries compensation and increased use of restitution.

A number of grass-roots lobby groups have also been influential in promoting awareness of victims' issues. Most notable of these is Victims of Violence, founded by Gary and Sharon Rosenfeldt, the parents of one of Clifford Olson's victims, and Canadians Against Violence Everywhere Advocating its Termination (CAVEAT), founded by Priscilla de Villiers, whose daughter was murdered.

There is currently no single, national "Bill of Rights" for victims of crime in Canada, largely because the jurisdiction over the components of the criminal justice system and the responsibility for meeting the needs of the victims of crime is shared by the federal, provincial, and territorial governments. In 1988, the Ministers of Justice from these jurisdictions endorsed the *Canadian Statement of Basic Principles of Justice for Victims of Crime*. These principles have served to guide the development of policy and legislation for the victims of crime at both the federal and provincial level. They are modelled on the 1985 United Nations *Declaration of Basic Principles of Justice for Victims of Crime*, which Canada co-sponsored. A 1999 report from the federal Standing Committee on Justice and Human Rights entitled *Victims' Rights—A Voice, Not a Veto* makes a number of recommendations regarding further amendments to the

**Postcrime victimization** or **secondary victimization** refers to problems in living which tend to follow from initial victimization.

Criminal Code to strengthen the voice of victims of crime. Most provinces and territories in Canada have enacted legislation to promote and protect the interests of victims.

The movement to recognize the needs and rights of victims and witnesses has led to the development of a variety of programs across the country. These programs can be found within various components of the criminal justice system and assist and support the individual in his or her involvement with the system as a victim. Most of these were not available as recently as the 1970s.

## theory versus reality  Canadian Statement of Basic Principles of Justice for Victims of Crime

In recognition of the United Nations *Declaration of Basic Principles of Justice for Victims of Crime*, Federal and Provincial Ministers Responsible for Criminal Justice agree that the following principles should guide Canadian society in promoting access to justice, fair treatment, and provision of assistance for victims of crime.

1. Victims should be treated with courtesy, compassion, and with respect for their dignity and privacy and should suffer the minimum of necessary inconvenience from their involvement with the criminal justice system.
2. Victims should receive, through formal and informal procedures, prompt and fair redress for the harm which they have suffered.
3. Information regarding remedies and the mechanisms to obtain them should be made available to victims.
4. Information should be made available to victims about their participation in criminal proceedings and the scheduling, process, and ultimate disposition of the proceedings.
5. Where appropriate, the view and concerns of victims should be ascertained and assistance provided throughout the criminal process.
6. Where the personal interests of the victim are affected, the views or concerns of the victim should be brought to the attention of the court, where appropriate and consistent with criminal law and procedure.
7. Measures should be taken when necessary to ensure the safety of victims and their families and to protect them from intimidation and retaliation.
8. Enhanced training should be made available to sensitize criminal justice personnel to the needs and concerns of victims and guidelines developed, where appropriate, for this purpose.
9. Victims should be informed of the availability of health and social services and other relevant assistance so that they might continue to receive the necessary medical, psychological and social assistance through existing programs and services.
10. Victims should report the crime and cooperate with the law enforcement authorities.

SOURCE: Department of Justice Canada, www.canada.justice.gc.ca/Orientations/victims/csbp_en.

CHAPTER 8
259
The Meaning
of Crime:
Social Process
Perspectives

_Police-Based Programs_  Many police services across Canada now have in-house victim services units.[66] Usually staffed by civilians and volunteers, these services are available 24 hours a day for immediate victim support. For example, in the case of a fatal car accident police officers can call upon their department's victim services unit to provide crisis intervention at the scene of the accident. Such services not only allow police offers to resume their duties but also ensure that the victim is supported by a trained professional. Many victim services units also use volunteers who represent various cultural, ethnic, and linguistic groups to help meet the specific needs of victims.

Some provinces have also established and funded independent crisis intervention services that provide victim support through referrals from police. In Ontario, the Victim Crisis and Referral Service (VCARS) is found in 20 centres across the province. Police may call upon the services of VCARS at any time.

_Court-Based Programs_  Most court-based victims programs assist those victims whose cases have resulted in prosecution. They are designed to assist the victim through the trial process, and most are located in the courthouse itself. The **Victim/Witness Assistance Programs** in Ontario provide services such as notification of court dates and adjournments, guided tours through the courtroom, explanations of court proceedings and emotional support throughout the trial, especially on the day(s) of victim testimony.[67] Many provinces also provide specialized court-based support programs for child victims and witnesses.

The recognition of the victim's involvement and the need for support throughout the court process has resulted in a number of provisions outlined in the Criminal Code of Canada. Section 722 allows victims to record a statement describing the emotional suffering, trauma, and/or financial hardship experienced as a result of their victimization. Known as a **victim impact statement**, these accounts are introduced into court after conviction and prior to sentencing. They are most common in cases of interpersonal victimization, and judges are expected to consider these statements in arriving at an appropriate sanction for the offender. The extent to which victim impact statements affect a judge's sentencing determination is debatable, and most victims do not submit one. Proponents of victim impact statements contend that they allow victims to have their say and feel involved in the criminal justice process, providing, for many, a cathartic emotional outlet.[68]

Other Criminal Code provisions for victims include publication bans. Subsection 746(3) states that judges can order that "the identity of the complainant or of a witness and any information that could disclose the identity of the complainant or of a witness shall not be published in any document or broadcast in any way." These bans can be imposed in specific types of cases only, such as those involving sexual assault, incest, extortion, or a sexual offence involving children. Contravention of a publication ban is a summary conviction offence.

In some instances, a trial judge may override the fundamental principle of justice that trials be public and issue an order to "exclude all or any members of the public from the courtroom for all or part of the proceedings" (s. 486(1)). Rarely done, this action is meant to allow for the "proper administration of justice" by allowing a victim or witness to testify free from stress or fear. These public exclusion orders are most often used in cases involving child witnesses.

**Victim/Witness Assistance Programs** counsel victims, orient them to the justice process and provide a variety of other services such as transportation to court, child care during court appearances, and referrals to social service agencies.

**Victim impact statement** a written document which describes the losses, suffering, and trauma experienced by the crime victim or by the victim's survivors. Judges are expected to consider them in arriving at an appropriate sentence for the offender.

Other provisions intended to facilitate the participation of witnesses include subsection 486(1.2), which permits a support person to be present in court with a witness under the age of 14 in sexual offence proceedings, and subsection 486(2.1), which permits a sexual offence complainant who is under the age of 18 to provide his or her testimony from behind a screen or by closed-circuit television. This provision has recently been expanded to include victims and witnesses in prostitution and assault cases. Subsection 715.1 permits, as evidence, a videotaped version of a witness's testimony in proceedings relating to sexual offences where the victim or witness was under the age of 18 at the time of the offence.

_Victims and Corrections_  Victim involvement with the criminal justice system can continue after the offender is convicted and sentenced. The federal Corrections and Conditional Release Act of 1992, for example, outlines the role of the victim in the parole process. In addition to those victims' rights highlighted in Box 8.2, the victim and/or any other interested party may attend a parole hearing, provided a written request has been made in advance of the hearing. Victims must travel to the location of the hearing and absorb any associated costs. Written transcripts of the hearing are made available upon request to those victims who cannot attend a hearing. In addition, some provinces have adopted legislation and procedures allowing the victim to remain informed of changes in the status of incarcerated offenders. In Ontario, the automated Victim Notification System provides victims with a personal identification number to access such information about their cases.

## Victims' Rights and the Parole Process

BOX 8.2

**_Can a victim's information be considered in conditional release decisions?_**
The Corrections and Conditional Release Act recognizes that victims have certain rights. The Board considers information from victims, especially that which can help to assess whether an offender's release may pose a risk to society. The Board is interested in information that will assist in assessing the offender's understanding of the effect of the offence and whether that person is likely to reoffend. In cases of statutory release, where the Board must decide whether to detain an offender, information about the harm suffered by victims is critical for the Correctional Services of Canada and the National Parole Board.

Information from victims is also important when it is directly relevant to assessing conditions necessary to manage a particular risk that the offender might present, and to the offender's release plans, especially if the offender will be near the victim or is a member of the victim's family. Victims are encouraged to provide this information as soon as possible after sentencing or before an offender becomes eligible for parole.

**_Will information from victims be kept confidential?_**
The National Parole Board and the Correctional Services of Canada are required by law to share with the offender any information that will be considered during the decision-making process. Information cannot be used if it is not shared with the offender. Exceptions to this rule are rare; they include extraordinary situations, such as the safety of a person, the security of a correctional institution, or the possible jeopardy of an ongoing investigation.

▶

CHAPTER 8

261

**The Meaning
of Crime:
Social Process
Perspectives**

### Who is a victim?

The Corrections and Conditional Release Act defines a victim as someone to whom harm was done or who suffered physical or emotional damage as the result of a crime. The law considered that relatives are victims when the victim has been killed or is unable to be responsible for some reason such as age or illness.

Victims may authorize someone to act for them should they prefer. The Board will recognize someone as an agent for a victim if the victim makes a written statement designating someone to that effect.

### How does someone request information about an offender?

Victims may write to request information from either the National Parole Board or the Correctional Services of Canada. If asked, the National Parole Board or the Correctional Services of Canada must release certain information to victims and may release certain other information.

Because the release of certain information about offenders is limited to victims as defined in the law, the request should clearly identify the offender and the crime committed. If guidance is needed, victims are invited to contact any of the offices of the National Parole Board or the Correctional Services of Canada.

A victim, or in some cases a victim's family, can request and will receive basic about an offender, including:

- when the sentence began and the length of the sentence; and
- the eligibility and review dates of the offender for unescorted temporary absences and parole.

More information may be released if the Chairperson of the National Parole Board or the Commissioner of the Correctional Services of Canada determines that the interest of the victim outweighs any invasion of the offender's privacy that could result from the disclosure.

Such information may include:
- the location of the penitentiary in which the sentence is being served;
- the date, if any, on which the offender is to be released on unescorted or escorted temporary absence, work release, parole, or statutory release;
- the date of any hearing for the purposes of a review for possible detention;
- any of the conditions attached to the offender's unescorted temporary absence, work release, parole, or statutory release;
- the designation of the offender when released on any temporary absence, work release, parole, or statutory release, and whether the offender will be in the vicinity of the victim while travelling to that destination;
- whether the offender is in custody and, if not, why not; and
- whether or not the offender has appealed a decision of the Board, and the outcome of that appeal.

In addition, when an offender has been transferred from a penitentiary to a provincial correctional facility, the name of the province in which the provincial facility is located may be disclosed.

### Is a victim or the family of a victim informed when a person convicted of a crime is granted conditional release?

No, not automatically. This information will be given only upon written request. Some victims prefer to have no further knowledge of the offender. A victim or a victim's family must ask for information.

▶ *Can victims receive ongoing information?*
Yes. Victims must make the request in writing and ensure that the National Parole Board
or the Correctional Services of Canada has their current address and telephone number.
They may then be informed of changes such as a move from one institution to another
or the grant of a conditional release.

*Can information be given to anyone other than victims?*
The same information that can be released to victims can also be given to certain other
people. However, they must satisfy the Chairperson of the National Parole Board or the
Commissioner of the Correctional Services of Canada that they suffered harm or physical or emotional damage because of an offender's act, whether or not the offender was
prosecuted or convicted for that act. If they have made a complaint to the police or the
Crown attorney, or an information was laid under the Criminal Code, then the person
will be formally recognized as a victim and given the same information that would be
given had the offender been convicted of the offence.

SOURCE: National Parole Board of Canada, Ottawa, "Parole: Balancing Public Safety and Criminal Responsibility," 1996, pp. 126–128.

**Restitution** a criminal
sanction, in particular
the payment of
compensation by the
offender to the victim.

*Victim Restitution* The victims' movement has also spawned a rebirth of the concept of restitution. **Restitution** is punishment through imposed responsibility—in
particular, the payment of compensation to the victim. Restitution encompasses the
notion that criminal offenders should shoulder at least a portion of the financial oblig-
ations required to make the victim whole again. Not only does restitution help make
the victim whole again, it places responsibility for the process back upon the offender
who caused the loss of wholeness initially. Advocates of restitution, which works
through court-imposed fines and garnishments, claim that, as a sentence, it benefits
society by leading to an increased sense of social and individual responsibility on the
part of convicted offenders.

   At one time in Canada, the responsibility for requesting restitution lay with the
victim. Many who were not aware of this option failed to petition the court and restitution was not ordered. Currently, a judge can unilaterally order restitution or do so
at the request of the Crown. Restitution can be so ordered as a stand-alone sentence or
as part of another, such as a probation order or a conditional sentence. These types of
sentences help ensure that beneficiaries of the restitution order receive payment. Failure to pay in either instance can lead to a breach of the sentence and incarceration.
Beneficiaries can also use civil courts to enforce a restitution order.

   A recent addition to the Criminal Code of Canada has extended the use of restitution to criminal cases involving criminal injury. Subsection 738(1) allows a judge to
impose a sentence of restitution to cover expenses to the victim relating to loss of income or support, costly dental work, physiotherapy expenses, etc. In addition, in the
case of an offence causing bodily harm to the offender's spouse or child in instances of
family violence, this subsection allows restitution to be ordered for readily ascertain-
able expenses incurred by the victim as a result of moving out of the offender's household, for temporary housing, child care, food, and transportation.

Section 737 of the Criminal Code of Canada requires a **victim fine surcharge** to be automatically imposed in addition to any other sanction handed down to an offender convicted of an offence in the Criminal Code or the Controlled Drugs and Substances Act. The revenue raised by this surcharge remains in the province or territory where it is imposed and is to be used specifically to fund programs and initiatives providing assistance to victims of crime. This provision further stipulates that the maximum victim fine surcharge is 15 percent of any fine imposed or, where no fine is imposed, is not to exceed $35. Proposed amendments to the Criminal Code would see this amount raised to $50 for an offence punishable by summary conviction and $100 in the case of an offence punishable by indictment. The sentencing judge may waive the victim fine surcharge where the imposition of the surcharge would cause undue hardship. Most provinces and territories have also enacted legislation imposing a surcharge on provincial offences such as highway traffic violations. This revenue is also used to fund victim programs and services.

> **Victim fine surcharge**
> a mandatory, judicial imposition of a monetary fine administered in addition to a criminal sentence and used to finance victim services.

## Policy Implications

As has been noted throughout this chapter, both offenders and victims are stigmatized through social processes involving the formal and informal imposition of labels. Removal of the stigmata would, at least theoretically, restore both to their precrime state.

Labelling theory, in particular, cautions against too much intervention, since it is often through contact with various types of rehabilitative programs that individuals become even further labelled. Even well-intentioned programs such as special education programs or support groups for released offenders can serve to label participants as "stupid" or "ex-con." Current restitution and court diversion programs are examples of policy initiatives that recognize the principles of labelling theory. Adult diversion projects or alternative measures for youth are designed to divert the offender away from formal contact with the criminal justice system, thereby avoiding the imposition of a label. For example, a man who is arrested for seeking the services of a prostitute but who has no previous criminal convictions may be ordered to attend "john school." Successful attendance means the offender has no further contact with the criminal justice system and is free of a criminal record. Diversion programs are usually joint initiatives involving the Crown's office and the local police service. Likewise, restitution initiatives are attempts to prevent the stigmatization of the offender. In lieu of the trial and court process, the offender is required to compensate either the victim or the community for the loss or for harm done. Since their inception, diversion programs have been surrounded by controversy. Whether they actually prevent the imposition of a negative label and thereby prevent future criminal activity is open to debate.[69]

Social learning perspectives have also had an impact on program initiatives dealing with offenders and those at risk of becoming offenders. These are based on the principle that since criminal behaviour and attitudes can be learned through association with criminal types, so can conventional values be learned by interaction with those holding them. Well-known programs such as "Night Hoops" or "After-4 Drop-ins" are aimed at "at-risk" youth and provide an opportunity for them to associate with positive role models. Well-known sports figures will often participate and deliver positive messages telling kids to "Stay in school" or "Say no to drugs." In Ottawa, Ontario, the Ottawa-Carleton Regional Police Service runs a youth centre in a neighbourhood once ridden with youth crime. They have reported a significant decrease in illegal activity in the neighbourhood since the centre's opening.

Closely linked to the notion of learned behaviour are those of commitment and attachment put forth by social control theorists. Not only do recreation programs run by such organizations as the Boys and Girls Club and the YM/YWCA promote positive learning, they help to develop a positive bond between individual participants and the program. Individuals, in turn, will not want to risk losing the privilege of being a member of the program if they break the rules. Similarly, educational programs such as Head Start work to socialize children at the preschool stage to help make their school experiences more enjoyable and thereby decrease the chances of early withdrawal. Social control theorists believe that a strong commitment to school, family, employment, and recreation—assuming these environments are all positive ones—can help decrease an individual's likelihood of succumbing to a criminal lifestyle.

Studies of victims' compensation programs seem to express a common caution: such programs can be effective provided they are intelligently managed and do not further expose victims to additional secondary victimization through less than effective bureaucracy. Moreover, money may not be as important to most victims as are practical assistance and fair representation within the justice system. Hence, legislation enhancing the rights of victims and local victims' assistance programs may be the best ways of channeling energies currently existing within the burgeoning victims' movement.

## Critique of Social Process Theories

Social process theories share some of the limitations of social-structural theories, discussed in Chapter 7. Most notable of these is the disregard for biological and/or psychological contributions to criminal behaviour; indeed, all these theories are concerned with the social reality surrounding individuals and their interaction with all or some segments of it. In addition, like social-structural theories the social process perspective fails to fully explain why some individuals who are surrounded by negative environments and poor role models manage to avoid becoming involved in criminal behaviour. How is it that some manage to resist the peer pressure to get involved in deviant activity? How are they able to desist from "learning" from what they see all around them? If socialization is so crucial to an understanding of criminal behaviour, how is it that crime rates fluctuate from region to region in Canada? Are youth, for example, in the western provinces, where crime rates are generally higher, socialized differently than those in the eastern parts of the country, where crime rates are generally lower?

**Summary** This chapter discussed a wide variety of perspectives, from social learning, social control, and labelling theories to the emergence of the victims' rights movement. We have used both the terms *social process approach* and *interactionist perspective* to classify the theories found here. More fundamental to each of this chapter's perspectives, however, is the concept of social meaning; this chapter might be appropriately titled "the search for social meaning."

CHAPTER 8
265
The Meaning
of Crime:
Social Process
Perspectives

When individuals interact with others, they naturally learn certain behaviours and the justifications for them. Social learning theories contend that excessive interaction with those who promote a criminal lifestyle rather than a law-abiding one will result, for most, in the pursuit of a similar way of life. In addition to engaging in antisocial behaviour, individuals can also learn the rationalizations needed to ignore conventional societal norms in favour of deviant ones. Similarly, social control theory holds that the bonds individuals form with positive role models or institutions prevent them from engaging in criminal behaviour. When these bonds become weak or break, individuals have "nothing to lose" by turning to antisocial behaviour.

When individual offenders are labelled criminal or deviant, the meaning that their presence holds for the group of which they are a part, as well as the personal significance of their own lives, have been inexorably changed. They will rarely be seen the same (in the predeviant state) again. In like fashion, when offenders internalize an acquired or imposed deviant self-conception, the meaning of their own lives changes and any future decisions they will make take on a new significance in light of the new self-image.

Finally, victims often find their lives dramatically modified by the victimization experience. Things previously taken for granted, such as evening strolls in the neighbourhood, may never seem the same again (especially if the person was the victim of a mugging or of a random act of violence). Hence, each perspective covered in this chapter examines the interaction that occurs between individuals, and looks closely at the interaction between criminals and their victims. We have learned from this chapter that social interaction is a process that is open to analysis, and that the ultimate outcome of any significant interaction is always a new experience or the reinterpretation of previous experiences—that is, the creation of new meanings.

# Discussion Questions

1. This book emphasizes a social problems versus social responsibility theme. Which of the theoretical perspectives discussed in this chapter (if any) best support the social problems approach? Which (if any) support the social responsibility approach? Why?

2. This chapter includes a discussion of the labelling process. Give a few examples of the everyday imposition of positive, rather than negative, labels. Why is it so difficult to successfully impose positive labels on individuals previously labelled negatively?

3. Compare and contrast the theories discussed in this chapter, citing differences and similarities between and among them. How, for example, does Reckless' notion of containment differ from Hirschi's idea of a social bond?

4. Do you believe that Sutherland's differential association approach, which contends that criminality is learned behaviour, provides any valuable insight into an explanation of deviant behaviour? If so, what is it? Do you believe that Sykes' and Matza's techniques of neutralization can also be learned? Can deviant behaviour be "unlearned"?

5. Review the *Canadian Statement of Basic Principles of Justice for Victims of Crime*. Do you believe victims in Canada should have more rights? Should the rights of victims be included in the Canadian Charter of Rights and Freedoms? Defend your position.

# Weblinks

**www.voices4children.org/**

Voices for Children. This group works with organizations and individuals to strengthen public commitment to the healthy development of children and youth.

**www.caveat.org/**

Canadians Against Violence Everywhere Advocating its Termination (CAVEAT). CAVEAT's mission is to contribute to the creation and maintenance of a just, peaceful society through public education, changes to the justice system, and ensuring the rights of victims.

**www.crcvc.ca/**

Canadian Resource Centre for Victims of Crime (CRCVC). The CRCVC is a national, nonprofit victims' rights advocacy group. Good links related to criminal justice sites and legislation.

**www.canada.justice.gc.ca/en/ps/voc/index.html**

Policy Centre for Victims' Issues. This Department of Justice site provides information on federal government initiatives concerning crime victims.

**www.hc-sc.gc.ca/hppb/familyviolence/index.html**

National Clearinghouse on Family Violence. Federal Department of Health site that provides extensive links to research on victims of violence and abuse. Extensive list of international, national, provincial, and local links.

**www.cfc-efc.ca/menu/eng013.htm**

Child and Family Canada. Public education site sponsored by 50 nonprofit organizations to provide resources on children and families. Extensive library of research papers.

## CHAPTER 9

# Social Conflict and Crime

Laws are like spiders' webs, which, if anything small falls into them, they ensnare it, but large things break through and escape.

—SOLON[1]

Our actions were not oriented toward intensive, wanton destruction but rather were carefully selected and carried out with great concern for political, economic, and human consequences.

—ANNE HANSEN[2]

## LEARNING OUTCOMES

After reading this chapter, you should be able to:

● Recognize the ways in which power conflict between social groups contributes to crime and criminal activity

● Understand the distinctions between a number of social conflict theories

● Consider those policy initiatives that reflect the social conflict approach

● Assess the shortcomings of the social conflict perspective

# Introduction

On March 11, 1990, a small Mohawk Aboriginal band erected a barricade along the border of the Mohawk Nation reserve of Kanesatake. The nearby city of Oka, Quebec was proceeding with plans to enlarge a golf course on 22 hectares of land known as "The Pines" that had been given to the city but was claimed by the Mohawks as a sacred native ancestral burial ground. Since the courts had rejected the Mohawks' claim to the land, the band perceived their only option to be a standoff. It lasted 78 days.

Initially, the barricade was guarded mostly by women and children. The standoff intensified, however, as the Mohawks of Kanesatake were joined by Mohawk natives from other reserves in Canada and the United States, some of whom belonged to a society of heavily armed Mohawk Warriors. The introduction of high-powered firearms and other weapons increased the tension between the Mohawks and authorities, represented largely by the Quebec provincial police force, known as the Sûreté du Québec (SQ). The city of Oka was successful in obtaining a court order to evict the Mohawks, and on July 10, 1990 about 100 SQ personnel attempted to enforce this injunction on behalf of the municipality. Armed Mohawks were positioned to one side in the woods while police equipped with gas masks and assault rifles advanced on the barricade. An armed conflict erupted, and hundreds of rounds of ammunition were fired from both sides, resulting in the wounding and eventual death of a 31-year-old SQ corporal. The standoff had reached crisis proportions, and each side blamed the other for the death of the police officer.

Thirty kilometers to the south of the Kanesatake reserve, Mohawks from the Kahnawake reserve were outraged by the actions of the police. In a show of support, they blocked off all roads into the reserve. These included two major highways, one of which led to the Mercier Bridge linking the city of Montreal to the residential neighbourhood of Châteauguay, which forced thousands of commuters to take a 2-hour daily detour. Threatening to "bring down the bridge" if there was another police assault at Oka, the Mohawks dug in. Over 100 chiefs from across Canada met at Kahnawake in a show of solidarity.

The crisis captured national attention, and throngs of media personnel transmitted interviews and pictures across the country. As the standoff continued throughout the summer of 1990, both sides in the conflict became more entrenched. Arms and ammunition were smuggled from native communities in the United States to bolster the Mohawk cause. Mohawk Warriors with monikers such as "Lasagna" and "Kadahfi" appeared before television cameras in army fatigues, with bandanas covering their faces. The 1 400 to 1 800 SQ forces were bolstered by 200 or so Royal Canadian Mounted Police officers throughout the duration of the crisis. As the standoff dragged on through the summer, with no progress made toward negotiating a settlement, then Prime Minister Mulroney called in the Canadian Armed Forces at the request of Premier Bourassa and the Quebec government. Approximately 1 000 military personnel took over police positions established at Kanesatake and Kahnawake. Numerous violent clashes erupted as each side stood its ground. Canadians witnessed scenes of armoured personnel carriers, barbed-wire barricades, and shouting matches between the two sides as the group of Mohawk Warriors resisted advances by the authorities. Eventually, on September 6, 1990 the Kahnawake Mohawks ended their occupation of the Mercier Bridge. On September 26, after often heated negotiations, the standoff ended when the Mohawk Warriors agreed to lift the barricade. The golf course has not since been expanded.

The Oka crisis cost the Canadian people $200 million, including the expense of extra policing and army intervention. Even though the incident at Oka ended relatively peacefully, it set off a wave of Aboriginal unrest across the country that saw native groups pitted against government and police authorities.

In a standoff at the Kanesatake reserve in Oka, Quebec, on September 1, 1990, a Canadian soldier comes face to face with a Mohawk warrior. SOURCE: F. Schmalleger, D. MacAlister, P.F. McKenna and J. Winterdyk, *Canadian Criminal Justice Today: An Introductory Text for the Twenty-First Century* (Toronto: Prentice Hall Allyn and Bacon, Canada, 2000), p. 6. *The Canadian Press/Shaney Komulainen.*

# Major Principles of Social Conflict Perspectives

This brief section serves to summarize the central features of the social conflict theories of crime causation. Each of these points can be found elsewhere in the chapter, where they are discussed in more detail. This overview, however, provides a guide to the rest of the chapter.

Most social conflict theories of crime causation make the following fundamental assumptions:

- Society is divided by conflict rather than integrated by consensus.
- Society is made up of groups based on political and economic power.
- Differences in social class, and in particular those arrangements within society which maintain class differences, is the focus for criminological study.
- Powerful groups make laws that reflect and protect their interests.
- Crime is an outcome of conflict between those who have and those who have not.

# Social Conflict Theories

**Conflict perspective**
an analytical perspective on social organization which holds that conflict is a fundamental aspect of social life itself and can never be fully resolved.

Social conflict theories place emphasis on social, economic, and political realities and place crime within this context. As with social process theories, the social **conflict perspective** focuses on the interaction between groups but views this interaction as one of conflict. Various groups within society, defined in terms of their political, economic or social standing, are seen to compete with one another to promote their own best interests.

Crime and criminal activity are the outcome of this struggle, according to social conflict theories. The creation and application of criminal laws is crucial to determining who becomes criminalized; social conflict criminologists see these roles largely filled by that segment of society holding the economic and political power. This segment uses the law as a means of controlling the dissatisfied and less powerful groups withing society while maintaining its position of power. As various groups struggle for power, conflict ensues, which promotes crime. Social conflict theorists are also concerned with the role of government and the state in producing crime, since what is considered acceptable and unacceptable behaviour is determined by state-sanctioned laws designed to set boundaries governing such behaviour.

Various theories found under the rubric of the social conflict perspective emphasize different root causes of the conflict. This chapter considers a number of these theories. *Radical criminology* is based on Marxist political thought and contends that current inequities in social standing and economic power are the main contributors to the reality of crime. *Critical criminology* is distinguished from radical criminology by its emphasis on a critique of the relationship between social classes; it is generally viewed as more reactive than the proactive approach taken by the radical criminological outlook. *Feminist criminology* sees the inequities that

*Theory in Perspective*
*Social Conflict Approaches*

---

**SOCIAL CONFLICT THEORIES.** Emphasize the power of conflict within society, based largely on inequalities between social classes.

**Radical Criminology.** Holds that the causes of crime are rooted in social conditions which empower the wealthy and the politically well organized, but disenfranchise those less fortunate.
**Period:**     1960s–present
**Theorists:**   Karl Marx, Richard Quinney, William Chambliss, Raymond Michalowski, George Vold, Austin Turk
**Concepts:**   Social class, bourgeoisie, proletariat

**Feminist Criminology.** A radical criminological approach to the explanation of crime that sees the conflict and inequality present in society based primarily on gender.
**Period:**     1970s–present
**Theorists:**   Freda Adler, Rita J. Simon, Kathleen Daly, Meda Chesney-Lind, John Hagan
**Concepts:**   Power-control, gender socialization, empowerment

**Peacemaking Criminology.** Holds that crime control agencies and citizens must work together to alleviate social problems including crime.
**Period:**     1980s–present
**Theorists:**   Harold E. Pepinsky, Richard Quinney
**Concepts:**   Compassionate criminology, restorative justice

**Left-realism Criminology.** A branch of radical criminology that holds that crime is a "real" social problem experienced by the lower classes.
**Period:**     1980s–present
**Theorists:**   Walter DeKeseredy, Jock Young
**Concepts:**   Radical realism, critical realism, street crime, social justice, crime control

---

exist within society as drawn along gender lines. The *left-realist* perspective moves away from a political-ideological explanation of crime and criminality toward the contention that crime is very "real," especially for marginalized segments of society. Finally, *peacemaking criminology* advocates the reduction of crime through the cooperative efforts of criminal justice agencies and the citizens they serve. A shortcoming of at least some of the theories is that they fail to appreciate the large number of problems that contribute to the reality of crime by limiting their focus to the conflict between classes.

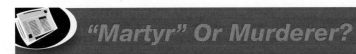

## "Martyr" Or Murderer?

### Abortion Protester's Death Sentence

The conflict perspective seems better suited to an understanding of many contemporary social issues, among them the heated battle between pro-lifers and pro-choice advocates over abortion, as the article in this box shows.

When Paul Hill used a 12-gauge shotgun to kill an abortion clinic's doctor, abortion rights supporters—and many foes—called him a monster.

Tuesday, Hill may have graduated from monster to martyr when he was sentenced to die in Florida's electric chair for the July murders of John Bayard Britton and his escort, James Barrett, in Pensacola.

"He'll be a good poster boy for murder in the future," said David Gunn, Jr., the son of a doctor killed in 1993 by another protester.

The National Right to Life Committee denounced violence. "The murders committed by Paul Hill were deplorable and reprehensible," says President Wanda Franz.

But radical abortion rights foes hailed Hill.

"He's a hero and a martyr in my book," says Christian Action Group's Roy McMillan of Jackson, Miss. "I believe in killing people in just wars ... and there's a war in the womb."

Now, "we are going to execute someone who simply did for a stranger something every father in America would do to protect his children."

Almost from the time he joined demonstrations outside Pensacola's abortion clinics, activists watched as the articulate, soft-spoken former minister and father of three grew more fervent in his protests.

First, his fetus posters became more graphic, his shouting more intense.

"Mommy, don't let them kill me!" he cried out to women at The Ladies Center clinic.

Then, in March 1993, when another protester shot and killed abortion doctor David Gunn in Pensacola, Hill stunned the Bible Belt community by proclaiming he was part of a group that believes in "justifiable homicide" to stop abortion.

The Gunn slaying, Hill said last week on *Eye to Eye With Connie Chung*, "literally changed my life."

The double murder occurred 17 months later. Britton's wife was wounded, too.

On *Eye to Eye,* Hill said he has no regrets: "I have done something that I think the Lord is pleased with. I know ... I'm going to heaven when I die."

Michael Bray, who served four years in prison in connection with the bombings of seven Washington, D.C.–area clinics, calls Hill an inspiration.

"If a martyr is one who dies for a just cause, yes," Bray said. "If he dies for doing what is good and right, yes. Therefore, I say yes."

Abortion rights activists say they're terrified such talk will provoke more violence.

"We are on red alert," says Eleanor Smeal of the Feminist Majority Foundation.

Smeal and others are urging the federal government to step up enforcement of a new law that makes it a crime to block access to clinics or threaten or harm workers. Hill also was convicted under that law.

Already, members of the new Republican-controlled Congress are considering ways to limit its scope.

"Those who commit violence ought to have federal penalties," says Rep. Chris Smith (R., N.J.). But the law goes too far, so "we're going to take a (new) look at it."

Barrett's son Bruce said Hill's sentence should send a powerful message. "It's real important that the state showed that this kind of violence is not going to be condoned, and the only way to do that is to give the maximum penalty," he said. Hill "shot my father in the face with a shotgun. He shot Dr. Britton in the head ... and he had planned to do it for a long time."

### DISCUSSION QUESTIONS

1. How is it that some people view Paul Hill as a common criminal, while others see him as a hero—even a martyr? How can otherwise law-abiding citizens condone the killing of abortion clinic workers?
2. What does the debate over abortion have to tell us about the role of law in society and about how laws are made and enforced?
3. What other issues can you identify that are officially law violations, but which have numerous proponents?

SOURCE: Mimi Hall, "'Martyr' or Murderer? Abortion Protester's Death Sentence Ignites Debate," *USA Today*, December 7, 1994, p. 3A. Copyright 1994, *USA Today*. Reprinted with permission.

## Radical Criminology

The conflict perspective is thoroughly entrenched in **radical criminology,** which is also diversely known as, or related to, schools of thought referred to as new, critical, or **Marxist criminology**. Radical criminology, which appeared on the North American scene in the 1970s, has its roots in the writings of nineteenth-century social utopian thinkers. Primary among them is **Karl Marx,** whose writings on the conflicts inherent in capitalism led to the formulation of communist ideals and, many would say, to the rise of communist societies the world over.

According to Marx, two fundamental social classes exist within any capitalistic society: the haves and the have nots. Marx termed these two groups the proletariat and the bourgeoisie. The **proletariat** encompasses the large mass of people, those who are relatively uneducated and without power. In short, the proletariat are the workers, whereas the **bourgeoisie** are the capitalists—the wealthy owners of the means of production (i.e., the factories, businesses, and other elements of a society's organizational infrastructure). Although Marx was German, the terms *proletariat* and *bourgeoisie* were taken from Marx's knowledge of the French language, and are in turn derived from Latin. In ancient Rome, for example, that city's lowest class was propertyless and were individually referred to as *proletarius*.

According to Marx, the proletariat, since they possessed neither capital nor the means of production, such as factories, land, or natural resources, must earn their living by continuously selling their labour. The bourgeoisie, on the other hand, are the

**Radical criminology** a perspective holding that the causes of crime are rooted in social conditions that empower the wealthy and the politically well organized but disenfranchise those less fortunate. Radical criminology is sometimes called **Marxist criminology.**

**Proletariat** in Marxist theory, the working class.

**Bourgeoisie** in Marxist theory, the class of people that owns the means of production.

capitalist class who, by nature of their very position within society, stand opposed to the proletariat in an ongoing class struggle. Marx saw such struggle between classes as inevitable to the evolution of any capitalistic society and believed that the natural outcome of such struggle would be the overthrow of capitalistic social order and the birth of a truly classless, or communistic, society.

## Early Radical Criminology

Radical criminology is the intellectual child of three important historical circumstances: (1) the ruminations of nineteenth-century social utopian thinkers, including Friedrich Engels, Georg Wilhelm, Friedrich Hegel, Karl Marx, George Simmel, and Max Weber; (2) the rise of conflict theory in the social sciences; and (3) the dramatic radicalization of North American academia in the 1960s and 1970s.

Central to the perspective of radical criminology is the notion of social class. Some authors maintain that "class is nothing but an abbreviation to describe a way of living, thinking, and feeling." For most sociologists, however, the concept of **social class** entails distinctions made between individuals on the basis of significant defining characteristics such as race, religion, education, profession, income, wealth, family background, housing, artistic tastes, aspirations, cultural pursuits, child-rearing habits, speech, accent, and so forth. Individuals are assigned to classes by others and by themselves on the basis of characteristics that are both ascribed and achieved. Ascribed attributes are those with which a person is born, such as race or gender, while achieved characteristics are acquired through personal effort or chance over the course of one's life and include such things as level of education, income, place of residence, and profession.

**Social class** distinctions made between individuals on the basis of important defining social characteristics.

The tomb of Karl Marx, in Highgate Cemetery, London, England. Marxist thought underpins the writings of many radical criminologists. How did Marxism influence criminology?
*Rex Features USA Ltd.*

Although Marx concerned himself with only two social classes, most social scientists today talk in terms of at least three groups: upper, middle, and lower class. Some have distinguished between five hierarchically arranged classes (the real upper, semi-upper, limited-success, working, and real lower) while further subdividing classes 'horizontally' according to ascribed characteristics such as race and religion.[3]

Conflict theorists of the early and mid-1900s saw in the concept of social class the rudimentary ingredients of other important concepts such as authority, power, and conflict. **Ralf Dahrendorf**, for example, wrote that "classes are social conflict groups the determinant of which can be found in the participation in or exclusion from the exercise of authority."[4] For Dahrendorf, conflict was ubiquitous, a fundamental part of and coextensive with any society. "Not the presence but the absence of conflict is surprising and abnormal," he wrote, "and we have good reason to be suspicious if we find a society or social organization that displays no evidence of conflict. To be sure, we do not have to assume that conflict is always violent and uncontrolled ... [and] we must never lose sight of the underlying assumption that conflict can be temporarily suppressed, regulated, channeled, and controlled but that neither a philosopher-king nor a modern dictator can abolish it once and for all."[5]

From Dahrendorf's perspective, power and authority were most at issue between groups, giving rise to class conflict. Dahrendorf also recognized that situations characterized by conflict are rarely static, and that it is out of conflict that change arises. For Dahrendorf, change could be either destructive or constructive. Destructive change brings about a lessening of social order, whereas constructive change increases cohesiveness within society.

Radical criminologists of today are considerably more sophisticated than their Marxist forebears. Contemporary radical criminology holds that the causes of crime are rooted in social conditions which empower the wealthy and the politically well organized, but disenfranchise those less fortunate. A well-known spokesperson for radical thinkers succinctly summarizes the modern perspective in these words: "what makes the behavior of some criminal is the coercive power of the state to enforce the will of the ruling class."[6]

**George Vold** was instrumental in popularizing radical criminology. In his 1958 work entitled *Theoretical Criminology*, Vold described social conflict as "a universal form of interaction" and argued that groups are naturally in conflict as their interests and purposes "overlap, encroach on one another and (tend to) be competitive."[7] He also addressed the issue of social cohesion, noting that as intergroup conflict intensified, loyalty of individual members to their group increased. "It has long been realized that conflict between groups tends to develop and intensify the loyalty of group members to their respective groups,"[8] Vold wrote. But Vold's most succinct observation of the role conflict plays in contributing to crime was expressed as follows: "The whole political process of law making, law breaking, and law enforcement becomes a direct reflection of deep-seated and fundamental conflicts between interest groups. ... Those who produce legislative majorities win control over the power," said Vold, "and dominate the policies that decide who is likely to be involved in violation of the law."[9]

In other words, from Vold's point of view powerful groups make laws, and those laws express and protect their interests. Hence, the body of laws that characterize any society is a political statement, and crime is a political definition imposed largely upon those whose interests lie outside of that which the powerful, through the law, define as acceptable. In his writings about conflict, Vold went so far as to compare the criminal with a soldier, fighting, through crime commission, for the very survival of the group whose values he or she represents. In Vold's words, "[t]he individual criminal is then viewed as essentially a soldier under conditions of warfare: his behavior may not be 'normal' or 'happy' or 'adjusted'—it is the behavior of the soldier doing what is to be done in wartime."[10] Vold's analogy, probably influenced by the fact he wrote in the wake of World War II, was meant to express the idea that crime was a manifestation of denied needs and values, that is, the cultural heritage of disenfranchised groups who were powerless to enact their interests in legitimate fashion. Hence, theft becomes necessary for many poor people, especially those left unemployed or unemployable by the socially acceptable forms of wealth distribution defined by law.

Another early conflict theorist, **Austin Turk,** said that in the search for an explanation of criminality, "one is led to investigate the tendency of laws to penalize persons whose behavior is more characteristic of the less powerful than of the more powerful and the extent to which some persons and groups can and do use legal processes and agencies to maintain and enhance their power position vis-à-vis other persons and groups."[11] In his seminal 1969 work, *Criminality and Legal Order,*[12] Turk wrote that in any attempt to explain criminality, "it is more useful to view the social order as mainly a pattern of conflict" rather than to offer explanations for crime based on behavioural or psychological approaches. Turk, like most other conflict criminologists, saw the law as a powerful tool in the service of prominent social groups seeking continued control over others. Crime was the natural consequence of such intergroup struggle because it resulted from the definitions imposed by the laws of the powerful upon the disapproved strivings of the unempowered.

## Radical Criminology Today

Two highly visible proponents of radical criminology today are **William Chambliss** and Richard Quinney. In 1971, Chambliss, along with Robert T. Seidman, published an intellectually renowned volume entitled *Law, Order, and Power*. Their work represented something of a bridge between earlier conflict theorists and the more radical approach of Marxists. Through its emphasis on social class, class interests, and class conflict, *Law, Order, and Power* presented a Marxist perspective stripped of any overt references to capitalism as the root cause of crime. "The more economically stratified a society becomes," Chambliss and Seidman wrote, "the more it becomes necessary for the dominant groups in the society to enforce through coercion the norms of conduct which guarantee their supremacy."[13] Chambliss and Seidman outlined their position in four propositions, as follows[14]:

- The conditions of one's life affect one's values and norms. Complex societies are composed of groups with widely different life conditions.
- Complex societies are therefore composed of highly disparate and conflicting sets of norms.
- The probability of a given group's having its particular normative system embodied in law is not distributed equally but is closely related to the political and economic position of that group.

- The higher a group's political or economic position, the greater the probability that its views will be reflected in laws.

Chambliss also believed that middle- and upper-class criminals are more apt to escape apprehension and punishment by the criminal justice system, not because they are any smarter or more capable of hiding their crimes than lower class offenders, but because of a "very rational choice on the part of the legal system to pursue those violators that the community will reward them for pursuing and to ignore those violators who have the capability for causing trouble for the agencies."[15]

By the 1970s, however, Chambliss's writings assumed a much more Marxist flavour. In an article published in 1975, Chambliss once again recognized the huge power gap separating the "haves" from the "have nots."[16] Crime, he said, is created by actions of the ruling class that define as criminal undertakings and activities that contravene the interests of the rulers. At the same time, he said, members of the ruling class will inevitably be able to continue to violate the criminal law with impunity, because it is their own creation.

By 1975, the Marxist flavour of Chambliss's writing had become undeniable. He began using Marxist terminology. "[A]s capitalist societies industrialize and the gap between the bourgeoisie and the proletariat widens," he wrote, "penal law will expand in an effort to coerce the proletariat into submission."[17] For Chambliss, the economic consequences of crime within a capitalistic society were partially what perpetuated it. "[C]rime reduces surplus labor," he wrote, "by creating employment not only for the criminals but for law enforcers, welfare workers, professors of criminology, and a horde of people who live off the fact that crime exists. ..."[18] Socialist societies, claimed Chambliss, should reflect much lower crime rates than capitalist societies because a "less intense class struggle should reduce the forces leading to and the functions of crime."

Although Chambliss provides much of the intellectual bedrock of contemporary radical criminology, that school of thought found its most eloquent expression in the writings of **Richard Quinney**. In 1974, Quinney, in an attempt to challenge and change social life for the better, set forth his six Marxist propositions for an understanding of crime, as follows[19]:

1. American society is based on an advanced capitalist economy.
2. The state is organized to serve the interests of the dominant economic class, the capitalist ruling class.
3. Criminal law is an instrument of the state and ruling class to maintain and perpetuate the existing social and economic order.
4. Crime control in capitalist society is accomplished through a variety of institutions and agencies established and administered by a governmental elite, representing ruling class interests, for the purpose of establishing domestic order.
5. The contradictions of advanced capitalism—the disjunction between existence and essence—require that the subordinate classes remain oppressed by whatever means necessary, especially through the coercion and violence of the legal system.
6. Only with the collapse of capitalist society and the creation of a new society, based on socialist principles, will there be a solution to the crime problem.

A few years later, Quinney published *Class, State, and Crime*, in which he argued that almost all crimes committed by members of the lower classes are necessary for the survival of individual members of those classes. Crimes, said Quinney—in fashion reminiscent of Vold's notion of the criminal as a soldier—are actually an attempt by the socially disenfranchised "to exist in a society where *survival* is not assured by other, collective means."[20] Quinney concluded that "[c]rime is inevitable under capitalist conditions ... because crime is "a response to the material conditions of life. Permanent unemployment—and the acceptance of that condition," wrote Quinney, "can result in a form of life where criminality is an appropriate and consistent response."[21] The solution offered by Quinney to the problem of crime is the development of a socialist society. "The *ultimate meaning* of crime in the development of capitalism," he writes, "is the need for a socialist society."[22]

Contemporary radical criminology attributes much of the existing propensity toward criminality to differences in social class, and in particular to those arrangements within society that maintain class differences. As Quinney puts it, "classes are an expression of the underlying forces of the capitalist mode of production. ..."[23] "Within the class structure of advanced capitalism," he writes, "is the dialectic that increases class struggle and the movement for socialist revolution." Table 9.1 depicts the class structure of the United States as Quinney portrayed it.

## Critical Criminology

Some writers distinguish between critical criminology and radical criminology, claiming that the former is simply a way of critiquing social relationships leading to crime, while the latter constitutes a proactive call for a radical change in the social conditions crime springs from.

Gresham Sykes explains **critical criminology** this way: "it forces an inquiry into precisely how the normative content of the criminal law is internalized in different segments of society, and how norm-holding is actually related to behavior."[24] As David A. Jones states in his insightful *History of Criminology*, however, "Sometimes, it may be difficult to distinguish 'critical' from a truly Marxist criminology. One basis, advanced by Marvin Wolfgang, is that 'critical' criminology is 'more reactive than proactive,' meaning that 'critical' criminology does not aim to overthrow the 'ruling class' so much as it may criticize the way it believes such a group dominates society."[25]

A cogent example of the critical perspective in contemporary criminology can be had in the work of Elliott Currie.[26] Currie claims that "'market societies'—those in which the pursuit of private gain becomes the dominant organizing principle of social and economic life—are especially likely to breed high levels of violent crime." Market societies, says Currie, are characterized by more than free enterprise and a free market economy. They are societies in which the striving after personal economic gain runs rampant and becomes the hallmark of social life. The conditions endemic to market societies lead to high crime rates because they undercut and overwhelm more traditional principles that "have historically sustained individuals, families and communities." North American society, and the United States in particular, is the world's premier market society, says Currie, and its culture provides "a particularly fertile

**Critical criminology** a perspective focused on challenging traditional understandings and on uncovering false beliefs about crime and criminal justice.

## Table 9.1

## Class Structure of the United States with Estimated Percentages of the Adult Population

| | |
|---|---|
| **Capitalist Class**<br>1.5% | Owns and controls production; wields state power |
| **Petty Bourgeoisie**<br>18.5% | Professionals, middle management, bureaucrats |
| **Working Class**<br>80% | **Technical and skilled working class, 25%**<br><br>*Technical*, 10%<br>   teachers<br>   nurses<br>   medical technicians<br>*Skilled*, 15%<br>   craftsmen<br>   clerical<br>   sales<br>   operatives<br>   transport<br>   industrial<br><br>**Unskilled working class, 55%**<br><br>*Unskilled*, 30%<br>   industrial labour<br>   service<br>   office<br>   sales<br>   clerical<br>*Reserve army*, 15%<br>   unemployed<br>*Pauperized poor*, 10% |

SOURCE: Richard Quinney, *Class, State, and Crime: On the Theory and Practice of Criminal Justice* (New York: David McKay, 1977), p. 77. Reprinted with permission.

breeding ground for serious violent crime." Similarly, the recent and dramatic rise in crime rates in former communist countries throughout Europe can be explained by the burgeoning development of new market societies in those nations. According to Currie, seven "profoundly criminogenic and closely intertwined mechanisms" operate in a market society to produce crime. They are:

1. The progressive destruction of livelihood," which results from the long-term absence of opportunities for stable and rewarding work—a consequence of the fact that market societies view labour "simply as a cost to be reduced" rather than as an asset with intrinsic value.
2. "The growth of extremes of economic inequality and material deprivation," which causes many children to spend their developmental years in poverty.

3. "The withdrawal of public services and supports, especially for families and children," resulting from the fact that "it is a basic operating principle of market society to keep the public sector small. ..."

4. "The erosion of informal and communal networks of mutual support, supervision, and care" brought about by the high mobility of the work force characteristic of market societies.

5. "The spread of a materialistic, neglectful, and 'hard' culture" that exalts brutal forms of individualized competition.

6. "The unregulated marketing of the technology of violence," including the ready availability of guns, an emphasis on advancing technologies of destruction (such as the military), and mass-marketed violence on television and in the media.

7. "The weakening of social and political alternatives," leaving people unable to cope effectively with the forces of the market society that undermine their communities and destroy valuable interpersonal relationships.

Currie suggests that as more nations emulate the 'market society' culture of the United States, crime rates throughout the world will rise. An increasing emphasis on punishment, and the growth of prisons systems, says Currie, will consequently be seen throughout most of the world in the twenty-first century.

## Critique of Radical-Critical Criminology

Radical-critical criminology has been criticized for its nearly exclusive emphasis on methods of social change at the expense of well-developed theory. As William Pelfrey explains, "[i]t is in the Radical School of Criminology that theory is almost totally disregarded, except as something to criticize, and radical *methods* are seen as optimum."[27]

Radical-critical criminology can also be criticized for failing to recognize what appears to be at least a fair degree of public consensus about the nature of crime, that is, that crime is undesirable and that criminal activity is to be controlled. Were criminal activity in fact a true expression of the sentiments of the politically and economically disenfranchised, as some radical criminologists claim, then public opinion might be expected to offer support for at least certain forms of crime. Even the sale and consumption of illicit drugs, however—a type of crime that may provide an alternative path to riches for the otherwise disenfranchised—is frequently condemned by residents of working-class communities.[28]

An effective criticism of Marxist criminology, in particular, centres on the fact that Marxist thinkers appear to confuse issues of personal politics with what could otherwise be social reality. As a consequence of allowing personal values and political leanings to enter the criminological arena, Marxist criminologists have frequently appeared to sacrifice their objectivity. Jackson Toby, for example, claims that Marxist and radical thinkers are simply building upon an "old tradition of sentimentality toward those who break social rules."[29] Such sentimentality can be easily discounted, he says, when we realize that "[c]olor television sets and automobiles are stolen more often than food and blankets."[30]

Marxist criminology has also been refuted by contemporary thinkers who find that it falls short in appreciating the multiplicity of problems that contribute to the

In October 1970, the Front de Libération du Québec (FLQ) kidnapped British diplomat James Cross and murdered Quebec cabinet minister Pierre Laporte to bring attention to their struggle for independence for French-speaking Quebec. The Canadian government responded by invoking the War Measures Act. How would the radical criminology perspective interpret the actions of the FLQ? *The Canadian Press.*

problem of crime. Some years ago, for example, Hermann Mannheim critiqued Marxist assumptions by showing how "subsequent developments" have shown that "Marx was wrong in thinking: (a) that there could be only two classes in a capitalist society ...; (b) that ... class struggle was entirely concerned with the question of private property in the means of production; (c) that the only way in which fundamental social changes could be effected was by violent social revolution; [and] (d) that all conflicts were class conflicts and all social change could be explained in terms of class conflicts. ..."

Mannheim went on to point out that the development of a semiskilled work force along with the advent of highly skilled and well-educated workers has led to the creation of a multiplicity of classes within contemporary capitalistic societies. The growth of such classes, said Mannheim, effectively spreads the available wealth in those societies where such workers are employed and reduces the likelihood of revolution.

Marxist criminology has also suffered a considerable loss of prestige among many would-be followers in the wake of the collapse of the former Soviet Union and its client states in Eastern Europe and other parts of the world. With the death of Marxist political organizations and their agendas, Marxist criminology seems to have lost some of its impetus. Many would argue that, in fact, the work of writers such as Quinney and Chambliss presaged the decline of Soviet influence and had already moved Marxist and radical criminology into new areas—effectively shedding the reigns of world communism and ending any association with its institutional embodiment in specific parts of the world. The work of Elliott Currie (discussed earlier in this chapter) and others, is now leading in a post-Marxist direction, while retaining a critical emphasis on the principles out of which radical criminology was fashioned.

## Feminist Criminology

**Feminist criminology**
a developing intellectual
approach that
emphasizes gender
issues and inequality in
the study of criminology

As some writers have observed, "Women have been virtually invisible in criminological analysis until recently and much theorizing has proceeded as though criminality is restricted to men."[31] Others put it this way: "Criminological theory assumes a woman is like a man."[32] Recently, however, advances in feminist theory have been applied to criminology, resulting in what has been called a **feminist criminology**. Other strands of feminist thought inform feminist criminology, including *liberal feminism, radical feminism, socialist feminism,* and *Marxist feminism.* Each of these perspectives argues that conflict in society is based on inequalities due primarily to gender, although they may vary on the degree to which this inequality exists. Early works in the field included **Freda Adler's** *Sisters in Crime*[33] and **Rita J. Simon's** *Women and Crime,*[34] both published in 1975. In these books, the authors attempted to explain existing divergences in crime rates between men and women as due primarily to socialization rather than biology. Women, claimed these authors, were taught to believe in personal limitations, faced reduced socioeconomic opportunities, and, as a result, suffered from lower aspirations. As gender equality increased, they said, it could be expected that male and female criminality would take on similar characteristics. Although Adler and Simon were instrumental in bringing the feminist perspective into theoretical criminology, their approach has not been validated by observations surrounding increased gender equality over the past few decades.

Early feminist theorizing may not have borne the fruit that some researchers anticipated, but it has led to a heightened awareness of gender issues within criminology. Two of the most insightful contemporary proponents of the usefulness of applying feminist thinking to criminological analysis are **Kathleen Daly** and **Meda Chesney-Lind.** Daly and Chesney-Lind have identified five elements of feminist thought that "distinguish it from other types of social and political thought."[35] They are:

1. Gender is not a natural fact but a complex social, historical, and cultural product; it is related to, but not simply derived from, biological sex differences and differing reproductive capacities.
2. Gender and gender relations order social life and social institutions in fundamental ways.
3. Gender relations and constructs of masculinity and femininity are not symmetrical but are based on an organizing principle of men's superiority and their social and political-economic dominance over women.
4. Systems of knowledge reflect men's views of the natural and social world; the production of knowledge is gendered.
5. Women should be at the centre of intellectual inquiry, not peripheral, invisible, or appendages to men.

In a similar, but more recent, analysis of feminist criminology, Susan Caulfield and Nancy Wonders describe "five major contributions that have been made by feminist scholarship and practice"[36] to criminological thinking: (1) a focus on gender as a central organizing principle of contemporary life; (2) the importance of power in shaping social relationships; (3) a heightened sensitivity to the way in which social context helps shape human relationships; (4) the recognition that social reality must be understood as a process, and the development of research methods that take this into account; and (5) a commitment to social change as a crucial part of feminist scholarship and practice. As is the case with most feminist writing in the area of criminology today, Caulfield and Wonders hold that these five contributions of feminist scholarship "can help to guide research and practice within criminology. …"

Feminism is a way of seeing the world—it is not strictly a sexual orientation. To be a feminist is to "combine a female mental perspective with a sensitivity for those social issues that influence primarily women."[37] Central to understanding feminist thought in its historical and contemporary modes is the realization that feminism views gender in terms of power relationships. In other words, according to feminist approaches men have traditionally held much more power in society than have women. Male dominance has long been reflected in the patriarchal structure of Western society, a structure that has excluded women from much decision-making in socially significant areas. Sexist attitudes—deeply ingrained notions of male superiority—have perpetuated inequality between the sexes. The consequences of sexism and of the unequal gender-based distribution of power have been far reaching, affecting fundamental aspects of social roles and personal expectation at all levels.

Various schools of feminist thought exist, with liberal and radical feminism envisioning a power-based and traditional domination of women's bodies and minds by men throughout history. **Radical feminism** depicts men as fundamentally brutish, aggressive, and violent and sees men as controlling women through sexuality by taking advantage of women's biological dependency during child-bearing years and their inherent lack of physical strength relative to men. Radical feminists believe, for example, that the sexual victimization of girls is a learned behaviour, as young males are socialized to be aggressive, resulting in male domination over females. They view society as patriarchal and believe that it is because of male control of the law that women are defined as subjects. Those young women who are sexually and physically exploited may then run away or abuse substances, thereby becoming criminalized; exploitation triggers the deviant behaviour. The elimination of male domination should therefore reduce crime rates for women and "even precipitate a decrease in male violence against women."[38]

**Liberal feminists**, although they want the same gender equality as other feminists, lay the blame for present inequalities on the development within culture and society of "separate and distinct spheres of influence and traditional attitudes about the appropriate role of men and women. …"[39] A recent book by Alida V. Merlo and Jocelyn M. Pollock,[40] for example, points out that feminists are often blamed in today's political atmosphere for the recent upsurge in crime because many, by entering or creating innovative family structures, have lowered what might otherwise be the positive effect of traditional family values on crime control. Liberal feminists call for the removal of the division of power and labour between the sexes. This, in turn, would eliminate inequality and promote greater social harmony.

**Socialist feminists**, who provide a third perspective, see gender oppression as a consequence of the economic structure of society and as a natural outgrowth of capitalist forms of social organization. Egalitarian societies, from the socialist point of view, would be built around socialist or Marxist principles with the aim of creating a society free of gender and class divisions. The present, capitalist social structure sees men committing violent street crimes, with women more likely to commit property and vice crimes.[41]

**Radical feminism**
a feminist criminology approach that views society as a patriarchy in which women are defined as subjects.

**Liberal feminism**
a feminist criminology approach that sees gender inequality being expressed in most spheres of influence.

**Socialist feminism**
a feminist criminology approach that views gender oppression as an obvious feature of capitalist societies.

**Power-control theory**
a perspective that holds
that the distribution of
crime and delinquency
within society is to some
degree founded upon
the consequences power
relationships within the
wider society hold for
domestic settings, and
for the everyday
relationships between
men, women, and
children within the
context of family life.

A fourth and complementary feminist perspective has been identified by Sally Simpson. She identifies it as an alternative framework developed by "women of color."[42] In Simpson's words, "[t]he alternative frameworks developed by women of color heighten feminism's sensitivity to the complex interplay of gender, class, and race oppression."

**John Hagan** built upon defining features of power relationships in his book *Structural Criminology*,[43] in which he explained that power relationships existing in the wider society are effectively "brought home" to domestic settings and are reflected in everyday relationships between men, women, and children within the context of family life. Hagan writes: "Work relations structure family relations, particularly relations between fathers and mothers and, in turn, relations between parents and their children, especially mothers and their daughters."[44] Hagan's approach has been termed **power-control theory,** and suggests that "family class structure shapes the social reproduction of gender relations, and in turn the social distribution of delinquency."[45] In most middle- and upper-middle-class families, says Hagan, a paternalistic model, in which the father works and the mother supervises the children, is the norm. Under the paternalistic model girls are controlled by both parents—through male domination and by female role modelling. Boys, however, are less closely controlled and are relatively free to deviate from social norms, resulting in higher levels of delinquency among males. In lower-middle- and lower-class families, however, the paternalistic model is frequently absent. Hence, in such families there is less "gender socialization and less maternal supervision of girls," resulting in higher levels of female delinquency.

In a work supportive of Hagan's thesis, Evelyn K. Sommers[46] recently conducted a series of four hour-long interviews with fourteen female inmates in a Canadian medium-security prison. Focusing on what led to violations of the criminal law, Sommers identified four common themes to explain the criminality of the women she interviewed: (1) economic and financial need; (2) drug involvement; (3) personal anger rooted in sexual and physical abuse or a sense of loss; and (4) fear. Because "need" was identified as the cause of lawbreaking behaviour by four of five women interviewed, Sommers concluded that women's criminality is based on two underlying issues: the effort to maintain connection within relationships (such as between mother and child), and a personal quest for empowerment (as single mothers are expected to be independent and capable of providing for themselves and their children).

In a cogent analysis that encompasses much of contemporary feminist theory, Daly and Chesney-Lind suggest that feminist thought is more important for the way it informs and challenges existing criminology than for the new theories it offers. Much current feminist thought within criminology emphasizes the need for gender awareness. Theories of crime causation and prevention, it is suggested, must include women, and more research on gender-related issues in the field is badly needed. Additionally, say Daly and Chesney-Lind, "criminologists should begin to appreciate that their discipline and its questions are a product of white, economically privileged men's experiences"[47] and that rates of female criminality, which are lower than those of males, may highlight the fact that criminal behaviour is not as "normal" as once thought. Because modern-day criminological perspectives were mostly developed by Caucasian middle-class men, the propositions and theories they advance fail to take into consideration women's "ways of knowing."[48] Hence, the fundamental challenge poised by feminist criminology is: Do existing theories of crime causation apply as well to women as they do to men? Or, as Daly and Chesney-Lind ask, given the current situation in theory development, "do theories of men's crime apply to women?"[49]

Other feminists have analyzed the process by which laws are created and legislation passed and concluded that modern-day statutes frequently represent characteristically masculine modes of thought. Such analysts have concluded that existing criminal laws are overly rational and hierarchically structured, reflecting traditionally male ways of organizing the social world.[50] Such statutes, some analysts suggest, need to be replaced by, or complemented with, "a system of justice based upon what are the specifically feminine principles of care, connection and community."[51]

In the area of social policy, feminist thinkers have pointed to the need for increased controls over men's violence toward women, the creation of alternatives (to supplement the home and traditional family structures) for women facing abuse, and the protection of children. They have also questioned the role of government, culture, and the mass media in promulgating pornography, prostitution, and sexual assault and have generally portrayed ongoing crimes against women as characteristic of continuing traditions in which women are undervalued and controlled. Many radical feminists have suggested the replacement of men with women in positions of power, especially within justice system and government organizations, while others have noted that replacement still would not address needed changes in the structure of the system itself, which is gender biased due to years of male domination. Centrists, on the other hand, suggest a more balanced approach, believing that individuals of both genders have much to contribute to a workable justice system.[52]

## Critique of Feminist Theory

Some would argue that in the area of theoretical development, feminist criminology has yet to live up to its promise. Throughout the late 1970s and 1980s, few comprehensive feminist theories of crime were proposed, as feminist criminology focused

Aileen Wuornos, accused female serial killer. Although some women are moving into areas of traditional male criminality, the number of women committing most forms of crime is still far lower than that of men. How does the criminality of women appear to differ from that of men? *Daytona Beach News/Sygma.*

instead on descriptive studies of female involvement in crime.[53] Although such data-gathering may have laid the groundwork for theory-building that is yet to come, few descriptive studies attempted to link their findings to existing feminist theory in any comprehensive way. Theory development suffered again in the late 1980s and early 1990s as an increased concern with women's victimization, especially the victimization of women at the hands of men, led to further descriptive studies with a somewhat different focus. Male violence against women was seen as adding support to the central tenet of feminist criminology that the relationship between the sexes is primarily characterized by the exercise of power (or lack thereof). Such singularity of focus, however, did not make for broad theory-building. As one writer explains the current state of feminist criminology, "[f]eminist theory is a theory in formation."[54] To date, feminist researchers have continued to amass descriptive studies, while feminist analysis has hardly advanced beyond a framework for the "deconstruction"[55] of existing theories—that is, for their reevaluation in light of feminist insights. A fair assessment of the current situation would probably conclude that the greatest contributions of feminist thought to criminological theory-building are yet to come.

Feminist criminology has faced criticism from many other directions. As mentioned previously, predicted increases in female crime rates have failed to materialize as social opportunities available to both genders have become more balanced. Similarly, other thinkers have pointed to fundamental flaws in feminist thought, asking questions such as, "If men have more power than women, then why are so many more men arrested?"[56] Where studies do exist,[57] gender disparities in arrest are rarely found, nor do sentencing practices seem to favour women.[58] The chivalry hypothesis of many years ago, under which it was proposed that women are apt to be treated more leniently by the justice system because of their gender, appears no longer operative today.[59]

Some critics even argue that a feminist criminology is impossible. Daly and Chesney-Lind, for example, agree that although feminist thought may inform criminology, "a feminist criminology cannot exist because neither feminism nor criminology is a unified set of principles and practices."[60] In other words, according to these authors, a criminology built solely on feminist principles is unlikely because neither feminist thought nor criminology meet the strict requirements of formal theory building. Even with such a caveat in mind, however, it should still be possible to construct a gender-aware criminology, that is, one that is informed by issues of gender and that takes into consideration the concerns of feminist writers. A "feminist-oriented criminology," say Caulfield and Wonders, is one that will transgress traditional criminology. "This transgression, or 'going beyond boundaries,'" they write, "must occur at a number of levels across a number of areas covered within criminology"[61] and will eventually move us toward a more just world.

## Peacemaking Criminology

Throughout much of history, formal agencies of social control, especially the police, officials of the courts, and correctional personnel have been seen as pitted against criminal perpetrators and would-be wrongdoers. Crime control has been traditionally depicted in terms of a kind of epic struggle in which diametrically opposed antagonists continuously engage one another, but in which only one side can emerge as victorious. Recently, however, a new point of view, **peacemaking criminology,** has come to the fore. Criminology as peacemaking has its roots in Christian and Eastern philosophies and advances the notion that crime control agencies and the citizens they serve should work together to alleviate social problems and human suffering and thus reduce crime.[62] Peacemaking criminology, which includes the notion of service, has also been called "compassionate criminology" and suggests that "[c]ompassion, wisdom, and love are essential for understanding the suffering of which we are all a part and for practising a criminology of nonviolence."[63]

Peacemaking criminology is a new undertaking, popularized by the works of **Harold E. Pepinsky**[64] and Richard Quinney[65] beginning in 1986. Both Pepinsky and Quinney restate the problem of crime control from one of "how to stop crime" to one of "how to make peace" within society and between citizens and criminal justice agencies. Peacemaking criminology draws attention to many issues, among them (1) the perpetuation of violence through the continuation of social policies based on dominant forms of criminological theory; (2) the role of education in peacemaking; (3) "commonsense theories of crime"; (4) crime control as human rights enforcement; and (5) conflict resolution within community settings.[66]

Commonsense theories of crime are derived from everyday experience and beliefs and are characteristic of the person-in-the-street. Unfortunately, say peacemaking criminologists, fanciful commonsense theories all too often provide the basis for criminological investigations, which in turn offer support for the naive theories themselves. One commonsense theory criticized by peacemaking criminologists is the "black-male-as-savage theory,"[67] which holds that African-American men are far more crime

**Peacemaking criminology**
a perspective that holds that crime-control agencies and the citizens they serve should work together to alleviate social problems and human suffering and thus reduce crime.

A homeless man in the inner city. Peacemaking criminology holds that the alleviation of social problems and the reduction of human suffering will lead to a truly just world, and thus reduce crime. What do you think? *Susan Tannenbaum/Impact Visuals Photo & Graphics, Inc.*

prone than their Caucasian counterparts. Such a perspective, frequently given added credence by official interpretations of criminal-incidence data, only increases the crime-control problem by further distancing African-Americans from government-sponsored crime-control policies. A genuine concern for the problems facing all citizens, say peacemaking criminologists, would more effectively serve the ends of crime control.

Richard Quinney and John Wildeman well summarize the underpinnings of peacemaking criminology with these words: "(1) thought of the Western rational mode is conditional, limiting knowledge primarily to what is already known; (2) each life is a spiritual journey into the unknown and the unknowable, beyond the ego-centered self; (3) human existence is characterized by suffering; crime is suffering; and the sources of suffering are within each of us; (4) through love and compassion, beyond the ego-centered self, we can end suffering and live in peace, personally and collectively; (5) crime can be ended only with the ending of suffering, only when there is peace and social justice; and (6) understanding, service, justice—all these—flow naturally from love and compassion, from mindful attention to the reality of all that is, here and now. A criminology of peacemaking—a nonviolent criminology of compassion and service—seeks to end suffering and thereby eliminate crime."[68]

Elsewhere Quinney writes: "A society of meanness, competition, greed, and injustice is created by minds that are greedy, selfish, fearful, hateful, and crave power over others. Suffering on the social level can be ended only with the ending of suffering on the personal level. Wisdom brings the awareness that divisions between people and groups are not between the bad and the good or between the criminal and the non-criminal. Wisdom teaches interbeing. We must become one with all who suffer from lives of crime and from the sources that produce crime. Public policy must then flow from this wisdom."[69]

Other recent contributors to the peacemaking movement include Bo Lozoff, Michael Braswell, and Clemmons Bartollas. In *Inner Corrections*,[70] Lozoff and Braswell claim that "[w]e are fully aware by now that the criminal justice system in this country is founded on violence. It is a system which assumes that violence can be overcome by violence, evil by evil. Criminal justice at home and warfare abroad are of the same principle of violence. This principle sadly dominates much of our criminology." *Inner Corrections,* which is primarily a compilation of previous works on compassion and prison experience, provides meditative techniques and prayers for those seeking to become more compassionate and includes a number of letters from convicts who demonstrate the book's philosophy.

In another recent work entitled "Correctional Treatment, Peacemaking, and the New Age Movement,"[71] Bartollas and Braswell apply New Age principles to correctional treatment. "Most offenders suffered abusive and deprived childhoods," they write. "Treatment that focuses on the inner child and such qualities as forgiveness and self-esteem could benefit offenders. Some New Age teachings tempered by the ancient spiritual traditions may offer offenders the hope they can create a future that brings greater fulfillment than their past. This changed future may include growing out of the fear of victimization, becoming more positive and open to possibilities, viewing one's self with more confidence and humility, understanding the futility of violence, and attaining emotional and financial sufficiency."[72] Many of these notions form the foundation of the restorative justice model. This model is discussed further in Chapter 12.

In a fundamental sense, peacemaking criminologists exhort their colleagues to transcend personal dichotomies to end the political and ideological divisiveness that separates people. They ask, "If we ourselves cannot know peace … how will our acts disarm hatred and violence?"[73] Lozoff and Braswell express the same sentiments this way: "Human transformation takes place as we change our social, economic and political structure. And the message is clear: without peace within us and in our actions, there can be no peace in our results. Peace is the way."[74]

## Critique of Peacemaking Criminology

Peacemaking criminology has been criticized as being naive and utopian, as well as for failing to recognize the realities of crime control and law enforcement. Many victims, for example, do not expect to gain much during the victimization process from attempting to make peace with their victimizers (although such strategies do occasionally work). Such criticisms, however, may be improperly directed at a level of analysis that peacemaking criminologists have not assumed. In other words, peacemaking criminology, while it involves work with individual offenders, envisions positive change on the societal and institutional level and does not suggest to victims that they attempt to effect personal changes in offenders.

# Left-Realist Criminology

Left-realist criminology, another recent addition to the criminological landscape, is a natural outgrowth of practical concerns with street crime, the fear of crime, and everyday victimization. **Realist criminology** insists on a pragmatic assessment of crime and its associated problems in everyday terms—that is, terms understandable to those people most often affected by crime: victims and their families, offenders, and criminal justice personnel. The test insisted upon by realist criminology is not whether a particular perspective on crime control or an explanation of crime causation complies with rigorous academic criteria, but whether the perspective speaks meaningfully to those faced with crime on a daily basis. As one contemporary source states, "for realists crime is no less harmful to its victims because of its socially constructed origins."[75]

Realist criminology is generally considered synonomous with **left realism**. Left realism, also called radical realism or critical realism, builds on many of the concepts inherent in radical and Marxist criminology, while simultaneously claiming greater relevancy than either of its two parent perspectives. Left realism also tends to distance itself from some of the more visionary claims of early radical and Marxist theory. Daniel J. Curran and Claire M. Renzetti portray left realism as a natural consequence of increasingly conservative attitudes toward crime and criminals in both Europe and North America. "Though not successful in converting many radicals to the right," they write, "this new conservatism did lead a number of radical criminologists to temper their views a bit and to take what some might call a less romanticized look at street crime."[76]

Some authors credit **Walter DeKeseredy**[77] with popularizing left-realist notions in North America, and **Jock Young**[78] is identified as a major source of left-realist writings in England. Prior to the writings of DeKeseredy and Young, radical criminology, with

**Realist criminology** an emerging perspective that insists on a pragmatic assessment of crime and its associated problems.

**Left-realism** a branch of radical criminology that holds that crime is a "real" social problem experienced by the lower classes.

its emphasis upon the crime-inducing consequences of existing power structures, tended to portray the ruling class as the "real criminals" and saw street criminals as social rebels who were acting out of felt deprivation. In contrast, DeKeseredy and Young were successful in refocusing leftist theories onto the serious consequences of street crime and upon the crimes of the lower classes. Left-realists argue that victims of crime are often the poor and disenfranchised who fall prey to criminals with similar backgrounds. They do not see the criminal justice system and its agents as pawns of the powerful but rather as institutions that could offer useful services if modifications were made to reduce their use of force and increase their sensitivity toward the public.

A central tenet of left realism is the claim that radical ideas must be translated into realistic social policies if contemporary criminology is to have any practical relevance. In a recent review of left-realism in Australia and England, concrete suggestions with respect to community policing models, for example, are indicative of the direction left-realists are headed. Instead of seeing the police as oppressors working on behalf of the state, left-realists recommend that police work with, and answer to, the communities being policed.[79] The major goal of left realism is, therefore, to achieve "a fair and orderly society" through a practical emphasis on social justice.[80] In general, left-realists are concerned with the reality of crime and the damage it does to the most vulnerable segments of the population.

### Critique of Left-Realist Criminology

Left-realist criminology has been convincingly criticized for representing more of an ideological emphasis than a theory. As Don C. Gibbons explains, "Left realism can best be described as a general perspective centered on injunctions to 'take crime seriously' and to 'take crime control seriously' rather than as a well-developed criminological perspective."[81] Realist criminologists appear to build upon preexisting theoretical frameworks, but rarely offer new propositions or hypotheses that are testable. They do, however, frequently suggest crime-control approaches which are in keeping with the needs of the victimized; policies promulgated by left realists understandably include an emphasis on community policing, neighbourhood justice centres, and dispute resolution mechanisms. Beirne and Messerschmidt summarize the situation this way: "What left realists have essentially accomplished is an attempt to theorize about conventional crime realistically while simultaneously developing a 'radical law and order' program for curbing such behavior."[82]

# Policy Implications

Some contemporary writers on radical criminology tell us that "Marxist criminology was once dismissed as a utopian perspective with no relevant policy implication except revolution. At best, revolution was considered an impractical approach to the problems at hand. Recently, however, many radicals have attempted to address the issues of what can be done under our current system."[83]

Most radical-critical criminologists of the current genre recognize that a sudden and total reversal of existing political arrangements within North America is highly unlikely. They have begun to focus, instead, on promoting a gradual transition to socialism and to socialized forms of government activity. These middle-range policy alternatives include "equal justice in the bail system, the abolition of mandatory sentences, prosecution of corporate crimes, increased employment opportunities, and promoting community alternatives to imprisonment."[84] Likewise, programs to reduce prison overcrowding, efforts to highlight injustices within the current system, the elimination of racism and other forms of inequality in the handling of both victims and offenders, growing equality in criminal justice system employment, and the like are all frequently mentioned as midrange strategies for bringing about a justice system that is more fair and closer to the radical ideal.

**Raymond Michalowski** well summarizes the policy directions envisioned by today's radical-critical criminologists when he says, "[w]e cannot be free from the crimes of the poor until there are no more poor; we cannot be free from domination of the powerful until we reduce the inequalities that make domination possible; and we cannot live in harmony with others until we begin to limit the competition for material advantage over others that alienates us from one another."[85]

Even so, few radical-critical criminologists seem to expect to see dramatic changes in the near future. As Michael J. Lynch and W. Byron Groves explain, "[i]n the end, the criminal justice system has failed as an agent of social change because its efforts are directed at an individual as opposed to social remedies. ... For these reasons, radicals suggest that we put our efforts into the creation of economic equality or employment opportunities to combat crime."[86]

## Summary

Politics and crime are inextricably intertwined. Sometimes the actions undertaken by government officials are themselves criminal, while on other occasions governments may act to shield law violators or even assist citizens in the violation of official dictums. More significantly, however, the very action of legislative bodies in defining crime through the making of statutory law reveals the crucial nexus between social organization and the use of law as a tool of the powerful. The form of social organization endemic to a society produces a set of intergroup relationships that ultimately define which individuals and which groups are empowered to make law. Those who find themselves excluded from such important decision-making processes will either find alternative paths to success or turn to other means to empower themselves.

## Discussion Questions

1. This book emphasizes a social problems versus social responsibility theme. Which of the theoretical perspectives discussed in this chapter (if any) best support the social problems approach? Which (if any) support the social responsibility approach? Why?

2. What is Marxist criminology? How, if at all, does it differ from radical criminology? From critical criminology?

3. Does the Marxist perspective hold any significance for contemporary Canadian society? Why or why not?

4. What have been the major contributions of feminist thinking to the field of criminology? Do you believe a feminist criminology is possible? Why or why not?

5. Describe peacemaking criminology. What are its central tenets? Do you believe that peacemaking criminology is realistic? Why or why not?

# Weblinks

**www.crimetheory.com/**
Teaching resource offered through the University of Washington. Follow the links to a good, albeit condensed look at radical criminology.

**www.inac.gc.ca/pr/pub/fnc/prg_e.html**
Indian and Northern Affairs Canada. Links to analysis of the Oka Crisis from the perspective of the federal government.

**www.canadianaboriginal.com/archives/**
Canadian Aboriginal News. Search the archives of the Canadian Aboriginal News for analysis of the Oka Crisis from a First Nations perspective.

**www.rcmp-grc.gc.ca/frames/rcmp-grc1.htm**
The community policing branch of the RCMP. Provides an overview of the principles of community policing as well as several RCMP initiatives.

**www.ledevoir.com/le_devoir/historique/90ans_qnau.html**
*Le Devoir* newspaper. Provides a good, historical French language overview of the FLQ crisis.

**www.amnesty.org**
Amnesty International. Amnesty International is a worldwide movement that campaigns to promote human rights.

CHAPTER 10

# Patterns of Crime

Crime has a thousand roots ... but a single outcome. It stems from fear and hatred, greed and corruption, deprivation and suffering. But it always ends with one thing: victims.

—PETER KENT, JOURNALIST[1]

There may be lies, damned lies, and statistics, but study after study tells the same, consistent story. Crime is down ... across Canada.

—MICHELE MANDEL[1]

## LEARNING OUTCOMES

After reading this chapter, you should be able to:

- Analyze the amounts and types of crime in Canada

- Distinguish between the myths and the reality of patterns of Canadian crime

- Recognize the usefulness of criminological theory in explaining crime

- Apply various theories to different classifications of crime

# Introduction

It was a crime spree that was as cunning as it was insidious. After 6 years and ill-gotten gains of over $1 million in stolen money and property, Ken Crawford was eventually apprehended in April 1998 by police in Ottawa, Ontario. Known as the "Locker Room Bandit," Crawford, 57, has the look of a respectable, middle-aged businessman. Since 1992, however, his "business" involved the theft of wallets, jewellery, and other personal possessions from health-club locker rooms across the country.

His crime spree began when Crawford, an out-of-work tool and die maker, tried to go back to school for retraining but was denied a student loan and was unable to get a part-time job to help pay for his tuition. Instead, he devised a plan that would get him the money he needed.

His scheme was simple and it worked hundreds of times over the 6 years that he was actively involved in crime. He would approach a health club and ask to try out the facilities, saying that he was interested in a membership. Once inside the locker room, he would select a wealthy-looking patron and wait until he went to work out. Out of his gym bag Crawford would produce a set of bolt cutters and a combination lock. After snapping the lock off the victim's locker and emptying it of the wallet and other valuable personal items, Crawford would re-lock the locker using the combination lock he had brought. When the unsuspecting victim returned, Crawford was long gone, buying himself valuable time as the victim struggled with his lock in vain. Using the personal identification in the wallet, Crawford emptied the victims' bank accounts and took cash advances using the credit cards. Police estimated he averaged about $5 000 cash for each job. When Crawford was apprehended, police found bolt cutters, 103 wallets, watches, jewellery, and thousands of dollars in cash in his home.

In return for pleading guilty to defrauding the public, possession of property obtained by crime, and possession of stolen credit cards, Crawford received a three and one-half year sentence. As he handed down his sentence, Judge Paul Bélanger told Crawford, "If you have talent, it is as a talented crook. But not that talented bearing in mind where you currently sit."[2]

# Classifications of Crime

A significant portion of this book has been devoted to examining a variety of explanations for why people commit crime. Chapter 2 provides an overview of the ways in which crime statistics are collected so that a picture of the incidence of crime and the number and types of criminals in a given period will emerge.

But what *types* of crime are committed in Canada? How many of each type occur annually? Typically, crimes are organized into categories, or **typologies of crime**. The Uniform Crime Reporting system (UCR) classifies crimes into the following categories: violent crime, property crime, other crime, traffic offences (as defined in the Criminal Code of Canada [CCC]), federal drug legislation offences, and other federal statutes violations. Categorization helps to identify patterns that may exist within these groupings and to focus discussion concerning motivation of the offender. For example, does the person who commits murder do it for reasons distinct from those of the person who breaks into someone's home and robs it?

This chapter examines three categories of crime: violent crime, property crime, and crimes against the public order such as prostitution and drug abuse. In addition to providing a snapshot of the incidence of crime committed in Canada for each of these categories, this chapter makes the link to theoretical explanations discussed in earlier chapters that might explain why these crimes are committed. Unless otherwise noted, all the 1998 statistics cited in this chapter are taken from 1998 UCR crime statistics.[3] Tables 10.1, 10.2, and 10.3 provide a statistical snapshot of the crime picture in Canada in 1998.

**Typologies of crime** classifications of crime useful in identifying patterns of criminal activity and motivations for criminal behaviour.

## Violent Crime

Violent crime incidents include homicide, attempted murder, sexual assault, other sexual offences such as incest, robbery, assault and abduction. The 1998 UCR reports that violent crime in Canada continues to decline. Compared to 1994, when the violent crime rate was 1 046 per 100 000 population, the rate of violent crime in 1998 was 975 per 100 000, showing a decline of 9 percent. Interestingly, within the categories of offences classified as violent crime, common assault account for 62 percent of the total number. Despite an overall lower rate of violent crime, anomalies exist within various regions of the country. For example, as Table 10.2 indicates, Saskatchewan and Quebec reported 3 percent increases in the violent crime rate in 1998, while Nova Scotia (–11%) and Newfoundland (–8%) showed the most significant decreases. New Brunswick, Alberta, Prince Edward Island, and Ontario remained stable. Overall, the western provinces recorded higher violent crime rates than did the eastern provinces, a pattern consistent with previous years.

### Homicide

In January 1998, James Blum pled guilty to second-degree murder in the death of his grandmother, Emma Blum. Blum, who was unemployed at the time and $715 behind in the rent for the Kitchener, Ontario apartment he shared with his common-law wife and their young son, claimed that he killed his grandmother as an act of mercy. He said he hit the 90-year-old woman two or three times on the temple with a magazine rack in the hope that this would be painless. Blum, who weighs 240 pounds, then stomped on her back, strangled her, and stabbed her in the neck to make sure she was dead. Marks on Emma Blum's hands, shoulders, and forearms indicated that she tried to fend off her grandson. James Blum claimed that, even though he deposited $228 taken from his grandmother just hours after the murder, he did not go to his grandmother's home to kill and rob her. Blum received a life sentence with eligibility for parole in 10 years.[4]

*continued on p. 300*

## Table 10.1

*Federal Statute Incidents Reported to Police, by Most Serious Offence, Canada, 1994–1998[a]*

| | 1994 | | 1995 | | 1996 | | 1997[b] | | 1998 | | Percentage Change (rate) 1997–1998[c] |
|---|---|---|---|---|---|---|---|---|---|---|---|
| | Number | Rate | Number | Rate | Number | Rate | Number | Rate | Number | Rate | |
| **Population** | 29 035 981 | | 29 353 854 | | 29 671 892 | | 30 003 955 | | 30 300 422 | | |
| Homicide | 596 | 2.1 | 588 | 2.0 | 635 | 2.1 | 586 | 2.0 | 555 | 1.8 | -6.2 |
| Attempted murder | 922 | 3.2 | 939 | 3.2 | 878 | 3.0 | 865 | 2.9 | 738 | 2.4 | -15.5 |
| **Assaults - Total (levels 1, 2, 3)** | **222 300** | **766** | **217 618** | **741** | **219 919** | **741** | **222 397** | **741** | **223 260** | **737** | **-0.6** |
| Level 1 | 181 577 | 625 | 178 934 | 610 | 181 545 | 612 | 183 087 | 610 | 183 440 | 605 | -0.8 |
| Level 2-Weapon | 37 725 | 130 | 35 921 | 122 | 35 626 | 120 | 36 665 | 122 | 37 209 | 123 | 0.5 |
| Level 3-Aggravated | 2 998 | 10.3 | 2 763 | 9.4 | 2 748 | 9.3 | 2 645 | 8.8 | 2 611 | 8.6 | -2.3 |
| Other assaults | 14 264 | 49 | 13 462 | 46 | 12 171 | 41 | 11 807 | 39 | 12 090 | 40 | 1.4 |
| **Sexual assaults - Total (levels 1, 2, 3)** | **31 706** | **109** | **28 234** | **96** | **27 026** | **91** | **27 013** | **90** | **25 493** | **84** | **-6.6** |
| Level 1 | 30 572 | 105 | 27 278 | 93 | 26 076 | 88 | 26 142 | 87 | 24 745 | 82 | -6.3 |
| Level 2-Weapon | 769 | 2.6 | 659 | 2.2 | 653 | 2.2 | 602 | 2.0 | 529 | 1.7 | -13.0 |
| Level 3-Aggravated | 365 | 1.3 | 297 | 1.0 | 297 | 1.0 | 269 | 0.9 | 219 | 0.7 | -19.4 |
| Other sexual offences | 3 818 | 13 | 3 494 | 12 | 3 343 | 11 | 3 650 | 12 | 3 459 | 11 | -6.2 |
| Abduction | 1 129 | 3.9 | 1 035 | 3.5 | 977 | 3.3 | 985 | 3.3 | 822 | 2.7 | -17.4 |
| **Robbery - Total** | **29 010** | **100** | **30 332** | **103** | **31 797** | **107** | **29 587** | **99** | **28 952** | **96** | **-3.1** |
| Firearms | 7 361 | 25 | 6 692 | 23 | 6 737 | 23 | 5 486 | 18 | 5 348 | 18 | -3.5 |
| Other weapons | 9 386 | 32 | 10 127 | 34 | 10 543 | 36 | 9 945 | 33 | 10 318 | 34 | 2.7 |
| No weapons | 12 263 | 42 | 13 513 | 46 | 14 517 | 49 | 14 156 | 47 | 13 286 | 44 | -7.1 |
| *Violent crime - Total* | *303 745* | *1 046* | *295 702* | *1 007* | *296 746* | *1 000* | *296 890* | *990* | *295 369* | *975* | *-1.5* |
| **Break & enter - Total** | **387 867** | **1 336** | **390 784** | **1 331** | **397 057** | **1 338** | **373 316** | **1 244** | **350 176** | **1 156** | **-7.1** |
| Business | 110 480 | 380 | 108 749 | 370 | 110 196 | 371 | 100 696 | 336 | 92 368 | 305 | -9.2 |
| Residential | 227 199 | 782 | 235 129 | 801 | 242 639 | 818 | 233 724 | 779 | 220 889 | 729 | -6.4 |
| Other | 50 188 | 173 | 46 906 | 160 | 44 222 | 149 | 38 896 | 130 | 36 919 | 122 | -6.0 |
| Motor vehicle theft | 159 469 | 549 | 161 696 | 551 | 180 123 | 607 | 177 130 | 590 | 165 799 | 547 | -7.3 |
| Theft over $5 000 ($1 000 prior to 1995) | 116 396 | 401 | 42 080 | 143 | 27 075 | 91 | 24 035 | 80 | 23 834 | 79 | -1.8 |
| Theft $5 000 and under ($1 000 prior to 1995) | 727 414 | 2 505 | 820 908 | 2 797 | 823 732 | 2 776 | 758 292 | 2 527 | 712 764 | 2 352 | -6.9 |
| Possession of stolen goods | 30 130 | 104 | 31 293 | 107 | 31 772 | 107 | 29 799 | 99 | 28 733 | 95 | -4.5 |
| Fraud | 103 243 | 356 | 103 964 | 354 | 102 052 | 344 | 96 964 | 323 | 94 575 | 312 | -3.4 |
| *Property crime - Total* | *1 524 519* | *5 250* | *1 550 725* | *5 283* | *1 561 811* | *5 264* | *1 459 536* | *4 864* | *1 375 881* | *4 541* | *-6.7* |
| Mischief | 396 904 | 1 367 | 380 041 | 1 295 | 365 830 | 1 233 | 341 854 | 1 139 | 325 884 | 1 076 | -5.6 |

*continued*

| | 1994 | | 1995 | | 1996 | | 1997[b] | | 1998 | | Percentage Change (rate) 1997–1998[c] |
|---|---|---|---|---|---|---|---|---|---|---|---|
| | Number | Rate | Number | Rate | Number | Rate | Number | Rate | Number | Rate | |
| Gaming and betting | 421 | 1.4 | 568 | 1.9 | 766 | 2.6 | 423 | 1.4 | 443 | 1.5 | 3.7 |
| Bail violation | 65 952 | 227 | 66 939 | 228 | 68 949 | 232 | 70 367 | 235 | 72 451 | 239 | 2.0 |
| Disturbing the peace | 51 213 | 176 | 51 401 | 175 | 54 563 | 184 | 57 704 | 192 | 64 995 | 215 | 11.5 |
| Offensive weapons | 18 898 | 65 | 17 571 | 60 | 16 400 | 55 | 16 103 | 54 | 16 735 | 55 | 2.9 |
| Prostitution | 5 575 | 19 | 7 170 | 24 | 6 397 | 22 | 5 828 | 19 | 5 985 | 20 | 1.7 |
| Arson | 13 509 | 47 | 13 156 | 45 | 12 830 | 43 | 12 693 | 42 | 12 952 | 43 | 1.0 |
| Other | 265 473 | 914 | 256 381 | 873 | 260 601 | 878 | 273 368 | 911 | 284 186 | 938 | 2.9 |
| *Other Criminal Code - Total* | *817 945* | *2 817* | *793 227* | *2 702* | *786 336* | *2 650* | *778 340* | *2 594* | *783 631* | *2 586* | *-0.3* |
| **CRIMINAL CODE WITHOUT TRAFFIC - TOTAL** | **2 646 209** | **9 114** | **2 639 654** | **8 993** | **2 644 893** | **8 914** | **2 534 766** | **8 448** | **2 454 881** | **8 102** | **-4.1** |
| Impaired driving[d] | 107 768 | 371 | 102 285 | 348 | 96 280 | 324 | 90 145 | 300 | 87 385 | 288 | -4.0 |
| Fail to stop/remain | 60 138 | 207 | 54 180 | 185 | 49 896 | 168 | 49 781 | 166 | 39 085 | 129 | -22.3 |
| Other C.C. traffic | 18 529 | 65 | 17 419 | 59 | 16 286 | 55 | 15 302 | 51 | 14 066 | 46 | -9.0 |
| *Criminal Code Traffic - Total* | *186 435* | *642* | *173 884* | *592* | *162 462* | *548* | *155 228* | *517* | *140 536* | *464* | *-10.4* |
| **CRIMINAL CODE - TOTAL** | **2 832 644** | **9 756** | **2 813 538** | **9 585** | **2 807 355** | **9 461** | **2 689 994** | **8 965** | **2 595 417** | **8 566** | **-4.5** |
| **DRUGS** | **60 153** | **207** | **61 613** | **210** | **65 729** | **222** | **66 593** | **222** | **71 293** | **235** | **6.0** |
| **OTHER FEDERAL STATUTES** | **40 525** | **140** | **36 121** | **123** | **34 274** | **116** | **35 204** | **117** | **34 981** | **115** | **-1.6** |
| **TOTAL FEDERAL STATUTES** | **2 933 322** | **10 102** | **2 911 272** | **9 918** | **2 907 358** | **9 798** | **2 791 791** | **9 305** | **2 701 691** | **8 916** | **-4.2** |

[a] Rates are calculated based on 100 000 population. The population estimates come from the Annual Demographic Statistics, 1998 report, produced by Statistics Canada, Demography Division. Populations as of July 1st: final intercensal estimates for 1994 and 1995, final postcensal estimates for 1996, updated postcensal estimates for 1997 and 1998.
[b] Revised figures.
[c] Percentage change based on unrounded rates.
[d] Includes impaired operation of a vehicle causing death, causing bodily harm, alcohol rate over 80 mg, failure/refusal to provide a breath/blood sample.

SOURCE: Sylvain Tremblay, "Crime Statistics in Canada, 1998" Statistics Canada, *Juristat*, Catalogue No. 85-002, vol. 19, no. 9 (1999), p. 16.

PART 3
298
**Crime in the Modern
World and the
Response to It**

## Table 10.2

### Selected Criminal Code Incidents, Canada and the Provinces/Territories, 1998[a]

| | Nfld. | P.E.I. | N.S. | N.B. | Qc | Ont. | Man. | Sask. | Alta. | B.C. | Yukon | N.W.T. | Canada |
|---|---|---|---|---|---|---|---|---|---|---|---|---|---|
| **Population** | 554 400 | 136 388 | 934 587 | 752 999 | 7 333 283 | 11 411 547 | 1 138 872 | 1 024 387 | 2 914 918 | 4 009 922 | 31 651 | 67 468 | 30 300 422 |
| **Homicide** | | | | | | | | | | | | | |
| number | 7 | —c | 24 | 5 | 137 | 155 | 33 | 32 | 64 | 90 | 3 | 5 | 555 |
| rate | 1.3 | —c | 2.6 | 0.7 | 1.9 | 1.4 | 2.9 | 3.1 | 2.2 | 2.2 | 9.5 | 7.4 | 1.8 |
| % change in rate[b] | 1.8 | —c | 0.0 | -37.4 | 3.4 | -14.1 | 6.3 | 27.7 | 2.1 | -23.4 | —d | —d | -6.2 |
| **Sexual assault (1,2,3)** | | | | | | | | | | | | | |
| number | 610 | 156 | 951 | 866 | 3 236 | 9 012 | 1 287 | 1 505 | 2 911 | 4 391 | 107 | 461 | 25 493 |
| rate | 112 | 114 | 102 | 115 | 44 | 79 | 113 | 147 | 100 | 110 | 338 | 683 | 84 |
| % change in rate[b] | -28.0 | 10.2 | -20.1 | -6.9 | 0.1 | -1.4 | -16.2 | -11.7 | -8.0 | -6.4 | -3.6 | -20.5 | -6.6 |
| **Assault (1,2,3)** | | | | | | | | | | | | | |
| number | 3 934 | 755 | 7 269 | 5 161 | 31 706 | 78 021 | 14 084 | 12 499 | 24 214 | 42 013 | 787 | 2 867 | 223 260 |
| rate | 723 | 554 | 778 | 685 | 432 | 684 | 1 237 | 1 220 | 831 | 1 048 | 2 329 | 4 279 | 737 |
| % change in rate[b] | -2.9 | -2.8 | -11.2 | 2.5 | 4.3 | -0.9 | -5.5 | 5.6 | 2.0 | -3.1 | -9.9 | 4.0 | -0.6 |
| **Robbery** | | | | | | | | | | | | | |
| number | 74 | 24 | 458 | 145 | 8 010 | 9 152 | 1 821 | 990 | 2 560 | 5 669 | 12 | 37 | 28 952 |
| rate | 14 | 18 | 49 | 19 | 109 | 80 | 160 | 97 | 88 | 141 | 38 | 55 | 96 |
| % change in rate[b] | 10.8 | 41.6 | 7.0 | 0.1 | -2.7 | -2.7 | -14.9 | 1.4 | 6.8 | -5.6 | -54.7 | -9.3 | -3.1 |
| **Violent crime - Total** | | | | | | | | | | | | | |
| number | 4 864 | 994 | 9 155 | 6 632 | 47 146 | 101 959 | 18 295 | 16 265 | 31 605 | 53 901 | 919 | 3 634 | 295 369 |
| rate | 893 | 729 | 980 | 881 | 643 | 893 | 1 606 | 1 588 | 1 084 | 1 344 | 2 904 | 5 386 | 975 |
| **% change in rate[b]** | -7.8 | 0.1 | -11.0 | 1.8 | 2.6 | -1.4 | -6.7 | 2.9 | 1.0 | -3.8 | -11.1 | -1.6 | -1.5 |
| **Breaking & entering** | | | | | | | | | | | | | |
| number | 4 479 | 700 | 9 118 | 5 574 | 97 774 | 101 126 | 16 023 | 17 813 | 29 861 | 65 457 | 608 | 1 643 | 350 176 |
| rate | 823 | 513 | 976 | 740 | 1 333 | 886 | 1 407 | 1 739 | 1 024 | 1 632 | 1 921 | 2 435 | 1 156 |
| % change in rate[b] | 17.9 | -21.6 | -1.9 | -8.7 | -6.2 | -7.7 | -5.0 | -5.6 | -6.7 | -10.2 | -19.9 | 0.2 | -7.1 |
| **Motor vehicle theft** | | | | | | | | | | | | | |
| number | 644 | 181 | 2 816 | 1 299 | 47 244 | 50 372 | 10 539 | 7 263 | 15 519 | 29 318 | 213 | 391 | 165 799 |
| rate | 118 | 133 | 301 | 173 | 644 | 441 | 925 | 709 | 532 | 731 | 673 | 580 | 547 |
| % change in rate[b] | 29.6 | -31.5 | 8.6 | -14.8 | -4.5 | -11.1 | -6.9 | 3.5 | -2.0 | -11.4 | 1.4 | 0.5 | -7.3 |
| **Other theft** | | | | | | | | | | | | | |
| number | 7 563 | 2 322 | 22 221 | 11 185 | 133 909 | 244 920 | 27 616 | 30 090 | 80 124 | 173 499 | 1 224 | 1 925 | 736 598 |
| rate | 1 389 | 1 702 | 2 378 | 1 485 | 1 826 | 2 146 | 2 425 | 2 937 | 2 749 | 4 327 | 3 867 | 2 853 | 2 431 |
| % change in rate[b] | -6.1 | -12.8 | 1.6 | -7.6 | -7.0 | -10.0 | -5.2 | -1.1 | -3.1 | -6.0 | -11.4 | 3.2 | -6.8 |
| **Property crime - Total** | | | | | | | | | | | | | |
| number | 14 512 | 3 747 | 37 964 | 21 181 | 298 821 | 440 912 | 58 762 | 62 287 | 143 471 | 287 816 | 2 210 | 4 198 | 1 375 881 |
| rate | 2 666 | 2 747 | 4 062 | 2 813 | 4 075 | 3 864 | 5 160 | 6 080 | 4 922 | 7 178 | 6 982 | 6 222 | 4 541 |
| **% change in rate[b]** | 2.8 | -13.7 | -0.2 | -8.0 | -6.1 | -9.2 | -5.6 | -2.3 | -2.4 | -7.6 | -14.2 | -1.2 | -6.7 |

continued

| | Nfld. | P.E.I. | N.S. | N.B. | Qc | Ont. | Man. | Sask. | Alta. | B.C. | Yukon | N.W.T. | Canada |
|---|---|---|---|---|---|---|---|---|---|---|---|---|---|
| **Population** | 554 400 | 136 388 | 934 587 | 752 999 | 7 333 283 | 11 411 547 | 1 138 872 | 1 024 387 | 2 914 918 | 4 009 922 | 31 651 | 67 468 | 30 300 422 |
| **Offensive weapons** | | | | | | | | | | | | | |
| number | 126 | 37 | 489 | 221 | 997 | 7 112 | 1 070 | 860 | 1 945 | 3 697 | 41 | 140 | 16 735 |
| rate | 23 | 27 | 52 | 29 | 14 | 62 | 94 | 84 | 67 | 92 | 130 | 208 | 55 |
| % change in rate[b] | -5.0 | -42.9 | 2.1 | -36.4 | -3.8 | 9.1 | -11.1 | 3.8 | -6.8 | 9.9 | -25.4 | -19.6 | 2.9 |
| **Mischief** | | | | | | | | | | | | | |
| number | 4 723 | 1 414 | 11 942 | 6 561 | 54 649 | 106 538 | 21 339 | 17 255 | 38 601 | 58 378 | 785 | 3 699 | 325 884 |
| rate | 868 | 1 037 | 1 278 | 871 | 745 | 934 | 1 874 | 1 684 | 1 324 | 1 456 | 2 480 | 5 483 | 1 076 |
| % change in rate[b] | 1.8 | -13.4 | -8.2 | 3.3 | -7.1 | -6.2 | -2.6 | 1.3 | -3.4 | -8.9 | -20.4 | 9.6 | -5.6 |
| **Other Criminal Code - Total** | | | | | | | | | | | | | |
| number | 12 218 | 3 820 | 28 956 | 18 845 | 125 095 | 258 252 | 43 828 | 48 504 | 88 528 | 145 144 | 2 576 | 7 865 | 783 631 |
| rate | 2 244 | 2 801 | 3 098 | 2 503 | 1 706 | 2 263 | 3 848 | 4 735 | 3 037 | 3 620 | 8 139 | 11 657 | 2 586 |
| % change in rate[b] | 7.5 | -3.4 | -5.2 | 6.4 | -4.1 | -1.0 | 1.0 | 8.5 | -1.2 | 1.0 | -13.4 | 11.9 | -0.3 |
| **CRIMINAL CODE - TOTAL without traffic offences** | | | | | | | | | | | | | |
| number | 31 594 | 8 561 | 76 075 | 46 658 | 471 062 | 801 123 | 120 885 | 127 056 | 263 604 | 486 861 | 5 705 | 15 697 | 2 454 881 |
| rate | 5 803 | 6 277 | 8 140 | 6 196 | 6 424 | 7 020 | 10 614 | 12 403 | 9 043 | 12 141 | 18 025 | 23 266 | 8 102 |
| % change in rate[b] | 2.7 | -7.9 | -3.6 | -1.3 | -4.8 | -5.8 | -3.5 | 2.2 | -1.6 | -4.8 | -13.3 | 4.9 | -4.1 |

[a] Rates are calculated on the basis of 100 000 population. The population estimates come from the *Annual Demographic Statistics, 1998* report, produced by Statistics Canada, Demography Division. Populations as of July 1st: updated postcensal estimates for 1997 and 1998.
[b] Percent change based on unrounded rates.
[c] Nil or zero.
[d] Figures not appropriate or applicable.
SOURCE: Sylvain Tremblay, "Crime Statistics in Canada, 1998," Statistics Canada, *Juristat*, Catalogue No. 85-002, vol. 19, no. 9 (1999), p. 17.

PART 3

300

Crime in the Modern
World and the
Response to It

## Table 10.3

### Persons Charged by Age Group and Gender, Selected Incidents, 1998

| | Age Group by Gender | | | | Total by Age Group | |
| | Adults | | Youth | | Adults | Youth |
| | Male | Female | Male | Female | | |
| | % | | % | | % | |
|---|---|---|---|---|---|---|
| Homicides[a] | 87 | 13 | 96 | 4 | 88 | 12 |
| Attempted murder | 88 | 12 | 96 | 4 | 88 | 12 |
| Assaults | 85 | 15 | 70 | 30 | 85 | 15 |
| Sexual assaults | 98 | 2 | 97 | 3 | 85 | 15 |
| Other sexual offences | 97 | 3 | 97 | 3 | 86 | 14 |
| Adbuction | 55 | 45 | 100 | 0 | 96 | 4 |
| Robbery | 91 | 9 | 85 | 15 | 64 | 36 |
| **Violent crime - Total** | **86** | **14** | **74** | **26** | **84** | **16** |

[a] These data are based on the Homicide Survey, CCJS.

SOURCE: Sylvain Tremblay, "Crime Statistics in Canada, 1998," Statistics Canada, *Juristat*, Catalogue No. 85-002, vol. 19, no. 9 (1999), p. 21.

**Homicide** when a person, directly or indirectly, by any means, causes the death of a human being. Homicide can be culpable or nonculpable.

**Murder** when a person intentionally causes the death of another human being or intends to cause bodily harm likely to result in death.

**First-degree murder** culpable homicide that is planned and deliberate.

**Second-degree murder** all murder that is not first-degree murder.

**Manslaughter** all nonintentional homicide.

**Infanticide** when a female considered disturbed from the effects of giving birth causes the death of her newborn child (under age 1).

**Serial murder** culpable homicide that involves the killing of several victims in three or more separate events.

The terms "homicide" and "murder" are often used interchangeably, but they are not synonomous. **Homicide** occurs when a person, directly or indirectly, by any means, causes the death of a human being. Homicide, therefore, can be either culpable or nonculpable. *Culpable homicide* is considered an offence under the Criminal Code of Canada and includes murder, manslaughter, and infanticide. *Nonculpable homicide* consists of justifiable and/or excusable homicide. Justifiable homicide includes legally authorized acts such as a police officer killing someone in the course of duty, while excusable homicide includes acts of self-defence, defence of others, or defence of property.

**Murder** (section 229 CCC) occurs when a person intentionally causes the death of another human being or intends to cause bodily harm likely to result in death. Murder is further classified into first-degree murder and second-degree murder. **First-degree murder** (defined in s. 231) describes culpable homicide that is planned and deliberate; or involves the killing of a peace officer such as a police officer or correctional worker; or occurs during the commission of another serious offence such as sexual assault, kidnapping, or hijacking. **Second-degree murder** (defined in s. 231) includes all murder that is not first degree. In other words, it is intentional and unlawful but not planned. **Manslaughter** (s. 234) is considered to be a nonintentional homicide committed in response to sudden provocation, as a result of impaired judgment due to alcohol or drug consumption, or as a result of recklessness or carelessness. **Infanticide** (s. 233) occurs when a female causes the death of her newborn child (under age 1) if her mind is considered disturbed from the effects of giving birth.

Serial murder and mass murder are two varieties of what is usually termed first-degree murder. Although most murderers kill only once in their lives, serial and mass murderers kill more than one person. **Serial murder** has been defined as culpable homicide that "involves the killing of several victims in three or more separate events".[5] These separate events are sometimes spread out over years. The Canadian serial killer Clifford Olson, for example, killed at least 11 young people aged 9 to 18 over a

Convicted murderer Paul Bernardo enters court in Kingston under heavy security. Bernardo was appealing his convictions in the deaths of two Ontario teenagers. *The Canadian Press/The Whig-Standard/Ian MacAlpine.*

9-month period in 1980–1981 in British Columbia. Between 1987 and 1990, Paul Bernardo committed at least 18 violent sexual assaults in Toronto and later went on to abduct, sexually assault, and strangle two teenaged girls in 1991 and 1992 in St. Catharines, Ontario. He was assisted in these murders by his wife, Karla Homolka, who subsequently testified against her husband. Allan Legère killed a grocery store owner in 1987 and went on to kill four other people in Miramichi, New Brunswick, terrorizing the rural community between 1987 and 1989 and earning him the nickname "The Monster of Miramichi." Other notorious serial killers include Jeffrey Dahmer, who killed and dismembered 15 young men in the 1980s; David Berkowitz, better known as "Son of Sam," who killed young men and women in New York City; Charles Manson, who ordered his followers to kill seven people in California; Ted Bundy, who killed many college-aged women; and the female serial killer Aileen Carol Wuornos, who killed six men who had picked her up as she hitchhiked through Florida.[6] Internationally infamous killers include Dr. Harold Shipman of Britain, who was convicted of killing 15 female patients and suspected in the deaths of 23 more; and Javed Iqbal, convicted of sexually assaulting and killing 100 street children in Pakistan and sentenced to die in the same way his victims died—by strangulation.

Similar to the serial killer is the spree killer, who kills a number of victims over a relatively short period. Andrew Cunanan, who killed fashion designer Gianni Versace and others in 1997, is an example. Cunanan's killing spree lasted 3 months and claimed 5 victims.

**Mass murder** is different from serial murder in that it entails "the killing of four or more victims at one location, within one event."[7] In 1989, in what became known as the "Montreal Massacre," Marc Lepine shot and killed 14 female students at the University of Montreal. Other mass murderers in Canada include Victor Hoffman, who, at age 19, killed 9 members of a family as they slept in their Saskatchewan farmhouse

**Mass murder** the illegal killing of four or more victims at one location, within one event.

PART 3
302
**Crime in the Modern
World and the
Response to It**

in 1967. Mark Chahal, a Vancouver accountant who shot dead his ex-wife and eight other members of her family at a home in Vernon, British Columbia in 1996; and Kevin Vermette, who shot three young men at a deserted campground in Kitimat, British Columbia in 1997. Other infamous mass murders include the 31 people killed in 1991 when a man smashed his pickup truck through a cafeteria window in Texas and shot lunch-goers to death; 21 killed at a McDonald's restaurant in California in 1984 by an out-of-work security guard; 16 school-aged children and their teacher killed in Dunblane, Scotland in 1995; and, in 1999, 12 high-school students and a teacher killed by 2 fellow students who marched through the halls of Columbine High School in Colorado targeting specific individuals.

Geographically, homicide rates increase from east to west in Canada. The Yukon Territory (which includes Nunavut) showed a homicide rate of 9.5 per 100 000 population in 1998, while the Northwest Territories registered a rate of 1.8 (actual homicides for these two jurisdictions were three and five, respectively). In absolute numbers, Ontario and Quebec led the country in 1998, with 155 and 137 homicides, respectively, although these rates, at 1.4 and 1.9, are about the national average. The lowest rates were found in Prince Edward Island (0.0) and New Brunswick (0.76).

Most provinces reported a decrease or no change in the number of homicides in 1998, with the largest decreases reported by British Columbia and Ontario. Among the nine largest metropolitan areas in the country, Winnipeg reported the highest rate (2.6), followed by Edmonton (2.4), and Vancouver (2.3). Both Ottawa and Hamilton had their lowest rates since 1981 (0.5 and 0.9, respectively).

In the United States, statistics indicate that persons accused of homicide have become increasingly younger over the past 10 years. In Canada, statistics show a different picture. The median age of those accused of homicide has actually been increasing. From 1974 to 1986, the median age of the accused was 26 to 27 years of age, increasing to 27 to 29 years of age since 1986.

Statistics reveal additional information about murder in Canada. Of the homicides in 1998 where an accused was identified, 40 percent of victims were killed by a spouse or other family member, and 45 percent were killed by an acquaintance; only 15 percent of murders were committed by strangers. Spousal homicides (spouses being defined as persons in registered marriages, common-law relationships, and separated or divorced persons) continued to account for 16 percent of all solved homicides. In 1998, 70 persons were killed by a spouse, 56 of whom were women. Other family-related homicides in 1998 included: 51 victims killed by a parent (34 by a father/stepfather, 17 by a mother), 20 by one of the children in the family, 9 by a sibling, and 21 by another relative. Of the 54 children aged 12 and under killed by parents, the majority (61%) were male. The number of infants under 1 year killed in 1998 almost doubled from the 13 in 1997, to 23 in 1998. Eighteen of these children were killed by parents (11 by the father, 6 by the mother, 1 by both parents). In 1998, 57 youths between the ages of 12 and 17 were accused of homicide, accounting for 12 percent of all persons charged with homicide.

Since 1979, firearms have been used in about one-third of all homicides each year. In 1998, this proportion fell to 27 percent. Of the 151 in that year, 70 (46%) were committed with a handgun, 51 (34%) with a rifle/shotgun, 14 (9%) with a sawed-off rifle/shotgun, 12 (8%) with a fully automatic firearm, and 4 (35%) with other types of firearms. Relatively strict gun control laws in Canada compared with the United States may be partially responsible for the decline in the number of homicides using a firearm (see Chapter 11 for a detailed look at Canada's firearm legislation). By comparison, American statistics indicate that 65 percent of all homicides involve the use of a firearm.[8] Of the remaining 73 percent of homicides in Canada in 1998, stabbings accounted for 33 percent (184), beatings 23 percent (126), strangulation/suffocation 11% (60), fire/burns 2 percent (12), poisoning 1 percent (6), and shaking (shaken-baby syndrome) 1 percent (6).

Various circumstance are associated with homicide in Canada. In 1998, 50 percent of those accused of homicide and 38 percent of victims had consumed alcohol and/or drugs at the time of the offence. As well, almost 33 percent of all homicide incidents in 1998 (173) occurred during the commission of another criminal offence. Thirty-two percent (56) of these were committed during an assault, 20 percent (34) during a robbery, 8 percent (13) during a sexual assault, 3 percent (5) as a result of a stalking, 2 percent (3) during a kidnapping/abduction, and 1 percent (2) during other violent offences. A further 5 percent (8) occurred as a result of arson, and 9 percent (16) during the commission of other property offences. Official statistics for 1998 also indicated that 10 percent of all persons accused of homicide were suspected by police of having mental or developmental disorders. This number may, in fact, be an underestimate, since police officers may not feel qualified to make such assessments (refer to Chapter 6 for a discussion of mental illness and crime).

## Sexual Assault

Former world heavyweight boxing champion Mike Tyson may be the most famous person to have recently served prison time for sexual assault. In 1991, Tyson was convicted of the hotel room rape of 18-year-old Desiree Washington and sentenced to 6 years in prison. Ms. Washington was participating in the 1991 Miss Black America pageant when she met Tyson and accompanied him to his room. Tyson was released from prison in 1995 and re-entered the world of professional boxing, only to be banned from the sport by the Nevada State Athletic Commission after he bit off part of Evander Holyfield's ear during a World Boxing Association heavyweight title rematch in Las Vegas in 1997.[9] In 1999, Tyson was again convicted for the assault of two motorists after a minor car accident and sentenced to one year in jail.

The Criminal Code of Canada distinguishes between three levels of sexual assault, according to the seriousness of the incident. These levels reflect amendments made to the Criminal Code in 1983. Prior to that year, section 143 of the Criminal Code defined rape to have occurred when "a male person has sexual intercourse with a female person who is not his wife (a) without her consent, or (b) with her consent if the consent (i) is extorted by threats or fear of bodily harm, (ii) is obtained by impersonating her husband, or (iii) is obtained by false or fraudulent representations as to the nature and quality of the act." Under this definition, the act was largely defined as one of sexual penetration, and the offender was presumed to be a male and the victim female. As well, under the legislation husbands could not be charged with raping their wives.

Currently, sexual assault legislation focuses on the violent nature of the act, rather than its sexual nature. **Sexual assault** is considered to be an assault committed in circumstances of a sexual nature such that the sexual integrity of the victim is violated.

**Sexual assault** an assault committed in circumstances of a sexual nature such that the sexual integrity of the victim is violated. The degree of violence used determines whether the sexual assault is level 1, level 2, or level 3.

PART 3
304
Crime in the Modern
World and the
Response to It

The current laws allow for the accused (including husbands) to be charged with sexual assault regardless of whether or not penetration occurred. As well, the offence has been "degenderized" such that perpetrators can be either male or female, as can victims. Critics charge, however, that it is overwhelmingly men who sexually assault women and that it has now been left to the discretion of the courts to determine what constitutes sexual assault, as opposed to common assault.[10] *Level 1 sexual assault* (s. 271, CCC) is the classification of least physical injury to the victim and can include unwanted sexual touching; *level 2 sexual assault* (s. 272) involves the use of a weapon or threats to use a weapon, or results in bodily harm; *level 3 sexual assault* (s. 273) is aggravated sexual assault, resulting in wounding, maiming, or disfiguring the victim, or endangering his or her life.[11]

**Date rape** is a term used to define sexual assault that occurs within the context of a dating relationship. It has received much attention recently, although it has undoubtedly occurred as long as there has been dating. According to recent studies, date rape is much more common than previously believed. Some authors suggest that date rape may occur when a male concludes that his date "owes" him something for the money he has spent on her.[12] A recent factor in the date rape phenomenon is the emergence of the "date rape pill," generally known as "rohypnol" and referred to on the street as "roofies," "roach," "ruffies," or "R2". These small white tablets have no taste or odour and when dropped into an unsuspecting victim's drink, make that person feel dizzy, disoriented, and nauseated until finally rendered unconscious. This state can last from 2 to 8 hours, and the victim often has little or no memory of what has happened in that interval.[13]

The *Violence Against Women Survey* (VWAS) conducted in 1993 revealed that only six percent of all sexual assaults were reported, and that the reasons for victims' hesitancy were varied. Some victims feel they are responsible for some aspect of their social relationship that led to the sexual assault, some are ashamed or embarrassed, in some cases victims may feel some concern for the offender and not wish to have him become the target of criminal prosecution—even if deserved.[14] Recent educational campaigns against date rape, found largely on college and university campuses, cite the slogan "No Means No" in an attempt to combat the notion that the dating game is one where the women hold the "prize" that men attempt to "win" and that when a woman says "No" she really means "Yes."

Statistics on sexual assault collected by the UCR are delineated according to the three levels of sexual assault. In 1998, 31 706 sexual assaults were reported nationwide under the UCR program, 96 percent of which were classified as level 1. In 1998, the rates for all three levels of sexual assault decreased from the previous year—level 1 sexual assault dropped by 6.3 percent, level 2 by 13 percent, and level 3 by 19.4 percent. Despite these declines, the 1998 rate of sexual assault of 84 per 100 000 population is still more than twice the rate reported in 1983, when the new definition of the offence was introduced (41 per 100 000). Refer to Chapter 2 for a discussion of the impact of crime definitions and crime rates. It is interesting to note that the sexual assault rate for females is effectively twice that indicated by the official figures, since any realistic tally of such crimes should compare the number of female victims assaulted with the number of females in the overall population (rather than to a count of the entire population, which includes males).

**Date rape** sexual assault that occurs within the context of a dating relationship.

Women who are physically and sexually abused often are not safe even in emergency shelters. Here police investigate the murder of a shelter resident by her estranged husband. Why do you think sexual assault is one of the most under-reported crimes in Canada? *The Canadian Press/LaPresse/Robert Nadon.*

Data from the UCR for 1998[15] indicate that 85 percent of victims of sexual assault were female. Thirty-three percent had been victimized by a casual acquaintance, 26 percent by a stranger, and 25 percent by a family member. Among male victims, 40 percent had been victimized by a casual acquaintance, 30 percent by a family member, and 14 percent by a stranger. Almost 60 percent of all sexual assault victims were younger than 18 years of age.

The sexual assault laws are applicable to all victims regardless of the age of the victim. In 1988, however, several new offences were created to deal with cases of sexual abuse involving children under 18 years of age. These new offences, referred to in the UCR as "other sexual offences," include sexual interference, invitation to sexual touching, sexual exploitation, incest, anal intercourse, and bestiality. Statistics from the UCR for 1998 show that 3 459 incidents of child sexual abuse came to the attention of police, a rate of 11 cases per 100 000 population.

Related to the offence of sexual assault is the offence of criminal harassment, often refered to as *stalking*. Legislation regarding this offence was first enacted in Canada in 1993. **Criminal harassment** (s. 264, CCC) is generally defined as "repeated following, watching or communicating with a person or someone known to them in a way that causes them to fear for their safety or for the safety of someone known to them".[16] Before the enactment of the criminal harassment legislation, stalkers could be charged either with uttering threats, intimidation, trespassing, indecent or harassing phone calls, or assault by threatening. Those fearing injury to themselves, their families or property could also have a *peace bond* laid against the accused. These measures, however, failed to adequately protect victims, since the accused usually had to threaten or physically harm someone before action could be taken. There also existed no means to deal with nonviolent harassing behaviour such as following or watching.

**Criminal harassment** also known as stalking, is the repeated following, watching, or communicating with a person or someone known to them in a way that causes them to fear for their safety or for the safety of someone known to them.

PART 3
306
Crime in the Modern
World and the
Response to It

Statistics from the UCR on criminal harassment show 7 472 reported incidents, or a rate of 25 per 100 000 population, in recent years.[17] Eighty percent of all victims of criminal harassment are female, while 88 percent of those accused of criminal harassment are males. In most cases, the offender is known to the victim; 39 percent of all female victims were stalked by ex-husbands, 24 percent by a casual acquaintance, and 17 percent by an ex-boyfriend. Other offenders include strangers (7%), other family members (4%), work acquaintances (3%), and husbands (2%). Male victims of criminal harassment are most commonly stalked by casual male acquaintances (46%), work acquaintances (11%), strangers (12%), ex-spouses (9%), ex-girlfriends (4%), and other family members (9%).

Twenty-five percent of criminal harassment incidents involved other offences. Some of these included uttering threats (24%), assault (22%), harassing phone calls (10%), mischief (8%), breach of probation (6%), bail violations (6%), and breaking and entering (6%).[18]

## Robbery

**Robbery** the unlawful taking or attempted taking or property that is in the immediate possession of another, by threatened or actual use of force or violence.

The crime of **robbery** (s. 343, CCC) is regarded as a violent personal crime because it is committed in the presence of a victim and involves threatened or actual use of force or violence in the commission of a theft or attempted theft from another person. Although some individuals mistakenly use the terms "robbery" and "break and enter" interchangeably (as in the phrase "my house was robbed"), it should be remembered that robbery is a personal crime and that individuals are robbed, not houses.

The 1998 UCR reports that 28 952 robberies came to the attention of the authorities across the nation that year, meaning that the robbery rate was 96 for every 100 000 people in Canada. This was a decrease of 3.1 percent from the previous year.

Fewer robberies involved the use of firearms in 1998, although robberies involving weapons other than firearms (such as knives) have been increasing. Robberies with no weapons constituted 46 percent of the total, those with a firearm accounted for 18 percent, while robberies using other weapons were about 36 percent of the total. Most robbery occurred against commercial establishments (56%), such as convenience stores (13%), banks and financial institutions (8%), gas stations (7%), and other establishments (e.g., restaurants and liquor stores (28%)). Transportation/storage facilities, nonprofit organizations, and public institutions were targets in 36 percent of the cases.[19]

In recent years, robberies of private residences have attracted attention. Commonly known as *home invasions*, this type of robbery is characterized by a forced entry into a private residence while the occupants are home and usually includes violence and extortion against the occupants.[20] While there is no official legal definition for this type of crime, some police services are reporting it specifically. Major metropolitan police departments, including those in Montreal, Toronto, and Vancouver, report that while home invasions constitute only 6 percent of the total number of robberies, they evoke a disproportionate amount of fear among victims and communities because they violate the safety and sanctity of one's home.[21]

Compared with other violent crime, robbery is more likely to involve younger people. In 1998, 36 percent of all robberies were committed by youth aged 12 to 17 years of age, while 16 percent of all violent crime was committed by this age group.

## Assault

**Assault** (defined in s. 265, CCC) involves the intentional or threatened application of force on another person without consent. The Criminal Code of Canada includes several categories of assault: *level 1 assault* (s. 266), or common assault, which is the least serious type of assault and includes behaviours such as punching, pushing, slapping, shoving, or threats by act or gesture; *level 2 assault* (s. 267), which involves the use of a weapon or results in bodily harm; *level 3 assault* (s. 268), which includes assaults that wound, maim, disfigure, or endanger the life of the victim; and *other assaults,* which involve use of force against a peace officer, unlawfully causing bodily harm, and discharge of a firearm with intent.

Of the 223 260 incidents of recorded assaults at levels 1, 2, and 3 in 1998, level 1 accounted for over 80 percent of all assaults and for 60 percent of all reported violent incidences. Overall, the rate of assault for 1998 (737 per 100 000 population) decreased by less than 1 percent from the previous year (741 in 1997).

The majority of assaults continue to be perpetrated by adult males, yet among youth aged 12 to 17, 30 percent of all assaults are committed by females. Unlike sexual assaults, victims of assault are as likely to be female as male. Females represented 52 percent of all victims of level 1 assault, while males made up 67 percent of all victims of level 2 assaults and "other assaults." Most female victims had been assaulted by a spouse or ex-spouse (42%), a casual acquaintance (18%), or a close friend (12%). Male victims, on the other hand, were assaulted most often by strangers (37%), followed by casual acquaintances (33%). Children under 18 assaulted by parents accounted for 3 percent of all assault victims in 1998—a figure that undoubtedly under-represents the actual occurrence of this type of assault (refer to Chapter 2 for a discussion of definitional concerns surrounding crime counting).

**Assault** the intentional or threatened application of force on another person without consent. The categories of assault include level 1—assault or common assault; level 2—assault involving the use of a weapon or that causes bodily harm; and level 3—assault that results in wounding or endangering the life of the victim.

## Theoretical Explanations of Violent Crime

Why do people commit acts of violence? What compels a man to sexually assault a woman or a youth to pick up a knife and and force a convenience store clerk to hand over the money in the till? While there are no easy answers to these questions, there are certainly a number of theoretical explanations commonly accepted within the field of criminology that might provide answers.

Cases of mass or serial murder, such as the 14 women killed by Marc Lepine in Montreal on December 6, 1989 or the 11 children killed by Clifford Olson between 1980 and 1981, often result in the temptation to examine the individual offender for clues. Surely people who kill others must have "something wrong with them" that compels them to commit these heinous acts. Chapters 5 and 6 examine a number of

Mass murderer Marc Lepine killed 14 female students at L'école polytechnique in Montreal. Which theories do you think work best to explain such violent criminal behaviour: those from the social responsibility perspective or those from the social problems perspective? *The Gazette.*

biological and psychological explanations of crime that can be applied to violent offenders. The biological theories found in Chapter 5 question whether certain individuals are predisposed to violence. Is the male sex drive, which has been developed through evolution to perpetuate the species, an explanation for man's sexual aggression toward women? Can naturally occurring levels of the male hormone testosterone be seen as a reason why males commit close to 90 percent of all violent crime in Canada? Chapter 6 outlines a number of psychological or neurological dysfunctions such as abnormal electroencephalograms, low intelligence, Attention Deficit Disorder (ADD) or Attention Deficit Hyperactivity Disorder (ADHD), as well as psychotic symptoms such as hallucinations, paranoia, and distorted views of reality that may account for criminal behaviour. Various personality disorders, including antisocial personality disorder—psychopathy in particular—are considered as possible causes for deviant sexual behaviour. Psychological theories emphasizing personality types look to Freudian analysis and contend that it is the *id*, or that aspect of personality from which drives, wishes, urges, and desires emanate, that causes the behaviour of rapists, for example. The hostile and sadistic feelings toward women many rapists tend to display are often considered to be rooted in psychotic or personality disorders.

An inability to deal with frustration is considered by some to contribute to aggressive behaviour. Chapter 6 recounts the case of Pierre Lebrun, who killed four fellow employees after years of taunting because of a speech impediment; this apparently caused him to "snap." Donald Lauzon, 19, who killed his 2-year-old daughter Samantha in August 1996 by repeatedly banging her head against the arm of a sofa, was at a loss to explain the anger that welled inside him and surfaced whenever he became frustrated. "The kid would do something and I would hit her," he is quoted as saying. "I wouldn't mean to actually use full force, but that's what would happen. I hit her. Kid would go flying. When it happened I'd freak out, I'd go 'Oh God. What did I do? I'm never going to do this again.'"[22]

Social learning theories assume that people learn how to behave by modelling themselves after others whom they have the opportunity to observe. Does a young person's exposure to violence in the home account for his or her future violent behaviour? Violence on television and in the movies has been cited as the cause of violence in some instances, most notably in the tragic 1993 case of James Bulger, aged 2, of Liverpool, England, who was abducted from a shopping mall, beaten to death, and dumped on a railway track by two 10-year-old boys, who claimed they got the idea after watching the same violent video several times the previous day. The individual responsibility perspective contends that it is the psychological makeup of each person that determines the way in which observed behaviour is absorbed, processed, and acted upon. Some individuals may be exposed to violence in the home and never become violent themselves, while others are compelled to model their behaviour on the actions, and even deviant actions, or others.

The same issues can be examined in the debate over whether or not those children who are abused physically or sexually in the home later go on to inflict harm on others. The link between family violence and future criminality is not a direct one, and there appear to be numerous other factors that need to be taken into consideration. Some criminologists argue that, while being abused as a child may increase the risk of future violence or criminality, there are many people who are victims of childhood violence who do not become violent adult offenders.[23]

In contrast to the individual responsibility perspective are those theories that fall under the social problems perspective. Discussed in Chapters 7, 8, and 9, these theories look to socialization and cultural factors as explanations for acts of violence. Are males raised to behave more aggressively? Are our cultural values responsible for sending a message to young males that the way to deal with stress and frustration is through the use of aggression? Well-known accounts of drivers who assault others as a result of what has become known as "road rage" suggest that perhaps societal tolerance for the use of violence to solve disputes has increased.

The feminist criminology perspective discussed in Chapter 9 would explain violence against women as resulting from societal inequalities due primarily to gender. The physical and sexual assault of women is a means by which males are able to maintain their dominance over women. Thus, the sexual victimization of girls is a behaviour learned by young males in a patriarchal society.

The subculture of violence theory in Chapter 7 is frequently cited as an explanation for acts of violence perpetrated by individuals from a certain subculture that promotes certain values or codes of conduct. For example, the expectation that young males defend their honour and reputation at all costs naturally leads to the use of violence, if that is what is necessary to achieve this end. Therefore, it is conformity to this set of values that leads to violence; violence is not seen in these subcultural settings as the result of deviant behaviour. This argument is used further to explain why victims of violence in these groups are usually members of the group and not outsiders. The account in Chapter 7 of the murder of Sylvain Leduc serves to illustrate this point.

PART 3

310

**Crime in the Modern
World and the
Response to It**

# Crime Rate Is Down:

## Violent Acts Are Changing Our Perspective

Winston Churchill once said, "We have nothing to fear but fear itself." He was, of course, referring to British involvement in World War II. Across Canada, fear of crime appears to be on the rise. Some researchers question whether this fear is more the result of media hype and politicians campaigning on law-and-order platforms than it is the logical consequence of any real rise in crime rates. What follows is a recent article from a Toronto newspaper that raises just such questions.

A woman is abducted off a busy north Toronto street by two men and beaten after being forced to withdraw money from a bank machine.

A Forest Hill couple is abducted, robbed and beaten by three men after their Mercedes is purposely bumped in Rosedale.

A Markham man is brutally beaten by two men on a TTC bus cruising a quiet stretch of North York while the driver and passengers do nothing to intervene.

And in a downtown courtroom, the city relives the murder of Alison Parrott and remembers the moment when we suddenly changed our view on the safety of this city.

It is difficult not to feel as if Toronto were going to hell in a handbasket, that this city we once knew has become a brutal stranger. "Violence seethes in big city," blared one *Sun* headline last week. And so it feels, that our safety has been compromised, our immunity to personal violence penetrated. Once, we imagined that living in a nice part of the city and keeping good company was enough to keep our families from harm.

But no more.

We are all potential victims, or so it feels. If you're not safe driving a nice car or leaving work at 6:30 P.M. at Yonge and Lawrence or riding a bus on Steeles Ave. W., then aren't we all vulnerable? When young women can be pushed in front of subway trains and mothers cut

down in drive-by shootings, where can the rest of us hide?

Fear not, say the social scientists, the statisticians, even Toronto Police brass. Take a Prozac and relax; the reality, or so statistics indicate, tell a much different story.

This past week, police announced that crime had dropped sharply in the first two months of this year compared to the same time in 1998.

### Prevention

In eight of the city's busier divisions, sexual assaults were down 55%, serious assaults down 41%, robberies down 42% and break and enters tumbled 31%.

Deputy chief Mike Boyd admits the bad weather may have been a contributing factor, but insists the drop has much more to do with community policing and its success at crime prevention. "I'm not sure the message is getting out that crime is on the decline," Boyd says from his office in police headquarters. "I'm not so sure the police are standing up on the soap box because we know things could take a turn and we don't want to leave people with a false sense of security. But we are noticing these reductions."

There may be lies, damned lies and statistics, but study after study tells the same, consistent story. Crime is down, not just here, but across Canada. While police credit community policing, experts like David Foot of *Boom, Bust and*

*Echo* fame attribute the decline to simple demographics: as the Baby Boom ages, there are fewer young men around in the 18-to-24 age group who account for a disproportionate amount of crime.

Whatever the explanation, Statistics Canada last summer reported the lowest general crime rate in this country since 1980, and a homicide rate that had fallen to its lowest level in almost three decades. In Toronto, the violent crime rate fell by 1.4% and the property crime rate by 9.1%, with an overall crime decline of 7.6%. StatsCan pronounced Toronto a safer city—statistically—than Winnipeg, Vancouver, Hamilton, Edmonton or even Ottawa.

A national survey in April's issue of Chatelaine concurs, again citing Toronto among the top five safest cities in the country. Its cross-Canada Safe Cities study reveals Canadians are more likely to be killed in Saskatoon than in Toronto, and are more at risk of property crime in Winnipeg.

Still critics call statistics a shell game, manipulated in a public relations exercise to make the numbers reinforce the effectiveness of community policing, the controversial change in philosophy adopted by Toronto Police several years ago.

"They say crime is on the decline but I don't believe it," ex-Toronto Police chief Bill McCormack told The Sun's Joe Warmington. "I believe enforcement is on the decrease. Violent crime is on the increase."

Much of it just might not be reported, many argue.

One victim made that point in a letter to the editor last summer after the StatsCan report on Canada's plunging crime rate: "If this is true, why do most Canadians believe the rates are rising and generally feel unsafe?" Bram Eedenburg asked in his letter. "Consider: If it were not for current paramedical and medical life-saving techniques the homicide rate would double overnight. Crimes previously unknown, or very rare, are becoming commonplace—carjackings, robberies of the disabled and the elderly, schoolyard bullying and violent crimes by children, road rage, gang-related shootings, acts of senseless and random violence such as drive-bys, hit-and-runs and subway pushings.

"Owing to language barriers, intimidation, fear, a prevailing sense of apathy, futility and a police force overwhelmed and suffering from burnout, many crimes go unreported," he argued. "I give myself here as a prime example. I have been mugged, victimized by several break-and-enter thefts and have had upwards of a dozen bicycles stolen. And I reported none of these."

### Don't trust polls

So despite all the numbers, Torontonians in opinion poll after opinion poll say they don't trust them. They're convinced Toronto is caught in the midst of a crime wave.

Last month, Toronto's new task force on community safety released its first report on the pulse of the city. They found the number one concern was "violence and fear of violence against children and young people."

The task force, co-chaired by Councillor Rob Davis, found a wide gap between the actual crime rate and Torontonians' fear of crime. That dichotomy was pointed out by Deputy Chief Bob Kerr at the launch of the task force. "He told us the more likely you are to be a victim of crime the less likely you are to fear crime," Davis recalled. "And the less likely you are to be a victim of crime, the more likely you are to fear crime."

### Elderly frightened

The task force study bears that out. In the suburbs, they found a high rate of fear but a lower incidence of crime, while people in the downtown core felt safer

PART 3

312

**Crime in the Modern
World and the
Response to It**

despite a crime rate that was actually higher. Only 71% in Scarborough said they felt safe to walk alone in their neighbourhood compared to 80% of the residents of Toronto. Yet the report said the highest crime rates were concentrated in downtown Toronto, with the east part of downtown, west central Toronto and the Junction/York area also showing higher than average levels of violent crime.

Most frightened are the elderly. A 1997 Angus Reid national poll found women aged 55 years and older were the most concerned that the amount of crime in communities had increased.

Once again, their fear is an inversion of reality—the elderly are the least likely victims of crime. Despite memorable stories about grannies being mugged by cowardly punks, young people are far more likely to be victims of crime than seniors. Yet while young men between 18 and 25 are the most likely to be either the perpetrators or victims of crime, they are the least fearful.

Similarly, we fear violence from strangers, yet most victims of violence actually know their attacker. In 1997, four times as many murder victims were killed by people they knew as by strangers, three and a half times as many sexual assault victims were attacked by people they knew as by strangers, and two and a half times as many non-sexual assault victims were assaulted by people they knew as by strangers.

Despite the mathematical probabilities on our side, many remain frightened and convinced the statistics are lying. Instinctively, we know, whatever the stats say, that we feel less safe now than we did as children. The 1997 Angus Reid poll found about 60% of Canadians believed crime had increased. More recently, a quality of life study last year by York University's Institute for Social Research found 43% of Torontonians were under the misguided impression the crime rate had risen.

So why are we so sure that violent crime is on the upswing?

"I think people watch a lot of American TV for one thing and one gets the feel from basically immersing oneself in the media that crime is rampant and on the increase," explains Paul Grayson, author of the York study.

Criminologists have long blamed the news media for sensationalizing crime and distorting our perception of how bad things really are to win readers and viewers.

Councillor Rob Davis also points to the media, but in a much less nefarious way. Unlike American cities our size—which might have 700 murders a year and where victims are just statistics—he argues Toronto's victims of violence loom so large because they are so rare.

"Because there are so few murders, the media are able to do such a good job of reporting on the lives and families of the victims and so crime becomes more personalized through the media," Davis notes. "And rightfully so, people feel a strong sense of indignation at any violent act partly because we have so few."

### Senseless

Politicians campaigning on law-and-order platforms also have reasons to indulge in some fear-mongering. Police unions looking for more officers and resources may also play the crime card. There is more to it, though.

Intuitively, we sense a difference in the kind of crime we're hearing about, a senselessness to the violence that we don't recall. Why in the world did those bank robbers kill Brampton teller Nancy Kidd while she lay on the floor? Why beat Winnie Ng after she had co-operated and given the robbers cash from the bank machine? Why break Schuyler Sigel's jaw?

Why pummel Rod McKeown until he was nearly blind when he was just minding his own business on a TTC bus?

"It's destroyed my faith in some human nature," McKeown says after surgery that may allow him to see again from his damaged eye in about a year. "It was a brutal, vicious attack. It wasn't random. He carefully aimed for my eye."

McKeown, a consultant returning home from a job at Queen's Park, says he has lived and survived the violence and crime of Glasgow and later Johannesburg. "When I came to Toronto everything seemed so gentlemanly and serene and to be whacked like this here is quite ironic.

"I never expected this would happen here. The city is an awful lot worse than it used to be."

The report by the Toronto task force on community safety seems to validate that fear. While the crime rate is down, the study says the proportion of violent crime is on the rise. Violent offences, which made up only 10.6% of all reported crime in 1987, rose to 13.5% in 1993 and 15% in 1997.

"There have been indications of the levels of violence in the past rising," admits Boyd. "And we've seen some new kinds of crimes like carjackings and home invasion robberies which cause a real concern. It's a different type of crime. It's something that's new and that causes real fear."

Real or imagined, fear of crime has far-reaching effects on our behaviour. The murder of Alison Parrott drastically changed the way we parented. Girls riding the subway alone at 11 years old would become rare; the demands for street-proofing, almost hysterical. It didn't matter that the murder of children, thankfully, remains a very rare occurrence.

### No eyes on street

The positive side of that anxiety is that our outrage and our intolerance for violence demands it be checked by our police and community. We refuse to be complacent about any level of crime.

There is a danger, though, as well. Fear can also be destructive and isolating.

The risk of having a misplaced sense of fear is that we adopt a fortress mentality, build gated communities and abandon our public spaces.

If we become so frightened we won't walk Yonge St. at night or take the subway, we ensure that crime will increase.

"It becomes a self-fulfilling prophecy," warns Councillor Davis of the city's safety task force. "If people do become afraid to walk, then the only ones who will occupy those sidewalks and public places will be criminals. And they'll know, as (famous urbanist) Jane Jacobs identified it, that there won't be any eyes on the street to report crime or detect these criminals."

And then we really will have more to fear than fear itself.

## DISCUSSION QUESTIONS

1. Why is it so difficult to agree on the true rate of crime? How does our definition of crime affect the rate of measured crime?
2. Do you think that the fear of crime is out of proportion to the rate of crime? How can the two be so disjointed?

SOURCE: Michele Mandel, "Crime Rate is Down: Violent Acts Are Changing Our Perspective," *Toronto Sun*, March 14, 1999. Reprinted with permission of the Toronto Sun Syndicate/Michele Mandel.

PART 3
314
**Crime in the Modern
World and the
Response to It**

## Property Crime

Property crimes are comprised of those unlawful acts perpetrated with the intent of gaining property, but do not involve the use or threat of violence. Included in this category are breaking and entering, theft, fraud, crime involving motor vehicles, arson, and possession of stolen goods.

The 1998 UCR reports 1.38 million incidents of property crime, or a rate of 4 541 per 100 000 population in that year, which represents a 7 percent drop from the previous year and the lowest recorded number since 1977. The rates of property crime declined in all provinces except Newfoundland in 1998. The greatest drops were recorded in P.E.I. (–14%), Ontario (–9%), British Columbia (–8%), and New Brunswick (–8%), while Newfoundland saw an increase of 3 percent. Overall, for 1998, B.C. showed the highest rate of property crime at 7 178 incidents per 100 000 population, while Newfoundland and P.E.I. recorded the lowest rates, at 2 666 and 2 747, respectively.

### Breaking and Entering

**Breaking and entering**
the unlawful entry of a
place to commit an
indictable offence.

**Breaking and entering** (s. 348, CCC) is one of the most common and serious of property offences. This crime constitutes an invasion of personal or work space and often results in the theft or destruction of property. While most break and enters are, strictly speaking, property crimes, the potential for personal violence is inherent. Breaking and entering a dwelling house carries a maximum penalty of life imprisonment (as compared with 10 years for breaking and entering of a place other than a dwelling house), reflecting the possibility of violent confrontations between the offender and the homeowner. In the UCR, police-reported breaking and entering is categorized into three different types: (1) residential—the breaking and enetering of a private residence, including single homes, garden homes, apartments, cottages, mobile homes, rooming houses, etc.; (2) business breaking and entering —the breaking and entering of a facility used for commercial or public affairs, including, for example, financial institutions, stores, and noncommercial enterprises such as government buildings, schools, churches, and nonprofit agencies; (3) other—the breaking and entering of private property structures such as sheds, detached garages, or storage and transport facilities. The UCR statistics include attempted as well as completed breaking and enterings.

In 1998, 350 176 incidents of breaking and entering were recorded, representing a rate of 1 156 per 100 000 population. This is a decrease of 7 percent from the previous year, in keeping with the consistent decreases since 1991. Sixty-three percent of all breaking and enterings were residential, while business breaking and enterings accounted for 26 percent (or a rate of 305 per 100 000). The remaining 11 percent included other locations such as sheds and storage facilities (for a rate of 122 per 100 000).

The type of property stolen from residences is quite different from that stolen from businesses. Audio/video equipment such as televisions, stereos, and VCRs typify the property stolen from residences. Other types of property frequently stolen from residences includes jewellery, money, cheques or bonds, personal accessories, machinery and tools, photographic equipment, office equipment, and bicycles. In comparison, thefts from breaking and enterings into businesses include money, cheques or bonds, office equipment, consumable goods (alcohol, cigarettes), audio/video equipment, machinery and tools, and personal accessories. Firearms were more frequently stolen from homes during a breaking and entering than from businesses. The majority of these were rifles and shotguns, while the minority consisted of restricted weapons.[24]

Data from the UCR suggest breaking and enterings involving violence occur in fewer than 5 percent of cases. Of these, the majority involved an assault, while others involved robbery, sexual assault, abduction, and criminal harassment. Almost all violent breaking and enterings occurred at a place of residence.[25]

Of those charged with break and enter in 1998, 60 percent were adults and 40 percent were youths aged 12 to 17. Within both these age groups, almost all of those charged were males (94 percent among adults, 90 percent among youth).

In keeping with the general trend of higher crime rates in the western provinces, the Yukon Territory, the Northwest Territories, and Saskatchewan recorded the highest rates of break and enter (2 435, 1 921, and 1 739 per 100 000, respectively) while Prince Edward Island and New Brunswick recorded the lowest rates, at 513 and 740, respectively.

## Theft

**Theft** (s. 322, CCC) is defined as the act of dishonestly taking property belonging to another person with the intention of depriving its owner of it either permanently or temporarily.[26] Specific categories of theft included in the Criminal Code of Canada are *theft of gas, electricity, or telecommunications* (cable television) (s. 326); *theft by husband or wife* (s. 289), and *theft of credit card* (s. 342). The severity of the theft is determined largely by the monetary value placed on the property taken. In 1995, the Criminal Code was amended to include *theft over $5 000* and *theft $5 000 and under* (prior to 1995, this amount was $1 000; prior to 1986, it was $200). Not included in the category are motor vehicle theft, fraud, or possession of stolen property. While the Criminal Code does include a section prohibiting the unauthorized use of computer facilities, the area of theft perpetrated using computers, such as theft of software or information obtained through online access, is one that will require further amendments.

In 1998, 736 598 incidents of theft accounted for about 33 percent of all Criminal Code incidents and over 50 percent of all property crimes. Of these, 97 percent were classified as theft $5 000 and under. This figure most likely under-represents the amount of theft that occurs: theft under $5 000 remains one of the crimes most under-reported by victims. It constitutes a rate of 2 352 incidents per 100 000 population, while the rate for theft over $5 000 stood at 79 per 100 000 for 1998. The overall theft rate was 7 percent lower than for the previous year and has been declining since 1991.

Over one-third of all thefts were thefts from motor vehicles (39%), while 13 percent were shoplifting incidents, 10 percent were bicycle thefts, and 38 percent were classified as "other." Compared with different types of offences, the number of females charged with theft $5 000 and under is quite high—30 percent of adults and 33 percent of youth aged 12 to 15. The majority of these females were charged with shoplifting (see Chapter 2 for a discussion on the strengthening correlation between female and criminal behaviour and the "feminization of poverty").

**Theft** the act of dishonestly taking property belonging to another person with the intention of depriving its owner of it either permanently or temporarily.

PART 3
316
**Crime in the Modern
World and the
Response to It**

**Motor vehicle theft** the
taking of a vehicle
without the owner's
authorization. A motor
vehicle is defined as a
car, truck, van, bus,
recreational vehicle,
semi-trailer truck,
motorcycle, construction
machinery, agricultural
machinery, or other
land-based motor
vehicle (such as a go-
kart, snowmobile, all-
terrain vehicle, or dune-
buggy).

## Motor Vehicle Crime

**Motor vehicle theft** is defined as the taking of a vehicle without the owner's authorization. A motor vehicle is defined as a car, truck, van, bus, recreational vehicle, semi-trailer truck, motorcycle, construction machinery, agricultural machinery, or other land-based motor vehicle (such as a go-kart, snowmobile, all-terrain vehicle, or dune-buggy).[27] Excluded from the category of motor vehicle theft is theft of airplanes, boats, trains, and spacecraft, which are counted as thefts over $5 000.

In 1998, 165 799 incidents of motor vehicle theft accounted for slightly more than 10 percent of all property crimes. At a rate of 547 per 100 000 population, this constitutes a 7 percent decrease from the previous year, yet this rate is higher than that for 1988. The 9 percent increase in the total number of vehicles registered in Canada between 1993 and 1997 accounts, in part, for the rising rate of motor vehicle thefts over the past decade.

Motor vehicle theft is a crime often associated with youth. Statistics from 1998 show that 42 percent of persons charged with motor vehicle theft were youth aged 12 to 17. Of these, 86 percent were male.

The rate of motor vehicle theft decreased between 1997 and 1998 in virtually every province and territory with the notable exception of Newfoundland, where it increased by 30 percent! Nevertheless, Newfoundland still reported the lowest rate of motor vehicle theft, at 118 per 100 000, while Manitoba and British Columbia reported the highest rates, at 725 and 731, respectively. Various explanations for such varied provincial rates could include very high rates of motor vehicle theft in Winnipeg (1 242 per 100 000) and Vancouver (1 331 per 100 000). Prevailing social or economic issues such as youth gang activity in Winnipeg and Vancouver's location favourable to the operation of car-theft rings may provide partial explanations for this.

Car-theft rings have become a reality in Canada in recent years as markets for stolen cars have expanded overseas. To be resold, the stolen vehicles must be made difficult to trace. This is usually done by altering or removing the Vehicle Identification Number (VIN). Altered VIN plates are sanded down and a new number etched in, or VIN plates are replaced with those matching cars considered "write-offs." Many of these accident wrecks are auctioned off by auto insurance companies. The cars are auctioned with the valid VINs still attached and bought by those involved in stolen-car rings. Lax regulations regarding the handling of wrecked cars in some provinces have meant that they have become virtual havens for illegal car-ring operators.[28]

Since the mid-1980s, another form of motor vehicle theft has captured the attention of the public. Known as *carjacking*, this violent form of motor vehicle theft involves the forced abdication of the vehicle by its owner to the felon. Usually armed with a weapon, the perpetrator will confront a car owner as he returns to his parked car, demanding the keys. Others who unwittingly leave their car running as they go into a store for a couple of minutes come out to find it gone. Still other victims are forced out of their cars as they wait at an intersection for a light to change. Another variation of carjacking involves "bumping" the victim's car from behind to get him or her to pull over in the belief there has been a traffic accident. Once out of the car, the perpetrator robs the victim of his or her vehicle and its contents. Currently in Canada, official statistics do not record carjackings as a separate incident; there is no Criminal Code section dealing with this offence. Most incidents of carjacking are dealt with as a robbery, since force or fear are typically used to steal the vehicle directly from the owner.

## Offences Involving Motor Vehicles

It is generally the responsibility of the provincial governments to regulate the use of roads and waterways within their jurisdiction. For example, speed limits, regulations regarding turns, and general "rules of the road" fall under the authority of each province. However, for those actions in which the use of a motor vehicle creates a risk of injury or death, the federal government uses its authority to make a federal law. The Criminal Code includes a number of offences addressing the use of motor vehicles, including: *dangerous operation of a motor vehicle* (s. 249); *failure to stop when involved in an accident* (s. 252); *driving while disqualified* (s. 259); and *impaired operation of a motor vehicle* (s. 253). Many of these Criminal Code offences are similar to offences outlined in provincial statutes; the Criminal Code offence is always considered a more serious one. The UCR records include only reported incidents that violate traffic offences identified in the Criminal Code.

In 1998, police reported 140 536 incidents involving Criminal Code traffic crimes, resulting in a rate 10 percent below that of the previous year (464 per 100 000 population compared with 517 in 1997). Impaired driving accounted for 62 percent of these incidents, while failure to stop or remain at the scene of an accident accounted for 28 percent, and driving while prohibited made up 10 percent.

The rate of **impaired driving** charges has been declining steadily since 1981. In that year, the rate was 859 per 100 000, while the 1998 rate was 295 per 100 000 (70 587 incidents), or a drop of about 65 percent. These changes resulted from a number of factors, including changes in public attitudes as well as trends in police enforcement measures such as R.I.D.E. programs (Reduce Impaired Driving Everywhere). Figure 10.1 illustrates this trend.

Of those charged with impaired driving in 1998, all but 1 percent were adults; among these, 90 percent were male.[29]

**Impaired driving** the operation of a motor vehicle by a person whose ability to operate it is impaired by alcohol or a drug. In the case of alcohol, impairment is said to occur when the concentration of alcohol in the person's blood exceeds 80 milligrams in 100 millilitres of blood.

### Figure 10.1

*Persons Charged with Impaired Driving, 1977–1998*

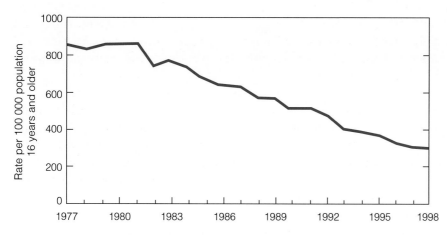

SOURCE: Julie Sauvé, "Impaired Driving in Canada," Statistics Canada, *Juristat*, Vol. 19, no. 11, Catalogue No. 85-002-XPE, p. 6.

PART 3

318

**Crime in the Modern
World and the
Response to It**

Fraud an attempt
through deceit or
falsehood to obtain
goods, services, or
financial gain without
legitimate rights. The
UCR defines three
categories of fraud,
namely, cheque fraud,
credit card fraud, and
other fraud, including
criminal breach of trust,
forgery, and insurance,
and telemarketing fraud.

## Fraud

**Fraud** (defined in s. 380, CCC), is characterized as an attempt through deceit or false-hood to obtain goods, services, or financial gain without legitimate rights. It can in-clude activities ranging from credit card theft to cheque forgery to telemarketing scams to complicated electronic money transfer schemes.[30]

Fraud is an immense area of concern, covering a wide range of illegal activities. For statistical purposes, the UCR defines three categories of fraud: *cheque fraud* is the fraudulent use of a cheque, traveller's cheque, money order, postal order, or any other promissory note; *credit card fraud* includes all offences involving the use and/or theft of a wide assortment of plastic cards and nonplastic coupons; *other fraud* includes criminal breach of trust, false pretenses, forgery, destroying or falsifying books or doc-uments, unauthorized use of computers, telemarketing fraud, insurance fraud, mail fraud, fraudulent manipulation of the stock exchange, etc.[31]

We will consider here the three categories of fraud defined in the UCR. Overall, total reported fraud offences have been declining, although some specific types have shown different patterns. Levels of police activity (use of "fraud squads"), reporting practices of victims, use of private security agencies by corporations, and overall changes in consumer activity may all influence rates of fraud.

In 1998, there were 94 575 police-reported incidents of fraud in Canada, for a rate of 312 per 100 000 population. (According to the UCR, a single incident can involve multiple fraudulent actions, so that one incident of credit card fraud may involve more than one illegal use of the card.) This represents an overall drop of 3 percent from the previous year, primarily due to a decrease in the rate of cheque fraud. Cheque fraud

Hockey czar Alan Eagleson shocked Canadian and American hockey fans when he was convicted of fraud in both Canada and the United States in 1998. Here Eagleson is shown leaving the Mimico Correctional Centre in Toronto after serving six months of an eighteen-month sentence. He was also sentenced to probation and a $700 000 fine by a U.S. court. Should white-collar criminals be punished the same as other offenders? *The Canadian Press/Frank Gunn.*

accounted for 35 percent of all fraud in 1998 (33 252 total, for a rate of 110 per 100 000), compared with 59 percent in 1988. Conversely, there was an 11 percent increase in the amount of reported credit card fraud between 1997 and 1998 (18 462 total, for a rate of 61 per 100 000). Like cheque fraud, fraud classified as "other" has declined in recent years yet still constitutes the largest number of frauds reported by police agencies: 45 percent in 1998. Of particular concern within this category of fraud is telemarketing fraud.

Arguments used to explain the overall decrease in the amount of fraud vary. Some explanations contend that the drop is real, since so many Canadians have turned to technology to complete financial transactions and have moved away from the use of cheques. Others hold that the downward trend is artificial, since more and more corporations are turning away from the public police and toward specially trained companies to assist with technologically complex frauds; the incidents detected by these private firms are not officially reported and recorded. New forms of fraud may also be simply more difficult to detect.[32]

As with most other crimes, males represent the majority of those charged with fraud (70%), and most of these are adults (93%). Female involvement in fraud, however, is relatively high when compared with other offences, second only to theft $5 000 and under. Among fraud offences, the proportion of women charged is highest for cheque frauds, at 33 percent.

## Credit Card and Insurance Fraud

### The Changing Nature of Credit Card Fraud

Losses due to credit card fraud are rising dramatically and are of great concern to the industry. Up until the early 1990s, most credit card fraud was based on lost or stolen cards. Since then, counterfeit and altered credit cards have surfaced as the newest type of credit card fraud. Although UCR police reported statistics do not specify the type of credit card fraud, the Canadian Banker's Association (CBA) reports that counterfeiting credit cards is one of the fastest-growing categories of fraud in Canada and around the world.

Counterfeit credit cards take on various forms. The basic principle behind each type of counterfeit credit card fraud is the theft of data, i.e., account numbers. These data, with the appropriate help of equipment such as embossing machines and laser copiers, is then used in various schemes. There are *"pure" counterfeit cards*, which are manufactured through a silk screen process and then encoded with actual credit card customer data. A second type involves the use of genuine cards (stolen or expired) that are *altered* and re-impressed (embossed and/or encoded) with different numbers. A third technique simply involves the use of an ordinary plastic card onto which a number if appended. This *white plastic fraud* is used for fictitious purchases which requires the collusion of a merchant or an employee. According to the 1993 Organized Crime Committee Report (OCCR) launched by the Canadian Association of Chiefs of Police (CACP), and the CBA, the production of high-quality "pure" counterfeit cards is the fastest growing type of counterfeiting activity.

▶

PART 3

320

**Crime in the Modern
World and the
Response to It**

▶

According to the CBA (1996), the theft, loss, and counterfeiting of cards were by far the most common types of credit card fraud, accounting for nearly all reported occurrences. Other types of fraud reported by the CBA include "non-receipts," whereupon a mailed card does not reach its destination; "fraudulent applications," which involves the impersonation of credit worthy applicants; "no card frauds," in which someone else's card number if utilized to make purchases via the telephone, mail, or Internet.

### Facts About Insurance Fraud

In June 1994, the Insurance Board of Canada-backed Canadian Coalition Against Insurance Fraud was founded to implement a series of actions to try and reduce the annual $1.3 billion cost of property and casualty insurance fraud. With its more than 60 members, the Coalition represents groups affected by fraud including the private insurance industry, police and fire services, consumer advocacy groups and public auto insurers. Actions aimed at curbing the high toll of insurance "scams" include public awareness, changing business practices, improved investigative and enforcement techniques, improved understanding of the problem, and changes to the legal and regulatory environment.

The Coalition defines insurance fraud as: *any act or omission with a view to illegally obtaining an insurance benefit*—in other words, any action where claimants receive money that they were not entitled to. The Coalition's efforts have produced the following:

- Insurance fraud includes a wide array of activities: completely fabricated claims, exaggeration or padding of genuine claims, false statements on insurance applications, and all types of internal fraud.
- Insurance fraud costs approximately $1.3 billion and an additional $1 billion per year in police and fire resources. Health costs to victims and fire fighters are other unmeasured costs.
- In North America, insurance fraud is estimated to be second to illegal drug sales in the source of criminal profits.
- All insurance fraud is a crime—including "opportunistic" actions like exaggerating a genuine claim.
- In a 1996 public opinion poll regarding insurance fraud, 43 percent of Canadians agreed it was easy to successfully defraud an insurance company; 78 percent understood that fraud had an impact on the cost of insurance; and 50 percent believe it was common to exaggerate claims.

SOURCE: Derek E. Janhevich, "The Changing Nature of Fraud in Canada," Statistics Canada, *Juristat*, vol. 18, no. 4, Catalogue No. 85-002, pp. 7, 11.

## Arson

**Arson** intentional or reckless damage to property by fire or explosion. This includes arson that causes danger to human life or damage to property and arson that results from criminal negligence.

**Arson** involves intentional or reckless damage to property by fire or explosion. The most serious form is *arson causing danger to human life* (s. 433, CCC), followed by *arson causing damage to property* (s. 434), and finally *arson by criminal negligence* (s. 346). It also includes the burning of property for fraudulent purposes, such as to claim insurance.

In 1998, police reported 12 952 incidents of arson, or a rate of 43 per 100 000 Canadians, registering a slight increase of 1 percent from the previous year. While the rate remained relatively stable for most of the country, there was a notable increase of 63 percent in Manitoba, due largely to a spate of arsons that have been plaguing the city of Winnipeg.

According to the UCR, the most common targets for arson were motor vehicles (28%), residences (27%), and noncommercial enterprises (24%). Youth aged 12 to 17 constituted 41 percent of those charged with arson, with 87 percent of these being male.

## Theoretical Explanations for Property Crime

The realities surrounding property crime are complex and belie the ability to pinpoint a simple explanation. Does the person who breaks into someone's home and steals the television and VCR do this for the same reason that someone else breaks into a car and rides around in it at high speeds?

The most obvious motivating factor in many cases of property crime appears to be greed, and many criminological theories have used this notion as a starting point. These theories fall under the social problems perspective heading, because they largely assume that property crime is the manifestation of a variety of underlying social problems, not the least of which is poverty. Theories such as the strain theory (discussed in Chapter 7) and the routine activities theory (Chapter 12) suggest that there is a desire to achieve a universal goal, which is defined in terms of money and the goods, services, privileges, and prestige it can buy. The opportunity to achieve this goal through legitimate means such as schooling and employment is restricted for some people, who then turn to illegitimate or criminal opportunities to do so. If the illegitimate opportunities outnumber the legitimate ones, the temptation for some to seek this "easy route" may become too great to resist. The increase in the amount of fraud being committed using credit cards over cheques may be explained using this theory, for example.

Still other theories contend that the commission of property crimes, including motor vehicle theft, breaking and entering, and shoplifting, all satisfy a need for excitement. The subcultural theories discussed in Chapter 7 maintain that material needs are often insufficient to explain the fascination with theft some people have. These theories suggest that crime is fun and is done to achieve a sense of status and belonging within a peer group.

The social process theories outlined in Chapter 8 look to the interaction between individuals as an explanation for criminal behaviour. What role, for example, does peer pressure and group behaviour have on the behaviour of some individuals? Can association with delinquent peers promote the learning of crimes such as theft and joyriding in stolen cars? The differential association theory suggests this is so. The social control theory outlined in Chapter 8 looks to the individual's attachment to positive role models, commitment to realistic goals, involvement in recreational and school activities, and belief in conventional values as a means of decreasing the likelihood of criminal behaviour. This theory suggests that those people, especially youth, who are bored and have no positive direction in life run a much greater risk of being attracted to crimes such as theft, shoplifting, arson, and vandalism.

## Crimes Against the Public Order

Included in the Criminal Code of Canada are a number of activities often referred to as *public order crimes* or *victimless crimes*. While it is debatable whether these activities do or do not victimize, it is generally agreed that though they violate prevailing morality, social policy, and public opinion, it *is* open to debate whether they should be classified as criminal. Such crimes against the public order traditionally refer to activities and behaviours involving sex (such as commercial sex, pornography, and erotic materials), activities involving the use, abuse, and sale of drugs and alcohol, and behaviours involving individual lifestyle choices, such as gambling and assisted suicide.

### Prostitution

**Prostitution** most commonly used to refer to the illegal activities of publically communicating with another person for the purposes of buying or selling sexual services, running a bawdy house, or living on the avails of prostitution of another person.

**Prostitution**, or the exchange of money for sex, is not illegal in Canada. What is illegal are the associated activities such as *publicly communicating with another person for the purposes of buying or selling sexual services* (s. 213, CCC) or *running a bawdy house* (s. 210) or *living on the avails of a prostitution of another person* (s. 212(2)).

Prostitution is a controversial issue, around which there seems to be little consensus as to the best means of dealing with it. While it is generally considered to be a voluntary activity and is therefore often classified as a victimless crime, there are serious health, social, legal, and community issues associated with it. Other forms of activity such as drug trafficking and use are often linked to it. Those neighbourhoods in which prostitutes ply their trade constantly struggle with the health and safety risks associated with discarded needles and condoms. Health concerns, such as the spread of sexually transmitted diseases, affect the prostitutes, their customers, and the families of customers.

Police round up women in a prostitute sweep. Do you think prostitution is a victimless crime? Why or why not? *The Canadian Press/Welland Tribune/Aaron Beaudoin.*

Statistics regarding prostitution are very closely tied to the law enforcement practices of any given police service and therefore vary across provinces and municipalities. In 1998, the rate of prostitution incidents reported to the police increased by 1 percent from the previous year. Most of these prostitution-related crimes involved communication with a person for the purpose of engaging in prostitution or stopping a vehicle for the same purpose. There has been a noticeable increase since 1993 in offences related to bawdy houses, including an increase of 19 percent from 1997 to 1998.

Fifty-three percent of the 5 490 individuals charged with prostitution-related crimes in 1998 were females. Of the males charged, it can be assumed that most were clients, although some were prostitutes themselves or were living on the avails of prostitution. Of those charged in 1998, official statistics indicate that only 3 percent were youth aged 12 to 17. It is generally believed that this number under-represents the actual number of youths involved in prostitution, since many in this age group are often diverted by police to social services rather than charged.

# The John School

In contrast to the numerous social studies carried out on prostitutes, relatively little research has focused on customers, who are the driving force behind the trade. A recent report, however, provides wide-ranging motives behind the market for commercial sex, gleaned from the literature and representing the observations of buyers, sellers, researchers, feminists and medical practitioners. Motives include social ineptitude (which precludes normal relationships); the desire to avoid the "hassle" of a relationship; the wish to assert dominance; the unavailability of the regular partner, or certain forms of sexual activity; curiosity; sexual addiction; and closet homosexuality.

Regardless of their motives, clients are being held increasingly responsible for their actions. This rising accountability lies behind the establishment of the "john school." Initially developed in San Francisco by a former prostitute and a police officer, the concept of the john school has recently been imported to Canada, where some police forces (e.g., in Toronto, Ottawa and Edmonton) have been carrying out pilot projects. When available, the option of attending a john school session may be offered to clients (i.e., "johns") arrested for the first time. A communicating charge is stayed or dropped in exchange for spending a few hours in a classroom setting, where the men are informed about the legal, medical and social ramifications of their activities.

Although these programs are still in their infancy, officials in San Francisco have reported a low rate of recidivism. This rehabilitative approach is cost-effective, since many of the speakers are volunteers and court costs are avoided; in some cities, school attendees are required to pay a fee or are asking for donations. Finally, community members feel that something tangible is being done to address the problem.

Several criticisms have been directed at the john school, however. Since customers dealing with prostitutes in indoor venues are rarely arrested for communicating, those dealing with street prostitutes are the most likely to be steered towards the school; furthermore, this option is not available to every client arrested. Also, there is no equivalent program for prostitutes at this time, although other interventions or facilities (such as safe houses) exist in some cities.

SOURCE: Doreen Duchesne, "Street Prostitution in Canada," Statistics Canada, *Juristat*, vol. 17, no. 2 (1997), Catalogue No. 85-002-XPE, p. 11.

PART 3
324
**Crime in the Modern
World and the
Response to It**

Recent public concerns have been raised about the ever-decreasing age of prostitutes. Incidents of children being recruited and sold into a life of prostitution in Asian countries such as Thailand, Japan, India, and the Philippines are well documented.[33] There are also concerns about youth involvement in prostitution in Canada. Sex tourism involves the promotion of travel packages to Canadians for the purpose of illegal sexual encounters, often with minors. This practice is one of increasing concern for law enforcement officers.

## Illicit Drugs

There is a correlation between illicit drug use and criminal activity, albeit a complex one. This examination of illicit drugs considers those related criminal activities contained in the Controlled Drugs and Substances Act (CDSA) of 1997. Essentially, the drug law is made up of two categories of offences: *supply offences*, which include the growing and distribution (trafficking and importing) of illegal and prohibited drugs, and *possession offences*, which include the purchase and use of illegal and prohibited drugs. The official number of recorded offences is obviously sensitive to enforcement and detection practices. An increase in the number of arrests and seizures does not necessariy indicate an increase in the population's use of illicit drugs, but rather may indicate an increased circulation of drugs or stepped up enforcement at national or international levels. Canadian government estimates for 1998 indicate that the illegal drug market in Canada generates $7 to 10 billion annually.[34]

There were 71 293 incidents (or a rate of 235 per 100 000) related to the CDSA reported in 1998. Cannabis offences made up 70 percent of these—68 percent for possession, 15 percent for cultivation, 15 percent for trafficking, and 2 percent for importation. This represented a 6 percent increase from the previous year. Similarly, the rate for heroin-related offences increased by 6 percent, while the rate for cocaine offences went up by 5 percent. Those drugs classified as "other" include drugs other than cannabis, heroin, and cocaine such as PCP, LSD, or ecstasy and controlled drugs such as amphetamines, barbiturates, and anabolic steroids; the rate of reported incidents climbed by 8 percent from 1997. Ninety percent of all persons charged with drug offences were adults, and the vast majority of these were male.

## Gambling

**Gambling** includes behaviours such as keeping a common gaming or betting house, betting or bookmaking, placing bets on behalf of others, promoting lotteries, and cheating at play.

Over the last 100 years, many forms of **gambling** and betting have become legal in Canada, including raffles and bingos for charitable purposes, parimutuel betting on horse races, games of chance at carnivals and fairs, and government-run lotteries, casinos, and video-lottery terminals. Some estimates indicate that gambling revenues in Canada totaled $4.8 billion in 1998, a 76 percent increase from 1992.[35] The Criminal Code of Canada does prohibit various forms of gambling, including: *keeping a* *common gaming or betting house* (s. 201, CCC), *betting or bookmaking* (s. 202), *placing bets on behalf of others* (s. 203), *promoting lotteries* (s. 206), and *cheating at play* (s. 209). Like illegal drug activities, there appears to be a link between gambling and other forms of criminal and deviant activity, such as drug and alcohol abuse, prostitution, and organized crime.

The UCR statistics for 1998 show a total recorded number of 443 instances of illegal gaming and betting, for a rate of 1.5 per 100 000 Canadians. This signified an increase of 4 percent from 1997. It is unlikely that these figures give a true picture of the criminal activity and social costs associated with gambling and dependance on it. Adult males were more likely to be problem gamblers than were women, yet those women involved in it were more likely to be young, single, unemployed, and undereducated.[36] The Criminal Intelligence Service Canada (CSIS) has initiated a national illegal gambling initiative in partnership with the Ontario Illegal Gaming Enforcement Unit. This partnership reported that in Ontario in 1998, 495 people were charged with 878 gaming-related offences.[37]

## Theoretical Explanations of Crimes against the Public Order

The radical criminology perspectives outlined in Chapter 9 contend that behaviours are deemed to be deviant or criminal by definition. Crimes against the public order are seen by many as examples of *conflict crimes*, or those behaviours around which there is much controversy within society as to their acceptance. Social conflict criminology would contend that laws against behaviours such as prostitution, gambling, and substance abuse are made by the powerful segment of society to ensure the subordination of those who engage in these activities. Feminist criminology, for example, would propose that, in the case of prostitution, women are conditioned to be subservient to men and are transformed into commodities to be bought and sold.

Many of the other social problem theories are useful to explain public order crimes. Refer to the differential association theory in Chapter 8; how can the crimes of prostitution and drug use be explained in terms of learned behaviour brought on through peer pressure? Similarly, social control theory, with its emphasis on strong bonds between the individual and the social order, might be applicable when explaining the criminal behaviour of bored and unfocused youth. Weak attachments to the family early on in life because of dysfunction within the home can compel many youth to flee and find refuge in the street, where prostitution and drug abuse are available options.

Individual responsibility theories can be seen to apply to public order crimes as well. For example, is it possbile that dependancy on alcohol and drugs has a genetic basis? Are addictive personality types passed on from generation to generation? Chapter 5 looks at some genetic roots of crime, while Chapter 6 examines theories of personality and asks whether there are certain personlity types that are predisposed to certain types of criminal behaviour. For example, does low self-esteem, poor self-image, and anxiety result in a personality that is prone to addiction?

PART 3
326
**Crime in the Modern
World and the
Response to It**

# Summary

Canada's police-reported crime rate for 1998 was the lowest since 1979. In fact, the crime rate has been decreasing for 7 years in this country and fell 4 percent between 1997 and 1998. All provinces reported a decline in their crime rate, with the exception of Newfoundland (+3%) and Saskatchewan (+2%). Of the 2.5 million Criminal Code incidents reported, violent crimes constituted 12 percent, property crimes 56 percent, and other offences such as prostitution, gaming and betting, and disturbing the peace 32 percent.

Given this look at the incidence of crime reported and counted in Canada, the question that remains, especially for criminologists is, why? Why do people feel compelled to violate our laws? How can this understanding of the root causes of criminal and deviant behaviour assist those who design and implement policies to combat crime? Should their efforts be focused on targeting the individual offender, seeking to "cure"him of his criminal "sickness?" Or should they look instead to the challenging social realities that so many offenders seem to have experienced and attempt to rectify them? Chapter 11 examines some recent legislative and policy initiatives undertaken in Canada to address crime. Nevertheless, there are no simple answers, and, despite the current downward trend, it is certain that crime and criminals will always be with us.

## Discussion Questions

1. This book emphasizes a social problems versus social responsibility theme. Which perspective best explains the reality of crime in this country? Is one perspective more appropriate when considering violent crime? Property crime? Crime against the public order?
2. Which of the categories of crime discussed in this chapter do you think has the most accurate crime count? Why?
3. From a study of the incidence of crime and of crime rates discussed in this chapter, do you feel that Canadians should fear the spread of crime? Why or why not?
4. How does the definition of a crime affect the counting of it? How do police enforcement activities affect the count?

## Weblinks

**www.statcan.ca/english/Pgdb/State/justic.htm**
Statistics Canada. National statistics on crime, victims, suspects, criminals, police, and the courts.

**www.canada.justice.gc.ca/en/ps/rs/index.html**
Federal Department of Justice. Research reports, statistical reports, and fact sheets on a variety of criminal justice issues.

**www.sgc.gc.ca/ehome.htm**
Solicitor General of Canada. National statistics on corrections, policing, and parole.

**www.acjnet.org/acjeng.html**
Access to Justice Network (ACJNet). ACJNet is an electronic community that brings together people, information, statistics, and educational resources surrounding Canadian justice and legal issues.

## CHAPTER 11

# Criminology and Social Policy

While the justice system is necessary to hold offenders accountable for their actions, it is only part of the solution to crime. A better solution is to prevent crime in the first place.

—NATIONAL CRIME PREVENTION COUNCIL[1]

Young people face a bewildering number of choices, or pathways, some positive, some negative. With little guidance and even less experience, they're forced to make critical choices about countless issues. And, not surprisingly, they often make bad choices.

—BARBARA HALL, CHAIR, NATIONAL STRATEGY ON COMMUNITY SAFETY[2]

## LEARNING OUTCOMES

After reading this chapter, you should be able to:

- Distinguish between the social problems approach and the social responsibilities approach to crime control

- Recognize and understand the various types of crime-control strategies

- Relate various crime-control strategies to recent Canadian crime-control policy initiatives

- Discuss the strengths and weaknesses of these and other recent Canadian crime-control policies

IMPORTANT TERMS

public policy

social policy

social epidemiology

nurturant strategy

protection/avoidance strategy

deterrence strategy

*Kriminalpolitik*

IMPORTANT LEGISLATION AND GROUPS

Firearms Act

National Strategy on Community Safety and Crime Prevention

National Crime Prevention Council

Crime Prevention through Environmental Design

Youth Criminal Justice Act

# Introduction

In the study of crime, as in many other areas, life often imitates art. On September 7, 1996, rapper Tupak Shakur, well known for his starring role in the movie *Poetic Justice,* was gunned down after leaving a Mike Tyson fight in Las Vegas. He died in hospital one week after being attacked. Shakur's violent past included a shooting that injured two off-duty police officers, a conviction on sodomy charges,[3] and a previous mugging, during which the rapper was shot four times. The mugging occurred in 1994 as Shakur was awaiting sentencing after being convicted of assault and battery in an attack on his former film director, Allen Hughes.[4] During his brief rise to stardom, Shakur's brand of "gangsta rap" was condemned by some, who charged that Shakur's violent lyrics had led a youth to kill a state trooper.

Six months after Shakur died, the Notorious B.I.G., or Biggie Smalls—another of gangsta rap's best known entertainers—was killed in a hail of gunfire. The 24-year-old B.I.G., whose given name was Christopher Wallace, was shot shortly after midnight on March 9, 1997, as he sat in the passenger seat of a GMC Suburban at a red light in downtown Los Angeles. He died in hospital a short time later. B.I.G., a former drug dealer and street hustler from New York, had burst on the gangsta rap scene in 1994 with his million-selling album *Ready to Die.*

About the time B.I.G. died, another infamous rapper, Snoop Doggy Dogg, and his bodyguard McKinley Lee, were acquitted of murder charges in the 1993 slaying of Phillip Woldermariam. Woldermariam, a member of the Venice Shoreline Crips, had been shot twice in the back after meeting with Snoop (whose birth name is Calvin Broadus). Others like Snoop have profited mightily by selling images of urban violence to mainstream youth. As a result of highly lucrative album sales, Snoop had no problem posting a $2 million bond following his arrest.[5] A $25 million wrongful death suit filed by Woldermariam's family was settled out of court in late 1996 for an undisclosed sum.

The violent exploits of gangsta rappers is replete with other examples. A few years before Shakur died, Flavor Flav (William Drayton), a singer with the group Public Enemy, was arrested for firing a .38-caliber pistol at a neighbour. By the time of Flav's arrest, Ice-T's song *Cop Killer* had been blamed in the 1992 shooting deaths of two police officers who were ambushed and killed by four juveniles. The juveniles continued to sing *Cop Killer* lyrics following their arrest.[6] *Body Count,* the Time-Warner album on which *Cop Killer* appears, was shipped to stores in a miniature body bag.

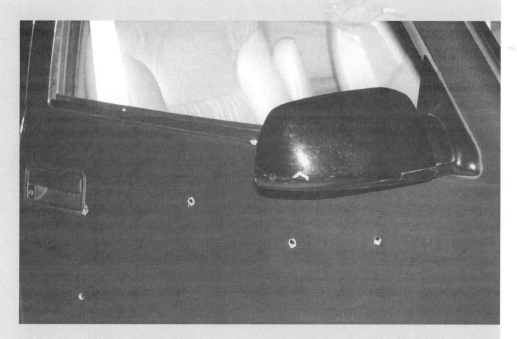

The car in which gangsta rapper Biggie Smalls, known as the Notorious B.I.G., was shot and killed in 1997. Some claim that violent themes in "ghetto rap" lead to crime. What do you think? *Mike Meadows/AP/Wide World Photos.*

One year later, rapper Dr. Dre (a.k.a. Andre Young) directed an 18-minute video of a Snoop performance called *Murder Was the Case.* Dre said he wanted to package the video with Oliver Stone's *Natural Born Killers.*[7] *Murder* and *Killers* were both quickly criticized by law enforcement organizations, parents' groups, and political leaders, who decried the lyrics of gangsta music.[8] Some radio stations began banning violent rap music soon after.

Gangsta rap and "hip hop" music have been condemned by many who claim that the lyrics promote antisocial and violent behaviour. But whether gangsta rap is indeed a cause of crime or merely a quasi-poetic rendering of the social conditions characteristic of many inner-city communities today, is less than clear. The real problems, some claim, lie outside rap music, not within it. Gangsta rap supporters suggest that rap may be the wake-up call needed to raise public awareness, thereby doing more to reduce violence than any government-sponsored program.

It should be noted that there is a current trend toward seeing rap and hip hop music as vehicles for social change. Groups such as Dead Prez, The Coup, and Public Enemy, for example, condemn sweat shops and the use of child labour.

# Crime Control and Public Policy

Pressure by some public groups to investigate the possible behavioural consequences of rap music in the hope that lawmakers will enact some sort of legislative control over the airing of offensive lyrics is one way that public policy can be influenced. Some understanding of how public policy—especially crime-control policy—is created is

Public policy
government-formulated
directives made on
behalf of the public
good to solve a problem
or achieve an end.

essential to the study of criminology. Before we consider a number of current public policies in the criminal justice area, a definition of the term *public policy* is in order. **Public policy** can be defined as "those standing directives, formulated by public organizations, on behalf of the public good"[9] or "a course of action that government takes in an effort to solve a problem or to achieve an end."[10] Other definitions contend that public policy is an expression of meaning: "A policy statement in the criminal justice system constitutes a declaration of social value, and it is upon the basis of the declared value that subsequent decisions are shaped."[11] Social values, in turn, are defined as ideals, customs, or institutions that society regards either positively (such as freedom) or negatively (such as cruelty). There are various types of public policy. Descriptors such as "social," "fiscal," "housing," "health," and "economic" can all be attached to the word "policy." Generally, policy dealing with issues of crime and its control fall under the rubric of social policy, which can be defined as policy "concerned with the betterment of social life, the amelioration of social ills, and the allocation of public money to accomplish that end."[12]

Analysts of public policy have observed that policies undergo five stages in their development[13]:

1. identification of the problem;
2. agenda setting or the prioritization of problems;
3. policy formation;
4. program implementation; and
5. program evaluation and reassessment.

The issue of policy-making in criminal justice in Canada has only recently become an area of concentrated interest for the field of criminology. There is debate within Canadian criminology circles as to the impact of criminological research on the development of public crime policy. As John Ekstedt and Curt Griffiths have noted, "Public policy-making in areas of critical social awareness has taken on the atmosphere of political 'campaigns' with all the attention to the marketing of ideas, the testing of public reaction, and the selling of policy positions normally associated with an election process. Governments seek to promote policies that can contribute to the common good without resulting in political disruption."[14] The outline in Box 11.1 illustrates this process by examining legislation introduced to address the public's concern with impaired driving. Others have made the comment that, "As all criminologists know, criminality is decided as much by legal and political authorities, and by their strategies of criminalization, enforcement, and control, as by criminals themselves."[15]

## Crime-Control Philosophies Today

Today's policy response to crime is twin pronged. One prong, that of crime control, defines crime as an issue of individual responsibility. The other sees crime and criminal behaviour as resulting from poor social conditions and dysfunctional social structures. In Chapter 1, we termed the first prong the "social responsibility perspective," while the second approach was called the "social problems perspective."

# The Birth of a Criminal Justice Policy in Canada

BOX 11.1

## Conception

*Behavioural Event Example*: Increase in reported incidence of drinking and driving and associated costs

## Gestation

Interested group (response from domain of public-at-large) critical mass established

*Bureaucratic Response*
- report
- control
- increase resources
- provide legal restraints

*Media Response*
- report
- sensationalize
- editorialize

*Political Response*
- reduce threat to political stability
- satisfy interests of public servants
- maintain equilibrium in government services (e.g., competition among ministries to obtain additional resources)
- respond to issue through media

## Birth

*Public Policy Example*: The government announces that it will establish a major initiative to combat drinking and driving. One million dollars will be committed through the Ministry of Health and the Attorney General. A director will be appointed to coordinate program development. Completion of "gestation" period requires:

1. the interest of bureaucracy
2. continuing (and mounting) pressure from groups that are (or appear to be) representatives of the public-at-large
3. continuing attention of the media
4. perceived threat to political stability

## Growth

Procedures for policy implementation established

*Education*
For example, good school programs on drinking and driving, including participation of law-enforcement and other agencies

*Law*
For example, increasing civil and criminal sanctions

*Regulation*
For example, "tightening up" on criteria to obtain a driver's licence

*Enforcement*
For example, breath-analysis testing, roadside checks; methods for monitoring of policy outcomes established

*Research*
Continuing data gathering and analysis of drinking and driving

*Program Evaluation*
Measuring cost-effectiveness and program efficiency in relation to program objectives

ENERGY SUSTAINED BEYOND INITIAL RESPONSE  ⟶

ENERGY NOT SUSTAINED
BEYOND INITIAL RESPONSE
⟶
No change in public policy or
bureaucratic energy devoted to the issue

SOURCE: John Ekstedt, "Canadian Justice Policy," in Margaret A. Jackson and Curt T. Griffiths, *Canadian Criminology Perspectives on Crime and Criminality,* Second Edition (Toronto: Harcourt Brace),1995, p. 309.

PART 3
332
**Crime in the Modern
World and the
Response to It**

Each of these perspectives sees the root causes of crime very differently and dictates a different approach to its resolution. Our American neighbours, for example, have embraced the social responsibility perspective, which is clearly reflected in their current criminal justice policies. The Americans have been "waging a war" on crime, criminals, and drugs since 1980, resulting in such legislation as the Comprehensive Crime Control Act (1984), the Omnibus Anti-Drug Abuse Act (1988), and the Violent Crime Control and Law Enforcement Act (1994). All of these pieces of legislation introduced harsher penalties and increased law enforcement powers. Currently, policies at both the state and federal level are becoming more and more focused on strict enforcement of existing laws and on strict punishments.[16] Prisons are being built apace, while tough legislation that will fill even more prisons is being passed at a feverish pitch. Americans are pushing their political representatives for the creation of conservative policy tools to deal with crime and the fear it engenders. At last count, there were some 1.8 million people incarcerated in the United States, or about 600 per 100 000 population (1 100 per 100 000 adult males!) In fact, the United States now imprisons more people than any other country in the world, and inmate populations continue to increase by 50 000 to 80 000 per year.[17]

Detractors of such "get-tough" policies claim that they may not provide the solution sought by those advocating them. They argue that those crime-control strategies that attempt to resolve the root causes of crime are more effective in the long run. "We know full well that the most serious and intractable types of crime have their roots in the very child welfare problems that are neglected as we trash through one ineffective war on crime after another," says one American commentator. "Political support for nurturant programs might be obtainable," he argues, "if we could reverse the vicious cycle of media sensationalism, short-sighted policy, and public impatience that encourages ineffective 'quick fixes' for crime."[18]

By way of contrast, the history of criminal justice policy in Canada is largely based on the social problems perspective. The "get-tough" approach to crime control has been decried by the current federal government and others as purely reactive and failing to address the underlying causes of crime and criminality. According to the former Federal Minister of Justice Allan Rock, "We do not think for a moment that violent crime is going to be resolved in this society by tinkering with statutes or changing Acts. The fact of the matter is that the criminal justice system itself is not going to end violent crime. It only deals with the consequences of the underlying social problems. It is crime prevention that must have at least the equal focus of the House of Commons."[19]

By addressing social problems and the need for improvements in the social infrastructure, the social problems perspective takes a *proactive* rather than *reactive* approach to the reality of crime. Within this context, recent Canadian crime policy initiatives have stressed crime prevention strategies. In a report entitled, *Working Together for Safer Communities*, written by the National Crime Prevention Council of the Federal Justice Department and Solicitor General of Canada, the following conclusion is presented: "While the justice system is necessary to hold offenders accountable for their actions, it is only part of the solution to crime. A better solution is to prevent crime in the first place. Each year Canadians pay billions of dollars for policing,

Prison weight-lifting bans, popular in some states, reflect a growing frustration with unsuccessful crime-control policies. Should recreational opportunities in prison be reduced? *Steve Lehman/SABA Press Photos, Inc.*

private security, courts, corrections and insurance. Canadians need to invest more time, effort and resources to deal with the social, personal and situational factors that lead to crime. The social development approach finds ways to help society deal with the underlying factors that determine community safety and result in crime."[20]

One new aspect of the social problems approach is its recasting in terms of social epidemiology. In terminology akin to the old social pathology approach of the Chicago school, some contemporary politicians and criminologists now view crime and the conditions that create it in terms of a disease model.[21] The word *epidemiology* refers to the study of epidemics and diseases, and the phrase **social epidemiology** has come to mean the study of social epidemics and diseases of the social order. Hence, the social epidemiologic approach holds that crime arises from festering conditions that promote social ills, and that individuals caught in an environment within which crime may be communicated display symptoms of this disease and suffer from its maladies. Crime becomes an illness, a social malady, but one that can be cured if the necessary resources could be dedicated to its treatment and eradication. Such thinkers advance solutions based on what is, in effect, a public health model. In keeping with the old health adage that "an ounce of prevention is worth of pound of cure," crime as a disease becomes a new kind of social problem—one that shifts responsibility for law violations away from individuals "afflicted" with criminality and toward the society that is ultimately responsible for their control.

**Social epidemiology** the study of social epidemics and diseases of the social order.

PART 3
334
**Crime in the Modern
World and the
Response to It**

Advocates of this "public health" approach have developed programs to deal with a number of criminal behaviours, most notably violence. In the words of the Pacific Center for Violence Prevention, located in the United States:

> Violence is a public health issue, and violence prevention is a public health mandate. Violence results in premature death, serious injury and disability in populations. These are the concern of public health agencies and advocates. The public health model suggests that efforts to prevent violence, like those to prevent injury and infectious diseases, should consider the interaction between host, agent and environment. The host for violent injury is the person who is at risk of harming or being harmed by himself or herself or another person. The agent for violent injury is the weapon, be it a gun, knife, fist, foot, broken bottle or baseball bat. The environment for violent injury has three components: physical, economic, and social. Examples of the physical environment of violent injury are dark streets, abandoned buildings, bedrooms, bar rooms and work sites. The economic environment of violent injury includes limited social, recreational and educational activities, high levels of poverty and unemployment, particularly among young males. The social environment of violent injury includes fear, hopelessness, sexism and racism. Comprehensive programs to prevent violence cannot ignore the interaction among host, agent and environment. Within the public health approach, efforts to prevent violence necessitate identifying and addressing the root causes of violence ...[22]

In Canada, the recent introduction of various pieces of legislation dealing with the registration and monitoring of firearms is an example of the public health model of crime prevention. Advocates of the gun control legislation believe that by more closely controlling the sale and use of firearms, violence using firearms can be controlled without first having to eradicate all the underlying social issues that contribute to gun violence. In other words, in the analogy of the public health approach, gun-related violence is symptomatic of a number of other issues, including socioeconomic factors and substance abuse, just as tuberculosis and venereal disease have been linked to poverty. The public health approach has been successful in controlling tuberculosis and venereal disease without really affecting the underlying contributing factor—namely poverty. In the same way, it is believed that gun control legislation will address violence by "treating" the symptom—gun ownership—without addressing the causes.[23] Box 11.2 provides an overview of recent Canadian gun control legislation.

There is much debate surrounding both gun control legislation, in particular, and, more generally, the public health approach to crime. Canadian gun owners believe that the legislation impinges upon their individual rights and freedoms. It serves only to make criminals out of law-abiding citizens, they argue, without significantly reducing the amount of gun-related violence.[24]

Further, according to Doctors for Integrity in Policy Research, "Treating crime as a disease—the essence of the 'public health' approach to gun violence—is as illogical and ineffectual as the converse, treating disease as a crime. We would mock any criminologist who advocated criminalizing disease by measures such as fines for obesity or jail time for tobacco-related emphysema. We would condemn the police if they invaded bedrooms to ensure the use of condoms in the crusade against AIDS."[25]

# A Brief History of Gun Control Legislation in Canada

BOX 11.2

*1934:*
- First real registration requirement for handguns is created.
- Records identifying the gun owner, the owner's address, and the firearm are required and are kept by the RCMP or police departments.

*1938:*
- Handguns have to be re-registered every 5 years.

*1951:*
- Registry system for handguns is centralized under the RCMP.
- Firearms are now required to have serial numbers.

*1968–1969:*
- Categories of "firearm", "restricted weapon", and "prohibited weapon" are created, allowing specific legislative controls for each category.

*1977:*
- Bill C-51 is enacted and comes into force in 1979.
- Bill C-51 includes requirements for Firearms Acquisition Certificates (FACs) and for Firearms and Ammunition Business Permits, both of which involve the screening of applicants and implementation of record-keeping systems.
- Provinces are given the option of requiring FAC applicants to take a firearms safety course.

*1991–1994:*
- Bill C-17 is enacted in 1991 and comes into force between 1992 and 1994
- Bill C-17 makes changes to the FAC, including:
    - —applicants required to provide a photograph and two references;
    - —mandatory 28-day waiting period for receiving an FAC imposed;
    - —mandatory requirement for safety training imposed;
    - —application form expanded to provide more background information; and
    - —a more detailed screening check of FAC applicants required.
- New requirements in Bill C-17 include:
    - —regulations for firearms dealers; and
    - —clearly defined regulations for the storage, handling, and transportation of firearms. By 1994, FAC applicants are required to demonstrate this by passing a firearms safety course test or receiving certification from a firearms officer.

*1995:*
- Bill C-68 is enacted.
- Major changes include:
    - —the creation of the **Firearms Act,** which removes the administrative and regulatory aspects of the licensing and registration of firearms from the Criminal Code;
    - —the Firearms Act regulates the manufacture, assembly, import, export, transfer, sale, lending, storage, transport, handling, possession, and registration of firearms in Canada;

▶

PART 3
336
**Crime in the Modern
World and the
Response to It**

▶

—the FAC is replaced with a new licensing system requiring licences for possession and acquisition of firearms and to buy ammunition; and

—all firearms, including shotguns and rifles, must be registered.

*1998:*

• The amended Firearms Act is brought into force, to be phased in over the next 5 years.

• Regulations in the Act include:

—all gun owners require a licence to possess or acquire a firearm or to buy ammunition by January 1, 2001. This licence must be renewed every 5 years;

—all firearms must be registered by 2003. To register, an applicant must first have a valid licence or valid FAC;

—safety checks are done on all applicants before a licence is issued;

—new applicants wanting to acquire firearms must take and pass the Firearms Safety Test;

—safe storage regulations require that all firearms be stored unloaded and made inoperable; and

—firearms brought into the country by visitors must be recorded at the point of entry.

SOURCE: Adapted from the Canadian Firearms Centre Web site, www.canadianfirearms.com.

## Types of Crime-Control Strategies

The dichotomous values that underlie modern-day policy-making reflect fundamental differences in philosophical and political orientations.[26] Even so, the range of effective crime-control alternatives available to reformers of any political bent is essentially limited to three types of strategies. These three strategies differ in terms of "strategic focus."[27] That is, they are distinguishable from one another "by whether they attempt to block opportunities for crime, alter the outcome of conscious or unconscious decision-making that precedes a criminal act, or alter the broad strategic style with which people approach many aspects of their lives."[28] The three strategies are

1. Nurturant strategies;
2. Protection/avoidance strategies; and
3. Deterrence strategies.

**Nurturant strategy** a crime-control strategy that attempts to forestall development of criminality by improving early life experiences and channelling child and adolescent development into desirable directions.

**Nurturant strategies** "attempt to forestall development of criminality by improving early life experiences and channeling child and adolescent development" into desirable directions. They "focus on prevention of criminality rather than its remediation or control."[29] Nurturant strategies include increased infant and maternal health care, child care for the working poor, training in parenting skills, enhanced public education, and better programs to reduce the number of unwanted pregnancies.

Nurturant crime-control strategies are largely aimed at improving the social conditions and experiences of youth such as these living in Toronto's Regent Park housing development. Do you think the focus on preventing crime through social development is an effective crime-control approach? *Dick Hemingway.*

A comprehensive crime-control strategy, say some criminologists, would be "a balanced mix of protection/avoidance, deterrence, and nurturant strategies."[30] Achieving the most effective balance in a politically sensitive world, however, is a difficult undertaking. In Canada, many crime-control initiatives emphasize the nurturant approach. Influential political constituencies, however, continue to press for crime-control measures that have protection/avoidance and deterrence strategies as their focus.

**Protection/avoidance strategies** "attempt to reduce criminal opportunities by changing people's routine activities, increasing guardianship, or incapacitating convicted offenders."[31] Incapacitating convicted offenders through incarceration or the use of electronic monitoring would be considered examples of protection strategies. Target hardening or opportunity reduction through the use of architectural design, crime prevention programs such as neighbourhood watch, and increased community policing provide examples of avoidance strategies.

**Deterrence strategies** "attempt to diminish motivation for crime by increasing the perceived certainty, severity, or celerity of penalties."[32] New and tougher laws, quicker trial court processing, harsher punishments, and faster imposition of sentences are all deterrence strategies.

**Protection/avoidance strategy** a crime-control strategy that attempts to reduce criminal opportunities by changing people's routine activities, increasing guardianship, or by incapacitating convicted offenders.

**Deterrence strategy** a crime-control strategy that attempts to diminish motivation for crime by increasing the perceived certainty, severity, or celerity of penalties.

PART 3

338

**Crime in the Modern
World and the
Response to It**

# Recent Crime-Control Policy Initiatives

## The National Strategy on Community Safety and Crime Prevention

In 1993, the Standing Committee on Justice and the Solicitor General tabled a report in Parliament that sent a clear message to the Government of Canada about crime control. It advised that traditional "police, courts, and corrections" approaches to crime and community safety are limited in their scope and stated that "[i]t is time to translate the rhetoric of crime prevention into policies, legislation and programs if we are to make real progress in our attempt to protect Canadians ..."[33]

The federal government responded in 1994 by introducing the **National Strategy on Community Safety and Crime Prevention.**[34] The objectives of the National Strategy are:

- to promote the integrated action of key governmental and nongovernmental partners to reduce crime and victimization;
- to assist communities in developing and implementing community-based solutions that contribute to crime and victimization, particularly as they affect children, youth, women, and Aboriginal people; and
- to increase public awareness of and support for effective approaches to crime prevention.

Referred to as "crime prevention through social development," this initiative is emblematic of a nurturant strategy.

Phase I of the National Strategy (1994–1997) set the groundwork for its national implementation. The creation of the **National Crime Prevention Council,** made up of 25 volunteers including child development experts, community advocates, academics, social workers, lawyers, police officers, doctors, and business people, facilitated the development of a plan to deal with the underlying causes of crime. With a mission to "develop strategies to empower individuals and their communities to improve their safety, security and well-being," the council identified children and youth as its immediate focus for a national crime-control policy. It concluded that the failure of Canadians to invest in the social development of children and youth has had serious implications in the areas of criminal activity and victimization. The council identified a number of factors that place children and youth at risk of engaging in criminal activity, including child poverty, inadequate living conditions, inconsistent and uncaring parenting, childhood traumas such as physical and sexual abuse, family breakdown, racism and other forms of discrimination, difficulties in school, delinquent friends, and living situations where there is alcohol, drug, and other kinds of substance abuse. It concluded that what is needed in Canada is "a comprehensive approach to systemic crime prevention through social development" to best address "the combination of social, systemic, personal and situational factors which place children and youth at risk and contribute to crime."

Building on the work of the National Crime Prevention Council, Phase II of the National Strategy was launched in 1998. From 1998 to 2003, the federal government will provide $32 million per year for crime prevention initiatives across the country, targeting those initiative that focus on children, youth, women, Aboriginal persons, and other at-risk groups, such as seniors, persons with disabilities, and ethno-cultural and other minority groups. The funding is to be allocated to three promotional streams. The bulk of the annual $32 million will be devolved to the Safer Communities Initiative ($28.8 million), under which there are four additional programs. The Community Mobilization Program ($17 million per year) is designed to fund local, community-based crime prevention activities. The Crime Prevention Investment Fund allocates $7.5 million annually to selected Canada-wide demonstration projects as well as research and evaluation of innovative crime prevention efforts. The Crime Prevention Partnership Program provides $2.3 million per year to support the involvement of national and international nongovernmental organizations that can directly contribute to community crime prevention efforts. The fourth program, the Business Action Program on Crime Prevention, supports the involvement of business and professional associations in corporate/community partnerships to prevent crime through its allocation of $2 million per year. The remaining $3.2 million is earmarked for the Promotion and Public Education Program, created to increase public awareness and assist those needing information on crime prevention solutions, and for the National Crime Prevention Centre, located within the Department of Justice and responsible for implementing the National Strategy in partnership with the Department of the Solicitor General of Canada. Box 11.3 highlights crime prevention projects from across Canada that have received funding from the Community Mobilization Program.

# Canadian Crime Prevention Projects

**BOX 11.3**

### ALBERTA

#### *Aboriginal Students (Stay in School) Project*

This group will provide spiritual, mental, emotional, and physical tools designed to help youth become upstanding citizens in the community. Keeping Aboriginal youth in school will not only help youth in their academic education, but also strengthen their dreams and hopes for the future. Ongoing support networks will be established with families, youth, and communities. Among these, elders, mentors, and role models will act as liaisons between young people, their families, and their schools.

> Métis Calgary Family Services Society
> 33086, 3919 Richmond Road SW
> Calgary, AB  T3E 7E2

### BRITISH COLUMBIA

#### *A Community with a Future*

The Whitevalley Community Resource Centre (WCRC) Society plans to focus on consensus building and changing community attitudes by incorporating the resiliency/asset

▶

PART 3
340
**Crime in the Modern
World and the
Response to It**

building model into the following four components: a Community Pride Campaign intends to decrease the amount of vandalism by fostering positive interactions between the business community and youth; a Know Your Neighbour component will improve the personal security of women and families by encouraging positive changes in community norms; workshops, employment, and networking opportunities will provide community youth with the opportunity to increase their personal skills; and the Zero Tolerance for Family Violence Program, initiated in 1995, will receive additional volunteer training, support, and counselling.

> Whitevalley Community Resource Society (WCRC) Society
> 2114 Shuswap Avenue
> P.O. Box 661, Lumby, BC  V0E 2G0

### MANITOBA
*Community Advocacy and Family Programs Development Project*
This project is composed of three distinct segments intended to provide support to recently released incarcerated individuals and their families through a drop-in centre approach. Libary Materials Development will provide participants with access to materials regarding Community Ministry with Ex-Offenders (CMEO) projects and provide a resource for volunteers. Family Development and Referral will offer leisure, life, and educational skills to participants and encourage their participation in self-help groups. The Community Support and Advocacy Service will focus on community outreach, volunteer training, circles of support for participants, volunteer development, and the tracking and evaluation of participants.

> Community Ministry with Ex-Offenders (CMEO)
> 700 Notre Dame Avenue
> Winnipeg, MB  R3E 0L7

### NOVA SCOTIA
*Activity-Based Parenting Skills Group for Men (Pilot Program)*
The goal of this program is to change the cycle of neglect and abuse by teaching men in conflict with the law skills that will help them become conscientious parents. Each session will have an academic component, a non-competitive activity to teach men how to play with children in a healthy, responsible manner, as well as a nutrition component.

> John Howard Society of Nova Scotia (The)
> 1657 Barrington Street, Suite 220
> Halifax, NS  B3N 2P8

### ONTARIO
*SKETCH The Working Arts Studio for Street-Involved and Homeless Youth*
The project will provide arts programming and job- and life-skills training for youth who are or have been street involved or homeless. SKETCH will integrate job- and life-skills development with artistic disciplines including visual art, drama, music, and creative writing to restore self-worth and invigorate participants' lives with purpose and direction. SKETCH will provide opportunities for street-involved youth to meet and work with community artists and seek to empower youth by: building self-esteem; building jobs and life skills; and encouraging youth to make healthy lifestyle choices and restore hope for the future beyond the streets.

▶ IMAGO on behalf of SKETCH
1087 Queen Street West
Toronto, ON  M6J 1H3

**QUEBEC**
*Alternative suspension: Une vision évolutive de l'école*
This project, which involves an alternative to suspension and a new approach to school,
will offer a program of activities for students in the secondary schools in a Montreal
neighbourhood who have been temporarily barred from classes, whether occasionally or
repeatedly. The activities will include problem-solving and active listening workshops
and group discussions on topics such as addiction and effective communication; also on
the agenda are trips to businesses and help with homework.

YMCA de Montréal
1441, rue Drummond
Montréal, QC  H3G 1W3

**YUKON TERRITORY**
*Family Fighting Group*
Family Fighting Group is an 8-week group for children aged 7–12 who have experienced
or witnessed family violence. The primary goals are to lower the anxiety levels of children, seek to validate the children's experiences, help them learn coping skills, teach them
healthy ways of resolving conflicts, help to develop positive social skills, and provide parents with an understanding of the effects of violence on their children.

Dawson Shelter Society
Box 784
Dawson City, YT  Y0B 1G0

SOURCE: Adapted from National Crime Prevention Centre Web site, www.crime-prevention.org, with permission.

## Crime Prevention Through Environmental Design

*Forget alarms. Forget stiff prison sentences. Even forget about police presence. One of the
best deterrents against crime is called CPTED.*

–PEEL REGIONAL POLICE SERVICE[35]

Indicative of the protection/avoidance approach to crime control is the notion of
**Crime Prevention Through Environmental Design** (CPTED). In 1971, C. Ray Jeffery's
work entitled *Crime Prevention through Environmental Design* introduced the concept
to North America.[36] It is based on the concept of *defensible space*, which holds that
crime can be prevented through proper residential and commercial architectural design
and the layout of the physical environment. The concept was introduced to Canada in
the early 1980s by the Peel Regional Police Service and has since been endorsed by a
great number of police services throughout Canada, including the RCMP, many of
whom have trained CPTED officers.

PART 3
342
Crime in the Modern
World and the
Response to It

The concept of CPTED has not been formally incorporated into any federal or provincial crime-control policies but has been widely incorporated into crime prevention plans at the municipal level. Local governmental crime prevention plans in Toronto and Edmonton include CPTED concepts, as does the mandate of the Peel Regional Police Service in Ontario. The municipalities of North York and Vancouver have both incorporated CPTED into their building codes and zoning bylaws. Its application is apparent in the design of various towns (Tumbler Ridge, B.C.), parks (Lethbridge, Alberta), shopping malls, schools, and public libraries.[37] A CPTED case study of the public library in Kitchener, Ontario is illustrated in Box 11.4.

## Kitchener Public Library: An Interior CPTED Case Study

BOX 11.4

### The Traditional Response

It had come to this. Police officers were again being asked to do permanent foot patrols through the main downtown branch of the Kitchener Public Library. If this weren't drastic enough, library officials wanted to build a police phone-in facility inside the main branch, in the faint hope that police officers would spend more time in this facility than their own major police division located just next door.

The incident that resulted in these demands occurred in the summer of 1995 when the library's third-floor stacks were used by an offender to approach a 15-year-old girl then masturbate and ejaculate in front of her. This was the most outrageous of the reported incidents, which included five other indecent acts, five thefts, one break-in, and seventeen miscellaneous calls for service.

### The CPTED Response

Crime Prevention Through Environmental Design (CPTED) is based on the belief that the proper design and effective use of the built environment can lead to a reduction in the fear and incidence of crime as well as an improvement in the quality of life. The conceptual thrust of the CPTED program is the manipulation of the physical environment for the purpose of influencing certain desired human behaviours. By exploiting lost opportunities for natural surveillance, access control, and territoriality, crime and loss are kept to a minimum through effective and efficient design.

With respect to the library, the layout of the book shelves paralleled the main third-floor corridor. This effectively limited natural surveillance of the book stacks to the first row of books and two cross aisles formed by regular breaks in the stacks. It also limited the natural surveillance potential of all corridor-based activities. These included a very busy elevator, stairway, and staffed information desk.

Adding to this problem was a natural surveillance void and "blinker" effect caused by an open second-floor ceiling along the right side of the stacks and the insular use of study carrels located along the rear.

An additional problem resulted from a permanently propped open and unalarmed exit door at the rear of the stacks. This provided superior escape opportunities for offenders while facilitating their unmonitored approach.

▶

### The CPTED Solution

In order to address this problem, it was necessary to provide for and exploit a number of lost opportunities for natural surveillance and access control. This necessitated:

- turning the library stacks perpendicular to the public corridor and circulation desk;
- installing a large mirror on the blank corridor wall opposite the circulation desk and newly arranged stacks;
- rearranging the study carrels from an unbroken, continuous row of units located at the end of the book stacks to a series of strategically placed, independent units that maximized natural surveillance of the aisles in the newly arranged stacks; and
- designating the secondary, rear stairwell as a fire route so that the door could be signed as a fire exit in the closed position and retrofitted with an alarm.

The first two recommendation were required to facilitate natural surveillance opportunities for staff and persons using the busy corridor that connects the old section of the library to the new.

The last recommendation was required to limit escape routes and increase the conspicuousness of anyone entering or leaving this area by "forcing" them to walk past a staffed area or sound a door alarm.

In addition to these measures, computerized catalogue terminals were placed near the cross aisles to generate activity and provide for natural surveillance.

### Net Impact

The net impact of the recommendations was the development of an easily monitored area which not only took full advantage of the many previously unexploited opportunities for natural surveillance but limited unsupervised access both into and out of the stacks.

### Cost

The project involved the movement and temporary storage of some 300 000 books. It was completed at an estimated cost of between $5 000 to $10 000 using part-time staff over a four-month period. Described as a "master stroke of coordination", it also involved partitioning off sections of the stacks to accommodate a coincident lighting upgrade that was undertaken at this time.

### Results

Police occurrences to the library as a whole dropped 39.5 percent from a high of 29 in 1995, the year of the CPTED audit, to 19 occurrences in 1997, the first full year after the CPTED retrofit. While impressive for a downtown library, the statistical drop understates the improvements to the problem area.

In this regard, there were no new sex offences in the problem area or the remainder of the library during 1997. In addition, staff noted that there "hadn't been any incidents" of any description to this area "for a good, long while."

Staff further noted a number of significant improvements to the way the area functioned. These included:

- wider aisles that resulted in improved mobility for people using strollers, scooters, wheelchairs, or staff carts; and
- improved lighting, signage and book display, particularly on the bottom shelves, and modest gain in shelf space.

▶

PART 3

344

Crime in the Modern
World and the
Response to It ▶

Collectively, this resulted in a "greater sense of space" and a "more open" and "dynamic" feel. It also resulted in comments that this section of the library was "easier to read," "felt more secure when working at the back", and "looked like a whole different place."

Perhaps the best comments came from Margaret Walshe, the Chief Executive Officer of the library. Ms. Walshe stated that the results were "well worth the investment of time and staff." Further, the lessons learned from this experience are now being applied to the design of new branches and representatives from neighbouring library boards have visited the library and were very impressed with the redesign.

SOURCE: Adapted from Peel Regional Police Crime Prevention Services Web site, www.peelpolice.on.ca, with permission of the Peel Regional Police.

Traditional "target hardening" crime prevention approaches have employed physical or artificial barriers such as locks, alarms, fences, gates, etc., to deny access to a crime target. The CPTED model recognizes that these traditional methods often tend to place constraints on use, access, and enjoyment of the "hardened" environment. As an alternative, CPTED focuses on *natural surveillance* (keeping potential intruders under observation), natural access control (decreasing the opportunity for crime), and *territorial reinforcement* (creating or extending the sphere of influence through physical design to develop a sense of ownership). Further, the CPTED model insists upon an assessment of the physical environment to be protected. The designated purpose of the space, the social, cultural, legal, or physical definitions that suggest desired and acceptable behaviours for it, and the appropriateness of the design in the productive use of the space are included in this assessment.[38]

The Crime Prevention Association of New Brunswick identifies the following CPTED tactics that can be employed in a variety of settings[39]:

*Neighbourhoods:*
- Minimize the number of entry and exit points on a block.
- Design roadways to discourage through-traffic.
- Maximize residents' ability to view public spaces.
- Encourage residents' use of public spaces.
- Provide appropriate lighting for streets, paths, alleys, and parks.
- Encourage residents to watch over each other.

*Houses:*
- Clearly delineate private property (e.g., yard, driveway) from public space (e.g., street, sidewalk) using shrubbery, alternate paving stone colour, and changes in grade.
- Use solid-core exterior doors.
- Use solid door frames with proper strike plates.

*Apartment Buildings:*
- Provide common spaces to ensure tenant interaction.
- Minimize the number of units sharing a common entrance.
- Equip shared entrances with an intercom.
- Ensure hallways are well-lit.
- Provide children's area that can be easily observed.
- Provide windows in laundry rooms that allow for surveillance in laundry rooms.

*Parking Lots and Garages:*
- Avoid enclosed, underground, multistorey garages.
- Install bright lights over driving lanes and parking spaces.
- Use paint to increase light levels.
- Control access and egress with automatic doors and gates.
- Avoid pillars and recesses that may hide offenders.

*Public Spaces:*
- Encourage use by legitimate users.
- Avoid locating dark and/or hidden areas near activity nodes.
- Install appropriate lighting.
- Avoid locating covered outdoor areas where loitering may be a problem.

Advocates of CPTED stress that it should only be considered part of a comprehensive approach to crime prevention. Modifications to the physical environment will only be effective if they complement community policing efforts and social programs that address some of the root causes of crime. One of CPTED's most ardent supporters, Greg Saville, claims that, "On the one hand, a CPTED that pretends to solve problems with physical designs alone, while ignoring the psychological response of those living there, is doomed to failure. … On the other hand, also doomed is a socio-psychological CPTED that ignores all the advances we have learned in architecture and urban design since the 1970s."[40] Saville insists that there must be a balance struck between the physical aspects of CPTED, such as access control, natural surveillance, etc., with psycho-social crime prevention strategies such as community-building, neighbourhood accords, school programs, and community policing. For Saville, initial analysis and diagnosis of the problem is crucial to striking that balance.[41]

## Youth Criminal Justice Act

One example of deterrence strategy, or an attempt to diminish crime by increasing the penalty, is the federal government's proposed **Youth Criminal Justice Act** (YCJA). Mounting public pressure on the government to deal with a perceived skyrocketing in the number of youths involved in crime, especially violent crime, has precipitated the overhaul of the existing Young Offenders Act. Media stories of youth involved in violent incidents have captured headlines across the country. In 1995, an Anglican

PART 3
346
Crime in the Modern
World and the
Response to It

clergyman aged 75 and his 70-year-old wife were beaten to death with beer bottles and a baseball bat at their home near Montreal by 3 boys aged 13, 14, and 15. In 1996, a group of Toronto youths aged 11 to 15 sexually assaulted a 13-year-old girl. In 1998, a 13-year-old girl and her 15-year-old boyfriend were convicted of murdering the girl's mother in Lethbridge, Alberta. Growing incidents of school violence also have the public demanding harsher penalties for young people who commit adult offences: in 1999, a 14-year-old boy and his 13-year-old friend were charged in Winnipeg, Manitoba, with threatening to bring pipe bombs and weapons to their school to get back at a substitute teacher they didn't like, and, in 2000, four students and one instructor were wounded in a knife attack at a high school on the outskirts of Ottawa, Ontario.

The Canadian Centre for Justice Statistics reports that the number of youths aged 12 to 17 charged with Criminal Code offences reached 106 984 in 1998, a rate of 4 363 offences per 100 000 youth.[42] Of those, 21 percent were charged with violent crimes, 51 percent with property crimes, and 29 percent with other Criminal Code offences. While the rate of youths charged with violent crimes fell by 1 percent in 1998 for the third consecutive year, the rate of youths charged with violent crimes remains 77 percent higher than it was a decade ago. The increase in youth violent crime is also markedly greater than that for adults; the adult violent crime rate has increased by 6 percent since 1988. Of those youths charged with violent offences, assault accounted for more than 84 percent of female youths charged and 68 percent of male youths charged. It is common assault that is largely responsible for the increase in youth violent crime, at 67 percent for females and 46 percent for males. By comparison, less than 1 percent of the youths charged with violent crimes in 1998 were charged with homicide. The 56 youths charged with homicide in that year represented 13 percent of all persons so charged. On average, 51 youths per year have been charged with homicide since 1988.

In May 1998, the Government of Canada released a Youth Justice Strategy, a component of which was the replacement of the Young Offenders Act (YOA) with the Youth Criminal Justice Act (YCJA) to more adequately reflect the reality of youth crime in this country. According to Justice Minister Anne McLellan, "Canadians want a youth justice system that protects society and instills values such as accountability, responsibility and respect. They want governments to help prevent youth crime in the first place and make sure that there are meaningful consequences when it occurs."[43]

The Declaration of Principle in the preamble to the proposed YCJA states that the protection of society is the primary objective of the youth justice system and is best achieved through prevention, meaningful consequences for youth crime, and rehabilitation. Moreover, youth would be held accountable for their actions and the consequences would reinforce respect for social values and encourage reparation for harm done to the victim and community. Highlights of the proposed Act include provisions that would

- allow an adult sentence for any youth 14 years or older who is convicted of an offence punishable by more than 2 years in jail, if the Crown applies and the court finds it appropriate in the circumstances;
- expand the offences for which a young person convicted of an offence would be presumed to receive an adult sentence to a new category of a pattern of serious violent offences. At present, only 16- and 17-year-olds accused of murder, attempted murder, manslaughter and aggravated assault are presumed to be subject to adult sentences;

- create an intensive custody and supervision sentence for serious violent offenders who suffer from mental illness, psychological disorder or emotional disturbance that will include an individualized plan for treatment and would require a court to make all decisions regarding release;
- maintain sentence lengths for first-degree murder (10 years) and second-degree murder (7 years);
- allow for and encourage the use of a full range of community-based sentences and effective alternatives to the justice system, such as victim compensation or retribution for youth who commit nonviolent offences;
- promote a constructive role for victims and communities, including ensuring they receive the information they need and that they have opportunities to be involved in the youth justice system (e.g., Victim Impact Statements permitted in youth court);
- permit tougher penalties for adults who willfully fail to comply with an undertaking made to the court to properly supervise youth who have been denied bail and placed in their care;
- permit the publication of names of all youth convicted of a crime who receive an adult sentence. Publication of the names of 14- to 17-year-olds who receive a youth sentence for murder, attempted murder, manslaughter, aggravated sexual assault, or repeat serious violent offences will also be permitted;
- allow the Crown greater discretion in seeking adult sentences and publication of offenders' names;
- give the courts more discretion to receive as evidence voluntary statements by youth to a person in authority, such as a police officer;
- require, in general, that youth be held in custody separately from adults to reduce the risk that they will be exposed to adult criminals;

This editorial cartoon reflects increasing public pressure on the federal government to overhaul the Young Offenders Act. *Ottawa Citizen*, March 12, 1999, p. A17. Reprinted with permission.

PART 3
348
**Crime in the Modern
World and the
Response to It**

- require all periods of custody to be followed by a period of controlled supervision in the community that is equal to one-half of the period of custody imposed, to support safe and effective reintegration; and
- require police to consider all options outside the formal justice system before laying a charge in the case of minor youth offences. The range of options would include verbal warnings from police, informal police diversion programs, and formal programs requiring restitution.

The implementation of the YCJA is part of a 5- to 6-year phase-in of the National Youth Justice Strategy, for which the Government of Canada has committed $206 million for the first 3 years. Critics of the YCJA claim that in an attempt to please everyone, the Act will please no one. Many groups feel that the YCJA is not hard-hitting enough, citing its failure to lower the age range of young offenders to 10 from the current age of 12. The proposed Act would provide considerable discretion in the area of punishment, recognizing that some provinces such as Alberta and Ontario want tougher penalties, while others, including Quebec, tend to rely on less heavy jail sentences for youth. For some, this weakens the YCJA. "If you commit a murder in British Columbia, you should face the same sanctions as in Ontario or anywhere else in the country," argues Reform Party Member of Parliament Chuck Cadman.[44] At the time of writing, the controversial YCJA is still being debated before the all-party Commons Justice Committee. The YCJA has yet to be voted on by the House of Commons and the Senate, and it is an open question whether it will be approved in its present form.

## Can We Solve the Problem of Crime?

In 1956, the European writer H. Bianchi[45] emphasized what he saw as the difference between criminology and what he termed *Kriminalpolitik*. Criminology, said Bianchi, should be considered a "metascience" or "a science of wider scope (than that of criminal law, jurisprudence, criminal justice, or corrections) whose terminology can be used to clarify the conceptions of its subdisciplines. Far from being a mere auxiliary to the criminal law," said Bianchi, "it is therefore superior to it."[46]

**Kriminalpolitik** the political handling of crime, or a criminology-based social policy.

For Bianchi and other writers of the time, the concept of **Kriminalpolitik** referred to the political handling of crime, or—as we might say today—a criminology-based social policy. Bianchi believed that if criminology were to remain pure, it could not afford to sully its hands, so to speak, with political concerns. Today, however, the image esteemed by criminologists and the expectations they hold for their discipline are quite different than they were in Bianchi's time. Many criminologists expect to work hand-in-hand with politicians and policy-makers, forging crime-control agendas based on scientific knowledge and criminological theorizing. Some would say that this change in attitude represents a maturation of the discipline of criminology.

Whether effective crime-control policies can ever be implemented, however, is another question. Central to any discussion of public policy development in Canada is the political reality of the country. Without going into a lot of detail on the impact of our decentralized, federalist political system, suffice it to say that the division of powers between the two levels of government in Canada—federal and provincial/territorial—has a profound impact on the creation and implementation of crime-control policy. Briefly, in criminal justice matters the federal government, through the Parliament of Canada, has exclusive jurisdiction to make criminal laws and set sanctions for their violation. The provinces and territories, on the other hand, are responsible for the implementation of the criminal laws, otherwise known as the administration of justice. There are a number of provincial/territorial statutes, such as those regulating liquor licensing and highway traffic, that are the sole responsibility of each individual provincial/territorial government. Needless to say, there is an overlap between the two governmental jurisdictions in the area of crime control, and, in many cases, joint decision-making mechanisms must be implemented before any policy can be developed—especially federal government initiatives with a national scope. Often referred to as federal/provincial/territorial conferences or task forces, these forums allow federal and provincial/territorial leaders to discuss issues of concern within the area of crime control. For example, the federal government is currently exploring strategies to manage high-risk offenders through potential amendments to the Criminal Code and provincial mental health legislation, through dangerous-offender provisions, and through a variety of mechanisms within the correctional system. The Federal/Provincial/Territorial Task Force on High-Risk and Violent Offenders has been struck to facilitate creation of this policy.

Matters of criminal justice are also dealt with at the municipal level of government. Essentially, municipalities are responsible for the enforcement of all laws and the creation of local bylaws.[47] In this way, a crime-prevention approach taken by a particular municipality through its police service may not necessarily dovetail neatly into crime-control approaches being taken at the provincial or federal levels.[48] In short, crime control is not as simple as implementing a federally developed policy across the country. Each level of government may interpret, implement, or challenge a policy, with the result that its uniform application from coast to coast often takes many years. The cost of a recent crime-control program, Phase II of the National Strategy on Community Safety and Crime Prevention (discussed earlier in the chapter), is shown in Box 11.5. Note some of the related costs listed in the box, such as the estimated annual costs associated with crime in Canada.

## The Costs of This, That, and the Other Things

**BOX 11.5**

- Amount of money invested each year in Phase II of the National Strategy on Community Safety and Crime Prevention: $32 million
- Average annual cost of keeping an offender in a federal institution (1995–96): $50 375
- Estimated annual cost of detaining a young offender (1995–96): $100 000
- Estimated total annual costs associated with crime and the criminal justice system in Canada (1996): $46 billion
- Operating costs of 411 Canadian shelters for abused women (1997–98): $170 million
- Amount that the theft of motor vehicles and their parts cost the insurance industry in Canada in 1996: $600 million
- Estimated costs due to fraudulent insurance claims in Canada in 1994: $1.3 billion

▶

▶

- Spending on justice services in Canada in 1994–95: $10 billion:
  on criminal prosecutions: $258 million;
  on youth corrections: $526 million;
  on legal aid: $646 million;
  on courts: $835 million;
  on adult corrections: $1.9 billion;
  and on police services: $5.8 billion.

- Estimated amount of the illicit street-drug trade in Canada in 1998: $18 billion
- Amount Canadians spent on tobacco products and supplies (1998): $5.8 billion
- Amount Canadians contributed to RRSPs in 1994: $20.9 billion
- Sales by Canadian wholesalers in the computer, packaged software, and electronic alarm system sector in 1996: $24.7 billion
- Amount Canadian consumers spent on food and beverages in 1998: $59.3 billion
- Amount Canadian consumers spent on motor vehicles in 1998: $86.4 billion
- Spending in Canadian retail stores in 1998: $246.8 billion

SOURCE: "National Strategy on Community Safety and Crime Prevention", *Prevention*, vol. 1, no. 1, Autumn 1999. Reprinted with permission of the National Crime Prevention Centre.

## Summary

Efforts to reduce crime, although well intentioned, are fraught with political uncertainties resting largely upon fundamental disagreements within Canadian society itself as to the sources of crime and the most appropriate means of combating it. One author summarizes the contemporary situation this way: "Lack of a unified criminological framework has fostered shortsighted, inconsistent, and ineffective crime-control policies. Theoretical ambiguity made it easier for policymakers to base their decisions on politics rather than science. Lacking a reasonable complete and coherent explanation of the causes of crime, they have been free to shift the focus of crime-control efforts back and forth from individual-level to macro-level causes as the political pendulum swung from right to left. This erratic approach hindered crime-control efforts and fed the desperate belief that the problem of crime is intractable."[49]

Although answers to the crime problem appear to face formidable obstacles, all may not be lost. Fundamental social changes including the development of high moral values through education, the elimination (or significant reduction) of poverty, increased opportunities for success at all levels, and decriminalization of certain offences may all be combined some day into a workable strategy for the management of criminal activity.

## Discussion Questions

1. This book emphasizes a social problems versus social responsibility theme. What types of anticrime social policies might be based on the social responsibility perspective? The social problems approach? Why?
2. What are the three types of crime-control strategies this chapter describes? Which comes closest to your own philosophy? Why?

3. Explain the social epidemiologic approach to reducing crime. In your opinion, is the approach worthwhile? Why or why not?

4. If you were in charge of government crime reduction efforts, what steps would you take to control crime in Canada? Why would you choose those particular approaches?

# Weblinks

**www.crime-prevention.org/ncpc**
National Crime Prevention Council. Information on crime prevention projects across Canada.

**www.peelpolice.on.ca/prevention/cpindex.htm**
Peel Regional Police Service. Access to numerous crime prevention articles, including many on CPTED.

**www.cpted.net**
International CPTED Association. This site is dedicated to creating a safe environment through the use of CPTED strategies. Links to the principles of CPTED.

**www.canada.justice.gc.ca/en/index.html**
Federal Department of Justice. Links to information on the Youth Criminal Justice Act.

## CHAPTER 12

# Future Directions in Criminology

The formal justice system tries too hard to do too much and needlessly disempowers parties, families, and communities, and robs communities of an invaluable community building block; active involvement in constructively resolving conflict.

—JUDGE BARRY STUART[1]

As we go forth into the future a world of crime as yet unknown awaits us.

—CYNTHIA MANSON AND CHARLES ARDAI[2]

## LEARNING OUTCOMES

After reading this chapter, you should be able to:

- Distinguish between a number of emerging theories of criminology

- Recognize the strengths and limitations of an integrated theory of crime causation

- Assess the shortcomings of emerging theories of criminology

- Appreciate the advantages of a multidisciplinary approach to the study of crime and criminals

- Discuss future challenges facing criminologists and criminal justice personnel

## IMPORTANT NAMES

| | | |
|---|---|---|
| William Tafoya | Dragan Milovanovic | Derek Cornish |
| Richter H. Moore, Jr. | Lawrence Cohen | Ezzat Fattah |
| Georgette Bennett | Marcus Felson | Gene Stephens |
| Stuart Henry | Ronald Clarke | |

## IMPORTANT TERMS

futurist
future criminology
futures research
environmental
　scanning
scenario writing
strategic assessment
postmodern
　criminology
deconstructionist
　theories

rational choice theory
routine activities
　theory
lifestyle theory
situational choice
　theory
situational crime
　prevention
target hardening
displacement
peace model

restorative justice
circle sentencing
　conferences
Victim-Offender
　Reconciliation
　Program
family group
　conferencing
community sentencing
　panels
community policing

# Introduction to the Future

Emile Durkheim once observed that crime and deviance are a natural part of any social world. Although the form of criminal activity varies with the nature of society, it is unlikely that any human future will be free of crime. People who study the future are called **futurists;** futurist criminologists try to imagine how crime will appear in both the near and distant future. **Future criminology** is the study of likely futures as they relate to crime and its control.

From our present point of view, multiple futures exist, each of which is more or less probable and each of which may or may not come to pass. In other words, the future contains an almost limitless number of possibilities, any of which might unfold but only a few of which actually will. The task of the futurist is to effectively distinguish between these impending possibilities, assessing the likelihood of each and making more or less realistic forecasts based on such assessments.

Some assumptions about the future, such as estimates of future world populations, can be based on existing and highly credible public or private statistics and mathematical analyses of trends. Others, however, are more intuitive and result from the integration of a wide range of diverse materials derived from many different sources. As one futurist explains, "Before we can plan the future, we must make some assumptions about what that future will be like. ... Assumptions about the future are not like assumptions in a geometry exercise. They are not abstract statements from which consequences can be derived with mathematical precision. But we need to make some assumptions about the future in order to plan it, prepare for it, and prevent undesired events from happening."[3]

Best known among groups that study the future is the World Future Society, which publishes *The Futurist,* a journal of well-considered essays about probable futures. Individual futurists who have become well known to the general public include Alvin

**Futurist** one who studies the future.

**Future criminology** the study of likely futures as they impinge on crime and its control.

PART 3
354
Crime in the Modern
World and the
Response to It

Toffler, author of the trilogy of futurist titles *Future Shock*,[4] *Powershift*,[5] and *The Third Wave*[6]; John Naisbitt, author of *Megatrends: Ten New Directions Transforming Our Lives*[7]; and Peter F. Drucker—who has written many books with futuristic themes, among them *Managing for the Future* and *Post-Capitalist Society*. Within criminology, the Society of Police Futurists International (PFI) represents the cutting edge of research into future crime-control policy. The PFI evolved from a conference of approximately 250 educators and practitioners representing most U.S. states and 20 different nations that was held at the FBI National Academy in Quantico, Virginia, in 1991. Members apply the principles of futures research to gain an understanding of the world as it is likely to be in the future.[8]

**Futures research** has been described as "a multidisciplinary branch of operations research" whose principal aim "is to facilitate long-range planning based on (1) forecasting from the past supported by mathematical models, (2) cross-disciplinary treatment of its subject matter, (3) systematic use of expert judgment, and (4) a systems-analytical approach to its problems."[9] In the words of PFI founder **William Tafoya**, "[f]utures research offers both the philosophy and the methodological tools to analyze, forecast, and plan in ways rarely seen" in crime-control planning. "Guided by insight, imagination, and innovation, a new perspective awaits criminal justice professionals willing to attempt creative new approaches to dealing with crime and criminals."[10]

Central to futures research are the techniques of environmental scanning, scenario writing, and strategic assessment.[11] **Environmental scanning** "is a systematic effort to identify in an elemental way future developments (trends or events) that could plausibly occur over the time horizon of interest"[12] and that might impact one's area of concern. In other words, it is impossible to predict the future without having some sense of what is happening now, especially where important trends are concerned. **Scenario writing** builds upon environmental scanning by attempting to assess the likelihood of a variety of possible outcomes once important trends have been identified. Scenario writing develops a list of possible futures and assigns each a degree of probability or likelihood. **Strategic assessment** provides an appreciation of the risks and opportunities facing those who plan for the future.

A comprehensive futures research approach, for example, might identify an important trend that shows affluent middle- and upper-class citizens fleeing cities and suburbs for the safety of enclosed residential enclaves surrounded by secure perimeters and patrolled by paid private security personnel. Many likely scenarios could then be envisioned, including a further decline in many North American cities as the moneyed classes abandon them, continued growth of street and property crimes in metropolitan areas, and rampant victimization of the urban working poor. Although crime-control strategies might be developed to counter the imagined threat to cities, many risks must be considered in any planning. A serious decline in the value of the dollar, for example, as experienced in the 1990s, may cause gated communities to unravel and may create a shortfall of tax dollars that would be needed to pay for enhanced policing in cities. The influx of new and large immigrant populations, likely to add to the burgeoning number of inner-city dwellers, could add another new dimension to overall crime-control planning.

**Futures research** a multidisciplinary branch of operations research whose principal aim is to facilitate long-range planning based on (1) forecasting from the past supported by mathematical models, (2) cross-disciplinary treatment of its subject matter, (3) systematic use of expert judgment, and (4) a systems-analytical approach to its problems.

**Environmental scanning** a systematic effort to identify in an elemental way future developments (trends or events) that could plausibly occur over the time horizon of interest, and that might impact one's area of concern.

**Scenario writing** a technique intended to predict future outcomes, and builds upon environmental scanning by attempting to assess the likelihood of a variety of possible outcomes once important trends have been identified.

**Strategic assessment** a technique that assesses the risks and opportunities facing those who plan for the future.

Such issues have been the concern of a number of outstanding thinkers in the field of criminology. Futurists who have made their mark on criminology include Georgette Bennett, Gene Stephens, William Tafoya, and Richter H. Moore, Jr. Their work and other emerging theoretical explanations for crime as well as new suggestions for crime-control policy are discussed in this chapter.

# Future Crimes

Murder, sexual assault, robbery, and other types of "everyday" crime which have become mainstays of contemporary criminological analysis will certainly continue to occur in the future, but other new and emergent forms of criminality will grow in frequency and number. Recently, for example, the president of a future-oriented "think tank" predicted that by the year 2025, "Socially significant crime—that is, the crimes that have the widest negative effects—in the advanced nations will be increasingly economic and computer based. Examples include disruption of business, theft, introduction of maliciously false information, and tampering with medical records, air traffic control, or national-security systems."[13] Another futurist predicts that "[t]he top guns of twenty-first-century criminal organizations will be educated, highly sophisticated, computer-literate individuals who can wield state-of-the-art information technology to the best advantage—for themselves and for their organizations."[14]

A police officer calls her base. Community policing, a strategy by which law enforcement officials stay in close touch with citizens, holds great hope for the future. What is new in community policing?
*Sidney/The Image Works.*

PART 3
356
**Crime in the Modern
World and the
Response to It**

In a wide-ranging overview of future crimes, **Richter H. Moore, Jr.** paints a picture of future criminality that includes many dimensions. Already present are elements of what Moore predicts: "computer hackers are changing bank records, credit accounts and reports, criminal-history files, and educational, medical, and even military records."[15] Identity manipulation, says Moore, will be a nexus of future criminality. "By the twenty-first century," he writes, "genetic-based records will include a birth-to-death dossier of a person and will be the method of criminal identification." The human genome project has made the complete mapping of human DNA a reality. Already the U.S. military is using genetic testing to provide unique identification codes to each of its soldiers. In the event of war, such codes will allow for the identification of human remains from as little as a single cell. DNA coding, unique to each of us, may soon form the basis for nearly foolproof identification technologies that will take the science of personal identification far beyond fingerprinting, blood-type matching, or photography. The science of bioengineering, however, which is now undergoing clinical trials in the treatment of various forms of disease, may soon be clandestinely employed for the illegal modification of human DNA, with the goal of effectively altering a person's identity. It is but one more step by which the theft of computer-based genetic identification records could make it possible for one person to effectively imitate another in our future society.

Moore describes many other crimes of the future. "By the next century," he says, "criminal organizations will be able to afford their own satellites." Drug trafficking and money-laundering operations could be coordinated through satellite communications, couriers and shipments could be tracked, and satellite surveillance could provide alerts of enforcement activity. Likewise, says Moore, "[p]rostitution rings will use modern technology to coordinate global activities," and children and fetuses may "become subject to unlawful trafficking." The illegal disposal of toxic materials, an activity that organized crime has already explored, may become even more profitable for criminal entrepreneurs as many more hazardous substances are produced in the face of ever-tighter controls. The supply of nuclear materials and military-quality armaments to "private armies … terrorists, hate groups, questionable regimes, independent crime groups, and individual criminals" will be a fact of life in the next century, as will the infiltration of governments and financial institutions by sophisticated criminals whose activities are supported by large, illegally acquired fortunes.

Another writer, **Georgette Bennett,** whose seminal book *Crimewarps*[16] was published in 1987 and helped establish the study of criminal futures as a purposeful endeavour, argues that society is about to experience major changes in what it considers criminal and in who future offenders will be. Some areas of change predicted by Bennett include:

- the decline of street crime, such as robbery and assault;
- an increase in white-collar crimes, especially high-technology crimes;
- increasing female involvement in crime;
- increased crime commission among the elderly;
- a shift in high crime rates from the "Frost Belt" to the "Sun Belt"; and
- safer cities, with increasing criminal activity in small towns and rural areas.

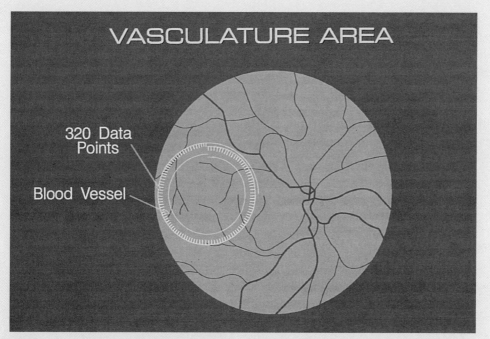

Diagram of a retinal image used for identification purposes. The security of sensitive sites and the accurate identification of personnel are being increasingly served by advanced technologies such as retinal imaging. Are such technologies foolproof? *Courtesy Eye Dentify, Inc.*

# The New Criminologies

Along with futures research, new and emerging criminological theories provide a picture of what criminology will be like in the years and decades to come. In an intriguing article entitled "Explaining Crime in the Year 2010,"[17] L. Edward Wells suggests that "[w]hen it comes to explaining crime, we seem to have an embarrassment of riches but a poverty of results." In other words, although many explanations for criminal behaviour have come and gone, "none has proven noticeably more effective in explaining, predicting, or controlling crime." That may be about to change, says Wells. Contemporary criminological theorizing is interdisciplinary and conservative in its approach to crime causation, and major changes in the premises upon which criminological theories are built are unlikely without significant ideological shifts or changes in basic components of the social structure such as the economy, the political system, or the family. Significant social change, however, can bring about the need for new theoretical formulations, says Wells. "Legal events in the 1960s and 1970s," for example, "changed abortion from a criminal act to a routine medical procedure. ..."[18] Similarly, an aversion to even minor forms of physical force may now be leading to a redefinition of crimes such as child abuse, spousal abuse, elder abuse, and sexual aggression. Hence, our basic understanding of criminal violence may be undergoing a fundamental modification that will require a concomitant change in our attempts to theorize about its causes.

PART 3
358
**Crime in the Modern
World and the
Response to It**

Wells sees similar possibilities for theoretical change about to be introduced by advances in scientific knowledge. Should the human genome project, for example, yield definitive evidence that some forms of aggression and violence are biologically grounded, it will provide the basis for an entirely new and emergent group of biological explanations for at least certain forms of criminal activity.

Wells makes a number of specific predictions about the future of criminological theorizing. He predicts, for example, that future explanations of crime will be[19]

1. more eclectic than past theories and less tied to a single theoretical tradition or discipline;
2. more comparative and less confined to a single society or single dominant group within society;
3. predominantly *individualistic* rather than collective, and *voluntaristic* rather than deterministic;
4. more applied and pragmatic in orientation;
5. more oriented toward explaining white-collar crime; and
6. reflective of a renewed appreciation for the biological foundations of human behaviour, with more theoretical substance assigned to biological and medical factors.

Unfortunately, from approximately 1960 until 1985 criminology suffered through several "dark decades" in which theory-building fell by the wayside as a generation of criminologists trained in quantitative analysis repeatedly tested existing ideas at the expense of developing new ones. In the mid-1980s, however, a new and dynamic era of theory-building was unleashed. Frank P. Williams and Marilyn D. McShane explain: "[a]s if the restraints on theory-building had created a pent-up demand, criminologists began exploring new theoretical constructs during the 1980s. Slowly at first, and then with great rapidity, theoretical efforts began to emerge."[20] Although space does not permit a detailed discussion of the various fast-growing new approaches, a few of the most significant ones will be discussed in the pages that follow.

## Postmodern Criminology

**Postmodern criminology**
a brand of criminology
that developed following
World War II, and that
builds on the tenets
inherent in postmodern
social thought.

Some significant, novel theoretical approaches now emerging within criminology are largely the result of postmodernist thought. Most such theories can be lumped together under the rubric of "postmodern criminology." **Postmodern criminology** applies understandings of social change inherent in postmodern philosophy to criminological theorizing and to issues of crime control.

Postmodern social thought, which developed primarily in Europe after World War II, represents "a rejection of the enlightenment belief in scientific rationality as the main vehicle to knowledge and progress ..."[21] Postmodernism epitomizes those societies that have entered a new age characterized less by an emphasis on industrialization and material production, and more by a concern with ideas, information, and individual needs. Hence, the new North American "information society" with its drift toward quasisocialism—which is so characteristic of postindustrial societies, rampant mass consumption, and overall technological sophistication—is one of the first truly postmodern societies to emerge in the world.

Postmodern criminology is not a single theory, but rather a group of new and emerging criminological perspectives that are all informed by the tone of postmodernism. At the cutting edge of postmodern criminology can be found novel paradigms with such intriguing titles as chaos theory, discourse analysis, topology theory, critical theory, constitutive theory, and anarchic criminology.[22]

All postmodern criminologies build on the belief that past criminological approaches have failed to realistically assess the true causes of crime and have therefore failed to offer workable solutions for crime control—or, if they have, may have been appropriate at one time but are no longer applicable to the postmodern era. Hence, much postmodern criminology is deconstructionist, and such theories are sometimes called deconstructionist theories.

**Deconstructionist theories** are approaches that challenge—often quite effectively—existing criminological perspectives, debunking them and working toward replacing them with approaches more relevant to the postmodern era. Bruce DiCristina,[23] for example, proposes one form of postmodern criminology that he calls "anarchic criminology." Anarchic criminology is "a criminology which embraces alternative methods and epistemologies, encourages imaginative solutions to social and criminal problems, and in the process continually undermines encrusted hierarchies of certainty, truth, and power."[24]

Two especially notable authors in the field of postmodern criminology are **Stuart Henry** and **Dragan Milovanovic**.[25] Their notion of a "constitutive criminology," rooted in phenomenological criminology, argues that crime and crime control are not "object-like entities" but rather constructions produced through a social process in which offender, victim, and society are all involved.[26]

A central feature of constitutive criminology is its assertion that individuals shape their world while also being shaped by it. Hence, the behaviours of those who offend and victimize others cannot be understood in isolation from the society of which they are a part. Individuals, however, tend to remain unaware of the role they play in the social construction of their subjective worlds and fail to realize that, at least to some degree, they are able to create new meanings while freeing themselves from old biases.

One area that well demonstrates constructionist notions is the sociology of law, which highlights the inherent interrelatedness between law and social structure. Milovanovic, for example, suggests the application of semiotics to the study of law.[27] *Semiotics* is a term akin to *semantics,* and both words derive from the Greek word *sêma,* meaning "sign." Milovanovic sees semiotics as especially useful in the study of law and criminology, because everything we know, say, do, think, and feel is mediated through signs—a sign being anything that stands for something else. Hence, language, gestures, sensations, objects, and events are all interpreted by the human mind through the use of signs. A semiotic criminology is concerned, therefore, with identifying how language systems (e.g., those of medicine, law, education, gangs, sports, prison communities, criminal justice practitioners, and criminologists) communicate uniquely encoded values. Such values are said to "oppress those who do not communicate meaning from within the particular language system in use" because they may prevent effective discourse with those in power.

The application of semiotics to the study of law can be illustrated by the phrase "mental illness." As a sign, this phrase is imbued with multiple—perhaps even contradictory—meanings. Two possible interpretations for what this sign represents would

**Deconstructionist theories** emerging approaches which challenge existing criminological perspectives to debunk them, and which work toward replacing them with concepts more applicable to the postmodern era.

PART 3

360
Crime in the Modern
World and the
Response to It

include a disease in need of treatment, and a person needing psychiatric services. Moreover, mental illness means something different in the law (wherein the proper phrase is "mental disorder") than it does in medicine or in the community. Different interpretations reflect different values, and these values can be traced to divergent interest groups. Moreover, as Milovanovic notes, the meaning of mental illness has changed over time—and continues to change.

Semiotics can also be applied directly to the notion of crime, as crime itself is a "socially constructed category," or sign. In the words of Henry and Milovanovic, crime "is a categorization of the diversity of human conflicts and transgressions into a single category 'crime,' as though these were somehow all the same. It is a melting of differences reflecting the multitude of variously motivated acts of personal injury into a single entity."[28] Such a statement, to the minds of constitutive criminologists, lays bare the true meaning of the word *crime*—effectively "deconstructing" it.

Crime should be understood, say Henry and Milovanovic, as an integral part of society—not something separate and apart from it. From this perspective, a kind of false consciousness, or lack of awareness, gives rise to criminal activity. "[C]rime is seen to be the culmination of certain processes that allow persons to believe that they are somehow not connected to other humans and society. These processes place others into categories or stereotypes and make them different or alien, denying them their humanity. These processes result in the denial of responsibility for other people and to other people."[29] Hence, from a constitutive point of view, crime is simply "the power to deny others," and crime is caused by "the structure, ideology and invocation of discursive practices that divide human relations into categories, that divide responsibility from others and to others into hierarchy and authority relations."

## Rational Choice Theory

**Rational choice theory** holds that criminality is the result of conscious choice, and predicts that individuals choose to commit crime when the benefits outweigh the costs of disobeying the law.

Strictly speaking, rational choice theory is not a postmodern approach, because it is primarily a modern version of classical deterrence theories which were discussed in Chapter 4. Nonetheless, rational choice theory, a product of the 1980s, contains a number of seminal new ideas. Proponents of the theory claim that it was a natural outgrowth of the realization that no existing criminological theory "contained an assumption of a rational, thinking individual."[30] **Rational choice theory** is built upon the assumptions of economists, many of whom view human behaviour—including that which is criminal—as the result of conscious choice. Rational choice theory is noteworthy for its emphasis on the rational and adaptive aspects of criminal offending, rather than on what other approaches might view as pathological aspects of the criminal event. Rational choice theory "predicts that individuals choose to commit crime when the benefits outweigh the costs of disobeying the law. Crime will decrease," according to such theories, "when opportunities are limited, benefits are reduced, and costs are increased."[31]

Two varieties of rational choice theory can be identified. One, which builds on an emerging emphasis on victimization, is called "lifestyle theory" or "routine activities theory." A second, which is largely an extension of the rational choice perspective, is called "situational choice theory."

**Routine activities theory** (also called **lifestyle theory**) was proposed by **Lawrence Cohen** and **Marcus Felson** in 1979.[32] Cohen and Felson suggested that lifestyles contribute significantly to both the volume and type of crime found in any society. The two believed that changes in the nature of North American society during the 1960s and 1970s—specifically increased personal affluence and greater involvement in social activities outside the home—brought about increased rates of household theft and personal victimization by strangers. Central to the routine activities approach is the claim that crime is likely to occur when a motivated offender and a suitable victim come together in the absence of preventative measures (which were sometimes termed "capable guardians"). Hence, "the risk of criminal victimization varies dramatically among the circumstances and locations in which people place themselves and their property."[33] For example, a person who routinely uses an automated teller machine late at night in an isolated location is far more likely to be preyed upon by robbers than is someone who stays home after dark. Lifestyles that contribute to criminal opportunities are likely to result in crime because they increase the risk of potential victimization.[34] Although noncriminal lifestyles at a given point in the life course are partly the result of unavoidable social roles and assigned social positions, those who participate in a given lifestyle generally make rational decisions about specific behaviours (such as going to a given automatic teller machine at a certain time). The same is true of criminal lifestyles. Hence, the meshing of choices made by both victims and criminals contributes significantly to both the frequency and type of criminal activity observed in society. See Box 12.1 for an examination of a Canadian geographic profiling system used to hunt criminals that is based on this notion of routine activities.

In a later work,[35] Felson suggested that a number of "situational insights" might combine to elicit a criminal response from individual actors enmeshed in a highly varied social world. Felson pointed out that "individuals vary greatly in their behaviour from one situation to another" and said that criminality might flow from temptation, bad company, idleness, or provocation. Convenience stores, for example, create temptations toward theft when they display their merchandise within easy reach of customers. Other authors[36] have defined the term *situation* to mean "the perceptive field of the individual at a given point in time" and have suggested that it "can be described in terms of who is there, what is going on, and where it is taking place."

**Situational choice theory** views criminal behaviour "as a function of choices and decisions made within a context of situational constraints and opportunities."[37] It suggests that the probability of criminal activity can be reduced by changing the features of a given social situation. **Ronald Clarke** and **Derek Cornish**, collaborators in the development of the situational choice perspective, analyze the choice-structuring properties of a potentially criminal situation. They define *choice-structuring properties* as "the constellation of opportunities, costs, and benefits attaching to particular kinds of crime."[38] Clarke and Cornish suggest the use of situational strategies such as "cheque guarantee cards, the control of alcohol sales at football matches, supervision of children's play on public housing estates, vandal resistant materials and designs, 'defensible space' architecture, improved lighting, closed-circuit television surveillance,"[39] and the like, as effective crime-preventative additions to specific situations—all of which might lower the likelihood of criminal victimization in given instances.

Routine activities theory (or lifestyle theory) a brand of rational choice theory suggesting that lifestyles contribute significantly to both the volume and type of crime found in any society.

Situational choice theory a brand of rational choice theory that views criminal behaviour as a function of choices and decisions made within a context of situational constraints and opportunities.

PART 3
362
**Crime in the Modern
World and the
Response to It**

# Geographic Profiling Online:
## Hot on a Killer's Trail

Rigel is a Canadian-made computer program that uses geographic profiling to hunt serial killers, repeat rapists, bombers, arsonists, and other major miscreants.

Rigel is at the core of an emerging crime-fighting field called geographic profiling. Instead of the traditional police approach of working outward from the crime scene to figure out where a criminal went, geographic profiling works inward to find out where the criminal came from. It has had impressive results.

As a test, Rigel was fed information about convicted serial killer Clifford Olson's 11 child murders. It pointed to a four-block area in Coquitlam, B.C., including his former street.

Late in the Paul Bernardo case, by using the locations of where teens Leslie Mahaffy and Kristen French were abducted and their bodies later found, Rigel pointed to the St. Catharines area town of Port Dalhousie where Mr. Bernardo and his wife Karla Homolka lived. Police were already closing in.

It worked again in the case of the Abbotsford killer wanted for murdering an Abbotsford, B.C. teenage girl and attempting to kill her friend. By giving Rigel the murder-scene location and the positions of telephone booths the killer used to make taunting calls to police, Rigel came incredibly close to pinpointing the home of Terry Driver.

Some day it could even be used to predict where a serial killer might strike next.

Rigel was invented by Kim Rossmo who overnight rose from a Skid Road beat constable to a detective inspector with Vancouver city police by coming up with the unique way to track down the likes of Hannibal Lector and Jeffrey Dahmer.

Named after the star in the constellation of Orion—the hunter—Rigel is a complex computer program that mathe-

**Investigators walk towards the house that was rented by Paul Bernardo in Port Dalhousie, Ontario, April 30, 1993.** *The Canadian Press/Jeff Chevrier.*

matically analyzes the hunting habits of serial criminals and points to where they most probably live.

Detective-Inspector Rossmo, a math whiz, came up with the idea in the late 1980s while working on the beat and beginning studies for his Ph.D. in criminology at Simon Fraser University. He even researched hunting techniques of lions on Africa's Serengeti plains.

In 1995, Vancouver police were the first in the world to open a geographic profiling unit under Rossmo's command. "Canada does not have a whole lot of money by comparison with the United States and Britain," he says. "So we have to be creative and innovative and more effective. To me, that's one of the most exciting parts of it."

Serial crimes, especially homicides and sex attacks, are investigative nightmares for police. Since serial killers often strike at random, there's no victim-killer relationship, which is the basic starting point for most homicide investigations. And because of their random, brutal nature, serial crimes can create intense public fear. That puts big pressure on police, who then assign considerable resources to the case. And that generates enormous lists of tips, witnesses and suspects to be checked out. Cases start suffering from information overload. In only 9 months, for example, the Bernardo murder case generated 3 200 suspects and 31 000 tips.

Rigel, in the hand of a skilled geographic profiler with a computer, math, and behavioural science background, helps find the needle in that haystack. But it will never replace a seasoned homicide sleuth.

About 20 years ago, Simon Fraser criminologists Patricia and Paul Brantingham came up with the idea of predicting where criminals were most likely to commit crimes based on where they lived, worked and played.

Detective-Inspector Rossmo, who studied under the husband-wife team, inverted that theory.

Rigel predicts where criminals are most likely to live, work or play based on where they commit crimes.

While serial killers and rapists often target victims randomly, where they attack is revealing. "Every time somebody makes a choice about something, we learn something about him," says the inspector.

Like the rest of us, criminals have defined geographic areas in which they go about their daily lives, including key "anchor" points such as home and work. Research into criminal behaviour has found most criminals won't commit crimes near home, for fear of being recognized and apprehended. That crime-free area around their home is called the buffer zone. Just outside of that is an area known as the comfort zone.

"When you leave your house and go to work, you drive the same couple of ways to work and use the same stores to pick up bread and milk, you have the place to go play basketball, whatever, all those things are in your awareness space," explains Ontario Provincial Police sergeant Brad Moore, who in 1998 graduated from extensive training to become one of the world's first geographic profilers.

"Criminals are the same. They're creatures of habit as well. So when they commit crimes, they commit crimes in areas they know, whether it's near their home or near their work. There's a comfort zone."

When a victim or opportunity intersects with a criminal's comfort zone, and at a time when he's ready to strike, a crime will usually occur.

The size of any one serial criminal's buffer and comfort zones is impossible to determine. But there are some clues among the vast body of research on criminal behaviour.

PART 3

364

**Crime in the Modern
World and the
Response to It**

Criminals who carry out acts with a certain level of sophistication and planning, such as bringing a murder weapon and removing it or hiding a body, are classified as "organized." And research shows organized criminals tend to travel farther from home to commit crimes than disorganized offenders.

That means they will have larger buffer zones than those of disorganized criminals.

To get a very basic idea of how Rigel works, place a small X, representing a criminal's home, on a piece of paper and draw a circle around it. The circle represents a 1-kilometre area around the home. Place a dot on a crime scene—somewhere within the circle. Draw another 1-kilometre circle around that dot. Draw a few more dots and circles.

In the end, they will all intersect around the crook's house.

In the case of a serial rapist terrorizing a city, Rigel studies the location of each rape site and, through some mathematical tricks, assesses the probability of every other point in the city being the rapist's home. It can take more than a million calculations.

Once it's done looking at each site, it will display a coloured map on a computer screen, with the highest probability areas marked in red.

If police already have a list of suspects, Rigel can cross-reference their addresses and quickly narrow down which ones live in the red zone so police can prioritize their next moves.

Or, if police have a partial licence plate number of a car used in a serial crime, Rigel's high-probability areas can be cross-referenced with postal codes and car registration databanks to look for a match.

Or, if police only have a description of a suspect, they can use Rigel's high-probability areas to tailor a direct-mail campaign and mail out a composite sketch of the suspect to everyone living in the area. Or they can target an area for increased patrols, or know where to go door-to-door for leads.

The program does have some limits. It won't be able to track serial criminals who have no "anchor" points, or ones who commit crimes across great distances. And because it's based on probabilities, it needs at least five crime-site locations to have any real precision. But the more locations, the greater its focus.

When police arrested British Columbia serial rapist John Oughton in the mid-1980s, they found coloured pins stuck in maps in his house indicating the locations of his 79 rapes.

Mr. Oughton was trying to make sure he kept his crime locales random so police couldn't pinpoint where he lived.

But when the 79 spots were later put into Rigel, a red, high-probability dot appeared precisely where Oughton's Vancouver apartment had once been.

"The hardest thing to beat is your habits," explains Sgt. Moore. "Even when you're trying to, sometimes unconsciously, you just can't."

SOURCE: Adapted from Ian MacLeod, "Hot on a Killer's Trail," *Ottawa Citizen*, January 25, 1998, p. B3. Reprinted with permission.

In brief, rational choice theorists concentrate on "the decision-making process of offenders confronted with specific contexts" and have shifted "the focus of the effort to prevent crime … from broad social programs to target hardening, environmental design or any impediment that would [dissuade] a motivated offender from offending."[40]

As mentioned earlier, rational choice theory is a modern version of classical deterrence theory. Earlier approaches, however, focused largely on the balance between pleasure and pain as the primary determinant or preventative of criminal behaviour. Rational choice theory tends to place less emphasis on pleasure and emotionality and more upon rationality and cognition. Some rational choice theorists have gone so far as to distinguish among the types of choices offenders make as they move toward criminal involvement. Involvement decisions have been described as "multistage" and are said to "include the initial decision to engage in criminal activity as well as subsequent decisions to continue one's involvement or to desist."[41] Event decisions, on the other hand, relate to particular instances of criminal opportunity such as the decision to rob a particular person or to let them pass. Event decisions, in contrast to involvement decisions which may take months or even years to reach, are usually made quickly.

In a recent study, Laura J. Moriarty and James E. Williams found that the routine activities approach explained 28 percent of property crimes committed in socially disorganized (high-crime) areas of a small Virginia city, and explained only 11 percent of offences committed in low-crime areas.[42] In the words of the authors, "this research demonstrates more support for routine activities theory in socially disorganized areas than in socially organized areas." Hence, although one could argue that the kinds of routine activities supportive of criminal activity are more likely to occur in socially disorganized areas, it is also true that the presence (or absence) of certain ecological characteristics (i.e., the level of social disorganization), may either increase (or reduce) the likelihood of criminal victimization. As the authors state, "those areas characterized by low socioeconomic status will have higher unemployment rates, thus creating a larger pool of motivated offenders. Family disruption characterized by more divorced or separated families will result in more unguarded living structures, thus making suitable targets more available. Increased residential mobility will result in more non-occupied housing, which creates a lack of guardianship over the property and increases the number of suitable targets."[43]

## Situational Crime Control Policy

Building upon the work of rational and situational choice theorists, Israeli criminologist David Weisburd describes the advantages of a situational approach to crime prevention. Weisburd points out that "Crime prevention research and policy have traditionally been concerned with offenders or potential offenders. Researchers have looked to define strategies that would deter individuals from involvement in crime or rehabilitate them so they would no longer want to commit criminal acts. In recent years crime prevention efforts have often focused on the incapacitation of high-rate or dangerous offenders so they are not free to victimize law-abiding citizens. In the public debate over crime prevention policies, these strategies are usually defined as competing approaches. However, they have in common a central assumption about crime prevention research and policy: that efforts to understand and control crime must begin with the offender. In all of these approaches, the focus of crime prevention is on people and their involvement in criminality."[44]

"Although this assumption continues to dominate crime prevention research and policy," says Weisburd, "it has begun to be challenged by a very different approach that

PART 3
366
**Crime in the Modern
World and the
Response to It**

seeks to shift the focus of crime prevention efforts." The new approach developed in large part as a response to the failures of traditional theories and programs. The 1970s, in particular, saw a shattering of traditional assumptions about the effectiveness of crime prevention efforts and led to a reevaluation of research and policy about crime prevention. For many scholars and policy-makers, this meant having to rethink assumptions about criminality and how offenders might be prevented from participating in crime. Others suggested that a more radical reorientation of crime prevention efforts was warranted. They argued that the shift must come not in terms of the specific strategies or theories that were used, but in terms of the unit of analysis that formed the basis of crime prevention efforts. This new crime prevention effort called for a focus not on people who commit crime but on the context in which crime occurs.[45]

**Situational crime
prevention** a social policy
approach that looks to
develop greater
understanding of crime
and more effective crime
prevention strategies
through concern with
the physical,
organizational, and
social environments that
make crime possible.

This approach, which is often called **situational crime prevention,** looks to develop greater understanding of crime and more effective crime prevention strategies through concern with the physical, organizational, and social environments that make crime possible.[46] The situational approach does not ignore offenders; it merely places them as one part of a broader crime prevention equation that is centred on the context of crime. It demands a shift in the approach to crime prevention, however, from one that is concerned primarily with why people commit crime to one that looks primarily at why crime occurs in specific settings. It moves the context of crime into central focus and sees the offender as but one of a number of factors that affect it. Situational crime prevention is closely associated with the idea of a "criminology of place," discussed in a box in Chapter 7.

Weisburd suggests that a "reorientation of crime prevention research and policy from the causes of criminality to the context of crime provides much promise." Says Weisburd: "At the core of situational prevention is the concept of opportunity ..." In contrast to offender-based approaches to crime prevention that usually focus on the dispositions of criminals, situational crime prevention begins with the opportunity structure of the crime situation. By opportunity structure, advocates of this perspective are not referring to sociological concepts such as differential opportunity or anomie, but rather to the immediate situational and environmental components of the context of crime. Their approach to crime prevention is to try to reduce the opportunities for crime in specific situations. This may involve efforts as simple and straightforward as **target hardening** or access control.[47]

**Target hardening** the
reduction in criminal
opportunity, generally
through the use of
physical barriers,
architectural design, and
improved security
measures, of a particular
location.

The value of a situational approach lies in the fact that criminologists have found it difficult to identify who is likely to become a serious offender or to predict the timing and types of future offences that repeat offenders are likely to commit. And, as Weisburd says, "legal and ethical dilemmas make it difficult to base criminal justice policies on models that still include a substantial degree of statistical error." Moreover, Weisburd adds, "If traditional approaches worked well, of course, there would be little pressure to find new forms of crime prevention. If traditional approaches worked well, few people would possess criminal motivation and fewer still would actually commit crimes."

Situational prevention advocates argue that the context of crime provides a promising alternative to traditional offender-based crime prevention policies.[48] They assume that situations provide a more stable and predictable focus for crime prevention efforts than do persons. In part, this assumption develops from commonsense notions of the relationship between opportunities and crime. Shoplifting, for example, is by definition clustered in stores and not residences, and family disputes are unlikely to be a problem outside of the home. High-crime places, in contrast to high-crime people, cannot flee to avoid criminal justice intervention; and crime that develops from the specific characteristics of certain places cannot be easily transferred to other contexts.

Another example can be had in robberies, which are seen as most likely to be found in places where many pedestrians stroll (such as bus stops and business districts), where there are few police or informal guardians (e.g., doormen), and where a supply of motivated offenders can be found nearby or at least within easy public transportation access.[49] Similarly, such places are not likely to be centres for prostitution, which would favour easy access of cars (and little interference by shopkeepers who are likely to object to the obvious nature of street solicitations), nor flashing, which is more likely to be found in the more anonymous environments of public parks.

Situational crime-control policy is most clearly manifest in the Crime Prevention Through Environmental Design (CPTED) concept, which is discussed in detail in Chapter 11.

## Critique of Rational Choice Theory

Rational and situational choice theories have been criticized for their overemphasis on individual choice and their relative disregard for the social and economic inequality of persons and groups. Likewise, rational choice theory seems to assume that everyone is equally capable of making rational decisions when, in fact, such is probably not the case. Some individuals are more logical than others by virtue of temperament, personality, or socialization, whereas others are emotional, hotheaded, and unthinking. Empirical studies of rational choice theory have added scant support for the perspective's underlying assumptions, tending to show instead that criminal offenders are often unrealistic in their appraisals of the relative risks and rewards facing them.[50] Similarly, rational and situational choice theories seem to disregard individual psychology and morality by their emphasis on external situations. Moral individuals, say critics, when faced with easy criminal opportunities, may rein in their desires and turn their backs on temptation.

The emphasis of rational and situational choice theories upon changing aspects of the immediate situation to reduce crime has been criticized for resulting in the **displacement** of crime from one area to another.[51] Target hardening,[52] a key crime-prevention strategy advocated by such theorists, has sometimes caused criminals to find new targets of opportunity in other areas.[53]

**Displacement** a shift of criminal activity from one spatial location to another.

## Restorative Justice

Postmodernism suggests that effective crime control in any future heterogeneous society can best be achieved by the adoption of a **peace model** based on cooperation rather than on retribution. The peace model of crime control focuses on effective ways of developing a shared consensus on critical issues that have the potential to seriously affect the quality of life. Such issues include major crimes like murder and sexual assault, but in future societies will also extend to property rights, rights to the use of new

**Peace model** an approach to crime control that focuses on effective ways for developing a shared consensus on critical issues that have the potential to seriously affect the quality of life.

PART 3
368
Crime in the Modern
World and the
Response to It

technologies, to the ownership of information, and so on. Relatively minor issues, including sexual preference, nonviolent sexual deviance, gambling, drug use, noise, simple custody claims, and publicly offensive behaviour will be dealt with fairly, but in ways that require few resources beyond those immediately available in the community.

The concept of restorative justice stems from these notions of cooperation and reconciliation rather than from retribution and punishment. The Canadian criminologist **Ezzat Fattah** has been a proponent of alternative forms of justice for several decades. In a 1995 article entitled, "Restorative and Retributive Justice Models. A Comparison," Fattah critically examines the ineffectiveness of the punishment model.[54] Citing per capita prison rates in the United States and punitive criminal justice practices in China and Singapore, Fattah asks whether the retributive approach really does effectively deter crime. He argues that the punishment model is a costly one, with incarceration being the most expensive sentencing option. Moreover, punishment serves only to treat human beings as a means to an end since it has little positive effect on those being punished. Even though the public and the victim may feel somewhat vindicated by a harsh punitive sentence, punishment, Fattah contends, does nothing to assist either in the healing process.

It is toward the goal of healing that the restorative justice approach reaches. **Restorative justice** is defined as

> an approach to justice that focuses on dealing with the harmful effects of crime by engaging victims, offenders and the community in a process of reparation and healing. The pain and suffering of victims is central to defining the harm that has resulted from the crime and the manner in which it is to be resolved. The community is active in offering support to victims and in holding offenders accountable for their crimes while giving the offenders the opportunity to make amends.[55]

Whereas the traditional adversarial system of justice defines crime as a violation of rules and a harm to the state, the restorative justice approach views crime as a harm done to the victim and the community. The adversarial system blames and punishes the offender and assumes a win-loss outcome; the restorative justice approach looks to a win-win outcome by focusing on the process of problem-solving, including the reintegration of the offender into the community and the preservation of his or her dignity.

Restorative justice models are not new. In Canada and the United States, Aboriginal groups have traditionally practised what is commonly referred to as **circle sentencing conferences**, which are based on traditional Aboriginal principles of peacemaking, mediation, and consensus-building. Sentencing circles involve participation by the judge, victim, offender, family or supporters, elders, and other justice and community representatives. Each has input, and the needs of each are considered equally important and worthy of representation. The conference results in sentencing recommendations, which are passed on to the judge with a view to ensuring the protection of the community, healing the victim, and the rehabilitating the offender. The judge may accept or reject the recommendations, and community members are responsible for ensuring that the eventual sentence is carried out.

**Restorative justice** a postmodern perspective which stresses remedies and restoration rather than prison, punishment, and victim neglect.

**Circle sentencing conferences** groups of community members who actively assist justice authorities by participating in discussions about available sentencing options and plans to reintegrate the offender back into the community.

The principles of restorative justice are reflected in community sentencing conferences such as the one shown here at the Aboriginal Ganootamaage Justice Service Centre in Winnipeg, Manitoba. Do you think this approach is "too soft" on offenders? Why or why not? *The Canadian Press/Winnipeg Free Press/Joe Bryksa.*

Circle sentencing conferences have been revived in many parts of Canada. Used extensively in the Yukon since the 1980s, they have become more widely used in other parts of the country, primarily in rural communities. The Peigan Nation Youth Traditional Justice circle on the Peigan Reserve near Lethbridge, Alberta was founded in the early 1990s and functions in the traditional manner. Adult and youth criminals can access the circle through pre- or post-charge diversion or even after a guilty plea is entered. The recommendations of the circle are forwarded to the Crown prosecutor, who then endeavours to have the presiding judge incorporate them into the court's final decision. In this way, the circle works in conjunction with the existing criminal justice system. Crown prosecutors screen cases coming through the courts and select those that appear suitable for referral to the circle. It is ultimately the circle's decision whether it wishes to accept any case. Interestingly, in cases where the Crown feels that a sentence of incarceration is warranted, the circle is advised of this at the time of referral. If the circle decides to accept the referral, it will often make a recommendation to the court that will not contradict the Crown's position, thereby ensuring that the court will not have to make a decision contrary to the wishes of the circle.[56]

The principles of restorative justice can be seen in a number of other Canadian criminal justice initiatives. The first **Victim-Offender Reconciliation Program (VORP)** was established by the Mennonite Community in Kitchener, Ontario in 1974, and the model spread rapidly, in various forms, throughout Canada, the United States, and Europe. By the early 1990s, there were 26 programs in Canada, over 120 in the United States, and more than 500 throughout Europe.[57] Based on mediation and alternative dispute resolution principles, the VORP involves face-to-face meetings

**Victim-Offender Reconciliation Program** a program that gives the offender the opportunity to meet face-to-face with the victim in the presence of a trained mediator in an attempt to reduce the victim's fears while establishing accountability and reparation for the crime.

**Family group conferencing** a forum for dealing with unanswered questions, emotions, and the victim's right to restitution and reparation resulting from a crime.

**Community sentencing panels** groups comprised of volunteers from the community who focus on restorative measures such as restitution, reparation, mediation and victim involvement.

**Community policing** a philosophy of policing involving proactive collaboration between the police and the community to prevent and respond to crime and other community problems.

between victim and offender, facilitated by a trained mediator, to discuss the events of the crime and its effects and reach an agreed-upon outcome. The program is usually used with young offenders, in the post-charge phase of the criminal justice process or as an alternative measure. The proliferation of community and neighbourhood justice centres has enabled expansion of VORPs and other similar mediation and dispute resolution programs that deal with both criminal and civil cases.

Since the inception of Victim-Offender Reconciliation Programs, restorative justice principles have been manifest in a number of other criminal justice initiatives. **Family group conferencing** provides a forum for dealing with unanswered questions, emotions, and the victim's right to restitution and reparation resulting from a crime. These conferences involve participation of the victim, offender, and their family members and supporters. **Community sentencing panels** are comprised of volunteers from the community and focus on restorative measures such as restitution, reparation, mediation, and victim involvement. These panels also consider crime prevention by addressing social factors that may contribute to crime. The principles of **community policing**, which emphasize a proactive approach to law enforcement through the establishment of partnerships with the community, can be seen to be compatible with much of the philosophy of restorative justice. The community policing approach has been formally adopted by the RCMP and the Ontario Provincial Police (OPP) and is practised by most police services across Canada.

The restorative justice philosophy has been embraced and endorsed by all levels of government in Canada as well as by voluntary and community organizations. The federal Departments of the Solicitor General and Justice, along with the National Parole Board and Correctional Services of Canada, are exploring the scope of restorative approaches and developing strategies for implementing them. The Restorative Resolutions Project (RRP), funded by the Solicitor General of Canada in 1993 and operated by the John Howard Society of Manitoba, provides community-based alternatives for offenders who are likely to be incarcerated. Located in Winnipeg, this project attempts to redress the harm done to victims and supervises offenders in the community. Offenders referred to the RRP must be facing a custodial sentence of at least 6 months, are required to enter a guilty plea, and are obliged to follow a community-based plan that includes meeting with the victim. Those charged with sexual assault or gang- or drug-related offences, or those who have been involved in incidents of domestic violence, are excluded. Once accepted into the program, RRP staff develop an individualized restorative plan that includes involvement of the victim and members of the community. If accepted by the judge, RRP staff implement the plan and provide the necessary services.

An evaluation of the Restorative Resolutions Project conducted in 1997[58] found that of the 297 referrals made between 1993 and 1997, 174 offenders met the selection criteria and were accepted into the program. In 91.4 percent (159) of these cases, the Crown's sentencing recommendation was incarceration for at least 6 months. Of these 174 referrals, only 10.3 percent (25) face-to-face victim-offender meetings were arranged; however, an additional 23.9 percent (58) of victims received written apologies from the offenders, and 78.6 percent of the victims wrote victim impact statements. Restitution was paid to one-half of the victims, for a total exceeding $130 000, and community service applied in 96.6 percent (168) of the plans. Recommendations for counselling or treatment services for the offender were made in 96.7 percent (168) of the plans. Fifty-four percent (94) of the RRP clients were followed for a 1-year period to measure recidivism rates. Of these, 5.3 percent (5) were convicted of a new offence. When compared with recidivism rates for offenders released from incarceration (16.7% recidivism rate) or sentenced to probation (17% recidivism rate), it appears that the Restorative Resolutions Project had a significant impact on those involved in the evaluation. The policy implications emerging from it, enumerated below, were quite clear:

1. Restorative justice programs such as the RRP can increase victim participation in criminal justice processing, produce significant restitution payments, and facilitate community service work from offenders.
2. Programs such as the RRP can divert offenders to the community and away from prison. These offenders are subsequently at lower risk for recidivism than offenders who undergo more traditional criminal justice processing.
3. Combining restorative justice practices with effective offender rehabilitation programming may produce benefits for the victim, the offender, and the community. Victims are given a voice in criminal justice processing, and the community benefits from reduced recidivism.

### Critique of Restorative Justice

The restorative justice approach has often been criticized for its vagueness of definition and direction. The term "community," for example, is an abstract one and has been used indiscriminately. Not all communities are clearly defined, nor are they all capable of engaging in partnerships that will sustain a restorative justice approach; for some, involving the community in restorative justice is seen as a "quick fix" for a crime issue that may require a more traditional approach. Some critics claim that the lack of due process and unclear legal procedures all serve to render the restorative justice approach ineffective. Concern around disparity of sentencing has been raised, especially if not all accused persons are afforded access to restorative justice programs. Whether or not power imbalances between those in positions of authority and the accused can be rectified to allow for the true implementation of restorative justice initiatives has been questioned as well. Finally, some critics charge that existing structural and legislative realities restrict or prevent widespread acceptance of the restorative justice approach.

## Theory Integration

The field of criminology today is rife with various theoretical explanations. Some are old, others are new. Many are complex, while a few are straightforward. Each theoretical approach is limited, although it may provide part of the explanation for why crime occurs or may offer a partial answer to the question of how to control crime. It may apply to only a certain type of offender, it may explain only a particular form of crime, or it may derive from only one philosophical or theoretical base.

Some have called the contemporary situation an embarrassment of riches, whereas others have compared it with the old fable of many blind men trying to understand an elephant—each "sees" only a small part of the overall picture. As a consequence, an

PART 3
372
**Crime in the Modern
World and the
Response to It**

emphasis on theory integration, with the ultimate goal of developing a unified theory of crime causation and prevention, began to emerge in the 1980s. Advocates of theory integration suggest that initial attempts at blending the propositions of different perspectives should begin at the level characteristic of those theories. In other words, theoretical approaches concerned with analyzing crime at the individual level (often called microlevel theories) might be integrated at the same time that sociological, political, and economic explanations (called macrolevel theories) are woven together. Finally, cross-level integration might be attempted.[59]

Other criminologists have developed rudimentary metatheories or theories about theories and the theorizing process, which they suggest may help to meld existing theories. Some metatheoreticians, however, have expressed the concern that we may integrate theories without first properly examining their worth and that, as a consequence, we may be left with highly elaborate integrated theories that are worthless.[60]

Unfortunately for advocates of integration, however, there seems "to be a consensus that there are too many problems for successful integration to take place. ..."[61] The reasons why successful integration can never occur, say Frank P. Williams and Marilyn McShane,[62] are (1) "crime is a very complex phenomenon," often determined and defined by whimsical legislative action and powerful interests; (2) "theories attempt to explain different pieces of the crime puzzle" and cannot be made to address all of its aspects; and (3) theories are "embedded in the assumptions we make about human nature and the way the world functions," and we all make different assumptions.

Einstadter and Henry summarize efforts at theoretical integration in criminology with these words: "The plain fact is that integrated theorizing does not lead to a more comprehensive understanding of crime or criminal etiology. Not only does the approach leave gaps between integrated theories, through which vital nuggets of the

Crimes against the environment have recently become an area of special concern to criminologists. Why have such offences only recently been recognized as crimes? *J. Muir Hamilton/Stock Boston.*

total reality of criminological explanation slip, but by presenting a range of theories as an integrated package, it tricks us into believing that a comprehensive coverage of criminological theory has been achieved."[63]

"Vital nuggets" of the reality of crime and justice can be found in such approaches as feminist criminology and black criminology, and advocates of theoretical integration are hard put to counter the ongoing development of such focused approaches. Some forms of feminist criminology, for example, even though they offer instructive insights, represent exclusive viewpoints which actively seek dismissal of much existing criminological thought—not integration with it. Similarly, other authors have advocated development of a black criminology to represent the experiences and felt needs of African-Americans and black criminologists.[64] Facing these developments, some feel that fragmentation of criminological theory, not integration, is the rule today.

Such critiques, however, may be overly harsh. One mistake made by advocates of theoretical integration is to assume that *all* existing theories must somehow be embraced and subsumed under *one* encompassing theoretical umbrella. A better strategy may be to work toward a multiple-theory approach that seeks the integration of only a few theories at a time. Multiple-theory formulations may provide the building blocks of larger and more comprehensive integrated theories in the future.

Sometimes a single organizing concept can help blend multiple perspectives, such as that identifying social support as a potential "organizing concept for criminology."[65] The author, Francis T. Cullen, contends that, "...both across nations and across communities, crime rates vary inversely with the level of social support. America," he says, "has higher rates of serious crime than other industrialized nations because it is a less supportive society." The idea of social support, says Cullen, is inherent in many criminological perspectives even though few theorists use the term directly. Cullen points to the ecological theories of the Chicago school, in which gangs were said to replace ineffectual families, as early examples of the social support thesis. Other research, including that on child abuse,[66] ethnographic studies of the "truly disadvantaged," and studies of welfare showing that "governmental assistance to the poor tends to lessen violent crime," adds credence to the social support thesis, argues Cullen. Because the concept of social support is capable of linking so many studies and so many other perspectives, it may truly hold value as an organizing or integrative concept in the field of criminology.

Cullen suggests that a "social support paradigm" (one holding that "social support [whether] delivered through government social programs, communities, social networks, families, interpersonal relations, or agents of the criminal justice system ... reduces criminal involvement") can serve not only as a useful integrative tool, but also "can provide grounds for creating a more supportive 'Good Society.'" Specifically, Cullen maintains, "the provision of social supports reduces criminogenic strains, fosters effective parenting and a nurturing family life, supplies the human and social capital needed to desist from crime, creates opportunities for prosocial modeling, strengthens efforts at informal and formal control, and reduces opportunities for victimization." Nonetheless, Cullen admits that an integrative theory of social support is a long way off. "Research must discern which of these hunches have merit," he says, "and to what degree."

Although we may not yet be able to see the practical promise of theoretical integration, work in the area has just begun. The door to this area will doubtlessly remain open a while longer. Box 12.2 provides an overview of several current integrated theories of criminology.

## Examples of Integrated Theories of Criminology[67]

BOX 12.2

**General Theory of Crime (GTC)**   *Michael Gottfredson, Travis Hirschi*

Integrates concepts from social control, psychological, sociobiological, routine activities, and rational choice theories. An individual's lack of self-control and propensity to impulsivity combined with weak bonds to the social order and the right criminal opportunities leads to crime and deviance.

**Social Development Model (SDM)**   *Joseph Weis, Richard Catalano, J. David Hawkins*

Integrates social control, social learning, and structural models of crime. The level of organization or disorganization within a given community will influence the ability of individuals to develop prosocial bonds, which, in turn, affects the likelihood that they will engage in future criminal behaviour.

**Elliott's Integrated Theory**   *Delbert Elliott, David Huizinga, Suzanne Ageton*

Integrates features from strain, social learning and social control theories. Those individuals who live in areas of social disorganization and who are poorly socialized at home face greater strain and are likely to form bonds with the delinquent rather than the social order. This, in turn, encourages and reinforces deviant and criminal behaviour.

## Policies of the Future

In a recent article, the eminent writer George F. Cole raised the question: "How can lawmakers, police, courts, and corrections begin to plan for the eventualities that lie ahead?" Cole concluded that "[i]t is essential that policy makers be given the best evidence as to prospects for future developments pertaining to the justice system and the broader socioeconomic and political context within which it will operate. Not all uncertainties about the future can be removed, but systematic and insightful exploration of the range of possibilities can provide a sounder basis for planning and a useful perspective on priorities for innovation."[68]

**Gene Stephens,** one of the best-known futurists to focus on crime in the past decade, observes that "[c]rime is increasing worldwide, and there is every reason to believe the trend will continue through the 1990s and into the early years of the twenty-first century."[69] In particular, observes Stephens, street crimes are escalating in formerly communist countries throughout Eastern Europe, and in other European nations such as those in Scandinavia and the United Kingdom. According to Stephens, the United States was one of the first nations to experience a rapid rise in criminality because, in many ways, it was the most advanced nation on the globe. The United States is a highly diverse, multicultural, industrialized, and democratic society that strongly supports individual freedoms and has fostered a strong sense of personal independence among its citizens.

Multiculturalism and heterogeneity, says Stephens, increase anomie, and previously isolated and homogeneous societies such as Japan, Denmark, China, and Greece are now facing a growing cultural diversity due to international migration, the expansion of new social ideals, and an increase in foreign commerce. "Heterogeneity in societies will be the rule in the twenty-first century," says Stephens, "and failure to recognize and plan for such diversity can lead to serious crime problems, especially in emerging multicultural societies."[70] Stephens's thesis is best summarized in this passage from his work: "The connection between crime and culture cannot be overemphasized: There are high-crime and low-crime cultures around the world. In the years ahead, many low-crime cultures may become high-crime cultures because of changing world demographics and politicoeconomic systems. In general, heterogeneous populations in which people have lots of political freedom (democracy) and lots of economic choice (capitalism) are prime candidates for crime unless a good socialization system is created and maintained."[71]

Homogeneous nations—in which citizens share similar backgrounds, life experiences, and values—produce citizens who are generally capable of complying with the wishes of the majority and who can legislate controls over behaviour, which are not difficult for most citizens to respect. In such societies, a tradition of discipline, a belief in the laws, and acceptance of personal responsibility are typically the norm.

Diverse societies, on the other hand, suffer from constant internal conflict, with much of that conflict focused on acceptable ways of living and working. Heterogeneous societies tend to place a strong emphasis on individualism, and disagreement about the law and social norms is rife. Characteristic of such cultures is the fact that lawbreakers tend to deny responsibility, "and violators go to great lengths to avoid capture and conviction." To highlight the difference between homogeneous and heterogeneous societies, Stephens points to the fact that in some highly homogeneous cultures, such as Japan, those who break norms will often punish themselves, even if their transgressions are not publicly discovered. Such self-punishing behaviour would be almost unthinkable in advanced heterogeneous societies such as Canada and the United States. As Stephens explains, "Some nations, such as the United States, face pervasive *anomie* due to their lack of restraints on human desires."[72]

Heterogeneity can arise in numerous ways, even within a society that had previously been relatively homogenous. One source of increasing and important differences in North American society today, for example, has been the growth of a technological culture that has produced two separate and distinct groups—the technologically capable and those who are incapable of utilizing modern technology. To these two groups we might add a third: the technologically aware, or those who realize the importance of technology but who, for whatever reason—be it age, lack of education, poverty, or other life circumstances—have not yet acquired the skills necessary to participate fully in what our highly technological society has to offer. In Stephens's words, "More people are turning to street crime and violence because they find themselves unprepared, educationally or emotionally, to cope with the requirements for success in the new era."[73]

Another reason why crime rates are high in increasingly heterogeneous societies, according to Stephens, is that such societies often display a lack of consistent childcare philosophies and child-rearing methods. "In some societies," says Stephens, "parents are seen as primarily responsible for their children, but all citizens share in that

PART 3
376
Crime in the Modern
World and the
Response to It

responsibility, since everyone's welfare is affected by the proper socialization of each child." In others, children are viewed as the parents' property, and little is expected of parents other than that they be biologically capable of reproducing. No requirements are set in such societies for parental knowledge, skills, income, education, and so on. Stephens describes child-rearing practices in such societies as "helter-skelter, catch-as-catch-can child care. ..." Lacking child-rearing standards in which the majority of members of society can meaningfully participate, heterogeneous societies tend to produce adults who are irresponsible and who do not adhere to legal or other standards of behaviour.

According to Stephens, future crimes will be plentiful, with countries around the world experiencing explosive growth in their crime rates. Many nations are now undergoing increased modernization, with many entering the postmodern era previously occupied solely by the United States. "[W]e can theorize," says Stephens, "that crime will be a growth industry in many countries as they find themselves gripped by the same social forces that have long affected the United States."[74]

Other authors have similarly attempted to describe crime-control issues that may face future policy-makers.[75] Richter H. Moore, Jr., for example, identifies the following seven issues that are likely to concern crime-control planners in the United States in the near future.[76] Many may also apply to the Canadian situation.

1. *New Criminal Groups:* According to Moore, "groups such as Colombian drug cartels, Jamaican posses, Vietnamese gangs, various Chinese groups, and Los Angeles black street gangs are now a much bigger concern than the Mafia." In Canada, the Nathanson Centre for the Study of Organized Crime and Corruption reports that the activities of outlaw motorcycle gangs, Asian-based triad groups, Russian/Eastern European groups, and indigenous Aboriginal gangs pose a significant threat to law enforcement officials.[77] See Box 12.3 for a further look at organized crime in Canada.

2. *Language Barriers:* According to Moore, "U.S. law-enforcement officials now find themselves hampered by a lack of understanding about the language and culture of some of the new criminal groups" operating in America. Cuban, Mexican, Colombian, Japanese, and Chinese criminals and criminal organizations are becoming commonplace, and such groups are increasingly involved in international communications and travel. In Canada, Asian-based and Eastern European groups pose the same challenges.

3. *Distrust by Ethnic Communities:* Recent immigrant groups have been slow to assimilate into North American culture and society. As a consequence, many of these groups hold strongly to native identities, distancing themselves from formal agencies of social control such as the police. As Moore points out, "[i]n many of their countries of origin, new immigrants see police as corrupt, self-serving individuals, a viewpoint often not without foundation." A distrust of police and government representatives is nearly instinctual for members of such groups, making the work of law enforcement within the context of immigrant communities challenging and often difficult.

4. *Greater Reliance on Community Involvement:* Moore observes that "[d]ue to the increasing costs of electronic surveillance, informant programs, undercover operations, and witness-protection programs, police are now encouraging community members to become more involved in their own security." The involvement of private citizens in the battle against crime may be the only

realistic solution to the problem. Neighbourhood watch groups, the use of community volunteers within criminal justice organizations, along with other neighbourhood self-help programs such as school and church-based education, all suggest the future of neighbourhood-based crime-control policy.

5. *Regulating the Marketplace:* Moore advises that decriminalization and legalization will become of increasingly greater concern to future legislators who will focus on "regulating the marketplace" for criminal activities such as gambling, drug trafficking, and prostitution.

6. *Reducing Public Demand:* Similarly, according to Moore, future crime-control policies will aim to reduce involvement in criminal activity "through better education" and other policies that will, over the long term, lower the demand for drugs and other illegal services.

7. *Increased Treatment:* Moore sees a greater emphasis in the future on the treatment rather than the punishment of all forms of criminality, including drug abuse, gambling, sexual assault, and other law-breaking behaviours.

---

# Organized Crime Groups and Activities in Canada

BOX 12.3

*Outlaw Motorcycle Gangs*: Of the 30 known outlaw motorcycle gangs in Canada, the Hells Angels are by far the most powerful and well-organized. The gang is comprised of 249 members in 16 chapters across the country. The Hells Angels are primarily involved in narcotics manufacture and distribution, firearms distribution, fencing stolen goods, auto theft, insurance and credit card fraud, extortion, debt collection, and smuggling. Other outlaw motorcycle gangs in Canada include the Apollos, the Los Bravos, the Rock Machine, Satan's Choice, the Vagabonds, Bacchus Motorcycle Club, and the Freedom Riders. The armed conflict between the Hells Angels and the Rock Machine continues to rage in Quebec—in 1998, there were 27 related homicides and 27 murder attempts.

*Asian-Based Organized Crime Groups*: These groups continue to be the primary suppliers of heroin to Canada and are increasingly involved in cocaine trafficking. They are also heavily involved in migrant smuggling and in violent crime such as home invasions, kidnapping, and extortion. They are expanding their involvement in credit card fraud schemes, loan-sharking, illegal gambling, prostitution, car theft, staged vehicle accidents, welfare and employment insurance fraud, and commodity smuggling. Asian-based criminal groups in Canada are dominated by Vietnamese-based gangs, particularly the Dai Huen Jai. Asian-based street gang violence is on the rise in many Canadian cities and involves such groups as the Red Blood gang and the Black Dragons.

*Eastern European-Based Organized Crime Groups*: Eastern European-based organized crime is expanding throughout Canada in both the range and level of criminal activity, although most of this activity continues to occur in the Toronto, Montreal, and Vancouver areas. These groups are involved in extortion, murder, prostitution, drug smuggling (cocaine, heroin, and steroids), tobacco and weapons smuggling, organized immigration fraud, organized theft of automobiles for illegal export, and various types of financial crime such as the manufacture and use of counterfeit currency as well as false identification documents. Eastern European organized crime groups are well-connected to their criminal counterparts in Russia, Europe, and the United States, and they function as integral constituents of large-scale international organized crime networks.

▶

PART 3
378
**Crime in the Modern
World and the
Response to It**

▶ *Aboriginal-Based Criminal Activity*: Much of this illegal activity is concentrated around the First Nations reserves that straddle the Canada-U.S. border in Quebec, Ontario, and New York State. Black market operations include the sale of firearms, explosives, drugs, cigarettes, and alcohol. Aboriginal street gangs continue to expand in the prairie provinces.

*Traditional Organized Crime Groups*: In Canada, Italian-based criminals are associated with one of three main organizations: the Sicilian Mafia, the Ndrangheta, or the Costa Nostra. The drug trade remains the primary activity of these groups, especially the sale of cocaine, hashish, and, increasingly, heroin. These organizations are also involved in gambling, money laundering, counterfeiting, and alcohol smuggling. Despite successful police operations against these traditional organized crime groups, they continue to be a threat in Canada.

*Other Organized Crime-Related Activity*: A number of other criminal activities are coordinated by organized crime groups. They include:
- the manufacture and distribution of child pornography and the sexual exploitation of children;
- environmental crime, particularly improper storage or disposal of hazardous waste;
- economic crime, including securities and telemarketing fraud, which is estimated to cost Canadians $5 billion per year; and
- the counterfeit products trade, especially the manufacture of clothing, software, and pharmaceuticals.

SOURCE: Compiled from information found in S.D. Porteous, *Organized Crime Impact Study* (Ottawa: Solicitor General Canada, 1998) and Canadian Intelligence Service Canada, *CSIC Annual Report on Organized Crime in Canada*, 1999, www.cisc.gc.ca.

# Summary
For all but the most astute, the future is difficult to presage. It is safe to assume, however, that the future will differ from the past, and that important differences in any future criminology will involve issues of theory formulation and crime-control policy. We can get some hint of what is to come by examining postmodern approaches. Although tending toward increased realism in their view of crime and criminal behaviour, these approaches generally advocate humane alternatives to traditional crime-control agendas. Some have termed such postmodern policies "restorative justice" and have suggested that crime-control programs of the near future must take into account both the suffering of victims and the inequities within society that promulgate criminality. Others, however, have complained that "postmodernism does not provide any practical guidance on policy. At most," such critics say, "it offers a basis for exposing possible pretenses and illusions in the pursuit of a just policy."[78] Postmodern criminology, because of its emphasis on deconstructionism, has also been criticized "for not valuing anything, and for a belief that 'anything goes.'"[79]

But those who perceive postmodern criminology as shortsighted fail to recognize that a new social order requires a new way of understanding it. Dragan Milovanovic, one writer whose work in the area is becoming increasingly important, believes that "[a]ffirmative postmodern criminology has emerged in the 1990s as a paradigm not only for deconstructing oppressive forms, but also for affirmatively reconstructing the new order."[80] Others point out: "It is still too early to evaluate the impact of postmodernism on criminology. Yet its influence is being felt in the increased questioning of traditional criminological concepts."[81] If early signs are any indication, postmodern criminology combined with the traditional approaches of the past appear to offer the best hope for coping with crime and for developing a truly just society in the twenty-first century.

## Discussion Questions

1. This book emphasizes a social problems versus social responsibility theme. Which perspective do you think will be dominant in the twenty-first century? Why?

2. Do you believe it is possible to know the future? What techniques are identified in this chapter for assessing possible futures? Which do you think holds the most promise? Why?

3. How does the situational approach to crime control differ from more traditional "offender-centred" approaches? Which, in your opinion, is more likely to deter crime? Why?

4. Describe the principles of restorative justice. What are its central tenets? Do you believe that restorative justice is a realistic approach to the administration of criminal justice in Canada? Why or why not?

5. What do we mean by the word *deconstructionist* in the context of new criminological approaches to crime explanation? Which of the emerging theoretical approaches outlined in this chapter would you classify as "deconstructionist?"

6. What is *postmodernism?* How has postmodernism affected criminology? What predictions for the future can we make based on an understanding of postmodernist approaches?

## Weblinks

**www.restorativejustice.org/**
Restorative Justice Online. This extensive site provides links to statutes, regulations, articles, and discussions concerning restorative justice.

**www.mcc.org/**
The Mennonite Central Committee. Links to restorative justice discussions.

**www.canada.justice.gc.ca/en/index.html**
The Federal Department of Justice site provides good links to restorative justice initiatives in Canada.

PART 3

380

**Crime in the Modern
World and the
Response to It**

**www.yorku.ca/nathanson/default.htm**
Nathanson Centre for the Study of Organized Crime and Corruption (York University). Extensive, current information on Canadian organized crime, with links to international sites.

**www.cisc.gc.ca**
Criminal Intelligence Service of Canada (CISC). Annual reports on organized crime in Canada.

**www.rcmp-grc.gc.ca/**
The RCMP site provides abundant information on organized crime in Canada and on the RCMP organized crime initiative.

# Notes

## Chapter 1

[1]Thomas Gabor, *Everybody Does It! Crime by the Public* (Toronto: University of Toronto Press, 1994).

[2]George B. Vold and Thomas J. Bernard, *Theoretical Criminology,* 3rd ed. (New York: Oxford University Press, 1986).

[3]Narrative materials in this section derive from Neal Hall, "All My Friends Betrayed Me" and "The Defence the Jurors Never Heard," *Ottawa Citizen,* March 20, 2000, p. A3; and Sandra Martin, "Murder in Victoria: Why Did Reena Virk Die?" *Chatelaine Magazine,* May 1998.

[4]"Aborigine Cleared of Death Curse Extortion," Reuters wire service, February 20, 1997.

[5]From the standpoint of the law, the proper word is *conduct* rather than *behaviour,* because the term *conduct* implies intentional and willful activity, whereas *behaviour* refers to any human activity—even that which occurs while a person is unconscious, as well as that which is unintended.

[6]Paul W. Tappan, "Who Is the Criminal?" in Gilbert Geis and Robert F. Meier, eds., *White Collar Crime* (New York: Free Press, 1947), p. 277.

[7]Edwin Sutherland, *Principles of Criminology,* 4th ed. (New York: J. B. Lippincott, 1947).

[8]Ron Claassen, "Restorative Justice: Fundamental Principles," Web posted at http://www.fresno.edu/pacs/rjprinc.htm.

[9]This is not entirely true. In common law jurisdictions, which are discussed shortly, a person can be arrested for serious violations of community standards even without an existing statute criminalizing the behaviour in question.

[10]"Kevorkian Gets Green Light in Libel Suit Against AMA," CNN online, May 28, 1997, http://cnn.com/US/9705/28/briefs/kevorkian/index.html.

[11]"Kevorkian Suggests Guidelines for Suicides," CNN Interactive online, January 14, 1997, http://cnn.com/US/9701/14/kevorkian/index.html.

[12]"Decriminalizing Drugs," *Ottawa Citizen,* April 12, 1997, p. B5 and "Decriminalizing Drugs II," *Ottawa Citizen,* April 14, 1997, p. A10.

[13]F. Schmalleger, *Criminology Today. An Integrative Introduction* (New Jersey: Prentice Hall, 1999), p. 11.

[14]*The American Heritage Dictionary* on CD-ROM.

[15]This list is not meant to be exclusive. There are many other journals in the field, too numerous to list here. See Chapter 3 for a more extensive list.

[16]In 1996, there were 59 090 police officers in Canada, compared to 82 010 private security personnel. Between 1991 and 1996, the number of private security personnel increased by 1 percent, while the number of police officers dropped by 4 percent. Karen Swol, "Private Security and Public Policing in Canada," *Juristat,* vol. 18, no. 13 (Ottawa: Minister of Industry, 1998).

[17]Integration and Analysis Program, "The Justice Factfinder 1997," *Juristat,* vol. 19, no. 7 (Ottawa: Minister of Industry, 1999).

[18]Sutherland, 1947, p. 1.

[19]Clarence Ray Jeffery, "The Historical Development of Criminology," in Herman Mannheim, ed., *Pioneers in Criminology* (Montclair, N.J., Paterson Smith, 1972), p. 458.

[20]Gregg Barak, *Integrating Criminologies* (Boston: Allyn and Bacon, 1998), p. 303.

[21]Jack P. Gibbs, "The State of Criminological Theory," *Criminology,* vol. 25, no. 4 (November 1987), pp. 822–823.

[22]Available through Sage Publications, Thousand Oaks, Calif.

[23]There are, however, those who deny that criminology is deserving of the name "discipline." See, for example, Don C. Gibbons, *Talking about Crime and Criminals: Problems and Issues in Theory Development in Criminology* (Englewood Cliffs, N.J.: Prentice Hall, 1994), p. 3.

[24]Charles F. Wellford, "Controlling Crime and Achieving Justice: The American Society of Criminology 1996 Presidential Address," *Criminology,* vol. 35, no. 1 (1997), p. 1.

[25]Gibbons, *Talking about Crime and Criminals: Problems and Issues in Theory Development in Criminology,* p. 4.

[26]Sutherland, 1947.

[27]Don M. Gottfredson, "Criminological Theories: The Truth as Told by Mark Twain," in William S. Laufer and Freda Adler, eds., *Advances in Criminological Theory,* vol. 1 (New Brunswick, N.J.: Transaction, 1989), p. 1.

[28]Barak, 1998, p. 5.

[29]Don G. Gibbons, "Talking About Crime: Observations on the Prospects for Causal Theory in Criminology," *Criminal Justice Research Bulletin,* vol. 7, no. 6 (Sam Houston State University, 1992).

[30]Gibbons, 1992.

[31]Raymond J. Michalowski, "Perspectives and Paradigm: Structuring Criminological Thought,"

in Robert F. Meier, ed., *Theory in Criminology* (Beverly Hills, Calif.: Sage, 1977), pp. 17–39.

[32]Roscoe Pound, *Social Control Through the Law: The Powell Lectures* (Hamden, Conn.: Archon, 1968), pp. 113–114.

[33]Although Pound's postulates originally made reference only to "men" we have here used the now-conventional phrase "men and women" throughout the postulates to indicate that Pound was speaking of all persons within the social group. No other changes to the original postulates have been made.

[34]Adapted from Michalowski, 1977.

[35]Adapted from Michalowski, 1977.

[36]"Fanning the Fire over Beavis, *USA Today,* October 15, 1993, p. D1.

[37]Department of Justice Canada and Solicitor General Canada, *Safer Communities. A Parliamentarian's Crime Prevention Guide* (Ottawa: Department of Justice Canada, Solicitor General Canada, 1996).

[38]*Safer Communities*, 1996.

[39]In 1996, the United States passed the *Telecommunications Act of 1996*, a subsection of which requires that all television manufacturers must install V-chips in every television set that is 13 inches or larger. (National Coalition on Television Violence, www.nctvv.org).

[40]"Film Scene to Be Cut After Fatal Imitation," *USA Today,* October 20, 1993, p. 1A.

[41]*Safer Communities*, 1996.

[42]Alfred Blumstein, "Making Rationality Relevant: The American Society of Criminology 1992 Presidential Address," *Criminology,* vol. 31, no. 1 (February 1993), p. 1.

[43]Angus Reid Group Inc., "Crime and the Justice System," www.angusreid.com, 1997.

[44]For an especially good discussion of this issue, see Theodore Sasson, *Crime Talk: How Citizens Construct a Social Problem* (Hawthorne, N.Y.: Aldine de Gruyter, 1995).

[45]Canada's National Strategy on Community Safety and Crime Prevention, www.crime-prevention.org.

[46]Megan's death led most states and the federal government to pass "Megan's Laws," requiring community notification when released sex offenders move into an area.

[47]Melanie Burney, "Megan's Law," Associated Press wire service, June 21, 1997.

[48]Angus Reid Group Inc., "Crime and the Justice System," www.angusreid.com, 1997.

[49]Nat Hentoff, "Justice Blackmun Reconsiders the Death Penalty," *Washington Post* wire service, December 11, 1993.

[50]For a good overview of this issue, see Wesley G. Skogan, ed., *Reactions to Crime and Violence,* The Annals of the American Academy of Political and Social Science (Thousand Oaks, Calif.: Sage, 1995).

[51]"Denny Beating," Associated Press wire service, December 8, 1993.

[52]For a good discussion of the social construction of crime, see Leslie T. Wilkins, "On Crime and its Social Construction: Observations on the Social Construction of Crime," *Social Pathology,* vol. 1, no. 1 (January 1995), pp. 1–11.

[53]For a parallel approach, see Terance D. Miethe and Robert F. Meier, *Crime and Its Social Context: Toward an Integrated Theory of Offenders, Victims, and Situations* (Albany, N.Y.: State University of New York Press, 1995).

[54]Joan McCord, "Family Relationships, Juvenile Delinquency, and Adult Criminality," *Criminology,* vol. 29, no. 3 (August 1991), pp. 397–417.

[55]Elizabeth Candle and Sarnoff A. Mednick, "Perinatal Complications Predict Violent Offending," *Criminology,* vol. 29, no. 3 (August 1991), pp. 519–529.

[56]Carol W. Kohfeld and John Sprague, "Demography, Police Behavior, and Deterrence," *Criminology,* vol. 28, no. 1 (February 1990). pp. 111–136.

[57]Leslie W. Kennedy and David R. Forde, "Routine Activities and Crime: An Analysis of Victimization in Canada," *Criminology,* vol. 28, no. 1 (February 1990), pp. 137–152.

[58]William G. Doerner, "The Impact of Medical Resources on Criminally Induced Lethality: A Further Examination," *Criminology,* vol. 26, no. 1 (February 1988), pp. 171–177.

[59]Doerner, 1988, p. 177.

[60]James F. Gilsinan, "They is Clowning Tough: 911 and the Social Construction of Reality," *Criminology,* vol. 27, no. 2 (May 1989), pp. 329–344.

[61]Jeff Ferrell, "Criminological *Verstehen:* Inside the Immediacy of Crime," *Justice Quarterly,* vol. 14, no. 1 (1997), p. 11.

[62]See, for example, Terance D. Miethe and Robert F. Meier, *Crime and Its Social Context: Toward an Integrated Theory of Offenders, Victims, and Situations* (Albany, N.Y.: State University of New York Press, 1995).

[63]For a good discussion of the historical development of criminology, see Don C. Gibbons, *Talking About Crime and Criminals: Problems and Issues in Theory Development in Criminology* (Englewood Cliffs, N.J.: Prentice Hall, 1994); Don C. Gibbons, *The Criminological Enterprise* (Englewood Cliffs, N.J.: Prentice Hall, 1979); and Leon Radzinowicz, *In Search of Criminology* (Cambridge, Mass.: Harvard University Press, 1962).

# Chapter 2

[1]F. Schmalleger, D. MacAlister, P.F. McKenna, J. Winterdyk, *Canadian Criminal Justice Today. An Introduction for the Twenty-First Century* (Toronto: Prentice Hall Allyn and Bacon Canada, 2000), p.29.

[2]A number of contemporary criminologists continue to study the effect of weather on crime. See, for example, Ellen G. Cohn, "The Effect of Weather and Temporal Variations on Calls for Police Service," *American Journal of Police,* vol. 15, no. 1 (1996), pp. 23–43; Ellen G. Cohn, "The Prediction of Police Calls for Service: The Influence of Weather and Temporal Variables on Rape and Domestic Violence," *Environmental Psychology,* vol. 13 (1993), pp. 71–83; Ellen G. Cohn, "Weather and Crime," *British Journal of Criminology,* vol. 30, no. 1 (1990), pp. 51–64; and Derral Cheatwood, "Is There a Season for Homicide?" *Criminology,* vol. 26, no. 2 (May 1988), pp. 287-306.

[3]B.J. Ennis and T.R. Litwack, "Psychiatry and the Presumption of Expertise: Flipping Coins in the Classroom," *California Law Review,* vol. 62 (1974), pp. 693–725.

[4]Canadian Centre for Justice Statistics, *The Juristat Reader. A Statistical Overview of the Canadian Justice System,* (Toronto: Thompson Educational Publishing, Inc., 1999), p. v.

[5]R.A. Silverman, J.T. Teevan, and V.F. Sacco, (eds.), *Crime in Canadian Society* (Toronto: Harcourt Brace, 1996), p. 62.

[6]Silverman et al., 1996, pp. 62–63.

[7]S. Tremblay, "Crime Statistics in Canada, 1998," *Juristat,* vol. 19, no. 9 (Ottawa: Minister of Industry, 1999).

[8]Canadian Centre for Justice Statistics, *Canadian Crime Statistics,* 1994 (Ottawa: Minister of Industry: 1995).

[9]Tremblay, 1999.

[10]Tremblay, 1999.

[11]Canadian Centre for Justice Statistics, *The Juristat Reader. A Statistical Overview of the Canadian Justice System* (Toronto: Thompson Educational Publishing Inc., 1999), p. 188.

[12]Solicitor General of Canada, "Victims of Crime," *Canadian Urban Victimization Survey* (Ottawa: Solicitor General Canada, 1983).

[13]J. Short and F. Nye, "Extent of Unrecorded Juvenile Delinquency: Tentative Conclusions," *Journal of Criminal Law, Criminology and Police Science,* vol. 49 (1958), pp. 296–302.

[14]M. LeBlanc and M. Fréchette, *Male Criminal Activity from Childhood through Youth: Multilevel and Developmental Perspectives* (New York: Springer-Verlag, 1989).

[15]For an overview of the reliability of self-report studies, see M.J. Hindelang, T. Hirschi, and J.G. Weis, *Measuring Delinquency* (Beverly Hills: Sage, 1981).

[16]For an excellent overview of the social dimensions of crime, see John Hagan and Ruth D. Peterson, *Crime and Inequality* (Stanford, Calif.: Stanford University Press, 1995); and James W. Messerschmidt, *Crime as Structured Action: Gender, Race, Class and Crime in the Making* (Thousand Oaks, Calif.: Sage, 1997).

[17]Persons accused refers to those involved in incidents "cleared by charge" and "cleared otherwise."

[18]Alfred Blumstein, "Violence by Young People: Why the Deadly Nexus?" *National Institute of Justice Journal,* no. 229 (August 1995).

[19]John J. Dilulio, Jr., "The Question of Black Crime," *The Public Interest,* Fall 1994, pp. 3–12.

[20]James Alan Fox, *Trends in Juvenile Violence: A Report to the United States Attorney General on Current and Future Rates of Juvenile Offending* (Washington, D.C.: Bureau of Justice Statistics, 1996); and Gary Fields, "Youth Violent Crime Falls 9.2%," *USA Today,* October 3-5, 1997, p. 1A (quoting James Fox).

[21]James Q. Wilson and Joan Petersilia, *Crime* (San Francisco, Calif.: Institute of Contemporary Studies, 1995).

[22]Wilson and Petersilia, 1995.

[23]Canadian Centre for Justice Statistics, *A Graphical Overview of Crime and the Administration of Justice in Canada* (Ottawa: Minister of Industry, 1999).

[24]Canadian Centre for Justice Statistics, "A Graphical Overview," 1999.

[25]Edna Buchanan, "You're Under Arrest," *New Choices for Retirement Living,* June 1994, p. 61.

[26]V. Sacco and H. Johnson, *Patterns of Criminal Victimization in Canada. General Social Survey Analysis Series,* (Ottawa: Minister of Supply and Services Canada, 1990).

[27]S. Besserer, "Criminal Victimization: An International Perspective," *Juristat,* vol. 18, no. 6 (Ottawa: Minister of Industry, 1998).

[28]R. Gartner and A. Doob, "Trends in Criminal Victimization," *Juristat,* vol. 14, no. 13 (Ottawa: Minister of Industry, 1995).

[29]S. Tremblay, "Crime Statistics in Canada, 1998," *Juristat,* vol. 19, no. 9 (Ottawa: Minister of Industry, 1999).

[30]Stephen E. Brown, Finn-Aage Esbensen, and Gilbert Geis, *Criminology: Explaining Crime and Its Context,* 2nd ed. (Cincinnati, Ohio: Anderson, 1996), p. 198.

[31]Elizabeth Cormack, "Women and Crime," in R. Linden (ed.), *Criminology: A Canadian Perspective,* (Toronto: Harcourt Brace Canada, 1996), pp. 139–175.

[32]Leanne Fiftal Alarid, James W. Marquart, Velmer S. Burton, Jr., Francis T. Cullen, and Steven J. Cuvelier, "Women's Roles in Serious Offenses: A Study of Adult Felons," *Justice Quarterly*, vol. 13, no. 3 (September 1996), pp. 432–454.

[33]Statistics Canada, *Violence Against Women Survey. Survey Highlights* (Ottawa: Minister of Industry, 1993).

[34]Frank Schmalleger, *Criminology Today: An Integrative Introduction* (New Jersey: Prentice Hall, 1999), p. 91.

[35]For a good review of the issues involved, see John Hagan, *Structural Criminology* (New Brunswick, N.J.: Rutgers University Press, 1989).

[36]Charles R. Tittle, Wayne Villemez, and Douglas Smith, "The Myth of Social Class and Criminality: An Empirical Assessment of the Empirical Evidence," *American Sociological Review*, vol. 43, no. 5 (1978), pp. 643–656; see also Charles R. Tittle, "Social Class and Criminality," *Social Forces*, vol. 56, no. 2 (1977), pp. 474–502.

[37]John Braithwaite, "The Myth of Social Class and Criminality Reconsidered," *American Sociological Review*, vol. 46, no. 1 (1981), pp. 36–57.

[38]Margaret Farnworth, Terence P. Thornberry, and Marvin D. Krohn, "Measurement in the Study of Class and Delinquency: Integrating Theory and Research," *Journal of Research in Crime and Delinquency*," vol. 31, no. 1 (1994), pp. 32–61.

[39]J. Hagan and B. McCarthy, "Street Life and Delinquency," *British Journal of Sociology*, vol. 43(4) (1992), pp. 533–561.

[40]Christine Wright, "Risk of Personal and Household Victimization, Canada, 1993," *Juristat*, vol. 15, no. 2 (1995).

## Chapter 3

[1]Hermann Mannheim, *Comparative Criminology* (Boston: Houghton Mifflin, 1967), p. 73.

[2]C. Murphy and P. Stenning, "Introduction," *Canadian Journal of Criminology*, vol. 41, no. 2 (April 1999), pp. 127–130.

[3]C. Murphy and P. Stenning, "Concluding Thoughts," *Canadian Journal of Criminology*, vol. 41, no. 2 (April 1999), pp. 321–323.

[4]Murphy and Stenning, 1999, p. 323.

[5]As discussed by Piers Beirne and Colin Sumner, "Editorial Statement," *Theoretical Criminology: An International Journal*, vol. 1, no. 1 (February 1997), pp. 5–11.

[6]Mannheim, 1967, p. 20.

[7]Don M. Gottfredson, "Criminology Theories: The Truth as Told by Mark Twain," in William S. Laufer and Freda Adler, eds., *Advances in Criminological Theory*, vol. 1 (New Brunswick, N.J.: Transaction, 1989), p. 3.

[8]Kenneth R. Hoover, *The Elements of Social Scientific Thinking*, 5th ed. (New York: St. Martin's, 1992).

[9]Hoover, 1992, p. 35.

[10]Bernard P. Cohen, *Developing Sociological Knowledge: Theory and Method*, 2nd ed. (Chicago: Nelson-Hall, 1989), p. 13.

[11]Cohen, 1989, p. 71.

[12]Susette M. Talarico, *Criminal Justice Research: Approaches, Problems and Policy* (Cincinnati: Anderson, 1980), p. 3.

[13]For a good review of secondary research, see J. H. Laub, R. J. Sampson, and K. Kiger, "Assessing the Potential of Secondary Data Analysis: A New Look at the Glueck's Unraveling Juvenile Delinquency Data," in Kimberly L. Kempf, ed., *Measurement Issues in Criminology* (New York: Springer-Verlag, 1990), pp. 241–257; and Robert J. Sampson and John H. Laub, *Crime in the Making* (Cambridge, Mass.: Harvard University Press, 1993).

[14]Sampson and Laub, 1993, p. 3.

[15]Murphy and Stenning, 1999, pp. 127–130.

[16]Donald T. Campbell and Julian C. Stanley, *Experimental and Quasi-Experimental Designs for Research* (Chicago: Rand McNally, 1966), p. 35.

[17]As identified in Campbell and Stanley, 1966, p. 5, from which many of the descriptions that follow are taken.

[18]Campbell and Stanley, 1966, p. 34.

[19]Frank E. Hagan, *Research Methods in Criminal Justice and Criminology* (New York: Macmillan, 1993), p. 103.

[20]Jeff Ferrell, "Criminological *Verstehen*: Inside the Immediacy of Crime," *Justice Quarterly*, vol. 14, no. 1 (1997), p. 11.

[21]William Foote Whyte, *Street Corner Society: The Social Structure of an Italian Slum* (Chicago: University of Chicago Press, 1943), pp. v–vii.

[22]Whyte, 1943, p. vii.

[23]Hagan, 1993, p. 192.

[24]Canadian Centre for Justice Statistics, *The Juristat Reader. A Statistical Overview of the Criminal Justice System*. (Toronto: Thompson Educational Publishing, Inc., 1999), p. v.

[25]Hagan, 1993, p. 218.

[26]Hoover, 1992, p. 34.

[27]Abraham Kaplan, *The Conduct of Inquiry: Methodology for Behavioral Science* (San Francisco: Chandler, 1964), p. 134.

[28]As reported in Kaplan, 1964, p. 145.

[29]Avshalom Caspim, Terrie E. Moffitt, Phil A. Silva, Magda Stouthamer-Loeber, Robert F. Krueger, and Pamela S. Schmutte, "Are Some

People Crime-Prone? Replications of the Personality-Crime Relationship Across Countries, Genders, Races, and Methods," *Criminology,* vol. 32, no. 2 (May 1994), pp. 163–195.

[30] Kaplan, 1964, p. 172.

[31] Mannheim, 1967, p. 87.

[32] Of course, as with almost anything else, qualitative data can be assigned to categories and the categories numbered. Hence qualitative data can be quantified, although the worth of such effort is subject to debate.

[33] Patrick J. Desroches, *Behind the Bars—Experiences in Crime* (Toronto: Canadian Scholars' Press, 1996), pp. 27–28.

[34] Ferrell, 1997, p. 10.

[35] Martin D. Schwartz and David O. Friedrichs, "Postmodern Thought and Criminological Discontent: New Metaphors for Understanding Violence," *Criminology,* vol. 32, no. 2 (May 1994), pp. 221–246.

[36] Ferrell, 1997, p. 8.

[37] Hagan, 1993, pp. 31–32.

[38] Hagan, 1993, p. 42.

[39] Carol LaPrairie, "The Impact of Aboriginal Justice Research on Policy: A Marginal Past and an Even More Uncertain Future," *Canadian Journal of Criminology,* vol. 41, no. 2 (April 1999), p. 249.

[40] LaPrairie, 1999, p. 250.

[41] The Campaign for an Effective Crime Policy, *The Impact of Three Strikes and You're Out Laws: What Have We Learned?* (Washington, D.C.: CECP, 1997).

[42] Lawrence W. Sherman, Denise Gottfredson, Doris MacKenzie, John Eck, Peter Reuter, Shawn Bushway, et al., *Preventing Crime: What Works, What Doesn't, What's Promising* (Washington, D.C.: National Institute of Justice, 1997).

[43] Fox Butterfield, no headline, *New York Times News Service* online, April 16, 1997, 7:06 EST.

[44] *Canadian Journal of Criminology,* vol. 41, no. 2 (April 1999), p. 326.

## Chapter 4

[1] Jeremy Bentham, *An Introduction to the Principles of Morals and Legislation (1789).*

[2] Cesare Beccaria, *Essay on Crimes and Punishments,* translated by Henry Paolucci (New York: Bobbs-Merrill, 1963).

[3] William Graham Sumner, *Folkways* (New York: Dover, 1906).

[4] L.J. Siegel and C. McCormick, *Criminology in Canada. Theories, Patterns and Typologies* (Toronto: ITP Nelson, 1999), pp. 447–448.

[5] Marvin Wolfgang, "The Key Reporter," *Phi Beta Kappa,* vol. 52, no. 1.

[6] Roman influence in England had ended by 442 A.D., according to Crane Brinton, John B. Christopher, and Robert L. Wolff, *A History of Civilization,* 3rd ed., vol. 1 (Englewood Cliffs, N.J.: Prentice Hall, 1967), p. 180.

[7] Howard Abadinsky, *Law and Justice* (Chicago: Nelson-Hall, 1988), p. 6.

[8] Edward McNall Burns, *Western Civilization,* 7th ed. (New York: W. W. Norton, 1969), p. 339.

[9] C. Brinton, J.B. Christopher, and R.L. Wolff, *A History of Civilization. Vol. I* (Englewood Cliffs, N.J.: Prentice-Hall Inc., 1955), p. 234.

[10] Brinton et al., 1955, p. 274.

[11] Referred to in official transcripts as Rudolf Franz Ferdinand Hoess.

[12] International Military Tribunal, "One Hundred and Eighth Day, Monday, 4/15/1946, Part 03," in *Trial of the Major War Criminals Before the International Military Tribunal, Volume XI. Proceedings: 4/8/1946–4/17/1946* (Nuremberg: IMT, 1943), pp. 398–400.

[13] Beccaria, 1963.

[14] Bentham, 1789.

[15] R. Martinson, "What works? Questions and Answers about Prison Reform." *Public Interest,* vol. 35 (1974), p. 25.

[16] See M.R. Chaiken and J.M. Chaiken, *Varieties of Criminal Behaviour* (Santa Monica, CA: RAND, 1982) and P.W. Greenwood and A. Abrahamese, *Selective Incapacitation* (Santa Monica, CA: RAND, 1982).

[17] See Canadian Sentencing Commission, *Sentencing Reform: A Canadian Approach* (Ottawa: Supply and Services Canada, 1987).

[18] T. Nouwens, L. Motiuk, and R. Boe, "So You Want To Know the Recidivism Rate," *Forum on Corrections Research,* vol. 5, no. 3 (1993), pp. 22–26.

[19] See, for example, W. C. Bailey, "Deterrence and the Death Penalty for Murders in Utah: A Time Series Analysis," *Journal of Contemporary Law,* vol. 5, no. 1 (1978), pp. 1–20; and "An Analysis of the Deterrent Effect of the Death Penalty for Murder in California," *Southern California Law Review,* vol. 52, no. 3 (1979), pp. 743–764.

[20] See, for example, B. E. Forst, "The Deterrent Effect of Capital Punishment: A Cross-State Analysis of the 1960s," *Minnesota Law Review,* vol. 61 (1977), pp. 743–764.

[21] Scott H. Decker and Carol W. Kohfeld, "Capital Punishment and Executions in the Lone Star State: A Deterrence Study," *Criminal Justice Research Bulletin* (Criminal Justice Center, Sam Houston State University), vol. 3, no. 12 (1988).

[22] *Ottawa Citizen,* December 4, 1996, p. A6.

[23]J. Braithwaite, *Crime, Shame and Reintegration* (Melbourne: Cambridge University Press, 1989).

[24]C. Goff, *Corrections in Canada* (Cincinnati, OH: Anderson Publishing Co., 1999), p. 4.

[25]S. Alberts, "Hanger's Cliffhanger," *Calgary Herald*, March 16, 1996, p. A3.

[26]Randy Martin, Rober J. Mutchnick, and W. Timothy Austin, *Criminological Thought: Pioneers Past and Present* (New York: Macmillan, 1990), p. 17.

[27]Martin et al., 1990, p. 18.

[28]Colman McCarthy, "Give the Boot to Boot Camps," *Washington Post* wire service, March 26, 1994.

## Chapter 5

[1]Karen J. Winkler, "Criminals Are Born as Well as Made, Authors of Controversial Book Assert," *Chronicle of Higher Education,* January 16, 1986, p. 9.

[2]As cited in David Jones, *History of Criminology: A Philosophical Perspective* (Westport, Conn.: Greenwood Press, 1986), p. 1.

[3]For a detailed description of the life of Robert H. Moormann, see John C. C'Anna, "Robert Henry Moormann," *Police,* April 1992, pp. 50–54, 86–88.

[4]C. Ray Jeffery, "Biological Perspectives," *Journal of Criminal Justice Education,* vol. 4, no. 2 (Fall 1993), pp. 292–293.

[5]C. Ray Jeffery, "Genetics, Crime and the Canceled Conference," *The Criminologist,* vol. 18, no. 1 (January/February 1993), pp. 1–8.

[6]Anastasia Toufexis, "Seeking the Roots of Violence," *Time,* April 19, 1993, p. 53. The leader of the opposition was Dr. Peter Breggin, director of the Center for the Study of Psychiatry in Bethesda, Maryland.

[7]C. Ray Jeffery, "The Genetics and Crime Conference Revisited," *The Criminologist,* vol. 21, no. 2 (March/April 1996), p. 3.

[8]Lee Ellis and Anthony Walsh, "Gene-Based Evolutionary Theories in Criminology," *Criminology,* vol. 35, no. 2 (1997), pp. 229–276.

[9] Ellis and Walsh, 1997, p. 230.

[10]Jeffery, "Biological Perspectives," p. 298.

[11]Konrad Lorenz, *On Aggression* (New York: Harcourt, Brace & World, 1966).

[12]Lorenz, 1966, p. 23.

[13]Lorenz, 1966, p. 38.

[14]Lorenz, 1966, p. 249.

[15]Lorenz, 1966, p. 225.

[16]Cesare Lombroso, "Introduction," in Gina Lombroso-Ferrero, *Criminal Man According to the Classification of Cesare Lombroso,* 1911; reprinted Montclair, N.J., 1972 by Patterson Smith, p. xiv.

[17]Charles Darwin, *Descent of Man: And Selection in Relation to Sex,* rev. ed. (London: John Murray, 1874), p. 137.

[18]Lombroso, "Introduction," in Lombroso-Ferrero, *Criminal Man According to the Classification of Cesare Lombroso,* p. xv.

[19]The term *positivism* appears to have its roots in the writings of Auguste Comte (1798–1857), who proposed the use of the scientific method in the study of society in his 1851 work, *A System of Positive Polity.*

[20]As cited in Hermann Mannheim, *Pioneers in Criminology,* 2nd ed. (Montclair, N.J.: Patterson Smith, 1972), p. 29.

[21]*Della Fossetta Cerebellare Mediana in un Criminale,* Institute Lombardo di Scienze e Lettere, 1872, pp. 1058–1065, as cited and translated by Thorsten Sellin, "A New Phase of Criminal Anthropology in Italy," *The Annals of the American Academy of Political and Social Science, Modern Crime,* 525 (May 1926), p. 234.

[22]The English language version appeared in 1895 as Cesare Lombroso, *The Female Offender* (New York: D. Appleton & Co., 1895).

[23]Marvin Wolfgang, "Cesare Lombroso," in Hermann Mannheim, *Pioneers in Criminology,* 2nd ed. (Montclair, N.J.: Patterson Smith, 1972), p. 254.

[24]Charles Goring, *The English Convict: A Statistical Study* (London: His Majesty's Stationary Office, 1913). Reprinted in 1972 by Patterson Smith, Montclair, N.J., p. 15.

[25]Goring, 1913, p.15.

[26]Earnest A. Hooton, *Crime and the Man* (Cambridge, Mass.: Harvard University Press, 1939), reprinted by Greenwood Press, Westport, Conn., 1972.

[27]Hooton, *Crime and the Man,* pp. 57–58.

[28]Hooton, *Crime and the Man,* p. 72.

[29]Hooton, *Crime and the Man,* p. 75.

[30]Hooton, *Crime and the Man,* p. 388.

[31]Ernest A. Hooton, *The American Criminal: An Anthropological Study* (Cambridge, Mass.: Harvard University Press, 1939).

[32]Stephen Schafer, *Theories in Criminology: Past and Present Philosophies of the Crime Problem* (New York: Random House, 1969), p. 187.

[33]William H. Sheldon, *Varieties of Delinquent Youth* (New York: Harper & Brothers, 1949).

[34]Sheldon and Eleanor Glueck, *Unraveling Juvenile Delinquency* (Cambridge, Mass.: Harvard University Press, 1950).

[35]D. Hill and W. Sargent, "A Case of Matricide," *Lancet,* vol. 244 (1943), pp. 526–527.

[36] Nanci Hellmich, "Sweets May Not Be Culprit in Hyper Kids," *USA Today,* February 3, 1994, p. 1A, reporting on a study reported in the *New England Journal of Medicine.*

[37] Hellmich, 1994., p. 1A.

[38] See, for example, A. R. Mawson and K. J. Jacobs, "Corn Consumption, Tryptophan, and Cross National Homicide Rates," *Journal of Orthomolecular Psychiatry,* vol. 7 (1978), pp. 227–230; and A. Hoffer, "The Relation of Crime to Nutrition," *Humanist in Canada,* vol. 8 (1975), p. 8.

[39] See, for example, C. Hawley and R. E. Buckley, "Food Dyes and Hyperkinetic Children," *Academy Therapy,* vol. 10 (1974), pp. 27–32; and Alexander Schauss, *Diet, Crime & Delinquency* (Berkeley, Calif.: Parker House, 1980).

[40] "Special Report: Measuring Your Life with Coffee Spoons," *Tufts University Diet & Nutrition Letter,* vol. 2, no. 2 (April 1984), pp. 3–6.

[41] See, for example, "Special Report: Does What You Eat Affect Your Mood and Actions?" *Tufts University Diet & Nutrition Letter,* vol. 2, no. 12 (February 1985), pp. 4–6.

[42] See *Tufts University Diet & Nutrition Newsletter,* vol. 2, no. 11 (January 1985), p. 2; and "Special Report: Why Sugar Continues to Concern Nutritionists," *Tufts University Diet & Nutrition Letter,* vol. 3, no. 3 (May 1985), pp. 3–6.

[43] A. Hoffer, "Children with Learning and Behavioral Disorders," *Journal of Orthomolecular Psychiatry,* vol. 5 (1976), p. 229.

[44] "Special Report: Does What You Eat Affect Your Mood and Actions?" *Tufts University Diet & Nutrition Letter,* vol. 2, no. 12 (February 1985), p. 4.

[45] Roger D. Masters, Brian Hone, and Anil Doshi, "Environmental Pollution, Neurotoxicity, and Criminal Violence," in J. Rose, ed., *Environmental Toxicology* (London and New York: Gordon and Breach, 1997).

[46] Peter Montague, "Toxics and Violent Crime," *Rachel's Environment & Health Weekly,* no. 551 (June 19, 1997).

[47] Alison Motluck, "Pollution May Lead to a Life of Crime," *New Scientist,* vol. 154, no. 2084 (May 31, 1997), p. 4.

[48] See Alexander G. Schauss, "Tranquilizing Effect of Color Reduces Aggressive Behavior and Potential Violence," *Journal of Orthomolecular Psychiatry,* vol. 8, no. 4 (1979), pp. 218–221; and David Johnston, "Is It Merely a Fad, Or Do Pastel Walls Stop Jail House Brawls?" *Corrections Magazine,* vol. 7, no. 3 (1981), pp. 28–32.

[49] Questions were raised, however, about the longterm effects of confinement in pink cells, and some researchers suggested that extended exposure to the color pink could generate suicidal impulses.

[50] See, for example, R. T. Rada, D. R. Laws, and R. Kellner, "Plasma Testosterone Levels in the Rapist," *Psychomatic Medicine,* vol. 38 (1976), pp. 257–268.

[51] "The Insanity of Steroid Abuse," *Newsweek,* May 23, 1988, p. 75.

[52] Dan Olweus, Mattsson Ake, Daisy Schalling, and Hans Low, "Testosterone, Aggression, Physical and Personality Dimensions in Normal Adolescent Males," *Psychosomatic Medicine,* vol. 42 (1980), pp. 253–269.

[53] Richard Udry, "Biosocial Models of Adolescent Problem Behaviors," *Social Biology,* vol. 37 (1990), pp. 1–10.

[54] Dan Olweus, "Testosterone and Adrenaline: Aggressive Antisocial Behavior in Normal Adolescent Males," in Sarnoff A. Mednick, Terrie E. Moffitt, and Susan A. Stack, eds., *The Causes of Crime: New Biological Approaches* (Cambridge: Cambridge University Press, 1987), pp. 263–282.

[55] Alan Booth and D. Wayne Osgood, "The Influence of Testosterone on Deviance in Adulthood: Assessing and Explaining the Relationship," *Criminology,* vol. 31, no. 1 (1993), pp. 93–117.

[56] Booth and Osgood, 1993, p. 93.

[57] Booth and Osgood, 1993, p. 93.

[58] Richard Udry, Luther Talbert, and Naomi Morris, "Biosocial Foundations for Adolescent Female Sexuality," *Demography,* vol. 23 (1986), pp. 217–227.

[59] "Drunk Driving Charge Dismissed: PMS Cited," *Fayetteville Observer-Times* (North Carolina), June 7, 1991, p. 3A.

[60] See D. Asso, *The Real Menstrual Cycle* (Toronto: Wiley, 1984)

[61] Anastasia Toufexis, "Seeking the Roots of Violence," *Time,* April 19, 1993, pp. 52–54.

[62] Richard Louis Dugdale, *The Jukes: A Study in Crime, Pauperism, Disease, and Heredity,* 3rd ed. (New York: G. P. Putnam's Sons, 1895).

[63] Arthur H. Estabrook, *The Jukes in 1915* (Washington, D.C.: Carnegie Institute of Washington, 1916).

[64] Henry Herbert Goddard, *The Kallikak Family: A Study in the Heredity of Feeblemindedness* (New York: Macmillan, 1912).

[65] Samuel Hopkins Adams, "The Juke Myth", *Saturday Review,* vol 38, no13, (1960) pp.48-49

[66] T. L. Chapman, "The Early Eugenics Movement in Western Canada", *Alberta History,* vol.25, (1977), pp.9-17. See also A. McLaren "The Creation of a Haven for Human Thoroughbreds", Canadian Historical Review, Vol. 67 (1986), pp.264-268.

[67] P. A. Jacobs, M. Brunton, and M. Melville, "Aggressive Behavior, Mental Subnormality, and the XYY Male," *Nature,* vol. 208 (1965), p. 1351.

[68] Biologists often define *karyotype* as "a photomicrograph of metaphase chromosomes in a standard array." The process of karyotyping typically involves drawing a small sample of blood.

[69] See David A. Jones, *History of Criminology: A Philosophical Perspective* (Westport, Conn.: Greenwood Press, 1986), p. 124.

[70] Many of which have been summarized in J. Katz and W. Chambliss, "Biology and Crime," in J. F. Sheley, ed., *Criminology* (Belmont, Calif.: Wadsworth, 1991), pp. 245–272.

[71] As reported by S. A. Mednick and J. Volavka, "Biology and Crime," in N. Morris and M. Tonry, *Crime and Justice: An Annual Review of Research,* vol. 2 (Chicago: University of Chicago Press, 1980), pp. 85–158; and D. A. Andrews and James Bonta, *The Psychology of Criminal Conduct* (Cincinnati: Anderson, 1994), pp. 126–127.

[72] T. Sarbin and J. Miller, "Demonism Revisited: The XYY Chromosomal Anomaly," *Issues in Criminology,* vol. 5 (1970), p. 199.

[73] Geoffrey Cowley and Carol Hallin, "The Genetics of Bad Behavior: A Study Links Violence to Heredity," *Newsweek,* November 1, 1993, p. 57.

[74] Johannes Lange, *Verbrechen als Schicksal* (Leipzig: Georg Thieme, 1929).

[75] Karl O. Christiansen, "A Preliminary Study of Criminality Among Twins," in Sarnoff Mednick and Karl Christiansen, eds., *Biosocial Bases of Criminal Behavior* (New York: Gardner Press, 1977).

[76] C. Ray Jeffery, "Biological Perspectives," *Journal of Criminal Justice Education,* vol. 4, no. 2 (Fall 1993), p. 300.

[77] Diana Kendall, Jane L. Murray, Rick Linden, *Sociology in Our Times,* (Toronto: ITP Nelson, 1997).

[78] Frank Schmalleger, *Criminology Today: An Integrative Introduction,* (New Jersey: Prentice Hall, 1999).

[79] D. Thomas, *Criminality Among the Foreign Born: Analysis of Federal Prison Population,* (Ottawa: Immigration and Employment Canada, 1992).

[80] Robert Silverman, Leslie Kennedy, *Deadly Deeds: Murder in Canada,* (Scarborough, Ont.: Nelson Canada, 1993).

[81] Mary Hyde, Carol LaPrairie, *American Police Crime Prevention* (Working Paper), (Ottawa: Solicitor General of Canada, 1987).

[82] Federal Bureau of Investigation, *Crime in the United States, 1996* (Washington, D.C.: U.S. Department of Justice, 1997), as computed by the author.

[83] See, for example, D. H. Fishbein, "The Psychobiology of Female Aggression," *Criminal Justice and Behavior,* vol. 19 (1992), pp. 99–126.

[84] Robbin S. Ogle, Daniel Maier-Katin, and Thomas J. Bernard, "A Theory of Homicidal Behavior Among Women," *Criminology,* vol. 33, no. 2 (1995), pp. 173–193.

[85] Ogle, Maier-Katin, and Bernard, 1995, p. 177.

[86] Ogle, Maier-Katin, and Bernard, 1995, p. 179.

[87] Arthur Fisher, "A New Synthesis Comes of Age," *Mosaic,* vol. 22, no. 1 (Spring 1991), pp. 2–9.

[88] Edward O. Wilson, *Sociobiology: The New Synthesis* (Cambridge, Mass.: The Belknap Press of Harvard University Press, 1975).

[89] Janet Zimmerman, "6 Held in Brutal Attack of Mich. Teens," *USA Today,* June 24, 1997, 3A.

[90] Wilson, 1975, p. 327.

[91] Sarah Blaffer Hrdy, *The Langurs of Abu: Female and Male Strategies of Reproduction* (Cambridge, Mass.: Harvard University Press, 1977).

[92] Research by Martin Daly and Margo Wilson of McMaster University in Hamilton Canada, as reported in Arthur Fisher, "A New Synthesis II: How Different Are Humans?" *Mosaic,* vol. 22, no. 1 (Spring 1991), p. 14.

[93] Arthur Fisher, "A New Synthesis II: How Different Are Humans?" *Mosaic,* vol. 22, no. 1 (Spring 1991), p. 11.

[94] John H. Beckstrom, *Evolutionary Jurisprudence: Prospects and Limitations on the Youth of Modern Darwinism Throughout the Legal Process* (Urbana, Ill.: University of Illinois Press, 1989).

[95] John Madison Memory, "Sociobiology and the Metamorphoses of Criminology: 1978–2000," unpublished manuscript.

[96] Memory, p. 33.

[97] See, also, Arnold L. Lieber, *The Lunar Effect: Biological Tides and Human Emotions* (Garden City: Anchor Press, 1978).

[98] James Q. Wilson and Richard J. Herrnstein, *Crime and Human Nature* (New York: Simon & Schuster, 1985).

[99] Karen J. Winkler, "Criminals Are Born as Well as Made, Authors of Controversial Book Assert," *The Chronicle of Higher Education,* January 16, 1986, p. 5.

[100] Winkler, 1986, p. 8.

[101] Jeffery, "Biological Perspectives," p. 303.

[102] Jeffery, "Biological Perspectives," p. 303.

[103] Julian V. Roberts, Thomas Gabor, "Lombrosian Wine in a New Bottle: Research on Crime and Race," *Canadian Journal of Criminology,* vol. 32, no. 2, (April 1990), p. 309.

[104] *Time,* April 19, 1993, p. 53.

[105]Lee Ellis and Anthony Walsh, "Gene-Based Evolutionary Theories in Criminology," *Criminology,* vol. 35, no. 2 (1997), pp. 229–230.

[106]Glenn D. Walters and Thomas W. White, "Heredity and Crime: Bad Genes or Bad Research?" *Criminology,* vol. 27, no. 3 (1989), pp. 455–485. See, also, P. A. Brennan and S. A. Mednick, "Reply to Walters and White: Heredity and Crime," *Criminology,* vol. 28, no. 4 (November 1990), pp. 657–661.

[107]Walters and White, 1989, p. 478.

# Chapter 6

[1]William R. Doerner, "The Man Who Hated Women," *Time,* December 18, 1989, p. 34.

[2]Karl Menninger, *The Crime of Punishment* (New York: Viking, 1968).

[3]"Police Fear Killings Span 10 Years," *USA Today,* July 26, 1991, p. 3A.

[4]"Mutilator 'Seemed So Normal,'" *Fayetteville Observer-Times,* July 28, 1991, p. 7A.

[5]"Doctor: Dahmer Wanted to Freeze-Dry a Victim," *Fayetteville Observer-Times,* February 13, 1992, p. 7A.

[6]"Psychiatrist: Dahmer Lacked Will to Stop," *Fayetteville Observer-Times,* February 4, 1992, p. 5A.

[7]"Dahmer: 936 Years for 'Holocaust,'" *USA Today,* February 18, 1992, p. 1A.

[8]Carlos Sanchez and Marylou Tousignant, "Jury Acquits Bobbitt; Discrepancies, Lack of Evidence Cited," *Washington Post* wire service, November 11, 1993.

[9]Sanchez and Tousignant, 1993.

[10]Barry Came, "Montreal Massacre," *Maclean's Magazine,* December 18, 1989, p. 14.

[11]Bruce Wallace, "The Making of a Mass Killer," *Maclean's Magazine,* December 18, 1989, p. 22.

[12]D. A. Andrews and James Bonta, *The Psychology of Criminal Conduct* (Cincinnati: Anderson, 1998), p. 93.

[13]See Adrian Raine, *The Psychopathology of Crime: Criminal Behavior as a Clinical Disorder* (Orlando: Academic Press, 1993).

[14]Cathy Spatz Widom and Hans Toch, "The Contribution of Psychology to Criminal Justice Education," *Journal of Criminal Justice Education,* vol. 4, no. 2 (Fall 1993), p. 253.

[15]Curt R. Bartol, *Criminal Behavior: A Psychosocial Approach,* 3rd ed. (Englewood Cliffs, N.J.: Prentice Hall, 1991), p. 16.

[16]For additional information, see S. Giora Shoham and Mark C. Seis, *A Primer in the Psychology of Crime* (New York: Harrow and Heston, 1993); and Frederic L. Faust, "A Review of *A Primer In The Psychology of Crime,*" in *Social Pathology,* vol. 1, no. 1 (January 1995), pp. 48–61.

[17]Nicole Hahn Rafter, "Psychopathy and the Evolution of Criminological Knowledge," *Theoretical Criminology,* vol. 1, no. 2 (May 1997), pp. 235–259.

[18]Nolan D. C. Lewis, "Foreword," in David Abrahamsen, *Crime and the Human Mind* (Montclair, N.J.: Patterson Smith, 1969), p. vii. Originally published in 1944.

[19]As noted by Nicole Hahn Rafter, "Psychopathy and the Evolution of Criminological Knowledge." See Richard von Krafft-Ebing, *Psychopathia Sexualis* (New York: Stein and Day, 1965), reprint of the original 1886 edition; and *Text-Book of Insanity* (Philadelphia: F. A. Davis Company, 1904). First German edition, 1879.

[20]Bernard H. Glueck, *Studies in Forensic Psychiatry* (Boston: Little, Brown, 1916).

[21]William Healy, *The Individual Delinquent* (Boston: Little, Brown, 1915).

[22]Early writings about the psychopath personality focused almost exclusively on men, and most psychiatrists appeared to believe that very few women (if any) possessed such traits.

[23]Ibid.

[24]Hervey M. Cleckley, *The Mask of Sanity,* 4th ed. (St. Louis: C. V. Mosby, 1964).

[25]Gwynn Nettler, *Killing One Another* (Cincinnati: Anderson, 1982), p. 179.

[26]A.A. Forth, S.D. Hart, and R.D Hare, "Assessment of Psychopathy in Male Young Offenders," *Psychological Assessment: A Journal of Consulting and Clinical Psychology,* vol. 2 (1990), pp. 342–344.

[27]Albert I. Rabin, "The Antisocial Personality—Psychopathy and Sociopathy," in Hans Toch, *Psychology of Crime and Criminal Justice* (Prospect Heights, Ill.: Waveland, 1979), p. 330.

[28]M.F. Belmore and V.L. Quinsey, "Correlates of Psychopathy in a Noninstitutional Sample," *Journal of Interpersonal Violence,* vol. 9 (1994), pp. 339–349 and C.S. Widom, "A Methodology for Studying Non-Institutional Psychopaths," *Journal of Consulting and Clinical Psychology,* vol. 45 (1977), pp. 674–683.

[29]R.D. Hare, *Psychopathy: Theory and Research* (New York: John Wiley & Sons, 1970).

[30]L.N. Robins, *Deviant Children Grow Up* (Baltimore: Williams and Wilkins, 1966).

[31]S.B. Guze, *Criminality and Psychiatric Disorders* (New York: Oxford University Press, 1976).

[32]American Psychiatric Association, *Diagnostic and Statistical Manual of Mental Disorders,* 2nd ed. (Washington: APA, 1968).

[33] American Psychiatric Association, *Diagnostic and Statistical Manual of Mental Disorders*, p. 43.

[34] S. Hodgins and G. Cote, "The Prevalence of Mental Disorders Among Penitentiary Inmates in Quebec," *Canada's Mental Health*, vol. 38 (1990), pp. 1–4.

[35] H. Prins, *Offenders, Deviants or Patients? An Introduction to the Study of Socio-Forensic Problems* (London: Tavistock, 1980).

[36] Hans J. Eysenck, *Crime and Personality* (Boston: Houghton Mifflin, 1964).

[37] Hans J. Eysenck, "Personality and Criminality: A Dispositional Analysis," in William S. Laufer and Freda Adler, eds., *Advances in Criminology Theory*, vol. 1 (New Brunswick, N.J.: Transaction, 1989), p. 90.

[38] Eysenck, *Crime and Personality*, pp. 35–36.

[39] Eysenck, *Crime and Personality*, p. 92.

[40] Eysenck, *Crime and Personality*, p. 53, citing J. B. S. Haldane, "Foreword," to Johannes Lange, *Crime as Destiny, A Study of Criminal Twins* (London: G. Allen & Unwin, Ltd., 1931), p. 53.

[41] David Abrahamsen, *Crime and the Human Mind* (Montclair, N.J.: Patterson Smith, 1969), p. vii. Originally published in 1944.

[42] P. Q. Roche, *The Criminal Mind: A Study of Communications Between Criminal Law and Psychiatry* (New York: Grove Press, 1958), p. 52.

[43] *The American Heritage Dictionary and Electronic Thesaurus* (Boston: Houghton Mifflin, 1987).

[44] *The American Heritage Dictionary and Electronic Thesaurus, 1987.*

[45] *The American Heritage Dictionary and Electronic Thesaurus, 1987.*

[46] *The American Heritage Dictionary and Electronic Thesaurus, 1987.*

[47] "Nationline: Book Thief," *USA Today*, August 1, 1991, p. 3A.

[48] Pauline Tam, "Not Criminally Responsible," *Ottawa Citizen*, October 29, 1996, p. C3.

[49] Nettler, 1982, p. 159.

[50] Nettler, 1982, p. 155.

[51] Abrahamsen, 1969, p. 99.

[52] Abrahamsen, 1969, p. 100.

[53] J. Dollard, L. Doob, N. Miller, O. Mowrer, and R. Sears, *Frustration and Aggression* (New Haven, Conn.: Yale University Press, 1939).

[54] Maria Bohuslawsky, "Troubled Killer Was Once Fired," *Ottawa Citizen*, April 7, 1999, p. C1.

[55] Andrew F. Henry and James F. Short, Jr., *Suicide and Homicide: Economic, Sociological, and Psychological Aspects of Aggression,* (Glencoe, Ill.: Free Press, 1954).

[56] Stewart Palmer, *A Study of Murder* (New York: Crowell, 1960).

[57] Abrahamsen, 1969, p. 26.

[58] Nancy Gibbs, "The Devil's Disciple," *Time*, January 11, 1993, p. 40.

[59] Seymour L. Halleck, *Psychiatry and the Dilemmas of Crime: A Study of Causes, Punishment and Treatment* (Berkeley: University of California Press, 1971).

[60] Halleck, 1971, p. 77.

[61] Halleck, 1971, p. 78.

[62] Halleck, 1971, p. 80.

[63] Halleck, 1971, p. 80.

[64] Halleck, 1971, p. 80.

[65] Arnold S. Linsky, Ronet Bachman, and Murray A. Straus, *Stress, Culture, and Aggression* (New Haven: Yale University Press, 1995).

[66] Linsky, Bachman, and Straus, 1995, p. 7.

[67] Albert Bandura, "The Social Learning Perspective: Mechanisms of Aggression," in Toch, *Psychology of Crime and Criminal Justice*, pp. 198–236.

[68] M. M. Lefkowitz, L. D. Eron, L. O. Walder, and L. R. Huesmann, "Television Violence and Child Aggression: A Follow-up Study," in G. A. Comstock and E. A. Rubinstein, eds., *Television and Social Behavior*, vol. 3 (Washington, D.C.: U.S. Government Printing Office, 1972), pp. 35–135.

[69] Jim Demers, "'I Am Gavin. How a Bright Kid with Excellent Self-Esteem Slaughtered His Whole Family," *Alberta Report*, December 6, 1993, pp. 18–22.

[70] Demers, 1993, p. 19.

[71] Demers, 1993, p. 22.

[72] Widom and Toch, 1993.

[73] Widom and Toch, 1993, p. 253.

[74] C. R. Hollin, *Psychology and Crime: An Introduction to Criminological Psychology* (London: Routledge, 1989), p. 42.

[75] Hollin, 1989, p. 254.

[76] "15-Year-Old Killer Feared Being Called a 'Little Punk,'" *Fayetteville Observer-Times*, December 26, 1993, p. 1A.

[77] *The American Heritage Dictionary and Electronic Thesaurus.*

[78] C. Ray Jeffery, *Criminology: An Interdisciplinary Approach* (Englewood Cliffs N.J.: Prentice Hall, 1990), p. 431.

[79] Chaulk (1990), 62 C.C.C. (3d)193 (S.C.C.).

[80] *R. v. Parks* (1992), 75 C.C.C. (3d) 287 (S.C.C.).

[81] S. Barnhorst and R. Barnhorst, *Criminal Law and the Canadian Criminal Code* (Toronto: McGraw-Hill Ryerson Ltd., 1996), p. 67.

[82] Halleck, *Psychiatry and the Dilemmas of Crime*, p. 213.

[83] *R. v. Swain* (1991), 63 C.C.C. (3d) 481 (S.C.C.).

[84]Minister of Justice and Attorney General of Canada, *Justice Communiqué*, January 30, 1992, p. 2.

[85]F. Schmalleger, *Criminology Today. An Integrated Introduction* (New Jersey: Prentice-Hall Inc., 1999), pp. 253–256.

[86]*Martin's Annual Criminal Code* (Aurora: Canada Law Book Inc., 1999), s. 672.5(2).

[87]M.A. Jackson and C.T. Griffiths, *Canadian Criminology. Perspectives on Crime and Criminality* (Toronto: Harcourt Brace and Co., 1995), p. 73.

[88]Pauline Tam, *Ottawa Citizen*, October 29, 1996, p. C3.

[89]See, for example, D. P. Farrington, "Childhood Aggression and Adult Violence: Early Precursors and Later Life Outcomes," in D. J. Pepler and K. H. Rubin, eds., *The Development and Treatment of Childhood Aggression* (Hillsdale, N.J.: Erlbaum, 1990), pp. 2–29; and R. E. Tremblay, B. Masse, D. Perron, M. LeBlanc, A. E. Schwartzman, and J. E. Ledingham, "Early Disruptive Behavior: Poor School Achievement, Delinquent Behavior and Delinquent Personality: Longitudinal Analyses," *Journal of Consulting and Clinical Psychology*, vol. 60, no. 1 (1992), pp. 64–72.

[90]R. Loeber, "Questions and Advances in the Study of Developmental Pathways," in D. Cicchetti and S. Toth, eds., *Models and Integration: Rochester Symposium on Developmental Psychopathology* (Rochester, N.Y.: University of Rochester Press, 1991), pp. 97–115.

[91]Joanne Laucius, "Pedophile's Trail of Destruction," *Ottawa Citizen*, April 28, 1999, p. B1.

[92]Jennifer L. White, Terrie E. Moffitt, Felton Earls, Lee Robins, and Phil A. Silva, "How Early Can We Tell? Predictors of Childhood Conduct Disorder and Adolescent Delinquency," *Criminology*, vol. 28, no. 4 (1990), pp. 507–528.

[93]Daniel S. Nagin and David P. Farrington, "The Stability of Criminal Potential from Childhood to Adulthood," *Criminology*, vol. 30, no. 2 (1992), pp. 235–260.

[94]Paul Gendreau, Tracy Little, and Claire Goggin, "A Meta-Analysis of the Predictors of Adult Offender Recidivism: What Works!" *Criminology*, vol. 34, no. 4 (November 1996), pp. 575–607.

[95]For one of the first and still definitive works in the area of selective incapacitation, see Peter Greenwood and Allan Abrahamsen, *Selective Incapacitation* (Santa Monica, Calif.: Rand Corporation, 1982).

[96]M. A. Peterson, H. B. Braiker, and S. M. Polich, *Who Commits Crimes?* (Cambridge: Oelgeschlager, Gunn and Hain, 1981).

[97]J. Monahan, *Predicting Violent Behavior: An Assessment of Clinical Techniques* (Beverly Hills, Calif.: Sage, 1981).

[98]J. Bonta, A. Harris, I. Zinger, and D. Carrière, "The Crown Files Research Project: A study of Dangerous Offenders," (Ottawa: Solicitor General of Canada, 1996).

[99]Jill Peay, "Dangerousness—Ascription or Description," in M.P. Feldman, ed., *Developments in the Study of Criminal Behavior*, vol. 2, *Violence* (New York: John Wiley & Sons, 1982), p. 211, citing N. Walker, "Dangerous People," *International Journal of Law and Psychiatry*, vol. 1 (1978), pp. 37–50.

[100]See, for example, Michael Gottfredson and Travis Hirschi, *A General Theory of Crime* (Stanford, Calif.: Stanford University Press, 1990); and Travis Hirschi and Michael Gottfredson, "Age and the Explanation of Crime," *American Journal of Sociology*, vol. 89 (1983), pp. 552–584.

[101]David F. Greenberg, "Modeling Criminal Careers," *Criminology*, vol. 29, no. 1 (1991), p. 39.

[102]D. A. Andrews and James Bonta, *The Psychology of Criminal Conduct* (Cincinnati: Anderson, 1998).

[103]Andrews and Bonta, 1998, p. 2.

[104]Andrews and Bonta, 1998, p. 2.

[105]Andrews and Bonta, 1998, p. 31.

[106]Andrews and Bonta, 1998, p. 349.

[107]Andrews and Bonta, 1998, p. 362.

[108]Robert R. Hazelwood and John E. Douglas, "The Lust Murderer," *FBI Law Enforcement Bulletin* (Washington: U.S. Department of Justice, April 1980).

[109]Hazelwood and Douglas, 1980.

[110]Anastasia Toufexis, "Mind Games with Monsters," *Time*, May 6, 1991, pp. 68, 69.

## Chapter 7

[1]Frank Tannenbaum, *Crime and the Community* (Boston: Ginn and Company, 1938), p. 25.

[2]Operation Go Home, www.childcybersearch.org/opgohome/gangs.htm

[3]P. Tam, "Driver in Battersby Killing Sent to Adult Jail," *Ottawa Citizen*, November 8, 1996, p. D1 and M. Blanchfield, "Crossed Paths," Ottawa Citizen, February 17, 1996, p. B2.

[4]Edwin M. Lemert, *Social Pathology*, (New York: McGraw-Hill, 1951), p. 3.

[5]For an excellent contemporary review of measuring the extent of social disorganization, see Barbara D. Warner and Glenn L. Pierce, "Reexamining Social Disorganization Theory Using Calls to the Police as a Measure of Crime,"

*Criminology,* vol. 31, no. 4 (November 1993), pp. 493–513.

[6]Lemert, 1951, p. 7.

[7]Peter Haggett, "Human Ecology," in Alan Bullock and Oliver Stallybrass, eds., *The Fontana Dictionary of Modern Social Thought* (London: Fontana, 1977), p. 187.

[8]W. I. Thomas and Florian Znaniecki, *The Polish Peasant in Europe and America* (Boston: Gorham, 1920).

[9]Clifford R. Shaw, et al., *Delinquency Areas* (Chicago: University of Chicago Press, 1929).

[10]David Matza, *Becoming Deviant* (Englewood Cliffs, N.J.: Prentice Hall, 1969).

[11]C.P. LaPrairie, "Community Types, Crime and Police Services on Canadian Indian Reserves," *Journal of Research in Crime and Delinquency,* vol. 25 (1987), pp. 375–91.

[12]C.P., LaPrairie, "Seen But Not Heard: Native People in the Inner City," in *City-By-City Differences. Inner Cities and the Criminal Justice System, Report 2, Aboriginal Justice Directorate* (Ottawa: Department of Justice, 1994).

[13]W. S. Robinson, "Ecological Correlation and the Behavior of Individuals," *American Sociological Review,* vol. 15, (1950), pp. 351–357.

[14]Robinson, 1950, pp. 351–357.

[15]Robert J. Bursik, "Social Disorganization and Theories of Crime and Delinquency: Problems and Prospects," *Criminology,* vol. 26, no. 4 (1988), p. 519.

[16]Stephen J. Pfohl, *Images of Deviance and Social Control* (New York: McGraw-Hill, 1985), p. 167.

[17]Lawrence W. Sherman, Patrick R. Gartin, and Michael E. Buerger, "Hot Spots of Predatory Crime: Routine Activities and the Criminology of Place," *Criminology,* Vol. 27, no. 1 (1989), pp. 27–55.

[18]Rodney Stark, "Deviant Places: A Theory of the Ecology of Crime," *Criminology,* Vol. 25, no. 4 (1987), p. 893.

[19]Stark, 1987, pp. 895–899.

[20]James Q. Wilson and George Kelling, "Broken Windows," *The Atlantic Monthly,* March 1982.

[21]Oscar Newman, *Architectural Design for Crime Prevention* (Washington, D.C.: U.S. Department of Justice, 1973). See also, Oscar Newman, *Defensible Space* (New York: Macmillan, 1972); and Oscar Newman, *Creating Defensible Space* (Washington, D.C.: Office of Housing and Urban Development, 1996).

[22]Oscar Newman, *Defensible Space: Crime Prevention Through Urban Design* (New York: Macmillan, 1972), p. 3. See also Ralph B. Taylor and Adele V. Harrell, "Physical Environment and Crime," National Institute of Justice, May 1996.

[23]Sherman, Gartin, and Buerger, 1989, p. 31.

[24]Peel Regional Police Service, www.peelpolice.on.ca/cepted.html

[25]Sherman, Gartin, and Buerger, 1989, p. 49.

[26]Thorsten Sellin, *Culture Conflict and Crime* (New York: Social Science Research Council, 1938).

[27]Rick Hampson, "Danish Mom Finds New York Doesn't Kid Around," *USA Today,* May 14, 1997, p. 3A.

[28]Although the practice may seem strange to Americans, the author, while teaching in Iceland, saw firsthand lines of unattended infants bundled into strollers awaiting their parents outside of restaurants and sports centers. The practice seems especially prevalent in Scandinavian countries, where the threat of child abduction is virtually unknown.

[29]Sellin, 1938, p. 68.

[30]Frederick M. Thrasher, *The Gang* (Chicago: University of Chicago Press, 1927).

[31]William F. Whyte, *Street Corner Society: The Social Structure of an Italian Slum* (Chicago: University of Chicago Press, 1943).

[32]Walter Miller, "Lower Class Culture as a Generating Milieu of Gang Delinquency," *Journal of Social Issues,* vol. 14, no. 3 (1958), pp. 5–19.

[33]Miller, 1958, p. 19.

[34]Miller, 1958, p. 8.

[35]Miller, 1958, p. 9.

[31]Miller, 1958, p. 9.

[36]Franco Ferracuti and Marvin Wolfgang, *The Subculture of Violence: Toward an Integrated Theory of Criminology* (London: Tavistock, 1967).

[37]Frank P. Williams III and Marilyn D. McShane, *Criminological Theory* (Englewood Cliffs, N.J.: Prentice Hall, 1988), p. 79.

[38]Ferracuti and Wolfgang, 1967, p. 151.

[39]Ferracuti and Wolfgang, 1967, p. 151.

[40]Jeffrey I. Ross, *Violence in Canada. Sociopolitical Perspectives* (Canada: Oxford University Press, 1995), pp. 195–196.

[41]For an excellent review of the literature, see F. Frederick Hawley, "The Southern Violence Construct: A Skeleton in the Criminological Closet," paper presented at the annual meeting of the American Society of Criminology, 1988.

[42]Bertram Wyatt-Brown, *Southern Honor: Ethics and Behavior in the Old South* (Oxford: Oxford University Press, 1983).

[43]John Hagan, "Structural and Cultural Disinvestment and the New Ethnographies of Poverty and Culture," *Contemporary Sociology,* vol. 22(3) (1993), pp. 327–31.

[44]Gwynn Nettler, *Explaining Crime* (New York: McGraw-Hill, 1984).

[45]Margaret Anderson, "Review Essay: Rape Theories, Myths, and Social Change," *Contemporary Crises*, vol. 5 (1983), p. 237.

[46]Emile Durkheim, *Suicide: A Study in Sociology* (New York: Free Press, 1897); reprinted and translated in 1951.

[47]Robert K. Merton, "Social Structure and Anomie," *American Sociological Review*, vol. 3 (October 1938), pp. 672–682; and Robert K. Merton, *Social Theory and Social Structure*, rev. ed. (New York: Free Press, 1957).

[48]Robert Merton, *Social Theory and Social Structure* (New York: Glencoe, 1957), p. 190.

[49]M. Beare, *Criminal Conspiracies: Organized Crime in Canada.* (Toronto: McClelland and Stewart, 1996).

[50]Richard A. Cloward and Lloyd E. Ohlin, *Delinquency and Opportunity: A Theory of Delinquent Gangs* (Glencoe, Ill.: Free Press, 1960).

[51]Cloward and Ohlin, p. 7.

[52]Cloward and Ohlin, p. 13.

[53]Cloward and Ohlin, p. 16.

[54]Cloward and Ohlin, p. 19.

[55]Cloward and Ohlin, p. 3.

[56]Cloward and Ohlin, p. 37.

[57]Cloward and Ohlin, pp. 12–13.

[58]Albert H. Cohen, *Delinquent Boys: The Culture of the Gang* (Glencoe, Ill.: Free Press, 1955).

[59]Cohen, 1955, p. 13.

[60]Donald J. Shoemaker, *Theories of Delinquency: An Examination of Explanations of Delinquent Behavior* (New York: Oxford University Press, 1984), p. 102, citing Cohen.

[61]Cohen, 1955, p. 121.

[62]Shoemaker, 1984, p. 105.

[63]Solicitor General of Canada, www.sgc.gc.ca/EFact/eyouthcr.htm.

[64]Robert, M. Gordon, "Criminal Business Organizations, Street Gangs and 'Wanna Be' Groups: A Vancouver Perspective," *Canadian Journal of Criminology*, vol. 42, no. 1 (January 2000), pp. 39–60.)

[65]Operation Go Home, www.cyberchilsearch.org/opgohome/gangs.htm.

[66]G. David Curry, Richard A. Ball, and Robert J. Fox, "Gang Crime and Law Enforcement Recordkeeping," National Institute of Justice, April 1994.

[67]G. David Curry, Richard A. Ball, and Scott H. Decker, "Estimating the National Scope of Gang Crime from Law Enforcement Data," National Institute of Justice, August 1996.

[68]National Gang Crime Research Center, *Achieving Justice and Reversing the Problem of Gang Crime and Gang Violence in America Today: Preliminary Results of the Project Gangfact Study* (Chicago: National Gang Crime Research Center, 1996).

[69]*Criminal Justice Newsletter,* vol. 19, no. 19 (October 3, 1988), p. 2.

[70]Telephone conversation with the Street Crimes Unit, Lost Angeles County Sheriff's Department, June 20, 1995.

[71]Telephone conversation with the Street Crimes Unit, Lost Angeles County Sheriff's Department, June 20, 1995.

[72]G. David Curry and Irving A. Spergel, "Gang Homicide, Delinquency, and Community," *Criminology*, vol. 26, no. 3 (1988), pp. 381–405.

[73]Curry and Spergel, 1986, p. 401.

[74]See Mary H. Glazier, a review of J. Mitchell Miller and Jeffrey P. Rush, eds., *Gangs: A Criminal Justice Approach* (Cincinnati: Anderson, 1996), in *The Criminologist,* July/April 1996, p. 29.

[75]Robert Agnew, "Foundation for a General Strain Theory of Crime and Delinquency," *Criminology,* vol. 30, no. 1 (1992), pp. 47–87.

[76]Agnew, "Foundation for a General Strain Theory of Crime and Delinquency."

[77]Raymond Paternoster and Paul Mazerolle, "General Strain Theory and Delinquency: A Replication and Extension," *Journal of Research in Crime and Delinquency,* vol. 31, no. 3 (1994), pp. 235–263.

[78]Robert Agnew and Helene Raskin White, "An Empirical Test of General Strain Theory," *Criminology,* vol. 30, no. 4 (1992), pp. 475–499.

[79]Agnew, "Foundation for a General Strain Theory of Crime and Delinquency.".

[80]Agnew, "Foundation for a General Strain Theory of Crime and Delinquency."

[81]Travis Hirschi, "Review of Delbert S. Elliott, David Huizinga, and Suzanne S. Ageton, *Explaining Delinquency and Drug Use*" (Beverly Hills, Calif.: Sage, 1985), in *Criminology,* vol. 25, no. 1 (February 1987), p. 195.

[82]Steven Schlossman et al., *Delinquency Prevention in South Chicago: A Fifty-Year Assessment of the Chicago Area Project* (Santa Monica, Calif.: Rand Corporation, 1984).

[83]J. Robert Lilly, Francis T. Cullen, and Richard A. Ball, *Criminological Theory: Context and Consequences* (Newbury Park, Calif.: Sage, 1989), p. 80.

[84]Lamar T. Empey, *American Delinquency: Its Meaning and Construction* (Homewood, Ill.: Dorsey, 1982), p. 243.

[85]Sibylle Artz, *Sex, Power and the Violent School Girl* (Toronto: Trifolium Books Inc, 1998), p. 24.

[86]Gwynn Nettler, *Killing One Another* (Cincinnati: Anderson, 1982), p. 54.

[87]James Q. Wilson, *The Moral Sense* (New York: The Free Press, 1993).

## Chapter 8

[1]Edwin M. Lemert, *Social Pathology: A Systematic Approach to the Theory of Sociopathic Behavior* (New York: McGraw-Hill, 1951), p. 284.

[2]Robert Reiff, *The Invisible Victim: The Criminal Justice System's Forgotten Responsibility* (New York: Basic Books, 1979), p. xi.

[3]"Killer's Admission to Law School Criticized," *Fayetteville Observer-Times*, September 12, 1993, p. 14A.

[4]"Killer's Admission to Law School Criticized."

[5]S. Brown, V. Creamer and B. Stetson, "Adolescent Alcohol Expectancies in Relation to Personal and Parental Drinking Patterns," *Journal of Abnormal Psychology*, vol. 96 (1987), pp. 117–121

[6]Gresham Sykes and David Matza, "Techniques of Neutralization: A Theory of Delinquency," *American Sociological Review*, vol. 22 (December 1957), pp. 664–670.

[7]Sykes and Matza, 1957, 664–670.

[8]Robert Agnew, "The Techniques of Neutralization and Violence," *Criminology*, vol. 32, no. 4 (1994), pp. 555–580.

[9]Agnew, 1994, pp. 555–580.

[10]Sheldon and Eleanor Glueck, *Delinquents and Nondelinquents in Perspective* (Cambridge, Mass.: Harvard University Press, 1968).

[11]John H. Laub and Robert J. Sampson, "Turning Points in the Life Course: Why Change Matters to the Study of Crime," *Criminology*, vol. 31, no. 3 (1993), pp. 301–325. See also, Robert J. Sampson and John H. Laub, "Crime and Deviance in the Life Course," *Annual Review of Sociology*, vol. 18 (1992), pp. 63–84.

[12]Robert J. Sampson and John H. Laub, *Crime in the Making* (Cambridge, Mass.: Harvard University Press, 1993).

[13]Marvin Wolfgang, Robert Figlio, and Thorsten Sellin, *Delinquency in a Birth Cohort* (Chicago: University of Chicago Press, 1972).

[14]Marvin Wolfgang, Terence Thornberry, and Robert Figlio, *From Boy to Man, From Delinquency to Crime* (Chicago: University of Chicago Press, 1987).

[15]Steven P. Lab, "Analyzing Change in Crime and Delinquency Rates: The Case for Cohort Analysis," *Criminal Justice Research Bulletin*, vol. 3, no. 10 (Huntsville, Texas: Sam Houston State University, 1988), p. 2.

[16]Marvin Wolfgang, "Delinquency in China: Study of a Birth Cohort," *National Institute of Justice Research Preview*, NIJ, May 1996.

[17]Lawrence E. Cohen and Richard Machalek, "A General Theory of Expropriative Crime: An Evolutionary Ecological Approach," *American Journal of Sociology*, vol. 94, no. 3 (1988), pp. 465–501; and Lawrence E. Cohen and Richard Machalek, "The Normalcy of Crime: From Durkheim to Evolutionary Ecology," *Rationality and Society*, vol. 6 (1994), pp. 286–308.

[18]Bryan Vila, "Human Nature and Crime Control: Improving the Feasibility of Nurturant Strategies," *Politics and the Life Sciences*, March 1997, pp. 3–21.

[19]Vila, 1997, pp. 3–21.

[20]See Stuart Greenbaum, "Drugs, Delinquency, and Other Data," in *Juvenile Justice*, vol. 2, no. 1 (Spring/Summer 1994), pp. 2–8.

[21]For another interesting analysis, see Robert J. Sampson and John H. Laub, *Crime in the Making* (Cambridge, Mass.: Harvard University Press, 1993).

[22]See Felton J. Earls and Albert J. Reiss, *Breaking the Cycle: Predicting and Preventing Crime* (Washington, D.C.: National Institute of Justice, 1994).

[23]Vila, 1997, p. 10.

[24]Frank Tannenbaum, *Crime and the Community* (New York: Atheneum Press, 1938), pp. 17–18.

[25]Lemert, 1951, p. 76.

[26]Lemert, 1951, p. 76.

[27]Howard Becker, *Outsiders: Studies in the Sociology of Deviance* (New York: Free Press, 1963).

[28]Becker, *Outsiders*, p. 1.

[29]Becker, *Outsiders*, p. 9.

[30]Becker, *Outsiders*, p. 147.

[31]M.A. Jackson and C.T. Griffiths, *Canadian Criminology: Perspectives on Crime and Criminality* (Toronto: Harcourt Brace Canada, 1995), pp. 261–263.

[32]Becker, *Outsiders*, pp. 37–38.

[33]Mike S. Adams, "Labeling and Differential Association: Towards A General Social Learning Theory of Crime and Deviance," *American Journal of Criminal Justice*, vol. 20, no. 2 (1996), pp. 147–164.

[34]Adams, p. 160.

[35]Randy Martin, Robert J. Mutchnick, and W. Timothy Austin, *Criminological Thought: Pioneers Past and Present* (New York: Macmillan, 1990), p. 368.

[36]Four papers have been released in the RISE series to date. They are: Lawrence W. Sherman and Heather Strang, *The Right Kind of Shame for Crime Prevention* (Canberra, Australia:

Australian National University, 1997); Heather Strang and Lawrence W. Sherman, *The Victim's Perspective* (Canberra, Australia: Australian National University, 1997); Lawrence W. Sherman and Geoffrey C. Barnes, *Restorative Justice and Offenders' Respect for the Law* (Canberra, Australia: Australian National University, 1997); and Lawrence W. Sherman and Heather Strang, *Restorative Justice and Deterring Crime* (Canberra, Australia: Australian National University, 1997).

[37]RISE Working Papers: *Introduction* (Canberra, Australia: Australian National University, 1997).

[38]Walter C. Reckless, *The Crime Problem*, 4th ed. (New York: Appleton-Century-Crofts, 1967).

[39]For a good overview of social control approaches, see George S. Bridges and Martha Myers, eds., *Inequality, Crime, and Social Control* (Boulder, Col.: Westview Press, 1994).

[40]Travis Hirschi, *Causes of Delinquency* (Berkeley: University of California Press, 1969).

[41]Hirschi, 1969.

[42]Michael Gottfredson and Travis Hirschi, *A General Theory of Crime* (Stanford, Calif.: Stanford University Press, 1990).

[43]See also Michael R. Gottfredson and Travis Hirschi, "Criminality and Low Self-Control," in John E. Conklin, ed., *New Perspectives in Criminology* (Boston: Allyn and Bacon, 1996).

[44]Werner Einstadter and Stuart Henry, *Criminological Theory: An Analysis of Its Underlying Assumptions* (Fort Worth: Harcourt Brace, 1995), p. 189.

[45]Hans von Hentig, *The Criminal and His Victim: Studies in the Sociobiology of Crime* (Archon Books, 1967), reprinted from the 1948 Yale University Press edition.

[46]As noted by Stephen Schafer, *The Victim and His Criminal: A Study in Functional Responsibility* (New York: Random House, 1968).

[47]Schafer, 1968, p. 384.

[48]Schafer, 1968, p. 385.

[49]Schafer, 1968, p. 399.

[50]Benjamin Mendelsohn, "Method to Be Used by Counsel for the Defence in the Researches Made into the Personality of the Criminal," *Revue de Droit Pénal et de Criminologie* (Brussels), Fall 1937, p. 877.

[51]See Henry Ellenberger, "Relations Psychologiques entre le Criminel et sa Victime," *Revue Internationale de Criminologie et de Police Technique* (Geneva), no. 2, 1954.

[52]Marvin E. Wolfgang, "Victim-Precipitated Criminal Homicide," *Journal of Criminal Law, Criminology and Police Science*, vol. 48, no. 1 (1957), pp. 1–11.

[53]Wolfgang, 1957.

[54]Thorsten Sellin and Marvin E. Wolfgang, *The Measurement of Delinquency* (New York: John Wiley & Sons, 1964).

[55]Rosa Casarez-Levison, "An Empirical Investigation of the Coping Strategies Used by Victims of Crime: Victimization Redefined," in Emilio Viano, ed., *Critical Issues in Victimology: International Perspectives* (New York: Spring, 1992).

[56]M. Bard and D. Sangrey, *The Crime Victim's Book*, 2nd ed. (New York: Brunner/Mazel, 1986).

[57]Elizabeth Kubler-Ross, *On Death and Dying* (New York: Macmillan, 1969).

[58]Richard Quinney, "Who Is the Victim," *Criminology*, vol. 10, no. 2 (1972), pp. 314–323.

[59]William G. Doerner, "The Impact of Medical Resources on Criminally Induced Lethality: A Further Examination," *Criminology*, vol. 26, no. 1 (February 1988), pp. 171–177.

[60]Doerner, 1988, p. 177.

[61]William Ryan, "The Art of Savage Discovery," in Adalberto Aguirre, Jr. and David V. Baker, eds., *Sources: Notable Selections in Race and Ethnicity* (Guilford, Conn.: Dushkin/McGraw-Hill, 1995).

[62]Steven Rathgeb Smith and Susan Freinkel, *Adjusting the Balance: Federal Policy and Victim Services* (Westport, Conn.: Greenwood Press, 1988), p. 13.

[63]V.F. Sacco and H. Johnson, *Patterns of Criminal Victimization in Canada* (Ottawa: Statistics Canada, 1990); and M. Baril, S. LaFlamme-Cusson and S. Beauchemin, *Working Paper No. 12. Crime Victims Compensation: An Assessment of the Quebec IVAC Program* (Ottawa: Policy Planning and Development Branch, Department of Justice, 1984).

[64]For a good review of the issues in the area, see Robert C. Davis, Arthur J. Lurigio, and Wesley G. Skogan, *Victims of Crime*, 2nd ed. (Thousand Oaks, Calif.: Sage, 1997).

[65]E.A. Fattah, *Understanding Crime Victimization* (Scarborough, Ont.: Prentice-Hall, 1991).

[66]J. Moylan, *Victim Services and Canadian Police Agencies—A Source Book* (Ottawa: Canadian Association of Chiefs of Police and Solicitor General of Canada, 1990).

[67]W. Jamieson and R.R. Ross, "An Evaluation of the Victim/Witness Assistance Programme, Ministry of the Attorney General of Ontario," *Canadian Journal of Program Evaluation*, vol. 6(1),(1991), pp. 83–96.

[68]A. Hatch Cunningham and C.T. Griffiths, *Canadian Criminal Justice, A Primer* (Toronto: Harcourt Brace Canada, 1997), p. 79.

[69]C.T. Griffiths and S. Verdun-Jones, *Canadian Criminal Justice* (Toronto: Harcourt Brace Canada, 1994), p. 559.

## Chapter 9

[1]Quoted in J.C. Hackler, *Canadian Criminology: Strategies and Perspectives* (Scarborough: Prentice Hall Allyn and Bacon Canada, 2000), p. 148. Solon, who lived from 640 to 559 BC, was known as one of the Seven Wise Men of Greece. He was a statesman, lawgiver, and poet, whose reforms included the end of slavery for debt, the replacement of the harsh draconian law code with a more humane one, and the end of exclusive aristocratic control of government. These, and other reforms, are considered to be the foundations of modern democracy.

[2]Anne Hansen was leader of the Squamish Five and received a life sentence for her involvement in the bombing of a Toronto nuclear weapons system manufacturer. Ten people were critically injured in the bombing and $3.8 million damage was done.

[3]Vance Packard, *The Status Seekers* (London: Harmondsworth, 1961).

[4]Ralf Dahrendorf, *Class and Class Conflict in An Industrial Society* (Stanford, Calif.: Stanford University Press, 1959).

[5]Ralf Dahrendorf, "Out of Utopia: Toward a Reorientation of Sociological Analysis," *American Journal of Sociology*, vol. 64 (1958), pp. 115–127.

[6]William J. Chambliss, "Toward a Political Economy of Crime," in C. Reasons and R. Rich, *The Sociology of Law* (Toronto: Butterworth, 1978), p. 193.

[7]George B. Vold, *Theoretical Criminology* (New York: Oxford University Press, 1958), p. 205.

[8]Vold, 1958, p. 206.

[9]Vold, pp. 208–209.

[10]Vold, p. 309.

[11]Austin Turk, *Criminality and Legal Order* (Chicago: Rand McNally, 1969), p. vii.

[12]Turk, 1969, p. vii.

[13]William Chambliss and Robert T. Seidman, *Law, Order, and Power* (Reading, Mass.: Addison-Wesley, 1971), p. 33.

[14]Adapted from Chambliss and Seidman, 1971, pp. 473–474.

[15]William J. Chambliss, *Crime and the Legal Process* (New York: McGraw-Hill, 1969), p. 88.

[16]William J. Chambliss, "Toward a Political Economy of Crime," *Theory and Society*, vol. 2 (1975), pp. 152–153.

[17] Chambliss, pp. 152–153.

[18] Chambliss, p. 152.

[19]Richard Quinney, *Critique of the Legal Order: Crime Control in Capitalist Society* (Boston: Little, Brown, 1974), p. 16.

[20]Richard Quinney, *Class, State, and Crime: On the Theory and Practice of Criminal Justice* (New York: David McKay, 1977), p. 58.

[21]Quinney, 1977, p. 58.

[22]Quinney, 1977, p. 61.

[23]Quinney, 1977, p. 65.

[24]Gresham M. Sykes, "Critical Criminology," *Journal of Criminal Law and Criminology*, vol. 65 (1974), pp. 206–213.

[25]David A. Jones, *History of Criminology: A Philosophical Perspective* (Westport, Conn.: Greenwood, 1986), p. 200.

[26]Elliott Currie, "Market, Crime, and Community," *Theoretical Criminology*, vol. 1, no. 2 (May 1997), pp. 147–172.

[27]William V. Pelfrey, *The Evolution of Criminology* (Cincinnati: Anderson Pub. Co., 1980), p. 86.

[28]For a good overview of critiques of radical criminology, see J. F. Galliher, "Life and Death of Liberal Criminology," *Contemporary Crisis*, vol. 2, no. 3 (July 1978), pp. 245–263.

[29]Jackson Toby, "The New Criminology Is the Old Sentimentality," *Criminology*, vol. 16 (1979), pp. 516–526.

[30]Toby, 1979, pp. 516–526.

[31]Don C. Gibbons, *Talking About Crime and Criminals: Problems and Issues in Theory Development in Criminology* (Englewood Cliffs, N.J.: Prentice Hall, 1994), p. 165, citing Loraine Gelsthorpe and Alison Morris, "Feminism and Criminology in Britain," *British Journal of Criminology* (Spring 1988), pp. 93–110.

[32]Sally S. Simpson, "Feminist Theory, Crime and Justice," *Criminology*, vol. 27, no. 4 (1989), p. 605.

[33]Freda Adler, *Sisters in Crime: The Rise of the New Female Criminal* (New York: McGraw-Hill, 1975).

[34]Rita J. Simon, *Women and Crime* (Lexington, Mass.: Lexington Books, 1975).

[35]Kathleen Daly and Meda Chesney-Lind, "Feminism and Criminology," *Justice Quarterly*, vol. 5, no. 5 (December 1988), pp. 497–535.

[36]Susan Caulfield and Nancy Wonders, "Gender and Justice: Feminist Contributions to Criminology," in Gregg Barak, ed., *Varieties of Criminology: Readings from a Dynamic Discipline* (Westport, Conn.: Praeger, 1994), pp. 213–229.

[37]Roslyn Muraskin and Ted Alleman, *It's a Crime: Women and Justice* (Englewood Cliffs, N.J.: Prentice Hall, 1993), p. 1.

[38]F.P. Williams III, and M.D. McShane, *Criminological Theory*, (Englewood Cliffs, N.J.: Prentice-Hall, 1994), p. 238.

[39]Carol Pateman, "Feminist Critiques of the Public/Private Dichotomy," in Anne Phillips, ed., *Feminism and Equality* (Oxford: Basil Blackwell, 1987).

[40]Alida V. Merlo and Joycelyn M. Pollock, eds., *Women, Law and Social Control* (Needham Heights, Mass.: Allyn and Bacon, 1995).

[41]Williams and McShane, 1994, p. 238.

[42]Simpson, 1989.

[43]John Hagan, *Structural Criminology* (New Brunswick, N.J.: Rutgers University Press, 1989), p. 130.

[44]Hagan, p. 13.

[45]Hagan, p. 13.

[46]Evelyn K. Sommers, *Voices from Within: Women Who Have Broken the Law* (Toronto: University of Toronto Press, 1995).

[47]Daly and Chesney-Lind, 1988, p. 506.

[48]Daly and Chesney-Lind, 1988, p. 506.

[49]Daly and Chesney-Lind, 1988, p. 514.

[50]For an intriguing analysis of how existing laws tend to criminalize women and their reproductive activities, see Susan O. Reed, "The Criminalization of Pregnancy: Drugs, Alcohol, and AIDS," in Muraskin and Alleman, *It's a Crime: Women and Justice*, pp. 92–117; and Drew Humphries, "Mothers and Children, Drugs and Crack: Reactions to Maternal Drug Dependency," in Muraskin and Alleman, *It's a Crime: Women and Justice*, pp. 131–145.

[51]Dawn H. Currie, "Feminist Encounters with Postmodernism: Exploring the Impasse of the Debates on Patriarchy and Law," *Canadian Journal of Women and the Law*, vol. 5, no. 1 (1992), p. 10.

[52]For an excellent overview of feminist theory in criminology, and for a comprehensive review of research regarding female offenders, see Joanne Belknap, *The Invisible Woman: Gender Crime and Justice* (Belmont, Calif.: Wadsworth, 1996).

[53]Such studies are still ongoing and continue to add to the descriptive literature of feminist criminology. See, for example, Deborah R. Baskin and Ira Sommers, "Female Initiation into Violent Street Crime," *Justice Quarterly*, vol. 10, no. 4 (December 1993), pp. 559–583; Scott Decker, Richard Wright, Allison Redfern, and Dietrich Smith, "A Woman's Place Is In the Home: Females and Residential Burglary," *Justice Quarterly*, vol. 10, no. 1 (March 1993), pp. 143–162; and Jill L. Rosenbaum, "The Female Delinquent: Another Look at the Role of the Family," in Muraskin and Alleman, *It's a Crime: Women and Justice*, pp. 399–420.

[54]Ronald L. Akers, *Criminological Theories: Introduction and Evaluation* (Los Angeles: Roxbury, 1994), p. 39.

[55]For additional insight into the notion of "deconstruction" as it applies to feminist thought within criminology, see Carol Smart, *Feminism and the Power of Law* (New York: Routledge, 1989).

[56]Daly and Chesney-Lind, "Feminism and Criminology," p. 512.

[57]See, for example, Darrell J. Steffensmeier and Emile Andersen Allan, "Sex Disparities in Arrests by Residence, Race, and Age: An Assessment of the Gender Convergence/Crime Hypothesis," *Justice Quarterly*, vol. 5, no. 1 (March 1988), pp. 53–80.

[58]Darrell Steffensmeier, John Kramer, and Cathy Streifel, "Gender and Imprisonment Decisions," *Criminology*, vol. 31, no. 3 (August 1993), pp. 411–446. Gender-based differences, however, have been discovered in some instances of probation-and parole-related decision making. See Edna Erez, "Gender, Rehabilitation, and Probation Decisions," *Criminology*, vol. 27, no. 2 (1989), pp. 307–327; and Edna Erez, "Dangerous Men, Evil Women: Gender and Parole Decision-Making," *Justice Quarterly*, vol. 9, no. 1 (March 1992), pp. 106–126.

[59]See, for example, Kathleen Daly, "Neither Conflict nor Labeling nor Paternalism Will Suffice: Intersections of Race, Ethnicity, Gender, and Family in Criminal Court Decisions," *Crime and Delinquency*, vol. 35, no. 1 (January 1989), pp. 136–168.

[60]Citing Allison Morris, *Women, Crime and Criminal Justice* (New York: Blackwell, 1987).

[61]Caulfield and Wonders, 1994, p. 229.

[62]For examples of how this might be accomplished, see F. H. Knopp, "Community Solutions to Sexual Violence: Feminist/Abolitionist Perspectives," in *Criminology as Peacemaking* (Bloomington: Indiana University Press), pp. 181–193; and S. Caringella-MacDonald and D. Humphries, "Sexual Assault, Women, and the Community: Organizing to Prevent Sexual Violence," *Criminology as Peacemaking*, pp. 98–113.

[63]Richard Quinney, "Life of Crime: Criminology and Public Policy as Peacemaking," *Journal of Crime and Justice*, vol. 16, no. 2 (1993), pp. 3–9.

[64]See, for example, Harold E. Pepinsky, "This Can't Be Peace: A Pessimist Looks at Punishment," in W. B. Groves and G. Newman, eds., *Punishment and Privilege* (Albany: Harrow and Heston, 1986); Harold E. Pepinsky, "Violence as Unresponsiveness: Toward a New Conception of Crime," *Justice Quarterly*, vol. 5 (1988), pp. 539–563; and Pepinsky and Quinney, *Criminology as Peacemaking*.

[65]See, for example, Richard Quinney, "Crime, Suffering, Service: Toward a Criminology of

Peacemaking," *Quest,* vol. 1 (1988), pp. 66–75; Richard Quinney, "The Theory and Practice of Peacemaking in the Development of Radical Criminology," *Critical Criminologist,* vol. 1, no. 5 (1989), p. 5; and Richard Quinney and John Wildeman, *The Problem of Crime: A Peace and Social Justice Perspective,* 3rd ed. (Mayfield, Calif.: Mountain View Press, 1991)—originally published as *The Problem of Crime: A Critical Introduction to Criminology* (New York: Bantam, 1977).

[66]All these themes are addressed, for example, in Pepinsky and Quinney, *Criminology as Peacemaking.*

[67]For a good discussion of this "theory," see John F. Galliher, "Willie Horton: Fact, Faith, and Commonsense Theory of Crime," in ibid., pp. 245–250.

[68]Quinney and Wildeman, *The Problem of Crime: A Peace and Social Justice Perspective,* pp. vii–viii.

[69]Richard Quinney, "Life of Crime: Criminology and Public Policy as Peacemaking," *Journal of Crime and Justice,* vol. 16, no. 2 (1993), abstract.

[70]Bo Lozoff and Michael Braswell, *Inner Corrections: Finding Peace and Peace Making* (Cincinnati: Anderson, 1989).

[71]Clemmons Bartollas and Michael Braswell, "Correctional Treatment, Peacemaking, and the New Age Movement," *Journal of Crime and Justice,* vol. 16, no. 2 (1993), pp. 43–58.

[72]Bartollas and Braswell, 1993.

[73]Ram Dass and P. Gorman, *How Can I Help? Stories and Reflections on Service* (New York: Alfred A. Knopf, 1985), p. 165; as cited in *The Problem of Crime: A Peace and Social Justice Perspective,* 3rd ed., p. 116.

[74]Lozoff and Braswell, 1989, p. vii.

[75]Werner Einstadter and Stuart Henry, *Criminological Theory: An Analysis of Its Underlying Assumptions* (Fort Worth: Harcourt Brace, 1995), p. 233.

[76]Daniel J. Curran and Claire M. Renzetti, *Theories of Crime* (Boston: Allyn & Bacon, 1994), p. 283.

[77]See M. D. Schwartz and W. S. DeKeseredy, "Left Realist Criminology: Strengths, Weaknesses, and the Feminist Critique," *Crime, Law, and Social Change,* vol. 15, no. 1 (January 1991), pp. 51–72; W. S. DeKeseredy and B. D. MacLean, "Exploring the Gender, Race, and Class Dimensions of Victimization: A Left Realist Critique of the Canadian Urban Victimization Survey," *International Journal of Offender Therapy and Comparative Criminology,* vol. 35, no. 2 (Summer 1991), pp. 143–161; and W. S. DeKeseredy and M. D. Schwartz, "British and U.S. Left Realism: A Critical Comparison," *International Journal of Offender Therapy and Comparative Criminology,* vol. 35, no. 3 (Fall 1991), pp. 248–262.

[78]See Jock Young, "The Failure of Criminology: The Need for a Radical Realism," in R. Matthews and J. Young, eds., *Confronting Crime* (Beverly Hills: Sage, 1986), pp. 4–30; Jock Young, "The Tasks of a Realist Criminology," *Contemporary Crisis,* vol. 11, no. 4 (1987) pp. 337–356; and "Radical Criminology in Britain: The Emergence of a Competing Paradigm," *British Journal of Criminology,* vol. 28 (1988), pp. 159–183.

[79]D. Brown and R. Hogg, "Essentialism, Radical Criminology, and Left Realism," *Australian and New Zealand Journal of Criminology,* vol. 25 (1992), pp. 195–230.

[80]Roger Matthews and Jock Young, "Reflections on Realism," in Jock Young and Roger Matthews, eds., *Rethinking Criminology: The Realist Debate* (Newbury Park, Calif.: Sage, 1992).

[81]Don C. Gibbons, *Talking About Crime and Criminals: Problems and Issues in Theory Development in Criminology,* (Englewood Cliffs, N.J.: Prentice Hall, 1994), p. 170.

[82]Piers Bierne and James W. Messerschmidt, *Criminology* (New York: Harcourt Brace Jovanovich, 1991), p. 501.

[83]Michael J. Lynch and W. Byron Groves, *A Primer in Radical Criminology,* 2nd ed. (Albany, N.Y.: Harrow and Heston, 1989), p. 126.

[84]Lynch and Groves, 1989, p. 128.

[85]Raymond J. Michalowski, *Order, Law, and Crime: An Introduction to Criminology* (New York: Random House, 1985), p. 410.

[86]Lynch and Groves, 1989, p. 130.

# Chapter 10

[1]Peter Kent, chapter 1, note 37; Michele Mandel, "Crime Rate Is Down: Violent Acts Are Changing Our Perspective," *Toronto Sun,* March 14, 1999, p. 32.

[2]Jeremy Mercer, "'Locker Room Bandit' Benched," *Ottawa Citizen,* March 6, 1999, pp. A1–A2.

[3]Sylvain Tremblay, "Crime Statistics in Canada, 1998," *Juristat,* vol. 19, no. 9 (Ottawa: Minister of Industry, 1999) and/or Canadian Centre for Justice Statistics, Canadian Crime Statistics, 1998 (Ottawa: Minister of Industry, 1999).

[4]Steve Cannon, "Grandson Gets Life in Prison For Murder of 90-Year-Old," *Ottawa Citizen,* January 10, 1998, p. E12.

[5]Bureau of Justice Statistics, *Report to the Nation on Crime and Justice* (Washington DC: U.S. Government Printing Office, 1988), p. 4.

[6]Frank Schmalleger, *Criminology Today. An Integrated Introduction* (New Jersey: Prentice Hall, 1999), p. 63.

[7]Bureau of Justice Statistics, *Report to the Nation on Crime and Justice*, 1988, p. 4.

[8]Frank Schmalleger, *Criminology Today. An Integrated Introduction* (New Jersey: Prentice Hall, 1999), p. 66.

[9]Schmalleger, 1999, p.66.

[10]See Elizabeth Cormack, "Women and Crime" in Rick Linden (ed.), *Criminology. A Canadian Perspective* (Toronto: Harcourt Brace Canada, 1996), pp. 139–175.

[11]Rebecca Kong,"Canadian Crime Statistics, 1996," *Juristat*, vol. 17, no. 8 (Ottawa: Minister of Industry, 1997).

[12]Frank Schmalleger and Ted Alleman, "The Collective Reality of Crime: An Integrative Approach to the Causes and Consequences of the Criminal Event," in Gregg Bank, *Varieties of Criminology: Readings from a Dynamic Discipline* (New York: Praeger Publishers, 1994).

[13]David G. Curtis, "Perspectives on Acquaintance Rape," *American Academy of Experts in Traumatic Stress*, www.aaets.org.

[14]Statistics Canada, *Violence Against Women Survey. Survey Highlights* (Ottawa: Minister of Industry, 1993)

[15]Integration and Analysis Program, "Sex Offenders", *Juristat*, vol. 19, no. 3 (Ottawa, Minister of Industry, 1999).

[16]Kong, 1997.

[17]Combined data from 1994–1995 are the most recent available. Reported criminal harassment incidents are counted regardless of whether or not it was the most serious violation in an occurrence or not. See Rebecca Kong, "Criminal Harassment," *Juristat*, vol. 16, no. 12 (Ottawa: Minister of Industry, 1996).

[18]Rebecca Kong, "Criminal Harassment," *Juristat*, vol. 16, no. 12 (Ottawa: Minister of Industry, 1996).

[19]Kong, 1997. Robbery statistics from 1996 are the most recent available that provide this breakdown.

[20]See note 16.

[21]Frederick J. Desroches, *Force and Fear: Robbery in Canada* (Toronto: ITP Nelson, 1995).

[22]Peter Hum, "Compassion for a Child Killer," *Ottawa Citizen*, December 28, 1999, p. B1.

[23]Cathy S. Widom, "The Intergenerational Transmission of Violence," in Neil Warner and Marvin Wolfgang (eds)., *Pathways to Criminal Violence* (Newbury Park, CA: Sage 1989.)

[24]Kong, 1997.

[25]Kong, 1997.

[26]Sherrie Barnhorst and Richard Barnhorst, *Criminal Law and the Canadian Criminal Code* (Toronto: McGraw-Hill Ryerson Ltd., 1996), p. 313.

[27]Julie Sauvé, "Motor Vehicle Theft in Canada, 1996," *Juristat*, vol. 18, no. 1 (Ottawa: Minister of Industry, 1997).

[28]Paul McKay, "Hot Cars. Inside Ontario's Auto-Wreck Racket," *Ottawa Citizen*, March 7, 1998, pp. A1–A2, B1–B3.

[29]For further information on impaired driving, see Julie Sauvé, "Impaired Driving in Canada, 1998," *Juristat*, vol. 19, no. 11 (Ottawa: Minister of Industry, 1999).

[30]Derek E. Janhevich, "The Changing Nature of Fraud in Canada," *Juristat*, vol. 18, no. 4 (Ottawa: Minister of Industry, 1998).

[31]Janhevich, 1998.

[32]See Karen Swol, "Private Security and Public Policing in Canada," *Juristat*, vol. 18, no. 13 (Ottawa: Minister of Industry, 1998) for an overview of recent trends.

[33]L. J. Siegel and C. McCormick, *Criminology in Canada*, (Scarborough: ITP Nelson, 1999), p. 427.

[34]S. Porteous, *Organized Crime Impact Study (Highlights)*, (Ottawa: Solicitor General of Canada, 1998).

[35]*CISC Annual Report on Organized Crime in Canada*, 1998, www.csis.gc.ca.

[36]Siegel and McCormick, 1999, p. 451.

[37]*CISC Annual Report on Organized Crime in Canada*, 1998, www.csis.gc.ca.

# Chapter 11

[1]National Crime Prevention Council of the Justice Department and the Solicitor General of Canada, "Working Together for Safer Communities," www.crime-prevention.org/ncpc.

[2]Barbara Hall, "Let's Prevent Youth Crime, Not React to It," *Ottawa Citizen*, May 5, 2000, p.E4.

[3]Although charged with sodomy, Shakur was convicted on three lesser counts of sexual abuse. See Samuel Maull, "Shakur Trial," Associated Press wire service, December 2, 1994.

[4]James T. Jones IV, "Real-Life Woes Beset Actor/Rapper," *USA Today*, February 11, 1994, p. 2A.

[5]$1 million for himself and another $1 million for his bodyguard. See "Prosecutors Mull Second Trial for Rapper," Reuters wire service, February 23, 1996.

[6]Dennis R. Martin, "The Music of Murder," *ACJS Today*, November/December 1993, pp. 1, 3, 20.

[7]Kendall Hamilton and Allison Samuels, "Dr. Dre's New 'Hood: Hollywood," *Newsweek,* August 22, 1994, p. 45.

[8]See, for example, Elizabeth Snead, "Dogg's 'Murder' Video has Plenty of Bite," *USA Today,* October 13, 1994.

[9]John Ekstedt, "Canadian Justice Policy," in Margaret A. Jackson and Curt T. Griffiths (eds.), *Canadian Criminology. Perspectives on Crime and Criminality* (Toronto: Harcourt Brace Canada, 1995), p. 311.

[10]James E. Anderson, *Public Policymaking: An Introduction* (Boston: Houghton Mifflin, 1990).

[11]Ekstedt, 1995, p. 308.

[12]Ekstedt, 1995, p. 312.

[13]Nancy E. Marion, *A History of Federal Crime Control Initiatives, 1960–1993* (Westport: Praeger, 1994), p. 3. For a more detailed analysis of the process by which crime control policies are created, see Paul Rock, "The Opening Stages of Criminal Justice Policy Making," *British Journal of Criminology,* vol. 35, no. 1 (Winter 1995).

[14]Ekstedt, 1995, p. 308.

[15]Jeff Ferrell, "Criminological *Verstehen:* Inside the Immediacy of Crime," *Justice Quarterly,* vol. 14, no. 1 (1997), p. 16.

[16]For an excellent discussion of the policies associated with law, punishment, and social control, see Thomas G. Blomberg and Stanley Cohen, eds., *Punishment and Social Control: Essays in Honor of Sheldon L. Messinger* (Hawthorne, N.Y.: Aldine de Gruyter, 1995).

[17]Eric Schlosser, "The Prison-Industrial Complex," *The Atlantic Monthly,* vol. 282, no. 6, December 1998, pp. 51–77.

[18]Bryan Vila, "Could We Break the Crime Control Paradox?" Paper presented at the annual meeting of the American Society of Criminology, Miami, November 1994 [abstract].

[19]From an address to the Standing Committee on Justice and the Solicitor General, 1993.

[20]National Crime Prevention Council of the Justice Department and the Solicitor General of Canada, "Working Together for Safer Communities," www.crime-prevention.org/ncpc.

[21]See Arthur L. Kellermann, "Understanding and Prevention Violence: A Public Health Perspective," National Institute of Justice, June 1996.

[22]Quoted in Frank Schmalleger, *Criminology Today. An Integrative Introduction* (New Jersey: Prentice-Hall Inc., 1999), p. 526.

[23]Vincent F. Sacco, and Leslie W. Kennedy, *The Criminal Event* (Toronto: ITP Nelson, 1998), p. 340.

[24]Canadian criminal justice statistics for 1998 indicate that the presence of firearms in violent crime has declined from 6.0 percent in 1994 to 4.8 percent in 1998. See Sylvain Tremblay, "Crime Statistics in Canada, 1998," *Juristat,* vol. 19, no. 9 (Ottawa: Minister of Industry, 1999).

[25]E.A. Suter, W.C. Waters, G.B. Murray, et al., "Violence in America: Effective Solutions," *Journal of the Medical Association of Georgia*, vol. 85, 1995, pp. 253–263.

[26]For an excellent up-to-date review of policy issues in the crime-control area, see James Houston and William W. Parsons, *Criminal Justice and the Policy Process* (Chicago: Nelson-Hall, 1997).

[27]Bryan Vila, "A General Paradigm for Understanding Criminal Behavior: Extending Evolutionary Ecological Theory," *Criminology,* vol. 32, no. 3 (August 1994), pp. 311–359.

[28]Vila, "Could We Break the Crime Control Paradox?"

[29]Bryan Vila, "Human Nature and Crime Control: Improving the Feasibility of Nurturant Strategies," *Politics and the Life Sciences,* March 1997, p. 10.

[30]Vila, "Human Nature and Crime Control," p. 11.

[31]Bryan Vila, "Human Nature and Crime Control," pp. 3–21.

[32]Vila, "A General Paradigm for Understanding Criminal Behavior."

[33]Report of the National Symposium on Community Safety and Crime Prevention, October 1993, www.crime-prevention.org.

[34]Information for this section has been obtained from the Federal Government's Web site dealing with this initiative, www.crime-prevention.org.

[35]From the Peel Regional Police Service Web site, www.peelpolice.on.ca/cpted/html.

[36]C. Ray Jeffery, *Crime Control Through Environmental Design* (Beverley Hills, CA: Sage, 1971).

[37]Crime Prevention Association of New Brunswick,"Safe Communities. Crime Prevention Through Environmental Design," www.cap.unb.ca.

[38]Peel Regional Police Service, "Want to Deter Crime? Think CPTED," www.peelpolice.on.ca.

[39]Crime Prevention Association of New Brunswick,"Safe Communities. Crime Prevention Through Environmental Design," www.cap.unb.ca.

[40]Greg Saville, "Balancing the CPTED Response," www.cpted.net.

[41]Saville, "Balancing the CPTED Response," www.cpted.net.

[42]All statistics on youth crime are from Josée Savoie, "Youth Violent Crime," *Juristat,* vol. 19, no. 13 (Ottawa: Minister of Industry, 1999).

[43]News Release, Department of Justice, Ottawa, March 11, 1999.

[44]Jim Bronskill and Janice Tibbetts, "New Law, but Same Controversy," *Ottawa Citizen*, March 12, 1999, p. A3.

[45]H. Bianchi, *Position and Subject-Matter of Criminology* (Amsterdam, 1956).

[46]Hermann Mannheim, *Comparative Criminology* (New York: Houghton Mifflin, 1965), p. 18.

[47]For an interesting look at jurisdictional complexities, see the discussion about the attempts to regulate lap dancing in Ontario in Alison Hatch Cunningham and Curt T. Griffiths, *Canadian Criminal Justice. A Primer* (Toronto: Harcourt Brace Canada, 1997), pp. 13–14.

[48]Ekstedt, 1995, pp. 307–329.

[49]Vila, "Could We Break the Crime Control Paradox?" p. 3.

## Chapter 12

[1]Barry Stuart, "Circle Sentencing: Turning Swords Into Ploughshares," in Burt Galaway and Joe Hudson, (eds.), *Restorative Justice: International Perspectives* (Monsey, N.Y.: Criminal Justice Press, 1996), pp. 193–206.

[2]Cynthia Manson and Charles Ardai, eds., *Future Crimes* (New York: Donald I. Fine, 1992), p. x.

[3]Joseph F. Coates, "The Highly Probable Future: 83 Assumptions About the Year 2025," *The Futurist,* vol. 28, no. 4 (July/August 1994), p. 51.

[4]Alvin Toffler, *Future Shock* (New York: Random House, 1970).

[5]Alvin Toffler, *Powershift: Knowledge, Wealth, and Violence at the Edge of the 21st Century* (New York: Bantam Books, 1990).

[6]Alvin Toffler, *The Third Wave* (New York: Bantam Books, 1981).

[7]John Naisbitt, *Megatrends: Ten New Directions Transforming Our Lives* (New York: Warner Books, 1982).

[8]Although this chapter cannot cover all future aspects of the criminal justice system, readers are referred to C. J. Swank, "Police in the 21st Century: Hypotheses for the Future," *International Journal of Comparative and Applied Criminal Justice,* vol. 17, nos. 1 and 2 (Spring/Fall 1993), pp. 107–120, for an excellent analysis of policing in the future.

[9]Society of Police Futurists International, "PFI: The Future of Policing" (brochure), no date.

[10]William L. Tafoya, "Futures Research: Implications for Criminal Investigations," in James N. Gilbert, ed., *Criminal Investigation: Essays and Cases* (Columbus, Ohio: Charles E. Merrill, 1990), p. 214.

[11]As identified by George F. Cole, "Criminal Justice in the Twenty-First Century: The Role of Futures Research," in John Klofas and Stan Stojkovic, eds., *Crime and Justice in the Year 2010* (Belmont, Calif.: Wadsworth, 1995).

[12]Cole, 1995.

[13]Cole, 1995.

[14]Richter H. Moore, Jr., "Wiseguys: Smarter Criminals and Smarter Crime in the 21st Century," *The Futurist,* vol. 28, no. 5 (September/October 1994), p. 33.

[15]Moore, 1994, p. 33.

[16]Georgette Bennett, *Crimewarps: The Future of Crime in America* (Garden City, N.Y.: Anchor/Doubleday, 1987).

[17]L. Edward Wells, "Explaining Crime in the Year 2010," in Klofas and Stojkovic, 1995, pp. 36–61.

[18]Wells, "Explaining Crime", pp. 48–49.

[19]Wells, "Explaining Crime", pp. 54–57.

[20]Frank P. Williams III and Marilyn D. McShane, *Criminological Theory,* 2nd ed. (Englewood Cliffs, N.J.: Prentice Hall, 1994), p. 257.

[21]Gregg Barak, "Introduction: Criminological Theory in the 'Postmodernist' Era," in Gregg Barak, ed., *Varieties of Criminology: Readings from a Dynamic Discipline* (Westport, Conn.: Praeger, 1994), pp. 1–11.

[22]For an excellent and detailed discussion of many of these approaches, see Dragan Milovanovic, *Postmodern Criminology* (Hamden, Conn.: Garland, 1997).

[23]Bruce DiCristina, *Methods in Criminology: A Philosophical Primer* (New York: Harrow and Heston, 1995).

[24]Jeff Ferrell, "Anarchy Against the Discipline," a review of Bruce DiCristina's *Methods in Criminology: A Philosophical Primer* (New York: Harrow and Heston, 1995), in the *Journal of Criminal Justice and Popular Culture,* vol. 3, no. 4 (August 15, 1995).

[25]See, for example, Stuart Henry and Dragan Milovanovic, *Constitutive Criminology: Beyond Postmodernism* (London: Sage, 1995); and Dragan Milovanovic, *Postmodern Criminology* (Hamden, Conn.: Garland, 1997).

[26]Milovanovic, 1997.

[27]Dragan Milovanovic, *Primer in the Sociology of Law,* 2nd ed. (New York: Harrow and Heston, 1994).

[28]Stuart Henry and Dragan Milovanovic, *Constitutive Criminology: Beyond Postmodernism* (London: Sage, 1995), p. 118.

[29]Werner Einstadter and Stuart Henry, *Criminological Theory: An Analysis of Its Underlying Assumptions* (Fort Worth: Harcourt Brace, 1995), p. 291.

[30]Frank P. Williams III and Marilyn D. McShane, *Criminological Theory,* 2nd ed. (Englewood Cliffs, N.J.: Prentice Hall, 1994), p. 221.

[31]Felton M. Earls and Albert J. Reiss, *Breaking the Cycle: Predicting and Preventing Crime* (Washington, D.C.: National Institute of Justice, 1994), p. 49.

[32]L. E. Cohen and Marcus Felson, "Social Change and Crime Rate Trends: A Routine Activity Approach," *American Sociological Review,* vol. 44, no. 4 (August 1979), pp. 588–608. Also, see Marcus Felson and L. E. Cohen, "Human Ecology and Crime: A Routine Activity Approach," *Human Ecology,* vol. 8, no. 4 (1980), pp. 389–406; Marcus Felson, "Linking Criminal Choices, Routine Activities, Informal Control, and Criminal Outcomes," in Derek B. Cornish and Ronald V. Clarke, eds., *The Reasoning Criminal: Rational Choice Perspectives on Offending* (New York: Springer-Verlag, 1986), pp. 119–128; and Ronald V. Clarke and Marcus Felson, eds., *Advances in Criminological Theory: Routine Activity and Rational Choice* (New Brunswick, N.J.: Transaction, 1993).

[33]Cohen and Felson, 1979, p. 595.

[34]For an analysis of the principles of routine activities theory in relation to crime prevention, see the January 1990 issue of the *Canadian Journal of Criminology,* entitled "Preventing Crime: Current Issues and Debates." For a test of routine activities theory as an explanation for victimization in the workplace, see John D. Wooldredge, Francis T. Cullen, and Edward J. Latessa, "Victimization in the Workplace: A Test of Routine Activities Theory," *Justice Quarterly,* vol. 9, no. 2 (June 1992), pp. 325–335.

[35]Marcus Felson, *Crime and Everyday Life: Insight and Implications for Society* (Thousand Oaks, Calif.: Pine Forge Press, 1994).

[36]Gary LaFree and Christopher Birkbeck, "The Neglected Situation: A Cross-National Study of the Situational Characteristics of Crime," *Criminology,* vol. 29, no. 1 (February 1991), p. 75.

[37]Ronald V. Clarke and Derek B. Cornish, eds., *Crime Control in Britain: A Review of Police and Research* (Albany: State University of New York Press), p. 8.

[38]See Derek B. Cornish and Ronald V. Clarke, "Understanding Crime Displacement: An Application of Rational Choice Theory," *Criminology,* vol. 25, no. 4 (November 1987), p. 933.

[39]Clarke and Cornish, *Crime Control in Britain: A Review of Police and Research,* p. 48.

[40]Werner Einstadter and Stuart Henry, *Criminological Theory: An Analysis of Its Underlying Assumptions* (Fort Worth: Harcourt Brace, 1995), p. 70.

[41]Daniel J. Curran and Claire M. Renzetti, *Theories of Crime* (Boston: Allyn & Bacon, 1994), p. 18.

[42]Laura J. Moriarty and James E. Williams, "Examining the Relationship Between Routine Activities Theory and Social Disorganization: An Analysis of Property Crime Victimization," *American Journal of Criminal Justice,* vol. 21, no. 1, 1996, pp. 43–59.

[43]Moriarty and Williams, 1996, p. 46.

[44]David Weisburd, "Reorienting Crime Prevention Research and Policy: From the Causes of Criminality to the Context of Crime," *NIJ Research Report* (Washington, D.C.: NIJ, June 1997).

[45]Material in this section comes from Weisburd, 1997.

[46]See P.J. Brantingham and P. L. Brantingham, "Situational Crime Prevention in Practice," *Canadian Journal of Criminology,* January 1990, pp. 17–40; and R. V. Clarke, "Situational Crime Prevention: Achievements and Challenges," in M. Tonry and D. Farrington, eds., *Building a Safer Society: Strategic Approaches to Crime Prevention, Crime and Justice: A Review of Research,* vol. 19 (Chicago: University of Chicago Press, 1995).

[47]Weisburd, 1997.

[48]See, for example, J.E. Eck and D. Weisburd, eds., *Crime and Place: Crime Prevention Studies,* vol. 4 (Monsey, N.Y.: Willow Tree Press, 1995).

[49]See L. Sherman, "Hot Spots of Crime and Criminal Careers of Places," in J.E. Eck and D. Weisburd, eds., *Crime and Place: Crime Prevention Studies,* vol. 4 (Monsey, N.Y.: Willow Tree Press, 1995); and L. Sherman, P. R. Gartin, and M.E. Buerger, "Hot Spots of Predatory Crime: Routine Activities and the Criminology of Place," *Criminology,* vol. 27, no. 1 (1989), pp. 27–56.

[50]Kenneth D. Tunnell, "Choosing Crime: Close Your Eyes and Take Your Chances," *Justice Quarterly,* vol. 7 (1990), pp. 673–690.

[51]See R. Barr and K. Pease, "Crime Placement, Displacement and Deflection," in M. Tonry and N. Morris, eds., *Crime and Justice: A Review of Research,* vol. 12 (Chicago: University of Chicago Press, 1990).

[52]For a good summation of target hardening, see Ronald V. Clarke, *Situational Crime Prevention* (New York: Harrow and Heston, 1992).

[53]For a good summation of studies on displacement, see R. Hesseling, "Displacement: A Review of the Empirical Literature," in R.V. Clarke, ed., *Crime Prevention Studies,* vol. 3 (Monsey, N.Y.: Willow Tree Press, 1994).

[54]E.A. Fattah, "Restorative and Retributive Justice Models. A Comparison", in H.H. Kuhne (ed.), *Festschrift fur Koichi Miyazawa* (Baden-Baden, Germany: Nomos Verlagsgesllschaft, 1995).

[55]J. Bonta, S. Wallace-Capretta, and J. Rooney, *Restorative Justice: An Evaluation of the Restora-*

*tive Justice Project, User Report 1998-05* (Ottawa: Solicitor General Canada, 1998).

[56]Robin Dann, *Restorative Justice Initiatives in South Eastern Alberta* (unpublished paper, 2000).

[57]Bonta et al., 1998.

[58]Bonta et al., 1998.

[59]For a more detailed discussion of theory integration, see Stephen F. Messner, Marvin D. Krohn, and Allan A. Liska, eds., *Theoretical Integration in the Study of Deviance and Crime: Problems and Prospects* (Albany: State University of New York Press), p. 1989.

[60]Joan McCord, "Theory, Pseudotheory, and Metatheory," in W. S. Laufer and F. Adler, eds., *Advances in Criminological Theory*, vol. 1 (New Brunswick, N.J.: Transaction, 1989), pp. 127–145.

[61]Williams and McShane, 1994, p. 265.

[62]Williams and McShane, 1994, 266–267.

[63]Einstadter and Henry, 1995, p. 309.

[64]See, for example, Katheryn K. Russell, "Development of a Black Criminology and the Role of the Black Criminologist," *Justice Quarterly*, vol. 9, no. 4 (December 1992), pp. 668–683.

[65]Francis T. Cullen, "Social Support as an Organizing Concept for Criminology: Presidential Address to the Academy of Criminal Justice Sciences," *Justice Quarterly*, vol. 11, no. 4 (December 1994), pp. 527–559.

[66]See, for example, Carolyn Smith and Terence P. Thornberry, "The Relationship Between Childhood Maltreatment and Adolescent Involvement in Delinquency," *Criminology*, vol. 33, no. 4 (1995), pp. 451–477.

[67]For a comprehensive overview of these and other integrated theories, see Larry J. Siegel and Chris McCormick, *Criminology in Canada* (Toronto: ITP Nelson, 1999), pp. 281–310.

[68]Cole, 1995, pp. 4–5.

[69]Gene Stephens, "The Global Crime Wave," *The Futurist*, vol. 28, no. 4 (July/August 1994), pp. 22–29.

[70]Stephens, 1994.

[71]Stephens, 1994.

[72]Stephens, 1994.

[73]Stephens, 1994.

[74]Stephens, 1994.

[75]For an interesting and alternative view of the future—one that evaluates what might happen if the insight provided by feminist perspectives on crime were implemented—see M. Kay Harris, "Moving Into the New Millennium: Toward a Feminist Vision of Justice," in Pepinsky and Quinney, *Criminology as Peacemaking*.

[76]Richter H. Moore, Jr., "Wiseguys: Smarter Criminals and Smarter Crime in the 21st Century," *The Futurist*, vol. 28, no. 5 (Sept.-Oct. 1994), p. 33.

[77]For a comprehensive look at the types and activities of various organized crime groups in Canada. refer to the Nathanson Centre for the Study of Organized Crime and Corruption Web site, www.yorku.ca/nathanson, or the Criminal Intelligence Service Canada (CSIS) Web site, www.cisc.gc.ca.

[78]Martin D. Schwartz and David O. Friedrichs, "Postmodern Thought and Criminological Discontent: New Metaphors for Understanding Violence," *Criminology*, vol. 32, no. 2 (1994), p. 237.

[79]Williams and McShane, 1994, p. 280.

[80]Dragan Milovanovic, "Postmodern Criminology: Mapping the Terrain," *Justice Quarterly*, vol. 13, no. 4 (December 1996), pp. 567–610.

[81]Williams and McShane, 1994, p. 297.

# Glossary

**Administrative law** regulates many daily business activities, and violations of such regulations generally result in warnings or fines, depending on their adjudged severity.

**Age of Reason.** See **Enlightenment.**

**Alloplastic adaptation** a form of adjustment that results from changes in the environment surrounding an individual.

**Anomie** a social condition in which norms are uncertain or lacking. Also see **Strain theory.**

**Antisocial** or **asocial personality** refers to individuals who are basically unsocialized and whose behaviour patterns bring them repeatedly into conflict with society.

**Applied research** scientific inquiry that is designed and carried out with practical application in mind.

**Arson** intentional or reckless damage to property by fire or explosion, including arson that causes danger to human life or damage to property due to criminal negligence.

**Asocial personality.** See **Antisocial personality.**

**Assault** the intentional or threatened application of force on another person without consent. The categories of assault include level 1—assault or common assault; level 2—assault involving the use of a weapon or causing bodily harm; level 3—assault that results in wounding or endangering the life of the victim.

**Atavism** a concept used by Cesare Lombroso to suggest that criminals are physiological throwbacks to earlier stages of human evolution. The term is derived from the Latin term *atavus,* which means "ancestor."

**Autoplastic adaptation** a form of adjustment that results from changes within an individual.

**Behaviour theory** a psychological perspective which posits that individual behaviour that is rewarded will increase in frequency, while that which is punished will decrease.

**Biological theories** (of criminology) maintain that the basic determinants of human behaviour, including criminality, are constitutionally or physiologically based and often inherited.

**Born criminals** individuals who are born with a genetic predilection toward criminality.

**Bourgeoisie** in Marxist theory, the class of people that owns the means of production.

**Breaking and entering** the unlawful entry of a place to commit an indictable offence.

**Broken windows thesis** a perspective on crime causation which holds that physical deterioration in an area leads to increased concerns for personal safety among area residents, and to higher crime rates in that area.

**Capital punishment** the legal imposition of a sentence of death upon a convicted offender; another term for the death penalty.

**Case study** an investigation into an individual case.

**Chicago school.** See **Ecological theory.**

**Circle sentencing conferences** groups of community members who actively assist justice authorities by participating in discussions about available sentencing options and plans to reintegrate the offender back into the community.

**Civil law** body of law that regulates arrangements between individuals, such as contracts and claims to property.

**Classical school** a criminological perspective operative in the late 1700s and early 1800s that had its roots in the Enlightenment, and that held that men and women are rational beings, crime is the result of the exercise of free will, and punishment can be effective in reducing the incidence of crime, as it negates the pleasure to be derived from crime commission.

**Code of Hammurabi** an early set of laws established by the Babylonian King Hammurabi, who ruled the ancient city from 1792 to 1750 B.C.

**Cohort** a group of individuals sharing certain significant social characteristics in common, such as gender, time, and place of birth.

**Cohort analysis** a social scientific technique which studies a population that shares common characteristics over time. Cohort analysis usually begins at birth and traces the development of cohort members until they reach a certain age.

**Common law** law originating from usage and custom rather than from written statutes. The term refers to nonstatutory customs, traditions, and precedents that help guide judicial decision making.

**Community policing** a philosophy of policing involving proactive collaboration between the police and the community to prevent and respond to crime and other community problems.

**Community sentencing panels** groups composed of volunteers from the community who focus on restorative measures such as restitution, reparation, mediation, and victim involvement.

**Conditioning** a psychological principle which holds that the frequency of any behaviour can be increased or decreased through reward, punishment, and/or association with other stimuli.

**Conduct norms** the shared expectations of a social group relative to personal conduct.

**Conflict perspective** an analytical perspective on social organization which holds that conflict is a fundamental aspect of social life itself and can never be fully resolved.

**Confounding effects** rival explanations, also called competing hypotheses, which are threats to the internal or external validity of any research design.

**Consensus model** an analytical perspective on social organization which holds that most members of society agree as to what is right and what is wrong, and that the various elements of society work in unison toward a common and shared vision of the greater good.

**Constitutional theories** those that explain criminality by reference to offenders' body types, inheritance, genetics, and/or external observable physical characteristics.

**Containment** those aspects of the social bond that act to prevent individuals from committing crimes and keep them from engaging in deviance.

**Containment theory** a form of control theory which suggests that a series of both internal and external factors contributes to law-abiding behaviour.

**Control group** a group of experimental subjects that is the subject of measurement and observation but is not exposed to the experimental intervention.

**Control theory.** See **Social control theory.**

**Controlled experiments** those that attempt to hold conditions (other than the intentionally introduced experimental intervention) constant.

**Correctional psychology** the aspect of forensic psychology that is concerned with the diagnosis and classification of offenders, the treatment of correctional populations, and the rehabilitation of inmates and other law violators.

**Correlates of crime** those variables observed to be related to criminal activity such as age, gender, ethnicity, and social class.

**Correlation** a causal, complementary, or reciprocal relationship between two measurable variables.

**Crime** human conduct in violation of the criminal laws of a province, the federal government, or a local jurisdiction that has the power to make such laws.

**Crime Prevention Through Environmental Design (CPTED)** a crime prevention model based on the design and use of a physical environment.

**Crime rate** crime per capita based on the number of recorded crimes calculated per 100 000 population.

**Criminal anthropology** the scientific study of the relationship between human physical characteristics and criminality.

**Criminal harassment** also known as stalking; the repeated following of, watching of, or communicating with individuals in a way that causes them to fear for their safety or for the safety of someone known to them.

**Criminal justice** the scientific study of crime, the criminal law, and components of the criminal justice system, including the police, courts, and corrections.

**Criminal justice system** the various agencies of justice, especially police, courts, and corrections, whose goal it is to apprehend, convict, punish, and rehabilitate law violators.

**Criminal law** the body of law that regulates actions which have the potential to harm interests of the provincial or the federal government.

**Criminality** a behavioural predisposition that disproportionately favours criminal activity.

**Criminalize** to make illegal.

**Criminaloids** a term used by Cesare Lombroso to describe occasional criminals who were pulled into criminality primarily by environmental influences.

**Criminologist** one who is trained in zthe field of criminology; also, one who studies crime, criminals, and criminal behaviour.

**Criminology** an interdisciplinary profession built around the scientific study of crime and criminal behaviour, including their form, causes, legal aspects, and control.

**Criminology of place.** See **Environmental criminology.**

**Critical criminology** a perspective focused on challenging traditional understandings and uncovering false beliefs about crime and criminal justice.

**Culture conflict** a sociological perspective on crime which suggests that the root cause of criminality can be found in a clash of values between variously socialized groups over what is acceptable or proper behaviour.

**Cycloid** a term developed by Ernst Kretschmer to describe a particular relationship between body build and personality type. The cycloid personality, which was associated with a heavyset, soft type of body, was said to vacillate between normality and abnormality.

**Dangerousness** the likelihood that a given individual will later harm society or others; it is often measured in terms of **recidivism,** or as the likelihood of new crime commission or rearrest for a new crime.

**Date rape** sexual assault that occurs within the context of a dating relationship.

**Deconstructionist theories** emerging approaches that challenge existing criminological perspectives to debunk them, and that work toward replacing them with concepts more applicable to the postmodern era.

**Defensible space** the range of mechanisms that combine to bring an environment under the control of its residents.

**Demography** the study of the characteristics of population groups (**demographics**); the characteristics of such groups are usually expressed in statistical fashion.

**Descriptive statistics** describe, summarize, or highlight the relationships within data that have been gathered.

**Deterrence** the prevention of crime. See also **General deterrence** and **Specific deterrence.**

**Deterrence strategy** a crime-control strategy that attempts "to diminish motivation for crime by increasing the perceived certainty, severity, or celerity of penalties."[1]

**Deviance** behaviour that violates social norms or is statistically different from the "average."

**Differential association** the sociological thesis that criminality, like any other form of behaviour, is learned through a process of association with others who communicate criminal values.

**Displacement** a shift of criminal activity from one spatial location to another.

**Ecological theory,** also commonly called the **Chicago school of criminology.** A type of sociological approach that emphasizes demographics (the characteristics of population groups) and geographics (the mapped location of such groups relative to one another) and sees the social disorganization that characterizes delinquency areas as a major cause of criminality and victimization.

**Ectomorph** a body type originally described as thin and fragile, with long, slender, poorly muscled extremities and delicate bones.

**Ego** the reality-testing part of the personality; also referred to as the reality principle. More formally, the personality component that is conscious, most immediately controls behaviour, and is most in touch with external reality.[2]

**Electroencephalogram (EEG)** electrical measurements of brain wave activity.

**Encryption** the process of encoding information, making it unreadable to all but its intended recipients.

**Endomorph** a body type originally described as soft and round, or overweight.

**Enlightenment, (the)** also known as the Age of Reason. A social movement that arose during the eighteenth century and built upon ideas such as empiricism, rationality, free will, humanism, and natural law.

**Environmental criminology** an emerging perspective that emphasizes the importance of geographic location and architectural features as they are associated with the prevalence of criminal victimization. (Note: as the term has been understood to date, environmental criminology is *not* the study of environmental crime, but rather a perspective that stresses how crime varies from place to place.)

**Environmental scanning** "a systematic effort to identify in an elemental way future developments (trends or events) that could plausibly occur over the time horizon of interest,"[3] and that might impact one's area of concern.

**Ethnic succession** the continuing process whereby one immigrant or ethnic group succeeds another through assumption of a particular position in society.

**Eugenics** the study of hereditary improvement by genetic control.

**Evolutionary ecology** an approach to understanding crime that draws attention to the ways people develop over the course of their lives.

**Experiment.** See **Controlled experiments** or **Quasi-experimental designs.**

**External validity** the ability to generalize research findings to other settings.

**Family group conferencing** a forum for dealing with unanswered questions and emotions, and the victim's right to restitution and reparation due to loss or injury resulting from a crime.

**Feminist criminology** a developing intellectual approach that emphasizes gender issues in the subject matter of criminology.

**First-degree murder** culpable homicide that is planned and deliberate.

**Focal concerns** the key values of any culture, and especially the key values of a delinquent subculture.

**Folkways** time-honoured customs. Although folkways carry the force of tradition, their violation is unlikely to threaten the survival of the group. See also **Mores.**

**Forensic psychiatry** that branch of psychiatry having to do with the study of crime and criminality.

**Fraud** an attempt through deceit or falsehood to obtain goods, services, or financial gain without legitimate rights. The UCR defines three categories of fraud, namely cheque fraud, credit card fraud, and other fraud including telemarketing fraud and criminal breach of trust, forgery, and insurance.

**Future criminology** the study of likely futures as they impinge on crime and its control.

**Futures research** "a multidisciplinary branch of operations research" whose principal aim "is to facilitate long-range planning based on (1) forecasting from the past supported by mathematical models, (2) cross-disciplinary treatment of its subject matter, (3) systematic use of expert judgment, and (4) a systems-analytical approach to its problems."[4]

**Futurist** one who studies the future.

**Gambling** behaviours such as keeping a common gaming or betting house, betting or bookmaking, placing bets on behalf of others, promoting lotteries, and cheating at play.

**General deterrence** a goal of criminal sentencing that seeks to prevent others from committing crimes similar to the one for which a particular offender is being sentenced.

**General theory** one that attempts to explain all (or at least most) forms of criminal conduct through a single, overarching approach.

**Hedonistic calculus** or **utilitarianism** the belief, first proposed by Jeremy Bentham, that behaviour holds value to any individual undertaking it according to the amount of pleasure or pain that it can be expected to produce for that person.

**Homicide** an act committed when a person, directly or indirectly, by any means, causes the death of a human being. Homicide can be culpable or nonculpable.

**Hybrid offence** a criminal offence that can be classified as an indictable or a summary conviction; the classification is usually made by the Crown attorney.

**Hypoglycemia** a condition characterized by low blood sugar.

**Hypothesis** 1. [a]n explanation that accounts for a set of facts and that can be tested by further investigation … 2. [s]omething that is taken to be true for the purpose of argument or investigation.[5]

**Id** the aspect of the personality from which drives, wishes, urges, and desires emanate. More formally, the division of the psyche associated with instinctual impulses and demands for immediate satisfaction of primitive needs.[6]

**Illegitimate opportunity structure** subcultural pathways to success that are disapproved of by the wider society.

**Impaired driving** the operation of a motor vehicle by a person whose ability to operate it is impaired by alcohol or a drug. In the case of alcohol, impairment is said to occur when the concentration of alcohol in the person's blood exceeds 80 milligrams in 100 millilitres of blood.

**Incapacitation** the use of imprisonment or other means to reduce the likelihood that an offender will be capable of committing future offences.

**Indictable offence** a serious criminal offence; specifically one that carries a maximum prison sentence of 14 years or longer.

**Individual rights advocates** those who seek to protect personal freedoms in the face of criminal prosecution.

**Individual rights and due process** the notion that criminal offenders have certain rights that must be defended against potential government excesses.

**Infanticide** an act committed when a female, considered disturbed from the effects of giving birth, causes the death of her newborn child (under one year of age).

**Inferential statistics** specify how likely findings are to be true for other populations, or in other locales.

**Informed consent** an ethical requirement of social scientific research which specifies that research subjects will be informed as to the nature of the research about to be conducted, their anticipated role in it, and the uses to which the data they provide will be put.

**Insanity (law)** a legally established inability to understand right from wrong, or to conform one's behaviour to the requirements of the law.

**Insanity (psychological)** persistent mental disorder or derangement.[7] Also, a defence allowable in criminal courts.

**Integrated theory** an explanatory perspective that merges (or attempts to merge) concepts drawn from different sources.

**Interactionist perspectives.** See **Social process theories.**

**Internal validity** the certainty that experimental interventions did indeed cause the changes observed in the study group; also the control over confounding factors that tend to invalidate the results of an experiment.

**Intersubjectivity** a scientific principle which requires that independent observers see the same thing under the same circumstances for observations to be regarded as valid.

**Juke family** a well-known "criminal family" studied by Richard L. Dugdale.

**Just deserts model** the notion that criminal offenders deserve the punishment they receive at the hands of the law, and that punishments should be appropriate to the type and severity of crime committed.

**Kallikak family** a well-known "criminal family" studied by Henry H. Goddard.

**Kriminalpolitik** the political handling of crime, or a criminology-based social policy.

**Labelling** an interactionist perspective that sees continued crime as a consequence of limited opportunities for acceptable behaviour, which follow from the negative responses of society to those defined as offenders.

**Law and order advocates** those who suggest that, under certain circumstances involving criminal threats to public safety, the interests of society should take precedence over individual rights.

**Learning theory** the general notion that crime is an acquired form of behaviour.

**Left-realism** a branch of radical criminology that holds that crime is a "real" social problem experienced by the lower classes.

**Liberal feminism** a feminist criminology approach that sees gender inequality being expressed in most spheres of influence.

**Life course theories** explanations for criminality that recognize that criminogenic influences have their greatest impact during the early stages of life, and hold that experiences which children have shape them for the rest of their lives.

**Lifestyle theory.** See **Routine activities theory.**

**Mala in se** acts that are thought to be wrong in and of themselves.

**Mala prohibita** acts that are wrong only because they are prohibited.

**Manslaughter** all nonintentional homicide.

**Marxist criminology.** See **Radical criminology.**

**Mass murder** the illegal killing of four or more victims at one location, within one event.

**McNaughten rule** a standard for judging legal insanity which requires that offenders not know what they were doing, or if they did, that they not know it was wrong.

**Mesomorph** a body type described as athletic and muscular.

**Monozyotic (or MZ) twins,** as opposed to dizygotic (or DZ) twins, develop from the same egg, and carry virtually the same genetic material.

**Moral enterprise** a term that encompasses all the efforts a particular interest group makes to have its sense of propriety enacted into law.

**Mores** behavioural proscriptions covering potentially serious violations of a group's values. Examples might include strictures against murder, sexual assault, and robbery. See also **Folkways.**

**Motor vehicle theft** the taking of a vehicle without the owner's authorization. A motor vehicle is defined as a car, truck, van, bus, recreational vehicle, semi-trailer truck, motorcycle, construction machinery, agricultural machinery, or other land-based motor vehicle (such as a go-kart, snowmobile, all-terrain vehicle, or dune-buggy).

**Murder** an act committed when a person intentionally causes the death of another human being or intends to cause bodily harm likely to result in death.

**Natural law** the philosophical perspective that certain immutable laws are fundamental to human nature and can be readily ascertained through reason. Man-made laws, in contrast, are said to derive from human experience and history—both of which are subject to continual change.

**Natural rights** the rights which, according to natural law theorists, individuals retain in the face of government action and interests.

**Neoclassical criminology** a contemporary version of classical criminology that emphasizes deterrence and retribution with reduced emphasis on rehabilitation.

**Neurosis** functional disorders of the mind or of the emotions involving anxiety, phobia, or other abnormal behaviour.

**Not criminally responsible by reason of mental disorder** (NCRMD) a finding that offenders are responsible for committing the offence with which they are charged but, because of their prevailing mental condition, should be sent to a psychiatric hospital for treatment rather than to prison. The maximum length of stay is predetermined.

**Nurturant strategy** a crime-control strategy that attempts "to forestall development of criminality by improving early life experiences and channeling child and adolescent development"[8] into desirable directions.

**Operant behaviour** behaviour that affects the environment in such a way as to produce responses or further behavioural cues.

**Operationalization** the process by which concepts are made measurable.

**Opportunity structure** a path to success. Opportunity structures may be of two types: legitimate and illegitimate.

**Panopticon** a prison designed by Jeremy Bentham, which was to be a circular building with cells along the circumference, each clearly visible from a central location staffed by guards.

**Paradigm** an example, model, or theory.

**Paranoid schizophrenics** schizophrenic individuals who suffer from delusions and hallucinations.

**Participant observation** a variety of strategies in data gathering in which the researcher observes a group by participating, to varying degrees, in the activities of the group.[9]

**Peace model** an approach to crime control that focuses on effective ways for developing a shared consensus on critical issues that have the potential to seriously affect the quality of life.

**Peacemaking criminology** a perspective that holds that crime-control agencies and the citizens they serve should work together to alleviate social problems and human suffering and thus reduce crime.

**Penal couple** a term that describes the relationship between victim and criminal. Also, the two individuals most involved in the criminal act—the offender and the victim.

**Phrenology** the study of the shape of the head to determine anatomical correlates of human behaviour.

**Pluralistic perspective** an analytical approach to social organization which holds that a multiplicity of values and beliefs exist in any complex society, but that most social actors agree on the usefulness of law as a formal means of dispute resolution.

**Positivism** the application of scientific techniques to the study of crime and criminals.

**Postcrime victimization** or **secondary victimization** refers to problems in living that tend to follow from initial victimization.

**Postmodern criminology** a brand of criminology that developed following World War II and that builds on the tenets inherent in postmodern social thought.

**Power-control theory** a perspective which holds that the distribution of crime and delinquency within society is to some degree founded upon the consequences that power relationships within the wider society hold for domestic settings, and for the everyday relationships between men, women, and children within the context of family life.

**Primary deviance** initial deviance often undertaken to deal with transient problems in living.

**Primary research** research characterized by original and direct investigation.

**Proletariat** in Marxist theory, the working class.

**Prostitution** the illegal activities of publicly communicating with another person for the purposes of buying or selling sexual services, running a bawdy house, or living on the avails of prostitution of another person.

**Protection/avoidance strategy** a crime-control strategy that attempts to reduce criminal opportunities by changing people's routine activities, by increasing guardianship, or by incapacitating convicted offenders.[10]

**Psychiatric criminology** theories derived from the medical sciences, including neurology, and which, like other psychological theories, focus on the individual as the unit of analysis. Psychiatric theories form the basis of psychiatric criminology. See **Forensic psychiatry.**

**Psychoanalysis** the theory of human psychology founded by Freud on the concepts of the unconscious, resistance, repression, sexuality, and the Oedipus complex.[11]

**Psychological profiling** the attempt to categorize, understand, and predict the behaviour of certain types of offenders based on behavioural clues they provide.

**Psychological theories** those derived from the behavioural sciences and that focus on the individual as the unit of analysis. Psychological theories place the locus of crime causation within the personality of the individual offender.

**Psychopath** or **sociopath** a person with a personality disorder, especially one manifested in aggressively antisocial behaviour, which is often said to be the result of a poorly developed superego.

**Psychopathology** the study of pathological mental conditions, that is, mental illness.

**Psychosis** a form of mental illness in which sufferers are said to be out of touch with reality.

**Psychotherapy** a form of psychiatric treatment based on psychoanalytical principles and techniques.

**Public policy** government-formulated directives made on behalf of the public good to solve a problem or achieve an end.

**Punishments** undesirable behavioural consequences likely to decrease the frequency of occurrence of that behaviour.

**Pure research** research undertaken simply for the sake of advancing scientific knowledge.

**Qualitative methods** research techniques that produce subjective results or results that are difficult to quantify.

**Quantitative methods** research techniques that produce measurable results.

**Quasi-experimental designs** approaches to research which, although less powerful than experimental designs, are deemed worthy of use when better designs are not feasible.

**Radical criminology** a perspective which holds that the causes of crime are rooted in social conditions that empower the wealthy and the politically well organized, but disenfranchise those less fortunate. Also called **Marxist** or **critical criminology.**

**Randomization** the process whereby individuals are assigned to study groups without biases or differences resulting from selection.

**Rational choice theory** holds that criminality is the result of conscious choice and that individuals choose to commit crime when the benefits outweigh the costs of disobeying the law.

**Reaction formation** the process in which a person openly rejects what he or she wants, or aspires to, but cannot obtain or achieve.

**Realist criminology** an emerging perspective that insists on a pragmatic assessment of crime and its associated problems.

**Recidivism** the repetition of criminal behaviour.

**Recidivism rate** the percentage of convicted offenders who have been released from prison and who are later rearrested for a new crime. Also see **Dangerousness.**

**Reintegrative shaming** that form of shaming, imposed as a sanction by the criminal justice system, that is thought to strengthen the moral bond between the offender and the community.

**Replicability** (experimental) a scientific principle which holds that the same observations made at one time can be had again at a later time if all other conditions are the same.

**Research** the use of standardized, systematic procedures in the search for knowledge.[12]

**Research design** the logic and structure inherent in an approach to data gathering.

**Restitution** a criminal sanction, in particular the payment of compensation by the offender to the victim.

**Restorative justice** a postmodern perspective that stresses "remedies and restoration rather than prison, punishment and victim neglect."[13]

**Retribution** the act of taking revenge upon a criminal perpetrator.

**Rewards** desirable behavioural consequences likely to increase the frequency of occurrence of that behaviour.

**Robbery** the unlawful taking or attempted taking of property that is in the immediate possession of another, by threatened or actual use of force or violence.

**Routine activities theory** (or **lifestyle theory**) a brand of rational choice theory which suggests that lifestyles contribute significantly to both the volume and type of crime found in any society.

**Scenario writing** a technique intended to predict future outcomes, and builds upon environmental scanning by attempting to assess the likelihood of a variety of possible outcomes once important trends have been identified.

**Schizophrenics** mentally ill individuals who are out of touch with reality and suffer from disjointed thinking.

**Second-degree murder** all murder that is not first-degree murder.

**Secondary analysis** the reanalysis of existing data.

**Secondary deviance** that which results from official labelling and from association with others who have been so labelled.

**Secondary research** new evaluations of existing information that has already been collected by other researchers.

**Selective incapacitation** a social policy that seeks to protect society by incarcerating those individuals deemed to be the most dangerous.

**Self-report study** a data collection method requiring subjects to reveal their own participation in criminal behaviour.

**Self-reports** research investigations of subjects in order to record and report their behaviours.

**Serial murder** culpable homicide that involves the killing of several victims in three or more separate events.

**Sexual assault** an assault committed in circumstances of a sexual nature such that the sexual integrity of the victim is violated. The degree of violence used determines whether the sexual assault is considered to be level 1, level 2, or level 3.

**Situational choice theory** a brand of rational choice theory that views criminal behaviour "as a function of choices and decisions made within a context of situational constraints and opportunities."[14]

**Situational crime prevention** a social policy approach that looks to develop greater understanding of crime and more effective crime prevention strategies through concern with the physical, organizational, and social environments that make crime possible.[15]

**Social bond** the rather intangible link between individuals and the society of which they are a part; created through the process of socialization.

**Social capital** the degree of positive relationships with other persons and with social institutions that individuals build up over the course of their lives.

**Social class** distinctions made between individuals on the basis of important defining social characteristics.

**Social contract** the Enlightenment-era concept that human beings abandon their natural state of individual freedom to join together and form society. Although, in the process of forming a social contract, individuals surrender some freedoms to society as a whole, government, once formed, is obligated to assume responsibilities toward its citizens and to provide for their protection and welfare.

**Social control theory** a perspective which predicts that when social constraints on antisocial behaviour are weakened or absent, delinquent behaviour emerges. Rather than stressing causative factors in criminal behaviour, control theory asks why people actually obey rules instead of breaking them.

**Social disorganization**   a condition said to exist when a group is faced with social change, uneven development of culture, maladaptiveness, disharmony, conflict, and lack of consensus.

**Social ecology**   an approach to criminological theorizing that attempts to link the structure and organization of human community to interactions with its localized environment.

**Social epidemiology**   the study of social epidemics and diseases of the social order.

**Social learning theory**   a psychological perspective that says people learn how to behave by modelling themselves after others whom they have the opportunity to observe.

**Social pathology**   a concept that compares society to a physical organism and sees criminality as an illness.

**Social policies**   government initiatives, programs, and plans intended to address problems in society. The "National Strategy on Community Safety and Crime Prevention," for example, is a kind of generic (large-scale) social policy—one consisting of many smaller programs.

**Social problems perspective**   the belief that crime is a manifestation of underlying social problems such as poverty, discrimination, pervasive family violence, inadequate socialization practices, and the breakdown of traditional social institutions.

**Social process theories,** also known as **interactionist perspectives**   emphasize the give-and-take that occurs between offender, victim, and society—and specifically between the offender and agents of formal social control such as the police, courts, and correctional organizations.

**Social relativity**   the notion that social events are differently interpreted according to the cultural experiences and personal interests of the initiator, the observer, or the recipient of that behaviour.

**Social responsibility perspective**   the belief that individuals are fundamentally responsible for their own behaviour and that they choose crime over other, more law-abiding, courses of action.

**Social-structural theories**   explain crime by reference to various aspects of the social fabric. They emphasize relationships between social institutions and describe the types of behaviour that tend to characterize *groups* of people as opposed to *individuals.*

**Social structure**   the pattern of social organization and the interrelationships between institutions characteristic of a society.

**Socialist feminism**   a feminist criminology approach that views gender oppression as an obvious feature of capitalist societies.

**Socialization**   the lifelong process of social experience whereby individuals acquire the cultural patterns of their society.

**Sociobiology**   "the systematic study of the biological basis of all social behaviour."[16]

**Sociopath.**   See **Psychopath.**

**Somatotyping**   the classification of human beings into types according to body build and other physical characteristics.

**Specific deterrence**   a goal of criminal sentencing that seeks to prevent a particular offender from engaging in repeat criminality.

**Statistical school**   a criminological perspective with roots in the early 1800s that seeks to uncover correlations between crime rates and other types of demographic data.

**Statute**   a formal written enactment of a legislative body.[17]

**Statutory law**   law in the form of statutes or formal written strictures, made by a legislature or governing body with the power to make law.

**Stigmatic shaming**   a form of shaming, imposed as a sanction by the criminal justice system, that is thought to destroy the moral bond between the offender and the community.

**Stigmatization**   the creation of an enduring label that taints a person's identity and changes him or her in the eyes of others.

**Strain theory** or **anomie theory**   a sociological approach that posits a disjuncture between socially and subculturally sanctioned means and goals as the cause of criminal behaviour.

**Strategic assessment** a technique that assesses the risks and opportunities facing those who plan for the future.

**Subcultural theory** a sociological perspective that emphasizes the contribution made by variously socialized cultural groups to the phenomenon of crime.

**Subculture** a collection of values and preferences that is communicated to subcultural participants through a process of socialization.

**Sublimation** the psychological process whereby one aspect of consciousness comes to be symbolically substituted for another.

**Summary conviction offence** a criminal offence that is less serious than an indictable offence; one that carries a maximum penalty of six months in jail.

**Superego** the moral aspect of the personality; much like the conscience. More formally, the division of the psyche that develops by the incorporation of the perceived moral standards of the community, is mainly unconscious, and includes the conscience.[18]

**Supermale** a male individual displaying the XYY chromosome structure.

**Survey research** a social science data-gathering technique that involves the use of questionnaires.

**Tagging** like **labelling,** the process whereby an individual is negatively defined by agencies of justice.

**Target hardening** the reduction in criminal opportunity, generally through the use of physical barriers, architectural design, and enhanced security measures of a particular location.

**Techniques of neutralization** culturally available justifications that can provide criminal offenders with the means to disavow responsibility for their behaviour.

**Testosterone** the primary male sex hormone; produced in the testes, its function is to control secondary sex characteristics and sexual drive.

**Tests of significance** statistical techniques intended to provide researchers with confidence that their results are, in fact, true and not the result of sampling error.

**Thanatos** a death wish.

**Theft** the act of dishonestly taking property belonging to another person with the intention of depriving its owner of it either permanently or temporarily.

**Theory** a series of interrelated propositions that attempt to describe, explain, predict, and ultimately to control some class of events. A theory gains explanatory power from inherent logical consistency and is "tested" by how well it describes and predicts reality.

**Trephination** a form of surgery, typically involving bone and especially the skull. Early instances of cranial trephination have been taken as evidence for primitive beliefs in spirit possession.

**Twelve Tables** early Roman laws written circa 450 B.C. that regulated family, religious, and economic life.

**Typologies of crime** classifications of crime useful in identifying patterns of criminal activity and motivations for criminal behaviour.

**Unicausal** having one cause. Unicausal theories posit only one source for all that they attempt to explain.

**Uniform Crime Report (UCR)** a summation of crime statistics tallied annually by the Canadian Centre for Justice Statistics (CCJS) and consisting primarily of data on crimes reported to the police and of arrests.

**Utilitarianism.** See **Hedonistic calculus.**

**V-chip** a device that enables viewers to program their televisions to block out content with a common rating. It is intended for use against violent or sexually explicit programming.

**Variable** a concept that can undergo measurable changes.

**Verstehen** the kind of subjective understanding that can be achieved by criminologists who immerse themselves into the everyday world of the criminals they study.

**Victim impact statement** a written document that describes the losses, suffering, and trauma experienced by the crime victim or by the victim's survivors. In jurisdictions where victim impact statements are used, judges are expected to consider them in arriving at an appropriate sentence for the offender.

**Victim fine surcharge** a mandatory, judicial imposition of a monetary fine administered in addition to a criminal sentence and used to finance victim services.

**Victim-Offender Reconciliation Program** a program that gives the offender the opportunity to meet face-to-face with the victim in the presence of a trained mediator in an attempt to reduce the victim's fears while establishing accountability and reparation for the crime.

**Victim-precipitated homicide** killing in which the "victim" was the first to commence the interaction or was the first to resort to physical violence.

**Victim-proneness** the degree of an individual's likelihood of victimization.

**Victim–witness assistance programs** counsel victims, orient them to the justice process, and provide a variety of other services such as transportation to court, child care during court appearances, and referrals to social service agencies.

**Victimization Survey** a survey first conducted as the Canadian Urban Victimization Survey in 1981 by Statistics Canada and then every five years since 1988 as part of the General Social Survey. It provides data on surveyed households reporting that they have been affected by crime.

**Victimogenesis** the contributory background of a victim as a result of which he or she becomes prone to victimization.

**Victimology** the study of victims and their contributory role, if any, in crime causation.

**Violent Crime Linkage Analysis System (ViCLAS)** a centralized computer bank containing details of violent crimes that assists police in recognizing patterns among violent offences and offenders.

## Notes to Glossary

1. Bryan Vila, "A General Paradigm for Understanding Criminal Behavior: Extending Evolutionary Ecological Theory," *Criminology,* vol. 32, no. 3 (August 1994), pp. 311–359.

2. *American Heritage Dictionary and Electronic Thesaurus* (Boston: Houghton Mifflin, 1987).

3. George F. Cole, "Criminal Justice in the Twenty-First Century: The Role of Futures Research," in John Klofas and Stan Stojkovic, eds., *Crime and Justice in the Year 2010* (Belmont, Calif.: Wadsworth, 1995).

4. Society of Police Futurists International, *PFI: The Future of Policing* (brochure), no date.

5. *American Heritage Dictionary and Electronic Thesaurus* on CD-ROM (text copyrighted 1987 by the Houghton Mifflin Company).

6. Ibid.

7. Ibid.

8. Bryan Vila, "A General Paradigm for Understanding Criminal Behavior: Extending Evolutionary Ecological Theory."

9. Frank E. Hagan, *Research Methods in Criminal Justice and Criminology* (New York: Macmillan, 1993), p. 103.

10. Bryan Vila, "Human Nature and Crime Control: Improving the Feasibility of Nurturant Strategies," *Politics and the Life Sciences,* March 1997, pp. 3–21.

11. *American Heritage Dictionary and Electronic Thesaurus.*

12. Abraham Kaplan, *The Conduct of Inquiry: Methodology for Behavioral Science* (San Francisco: Chandler, 1964), p. 71.

13. Fay Honey Knopp, "Community Solutions to Sexual Violence: Feminist-Abolitionist Perspectives," in Harold Pepinsky and Richard Quinney, eds., *Criminology as Peacemaking* (Bloomington: Indiana University Press, 1991), p. 183.

14. Ronald V. Clarke and Derek B. Cornish, eds., *Crime Control in Britain: A Review of Police and Research* (Albany: SUNY Press), p. 8.

15. David Weisburd, "Reorienting Crime Prevention Research and Policy: From the Causes of Criminality to the Context of Crime," *NIJ Research Report* (Washington, D.C.: NIJ, June 1997).

16. Edward O. Wilson, *Sociobiology: The New Synthesis* (Cambridge: The Belknap Press of Harvard University Press, 1975).

17. Henry Campbell Black, *Black's Law Dictionary,* 6th ed. (St. Paul: West Publishing Co., 1990), p. 1410.

18. Ibid.

# Name Index

Page numbers in *italics* indicate photographs.

# Subject Index